JUN 22 1970

UNIVERSITY OF CONNECTICUT — GROTON, CONN. — SOUTHEASTERN BRANCH LIBRARY

MAN in Western Civilization

VERN L. BULLOUGH
San Fernando Valley State College

HOLT, RINEHART AND WINSTON, INC.
New York   Chicago   San Francisco   Atlanta
Dallas   Montreal   Toronto   London   Sydney

Maps on pages 8 (detail), 48, 136, 142, 168, 221, 275, 332, 423,
and 445 are from *A History of World Civilization,*
Volumes One and Two, edited by Max Savelle.
Copyright © 1957 by Holt, Rinehart and Winston, Inc.
Reprinted by permission of
Holt, Rinehart and Winston, Inc.

Copyright © 1970 by Holt, Rinehart and Winston, Inc.
All rights reserved
Library of Congress Catalog Card Number: 74–95788
SBN: 03–077015–7
Printed in the United States of America
1 2 3 4 5 6 7 8 9

to David,
and to James, Steven, Susan,
and Robert

Preface

At best, textbooks are only an introduction to the study of history. They establish an elementary frame of reference for the reader, who must fill in the details and even supply interpretations. Unfortunately, however, history textbooks are too often regarded as primary sources, especially by the beginning history student. Though it is hoped that this text has kept factual inaccuracies to a minimum, no individual or even a group of individuals can claim to know all that has taken place in the past. Moreover, in sketching an outline of Western civilization, it is necessary to simplify, to make some events seem less complex than they were, and to pass over many events and figures simply because to include them would make the text unwieldly and unreadable.

History textbooks best serve their purposes if the reader keeps in mind that they represent only an elementary summation of a multi-stepped process in the writing and study of history. History starts with and is based upon the primary source materials: the surviving objects, manuscripts, and oral materials of the past. When the historian begins to examine these materials, however, judgment enters the picture. He must then apply some sort of test to distinguish the authentic sources from those that are not authentic or even actual forgeries. The process still leaves him with records that are often contradictory, incomplete, or lacking in the kind of information he wants, but from these he must extract a credible testimony, and weave this into a meaningful narrative. Though history is based upon a collection of facts, all historians need not interpret these facts in the same way.

This is because the facts of history are facts of meaning and cannot be seen, felt, tasted, heard, or smelled. Rather, they are symbolic or representative of what was once real but now has no objective reality. In other words, they exist only in the observer's — the historian's — mind. To be studied objectively, a thing must have an independent existence outside the human mind. Unfortunately, however, recollections, which are the basis of history, can only be products of the mind. Memories are abstract images, not realities, and reconstructions of others' memories are likely to be even more abstract. The historian can do little more than project mental images of the past using his own experience as a guide. History, therefore, is a subjective process. While the historian can try to get as close to the truth about the past as constant correction of his mental images will allow, all historians recognize that the complete truth has in fact eluded them. Only when we find relics of human happenings — documents, manuscripts, potsherds, coins, ruins, portraits, or other archeological or anthropological remains — do we have objects to study, but even these objects are never the happenings or events themselves.

Obviously, then, the job of the historian is to re-create an image of the past on the basis of the evidence that has been recovered. This re-creation, of course, differs from one historian to another and from one generation to the next. Students can better understand the problems of the historian by dipping into the reference works, the monographs, and even some of the primary source materials listed in the bibliography. This book has deliberately been kept as short as possible in order to encourage such reading. If this text can serve as an initial guide, it will have fulfilled its purpose.

This book originally grew out of conversations with Stephen V. Fulkerson and in a sense he is as much responsible for it as I am though he does not wish to be listed as a co-author. Kenneth Culver of Holt, Rinehart and Winston encouraged me to go ahead with the project, and Clifford Snyder proved to be a most helpful and patient editor. Mrs. Jeanette Johnson helped with the final editing and saw the manuscript through the press. The manuscript was read in whole or in parts by Emil Lucki, Judith Zacek, Allen Dirrim, Darrel Morse, Marjorie Berlincourt, Earle Field, Morris Slavin, and numerous times by my wife, Bonnie Bullough. Betty Drew and Joy Thornbury did the final typing.

Vern L. Bullough

Northridge, California
October 1969

Contents

Prologue

Most beginning history students suppose that history is primarily a chronological exercise of remembering dates. While historians utilize dates, they do so only as a convenient means of measuring time. Any system for keeping track of time, however, is only an invention and is not fixed by any immutable law. The beginning of a year is whenever men decide it shall be: in early spring, as was the practice in English-speaking lands at the time George Washington was born; in early fall, as in the calendar used by many Jews; or, as among Islamic peoples, at the end of twelve lunar months totaling no more than 355 days. The latter system makes every new year ten or eleven days earlier than the previous one, so that while Americans are counting thiry-two years, the Muslims are counting thirty-three.

The problems of measuring time were not immediately apparent to primitive man, and it took many centuries for him to fully realize what they were. It was easy enough to count the days, but the number soon became large and unwieldy. The next logical step in many societies was to count the changes in the lunar cycle, but the phases of the moon do not correspond with those of the sun. Since the moon takes some twenty-nine and one-half days to complete its cycle, various methods were developed to reconcile the lunar phases with the solar phases. The Jewish calendar resolved this problem by adding some seven extra months, called intercalary months, over a nineteen-year period. Julius Caesar in his reform of the calendar ignored the phases of the moon entirely (as had the Egyptians many centuries earlier) by giving the odd-numbered months thirty-one days and the even-numbered months, with the exception of February, thirty days. This system

1

gave 365 days, and by adding an extra day to the month of February every four years — an intercalary day — a close approximation was achieved between the calendar year and the actual year. Unfortunately, a discrepancy of about eleven minutes still remained, which led to an increasing distortion of the calendar. As a result, Pope Gregory XIII in 1582 dropped ten days out of that year and required that thenceforth the years ending in hundreds should not be leap years unless they were divisible by 400. This system, in substance, gave us the present-day Gregorian calendar.

Months have names, as do the days of the week, but years ordinarily do not. Instead, they bear numbers, usually dating from some special occasion. Medieval English statutes dated from the accession of a king; the first Roman year began with the legendary founding of the city; the Greeks utilized the year of the first Olympic games; and the Jews went back to creation. The Muslim era began with the flight of Muhammad from Mecca in the year 622 of the Christian era, usually abbreviated A.D. for the Latin words *anno domini*, the year Jesus was born. Even this date is a miscalculation, however, for historians now realize that Jesus was born several years before this. Nevertheless, the system is a convenient and widely used chronological scheme. Dates before the Christian era, usually noted B.C., are accurate for several hundred years back in the Mediterranean region, and through dependence upon the annals of the Assyrian kings, for several centuries further back. Up to this period, all dates are approximate, and even these approximations have changed radically within the last two decades. For the second millennium (2000–1000 B.C.), the approximations of historians can be accepted as reasonably accurate. For the third millennium (3000–2000 B.C.), uncertainty increases to the point where authorities can do little more than guess in which century some known happenings actually occurred. The fourth millennium (4000–3000 B.C.) goes back into what is properly called prehistory, when even the events themselves become obscure.

Students of prehistory rely for the most part on relative chronologies. They know the sequences of happenings and periods without knowing much of the duration of a period in years. An archeologist, for example, knows from a certain style of pottery that the people who made it lived before the bow and arrow came into use because no arrowheads have been discovered at the same place or level as that in which the pottery was found. The best known relative chronology picks up the story of mankind in the Old Stone Age and carries it through the New Stone Age to the Copper, Bronze, and Iron ages. The Bronze Age has been dated with some accuracy in the eastern Mediterranean lands from about 3000 to 1000 B.C. With the Iron Age it is possible to begin dating by the B.C. and A.D. method.

part one

THE BEGINNINGS

1

The Beginnings
of Civilization

History is a form of literature. It is also one of the social sciences. In the past, however, history has most often been more literary than scientific. This book aims at being both. It attempts to explain within the pages of a short volume how civilized society in Europe first developed and then evolved over the centuries into the form that has come to be known as Western civilization. European civilization was erected on an Oriental foundation, and it still owes more to Asia and Africa than most Western people realize or are usually willing to acknowledge. Moreover, throughout much of history, the development of European civilization has been much less impressive than that of many eastern civilizations. In fact, it has only been since the fifteenth century that European society and culture rose to a position of dominance in the world — a dominance that today is being challenged by various segments of the non-Western world.

Essentially, history is based upon written records. Thus, in a narrow and technical sense at least, there was no history until late in his development man acquired writing skills and began to keep records. For the period before written records, most of our information comes from tools, building materials, weapons, pottery, and other remains found in archeological excavations. Large quantities of such materials have been collected, particularly since the eighteenth century. Gradually we have begun to understand something about the beginnings of civilization, although many of the explanations put forth in the past are no longer accepted. In recent years, new scientific techniques for dating archeological finds or for interpreting artifacts have enabled historians to correct some of their earlier assumptions, although there is still only limited agreement about what happened.

EARLY MAN

All investigators agree that for much of his life on earth — and no one is prepared to say with much precision just how long this has been — man has gathered together in tribes. Since tribal life still survives in many places throughout the world, it is possible to gain insight into the nature of such a life even though we do not know the details of how prehistoric man lived. In general, we can assume that early tribal societies were stable and resistant to change. Members were related either by kinship ties or by ritual ones. The smallness and closeness of tribal society tended to limit both the variety and the extent of the enterprises that could be organized and pursued. Traditional activities were carried out with efficiency, but tasks demanding new or different approaches were undertaken only with reluctance or under extreme pressure. As a result, we can assume that long periods of time elapsed during the prehistoric era when improvement was slow and radical change was almost nonexistent. This is not meant to imply that pre-

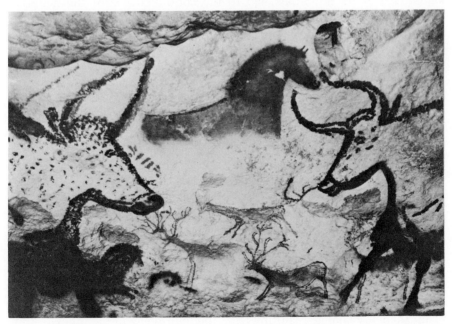

Prehistoric cave painting from Lascaux. (French Government Tourist Office)

historic man was stagnant but only that he usually developed and perfected what he knew before he attempted anything different. Because of his stone work, primitive man is generally known as Stone Age man, just as he is also known as a cave man because some men lived in caves. It should be emphasized that within the limits of his knowledge, ancient man was remarkably skilled. From the first invention or discovery of the possibilities of stone, his tools and equipment became more and more ingenious. Stone jugs and vases have been found of such excellent quality and workmanship that they cannot be surpassed even with the use of modern stonecutting equipment. Stone Age man was also creative. The representations of animals which have survived in the caves of southern France and northwestern Spain for some 20,000 years are not only technically sophisticated but also intensely expressive.

In his way Stone Age man was also a scientist and an engineer. After discovering how to control fire, he used it not only for cooking and for protection but also for making pottery. He found out how to make cloth and eventually began to work with metals. The first metallurgist, curiously enough, lived in the Stone Age. The development of copper technology is considered to have brought man out of the Stone Age, although in actuality the availability of stone, together with a knowledge of its potentials, led to the continued use of the material until as late as the middle of the first millennium B.C.

THE DEVELOPMENT OF AGRICULTURE

Undoubtedly, prehistoric man's most significant accomplishment was the development of agriculture. Throughout most of the long period of the Stone Age, man was a hunter, a fisherman, a food gatherer. Only in the last few thousand years of his prehistory did he develop ways of producing his food instead of catching it or helping himself to what he could find. These agricultural advances brought such radical changes in man's way of life that historians speak of them as representing a revolution. This turning point is sometimes called the agricultural revolution, although it is more often referred to as the Neolithic Revolution because it occurred in the Neolithic period, the technical name for the New Stone Age. The Neolithic period was broken off and separated from the Paleolithic, or Old Stone Age, because of the notable excellence of its stone work. Sometimes an intermediary period between the two periods, called the Mesolithic, is recognized, but the shift from food gathering to food production is far more significant than any change resulting from the improvement of stoneworking techniques.

The development of agriculture is still the subject of much conjecture. It is generally assumed that men began to harvest crops before they actually began to plant anything. In the course of their travels, food-gathering peoples cut and thrashed wild grains. Similarly, in desert regions, the date palm growing in the oases quite naturally became a source of food. Man's next step was to throw seed along the way as he traveled, hoping to harvest on his return. More effective farming was closely related to the domestication of animals. The first domesticated animal is believed to have been the dog, which more than likely domesticated itself. The dog made itself at home among men, was accepted, tolerated, and utilized. The Eskimo made it a draft animal; other food-gathering peoples employed it in hunting, and most did not hesitate to eat it when no better food was available. Other animals known to have been domesticated by early farmers included the cow (and the water buffalo), the cat, the goat, the sheep, the pig, and the ass, as well as various birds. The ox was rather easily taught to draw a load with a minimum of equipment, and this fact might have led to the development of the plow, an important factor in the agricultural revolution. The placidity of the ox was also a major element in the invention of the wheel for transportation. Two other domesticated animals often associated with ancient peoples, the horse and the camel, were nonagricultural animals and were not widely used until after 2000 B.C. In fact, until the invention of the horse collar and the saddle in medieval times, the full potential of the horse was not realized. Instead, the horse was kept primarily for sport (racing) and for war.

THE APPEARANCE OF CITIES

With the appearance of cities during the fourth millennium B.C. — about 5000 years ago — civilization began. Where and when cities first appeared is still a matter for scholarly debate, but among the earliest, and the most important for Western civilization, were those in the river valleys of the Near East (sometimes called the Middle East), particularly in the area that extends from modern Egypt to modern Iraq. One group of cities was centered in southern Iraq, a region traditionally known as Mesopotamia from the Greek description of it as "the land between two rivers," the Tigris in the east and the Euphrates in the west. In ancient time, each river had a separate mouth flowing into the Persian Gulf, but today they are united and run through a swampy delta which extends out into the gulf. Better known even than the civilization of Mesopotamia is that of the lower Nile valley. Here appeared the strong and unified kingdom of "the two lands," Upper Egypt in the narrow valley south of present-day Cairo, and Lower Egypt, the delta region. The people in both the land between the two rivers and in the two lands along one river left many records, including a literature that deals with their long and successful mastery of their

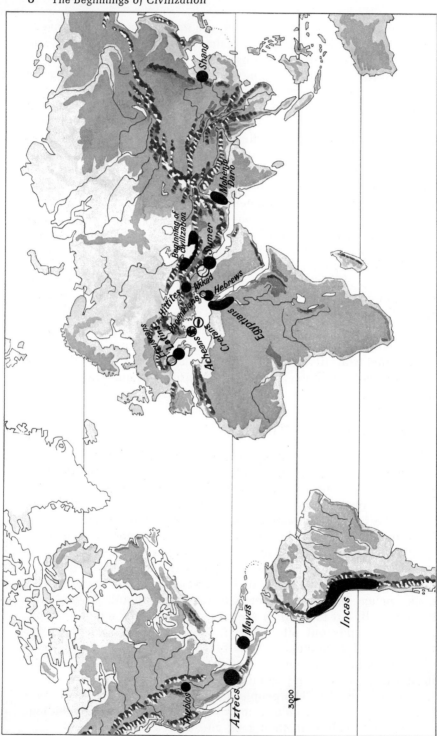

Early foci of civilization.

river valley environment. We know the names of people, of cities, of gods, of enemies; we have narrations of events and of myths; and for the first time, we have insights into ways of thought and living in the long evolution of mankind. With the help of the archeologist, the anthropologist, and the linguist, as well as the meteorologist and the geographer, the historian is in a position to begin the study of civilization.

We know more about the beginnings of civilization in early Mesopotamia than in Egypt, largely because the lower Euphrates has wandered about a good deal throughout its history. When the Euphrates changed its channel, cities that were once on its banks were deserted. They soon became lonely mounds standing isolated in the desert, remote from other settlements and undisturbed by anyone until the modern-day archeologist arrived to conduct systematic explorations. The Nile, except in the delta, runs in the same channel today that it always has, so prospective archeological sites are still inhabited, although modern industrial projects such as the Aswan dam are destroying many. In the delta area, old sites are covered by the accumulated sediment of thousands of years of flooding, making digging expensive and time-consuming even when a comparatively deserted area can be found.

The nature of ancient writing is also responsible for preserving information about Mesopotamia in the earlier periods. The inventors of writing in Mesopotamia were a people known as Sumerians in the lower delta area. Curiously, they appear to have been relatively recent immigrants who came from an unknown place, perhaps Iran, around 4000 B.C. Sumer at that time was uninhabited or only sparsely inhabited by hunters and fishermen, who found the lush swamplands an easy place to catch a food supply. By 3000 B.C. the Sumerians were building cities and had developed a writing system. They kept their records on clay tablets that have proved surprisingly durable. Thousands upon thousands of these tablets have been dug out of the earth, and even some that have been found in water can be dried out and read. The Egyptians, on the other hand, wrote mostly on papyrus, a kind of paper made from a plant of the same name that grew abundantly in the swamps. As paper goes, papyrus was durable, but the quantity of Egyptian writing that has survived from early times does not approach what has survived from Sumerian civilization.

WHY CITIES DEVELOPED
IN THE NEAR EAST

Before cities could develop, it was necessary for man to settle down, to stay in one place. Since most of the first cities appeared in desert regions, it is quite possible that the drying up of previously well-watered terrain forced men to congregate in river valleys where they had to organize themselves into communities to survive. Unfortunately, we do not yet know how ancient the deserts are nor how rapidly they evolved. We know, however, that deserts were important to the development of cities. The mere existence of large desertlike areas tended to keep people from traveling as far in search of food as they might otherwise have done. The desert climate along the 30th parallel, with its high temperature and short winter season, provided ideal growing conditions when and if adequate water was available. The large rivers of Egypt and Mesopotamia furnished the necessary water, and the periodic floodings kept the soil fertile. In addition, desert lands were easily cleared, since they lacked the heavy forest or brush which existed in other areas. The problem in desert areas was to keep the crops watered in the dry season. This necessity to irrigate forced a more complex organization on society, making men reluctant to move on to a new place within a few years.

The Nile was particularly suited to irrigation since it was regular in both the degree and the time of its flooding. The Egyptian farmer could count on the river rising soon after the middle of June and receding by October, right in the middle of the growing season when it was most essential to have adequate water. This regularity of the Nile derived from the fact that its sources were dependent upon the seasonal monsoon rains of central East Africa. Thus in the Nile valley it was possible with an organized society to plant crops in the receding flood water caught in man-made catch basins. During the rest of the year, the Egyptians irrigated their crops by lifting water from especially dug canals or from the river itself by buckets or by water wheels driven by human and sometimes animal power.

The Tigris and Euphrates rivers were less regular, more difficult to control. Both rose in the highlands of modern Turkey, fed by snow that melted gradually in some years and more rapidly in others. The Tigris especially, joined by several tributaries within two or three hundred miles of its mouth, often went out of control. The Nile, on the other hand, had no tributaries for over 1000 miles, and the natural barricades (the cataracts) moderated the force of the flood.

The agricultural revolution that made possible the more settled life also led to the production of a food surplus, a requisite for the development of cities. As long as man relied on hunting and fishing, the product of his efforts could not be preserved for any great length of time. Even a pastoral people could keep a supply of food available only as long as they could feed their animals. This problem had necessitated a migrant society where possessions were limited. When men turned to raising grain crops and settled down, they could store their surplus in bins and granaries and acquire possessions. The result was not only a greater population concentration but also a rapid increase in trade and commerce, particularly in the river valleys where communication and transportation were fairly easy. Trade, in fact, was a necessity, since however rich agriculturally these desert areas were, they lacked such resources as metal, timber, and even stone. To gain these scarce items, men used their surplus labor in manufacturing and began to buy or sell commodities. An inevitable result was the specialized workman, who practiced his trade or craft to the exclusion of other duties. Such concentration led to the development of the ever more specialized skills and techniques necessary for the production of high-quality merchandise which could be shipped abroad in exchange for raw materials and other commodities not available locally.

Unfortunately, the wealth made possible by surplus crops also attracted invaders who wanted to share or to control. Indeed, the archeological records of the ancient Near East are replete with evidence of captured and burned settlements. This constant threat of invasion forced the inhabitants of settled areas to draw closer, to organize themselves into ever more effective political units, in order to defend themselves. The result was the walled city, especially in Mesopotamia, which further concentrated activities such as manufacturing, trade, and the building of shrines. The more sophisticated organization necessary for the functioning of such communities soon enabled these people to dominate the surrounding countryside, which then came under their protection. All of these advances necessitated the keeping of records, which in turn led to the development of writing.

2

Gods, Kings, and Ancient Empires

Sumerian culture expanded rapidly until it came to dominate much of southern Iraq. This dominance, from the time when we can first begin to make something of their earliest written records until their language ceased to be spoken, lasted about a thousand years. Sumerian influence, however, continued long after the Sumerians had disappeared. The circle has 360 degrees and there are twelve hours in a day because the Sumerians said so, and so far no one has made it otherwise.

THE SUMERIAN CITIES

Although the population within the walled area seldom reached 20,000 people, the Sumerian cities were forerunners of the modern urban complex. Traditionally regarded as the home of Abraham, the best known of the ancient cities is Ur, located where the Euphrates then had its outlet. About 100 miles upstream was Kish, which was difficult to identify as a Sumerian city because it was actually located in Akkad, the home of the Semitic-speaking Akkadians, the linguistic ancestors of the modern Arabs and Jews. In all likelihood the Akkadians originally differed in both appearance and customs from the Sumerians, although their civilization became almost totally Sumerian. Further north lay Sippar and Eshnunna, both Akkadian, while Lagash, Nippur, Ereck (or Uruk), and Eridu were Sumerian. Mari in the west was a Sumerian outpost amidst a sea of Semites, as was Assur on the Tigris in the region that later produced the Assyrians.

At first these cities were small independent city-states ruled more or less democratically. This tentative democracy soon yielded to rule by war chiefs in alliance with the priestly class. Though every city had several different orders of priests, each dedicated to a different god, one priesthood and one deity always had precedence. In part, the prosperity of the city was dependent upon the good will of the god or gods. Great effort went into building elaborate ziggurats, man-made mountains with temples at the top. Attached to each temple was a complex of warehouses, factories, and houses for the scholars, priests, and slaves; these structures were surrounded by the city and by the irrigated land which yielded the resources necessary to support the god's establishment. Since the whole system was dedicated to gaining the approval of one god in particular and as many others as possible, and since landownership gravitated to the priesthood of the temples, the term "temple economy" is used to describe it.

Though we may find it difficult to understand a system that devoted so much of its energy to religious purposes, the Sumerian temple economy in its way fostered the development of conditions that made city living possible. In the beginning urbanization was radically different from the tribal society that had existed before. One of the first effects of the growing urban economy was the weakening of old patterns of kinship. People whose past experiences had been entirely regulated by conditions of birth found themselves in a new kind of society in which men were organized according to skill and occupation. This division of labor was and is a part of city life, although the longer cities existed the less radical the innovation seemed. Unfortunately, the advantages of a division of labor did not benefit all individuals equally. In fact, the first effect of urbanization on most people was to make them subject to a variety of forces over which they had little or no control. Many of their activities were regulated by the decisions of a few people who did not always possess either wisdom or good intentions. It was easier for men to accept these new arrangements as the acts of gods, an explanation that had also served a tribal society but that now became much more complex as an elaborate priesthood developed. Numerous gods and temples allowed contradictory actions to be explained in terms of competition among the rival gods.

The ability of the Sumerians to produce surplus crops meant that more men could be freed from farming to build, to fortify, and to beautify, as well as to trade. Relocated inside city walls, these people developed and perfected various specialized trades and crafts that were passed on to younger generations. The conversion of agricultural wealth into fabricated commodities meant that the new products could be traded or exchanged for other commodities and needs. One specialist who emerged was the scribe who kept track of the increasingly complicated transactions that took place in the city.

MUD AS A BUILDING AND WRITING MATERIAL

Sumerians were an inventive people. Lacking an adequate supply of timber and stone, they converted mud into sun-dried brick for use as building material. Walls made of such brick had the necessary thickness to support the heavy earth-covered roofs used by these people and in a hot country had the additional advantage of being reasonably cool. Sometimes the exteriors of buildings were protected from the rain by setting baked brick in asphalt, a substance also used for paving. Fuel, however, was scarce, and since most of what was available was reserved for the potters and metal workers, fired brick was not very plentiful.

Mud also served as a writing material; the clay tablet was, in fact, a small brick. Holding such a tablet in one hand, the scribe, using a reed with a triangular-shaped point for a stylus, covered the face with small,

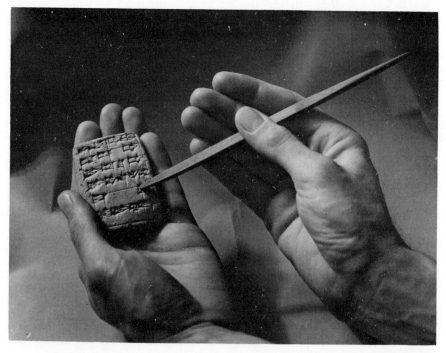

Demonstration of cuneiform writing, using a wedge-shaped stylus on a clay tablet. (Courtesy of the Oriental Institute, University of Chicago)

three-cornered signs. From this style the script is called cuneiform (Latin for wedge-shaped). Its utility is evident from the fact that it served as a common type of writing in the area for some 2500 years. The script began as a type of picture writing, and while it always retained certain pictographic elements, its most significant feature was the use of signs to represent syllables. Words could be "spelled out" by combining the proper syllables. Unfortunately, cuneiform did not progress sufficiently to develop an alphabet; thus learning to write remained the province of the specialist, who had to memorize several hundreds of these syllable symbols.

WAR AND KINGSHIP

To the ancient city-states of Mesopotamia, who were either fighting against one another or against the numerous intruding barbarians, war was seemingly endemic. As warfare grew in ferocity and deadliness, power in the cities ultimately fell to men who could command the troops, hold their loyalty, and keep them profitably occupied. In the records, a man of this type is called a *lugal*, a great man, or sometimes an *ensi*, a governor. We may, without being inaccurate, call such men kings. Success in the military field led to control of ever-larger areas, called empires, which were centered around the bigger or more prosperous cities.

Excavation of these cities in recent years has led to the accumulation of information about their leaders. Where we are able to give these men distinctive personalities, we find that they were not only conquerors but law-givers — a not unnatural combination, since a uniform law worked to hold the conquests together. The surviving ancient law codes shed considerable light on the problems of the time as well as on the individual conquerors. One of the earliest lawgivers was Urukagina of Lagash, but much better known is the Akkadian empire builder Sargon, who lived somewhat later. Sargon's kingdom, established about 2350 B.C., included a diversity of peoples, although it is not possible to say how large it actually was. This "first empire" survived for nearly 150 years, after which it fell to an invasion of the Guti people from the mountains east of Mesopotamia. In about 2050, rulers first of the city of Lagash, then of the city of Ur, laid the foundation for another Sumerian empire that is known as the Empire of the Third Dynasty of Ur. After about a century, it too fell prey to foreign invaders, this time the Amorites.

The Amorites came from Amurru, literally the lands of the west. Historians tend to look upon them as one more set of desert people who were attracted by the better-watered and more civilized regions of the fertile crescent, the steppe lands stretching from Jerusalem north through Syria, eastward across the Euphrates, and south beyond the Tigris. A few of these invaders moved into Egypt, but since Egypt could be reached only by crossing long stretches of desert, most of the migrant peoples followed the easier path into the Tigris-Euphrates valley. Like other invaders, the Amorites soon acquired the trappings of civilization, adopting Sumerian mythology and technology and changing from invaders to promoters and defenders of civilization. The center of Amorite power was the city of Babylon, which became the center of an empire larger than any that had preceded it and which gave its name to the whole area. The most famous ruler of the Babylonian Empire was Hammurabi, whose collection of laws represents the outstanding achievement of the period. These laws were carved into a column seven feet high of black diorite that was uncovered in 1902 by a French archeological team.

The publicity that resulted from this discovery gave Hammurabi, his empire, and his laws somewhat more attention than they warrant. His empire was not very durable, and while his laws are the most complete that have come down to us, they were certainly not the earliest. The laws are significant, however, because they represent a sophisticated approach to problems in their attempt to impose social order by establishing uniform procedures and policies.

The same kind of sophistication is evident in the literature of the Sumerians, who early produced epics, tales, love poems, and annals, as well as more specific medical prescriptions, mathematical texts, and law and trial records. The great pieces of Sumerian literature, however, were composed during the twelfth and eleventh centuries B.C., long after the fall of Hammuraki's empire. This is the period when the two epics *Enuma Elish* and *Gilgamesh* were written, both of which are literary masterpieces. The *Enuma Elish*, the story of creation, explains how Marduk shared in the creation of the universe and became the supreme god in Babylonia. Though later conquering peoples substituted other gods for Marduk, the epic remained an essential part of the culture of Mesopotamia. The *Gilgamesh* deals with even more important issues than the *Enuma Elish* as it examines the question of why man must suffer and die. The story of the flood in the narrative appears later in the story of Noah, but the moral is quite different from the Biblical one. The conclusion of the *Gilgamesh* is that all men must die and only by his own efforts can man survive at all.

The Sumerians also demonstrated skill in their arts and handicrafts. Their accomplishments in this area are particularly evident in their cylinder seals and carved gem stones. The metal work of these people also reflects their artistic sensibility. They seem to have been most effective in miniature work, however, although perhaps we are more conscious of this technique because it has survived while somewhat larger works of art were very likely destroyed during the constant periods of invasion and war. Indeed, the only architectural structures that have survived so that we can reconstruct them are the ziggurats.

THE CIVILIZATION OF EGYPT

Contemporary with the Sumerians and Akkadians in Mesopotamia was the Pyramid Age of Egypt, otherwise known as the Old Kingdom, which extended from about 2700 to 2200 B.C. Egyptian civilization was quite different from that of Mesopotamia, and part of the difference can be explained by the geographical setting. Egypt was more naturally defensible, so that it had long periods of peace. The regularity of the Nile made irrigation much simpler than in the Tigris-Euphrates valley. Moreover, observers stationed upstream could predict the height the flood would reach, thereby making possible large-scale governmental organization to prepare for the rising water. The deserts hemming in the Nile valley made centralized control seem a logical development, since the population was concentrated in a narrow cultivated strip. Most of the needs of an ancient people were near at hand, or not too far away by boat, so that the cities did not become as commercially dominant or as strong as they did in Mesopotamia. The major scarcities in Egypt were copper, which it had to import from the Sinai Peninsula or Cyprus, and timber, which it received from Syria. The organization of the large-scale ventures that were necessary to ship quantities of these materials over such distances was usually beyond the capacity of any one city. All of these geographic factors tended to foster one-man rule in the person of the pharaoh. The title pharaoh comes from an Egyptian term referring to the monarchy as the "great house." Manetho, a priest who wrote a history of Egypt in Greek in about 300 B.C., recorded the rule of some thirty successive dynasties of pharaohs. We now know that many of these dynasties were not successive, in fact, that in some periods several dynasties in various parts of the country were in power at the same time. Yet despite these inaccuracies, Manetho's system of indicating divisions of Egyptian history is still in use.

Manetho believed that the first king of the first dynasty was Menes. We know little about Menes, or for that matter about the sixteen or eighteen other rulers who make up the first two dynasties. Both dynasties preceded what we call the Old Kingdom. We do know that it was during the period of these rulers that two kingdoms, a southern one in the Nile valley and a northern one in the delta, were brought together under the ruler of the southern kingdom to establish a single state. Unification for Egypt appears to have been a painful process, one that however inevitable and logical it seems to us, may have resulted from the activities of foreign adventurers who earlier had made contact with Sumer. If we accept this possibility, we can resolve several matters concerning early Egyptian civilization that puzzle modern historians, for example, why Sumerian-type cylinder seals have been found in Egypt, why the Egyptians utilized brick in ways reminiscent of the Sumerians, and why Egyptian writing appeared almost fully formed without any evidence of earlier development. All we can now say for certain is that regardless of how unification occurred or how Sumerian influences reached Egypt, the Egyptians soon developed an unexampled prosperity that led them to believe they were a particularly fortunate people.

THE PYRAMID BUILDERS

With only slight exaggeration we can say that the Old Kingdom Egyptian could imagine no problem that had not been solved. He knew with almost absolute certainty that his way was the right way, and this attitude is reflected in both his religious and his political beliefs. The ruler of Egypt was not the high priest of the god, he was a god. Divinity to the Egyptians, however, did not imply a necessary perfection of behavior but rather possession of superior abilities. The Egyptians did not make the modern distinction between the human and the divine, nor did they differentiate between the animate and the inanimate. The Nile was as much a living thing as a palm tree or a bird. The pharaohs who united the two lands (and who wore a double crown to symbolize this achievement) were worshipped as gods who had brought stability, security, and prosperity to Egypt.

By the third dynasty, the Egyptians had attained an impressive mastery over their environment. Their influence extended up the Nile to modern Sudan, west into Libya, and eastward into Asia to include Sinai and the coastal parts of Palestine and Syria. They had access to resources that were not available in their own valley, and they had perfected their skills in working with metal, textiles, wood, and especially stone. They had the ingenuity to manufacture a kind of paper out of the readily available papyrus reed; they were able to set their pyramids with geometrical precision; they could handle monoliths weighing hundreds of tons without wheeled vehicles, axles, cranes, or pulleys; and they could quarry, dress, and carve many varieties of stone, including granite. Politically they demonstrated an organizational ability unmatched by their contemporaries, perhaps best evidenced in the building of the pyramids, which required the coordinated labor of thousands and thousands of men. Particularly important to modern students is the Egyptian writing system, based on hieroglyphs (Greek for "sacred carvings"), which when it was deciphered in the nineteenth century opened up a direct channel of communication with the past.

The characteristic architectural structure of Egypt is the pyramid, yet the pyramid was only one of several types of tombs built by these people. The largest pyramids were built during the third and fourth dynasties (2700–2500 B.C.), but smaller ones were also built in later times. Best known of the several dozen pyramids that have survived is a complex of three in the Cairo suburb of Giza near the site of ancient Memphis. These three were built within seventy years of each other in the fourth dynasty. Largest of the group is the pyramid of Khufu, called Cheops by the Greeks, the second pharaoh of the dynasty. Originally 482 feet high, it covers thirteen acres and contains about 2,300,000 blocks of stone averaging two and a half tons each. Even more impressive than its size is the accuracy of the workmanship and the engineering skill that went into its construction. The base, for example, is almost perfectly square, oriented to the points of the compass almost with jeweler's precision.

Though meant as tombs, the pyramids were also part of a temple complex. In the construction of the temples the Egyptians solved the architectural problem of spanning or roofing over a large area. Most of the early temples had a long and narrow hall (sometimes two), the roof of which was supported by pillars that towered over the main walls. This arrangement resulted in clerestory that left room for win-

Egyptian temple, XIX Dynasty (1350–1205 B.C.). Model of Hypostyle Hall, Temple of Karnak. (The Metropolitan Museum of Art, Purchase, 1890, Levi Hale Willard Bequest)

dows between the two roof levels. Behind the temple was a series of small sanctuaries containing statues of the *ka*, the vital force or personality present in men during life and after death. The *ka* statues were given individualized features, but otherwise, unless the subject had some outstanding physical characteristic (such as obesity), they were highly stylized figures in stiff frontal poses. Many of the tombs surrounding the pyramids also included highly colored wall paintings, which were somewhat more natural that the statuary, probably because artists were used to painting decorations in houses. Still they were stylized. Painted figures were shown with face in profile, though the eyes were full face and the shoulders were to the front. Hips and legs were then in profile, making an impossible pose but one that is repeated over and over. Death and perspective were totally absent in Egyptian painting; people of higher rank or importance were always shown larger than lesser persons, with a pharaoh towering over all.

Each temple complex included lands, and each was staffed by priests and other officials who maintained temple services. The largest of the temple structures was centered around the oldest pyramid, the stepped pyramid of Zoser, a pharaoh of the third dynasty. Some pharaohs had two pyramids as well as other tombs built in various sections of Egypt. Those that were not actually used for interment are called cenotaphs. Tomb building, in fact, was an obsession for the Egyptians. They were so certain that life in the next world would be as full and satisfying as life in this one that they equipped their tombs with their valued possessions. Because of this practice, modern man has been able to learn a great deal about how the Egyptians lived and what they believed.

The ancient Egyptian does not appear to have been a particularly curious person. He liked this world enough to hope it would go on forever, and probably for this reason he took little interest in speculative or philosophical reasoning. He expected his pharaoh to create all of the excellent features of this life in the next. Since the Egyptian of the Old Kingdom trusted his ruler in all worldly matters, he seems to have had no difficulty in believing the pharaoh would competently manage affairs in the hereafter. The loyal subject who had conscientiously served his lord and himself to the benefit of both could expect to do so forever and ever. In such a system, death thus lost some of its sting.

DISINTEGRATION OF THE OLD KINGDOM — RISE OF THE MIDDLE KINGDOM

The Egyptian's comfortable viewpoint was rudely shaken when the Old Kingdom disintegrated soon after 2000 B.C. at the end of the sixth dynasty. While the details of this downfall are obscure, the reasons seem clear. Even though kings may be thought divine, some are clearly better than others. Disputed successions or even lack of successors allowed related families or other notables to establish themselves locally as privileged magnates with hereditary exemptions from royal interference. A succession of weak monarchs gradually lost their power as well as their revenues. Moreover, the continual erection of tombs and temples, together with the necessary endowments, built up a burdensome drain on finances. The disintegration of the monarchy so shook the faith of the Egyptians that never again did they feel as confident or as certain as they had in the Old Kingdom. There was always the possibility that the god-king who could fail in this world might do so in the next. It was even possible for such a god to forget his faithful retainers and loyal subjects. An obvious next step was for the individual to do something about his own salvation instead of depending upon his ruler. Wealthy Egyptians began to build elaborate tombs and chapels of their own, while the poor were perhaps fortunate only in having little time to worry about such matters.

Egypt was once again reunited around the year 200 B.C. by the hereditary princes of Thebes in Upper Egypt (near modern Luxor) who established the eleventh dynasty. The 200-year reign of six pharaohs of this and the twelfth dynasties is known as the Middle Kingdom. Never so powerful as the Old Kingdom monarchs — though the nobility was far more powerful — the rulers of the twelfth dynasty nevertheless re-established the Sinai mining operations and reopened the country's trade connections on the Mediterranean and Red seas and south into Nubia. The architectural achievements of the Middle Kingdom are not particularly impressive, although tombs, temples, and pyramids continued to be built, with many more tombs erected for individuals than in the preceding period. Particularly striking is the relief sculpture and painting in the tombs, which were also filled with small-scale figures of men, boats, animals, and buildings that were carved and colored with exacting realism. Glassmaking also developed, and artists used the medium to make small statues. The dominant achievement of the period, however, was in literature, and the Middle Kingdom is considered to be the golden age of ancient Egyptian literature. Letters and hymns abound, but the most interesting literary survivals are the examples of the so-called wisdom literature advising listeners how to get ahead, much in the manner of Benjamin Franklin later in America. Many such sayings were ascribed to Ptahhotap, an Old Kingdom figure around whom had gathered many legends. Also popular were tales of adventure and magic that were composed not only for entertainment but for moral education and indoctrination. One of these, *The Two Brothers,* is reminiscent of the Biblical story of Joseph, while another brings to mind the adventures of Sinbad the Sailor. As wealth accumulated, arts and manufacturing flourished, and Egyptians began once again to hope that the good life would prove permanent.

INNOVATION AND INVASION

During the period of the second millennium, when Hammurabi was king in Babylonia and the Egyptian twelfth dynasty was in its prime, civilization in Egypt and Mesopotamia seemingly found a groove in which it ran for centuries. Further innovation seems to have been forced upon these areas by outsiders rather than to have come from indigenous needs or impulses. As internal problems mounted, there was a growing spirit of hopeless resignation coupled with a determination to cling to past glories rather than to strive for new ones, to find refuge in the next world rather than to face the reality of this one.

Time after time there were rude awakenings as new groups of invaders moved into the settled lands. In the first half of the second millennium appeared the Indo-European–speaking peoples, the ancestors of modern Europeans as well as the Aryans of India. We know that these invaders came from central Asia or eastern Europe, bringing with them the use of the horse and chariot in warfare. This gave them a tactical advantage until the peoples whom they threatened adopted this new weapon also. Some of the horse and chariot people, called Hyksos by the Egyptians, took possession of Syria and Palestine in about 1750 B.C. and then followed this conquest by taking Egypt itself, or at least the northern part of Egypt. Another group, the Kassites, gained control over Babylonia, where they retained power for nearly four centuries, until about 1200 B.C. We know a great deal more about the Kassites than about the Hyksos, largely because they became closely integrated into Sumerian civilization and adopted it as their own. A third horse-owning people were the Hurrians, who created a kingdom called Mitanni, which included Assyria and territory at least as far to the west as the Euphrates. In 1365 B.C., the power of the Hurrians was broken by the Hittites, still another group of invaders who settled in Anatolia.

THE HITTITES

The Hitties were more successful than the Hurrians, the Kassites, and the Hyksos in preserving a cultural identity, in part because they occupied lands that had not previously been organized under any central administration. Their capital was Hattusas, near present-day Boghazkeui in the north central part of Anatolia. Though the Hittites had captured Babylon in about 1590 B.C., they were soon supplanted in that area by the Kassites. From this and other contacts, however, Mesopotamia became a dominating influence on the Hittites. They borrowed the cuneiform script, wrote on clay tablets, and developed religious ideas as well as law codes similar to those of the Akkadians and Sumerians. Their art and architecture, however, are uniquely their own. Particularly remarkable are their stone fortresses.

The Hittite empire, which lacked any real geographical identity, survived only because of the skill of these people in war and government. In spite of the fact that their agricultural production was not very great and that as a people they were not very populous, the Hittites remained a power for some two centuries. Shortly after 1200 B.C., however, their main Anatolian territories were overrun by other groups of newcomers. Several small Hittite centers survived in northern Syria for some centuries until they were conquered by the Assyrians. It has only been during the past few decades that historians have come to recognize the importance of the Hittites, and this realization has forced a reassessment of previous suppositions about the Near East. One major shift in thinking was brought about when linguists discovered that the Hittites spoke an Indo-European language. This discovery meant that Indo-Europeans had appeared much earlier in the Near East than had previously been assumed and had played an influential role in civilizing these areas instead of just conquering them. Eventually all of the ancient centers of civilization came under the control of one or another group of Indo-Europeans, either the Persians, the Greeks, or the Indo-Iranians (the Aryans of India).

THE EGYPTIAN EMPIRE

Egypt itself dominated much of the Near East during the Hittite period of influence. In the first quarter of the sixteenth century B.C., a native Theban prince of the seventeenth dynasty named Ka-mose managed to adopt the weapons of the Hyksos and begin the task of reuniting Egypt. His successors of the eighteenth dynasty succeeded not only in expelling the foreign invader but in launching punitive expeditions beyond the Egyptian frontiers into Syria. In about 1450 B.C., under the leadership of Thut-mose III, the Egyptians took possession of Palestine and Syria, establishing direct royal control in that area for the first time. This outward expansion of Egypt during the New Kingdom or Empire period forced the Egyptians to change their outlook toward the non-Egyptian world.

Up to this time the Egyptians had not been a military people and regarded war only as an occasional adventure. Conquest and the wide-flung obligations and contacts that it implied were alien to the Egyptian experience. Moreover, Egypt's expansion coincided with a period when the Egyptians were beginning to doubt the power and good will of their pharaoh god to watch over the land. Perhaps as a result of this disenchantment, the Empire period was marked by a pervasive restlessness and anxiety. Babylonians and Hittites adjusted to a world permeated by threats and haunted by danger, but there was nothing in the Egyptian background to prepare them for this type of living. They lacked the laws as well as the complex administrative procedures to cope with the problems of alien peoples. To cover this weakness they erected an empressive facade.

Under such conditions the Empire was a paradox, representing both the brilliant and the dismal. Temples and tombs were built with a magnificence never before attempted. The largest of these, the great temple at Karnak (modern Luxor), was continually expanded until Roman times, when it covered some sixty-two acres of ground. Still standing today is a forest of heavy columns of different ages and design. Unfortunately, the buildings of the empire at times seem as if they were shallow boasts of past greatness, since they were often carelessly designed and the parts that did not show were shoddily executed. Even the pharaohs seemed to imply that it was only form that mattered, for they robbed their predecessors' monuments to build their own, which in turn were robbed by both their contemporaries and their successors. Only the tomb of the young Tutenankh-amen was undisturbed until our own time.

Until this period, Egyptian society had always been characterized by a strong adherence to principles of right, best expressed by the Egyptian word *ma'at,* meaning "right thinking," that is, thinking which is in harmony with Egyptian concepts of the functioning of the universe. In an earlier Egypt, a man "thought right" because there was no cause for him to think otherwise; everyone knew what was expected of him, and the relative stability of Nile civilization did not encourage change. In the Empire period, as a result of greater diversity, as well as because of a continued insistance on outmoded principles, *ma'at* became almost irrelevant as each person defined the term according to his own interest. Though the Egyptians officially denied this was happening, everyone who had an opportunity to do so tried to equip himself for his own passage beyond the grave instead of depending upon the pharaoh. Under these conditions, *ma'at* was little more than a facade behind which the ills of the Empire progressed without remedy or hindrance until only a shell of greatness remained.

AKH-EN-ATON

The one attempt to change existing conditions was the rather curious religious movement led by Amenhotep IV, whose queen was the famous Nefertiti. Several years after his accession (about 1350 B.C.), Amenhotep, the beloved of the god Amen, moved his capital from Thebes to Akhet-aton, or Amarna, about 200 miles down river. At the same time he changed his name to Akh-en-aton, signifying his devotion to something called the Aton, which still remains somewhat mysterious and beyond our understanding. Much interest has been shown in the religious changes of Akh-en-aton, partly because some early scholars saw them as an attempt to establish a "true" monotheistic religion in Egypt, a sort of forerunner of Judaism. As scholars delved deeper into the period, it became clear that this was not the case; in fact, Akh-en-aton's motivations were probably as much political as religious. The most impressive effect of his short-lived challenge to the status quo was in art, especially painting, which made a radical shift toward a more naturalistic representation of royalty, a subject that until then had been regarded as sacred. Instead of the massive austerity and the formidable presence of the earlier representations, members of the royal family were now shown engaged in everyday domestic activities. The new principles of Aton, whatever they were, did not long survive their founder, who died in middle age without leaving a son to succeed him. His son-in-law, a child by the name of Tut-ankhaton, was taken back to Thebes from Amarna by opponents of Akh-en-aton. Before he died eight years later he had changed his name to Tutenankhamen, formally marking the end of the Amarna "reformation" and the re-establishment of Amen and his priests.

EGYPT AFTER AKH-EN-ATON

During the reign of Akh-en-aton, Egypt's Asiatic empire began to crumble. The rising Hittite power easily weaned the nearby states of North Syria from dependence on the pharaoh, while desert tribes, always prone to harass frontier outposts, stepped up their attacks on the extended frontiers until Egyptian influence in Palestine was reduced to almost nothing. A revival began under Seti I, a king of the early nineteenth dynasty, who temporarily restored Egyptian power in Palestine as well as in parts of Syria. His successor was Ramses II, the pharaoh who according to tradition was the oppressor of the Hebrews at the time of Moses. Even in ancient times Ramses became an almost legendary figure. He was noted for his great building schemes that resulted in the erection of a number of grandiose temples and monuments to serve as reminders of his glory. While he boasted of much more than he actually accomplished, Ramses nevertheless managed to secure a permanent peace between the Hittites and the Egyptians.

A few years after his death, in about 1250 B.C., Egypt overcame a dangerous invasion from the west, the effort in part at least of a movement of marauders known as the Sea Peoples. Egyptian and Hittite records both refer to these invaders, and they seem to have been the cause of the overthrow of the Hittites. Egypt was more fortunate, although the attacks lasted into the reign of Ramses III, a king of the twentieth dynasty, who defeated a combined land and sea operation from the direction of Asia that also included people known as the Peleste (or Philistines in the Bible). Though none of the Peleste penetrated Egypt, they secured a foothold in Palestine and gave their name to that region.

Ramses III, the last pharaoh of any major significance, was murdered in about 1165 B.C. after some thirty years of rule. Egypt then entered into a period of troubles. The army, comprised in large part of foreign mercenaries, contended for power with the Theban priesthood, grown richer and more powerful than the government itself. Foreign kings from Libya reigned in various parts of the land for two centuries, followed in the eighth century B.C. by Ethiopian rulers, who were in turn

Head of a king, probably Ramses II, wearing the war helmet. Egyptian, XIX Dynasty, broken in ancient times from a life-sized statue. (The Metropolitan Museum of Art, Rogers Fund, 1934)

conquered by the Assyrians in 670 B.C. After this period came the "Saitic" revival of the twenty-sixth dynasty, when a line of pharaohs from the delta city of Sais expelled the foreign rulers and united Egypt. This last bit of glory lasted about a century until the arrival of the Persians in 525 B.C.

THE ASSYRIANS

While Egypt built only one empire, the peoples of the Tigris-Euphrates region saw the coming and going of several, but none of the conquerors were as feared as the Assyrians. Originally part of the Akkadian Empire, the Assyrians had remained little noticed until the Amorites under Hammurabi had forced a redirection in trade routes through Assur, the chief city of the Assyrians. Any people in control of this trade commanded great resources, but not until the destruction of the Mittanian rule by the Hittites did Assyrian influence begin to increase. Predominance was assured when the Assyrians developed an effective military machine armed with iron weapons.

War had always been part of the life of the Assyrians. In an exposed and unprotected homeland, they had to be good fighters in order to survive. By the ninth century they had learned how to employ iron weapons effectively, one of the first peoples to do so. Once the process for making iron had been invented in eastern Anatolia, it was found that iron was cheaper and made better-cutting implements than copper or bronze. The Assyrians learned from their subject peoples how to employ mounted horsemen as a supplement to chariots and archers, and they also developed special siege machinery for capturing fortified towns. All of these military innovations worked to the advantage of offensive operations. The Assyrians quickly learned that war could be a profitable enterprise. Their empire grew larger than any that had preceded it, extending over all of Mesopotamia, into northeastern Anatolia (Armenia), throughout the whole of Syria and Palestine, and for a time into Egypt. The wealth of the subject territories was carried to Assyria, where it was used to rebuild the cities in a magnificent style.

Once the Assyrians had conquered an area, they did not hesitate to practice wholesale deportation and dispersion of subject peoples to keep down possible rebellion. Either for their own edification or to frighten subject peoples, they filled annals with gory accounts of executions and mass mutilations. Still, they temporarily brought the Near East under unified control, and the result was increased trade and the growth of wealth and luxury.

Much of the Assyrian wealth went into buildings and art. The palaces and temples built by the Assyrian kings, especially those at

Nineveh, the capital established by Sennacherib around 700 B.C., were treasure houses, their walls carved with pictures and texts recording the feats of the kings in warfare and hunting. Carved ivory reliefs were also made in quantity. Assyrian artists were particularly adept at portraying animals, and many of their huge human-headed winged bulls are now in Western museums. The engineering knowledge that was applied to war could also be applied to peacetime tasks, and the Assyrians proceeded to systematically lay out and construct new cities. Even though they often seemed to their contemporaries to be destroyers of civilization, they ended up as its preservers. Indeed, even the Assyrian practice of mass deportation increased the spread and assimilation of new ideas and customs. The Assyrian ruler Assurbanipal is particularly important for the great library he established at Nineveh, in which he attempted to gather together the whole body of cuneiform writing to consolidate the literary heritage of Babylonia. The discovery of this library in 1853 and the subsequent transfer to the British Museum of 22,000 tablets have provided modern scholars with a prime source of information about the ancient world.

After the death of Assurbanipal the Assyrian Empire disintegrated. Citizen farmers had in the beginning furnished the main strength of the army, but as the empire expanded, more men were required to police and govern the conquered lands than the Assyrians had. Though the Assyrians did not hesitate to meet revolt with mass extermination, their opponents grew more numerous, and in 612 B.C. they were defeated by the accumulated might of their neighbors and former subjects. The leaders in the overthrow were the Babylonians, assisted by some Indo-European allies, mostly Medes from Iran. Assyrian history ended abruptly and almost completely. This was partly due to a revival of power in southern Mesopotamia, but also partly to a conscious rejection of Assyrian methods and ideas on the part of their former subjects. The Assyrians, however, had demonstrated the economic advantage of a large political unit, and their various successors tried to unite the ancient Near East again but without rousing the antagonism that the Assyrians had.

NEO-BABYLONIAN EMPIRE

Succeeding the Assyrian Empire in Mesopotamia was the Second Babylonian, sometimes called the Neo-Babylonian, or in the Bible as well as in older history books, the Chaldean Empire. Within a few years this empire had absorbed most of the Assyrian territories in western Assia. The second king of the Neo-Babylonian dynasty was Nebuchadnezzar, more correctly called Nebuchadrezzar, who is still remembered for taking many Jews back to Babylon after he had conquered Palestine and Syria. With his wealth he made Babylon even more magnificent than Nineveh had been, and the city became the home of one of the seven wonders of the ancient world, the famous hanging gardens. Babylon also had the largest population, covered the greatest area, and boasted the strongest walls of any city up to its time. Although the Persian capture of the city in 539 B.C. made its days as capital of an empire short, Babylon continued to be an intensely urban, culturally stimulating place to live. None of the kings of Neo-Babylonia Empire was able to extend his control as far as the Assyrians had done, nor did any of them seem to realize the rising dangers from their former allies, the Medes and the Persians.

THE PERSIANS

It was Indo-European–speaking inhabitants of Iran, known as the Persians, who attained the apex of imperialism in the ancient Orient. These people, who lived in the area around the Persian Gulf, adjacent to ancient Elam, had nominally been vassals of the Medes, a closely related people who had a large kingdom in western Iran and eastern Anatolia. Under the leadership of Cyrus the Great, a king who was a gifted soldier and organizer, the Persians incorporated the Medes in 550 B.C. and moved across Anatolia to the Aegean Sea, destroying the kingdom of Lydia and conquering a group of Greek cities on the coast. Still another Indo-European people, the Lydians, had settled near valuable deposits of electrum, a natural alloy of gold and silver. By casting small pieces of metal in standard weights with the appropriate value stamped on each, they became among the first, if not the first, people to use coins, and their invention spread rapidly.

After annexing Babylon, Cyrus moved eastward to the borders of modern India and northward into the steppes of southern Siberia (Russian Turkestan). His empire thus became nearly three times the size of the old Assyrian Empire, and it grew still larger with the annexation of Syria, Palestine, and finally Egypt. Within a few years of Cyrus' death there were widespread revolts, but Persian control over this enormous empire was reasserted by Darius the Great, a successor of Cyrus who ruled for forty years. Despite its huge size, its diverse peoples, the primitive and backward character of many of its inhabitants, and numerous other seemingly insurmountable obstacles to unity, the Persian Empire remained intact for a century and a half following Darius' death; it was finally overthrown by the military genius of Alexander the Great.

The Persians offer a startling contrast to the Assyrians. Characteristic of Persian rule was a judicious policy of conciliation. Cyrus, as a grandson of the king of Media, was able to lay legitimate claim to the rulership of that kingdom. Perhaps influenced by the success of his policy in Media, Cyrus endeavored to present himself as a superior ruler, a magnanimous overlord, a bringer of order and stability into each territory he conquered. Persian conquerors did not burn down cities, ravage, plunder, or massacre, nor did they attempt to arrogate to themselves all of the privileges of conquerors. Not only did they honor the gods of other groups but they allowed conquered peoples considerable autonomy in managing their local affairs.

Darius the Great modified the character of Persian rule by restricting the top administrative and military posts to Persians. Because the empire was so large — and the Persians not very numerous — individual Persians could acquire great wealth as administrators. To prevent any single official from becoming as powerful as the king, the empire was divided into·provinces, each under the authority of an official called *satrap* who represented the king. A second royal official commanded the military forces, while a third collected the king's revenues. To further weaken the *satrap,* his secretary was appointed by the king. In addition, a system was set up whereby royal representatives traveled throughout the empire as inspectors. To facilitate the coming and going of these inspectors, as well as to speed up the movement of troops to trouble spots, the Persian monarchs became major road builders. Their roads, which in part were based on earlier Assyrian ones, were equipped with post stations to supply horses and other needs to the royal couriers. The roads also facilitated trade and commerce, which not only increased wealth but also helped to spread the material and intellectual achievements of the old urban centers of Mesopotamia and Syria. No empire before, and few since, have approached the Persian Empire in the extent of benefits achieved for subject populations.

Historians have often pondered why the Persians, who had less experience with civilization than numerous other peoples in the ancient Near East, could have been such able managers of a civilized society. One explanation is the influence of the Zoroastrian religious ideals on Persian conduct. Zoroastrianism was based on the teachings of Zoroaster, an almost legendary Iranian who might have lived about 600 B.C. Before Zoroaster the Persians, like other ancient pagans, worshipped numerous gods who differed in various ways, but each of them represented both good and evil. In contrast to this view, Zoroaster's approach was to classify all gods into two groups, the good ones and the evil ones (demons); he then made the rather logical recommendation that men serve the good ones. Usually this Zoroastrian dualism is expressed as the contrast between light and darkness, each of which is striving for mastery. Man's business in the world was to work for the better cause — though obviously which cause is the better is not always easy to determine. To make a wise choice a man must exercise judgment, and since there should be some sort of reward for those who choose right and punishment for those who choose wrong, a system of rewards and punishments was implicit. Ultimately, this could mean that man would be urged to be good, that he would choose right not out of conviction but for fear of the consequences. Whether because of conviction or for hope of salvation, the Persians turned out to be sane and effective rulers.

3

The Hebrews

The ancient Hebrews, the people of the Bible, are at the same time very well known to us and very poorly understood by us. The cause of this paradox is the Bible itself, which, while it describes in detail how its authors felt about the world, does not always say who was doing the thinking or in what period a particular episode was being recorded. Our lack of understanding is further complicated by the fact that the Bible has been revised, recopied, and tampered with. While many Egyptian and Babylonian records remain today as they were carved into stone walls, inscribed on clay tablets, or preserved on papyrus in the dry climate of Egypt, the original records of the ancient Hebrews have long ago vanished. Only copies of copies remain. Moreover, the Bible is highly selective. Its transmitters, who were for the most part parochial in outlook, chose to include some episodes and to neglect others, to ignore or repress certain incidents and to edit carefully the remaining ones. Thus, though we can draw independent judgments about the Babylonians or the Egyptians from archeological remains, with the ancient Hebrews we are forced to think more or less as the Hebrews did.

HEBREW ORIGINS

Palestine, also called Israel or the Holy Land, is Egypt's nearest neighbor in Asia. Beyond it to the north lies Syria, a larger and richer territory that often exercised dominion over it. In the Old Testament, Palestine is usually called Canaan and its people Canaanites. The

Bible emphasizes, however, that the Hebrews, who also lived in this area, were not Canaanites but rather Israelites. Unfortunately for modern scholars, in ancient times the terms "Hebrew" and "Israelite" did not always mean the same thing. When Abraham's descendants first made claim to being "Hebrews," the term seems to have meant "wanderers." Later, when they had become a settled people, the Hebrews were identified as the people who spoke Hebrew. Linguistically, however, Hebrew was the same as Canaanite, a fact that makes the whole situation a matter of scholarly debate.

An increasing number of scholars now believe that "Israel" started out as a geographic term, derived from the name Jezreal, the city that was the first Palestine home of the wandering people who came to be called Israelites. Originally these early Israelites were Indo-European participants in the Hyksos and Hurrian migrations who chose to settle down in Palestine and adopt the local Semitic language and culture. They retained a sense of being somewhat different from the original Canaanites, however, and it is just this sense of being different that has caused so much confusion concerning their origins.

EGYPTIAN INFLUENCE

It seems that the Hebrews would naturally have been strongly influenced by Egypt, their powerful neighbor and sometime ruler of Palestine. While there were some direct borrowings from Egypt, the Hebrews felt antipathy to most things Egyptian. This hostility is evident in the Old Testament accounts of the Hebrews being forced to live and work in Egypt against their will. Though the Biblical narrative may be exaggerated, there is no reason to doubt that a least some Hebrews were held as slaves in Egypt for long periods of time. Moreover, these captives would have become subject to even more oppressive conditions in the thirteenth century B.C. when Egypt was threatened by internal dissension and external invasion. At any rate, the tyranny of the pharaoh became part of the Hebrew tradition.

The man who is credited with terminating Egyptian oppression was Moses, whose career has been overlaid with folklore: he was a worker of miracles, a man of the people but also a prince raised in the Egyptian royal household, an exile who had lived for many years in the desert, a prophet. Moses is almost unique among ancient heroes in that instead of leading his people to victory he led them to freedom, first to the Sinai Peninsula and then eventually, under his successors, to Canaan, the promised land. In the process, Moses taught the Israelites the worship of Yahweh and provided them with the Mosaic code, a vast body of law more influenced by Canaanite and Mesopotamian principles than Egyptian.

THE STRUGGLE FOR PALESTINE

The next stage in Hebrew history remains obscure. Historians think that the whole area of Palestine and Syria was undergoing a period of anarchy as a result of the decline of Egyptian control. Several different factions of peoples struggled to become dominant. Among these were the Philistines (also known as Peleste), an Indo-European–speaking people whose possession of iron weapons, coupled with a strong military tradition, tended to give them an advantage over the native inhabitants. During the eleventh century they controlled all of Palestine except for some of the hill country in the general area of Jerusalem. Along the northern coast were the Phoenicians, who had access to the valuable cedars of Lebanon. They were skilled in shipbuilding, glassmaking, and the manufacturing of textiles. The Phoenicians were particularly renowned for their purple woolens, the dye for which they derived from a shellfish. From their ports of Tyre and Sidon, the Phoenicians sent out colonies into the western Mediterranean, establishing numerous cities, the greatest and most famous of which was Carthage, and into the Atlantic, where they established Cadiz in what is now Spain.

Closely related to the Phoenicians were the Aramaeans, groups of Semitic-speaking desert nomads who had turned from wandering and plundering to commerce and urban living. These people became dominant in eastern Syria in the twelfth century, where they developed Sumerian-type city-states, including Samal, Damascus, Hamath, and Arped. The Aramaeans (or perhaps it was the Phoenicians) invented the alphabet, a development that made both writing and reading much simpler to learn. Aramaean business and professional men soon secured such a monopoly of communication through their utilization of this invention that Aramaic continued to be written and spoken long after the Aramaean state had disappeared.

ISRAEL

Against this background the Hebrews began their slow and difficult conquest of Canaan. During the long periods of invasions, battles, and settlement, there was a blending of the migrants from Egypt with the older inhabitants of the area into tribal units. Leaders of these units were called judges. As the Hebrews consolidated their occupation, they were faced with more powerful enemies in the form of the Philistines, and it was this threat that forced them to consolidate their forces under one man, a king. The founding of the kingdom of Israel took place somewhere around 1025 B.C. among a small faction of mountain people known as the tribe of Benjamin. King Saul was the first acknowledged monarch, and for most of his reign he fought the Philistines in an effort to maintain his kingdom's independence. Saul was succeeded by his rival David, who had so strongly opposed him that he had gone into exile and served as a Philistine commander. After several years of fighting, David emerged as undisputed king of Israel. The eastern and southern nomads were brought under his jurisdiction, and through cultivating good relations with the Phoenicians, the kingdom began to prosper. The seizure of Jerusalem from its Canaanite inhabitants gave David a strong, fortified capital, where his son and successor, Solomon, constructed a palace and a temple. After Solomon's death, the northern two-thirds of the kingdom seceded.

The northern kingdom, which kept the name Israel, is sometimes referred to as Samaria from its leading town of that name. It was the most advanced culturally of the two kingdoms, closer to Phoenicia (and other civilized areas), more fertile, and better watered. Much of its importance came from the fact that two caravan routes, one from the Red Sea to Tyre and Sidon and one from Damascus to Egypt, crossed each other within its borders. As a result, Israel was more open to outside influences as well as to covetous conquerors. Still, the kingdom managed to survive as a separate state until 722 B.C., when it was destroyed by the Assyrians and its peoples dispersed. Judah, the much smaller southern kingdom, escaped the horrors of Assyrian occupation because of its comparative isolation. Centered in the mountainous region west of the Dead Sea near Jerusalem, Bethlehem, and Hebron, it managed to survive as a separate kingdom until 587 B.C., when it fell to the Babylonians, who took thousands of its people into exile. It is from "Judah" that the term "Jew" derives.

The destruction of the Jewish kingdoms is the low point in Hebrew history. In spite of their political setbacks, however, the Jews kept the concept of Israel alive, and after 539 B.C., when Cyrus the Great captured Babylon and permitted the Jewish captives to return home, the Israelites displayed new vigor. Although they were no longer an independent people, they rebuilt the city of Jerusalem along with its temple. In this atmosphere Judaism grew to maturity as a religion.

THE JEWS AND JUDAISM

Today the nation of Israel is no larger than the state of Vermont. In the days of David and Solomon, when the entire Jordan Valley was included, the country was not quite twice as large, but its free population did not exceed three-quarters of a million people. Despite its small size, its modest material achievements, and its comparatively short-lived political independence, Israel significantly affected Western civilization. The genius of the Hebrew people is captured in their literature, which represents one of the great achievements of ancient man.

The importance of Hebrew literature is ordinarily thought to be religious. Our present-day use of the term "religious," however, fails to convey exactly what the Hebrews were attempting to do. It is often said, for example, that the purpose of religion is "salvation," yet salvation did not play an important role in Judaism. Judaism, instead, was founded on the belief that the Jews were a chosen people of a particular god, a god originally associated with the southern desert, Mt. Sinai, and the Exodus from Egypt. Acceptance of this fact signified that the religion predated the formation of the kingdom, making the foundation of Israel a sacred enterprise. While this sacred project never flourished for very long, the Hebrews still claimed to have a special destiny under the protection of Yahweh. The concept of Yahweh probably originated with Judah itself, but his advocates attempted also to make him the god of the patriarchs, to associate him with the entire people. Since each generation altered somewhat the thinking of its predecessors, whatever principles Moses had taught his people were changed or reinterpreted by later prophets to meet changing conditions. The Jewish refugees from captivity in Babylon naturally viewed religion quite differently than the earlier refugees from Egypt.

Judaism is usually credited with the development of ethical monotheism. Monotheism, however, does not necessarily represent the first step away from paganism. In fact, it appears that the worship of Yahweh in early Israel was not originally monotheistic, whatever it eventually came to be. Other gods were taken for granted. Yahweh was a national god like Melcart of the Phoenicians or Milcom of the Ammonites. While Yahweh had promised to guide and to protect the refugees from Egypt, the land had other gods who were not to be neglected. Neither is monotheism necessarily superior to paganism in developing moral conduct. The dualistic Persians, for example, had a highly developed moral sense. Monotheism can be, and in this case should be, regarded as a consequence of a people's experience, growth, and development of ideals.

In the case of the ancient Hebrews, the development of religion was aided by the fact that these people had an almost unique historical sense that led them to keep a record of their past. While Biblical history is filled with legends and fables, as well as sermons, these are historical materials. Even modern history, after all, can be and often is inaccurate. Moreover, the ancient Hebrew had fewer materials available to him than we do to aid him in judging his past. Generally, Old Testament writers were harsh in their judgments of the contemporary scene. This attitude is perhaps a reflection of the Judaean point of view, since Judah felt far more keenly than Israel the division of the kingdom; moreover, the writings that have survived have more often been those of Judah. For both kingdoms the course of events must have been dismal, since in the end both were destroyed. Their destruction implied that something had gone wrong with God's sacred enterprise. How could the Jews continue to believe in their unique destiny if their kingdom no longer existed? They did so by elevating God to greater power and omniscience, a being that could not be fully comprehended by men. The implication was that man must have greater faith because it was he himself, not God, who had erred.

Through coming to believe in a great God, the ancient Jews could also believe that a divided or destroyed Israel had some purpose that ordinary human beings could not understand. This developing monotheism had far-ranging moral and ethical implications. As the omnipotent God assumed greater responsibilities, other gods now became insignificant or disappeared. Gradually the jealous, quarrelsome Yahweh who led the tribes of Israel to victory (at least sometimes) underwent significant changes.

Giving birth to this reinterpretation were the prophets, men who spoke God's word or who possessed insights into divine understanding. In a sense, the prophets were descendants of the fortune-tellers who had once made a living reading the portents of things to come. They were far more sophisticated than their early prototypes, however, because they realized that they had to understand the present before they could know the future. The prophets insisted on knowing what man was and what he should or should not do, and they came to believe that what a man does has consequences for all man. Men who were to rule, to command, or to succeed must meet certain standards. Success did not come from calling to the right god or making the appropriate sacrifice but from coming to terms with oneself.

Mature Judaism, then, was quite different from the simple faith of a pastoral people. It had evolved from polytheistic paganism through wars and disasters over many centuries. Judaism came to reflect the difficulties of people in coping with the problems associated with civilization — government, national defense, foreign affairs, the masses of poor. The famous peroration of Amos (eighth century B.C.) clearly deals with the problems of an "affluent society":

Hear this, you who trample upon the needy,
and bring the poor of the land to an end
saying, 'when will the new moon be over,
that we may sell grain?
And the Sabbath,

that we may offer wheat for sale,
that we may make the ephah small and the shekel great
and deal deceitfully with false balances,
that we may buy the poor for silver
and the needy for a pair of sandals,
and sell the refuse of the wheat?'

In seeking answers to the problems of civilization, Judaism demonstrated a sophisticated, cosmopolitan character. From Egypt it had derived a sense of nationhood, a feeling for ethics, and a concept of ethnic superiority. Later, through contact with Assyrian power and Babylonian culture and through linguistic similarities, Israel, like other Near Eastern countries, became indebted to Mesopotamia. The influence of Babylon is nowhere more apparent than in the Judaic concern for law. Yet Hebrew law was more Hebrew than anything else, in large measure because Israel had its own peculiar object, national survival, in developing its law.

As first Assyria, then Babylonia, and finally Persia swept away the little countries of southwestern Asia, the Hebrews came to believe that such happenings were not just random affairs. They saw them as linked to a purposeful sequence, proof positive of divine management in which men had to play a part. Israel failed because it had not walked in the ways of the Lord. The damage could be repaired only when men determined to follow the laws of God. Judaism became a religion of laws, based on the Mosaic code. Simply stated, the purpose of that law was the regulation of personal conduct in the light of God's commandments. Failure to do so would bring divine disfavor on the community. The individual's hopes and expectations lay with the perpetuation of an orderly and organized society, with the welfare of future generations. After considerable confusion and contradiction, the Hebrews had developed a religious ideal that had great survival value. Its major orientation centered about a mystical essence constituting a common ideal, patriotism. At the same time, Judaism reflected a great awareness of social morality. The Judaic idea that men cannot serve themselves unless they also take the community into consideration was later to exert a major influence on Western civilization.

Supplemental Reading
for Part One*

Precivilization

Braidwood, Robert, *Prehistoric Men* (Scott, Foresman).
Childe, V. Gordon, *Man Makes Himself* (Mentor).
Childe, V. Gordon, *What Happened in History* (Penguin).
Cole, Sonia, *The Prehistory of East Africa* (Mentor).
Hawkes, Jaquetta, *Prehistory* (Mentor). This is part I of volume I in the UNESCO *History of Mankind*. It is difficult reading but incorporates the latest scholarship.
James, E. O., *Prehistoric Religion* (Barnes & Noble).
Kuehn, Herbert, *Rock Pictures of Europe* (October).
Leakey, L. S. B., *Adam's Ancestors: The Evolution of Man and His Culture* (Harper & Row). The best brief account of paleolithic man, his evolution and culture.
Malinowski, B., *Crime and Custom in Savage Society* (Littlefield).
Myron, R., *Prehistoric Art* (Pitman).
Oakley, K. P., *Man the Toolmaker* (Chicago).
Redfield, Robert, *The Primitive World and Its Transformation* (Cornell).
Wingert, P. S., *Primitive Art: Its Tradition and Styles* (World).
Wooley, Sir Leonard, *The Beginnings of Civilization* (Mentor). A continuation of the UNESCO *History of Mankind* of which Jaquetta Hawkes' is the first part.

FICTION

Fisher, Vardis, *The Golden Rooms* (Pyramid). Fisher did a whole series of novels on primitive man.

Ancient Near East

GENERAL

Albright, W. F., *From the Stone Age to Christianity* (Anchor).
Childe, V. Gordon, *New Light on the Most Ancient East* (Norton).
Cottrell, Leonard, *The Anvil of Civilization* (Mentor).
Frankfort, Henri, ed., *Before Philosophy* (Penguin). A reprint of a 1964 symposium on the intellectual adventure of ancient man.
Frankfort, Henri, *The Birth of Civilization in the Near East* (Anchor).

* All books listed here and in other Supplemental Reading sections are available in paperback editions.

Gaster, T. H., *Thespis: Ritual, Myth and Drama in the Ancient Near East* (Harper & Row).

James, E. O., *The Ancient Gods* (Putnam).

Lampl, P., *City Planning and Architecture in the Ancient Near East* (Braziller).

Lloyd, Seton, *Art of the Ancient Near East* (Praeger).

Mellaart, J., *Earliest Civilizations of the Near East* (McGraw-Hill).

Moscati, Sabatino, *Ancient Semitic Civilizations* (Putnam).

Moscati, Sabatino, *The Face of the Ancient Orient* (Anchor).

SUMER AND THE TIGRIS EUPHRATES VALLEY

Chiera, Edward, *They Wrote on Clay* (Chicago).

Contenau, G., *Everyday Life in Babylon and Assyria* (Norton).

Kramer, S. N., *History Begins at Sumer* (Anchor).

Lloyd, Seton, *Foundations in the Dust: The Story of Exploration in Mesopotamia* (Penguin).

Mallowan, M. E., *Early Mesopotamia and Iran* (McGraw-Hill).

Oppenheim, A. Leo, *Ancient Mesopotamia* (Chicago). Difficult reading but invaluable.

Wooley, Sir Leonard, *The Sumerians* (Norton).

Wooley, Sir Leonard, *Ur of the Chaldees* (Norton).

EGYPT

Aldred, C., *Egypt to the End of the Old Kingdom* (McGraw-Hill).

Breasted, J. H., *Dawn of Conscience* (Scribner). A classic.

Breasted, J. H., *History of Egypt* (Bantam). Still worth reading but somewhat outdated.

Desroches-Noblecourt, C., *Introduction to Egyptian Wall Paintings from Tombs and Temples* (Mentor).

Edwards, I. E., *Pyramids of Egypt* (Penguin).

Emery, W. B., *Archaic Egypt* (Penguin).

Gardiner, Sir Alan H., *Egypt of the Pharaohs* (Oxford).

Steindorff, G. and Seele, K. C., *When Egypt Ruled the East* (Chicago).

White, J. M., *Everyday Life in Ancient Egypt* (Putnam).

Wilson, J. A., *Culture of Ancient Egypt* (Chicago).

HITTITES

Gurney, O. R., *The Hittites* (Penguin).

PHOENICIANS

Harden, Donald, *The Phoenicians* (Praeger).

PERSIANS

Frye, R. N., *Heritage of Ancient Persia* (Mentor).

Olmstead, A. T., *History of the Persian Empire* (Chicago).

ISRAEL AND JUDAISM

Albright, W. F., *The Archaeology of Palestine* (Penguin).
Albright, W. F., *Biblical Period From Abraham to Ezra* (Harper & Row).
Bickerman, E., *From Ezra to the Last of the Maccabees* (Schocken).
Chase, Mary E., *Life and Language in the Old Testament* (Norton).
De Burgh, W. G., *The Legacy of the Ancient World* (Penguin).
Ehrlich. E. L. and T. J. Barr, *Concise History of Israel: From Earliest Times to the Destruction of the Temple* (Harper & Row).
Gray, J.. *Archaeology and the Old Testament* (Harper & Row).
Kenyon, K. M., *Archaeology in the Holy Land* (Praeger).
Meek, T. J., *Hebrew Origins* (Harper & Row).
Orlinsky, *Ancient Israel* (Cornell).
Rowley, H. H., *The Old Testament and Modern Study* (Oxford).
Wellhausen, J. H., *Prolegomena to the Study of Ancient Israel* (World). Somewhat outdated but interesting.

SOURCE READING

The Bible
Duchesne-Guillemin, J. and M. Henning, eds., *Hymns of Zarathustra* (Beacon).
Gaster, T. H., *The Dead Sea Scriptures in English Translation* (Anchor).
Gordon, Cyrus, *Hammurabi's Code* (Holt, Rinehart and Winston).
Hooke, S. H., *Middle Eastern Mythology* (Penguin).
Kramer, Samuel, *Mythologies of the Ancient World* (Doubleday).
Kramer, Samuel N., *Sumerian Mythology* (Harper & Row).
McNeill, William H. and Sedlar, Jean, *Ancient Near East* (Oxford).
McNeill, William H. and Sedlar, Jean, *The Origins of Civilization* (Oxford).
Sandars, N. K., translator, *Epic of Gilgamesh* (Penguin).

FICTION

Waltari, M. T., *The Egyptian* (Pocket Books). A novel based on the "Story of Sinuhe."

part two

CLASSICAL MEDITERRANEAN CIVILIZATION

4

The Greeks:
Beginning and Expansion

To modern man it sometimes seems as if the Greeks started every-thing. Their books appear to cover the whole range of thinking. In epic, lyric, and dramatic poetry they set the standards by which modern accomplishments are still judged. They established the art and craft of history. In philosophy, they raised many of the major questions about man which we are still seeking to answer. In art, particularly in sculpture, they established the ideals that guide us still. Even in science, the Greeks, building on the knowledge of earlier cultures, contributed to the theoretical development of mathematics and astronomy and laid the foundations for physics and medicine. In other fields, such as engineering, they provided the framework for later innovations by the Romans. In fact, the accomplishments of the Greeks and the Romans so impressed our forefathers that classical studies — the study of Greek and Roman literature, history, and thought — became the basis of the curriculum in the secondary school and even in the university.

While we no longer emphasize classical training — indeed, few graduates of American colleges can read Latin or Greek — the fascination of the Greeks remains. How did they accomplish so much? Historians have not yet been able to offer a complete answer to this question. We know, however, that Greek society and culture did not develop in isolation but were profoundly influenced by neighboring civilizations, particularly that of Crete. Crete represented a mixture of ideas and concepts from the older civilizations of Asia and Africa, so that the

44

early Greek accomplishments were in part dependent upon the advances of their predecessors. Long after they had forgotten the details of their past, the Greeks kept alive the memory of this period of Cretan influence through stories centering around the legendary King Minos. It was this legend that led Sir Arthur Evans, who began excavations on Crete in the beginning of the twentieth century, to call the Cretan period the Minoan civilization.

THE MINOAN CIVILIZATION

Crete in ancient times was a more fertile area than it is today, and the island grew wealthy on the basis of its agricultural output of grain, olives, and grapes, the famous triad of crops that later spread throughout the classical world. An island home serves as a natural incentive for people to explore the surrounding sea, and the Cretans soon turned to trading with their various mainland neighbors. They became known for their manufactured products, particularly their bronze ware, which has been found throughout the Near East. Bronze is made from copper, which was available at several places in the Near East, and tin, still a comparatively rare metal, which was found in Spain, England, and other far off places. Bronze making, therefore, indicates the existence of widespread trade. Using the wealth accumulated from this commerce, the Cretans built great unwalled cities around luxurious palaces, particularly in the period 2000–1400 B.C., the height of the Minoan age of glory.

The most damaging enemy to early Minoan civilization was not man but nature. Earthquakes shook the island several times, each time destroying man-made structures at Knossus, Phaestus, Gournia, and other key settlements. Time and again the Cretans rebuilt, often on an even grander scale. The wealth of the civilization is most evident in the ruins of Knossus, the dominant city during the Minoan period. Evans there uncovered and partially reconstructed a many-storied rambling complex of buildings that he called a palace. Included within the complex were a maze of storerooms, guard rooms, apartments, a throne room, and the most notable feature of all, the royal bathroom. Evans was so impressed with the network of pipes and drains in the palace that he attributed the invention of flush toilets to the Cretans and said that they achieved standards "obtained by few nations even at the present day."

The attitudes and beliefs of the Minoans are known to us primarily through their art, which is much more naturalistic than other ancient art. On the basis of a study of frescoes and polychrome pottery, historians believe that Cretan women enjoyed a favored position in society. There are numerous portrayals of them in hoop skirts with

"La Parisienne," fresco fragment from Knossos, 1500–1400 B.C. (Photo by Vern L. Bullough)

wasp waists, tight-fitting bodices, and almost modern hair styles. A French archeologist, unaccustomed to seeing such beautiful women in ancient art, said that the women in one fresco seemed so modern and so fashionable that they looked like Parisians. To complicate the problem of interpretation, however, the men are also portrayed with wasp waists, something far more difficult for the male to achieve than the female. The answer may be that men habitually wore a waist cincher of some sort, or that the paintings were symbolical rather than actual representations. Since the double ax was so important to the Minoan religion, there is always the possibility that the wasp waists represent such an ax in human form.

Minoan fresco painting was dominated by athletic scenes: boxing matches, various forms of acrobatics, and particularly by an activity that has been described as bull leaping. Women and men are shown grasping a bull by the horns and then turning somersaults or leaping over its body. Some modern cattlemen have claimed that such gymnastics would be impossible to perform because of the way a bull holds its head. If this is the case, the paintings might well represent a religious myth, since the bull was a highly regarded religious symbol not only in Minoan religion but in most of the religions of the Near East.

The chief deity of Crete, however, was female, a deity similar to the Earth Mother or the goddess of fertility found in other cultures. Before most civilizations were far advanced, these female deities had usually been subordinated to male gods, but on Crete the female deity remained dominant. Unlike other Near Eastern deities, the Cretan goddess, who predated the city, did not demand special temples. Instead, she could be worshipped in one's home or in various sacred places on the island. Some historians believe that the women pictured in the frescoes might be priestesses, a view that is supported by the fact that the statuettes of the goddess show her dressed in the same way as the women except that her hair is covered. Even if this view proves to be valid, it seems safe to say that Minoan religion was never as well organized as in other Near Eastern societies, nor was the priesthood as dominant. In fact, the Cretans seem to have enjoyed considerably more freedom than either the Egyptians or the Babylonians. Perhaps in a commercial economy it was more difficult for rulers to become as despotic as they could in an agricultural society, since businessmen or merchants could seek homes elsewhere if the government proved to be too restrictive. An enterprising trading people are also less likely to be isolated in their thinking and more open to new ideas than a rural people.

The commercial basis of Minoan society is attested to by the large number of surviving clay tablets. Most of the tablets seem to be business accounts or inventories, and nothing has yet been found resembling the collections of law in the early records of Mesopotamia or the religious narratives of Egypt. Historians have identified three different forms of Minoan writing. The oldest, a pictographic or hieroglyphic type, was transformed into a cursive form of writing called linear A; the third form, or linear B, was deciphered by Michael Ventris nearly two decades ago. Linear B tablets have been found on the island only in Knossus, and they have also been found in Mycenae and other cities on the Greek mainland. Ventris demonstrated that linear B was actually a Greek language, a fact that has re-emphasized the ties between the Minoan and the Greek civilizations.

MYCENAEAN CULTURE AND THE DECLINE
OF CRETE

The first Greeks had entered Greece from the north around the beginning of the second millennium as part of a general Indo-European

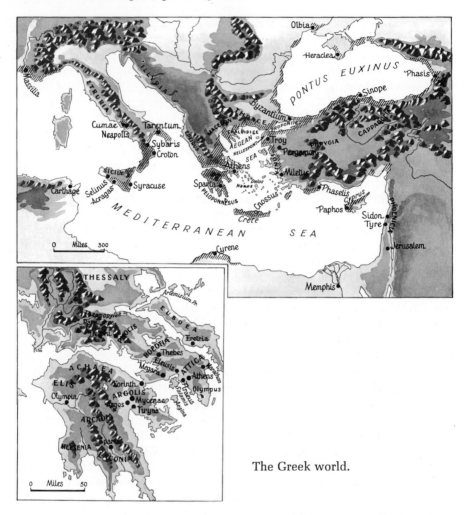

The Greek world.

migration. They had gradually erected great fortified centers at Mycenae, Pylos, Tiryns, and elsewhere. Their most important center was
Mycenae, and from it they are usually called the Mycenaean Greeks.
During their expansion, these Greeks made contact with the civilization
of Crete, particularly the city of Cnossus. Through this contact the
Greeks adopted a modified form of Minoan writing, linear B, and patterned their art and architecture after Cretan models. Unlike either the
Minoans or their own descendants, these early Greeks did not build
cities. Instead, they erected heavily walled fortresses that served as
bases for their conquering expeditions. One group of wandering Greeks
captured the unwalled Knossus around 1500 B.C., drawing the city

still further into the Greek sphere of influence. The loss of Knossus began the decline of the Minoan period in Crete, and the island's greatest era ended completely about a century later. Scholars are not fully agreed on the reasons for the sudden decline of Crete, but there is a general belief that the cities were attacked by masses of sea raiders, the same Sea Peoples who caused so much devastation on the nearby mainlands of Asia and Africa. Civilization on Crete continued to exist, but the raids, coupled with recurrent earthquakes and the loss of trading markets as iron began to replace bronze, encouraged the Cretans to withdraw into the interior of the island, and they were no longer a major factor in the Mediterranean power struggles.

The mainland Greeks were comparatively unaffected by these raids, in part because they were protected by their walled forts but also because they joined with the raiders. The Mycenaeans quickly moved to supplant the Cretans. Greek-speaking settlements were established throughout the Aegean Sea on Rhodes, Cyprus, Crete, in Asia Minor, and even in the western Mediterranean. This colonization brought vast wealth to the people of the Greek mainland, who now had direct contact with many different peoples and cultures. The Mycenaean culture, which dominated the mainland as well as much of the Aegean, is even now identifiable from the remains of the great palace fortresses. The greatest of these fortresses, that at Mycenae, had walls some twenty feet thick. Later Greeks were so impressed with the size of the walls, as well as with the stones used to build them, that they came to believe the structures had been erected by the Cyclops, the one-eyed giants of Greek myth. Entry into the Mycenae fort was through the lion gate, a nine-foot passage formed by four great monolithic stones and so named because the top stone was decorated with two carved lions. At Mycenae and elsewhere in early Greece, excavations have confirmed the uses of Minoan forms and motifs in the art and architecture even though the subject matter is quite different from that of the Minoans. Mycenaean gold and silver work is particularly outstanding. When some of the exquisitely carved or molded pieces were first uncovered by Heinrich Schliemann at the end of the nineteenth century, historians were forced to re-evaluate the whole of early Greek civilization. The pottery, the carved gems, and even the tombs, particularly the famed beehive tombs at Mycenae, all attest to the creative genius of these early Greeks.

The Greeks of the Mycenaean period seem to have failed because of their inability to unite except in order to launch raiding expeditions, such as that against Troy, the rich city that controlled much of the commerce from the Black Sea. The heavily fortified centers themselves are testimony that war was an integral part of the lives of these early Greeks. Even after they were threatened by another Indo-European invasion, there is little evidence that the Greeks united. This new wave of invasions, which lasted for some 300 years, brought the Dorians into the peninsula. Though a Greek-speaking people, the Dorians were more backward, less sophisticated, and not yet literate. The initial effect of their appearance was not only to destroy the Mycenaean strongholds but to force a mass migration throughout the Near East. Many of the Greeks from the older settlements moved to Asia Minor, where they became known as Ionian Greeks. Some of them moved to the area around Athens, which was not so hard hit by the Dorians. Others moved to wherever they found little resistance. Such a mass migration was possible because the Hittite Empire, once the great power in Asia Minor, had been destroyed by the movements of the Sea Peoples, while Egypt, another of the great powers, had lost control of its Asiatic possessions. As part of this changing scene, various small states such as Israel, Phoenicia, Aramaea, Lydia, and individual Greek cities grew and prospered until they were threatened by the emergence of Assyrian power.

THE DARK AGES

The period in Greek history that followed the Dorian invasion is called the Dark Ages, both because many earlier achievements seemingly disappeared and because we know so little about what happened during this time. The use of writing, never very common in the Mycenaean world, was lost to the Greeks. Rulers of the palace had used the written word to keep official records, and most people probably were not unhappy about the disappearance of the writing, which they could not understand. The weakening of the power of the Mycenaean kings also brought changes in the nature of Greek art as the artists lost their royal patrons. Since civilization is in part dependent upon a solid social and political framework, the period of the mass migrations was characterized by a decline in production and commerce, a decrease in material wealth and cultural achievements, and a drop in the general population.

Periods of anarchy and confusion, even though they can be frightening to the people of the time, may in the long run prove to be periods that encourage innovation and creativity, simply because the old ways of doing things no longer seem to work. People become more willing to experiment, to change, to modify; in fact, they are often forced to do so in order to survive. Innovation in Greece was further encouraged by the fact that the invaders were not totally alien to the inhabitants. They were Greeks who spoke a dialect that others could understand and who had enough of the common tradition for Greek to identify with Greek. Thus no impossible barriers were erected between the invaders and invaded, but instead there existed possibilities for mutual adjustment to altered conditions. Some of these changes can be documented, such as those in burial customs, or in the nature and design of pottery. These are changes that left material remains for the modern archeologist to interpret. Other changes are hinted at in Greek legend and tradition, but, since these sources are notoriously difficult to interpret, modern scholars are not always in agreement concerning what is significant. At any rate, through some processes that are not yet fully understood, Greek culture appears to have been quite different at the end of the Dark Ages from what it had been in the Mycenaean period. Kings were no longer so important. The Greeks had learned to write again, but in a different way. They had made contact with the Phoenician alphabet and had modified it to suit their own language. The new writing was so different from the old that scholars did not recognize that the two forms were used for the same language until Ventris proved it in 1952.

THE POLIS

It was during this period of innovation that the unique political institution of the Greeks was developed — the city-state. "City-state" is a modern political term, however, and not really descriptive of the Greek institution. The Greek term is *polis*, and it was in the polis that Greek culture flowered and reached maturity. To the Greeks of Aristotle's time, the fourth century B.C., the polis was an ideal form of government — even of existence; a good life outside it was impossible. Aristotle went so far as to say that "man is an animal whose nature it is to live in a polis." While other peoples had built cities long before the Greeks, the Greek city was different from earlier ones, and its uniqueness helped to change the nature of Greek thinking.

It ought to be easy to explain the special nature of the Greek polis as a natural outgrowth of the geographical setting of Greece and the economic conditions of the time. Greece, with its mountainous valleys, would seem to demand small units. Unfortunately, the geographical arguments yields only a partial explanation, because many of the plains had several cities while some city-states covered several valleys. Other mountainous areas, for example, Macedonia, did not develop true city-states. Economically, the Greek city-state was almost self-sufficient, as much out of necessity as out of choice, since transportation was difficult except by water and it was not until the eighth century that the Greeks once more turned to the sea for commerce. Moreover, the largest and most successful city-states were those such as Athens that were the least self-sufficient. Perhaps the ultimate explanation lies simply in that ambiguous concept we sometimes call the Greek character. The

Greeks were gregarious people who preferred to live in urban units and walk to their farms rather than live on the farms and walk to the city.

The polis was a true community; its affairs were the concern of all its citizens. With this growth of community consciousness certain changes were required in Greek political philosophy and outlook. Historians are fairly certain that the various city-states had their beginnings around a citadel or a stronghold. Known as an *acropolis*, this fortress remained the religious center as the cities developed. A citadel usually implies a king, and the Greeks did have kings, but their role was not the same as it was in other cultures. Rather, the monarch acted in the name of the people — a distinction that made it fairly easy for him to be replaced subsequently by a council of landowners, by the heads of various noble families, or by a gathering of all citizens without altering in any radical way the concept of Greek government. From such beginnings the polis came to mean the whole communal life of the people — political, cultural, moral, economic, and religious. To the Greeks the polis was an active institution that trained their minds and shaped their character. It was the instrument by which the law was observed and by which man was saved from chaos. Thus while the Greek earned his living through his individual efforts, and in the process brought about great inequities in wealth and position, such individualism had no part in his recreation, his religion, his art, his games, or his entertainments, all of which were communal.

HOMER

The chief literary guides we have to this period of darkness and innovation are the two narrative poems attributed to Homer, the *Iliad* and the *Odyssey*. Who Homer was, whether such a person ever existed, or whether there were several persons collectively known as Homer are matters upon which scholars are not agreed. The poems themselves recount the story of the fall of Troy and its aftermath. While this event did have some basis in fact, the main historical value of the poems is their description of the Greek social organization and the conditions that prevailed in the ninth century, the time when the poems began to receive their final form. Although the narratives shed little light on the beginnings of the polis, they aid us in understanding Greek religion, for to his countrymen Homer served as both a textbook and a Bible. Children learned their Greek by reciting Homer's poems and at the same time acquired a knowledge of the gods. Although Homer did not make up the stories of the gods, he, along with Hesiod, tended to establish the official form of the Greek myths, to which each individual city added its own interpretations. Much more than stories of the gods or social histories of ninth-century Greece, however, the poems are literary masterpieces. Woven into the tales of wars, battles, and the difficulties of man with his gods are powerful dramas of human foibles and human tragedies.

THE GREEK GODS

Compared to the mature religious concepts of the Hebrews and the Persians, the religious beliefs of the early Greeks seem crude and primitive. The gods act like glorified human beings who have achieved immortality, eternal beauty, and great powers over nature, but in other ways they have the pains and passions of men. That this characterization was not just the product of Homer's poetic license is indicated by the fact that the eighth-century poet Hesiod portrayed the gods in much the same way.

Perhaps the gods seem confusing because both Homer and Hesiod were poets rather than theologians or philosophers. More likely, however, the explanation lies in the nature of the Greek belief in the gods. To the Greeks there was a real distinction between theology and morality. Proper worship of the gods was carried out in order to secure control over external factors that normally men could not control. On the other hand, however, man himself had to arrive at morality. Thus the nature of morality became one of the major problems for the Greek philosophers. The gods are also confusing because as a kind of Greek nationalism developed in the Dark Ages, there was an attempt to give unity to the various rival gods, to combine them into families or into a family council, and to ascribe to them experiences that matched those of the Greeks themselves. Viewed in this way, the religion of Zeus as centered on Mt. Olympus becomes an attempt to tie various competing cults together. Scholars have shown that Zeus started as a Dorian god, that Poseidon was a hold over from the Minoan civilization, and that Aphrodite was an import from Babylon. Some gods, such as Apollo, started out as purely local gods but achieved so much influence that they worked their way into the pantheon, a rather loose association usually dominated by twelve gods. The easiest way to amalgamate a local god was to have him become a descendant of Zeus through one of the latter's many amorous affairs with goddesses or mortal women. The loose sexual mores of the Greek gods can in part be explained as an attempt to incorporate various competing gods into the same family. Descent from Zeus became an honored background for a god or hero (the semigod), in much the same way that many Americans claim descent from passengers on the Mayflower.

The Olympians, on the whole, do not seem to have been very difficult for their worshippers to satisfy. As long as their altars were properly maintained and supplied, the gods rendered service to men. Moreover, they demanded no higher standards of morality from men than they imposed upon themselves. Since the Greeks possessed no religious books except poetry and no dogma except mythology, there was no need for a privileged priestly cast to serve as the special servants of the gods. Religious ceremonies, emphasizing the concept of the Greek polis, were conducted by civic officials as a state function.

Lacking an organized clergy or church for their competing versions of the gods, none of whom was particularly concerned about the quality of human morality, the Greeks could be somewhat more objective in analyzing their religion than the Hebrews, the Egyptians, or even the Persians. For example, the early philosopher Xenophanes was able to point out that if oxen or horses had hands "and could paint with their hands, and produce works of art as men do, horses would paint the forms of the gods like horses, and oxen like oxen, and make their bodies in the image of their several kinds."

Yet many Greeks sought to find more in the next world than the abode of the shades offered by the Olympian gods. As a result, other gods who had not originally appeared in the pantheon, such as Dionysus, or who had only minor roles, such as Demeter, came to be favored by large numbers of believers. We can trace the changes in some of these gods: none was more radical than that of Dionysus, who started out as a female god and ended up as a male.

PHILOSOPHY AND SCIENCE

Some Greeks attempted to find the truth about the universe not through seeking new mythologies or reviving old ones but through reasoning about the nature of human experience. Undeterred by a rigid theology, they could ask questions and even offer tentative answers to questions that modern man is still seeking to answer: How did the universe begin? Is change or permanence the more real? What is the purpose of man's existence?

Even though they were Greeks, most of these early philosophers or scientists came from settlements in Asia Minor and other fringes of the Greek world rather than from Greece itself. They are important because the records they left — though only traces remain — represent the first permanent documentation of philosophical thought in Western civilization. These early thinkers, however, were different from the modern philosopher and the modern scientist in that they preferred to develop theories, which might be based upon reason but not usually upon the slow amassing of data from observation and the testing of facts that is the method today. They were good observers of life, however, and since they lived and observed in every part of the Greek world, they knew and transmitted many concepts and ideas from non-

Greek cultures. They incorporated Babylonian astronomy, Egyptian geometry, and other more general knowledge into their theories. The first such thinker known to us was Thales of Miletus in Asia Minor. Like many later innovators, he is remembered not so much for the answers he offered but for the questions he asked. He wanted, for example, to find out what substances make up the world. Basically, the question is useless because the answer serves no immediate purpose. Yet by asking such questions mankind has been able to advance. Thales's answer to his question was water. Water, after all, is ubiquitous; it falls from the sky; it gushes out of the earth; it can be solid, liquid, or gas. But his answer was important because it said that the world is made up of only one basic element. No matter how complicated nature might appear, it had to be not only rational but also simple. While we do not accept Thales's answer, we still search for the rational explanation.

Like many other answers, Thales's explanation really satisfied no one but himself. Those who followed him in Miletus, such as Anaximander and Aneximenes, gave different answers. Other Greek philosophers in Asia Minor, Greece, Sicily, southern Italy, and elsewhere held still other views. Fire had its advocates, as did mist, while some argued for a combination of earth, water, mist, and fire. Some, such as Pythagoras, sought the answer in mathematics, while others advocated pluralistic answers such as seeds, and Democritus believed the explanation lay in something called atoms, although he did not mean what modern scientists mean when they speak of atoms.

GREEK EXPANSION

The variety of answers that were offered to the basic questions reflect the diversity of the Greek world. It was also an expanding world. Earlier the Mycenaean Greeks had made contact with and had established settlements in much of the eastern Mediterranean, and it is possible that the first wave of expansion at the end of the Dark Ages resulted from a renewed contact with some of these earlier cities. The strength and influence of the renewed expansion are evident in the continued use of Greek place names throughout the Mediterranean. Established in the wave of expansion that took place in the eighth, seventh, and sixth centuries were such cities as Massilia, now Marseilles; Nikaia, now Nice; and Neapolis, the new city, which today is Naples. Another wave of expansion began with Alexander the Great, an expansion still commemorated by Alexandria in Egypt, while a still later wave dates from Roman times. Sebastopol in Russia is the Greek name for the "City of Augustus."

One explanation for the widespread expansion is that the Greek cities on the peninsula were overpopulated. The polis at best could not become very large or it would lose the unique qualities that the Greeks believed were essential to their cities. In addition, the majority of the citizens in the Greek city-states were farmers. Since primogeniture had not yet developed, families who had to divide their original family plot among many sons found their lands shrunken to the point where efficient farming was impossible. Under such conditions, larger estates often assumed control over the small parcels of land, in fact if not in law, so that an increasing number of Greeks were without land. There was thus much agitation for the redistribution of land, and rather than face the problems of redistribution, an increasing number of cities turned to colonization as an alternative. A standard pattern emerged in the eighth and seventh centuries for establishing a colony. An official leader chosen by the mother city to plant a new colony would supervise the distribution of new lands among the colonists and be honored as the founder. No more than one male member from each family was allowed to join the colony, and since this limited the number of available colonists in any one city, several cities often joined together to furnish the first settlers. The oracle at Delphi, which had become a national shrine during the Dark Ages, was consulted about a site. The priestesses of the shrine, after breathing the noxious odors that came out of the earth at Delphi, mumbled something which the attending priest translated into suitably ambiguous terms. The advice given by the oracle would usually fit any number of locations or conditions. Armed with the blessing of the gods, the colonists then set out for the new area, settling down wherever they found the least opposition.

As these new colonies proliferated, the nature of Greek civilization underwent change. While the ties between the colony and the mother city were regarded as religious and sentimental, trade also developed, for the home city might have commodities that the colonists wanted, or vice versa. Moreover, the colonists were forced to meet new conditions and new peoples and to challenge the old ways of thinking and of doing things. It was therefore no accident that most of the creative thinking took place at first in the colonies rather than in the settled peninsula of Greece. The colonies were also conscious of their Greek heritage, and it was as a result of the need to maintain contact with this tradition that the Olympic games and similar events were established. Perhaps even the philosophers began asking their questions as an attempt to maintain some sort of unity in the midst of all of the diversity of the Greek world.

5

The Greeks:
The Age of Athens

Colonization had a decisive effect upon the Greek imagination, but it provided only a temporary answer to the growing problems that faced the homeland. As the number of outlying settlements increased, and the more desirable locations for new colonies diminished, other solutions to the problem of overpopulation became necessary. To complicate matters, the economic inequities among the Greek citizens were accentuated by the introduction and growth of a money economy, which not only facilitated trade but made hoarding easier. Unlike grain or oil, money was not subject to spoilage or to leakage, nor did it take up much space. Money could also be utilized to bring in more money. When the small landowner suffered a bad year, he might have to borrow to tide him over until he could recover. Whereas previously he had borrowed a certain amount of grain that he could repay when the crops were good, he now borrowed money — or else the materials he borrowed had to be repaid in money. This meant that the poor farmer borrowed when the price of grain and other necessities was high due to scarcity. When he attempted to repay the loan during the good years, prices were lower because food was plentiful. It might therefore take several years for him to overcome the debts of a bad year, and when several bad years came in succession, he usually found it impossible to ever recover.

When the peasant failed to pay, he first forfeited his land and then his personal freedom. He was sold into bondage by his creditors so that they could recoup their investment. Such a system led to a growth in slavery and forced succeeding generations of peasants into increasingly bitter competition with the cheap labor force of the large landowner who controlled the slaves.

When the peasant turned to the state for support, he found it was run by the very people against whom he had a grievance — the aristocrats. This group, composed primarily of the large landholders, controlled the army, dominated the old tribal units, and furnished the priests and officials of the state. Since the power of the aristocrats grew during times of stress, the aristocratic councils also usurped the power of the kings in many Greek cities. In cities where kings still ruled, aristocratic members of the council acted as their key advisers. Everywhere this class also supplied the judges for the court. While the aristocrats were not particularly wicked men, they were understandably reluctant either to weaken their own position in society or to forget the debts that were owed to them.

The situation was ripe for a revolution, and this revolution was facilitated by a challenge to the long-time military supremacy of the nobility. One of the original reasons for the existence of the aristocratic nobility was that it constituted the key fighting force. Since each soldier had to supply himself with arms, only the aristocrat could provide the necessary horses and equipment used in chariot warfare. For the same reason, even the heavy, armed infantry was made up mostly of nobles. With the growth of a money economy, however, there began to develop a merchant class. The emergence of this class coincided with the introduction of a new type of infantry fighting, the hoplite, where the individual soldier subordinated himself to the group. Each hoplite infantryman carried a huge shield in his left hand and a spear in his right. He charged in a formation, a practice that had evolved from the fact that the shield covered only his left side. The right side was protected solely by the shield of the person next in line. Hoplite tactics demanded larger and more sophisticated armies than the old individualistic combat methods. The result was that the members of the merchant class, and even some peasants, became part of the army.

THE TYRANTS

These new army men demanded that the rights of government be extended to include them. To enforce this demand, they were willing to form an alliance with the discontented masses. At such a critical juncture, an ambitious leader served by an army could successfully challenge the old aristocratic council for leadership. In Greek history, these challengers to the old regime were called tyrants. Essentially, a tyrant was a man who made himself a dictator in defiance of whatever constitution then existed. He justified his seizure of power on the ground that he alone was able to provide the kind of government that could effectively meet some crisis that had developed. Tyrants were not necessarily bad or evil rulers, although some were, but essentially soldiers who ruled, at least in part, by appealing to the masses against the aristocrats. Nearly all of them gained power through usurpation, although some were called to power by the ruling oligarchic faction, often to forestall the rise of a rival tyrant.

Among the first tyrants to rule in Greece was Cypselus of Corinth, in the middle of the seventh century B.C. His reign marks the beginning of the Age of Tyrants, which lasted until the end of the sixth century when the tyrants were expelled from Athens. The rule of tyrant families did not usually last for more than two or three generations, by which time the members were overthrown or assassinated or their type of rule replaced by some other. Conditions within the Greek cities, however, were no longer what they had been before the tyrants made their appearance. The power of the aristocrats was usually much weaker; in fact, in some states, tyranny actually seems to have served as an intermediate step in the emergence of democratic government. In other cities, tyranny led to revolution and counterrevolution, the conflict serving to destroy whatever prosperity and well-being the city had achieved. Mass confiscation of land by a tyrant who favored the poor was matched by the repression of the poor when the aristocrats returned to power.

SPARTA

The one Greek city that managed to remain aloof from many of these problems was Sparta, but Sparta was unique in most ways. The city had originally been established by the invading Dorians, who, after conquering the plains of Lacedaemon in the Peloponnesian peninsula, attempted to set themselves apart from the conquered population. This decision meant that this chief city of the plains became a fortress in the midst of a hostile people. The Spartans were the rulers and the citizens, while the indigenous inhabitants became either *perioeci* (neighbors), who had no political rights but who could own and inherit property, or *helots*, who were regarded as slaves. The *perioeci* eventually became the businessmen and merchants of the Spartan community, while the *helots* worked the land, contributing half of their produce to the citizens to whom they were assigned.

In spite of this beginning, Sparta went through its own land crisis. Like the other Greek city-states, it at first sent out colonies. The Spartans, however, soon found another solution more to their temperament — conquest. After a long and involved war, the neighboring territory of Messenia was annexed, a land and people almost equal in size and numbers to Sparta. In the long run, this conquest made Sparta the dominant power in the Peloponnesian peninsula, but in the meantime, it brought the problem of dealing with conquered peoples. The Spartans elected to keep the new territory in permanent subjugation, with its people as state slaves. This decision, undoubtedly influenced by earlier Spartan trends, was a momentous one, since it meant that a small number of people must control a much larger number. With today's weapons of war, such dominion can be accomplished rather easily, but in the classical world where fighting was still very much a man-to-man enterprise, the task was a formidable one.

It was on this scene that the semilegendary figure of Lycurgus appeared. He formulated 'a constitution based on the philosophy that every individual must subordinate his own needs to those of the state, and he sought to turn every free-born Spartan into a professional soldier. Spartans were forbidden to engage in agriculture, trade, the professions, or even the arts; rather, they must become and remain soldiers. Spartan soldiers, however, did not usually go to war against far-off states. Their purpose was mainly to suppress revolts, to maintain Spartan domination in the peninsula, and to guard the city-state from attack by its immediate neighbors.

Human nature has remarkable capacities for self-delusion. Children who are taught untruths long enough, and who are never allowed to question the official interpretation, tend to believe what they have learned and to act accordingly, even when they are adults. In such a system, the problem is to keep outside contact to a minimum, and for this purpose Sparta established the original iron curtain. Life was regulated from the cradle to the grave. Since the first requirement for a would-be soldier is physical stamina, the totalitarian regime allowed weak infants to die. While still at his mother's side, the child was told that fighting was good and that to come back from war without a shield, which implied desertion, was worse than death. Parental approval was replaced by peer-group approval as the child matured. At seven, a boy was taken from his mother and placed in the state dormitories, where he remained until he was thirty. Flogging was routine. Endurance, fortitude, self-denial, and patriotism were instilled under all sorts of extreme conditions. At eighteen, the Spartan boy entered the "secret corps," whose business it was to spy on the serfs and others. Dangerous persons among the helots were liquidated. Tradition has it that on one particular occasion the Spartans eliminated some 2000 of them. Finally, the Spartan became a citizen, but obviously he no longer questioned; he merely obeyed. Girls, although separated from the boys and not eligible for citizenship, were brought up to value the same character traits and the same emphasis on physical stamina.

While the Spartans had earlier been poets and musicians, once the

Lycurgan constitution was accepted literature, rhetoric, poetry, and even music, except as they had to do with physical conditioning or fighting, were ignored. The Spartans often won the athletic events at the Olympic games, but their intellectual life was stagnant. To make certain that it remained so, the city adopted a heavy iron currency that was valueless beyond the frontiers, and every effort was made to keep the citizens at home. Foreigners, who might bring new ideas into the closed society, were periodically expelled. Literacy, which might encourage an inquiring mind, was limited and discouraged.

In spite of these efforts — or perhaps because of them — the Spartans lived with fear. Such fear was understandable, since an estimated 8000 adult males ruled over a subject population of more than 200,000 people. Thus change of any kind had to be considered potentially dangerous. Sparta was not a conservative state; it was a reactionary one. Any relaxation of the guard, any move toward change, would lead to all sorts of troubles. Though the Spartans did change, they did so slowly and unknowingly. They never discarded anything, even in their constitution. The city had two kings simply because the Spartans could never remember when they did not have two. These kings commanded the armed forces abroad, but since kings at home might pose a danger, they held no domestic power. Internal affairs were supervised by five overseers (*ephors*) chosen annually by ballot from among the older citizens. Guiding the actions of the *ephors* was the aristocratic council of old men, the *gerousia*, no member of which was less than sixty years of age. Obviously, those Spartans who had lived to be sixty, accepting such a way of life for all that time, would be reluctant to change it. Within very narrow limits, Sparta was also a democracy. All citizens could vote in the assembly, although they could not debate the issues. The decision went in favor of the side that shouted the loudest.

Notwithstanding its reactionary character, Sparta was much admired by other Greeks. This admiration stemmed in part from the power and prestige of the city and in part from the belief that Spartan citizens had imposed their harsh existence upon themselves. Other Greeks reasoned that the Spartans could change their system if they wanted it changed, and they admired the Spartans because their laws and institutions trained them to the devotion of the polis, the highest of Greek ideals. Moreover, Sparta was not particularly imperialistic. Its army did not dare to leave home for any length of time or to risk defeat of a large force because the helots might rebel or the citizens become contaminated with foreign ideas. Admiration of Sparta continues to this day. The very word "Spartan" now means self-sacrifice, while "laconic," derived from "Laconia," the Latin name for the plains of Lacedaemon, means a person of few words.

ATHENS

If Sparta represented one extreme of the Greek world, Athens represented another. The other Greek city-states were somewhere in between these two. We know a great deal about Athens, and, in fact, what we know about all the other cities, including Sparta, is in the main derived from Athenian sources. Athens in the fifth century came to dominate the Greek world, politically at first and then intellectually and culturally. Most of the Greek literature we have comes from Athens, and since the citizens of Athens were most intimately involved with Sparta, the image we have of Sparta represents the Athenian viewpoint. We cannot really gain a true picture of the Greek world by looking at these two states any more than we can gain a true picture of the modern world by looking at the United States and China from the American view. If, however, each city-state is thought of as unique, but with certain underlying similarities to other city-states, even a study of extremes can be useful.

The greatness of Athens was due to the fact that the city was usually able to adjust in a comparatively peaceful way to the changing conditions in the Greek world. This flexibility gave it a great advantage over most of its rivals. While Athens had tyrants, even Athenian tyrants seem to have been somewhat less drastic in their methods than tyrants elsewhere. In times of crisis, the Athenians seem to have been able to deal with social troubles as reasonable people acting together to avoid violence. In times of great stress, the privileged class in Athens usually managed to come forth with a type of leadership willing to discuss the need for change and even to initiate it. Thus in Athens there was an awareness of common interests among the various classes, a rarity in other Greek city-states.

This ability to compromise was first evidenced in the amalgamation of the people of Athens. Unlike Sparta, where unification had been accomplished by conquest, the people of Attica seem to have come together under Athenian dominance through peaceful agreement. Unrest plagued Athens in the seventh century, just as it did other areas, and after an abortive rising aimed at establishing a tyranny, the aristocrats designated one of their members, a (perhaps) legendary Draco, to tackle the problems. In 621 B.C., Draco tried to solve Athenian difficulties by writing down the laws of the community. Though his laws confirmed the privileges of the aristocratic group to which he belonged, the mere fact that they were written down tended to remove some of the power of the aristocrats to interpret the law as well as to make the more disputed actions subject to the authority of the court. Moreover, Draco's appointment set a precedent for attacking the formidable problems facing Athens. Within a generation (about 594 B.C.), the Athenians again appointed an aristocrat to deal with the growing problems, this time one who had been critical of existing policies, a man by the name of Solon.

Solon was no radical revolutionary but a cautious innovator and compromiser who was at the same time a poet, public servant, philosopher, and businessman. He believed that many Athenian difficulties stemmed from the fact that the city attempted to be self-sufficient agriculturally when the soil of Attica was not really suitable for the grain that was so much a part of the Greek diet. To solve this problem, Solon encouraged specialization, particularly agricultural specialization in olives and grapes. Olives were not only a food, they were the source of the oil essential for lighting and cooking. Grapes provided the wine which most of the Greek world drank instead of water. These crops demanded allied industries. Athenian pottery makers, who had already reached a high level of skill and artistry, as well as the boat builders, easily increased their production to meet the demand for containers to ship oil and wine to other parts of the ancient world. To aid manufacturing, an area in which the Athenians were not so proficient, Solon encouraged foreign craftsmen to settle in Athens by promising them Athenian citizenship. To be certain that the new crafts would be kept alive, he insisted that each father teach his son a trade. All of the new products were sold for money, with which the Athenians purchased the necessary grain to supply the growing population. This meant that Athens became more and more a commercial capital. Unlike most cities, Athens was no longer self-sufficient and so could not afford to be isolationist or provincial in politics. Instead, it became progressive and innovative.

Solon effected other reforms, although they were somewhat less imaginative. He limited the size of estates without altering the system of land tenure. He put an end to enslavement for debt and brought home Athenians who had been sold abroad into slavery, but he made no move toward expropriation of creditors. He extended membership in the assembly to include all citizens, but he left the selection of the executives (*archons*) in the hand of a restricted group. He did, however, make the holding of this office dependent upon property qualifications rather than on birth. This practice, which allowed some of the richer merchants who had previously been excluded to qualify, eventually brought some changes in the Council of the Areopagus, the aristocratic council to which the *archons* retired after serving their one-year term. Politically, Athens remained an oligarchy, but a much less oppressive one than it had been before Solon. After some twenty years of service, Solon retired to travel — and to give his reforms a chance to work without him.

Once change had begun in Athens it gathered momentum. Athenians, realizing that things could be better managed, demanded that other improvements be made rapidly. With Solon no longer in control, factionalism broke out between the citizens of the coast (the merchants) and those of the plain (the nobles). A noble relative of Solon's, Peisistratus, took advantage of these disputes to build a party of the mountains (the poorer peasants). With support from some elements of the other two classes, he was able to make himself tyrant of the city (about 560 B.C.). Though twice expelled, Peisistratus eventually emerged triumphant and remained dominant until his death in 527 B.C. Once established, he effected some drastic economic reforms. He sent those who resisted his rule into exile, confiscating their land and distributing their property to the poor. This kind of action forced the growth of democratic tendencies. Equally important, Peisistratus reorganized the religious festivals, particularly that of Dionysus, giving public status to a new art form, the tragic drama. He also helped to preserve epic poetry by incorporating recitals of Homer into other Athenian festivals. Such encouragement did much to set Athens on the way to future literary and cultural dominance.

While Peisistratus maintained the political reforms of Solon, enlarged the role of the poor, and brought political stability to Athens, he did not solve the problem of finding an adequate successor to himself. Even a benevolent tyrant like Peisistratus did not find it easy to transfer power. While his sons Hipparchus and Hippias succeeded him on his death, they were not as capable as their father. Hipparchus was assassinated in the aftermath of a homosexual love affair, while Hippias in 510 B.C. was exiled, bringing the Age of Tyrants to an end in Athens.

The last years of the sixth century were a confused period for the Athenians. Despite its growing democratic tendencies, the city was still dominated by a handful of powerful figures. In the struggle for leadership that followed the exile of Hippias, a new artistocratic leader of the people, Cleisthenes, emerged. He completed the reform of the constitution, realigned the citizens into new political patterns to cut down the old economic and tribal animosities, included aliens on the citizenship rolls, and increased the power of the assembly until it was the sole and final legislative body.

THE PERSIAN WARS

Though Athens continued to be vexed by internal dissension, its citizens could devote their energies toward making their city one of the leading powers of the Greek world — a position that enabled it to assume the leadership in the struggle against the Persians, who had reached the Aegean Sea with the conquest of Lydia in 548 B.C. With this conquest the Ionian Greeks in Asia Minor fell under Persian control. While the Persians were comparatively benevolent rulers, the fact that just across the Aegean other Greeks were wholly free served as a constant reminder to the Ionians of their fate. Galled by their loss of independence, they rose in revolt in 499 B.C. Both Athens and Eretria sent ships to aid the insurgents; the rest of the Greeks found various reasons for not interfering. Even though the revolt was crushed, the Persians recognized that they could not keep peace in Asia Minor until the two offending cities had been punished.

The Persian king Darius dispatched a punitive expedition against Athens and Eretria in 490 B.C. Athens was not totally unprepared, since under the competitive leadership of Themistocles, who emphasized the navy, and Miltiades, who supported the army, the city had begun to make preparations. War, however, particularly defensive war, was costly and Athens lacked the resources to build an adequate war machine. Unlike today, a government then could not go into debt by borrowing money against future income to pay for the cost of a war. Cities had to use current resources for their equipment, and, when these were exhausted, they usually had to surrender. Most Greek city-states were reluctant to imperil their own defenses in order to come to the aid of Athens and Eretria. Instead, they consoled themselves with the thought that the two cities had created their own difficulty when they sent aid to the Ionians. Even Sparta, which had power to spare and was determined not to submit to Persia, delayed sending troops. As a result, when Eretria was captured through treachery, the Athenians were left virtually alone to meet the Persians. The Athenians survived this threat, much to their own surprise, by winning a famous battle on the nearby plain of Marathon in eastern Attica. Their victory was due to the fact that their heavily armed hoplite was more than a match for the lightly armed Persian troops. Soon after the defeat, the Persian expedition withdrew to Asia. For the time being, Athens was saved.

To the Athenians, Marathon was a tremendous victory; to the Persians, it was probably regarded as a temporary failure. Instead of sending another punitive expeditionary force, the Persians would now have to mount a full-scale invasion of Greece. They began preparations for just such an invasion, but it was delayed for several years, first by the death of Darius, then by a revolt in Egypt, and finally by the logistics of moving across the Aegean an army of the size they believed necessary.

Most Greeks realized that their victory at Marathon was temporary, that the Persians would come again, this time to conquer all of Greece. The rather surprising thing is that little was done to prepare for this eventuality. The Greeks enjoyed life as long as they could, apparently reconciled to submission if conquest became inevitable. Many Athenians also seemed ready to accept the inevitable, but luck or the gods were on their side. The miners at Laurium, the site of the Athenian state mines, uncovered a rich vein of silver, bringing the unexpectedly pleasant problem of deciding what to do with the sudden wealth. Many people proposed that the silver be distributed among the Athenians. Themistocles, who was still active, persuaded the people to use the money to build a fleet. This, he argued, would help Athens defeat the island (and city) of Aegina, a commercial rival. While Themistocles probably had the forthcoming war with Persia in mind, he had to put his plea for defense money in more immediate and tangible terms, arguing that the conquest of Aegina would bring the Athenians even greater wealth.

The Persians launched their campaign in the spring of 480 B.C. with a massive land and sea force that crossed the Hellespont and invaded Greece on the northern coast. Individual cities in the path of the advance had no choice but to come to terms, since resistance would have been useless without any organized plan of opposition. Many of them actually preferred their chances under the Persians to risking an alliance with traditional enemies. Elsewhere in Greece, the Spartans, both by their power and their example, could compel a certain unity of action, while the Athenian fleet, the largest in Greece, could draw support from other maritime communities. The Greeks planned to hold up the Persian advance at Thermopylae, which controlled a narrow pass into central Greece. To hold the passage, the Spartans sent some irregulars plus only 300 first-line soldiers under the command of one of their kings, Leonidas. A fleet collected under Athenian leadership from a dozen cities guarded the coast to prevent troops from being landed in the rear of the defenders. The forces of the Spartan king were betrayed to the Persians by other Greeks, and when Leonidas realized this he sent his auxiliaries home. In a heroic battle, the Spartans fought and died to the last man rather than be captured. While this battle gave the Spartans a prominent role in song and story, it also let the Persians into the heart of Greece.

The navy then withdrew to Athens, where it ferried much of the population to the nearby island of Salamis. When the Persians took and burned most of Athens, much of the allied fleet appeared willing to disband. To prevent this, the Athenian commander purposely allowed the Persian navy to bottle up all the Greek ships in the bay so that they had no choice but to stay together and fight. This version of the story is the one given us by Herodotus, who wrote more than forty years later. In the ensuing contest, the Greeks won a signal victory that gave them control of the Aegean and that threatened the Persian communications. The Persian king Xerxes, the successor of Darius, fearing that the defeat might also be a prelude to uprisings in Asia, quickly returned home with most of his army. This still left a considerable force to winter in northern Greece, but when it returned to Attica in the following spring, it was met and defeated by a Greek army under Spartan leadership at nearby Plataea. The final *coup de grace* was given by a naval victory won under Athenian leadership at Mycale on the Ionian coast in 478 B.C. The Persian menace was no more.

THE ATHENIAN EMPIRE

Victory left many problems. Several Greek cities were still under Persian control. Should they be liberated by carrying the war to Persia? There was also the danger that Persia would come back again. Should the Greeks prepare for this expected return by some form of concerted action? The Spartans, by the very nature of their state, voted to retire with honor. Athens, however, assumed the leadership of the forces working for full emancipation from the Persian yoke. The Athenians organized a naval confederacy with headquarters on the sacred island of Delos. Maritime cities contributed a fixed number of men and ships, or, if they preferred, since some might have use for their ships and others were assigned only a portion of a ship, they contributed money. As the subject cities were liberated, they were incorporated into the league. Slowly, almost imperceptibly, the league became an Athenian empire. Part of the reason was simply administrative convenience. The league's treasury, for example, was transferred to Athens, where it would be safer from sudden Persian naval attack. Commercial disputes between league members were referred to the Athenian courts, a logical and efficient way of solving a problem, but one that again increased Athenian dominance. More and more member cities contributed money rather than ships or men, leaving the Athenians to man the fleet and making the league navy more and more an Athenian one. In addition, since Athens was a democracy, or on the road to becoming one, it worked to encourage democratic trends among other cities, thereby antagonizing the conservative aristocrats throughout the league.

The money that the league members paid into the treasury had a way of ending up in the pockets of Athenians. In part this result was natural, since those who manned the ships had to be paid, but the Athenians also used the gold to rebuild, enlarge, and improve their own city. Citizens of Athens rationalized their action by claiming that the gold statues and other ornamentation of these buildings could be easily reclaimed and used in time of need. Though this was true, the gold was still in Athens and not elsewhere. Poets, sculptors, and other artists came there seeking patronage from the state. This period represented the city's golden age, also known as the Age of Pericles, after the dominant political leader of the day. Since the navy by its nature depended upon the unglamorous drudgery of the common oarsman, and since Athens was primarily a naval power, the growth of the navy contributed to an extension of democracy. Those who fought for the state demanded some say in its affairs. Pericles introduced the practice of paying for attendance in the assembly and the law courts, an innovation that encouraged greater participation in government on the part of the lower classes. To emphasize the concept that one Athenian, even though poor, was equal to the next, the procedure of annual election by lot had been devised. The assumption behind this practice was that the gods or the fates would choose one man over another, but at least the choice would not be determined by wealth. Election by lot, however, meant that there was a continual changeover in office and continuity was lacking. To impose some sort of stability, the Athenians left one group of officers, the generals (*strategoi*), to be elected by the people themselves. Since re-election to this office was possible, the generals became the actual leaders of Athens. Pericles, in fact, held power by reason of his continuous re-election as a general.

In spite of these reforms, Athenian democracy was incomplete. Though it was the most democratic of the Greek city-states, it would not meet the modern definition of a democracy. The Athenian economy was based upon slaves, many of whom were wartime captives. While later Greeks felt that no Greek should be a slave, no Greek ever saw anything wrong with having non-Greeks serve in that capacity. Women were excluded from voting and from government itself. Pericles, the great democratic leader in Athens, the lover of the illustrious courtesan Aspasia, stated, "The less heard of women in male company the better, whether for good or ill." Women of the better classes were confined to the female quarters of the home, where they lived in Oriental exclusion. Working class or peasant women could circulate somewhat more freely, but the women with the most independence were the courtesans. This group, however, probably lost as much as it gained, since the children of prostitutes were barred from citizenship and were not acceptable to the married women of the community. Though women undoubtedly had a great deal of power over their children and even over their husbands, they lacked formal standing in the political life of the state.

Democratic Athens could at best be described as a limited democracy. The adult male population of the city has been estimated at approximately 50,000 citizens, 25,000 resident aliens, and 55,000 slaves. Thus only slightly over one third of all males were eligible to participate in the full democratic life. While it can be argued that resident aliens received better treatment in Athens than elsewhere and that the life of the slave, except in the state mines, was not particularly arduous, it should be remembered that the greatness of Athens was built in part upon an increasingly restive empire, upon domestic slavery, and that it was an all-male affair.

ATHENIAN CIVILIZATION

It is a truism that wealth brings leisure and leisure brings time for the pursuit of learning and the arts. While not all wealthy cities or countries have produced great artists or writers, it is certainly easier to secure recognition for one's talents in such an environment than in a poverty-stricken one. The rise of Athens had a notable effect upon Greek culture, a culture increasingly centered in Athens. It is an unhappy commentary upon human achievement that great accomplishments of the past have often been the work of a minority of men who have been supported by an unwilling slave population while the few enjoyed leisure to pursue the arts.

When Solon first began to effect his reforms, the dominant form of literature was lyric poetry that was sung either as a solo or in chorus. Solon himself, was a poet of the first rank — in fact, part of his success was due to his ability to convey his message through poetry. Lyric poetry, at least at this stage of its development, was the most sophisticated form of expression among a still predominantly illiterate people. While we know the names of many of these poets, and they seem to have come from all parts of the Greek world, we usually have only fragments of their writings: Terpander, Alcman, Sappho, Pythemus, Archilochus, and others. Many of their poems were eventually written down, but the only one whose work has survived in any quantity is Pindar, whom the Greeks regarded as the greatest of their lyric poets.

With the rise of Athens, a new form of poetry, the poetic drama, came to the front. When Peisistratus reorganized the Dionysian festival, he gave birth to Greek tragic drama. Originally the festival of Dionysus had included a "dithyram," in which a chorus sang and mimed a lyric poem around a wooden altar. Thespis, a semilegendary Athenian, added something new to this performance by introducing an actor who wore a mask and costume and impersonated some character in the narrative. As the dramatic festival evolved under the partronage of Athens, the chorus became less important while the actors or speechmakers tended to assume the roles of real persons. The great age of tragic drama came in the fifth century, the period of the greatest Athenian prosperity.

Greek audiences were already familiar with the story that took place on the stage. This fact makes Greek drama particularly important to the historian, because by comparing different treatments of the same theme, he can gain an insight into the changes that were going on in society. Tragedies by three great Athenians of the fifth century have survived: those of Aeschylus, Sophocles, and Euripides. Each made some innovation in the drama: Aeschylus introduced a second actor, Sophocles a third, and Euripides lessened the importance of the chorus. Each, however, differed from the others in more important ways. Some seven of Aeschylus' seventy plays survive. In them the gods still remain dominant and on stage. His heroes cannot escape from their fate, but their greatness is in how they meet destiny. Aeschylus believed that men should accept fate and suffer their punishment without questioning the gods. Sophocles, a younger contemporary of Aeschylus, was the most successful playwright of the period, since he won more festival prizes than any other. While only seven of his hundred or so plays survive, they demonstrate that he took the same themes as Aeschylus but tended to give universal significance to individual emotions. The gods moved into the wings in order for man to assume more importance. Sophocles was concerned with the ethical relations of man to the gods, with individual behavior and its relation to the general welfare. The last of the great trio of tragic writers was Euripides, who, though younger than Sophocles, died at the same time. Euripides broke away from the traditional modes of treatment. In contrast to Sophocles, he appears to have questioned what was going on in Athens in his time. He probed the conflict between love and duty and between loyalty and honor as they affected an individual's character. Traditional religion in his drama was treated in a negative, skeptical, and critical manner, and he was less concerned with whether the gods existed than he was with the effect of belief on individual character.

In his skepticism, Euripides seems to represent the Sophists, a group of fifth-century Athenian thinkers. Attracted both by the wealth and the comparative tolerance of the city, the Sophists reoriented philosophy. Though they despaired of finding full answers to the basic questions that Thales and others had asked earlier, they clung to the same essential materialism and sought knowledge particularly related to the practical problems of life. Since most of the Sophists were strangers to Athens, they suffered as outsiders. Because they questioned the ancient gods and teachings, they were accused of being atheists. Convinced that truth was relative, not absolute, they were accused of undermining the fabric of society. They were not so much a sect, since they disagreed among themselves, as they were teachers and innovators who brought new ideas to public attention by forcing the Athenians, often against their will, to examine their beliefs. In the process, they laid the foundation for much of the thought of the later Greeks, and by their emphasis on rhetoric, they changed the nature of literature. Laws to the Sophists were not made by the gods but by men, and the best laws were those made by the many to restrain the powerful few. Man, in the words of the Sophist Protagoras, was "the measure of all things." Before man could understand the gods or the universe, he had to understand himself. Later Sophist thinkers disagreed with the earlier ones, and while Socrates, for example, believed that right was absolute and eternal, he too forced the Athenians to reassess themselves.

THE PELOPONNESIAN WAR

Only a secure society is free enough to allow the necessary self-criticism that was the foundation of Sophist thought. As Athens entered into a period of trouble, Athenians became less inclined to tolerate such questioning. The city had grown to dominate the Greek world through its league and in the process had aroused powerful antagonisms. With the menace of Persia seeming more and more distant and Athens growing richer and richer, citizens of other league cities wanted to get a share. Others not in the league were fearful that Athenian expansion might eventually include them. Aristocratic factions feared the spread of democratic influence would further weaken their prospects.

Even though the Athenians perhaps looked upon themselves as the benevolent leaders of a league against Persia, some cities wanted to escape from the confederation. When they tried to withdraw from what had originally been a voluntary association, they found Athens was willing to use force to make them stay. The Athenians justified their actions with the belief that if the league fell apart, the old menace of Persia would appear again. Most Greeks could no longer be persuaded by this argument, however. Instead, they demanded to know by what right Athens claimed to direct Greek affairs. Increasingly they turned to Sparta to counter Athenian pretensions. When the Athenians forbade the citizens of Megara, allies of Corinth, the right to trade in the markets of Athens or the league cities, the Spartans, prodded by the Corinthians and some others, issued an ultimatum, which the Athenians rejected. The so-called Peloponnesian War that followed lasted on and off for some twenty-seven years, from 431 to 404 B.C.

The tragedy of the war, which involved most of the Greek world, was that democratic government proved incapable of keeping the struggle within a proper focus. Athens several times had victory in sight only to throw it away for some purposeless adventure, such as an attempted conquest of Syracuse in Sicily or the slaughter of the inhabitants of Melos — not to mention the execution of Athenian generals who unhappily belonged to the wrong faction. The Athenian assembly set one policy one day only to reverse it the next when a new demagogue made a different speech. The irony of it all was that Persia, which had been virtually excluded from the Greek world, was now urged to intervene, first by one faction and then another, and in turn, Persian domination over the Greeks in Asia Minor was recognized. In the end, it was the financial support of the Persian king that eventually allowed Sparta to win. Increasingly, the war became a sea war, the most costly of ancient wars, and exactly the type in which Athens originally had every advantage. Yet the Spartans won by laying siege to Piraeus, the port of Athens. After some four months, the Athenians surrendered in 404 B.C. on the victor's terms: destruction of the long walls to the port and its defenses, surrender of the remaining warships, and obedience to Sparta in foreign policy. Actually, the Spartan terms were generous as compared with the demands of their allies, some of whom wanted Athens totally demolished. Tired of war, and under Spartan occupation, the Athenians experienced an antidemocratic reaction that lasted for several months. The government fell into the hands of a commission of thirty, known as the thirty tyrants, who were supported by a Spartan garrison. This group set up a reign of terror, executing hundreds of people, driving thousands of others into exile, and confiscating great blocks of property that they then diverted to their own use. The exiles returned as soon as the Spartan army left, and with the support of the populace, overthrew the tyrants. Though a Spartan army again threatened, peace was maintained when the new democratic rulers arranged a general amnesty for all citizens except a few magistrates and those of the thirty tyrants who still survived. Much of the fury of a people who had suffered through the war and the period of tyranny was directed at one man, Socrates. Socrates was charged with being a Sophist, with corrupting the youth, and with encouraging through his teachings the scandalous behavior of the aristocrats, as well as being blamed for most of the other ills that had befallen Athens. For these crimes he was condemned to death.

THE AFTERMATH

A society that has lived through tragedy does not necessarily appreciate seeing more of it enacted on the stage. When life itself is cruel and harsh, the emotions aroused by tragic drama become almost unbearable. The death of Euripides and Sophocles in 406 B.C. coincided with the defeat of Athens, and with them tragic drama also died. People wanted to laugh rather than to cry, to forget rather than to remember. Comedy replaced tragedy, although it too was associated with the festival of Dionysus. While like tragedy comedy was musical, its spirit was exultant, satiric, ribald, and farcical. The first great period of comedy was that dominated by Aristophanes, who started writing when both Euripides and Sophocles were active. Some eleven of his plays have survived. Aristophanes was a conservative in an age of ferment. He attacked imperialism, which many Athenians had equated with the cause of their defeat; he attacked war, which had caused so much Athenian suffering, and suggested in his famed comedy *Lysistrata* that the only way to keep men from fighting was for women to deny sexual contact to the warring male. As a true aristocrat, Aristophanes ridiculed the low-born who had risen to high positions in society, and he pictured a whole parade of them from a leather seller to a sausage dealer as blustering braggarts. He even ridiculed the new thought of Euripides. In *The Frogs,* he has Aeschylus, the man who respected the gods, emerge as a greater dramatist than the iconoclastic Euripides. Quite naturally he made fun of Socrates.

The comedy of Aristophanes is deadly serious. While it employs slapstick and lampoon and contains unexpected situations and unforseen events, it is basically a comedy with a message. Aristophanes opposed the changes that had taken place in Athens and tried to get Athenians to return to the old attitudes which he valued. Even comedy of this kind was too serious for the Athenians, who desired only to be entertained and not to be reminded of their past misfortunes. The comic form soon changed to a light situation-type comedy.

During the same period, prose was also developing as a literary form. The mere fact that prose, which is meant to be read, not recited, grew in importance in the fifth century proves that literacy was increasing, that Periclean democracy was reaching more and more people. As a typical aristocrat, Aristophanes made fun of this development, but it was an important phenomenon that helped change the nature of literature.

One of the earliest forms of prose writing was history. The first surviving work among the Greeks that can be described as history is that of Herodotus, who lived and wrote in the fifth century B.C. Herodotus is fascinating reading to us today. He combines the naïve with historical shrewdness; he is amiable and garrulous. Herodotus had traveled widely and he reported what he saw in religions, governments, and peoples. If he is not the first historian, he is certainly the first anthropologist. His main theme was the clash between the Greeks and the Persians. To explain it he was compelled to write both a history of Greece and an explanation for the rise of Persia, including its ascendancy over all its predecessors, including the Egyptians and the Babylonians. His bias was in favor of moderation and against excess, he felt that this was what the gods favored also.

The growing literary sophistication of the Greeks can be appreciated by comparing Herodotus with his younger contemporary Thucydides.

Thucydides' history is much more narrowly conceived and he is more difficult to read. He did not want to distract the reader from the seriousness of his theme, the story of the Peloponnesian War. His main interest was to explore the significance of economic and personal factors in shaping history. To him the Peloponnesian War was a tragic drama, the tragedy of Athens and imperialism. Imperialism meant that Athens must expand or perish, and, according to Thucydides, it was the constant need to renew itself that caused Athens to lose all that it had gained.

In spite of defeat, Athens retained dominance in the arts. Though the city no longer played a central role in Greek politics, it once again, after venting its anger on Socrates, became a haven for the artist and the thinker. It is for its intellectual and cultural contributions to Western civilization, rather than for its political dominance in the Greek world, which lasted only a brief moment in history, that Athens has retained its importance.

6

Greece under Stress

The Peloponnesian War marked the beginning of the end for the Greek city-state system of government and allowed the entrance of outside powers, first Persia and then Macedonia, into the affairs of Greece. Some modern historians have equated this period of Greek history with that of Europe after World War II, with Russia and the United States acting as the two outside powers. Though such a comparison is interesting, in the long run it is of little value except to serve as a reminder that the Greeks experienced many of the same problems that we have. Even though Athens had been defeated, the Athenians had demonstrated that some sort of union or federation was the key to greater prosperity and security in the Greek peninsula. Sparta, ignoring this fact, and encouraged by Persia, attempted to turn the clock back to the time when each city was self-sufficient and independent of any other. In part, the Spartan reaction was due simply to innate conservatism, but the Spartans, with their Persian allies, tended to regard any coalition or league as a threat either to themselves or to Persian control of the Ionian Greeks in Asia Minor. As a result, once the Spartans had achieved victory, they broke up long-standing alliances, intimidated the smaller states, which had difficulty surviving as independent units, and did not heistate to use force even against former friends and allies who attempted to form a league. Those Greeks who had originally hailed the Spartans as liberators from the threat of Athenian dominance were soon alienated and in rebellion.

Instead of securing peace in the peninsula, Spartan tactics increased the number of wars. The natural rivalry among the cities, unchecked by economic or political alliances, was made even more devastating by Persian encouragement. The Persians continually intervened in local wars, supporting first one side and then the other, sometimes both, in order to keep the Greeks fighting among themselves. The Greeks of the fourth century, due in large measure to a change in the nature and composition of armies, also seemed more willing to go to war than their predecessors. Earlier Greek armies had largely been made up of citizen-soldiers; in the fourth century, they became professional. The long, drawn out Peloponnesian War had caused great destruction, uprooting men from their farms, from their jobs, and from their old ways of life, and when the war was over, they had nothing to return to. Many became mercenaries, selling their fighting talents to the highest bidder, whether Greek or Persian. Since the Persians were willing to support local wars, many Greek cities were perfectly willing to authorize a war that did not cause undue financial burdens or in which few citizens would have to serve in the army, since there was always a chance of gaining territory or booty.

Mercenary soldiers were only one symptom of a growing specialization in Greek life. At its best, the Greek polis had been the creation of amateurs. In the fourth century, with the advances in learning, the growing militarism, and the complexity of political decisions, specialists were required to run things, people who had acquired a special competence in particular areas. Sparta early had specialized in military affairs, but the conservative character of the Spartans precluded change, and the Spartan army was finally defeated by Thebes in the fourth century simply because the Thebans increased the number of men in one wing. Because it was unwilling to change its own tactics, the Spartan army was thrown into a quandary by this slight innovation. Though Thebes emerged as the dominant power within Greece, it was still not strong enough to prevent local feuds, and Persian interference was not stopped.

THE RISE OF MACEDON

The more the Greeks fought and disputed among themselves, the less able they were to defend themselves from outsiders, thus preparing the way for unification under the domination of Macedon. Though forced, this unification was not entirely unwanted. Ordinary people grew increasingly tired of the wars; they resented the Persian influence in Greek affairs, and they realized the wars were destroying Greece. A growing number of them seemed willing to sacrifice the independence of their cities in order to achieve peace, although few of them would have welcomed foreign conquest. As Macedonian influence spread, some of the Greeks tried to organize an opposition, particularly the famed orator Demosthenes of Athens. Demosthenes ultimately failed, because, as he complained, the Greeks had lost interest in their native cities. Loyalty to the polis had so far given way to the feeling of being Greek that even many Athenians were willing to accept Philip of Macedon as sovereign if he could bring greater political stability.

At the beginning of the fourth century, Macedon was on the fringe of the Greek world. It was tribal, it had a king, it lacked real cities; in effect, it had all the trappings the Greeks regarded as barbarian. The Macedonians, however, had an important military potential. Unlike most of the Greeks, they had a strong cavalry, their population and resources were more than equal to those of any individual Greek city, and their assets had recently been increased by the discovery of a new gold mine. What they needed was a leader, one who could bring peace to the various warring factions within Macedon. The man who managed to achieve this was Philip, who emerged as king of Macedon in 359 B.C. after a round of family assassinations. Intelligent, able, and ambitious, Philip had spent some years in Thebes as a youth, long enough to learn about the new Theban military tactics and to discern the major weaknesses of the Greek cities. Using the Theban innovations as a starting point, Philip developed an even more maneuverable formation, the Macedonian phalanx, which dominated the military scene until supplanted by the Roman legion. Philip also embraced the idea of unifying the Greeks not merely as a conqueror but as the organizer of a new expedition against the Persians.

His approach not only exploited Greek resentment of the Persians but also took into consideration the internal weaknesses of the Persian Empire, which no longer was the power it had once been. That Persian power was beginning to decline is evident from the writings of Xenophon, who along with thousands of other Greek mercenaries had been hired by the Persian prince Cyrus the younger in an attempt to overthrow his brother Artaxerxes II. After marching into the heart of the empire, the Greeks fought and defeated the Persian army of Artaxerxes, but Cyrus was killed in the battle. Thus the victorious troops, over 10,000 of them, found themselves 1000 miles from home, surrounded by Persians, and with no clear plan of action. Determined to return to Greece, they successfully did so under the leadership of Xenophon, who later recorded this adventure in his *Anabasis*. The *Anabasis* came to be widely read, not just for its epic qualities, but for the light it sheds on the Persians, whose weaknesses enabled the poorly supplied band of Greeks to survive. The possibilities were not lost on Philip.

Philip, moreover, was in a better position to act than most people who read Xenophon's story. He was a king with considerable resources; he was also a military and political genius with few scruples, willing to use bribery, trickery, or force to achieve his ends. First he had to unite the Greeks. His persistent interference in the affairs of various warring cities finally provoked an alliance of Athens and Thebes against him, but the combined armies were defeated by the Macedonians in the battle of Chaeronea in 338 B.C.

This defeat led to the formation of the league of Corinth, in which each city-state was theoretically autonomous but united with the others for military action. In reality, however, Philip dominated Greece, a situation that became apparent, when at his own insistence, he was elected general of the league and its members promised to support his campaign against Persia. Before he could take any further action, he was assassinated. Many of the Greek cities took the opportunity provided by Philip's murder in 336 B.C. to break free of Macedonian control, but they failed to reckon with Alexander, Philip's son and successor, known as Alexander the Great.

ALEXANDER THE GREAT

Though he was only twenty years of age, Alexander proved to be more than a match for his contemporaries, regardless of their age. Within a few months he had stamped out an insurrection in Thessaly, secured his northern frontier on the Danube, and marched into Greece, where he captured and destroyed the city of Thebes, which, supported by Persian gold, had attempted to lead the insurrection. He then settled down to the invasion of Persia. His first step was to establish himself as a liberator, not just a conqueror. The Greek cities in assembly at Corinth were persuaded to award him the title of general in chief of the Hellenes, protector of Greece, a propaganda device aimed at the Greeks living under Persian rule in Asia Minor.

In 334 B.C., with less than 40,000 troops and only a limited supply of equipment and money, Alexander crossed the Hellespont. Though the Persians might theoretically have raised an army of about a million men to meet him, most of these would have been untrained levies and difficult to assemble, since no ancient power had the facilities or the resources for maintaining a large standing army. To gain time while the levies were brought together, it was standard Persian practice to employ mercenaries, usually Greeks, who could not always be trusted when facing other Greeks. Moreover, the number of available Greek mercenaries had been reduced because many had enlisted under Alexander's banner. Also, though Alexander's army was only moderate in size, large numbers might have proved a weakness because they would have been impossible to supply and difficult to support from the countryside.

The real deficiency of the Macedonian force was its navy. Alexander had only sixty ships, while the Persians could command the Aegean through their mastery of Phoenician sea power. The lack of a navy therefore dictated Alexander's strategy. He began at the Granicus River by defeating the troops immediately available to the Persian defenders of Asia Minor, after which he turned to occupying the coastal cities so as to deny the Persians the use of ports for their shipping. Few important military operations were involved in these early efforts, which consisted mainly of setting cities free of their Persian governors and putting Macedonian generals in their place.

In the second year, another battle took place near the town of Issus, in the border country between Syria and Anatolia. It seems clear that Alexander might have been impeded more effectively by some type of harassment or delaying tactics than by frontal assaults. Such a strategy would have required a strong leader, however, and it is apparent that the Persian king Darius III was notably lacking in competence. He had made little preparation for the Macedonian attack even though it had been imminent for several years. At Issus, Darius demonstrated little understanding of war, yet he lacked both the wisdom to consider good advice and the courage to endure combat. He attempted to stem the twenty-five or thirty thousand armed and skillfully led Greek and Macedonian soldiers with about the same number of troops, many of whom were not yet ready for battle. When Alexander personally led a picked cavalry detachment in a charge that scattered some second-string infantry, Darius simply mounted his chariot and fled, an act that may have turned the tide against him.

By his victory at Issus, Alexander came into possession of much of Darius' personal property, together with his wife, mother, and two daughters. The captives were treated with honor while the property relieved Alexander of his major financial problems. The next operation was to secure the Phoenician coast, accomplished after an arduous seven-month siege of Tyre. Alexander then moved on to Egypt, which fell easily. By midsummer of 331 B.C., he had returned to Syria, from where the advanced across the Euphrates and Tigris rivers. Near the village of Guagamela in Assyria, he won his most momentous victory against the largest and best force that the Persians could put in the field, a force considerably outnumbering his own troops. Darius again fled the scene, only to be assassinated shortly thereafter. Alexander then usurped the throne as king of kings, the traditional Persian title. Abandoning the role of both conqueror and liberator, he now became king of the Persians, treating Macedonians, Greeks, Persians, and others alike.

Alexander devoted the next nine years to establishing his authority throughout Iran and eastward, first into central Asia and then to the borders of India before he returned to begin the formidable task of governing his conquests. What he might have achieved in the area of administration must remain unknown, for a year later he fell ill and died (323 B.C.), not yet thirty-three years old. Since he had made no arrangements for a successor, his vast domain was soon divided up by his generals into a collection of more or less hostile kingdoms.

THE HELLINISTIC KINGDOMS

The two centuries from the appearance of Alexander to the emergence of Roman predominance in the eastern Mediterranean are called the Hellenistic period in order to distinguish the era from the earlier and purely Greek or Hellenic age. The Hellenistic period was dominated by the three great powers of Egypt, Macedonia, and Seleucia. Egypt, which had been seized by the army general Ptolemy, was by far the most successful of these successor states. This ancient kingdom had been given renewed vigor both by Alexander's destruction of the Phoenician naval supremacy and by his establishment of a new and superior trading center in the western delta, the city of Alexandria. By steering clear of most of the wars that marked the Hellenistic rivalry, Ptolemy and his successors managed to make their kingdom the commercial center of the eastern Mediterranean. Macedonia remained a powerful state under the control of the descendants of Antigonus, another of Alexander's generals, who also dominated Greece. Most of Asia fell to Seleucus, another general, who soon lost the eastern territories to a new people, the Parthians. Increasingly, the Seleucids were restricted to Syria, but their capital city of Antioch on the Orontes River became Alexandria's most important rival. Growing in importance as a buffer between the Antigonid and Seleucid states was the kingdom of Pergamum in Asia Minor. This small country, centered around the city of Pergamum, achieved considerable properity and influence under the rule of the Attalid family.

Alexander's conquests had reunited the various parts of the ancient Near East under Greek control. Greek learning, already well advanced, was now fortified and strengthened by renewed contact with the East, the original source of much of the existing knowledge. Economically, the conquest removed the barriers between the various parts of the Near East, and the release of the Persian gold hoards caused a tremendous growth in trade as well as a sudden inflation of prices. As political conditions became more stable, some of this trade declined, but neither Greek thought nor Greek life was ever again contained within the concept of the polis.

Athens, the city that dominated the intellectual life of the fifth century, was gradually supplanted by Alexandria, Pergamum, and Antioch, although much of the achievement in these other cities was the outgrowth of Athenian accomplishments. For this reason, Athens, in spite of its political insignificance and its lack of resources, managed to retain importance as the titular center of education and learning until well into the Christian era. The resources of Egypt, of Asia Minor, and of the Seleucid Empire, however, increasingly attracted scholars and scientists to Alexandria, Pergamum, and Antioch.

SOCRATES AND PLATO

Old ideas had already been challenged by the Sophists, and this challenge was reinforced by the turmoil of the last part of the fifth century and the collapse of the city-state in the fourth century. The Greeks no longer felt the certainty and confidence they once had. It did not seem as though the problems of the Hellenistic period could be solved with answers based upon the old gods and the old dogmas. Many Greeks looked to the mystery religions of the East, while a few attempted to find reasoned explanations for man's condition. The most important person in the latter group, at least to future generations, was Socrates, the man whom the Athenians put to death during their time of troubles. Just exactly what Socrates taught is not always possible to determine. He left no written work, and the portrayals we have of him by the fourth-century writers Xenophon, Aristophanes, and Plato differ radically. It is the Socrates of Plato who has become famous, the heroic figure continually searching for truth, the man of unswerving moral integrity with a determined belief in reason as the answer to man's problems. Plato's Socrates is an admirable person, one who has been respected by generations of readers for living up to his beliefs. In a sense, however, Socrates is almost too heroic, too good; at times he appears to be a god rather than a mortal.

Plato himself was a dramatist, and he abandoned playwriting for philosophy only after coming under the influence of Socrates. His philosophical writings retained the dramatic qualities essential to a successful play, however. In fact, the dramatic quality of his dialogues makes it difficult to decide just what Plato himself believed. In his earlier writings, in which Socrates is the chief protagonist, the latter seems clearly to be the embodiment of Plato's ideas. In the later dialogue, this same viewpoint is more difficult to identify. At the base of Plato's philosophy was the conviction that the prime essence of anything is the idea of it, from which derives the philosophical term "idealism." Plato's ideas were universal concepts such as beauty, justice, goodness, and truth. Plato, and also Socrates, believed that these universals were real, that they existed as absolutes. These absolutes were known to the *nous*, a Greek word for what we might loosely call the soul. Philosophy to Plato consisted in trying to discover the true nature of these universals. Before man could understand them, he had to question, to toss out preconceived ideas, to penetrate to the fundamentals; then and only then could he arrive at the universals. Plato went one step further, stating that once man knew what was good, he would not choose anything else.

Plato felt keenly the chaos of the age in which he lived. He was an aristocrat in a democratic city, a conservative in an age of change. In his search for the truth, for the good life, he examined Greek educational and political systems and inevitably found them wanting. A better society would have been the one he described in his most famous dialogue, the *Republic*. His ideal state was controlled by philosopher-kings (whom he called guardians), who devoted themselves to investigating the nature of human problems and then acting upon the truths they found. The rest of society was dedicated to the support of these rulers by a rigid class stratification. In effect, his *Republic* was an intellectualized and somewhat humanized version of Sparta.

As all of his candidates disappointed him, Plato later despaired of ever achieving a rule by philosopher-kings. In his *Laws,* he argued that since his kind of utopia was not possible, the best system would be a state ruled by laws, but even here his recommendations were

Plato and Aristotle, detail from Raphael's fresco, the "School of Athens." (Alinari–Art Reference Bureau)

extremely conservative. In a sense, however, Plato was also a radical. Like any good philosopher, he challenged much of the conventional wisdom of his day. He wondered, for example, whether women were capable of performing the same work as men, and he believed that except for fighting they could and should. In part at least, Plato also laid the basis for the eventual revolution in science, which, although long delayed, utilized the Platonic method of applying mathematical concepts to abstract thoughts. He believed that knowledge could come only through a life given to intellectual striving, yet before one could venture into the unknown it was necessary to understand conceptual constructs based on mathematics. Plato also believed in the immortality of the soul and evolved a sort of intellectual monotheism, concepts so valued by later Christians that they believed Plato must have been a Christian even though he lived several centuries before Jesus. At any rate, Plato early entered the pantheon of Christian saints.

ARISTOTLE

An innovator in education, Plato established the academy, a school devoted to carrying on his teachings. For almost a thousand years, the academy was a sort of institute for advanced studies which performed the valuable function of allowing scholars to work together to the common advantage. Basically, Plato was a teacher, and the mark of a great teacher lies mainly in his ability to inspire others. If for no other reason, Socrates was a great teacher because he inspired Plato, whose monument, in turn, was Aristotle. By any definition of accomplishment, Aristotle must be classed as one of the most influential persons in the history of human thought. We accord him this honor despite the fact that we have only a partial knowledge of what he thought, believed, and wrote.

As far as we can tell, everything that Plato wrote has been preserved, a fact that makes him unique among the ancients. On the other hand, none of what Aristotle himself wrote for publication has survived. Instead, we have only his lecture notes or notes taken down by his students. For this reason, Aristotle is difficult to understand; he seems to be obtuse, detailed, and at the same time compact. He takes effort while Plato is almost too easy. Aristotle explored nearly every subject, and his ideas have been grouped into eight major fields: logic, metaphysics, ethics, aesthetics, biology, psychology, physics, and political philosophy.

Logic rightfully belongs first in the list because Aristotle was the inventor of logic. His systematic approach to the problem of discriminating between truth and fallacy made possible new ways of thinking, not just once in the history of civilization but several times because for long periods knowledge of the science was lost. Aristotle also founded metaphysics, so named because in the later collections of his works, this monograph followed the one on physics. In it Aristotle not only modified the Platonic concept of universals but developed the idea of causation. He argued that for anything to be completed there were four basic causes: the material, the formal, the efficient, and the final. This idea was a decisive influence on Christianity, although Aristotle's effect was felt several centuries later than Plato's.

Aristotle's father was a physician in the employ of Philip of Macedon. He sent his son to study under Plato at the academy, after which Aristotle returned to Macedon as tutor to the young Alexander. Alexander later helped his teacher set up his own school in Athens, the lyceum, which rivaled 'the academy in influence. The support of such a powerful figure enabled Aristotle to assemble literary and biological materials for study, and in particular to study the actual constitutions of cities. His treatise on politics, for example, was based on objective inquiry rather than simple reason or intuition and was designed to find out what kinds of governments existed. He classified the various kinds of governments, described them, and drew his conclusions. For Aristotle, monarchy was the best form of rule, although he noted that it often turned into autocracy, the worst form. He believed timocracy, a rule based upon property, to be much less desirable than monarchy, but he felt that its perversion, democracy, was preferable to autocracy. In much the same way, Aristotle analyzed poetry, biology, ethics, physics, astronomy, and other subjects. He was at his best as an assembler of knowledge who attempted to reject the specious and the spurious, and with Aristotle ancient science was codified. Truth among the Greeks was never so much *discovered* by purposeful research as it was *uncovered,* or found lying around, so to speak, hidden by a clutter of error, superstition, or deliberate misrepresentation. A scientist thus became something of an assayer, skilled at knowing when the treasure was genuine and when it was only fool's gold.

HELLENISTIC SCIENTISTS

Aristotle had demonstrated what could be achieved when a small part of the resources of an Alexander were used to support intellectual efforts. The lesson was not entirely lost upon that monarch's successors. In Alexandria, the Ptolemies built and supported the famous museum and library. Similar institutions took shape in Pergamum and in Antioch, while Athens maintained its academy and lyceum.

The Alexandrian conquests had brought the Greeks into contact with other learning, which resulted in an outpouring of scientific achievement, particularly at Alexandria. In the third century, Euclid of Alexandria summarized the existing knowledge of geometry, much of it based upon Egyptian accomplishments. Other Greeks turned to astronomy, where their ideas were influenced by the astronomical discoveries of the Babylonians and the speculations of earlier Greeks such as Pythagoras. Astronomers attempted to calculate the circumference of the earth, its motion, and other factors. One Greek thinker, Aristarchus of Samos, in a sense anticipated the Copernican theory by holding that the earth rotated daily on its axis and moved in orbit around the sun. His ideas were rejected by other astronomers in favor of what they believed to be the more logical geocentric universe theory, based in part upon Aristolelian concepts, in which the sun moved around the earth. Geometry, astronomy, mathematics, and medicine were the main areas of interest for Hellenistic scientists, who continued their work into the Roman period. In medicine, Hellenistic physicians collected the treatises that go under the name of Hippocrates, a semilegendary figure from fifth-century Cos. Other physicians at Alexandria and elsewhere laid the foundation through dissection for anatomy and also for physiology and pharmacology. The new Hellenistic centers, in addition, collected works by ancient Greek writers, preserving copies of old manuscripts. It is largely as a result of such efforts at Pergamum and Alexandria that what we have of Greek learning was eventually transmitted to the modern world.

THE SEARCH FOR PEACE OF MIND

Other Greek thinkers were less concerned with scientific problems. Instead, they sought solace for the spirit, a way to free the individual from the growing uncertainties and worries of his life on earth. Those who offered a means of finding such peace are conventionally grouped by schools: the Cynics, the Skeptics, the Stoics, and the Epicureans.

All of the systems that evolved reflect the dislocation of the Greek world in the fourth and third centuries B.C. The Cynics, alienated by contemporary society, believed that happiness could be found only by renouncing physical and social pleasures and returning to nature. The wise man was the person like Diogenes who lived in a tub and cultivated rudeness, demonstrating his independence of life's superfluities. The Skeptics emphasized the impossibility of knowing truth. Since man could know only what his senses tell him, and since these could not reveal reality, the only way to achieve spiritual tranquillity was to suspend judgment on all matters — a most undogmatic approach to life, but one that left a person totally passive.

Obviously the solutions of the Cynics and the Skeptics could have no more than limited appeal. In a sense, these groups represented the "hippy" element in society, an element that may, nevertheless, have forced some men to think through the purpose of life and face up to the difficulties of existence. More appealing answers, at least for those who looked to philosophy, were given by the Stoics and the Epicureans. Stoicism was a third-century movement built around the teachings of Zeno, Cleanthes, and Chrysippus. Though influenced by the teachings of the Cynics, the Stoics had greater faith in the individual to mold his own personality and to surmount his misfortunes. Stoicism taught that man should rise above his emotions rather than be controlled by them. Accomplishment was less important than genuine effort. Every man, regardless of his occupation, whether slave or free, should pursue his calling with dignity and effort. The chief purpose in life was the pursuit of virtue, and virtue could be attained only through reasoned actions and individual effort. A man was to be judged for himself, not for what group he belonged to nor by where he was born. In their emphasis upon individualism, the Stoics also achieved a kind of cosmopolitanism, since they believed that beneath appearances all men are brothers and all have the potential of achieving virtue. Stoicism, however, still had the effect of encouraging a passive acceptance of society as it was rather than urging men to try to improve their situation.

Epicureanism, which rivaled Stoicism, emphasized enlightened self-interest. To Epicurus, the founder of the movement, the most important thing in life was happiness growing out of the pursuit of pleasure and the avoidance of pain. Pleasure, however, was subject to careful discrimination. Epicurus taught that man should seek enduring pleasures rather than temporary ones. The pleasures of wine or of sex, for example, could not compare, he thought, to the lasting pleasures of the mind. To Epicurus, the wise man was the man who examined the reasons for all his choices and who then ignored petty pleasures or vain opinions, which were the source of confusion. Still, like Stoicism, Epicureanism was an encouragement to accept the world as it was rather than to try to change it.

RELIGION

Both Stoicism and Epicureanism assumed that men possessed a measure of reason and detachment, and both philosophies attempted to achieve peace of mind through contemplation. Most people, however, were too pressed by the world's innumerable tragedies to have time for contemplation. Instead, the mystery cults, with their assurances of rebirth, regeneration, and immortality, had much wider appeal. These cults were restricted to members, or persons who had acquired access to them through a prescribed course of purification to a mysterious providence. Each cult had sacramental rituals that distinguished it from others and through which members achieved a sense of communion with their deity as well as a purgation of sin. While Socrates and Plato had reasoned a necessity for some sort of afterlife — indeed, Socrates was willing to die because of this belief — most people wanted more tangible support for the idea of life after death than philosophical arguments. The Alexandrian conquests brought the Greeks into contact with Mithraism (an offshoot of Zoroastrianism) from Persia, with Judaism, with the fertility cults of Syria, and with various Egyptian religions such as that centered about Osiris and Isis. Gradually these religions were imported into Greece, where they joined the earlier Greek cults associated with Dionysus and Eleusis. In the Dionysian cult, the god, though destroyed and dismembered, was eventually resurrected, a symbol of what could happen to his followers. Similar themes were to be found in the other mystery religions, although since the rites were always observed with great secrecy, it has never been easy for the historian to explain the differences among them. Interpretation is also complicated because these cults made their greatest appeal to the lower classes, the least literate group in society.

GREEK ART

The significance of religion in the Greek world is most evident to us from the architectural and other artistic survivals. The largest collections of Greek buildings still standing are those in the sanctuary cities of Olympia, Delos, and Delphi and in the temple complexes of cities like Athens. Greek temples were built to be seen, not for worship. Each was a creative triumph. The Greeks understood the distortions of the human eye, and their architects took this into account to obtain a visual effect. For utilitarian purposes, however, the temples were not particularly outstanding. Inside they were often dark and damp, indicating that the Greeks lacked the engineering abilities of the Egyptians or even of their own Mycenaean ancestors. Visitors today are impressed with the marble purity of the Greek temples, but the remains look quite different from what they once did. The relief sculptures were originally painted, often quite brightly, and they would probably be considered garish by present-day standards.

Like Greek literature and philosophy, Greek art reflects the changes that took place in Greek society over the years. The first Greek temples seem to have been influenced by Egyptian models, as was early Greek sculpture. In fact, sculpture and architecture were so closely identified that it is necessary to discuss them together. Like the Egyptian models, the early sculpture, usually called archaic, was dominated by block-like figures in rigid frontal poses. Most of the early sculptors and architects are unknown to us, but as Athens grew in importance in the fifth century, individual personalities began to appear. The most famous of Athenian sculptors was Phidias, who supervised the construction and embellishment of the Parthenon. It was he who carved the gigantic ivory and gold figure of Athena that dominated the temple, which is known to us only through small copies. Phidias also designed and executed most, if not all, of the figures on the Parthenon frieze now preserved in the British Museum.

In general, the art and architecture of the fifth century give a feeling of serenity that is not present in the emotional and sentimental survivals of the fourth and third centuries. By the fourth century, heroic religious sculptures were no longer in demand, since no city was wealthy enough to build on the lavish scale of Athens. Elaborate public works, such as the Acropolis buildings in Athens, gave way to private commissions of tombs or other commemorative monuments. New in the art of this period was the unclothed female figure, introduced by Praxiteles in his "Cnidian Aphrodite." The change in emphasis is best represented by the sculptor Scopas, whose most famous work was the Mausoleum of Halicarnassus. Built by Queen Artemisia as a memorial for her husband Mausolus, the work is decorated with a series of figures that express quiet but intense sorrow. With the advent of Alexander, individual portrait sculpture became increasingly common as rich and powerful individuals could become personal patrons. Lysippus, the official portraitist of the conqueror, was one of the leading artists. After the death of Alexander, the centers of art shifted. Pergamum, for example, became important for figures of rather sensational realism such as the "Dying Gaul" or the famed Pergamum Altar, now in the Bode Museum in Berlin. Sculptors at Alexandria produced a series of personality portraits, often of ordinary people such as street urchins or an old market woman. The idealized figures of the fifth century had become more realistic in the fourth century and almost caricatures in the third.

GREECE IN THE THIRD
AND SECOND CENTURIES

By 300 B.C., Greece itself was no longer particularly important. While its cities, subsisting under the shadow of Macedonia, still reflected an aura of grandeur, large numbers of Greeks moved to where opportunities were greater — Italy, Egypt, Syria, Anatolia, and even India. In these new places they lived in the large cities as the socially dominant, ruling, and commercial classes, a status they had gained through their knowledge, skill, and resourcefulness. Almost for the first time, the Greeks seemed to demonstrate a spirit of comradeship that transcended political boundaries, a spirit that led to a cooperation in the international sphere which they had never been able to attain in their homeland.

In spite of the fact that the Hellenistic world was fairly prosperous and enjoyed considerable stability, it was also characterized by slavery, desperate poverty, exploitation, tyranny, and insecurity. Increasingly, the individual was forced to look to his own devices, since he could expect less and less from his community. It is not surprising, therefore, that Hellenistic culture was less than satisfying to large numbers of people. Many disillusioned Greeks attempted to escape from the actualities of their lives by cultivating other-wordly interests or by seeking serenity in the mystery cults of the East.

Against this background the new power of Rome made itself felt soon after 200 B.C.

7

The Rise of Rome

The rise of the comparatively backward and inconsequential people from the village of Rome to eventual control of the Mediterranean seaboard is one of the great success stories of all time. By examining the factors that led to the growth of Rome, we can better understand why earlier empires such as the Persian or the Assyrian, for which source materials are much more nebulous or even nonexistent, also developed. The story of Rome, however, poses special problems because its later history changed from one of triumph to one of tragedy. Roman history is the kind of material out of which sermons are made, with each pulpit interpreting the cause of the Roman success or failure to suit its own moral. Even historians find it easier to say what happened rather than to explain why it happened.

Geographically, Rome enjoyed a slight advantage over most of its potential rivals in Italy. It was located near the northern edge of Latium, one of the most fertile agricultural plains of the mountainous Italian peninsula. It was some fifteen miles inland on the Tiber, the most important river of central Italy, near a key river ford and a road junction. Since ancient ships could go up the Tiber to Rome but no further, the site not only offered protection against a sudden attack by pirates but it also had the potential of serving as a transshipping center. Italy, however, was located in the western Mediterranean, and this fact enabled Rome to develop with comparatively little interference from the great powers in the East. By the time Rome became dominant in the Italian peninsula, it had the resources and the organizational ability to defeat Carthage, its chief rival in the West. Rome then became the major military power on the Mediterranean and ended up conquering all of the territories that bordered this great inland sea.

According to mythology, Rome was settled on a cluster of hills by the followers of Romulus and Remus, descendants of Aeneas who had fled to Latium from Troy. Romulus, after killing Remus, became king of the city in 753 B.C. The Romans later dated events by this legendary year, using A.U.C. (*ab urbe condita*), literally "from the founding of the city," a system that served the same function as A.D. and B.C. today. Romulus, in order to obtain wives for his followers, invited some neighboring Sabines to a feast, whereupon the Romans killed the men and seized the women. After other similar adventures, Romulus died and was succeeded by six more kings, some of whom were Etruscan. The legend is important because it tells something of what the Romans believed, at least for a time, although historically it has little value. Along with most of the peoples of the Italian peninsula, the Romans had entered Italy as part of the general migration of Indo-Europeans at the beginning of the Iron Age. Later, other immigrants, such as the Etruscans, also settled in Italy, and for a time the Etruscans controlled Rome.

THE ETRUSCANS

Most scholars believe that the Etruscans were eighth-century B.C. emigrants from Asia Minor, whose culture had come under the same influences as that of the Greeks of that time. But though we have excavated many of their settlements, the people themselves remain a mystery, largely because the Etruscan language has not yet been deciphered. Even though linguists can read numerous words and know the general principles upon which the language was constructed, they are unable to go further because of the paucity of surviving records. With their superior weapons, organizational ability, and sophisticated city-state system of government, the Etruscans soon gained dominance in that part of the Italian peninsula known today as Tuscany (the area around Florence). Many of the city-states organized themselves into a loose confederation which expanded southward to include Rome, where Etruscan civilization had a lasting effect on art and architecture and particularly on written Latin. It was the Etruscans who developed the modified Greek letters which evolved into the Latin alphabet.

THE ROMAN REPUBLIC

Even though the Etruscans made Rome the dominant city-state in the plains of Latium, the Romans were restive members of the confederation. In about 509 B.C., they deposed their Etruscan king, withdrew from the confederation, and established a republic. This act of independence not only subjected the Romans to the possibility of retaliation but also made them prey to invasion by other enemies no longer deterred by Etruscan power. In effect, Rome could exist as an independent power only by becoming a military state. In this respect the Romans resembled the Spartans, although they remained much more open-minded and adaptable.

The strength of the early Roman army lay in its citizen-soldiers, who, as soon as a battle was over, returned to cultivate their farms. Each citizen had to furnish his own equipment according to his income, which meant that the rich served as horsemen while the less wealthy were infantrymen. To make certain that burdens were correctly distributed, the Romans took periodic censuses, after which each man was assigned to an appropriate class in the army. The great virtue of the system lay not in any particular military genius, although the Roman legion soon became the most adaptable unit of any ancient infantry, but rather in the reluctance of the army to admit defeat. With time out for planting and harvesting, the civilian soldier could fight on for years.

The first stage in Roman expansion, the elimination of Etruscan strongholds from the plains of Latium, lasted over a hundred years. It was during this period that the Romans demonstrated the ability to win and hold allies that played such a large part in their ultimate supremacy over the other Italians. To gain supporters during the various wars, Rome drew up formal agreements of alliance with other cities, each one slightly different from any other, so that no two allies ever had quite the same disagreement with Rome. Since Rome, like Athens, was usually the most influential partner in any alliance, it soon came to dominate all of them through control of their foreign policy. Unlike the Athenians, however, the Romans were usually willing to share the fruits of their alliances and eventually even recognized their allies as Roman citizens. Though Rome was undoubtedly enriched by the booty of successful wars, so were those parts of Italy that took the Roman side.

Alliances also served as a pretext for further expansion once the Etruscan threat was removed. The enemies of the allies became the enemies of Rome, and because Italy lacked any real unity in the early years of the republic, local wars were a regular occurrence. Moreover, the alliance system allowed the Romans to delude themselves with the idea that they never went to war for any offensive purpose but merely to protect their own borders. They conveniently neglected to remember that their frontiers were always expanding either through alliance or conquest, and, like many more modern states, they soon were fighting in areas far removed from their homeland.

ROMAN INTERNAL REFORM

During the early period of expansion, the Romans also modified their internal constitution. Fearful of again having a strong monarch, the patricians, or the heads of the aristocratic families, attempted to distribute royal power. Religious authority was assigned to a chief priest (the *pontifex maximus*) who became head of the state religion. Judicial and executive powers were divided between two officials, usually called *consuls,* who were elected to serve one-year terms. To further weaken their potential for strong rule, each consul had a veto over the plans of the other. The patricians, however, recognizing that in time of crisis such veto power might be dangerous, provided in the constitution that the *senate* could replace the consuls with a single dictator for short periods of time. Real power at all times was held by the senate, nominally a council of elders (*senex* means "old man"), but restricted to the patricians.

The most obvious difficulty with the system was that the common citizens, the *plebeians* or *plebs,* had no voice in public affairs. Moreover, they lacked legal protection. Rome soon found itself involved in the same kinds of struggles that in the Greek cities had led to the emergence of tyrants. In Rome, however, the patricians proved more amenable to change, and the plebeians were better able to secure their demands. In a state more or less continually involved in war, as Rome had come to be, the plebeians by refusing to serve in the army could force the patricians to negotiate. Such an undertaking required organization, and the plebeians formed an unofficial union among themselves and elected *tribunes* to present their demands to the aristocracy. To protect the tribunes from possible retaliation, the plebeians swore to regard them as sacrosanct, which implied that anyone who manhandled a tribune would be subject to assassination. Then, by periodically threatening to secede from the state (but never in time of war), the plebeians forced through a whole series of reforms. Their first gain was the codification of law, followed by land redistribution, the right to hold political office, and the right of plebeians to intermarry with the aristocrats. Finally, the plebeian union itself was recognized as a legal legislative body known as the tribal assembly, or the *comitia tributa*. This recognition was granted only on condition that aristocrats be allowed to become members and that the number of tribunes be increased. Since each tribune had veto power over the other, the revolutionary potential of the plebeian organization was weakened, although the *comitia tributa* was given the right to initiate legislation.

The Roman ability to compromise, so apparent in these negotiations between segments of the populace, tended to set Rome apart from most of its neighbors. It also enabled the aristocrats to maintain their control of the state by incorporating the leadership of the plebeians into the power structure. Since offiholders did not receive a salary, only the richer — and usually less radical — plebeians could hold office, and often these men had more in common with the patricians than with the poorer plebeians, particularly after the removal of the artificial barriers that had separated the rich plebeians from the aristocrats. The one gain the poor plebeian had made was his right to vote for various officers, and periodically a reformer who represented his interests managed to be elected.

DOMINATION OF THE MEDITERRANEAN

Social inequities at the beginning of the third century were not as noticeable as they became later, since Rome was not yet a particularly rich state. As the Roman state expanded, the gap between the rich and the poor widened because the wars brought vast amounts of booty to the victors, particularly to the officers of the state. Though the Romans were comparatively benevolent conquerors, the wealth they acquired after their conquest of the Greek colonies in southern Italy forced a change in the whole nature of the state.

Like Greeks elsewhere, those in Italy were continually fighting among themselves, ignoring the growing Roman colossus until they found it on their doorstep. In 280 B.C., the city of Tarentum, fearful of further Roman advance, imported the soldier-adventurer Pyrrhus, the king of Epirus in northwest Greece, along with a large band of mercenaries, to do battle with the Romans. Pyrrhus defeated the Romans in two costly battles (Pyrrhic victories), but his success caused the Greeks of southern Italy to be more fearful of him than of the Romans. Denied further support, Pyrrhus then moved to Sicily, where he began clearing the island of Carthaginians. Rome, angered by Greek support of Pyrrhus, started moving into southern Italy, whereupon the fearful Greeks immediately recalled Pyrrhus. This time the Romans defeated Pyrrhus and the latter abandoned Italy for a new campaign in Macedonia. Tarentum soon surrendered to the Romans and became an allied city whose foreign policy was controlled by Rome. The other Greek cities in southern Italy followed suit, so that by 265 B.C. the whole peninsula south of the Arano and Rubicon rivers was under firm control of Rome.

ROME VERSUS CARTHAGE

The domination of southern Italy made Rome one of the great powers in the Mediterranean world, along with Egypt, Macedonia, the Seleucid kingdom, and Carthage — and a possible threat to them all. The closest, and for that reason the most threatened, was Carthage, located on the coast of North Africa. This former Phoenician colony had grown rich from its naval and commercial control over the western Mediterranean, and it dominated much of North Africa, Sicily, and Spain. During the early centuries of Roman expansion, the Carthaginians had been friendly and helpful, in part because the Romans had not been particularly interested in commerce or trade. In fact, the Roman patricians, who looked with disdain upon business, had been perfectly content to let the Carthaginians control what little foreign trade existed in Rome. With Roman domination of the Greek colonies in southern Italy, however, Greek commercial policies now became Roman, resulting in a rapid deterioration in relations between Rome and Carthage. The first clash was over Sicily, where the Greek allies of Rome and the Carthaginians had competing interests.

Growing out of this clash in Sicily were three Punic Wars, so called from the Latin name for Phoenicians. Since the struggle of the two great western powers quite naturally involved the interests of the other great powers, the Punic Wars also coincided with Roman involvement in four Macedonian Wars, as well as a war with the Seleucid monarchs, and direct intervention into Egypt. Rome also began to expand into Gaul.

The Punic Wars, which were fought between 265 and 146 B.C., finally ended with the conquest and destruction of Carthage. The first Punic War, which ended in 241 B.C., made Rome a naval power and gave the Romans control of Sicily. Shortly after this, Rome also occupied the islands of Corsica and Sardinia, which the weakened Carthaginians, then involved in an army revolt, were unable to prevent. The second Punic War, which lasted from 218 to 201 B.C., was the greatest military challenge that Rome had ever faced. Led by Hannibal, a Carthaginian army invaded Italy, lived off the country, and remained undefeated in the very heart of Roman power for more than a dozen years. In spite of the circumstances, only a few of Rome's allies deserted to Hannibal. The war was finally won by sheer endurance and the resourcefulness of the senate in sending military expeditions directly into enemy teritory in Spain and Africa. The Carthaginian government, which had never given sufficient material support to Hannibal, was forced to recall the victorious general, who then met defeat under the walls of his own city. From this war Rome acquired Carthaginian Spain, the source of Hannibal's power — most of which it then had to conquer. With only a portion of its African territory left, Carthage enjoyed about a half century of peace until the Romans decided to destroy it. The third Punic War dragged on for three years before Carthage was finally carried by storm and almost wholly obliterated. The region was annexed as the Roman province of Africa.

Macedonia first intervened on the side of Carthage during the second Punic War. The outcome, after some four wars, was annexation, which also gave Rome control of the affairs of Greece. Initially, Rome had declared that the Greek cities should be free, but the Greeks soon realized that this freedom had severe limitations. Any city that showed signs of being independent was subject to harsh treatment. The Seleucid Empire, after having lost much of its eastern territory to the Parthians, found itself restricted after a war with Rome to the area around Syria. Egypt managed to retain a measure of independence as a kind of client state, whereas Pergamum in Asia Minor, which had grown prosperous as an ally, was willed to the Romans in 133 B.C. Its ruler, Attalus II, the last of his family, had become convinced that Roman conquest was inevitable.

THE EFFECTS OF CONQUEST

So rich did Rome become from the loot and plunder of these wars that after 167 B.C. all Roman citizens could live free of direct taxation. When Macedonia was annexed, for example, shiploads of sculpture and other works of art were brought to Rome along with quantities of other types of booty. Conquest also brought slaves — so many, in fact, that the Romans were averse to having slaves wear a distinctive costume lest they realize their numbers and attempt to overthrow the government.

Not all citizens shared equally in this prosperity, however, nor did the Roman allies receive what they regarded as their just portion. Instead, the divisions between the rich and the poor widened, and there emerged new grounds for friction between Rome and the other Italian cities. The small landed proprietors who had been the bulwark of an earlier Rome found themselves threatened with extinction, unable to sustain the increasing demand for military service. Since most wars were fought outside Italy, it meant that armies could no longer be disbanded in the autumn and reassembled for the summer campaigns as had once been the case. Instead, the soldier had to remain in Spain, Greece, or elsewhere, for several years, and when he returned to his land he often found his fields deserted and neglected. Even if his wife and family had managed to hold the farm together, the veteran discovered that he had to compete with the large slave-run estates (latifundia) owned and controlled by the wealthy. Inevitably, many soldiers, unwilling or unable to work their farms under the new conditions, abandoned the countryside and moved to Rome in the hope of getting a greater share of the benefits of empire. Plunder at best could provide little more than a temporary subsistence; in the meantime, these men had to survive in a city that had little industry and few jobs. Rather than attempting to provide a long-term solution to the problem of this mass influx of unemployed citizens, the government merely tried to quiet discontent by providing grain doles and some form of entertainment (bread and circuses). Even more dangerous to Rome was the fact that when they abandoned their farms, the peasants were more or less lost to the army, since the Roman census was based upon landed wealth. As a result, even though population increased and Rome became extremely wealthy, the number of persons eligible to serve as soldiers declined.

With most officials more and more involved in the ruling of an empire, these growing internal difficulties were ignored. Roman imperialism itself changed radically once the army moved beyond Italy. Traditional means of communication and transportation were too primitive for the city to rely upon the independent ally system that had been developed for Italy. Moreover, the possibilities of exploitation of the conquered peoples encouraged the development of different methods of administration. Beginning with the annexation of Sicily, Rome converted the newly conquered areas to provinces. Within each province there might be colonies of citizens and some old-style allied cities, but most of the people resided in various kinds of subject cities, all of which had to pay taxes to Rome. Supervising the administration of the province was a Roman governor, appointed by the senate from the retiring consuls and other officeholders. The governors had almost absolute power in a province, subject to no control but that of the senate. Because Roman administration was still not well organized, with even the collection of taxes an individual enterprise, the governors could and did become rich simply by helping themselves to some of the revenue or by charging for their judicial opinions. Theoretically, provincials who were harshly exploited could appeal to the senate for relief, but since the senate had appointed the governor in the first place and contained a good number of former governors, none but the most indiscrete was ever punished. The growth of this type of provincial government radically changed the nature of politics within the city of Rome itself, simply because the only way to become a provincial governor was to run for office in Rome. The office of consul, for example, which had earlier been regarded as an honor even though its holders had to pay for certain public functions, now became the possible source of great wealth, and ambitious candidates were willing to spend large sums of money to be elected. The unemployed Roman citizen was the beneficiary of this situation when he discovered that the properly managed sale of his vote in the annual elections could provide him with a good supplemental income.

Roman administration was weak because, first of all, it was ill adapted to ruling a growing empire; rather, the system had been designed to rule a medium-sized city-state, and the Romans refused to recognize that their world had changed. Rather than developing a paid civil service to administer the empire, the Romans relied upon individual enterprise. Such tasks as the collecting of taxes in the provinces, the supplying of troops in the field, and the operation of state mines were contracted out to private groups through public bidding. Persons who bought the right to undertake such contracts were called publicans. When a job was beyond the financial resources of a single man, several publicans came together to form joint stock companies with limited liability. While the concept of limited liability held great potential for the future of business, its functioning within the state administration proved harmful. It naturally meant that the individuals acting in behalf of the government were not particularly interested in the problems of government nor in the welfare of the people, but primarily in getting a good return on their investment. Any amount they collected over their bid belonged to them. Often they were more than willing to cut corners wherever and whenever they could, and they were equally willing to resort to pressure and influence. A cooperative Roman governor could easily make the difference between a profit and a loss, and the publicans were never unwilling to share a percentage with an official. Since Roman patricians were barred by law from business activities, many publicans became rich enough to create a new middle class called the equestrians or *equites* because they were classified in the census as being able to afford horses for service in the cavalry.

Dissatisfaction grew among the allies who had shared in the original spoils of conquest, who now realized that they were not getting any of the profits of administration. The allied leaders demanded citizenship so that they too could become wealthy publicans or provincial governors, while the allies themselves wanted a greater share of the riches. Ordinary Romans who earlier might have been willing to grant citizenship to the allies now became reluctant to do so because they foresaw that additional numbers could only reduce the weight of their own votes in the elections. The publicans did not want competition, and the patricians had never welcomed additions to their class.

ART AND LITERATURE

Quite obviously, in spite of themselves the Romans were changing. Nowhere is their changing character more evident than in their art and literature. The early Romans had demonstrated no particular bent for literature, probably because the creative energies that might have gone into aesthetic pursuits were directed toward military and governmental affairs. In fact, the first true Roman writer was a Greek, Livius

Andronicus, who was brought to Rome in 272 B.C. after the capture of Tarentum. He became a schoolteacher, but without textbooks. To make up for this lack, he began to translate Homer into Latin. He also produced adaptations of Greek tragedies and comedies, playing some of the roles himself, and thereby formally established Latin drama.

Though Latin literature was strongly influenced by Greek models, the Romans soon managed to make Greek forms their own, as is apparent in the Latin comedy writers of the second century B.C., Plautus and Terence. Both of these writers testify to the growing importance of Rome as a literary and cultural center, since neither was a native Roman. Plautus, or more technically Titus Maccus Plautus, moved to Rome at an early age, where he learned Latin as a supplement to his native Umbrian. Like Aristophanes, he was critical of the ways and thought of his contemporaries, and the Romans, anxious about themselves but certain of their future, flocked to his plays. Though his criticism was expressed in ribald and earthy language, he enjoyed such popularity that later writers tried to attribute their own efforts to him. Terence, the other great Latin dramatist, was neither Roman nor Italian but a slave brought to Rome from Africa. He took his name, Publius Terentius Afer, from his former owner and patron, whose name was Terentius. Terence's comedies are more sophisticated than those of Plautus and depend much more upon purity of diction and a sly wit rather than boisterous humor. In fact, the comedies of Terence mark the beginnings of a change in Roman drama, with the form eventually becoming "closet" drama, or plays written to be enjoyed in the quiet of the study rather than as performances on the public stage. The ultimate result was that Roman drama became the preserve of the aristocrats rather than of the common man.

Just as the Romans mastered the Greek dramatic style, they also began to imitate and then perfect other forms derived from Greeks. In the great narrative poem the *Annals*, Quintus Ennius, a native of Italy, recounted in a Latin imitation of the Greek hexameter the history of Rome from its beginning until the time of his death in the middle of the second century B.C. Ennius was more original in his satire, in which he made a plea for reform, by making fun of the contradictions in the society he saw around him. The poet Lucilius, a member of a prominent Roman family, took up where Ennius left off, giving satire the spontaneity, topicality, and ironic wit that made it a uniquely Latin form of literature.

Latin prose developed somewhat more slowly, partly because of the comparative unsophistication of the Latin language as a medium of expression but also because Greek became the second language of educated Romans. Hellenism, which had started with Livius, became the fashion when such influential figures as Publius Cornelius Scipio, usually known as Scipio Africanus from his successful conquest of Carthage, adopted and encouraged all things Greek. Greek slaves were employed to teach children and special Greek schools were opened. Since the Romans still believed that education was best left to a child's parents, schools were privately operated, though most of the leading families sent their children to Greek schools, and many Romans even took to writing in Greek. The Roman senator Fabius Pictor compiled a history of Rome in Greek during the second century B.C., although his choice of language was only partly due to the inadequacies of Latin; Pictor's main objective was to allay Greek fears about Roman ambitions.

Not all Romans were impressed by the sudden influx of Greek models and ideas. To some it seemed to threaten all that was Roman. The leaders of the anti-Greek school was Marcus Porcius Cato, usually called Cato the Censor, a Roman superpatriot and xenophobe, hostile to anything foreign. To overcome the dominance of Greek texts and teachers, he wrote practical handbooks in Latin on all subjects in the curriculum. If his one surviving work, his treatise on agriculture, is a fair sample of his thinking, he appears to have been something of a reactionary. Cato was also an ambitious politician intent on expressing popular views, and much of his success depended upon an almost paranoid fear of anything that was not Roman. In spite of such sentiments, Greek influence grew ever more pervasive. The founder of Roman historical writing, for example, was Polybius, a Greek who was brought to Rome in 167 B.C. as a hostage. Polybius' work, in Greek, attempted to account for the establishment of Roman supremacy in the Mediterranean, and it became the model for later Latin historians.

The great Latin literary achievements of this period were in poetry, and the two great poets were Lucretius and Catullus, both of whom lived in the first century B.C. Lucretius made the Latin hexameter developed by Ennius into a poetic force of impressive vitality. He was even able to make a scientific essay, *On the Nature of Things*, into a poetic masterpiece. Catullus was concerned with more personal matters. His love poems are particularly moving, especially those about his beloved, a married woman whom he called Lesbia. Obviously, Catullus' relationship with Lesbia was tempestuous, for his poems trace every step in their quarrels and reconciliation. His famous verses beginning, "I love her and I hate her" capture the feelings of quarreling lovers everywhere.

RELIGION

Greek influence also permeated Roman religion, which originally had been heavily oriented toward ancestor worship and respect for the customs of the past. The effect of the traditional religious beliefs had been to make the Romans more conservative than the Greeks, more inclined to accept authority and less inclined to challenge the habitual way of doing things. Each family, household, and even field had its own nebulous spirits and gods, which only began to take on definite personalities and physical features during the early republican period. With the translation of Homer into Latin, the trend was accentuated as old Roman gods came to be almost interchangeable with those of the Greeks: Jupiter was a Roman Zeus, while Neptune was equated with Poseidon, Minerva with Athena, and Mercury with Hermes; some gods such as Apollo retained the same identity in both cultures. Besides importing the Olympic deities, the Romans also collected gods from wherever they went, on the assumption that the new gods might help Rome in one way or another. Under this influx, the old family cults began to decline and were replaced in part by the state cults, in which selected officials served as leaders. Although the official state cults dwarfed the old family religion in the magnificence of their temples and their organized priesthood, the Roman himself was never really satisfied with these changes in his ancient beliefs, and the result was a growing restlessness evident throughout the late republic. This restless spirit was undoubtedly given fuel by the appearance of Greek philosophy, which undermined many traditional Roman assumptions. A Latin advocate of the philosophy of Epicurus, Lucretius argued in *On the Nature of Things* that man made his greatest error in trying to see the hands of the gods behind natural phenomena. It is no wonder that the masses of Rome began to seek solace in the various mystery cults that had become so widespread in the eastern Mediterranean, while the upper classes turned to Stoicism or Epicureanism.

ART

Roman sculpture to all intents and purposes was Hellenistic. Wall painting, however, was more influenced by Etruscan rather than Greek models. In general, the Roman patrons preferred busts or portraits of themselves, a preference which allowed the artist in Rome to give his works a greater individuality than was usual in Greece. At the same time, the Romans commissioned copies of famous Greek works. This affinity for Greek art on the part of the Romans served to preserve replicas of many Greek originals which have since perished, but it did not encourage a unique or independent Roman contribution. In fact, most Roman artists and craftsmen were Greeks who were brought to Rome, either from the south of Italy or from the eastern Mediterranean.

Roman architecture was much more original, and the Roman innovation of the arch and the dome was the foundation of a creative Latin style. In the republic much genius was also expanded in technical fields such as in building aqueducts, bridges, and highways, original Roman engineering achievements that owed little to Greece.

THE FAILURE OF THE REPUBLIC

By the middle of the second century B.C., it was clear that the old Roman methods were being supplanted by new and different ones, that the old city-state government was inadequate for an empire, and that the influx of wealth as well as ideas had altered the Roman way of life. Yet the Romans were reluctant to admit that change was needed. Believing that they had become great and powerful by adhering to their old constitution and traditions, they also tended to feel that to change anything would be to evidence disloyalty. This sentiment was reinforced by the fact that persons enjoying privileges under the existing establishment felt threatened by any change. Instead of going along with change, even reluctantly, as earlier had been the case, the Roman ruling class had now developed a vested interest strong enough

Etruscans, scene from fresco in the tomb of the Leopardi, Tarquinia. (Alinari–Art Reference Bureau)

to prevent any kind of legislative innovation, leaving only the possibility of more radical, less peaceful action.

The difficulties of achieving peaceful reform were exemplified by the experience of Tiberius and Gaius Gracchus. Though the brothers were members of the senatorial aristocracy, they believed that the only chance to change things was to ignore the senate and work directly with the people as tribunes. It was as a tribune that Tiberius, the elder, proposed a land redistribution program in 133 B.C. Such a plan, he believed, would add to the army levies, give stability to city life by moving many of the poorer citizens to the country, and re-create the conditions for individual self-reliance present in the earlier republic. Even though the landowners were promised reimbursement for any land that might be taken from them, they opposed the scheme with every means at their disposal. When legal obstructions failed, some of the more hostile had Tiberius assassinated. A few years later, his younger brother was elected tribune. Gaius attempted to extend the program for land reform and, in addition, promised citizenship for many of the allies, better judicial procedures for the provinces, and much else. He too was killed.

The failure of the Gracchi to achieve reform by political methods proved disastrous. Within half a century Italy was torn by a civil war between Rome and many of its Italian allies, a war that ended only when the Italians were given the very citizenship that had been called for by Gaius Gracchus. Moreover, unwilling to make the land redistribution necessary to preserve the old methods of recruiting an army, the Romans were finally forced to drop land holding as a requirement for military service or face military defeat. The result was a large-scale enlistment of the urban proletariat, who were more interested in the opportunities for pillage than in serving a republic that had offered them so little. Thus the general who demonstrated success in battle could easily become a successful politician by exploiting the votes and hopes of his veterans. The rise of these politician-generals was facilitated by the employment of force to eliminate rivals such as Tiberius and Gaius. It was perhaps inevitable that those persons who controlled the army would come to dominate the city.

THE RISE OF THE GENERALS

The first successful general-politician was Gaius Marius, a well-meaning if somewhat confused figure, who at the end of the second century B.C. brought the new kind of army into politics. Marius allied himself — and his army — with the *populares*, a political party determined to limit upper class prerogatives. This party of the "common" man was opposed by the *optimates*, the party of the "best" people. As

Marius grew in power and influence, the *optimates*, including most of the senators, turned to a rival general, Sulla. Both men needed a continuing succession of military victories to retain their followers, and, in the jockeying for command, Sulla had a natural advantage because of his alliance with the senate. After demonstrating his superiority in a military trial of strength with Marius, Sulla imposed a dictatorship upon Rome. Though his actions convincingly marked the end of the republic, Sulla seems to have believed that he was only restoring the old constitution. After proscribing or executing most of the leadership of the *populares*, he so organized the government that the *optimates* and the senate had almost total control of the city, and thus of the empire. He made little effort to alleviate the economic and social discontent that underlay most of Rome's difficulties.

POMPEY AND CRASSUS

No sooner had Sulla died in 78 B.C. than his subordinates proceeded to throw aside his new constitution. One of these was his lieutenant, Gnaeus Pompeius, better known as Pompey, who first achieved independent military success as a commander in Spain against an antisenatorial general. While Pompey was fighting in Spain with senatorial backing, a major slave revolt began sweeping Italy. Between 73 and 71 B.C., the rebellious slaves, led by the famed gladiator Spartacus, were able to defeat the several armies sent against them. In desperation the senate established a special military unit under the command of another of Sulla's lieutenants, Marcus Licinius Crassus. Crassus crushed the rebellion just as Pompey returned victorious from Spain. Both generals then demanded the right to serve as consuls. The senate, suddenly fearful of their ambitions, attempted to prevent them from being candidates. Crassus and Pompey, however, refused to disband their troops, and after intimidating the senate made an alliance with the remnants of the *populare* party, which resulted in their election. Once again force had prevailed.

CICERO AS POLITICIAN AND WRITER

Not all Roman political figures were successful generals. The orator and rhetorician, of which Marcus Tullius Cicero is the outstanding example, occasionally could rival the military man for weight and influence in public affairs. Cicero, who is today remembered for his great Latin style, first made his reputation by successfully prosecuting a Roman governor of Sicily. Even in a corrupt society this governor was still notorious. During his three-year term as governor, he had managed to pocket the equivalent of about two million dollars — this in a period when most Romans earned under a hundred dollars a year.

The governor explained quite openly that the profits of his first year went to pay the debts contracted to land the post, those of the second to bribe his jurors, and that he himself only retained the third year's revenue. Cicero had been hired by the Sicilians as their advocate, and his eloquence won the case. He was soon the leading lawyer of Rome. From this position he moved into the senate, where he became the spokesman for the preservation of the republic, even if that meant senatorial dominance. Although he recognized the need for reform, he believed that it could come successfully only from within the system.

Cicero is most important to posterity not as a politician, which he was, but as an orator and writer. He helped to create a more flexible Latin, through which he achieved an almost orchestral variety of emotions, ranging from tenderness to hatred. While to modern readers he sometimes appears to be verbose, his purpose was not so much to tell a story as to influence his audience in order to win a case. The Gracchi, Crassus, and Julius Caesar were also orators of note, but Cicero went beyond political oratory to become the greatest man of letters during the last trials and tribulations of the republic. In his later years, he undertook the task of making Hellenistic philosophy available in Latin. His urbane, tolerant, and undogmatic approach has given him influence over Western literature. It was through him that Greek Stoicism eventually achieved a vogue among the Roman upper classes, although in practice such beliefs seem to have had little effect in the Roman political arena. It is also through the efforts of Cicero that we know about many of the Greek philosophical writers after the time of Plato and Aristotle.

THE RISE OF JULIUS CAESAR

In the final analysis, however, it was not the orators or the writers who held the key to Rome. Rather, it was the generals. While Cicero tried to uphold the corrupt republic, Pompey and Crassus continued to compete against each other for the successful commands, much as Sulla and Marius had earlier done. In this struggle, Pompey was the more successful, and Crassus, unable to compete in military terms, was able to console himself by becoming the richest man in Rome and by serving as the political patron of the equestrians. To counter the military success of his opponent, Crassus backed various potential rivals, notably and most successfully Gaius Julius Caesar. Caesar was descended from an old Roman patrician family, but his aunt had been the wife of Marius, and his wife was the daughter of a prominent *populare* leader. When Sulla emerged triumphant, Caesar gave up his property and prudently went into exile, returning only after the dictator's death to begin building his political fortunes.

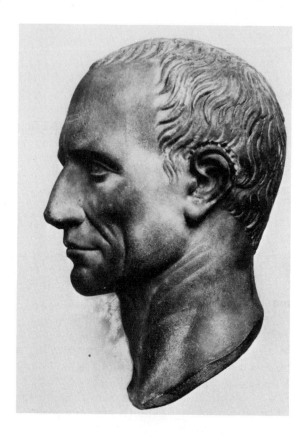

Julius Caesar. (Courtesy
of the Trustees of the
British Museum)

In the meantime, Pompey had gone from one triumph to another. He reached the heights of his success during his five-year campaigns in Asia Minor and Syria, which resulted in the extension of Roman control over most of the East. Since he had generously spread the spoils of his victories among all levels of society, Pompey was extremely popular. To the senate, however, he was a possible threat who had to be put in his place. When Pompey returned from Syria as one of the most successful conquerors in Roman history, he requested ratification of the political arrangements he had made in the East, as well as land for his veterans. Emboldened by the fact that Pompey had disbanded his troops, the senate, determined to weaken his position, summarily refused to act. Pompey was not the only one who had been thwarted by recent senate action. Crassus had attempted to renegotiate a tax contract in Asia, but the senate had also refused his request. This rejection so threatened the political power of Crassus that he was more than willing to join with Pompey, who was both his former ally and his ex-enemy, to gain his ends. The man who brought the two together was Caesar, then serving as consul, who desperately wanted a chance to command troops of his own. In 60 B.C., the three men drew up a five-year agreement among themselves, which they later renewed for a second five years. These ten years are usually called the period of the First Triumvirate, the rule of the three men. The initial result of the agreement was to give Caesar a military command in Gaul, Pompey land for his veterans and confirmation of his actions in the East, and Crassus the right to renegotiate the tax contract in Asia. The long-term result was to make the three virtually dictators of Rome — and to stimulate their underlying rivalry.

Caesar soon departed for Gaul, where he spent ten years extending Roman control over the area that today is France; at the same time, he took pains to win popularity in Rome by sending back large quantities of plunder. Crassus, jealous of both Pompey and Caesar, managed to be appointed general of a campaign against the Parthians, successors to the Persians and the Seleucids in control of Mesopotamia. He was defeated and killed while fighting in 53 B.C. This left Pompey, who, growing fearful of the increasing popularity of Caesar, reconciled himself with a frightened senate to oppose Caesar. Matters came to a head in 50 B.C. when Caesar's command in Gaul ended. By preventing Caesar from running for office and denying him an extension of his command, Pompey and the senate laid the groundwork for bringing Caesar to trial. Fearful of the results of such a trial, Caesar refused to disband his army. Instead, when his term was up, he crossed the boundary between Italy and Gaul, the Rubicon River, on January 7, 49 B.C., in open revolt against the state.

Pompey and the senate, even though they had precipitated Caesar's actions, were quite unprepared for the speed with which he moved. Much to their surprise, most of the northern Italian cities seemed perfectly willing to accept Caesar without a fight after he convinced them he was not in revolt against Rome but only against Pompey. Unable to meet Caesar on the battlefield, Pompey and his senatorial allies withdrew from Italy to gain time. This decision proved costly, since it enabled Caesar to seize command of the government and to provide himself legal authorization for anything he wished to do. It also gave him control of the Roman treasury, which he used to finance his actions. After pacifying Italy and Spain, Caesar marched off to Greece against Pompey's forces. When Caesar again emerged victorious, Pompey fled to Egypt, where he was put to death by the Egyptians.

CAESAR IN POWER

Caesar then proceeded to settle matters in the eastern Mediterranean, although he was held longer in Egypt than he planned because of both a rebellion and an affair with Cleopatra. His stay in the East temporarily allowed some of his senatorial opponents to recoup, but he quickly regained his control. He then began the process of remaking the Roman republic. If his first actions are any indication, he planned a rather radical reorganization. He sent out a great number of colonists in order to reduce the recipients of the grain dole in Rome. He reformed local government throughout Italy by dividing the peninsula into municipal areas, each of which was governed by local officials. He increased the size of the senate and brought new men in to make it more representative. He laid plans for a long overdue codification of the Roman law. The most permanent of his accomplishments was his transformation of the old lunar calendar into a solar one based upon the calculations of the Greek astronomer Sosigenes of Alexandra.

Caesar's efforts at reform were handicapped because his position was not quite clear. He controlled Rome because he controlled the army; any permanent achievement would depend upon consolidating his own legal position. His willingness to scrap the old Roman constitution, which was not really suited to the governing of an empire, horrified many, and some of his most vociferous opponents were fearful that he wanted to become king. Most of these antagonists earlier had been supporters of Pompey or the senate, but Caesar had pardoned them and restored their full rights. This act of clemency, however, did little to lessen their suspicions of Caesar. They regarded him as an autocratic dictator who had destroyed the republic, tending to forget that the republic had long been little more than a corpse. So far removed from reality were some of these opponents that they thought the republic could be restored by removing Caesar. The result was his assassination on the ides of March (March 15), 44 B.C., as he entered the senate chamber.

THE SECOND TRIUMVIRATE

Whether the assassins were tyrannicides who killed a tyrant or murderers who killed an essential reformer is still a matter of some debate. Regardless of what they were, they had failed to make any plans for what might happen after Caesar's death. Their very naivete convincingly demonstrates the bankruptcy of the political leaders of the republic. Within a year, a new triumvirate, composed of Octavian, the nephew and adopted son of Caesar, Marcus Antonius (Mark Antony), and Lepidus, both formerly lieutenants of Caesar, was in control of Rome. A resort to proscription soon eliminated those with any sympathy for the assassins, as well as most of those who still believed the republic had a future. Included in this second group was Cicero, who was removed because he had made the unfortunate mistake of having Antony as an enemy.

Like the alliance of Caesar, Crassus, and Pompey before, this second triumvirate was rent with dissension. Within a few years, Lepidus was set aside, and the remaining two men divided the empire between them. Antony, who thought himself the dominant partner, took control in the East while Octavian had the West; they shared Rome. Antony moved to enhance his prestige even further by a war against Parthia, an effort that proved disappointing; he then became involved with Cleopatra in Egypt. While this involvement undoubtedly had political motivations, it also became, at least for Antony, an affair of the heart. Octavian in the West made political capital out of it, convincing the Romans that Antony's real intention was to establish a foreign queen in Rome. The ultimate result was a trial of strength between the two at the battle of Actium in 31 B.C. Antony was defeated, and hearing a rumor of the death of Cleopatra, he killed himself. Cleopatra, very much alive, tried to make a new alliance with Octavian, but when it was refused, she too committed suicide, after recovering the body of the dead Antony. Octavian was now unchallenged. He picked up the task of remaking the Roman government but in a much more cautious way than his adopted father Caesar had attempted. Rome had demonstrated that it could conquer the Mediterranean world; it now had to demonstrate that it could govern it. The bringing together of the various threads of Mediterranean civilization was the great contribution of Rome to Western civilization.

Supplemental Reading
for Part Two

General

De Burgh, W. G., *The Legacy of the Ancient World* (Penguin).
Farrington, B., *Science in Antiquity* (Oxford).
Fustel de Coulanges, Numa, *The Ancient City* (Doubleday). A classic over a hundred years old but with many valuable insights.
Glover, T., *The Ancient World* (Penguin).
Hadas, Moses, *Ancilla to Classical Reading* (Columbia).
Kahane, P. P., *Ancient and Clasical Art* (Dell).
Marrou, H. I., *A History of Education in Antiquity* (Mentor).
Rose, H. J., *Religion in Greece and Rome* (Harper & Row).
Scullard, Howard H. and A. A. Van der Heyden, *Shorter Atlas of the Classical World* (Dutton). A handy reference work.
Seltman, C. T., *Women in Antiquity* (Macmillan).

Greece

Agard, Walter, *What Democracy Meant to the Greeks* (Wisconsin).
Andrewes, Antony, *The Greek Tyrants* (Harper & Row).
Barker, Ernest, *Greek Political Theory: Plato and His Predecessors* (Barnes & Noble).
Boardman, John, *Greek Art* (Praeger).
Boardman, John, *The Greeks Overseas* (Penguin).
Bowra, Sir Cecil, *Ancient Greek Literature* (Oxford).
Bowra, Sir Cecil, *The Greek Experience* (Mentor).
Burn, A. R., *Alexander the Great and the Hellenistic World* (Macmillan).
Burn, A. R., *The Lyric Age of Greece* (Funk & Wagnalls).
Burn, A. R., *Pericles and Athens* (Macmillan).
Carpenter, Rhys, *Discontinuity in Greek Civilization* (Norton).
Carpenter, Rhys, *Folk Tale, Fiction and Saga in the Homeric Epics* (California).
Chadwick, John, *The Decipherment of Linear B* (Random House).
Clagett, Marshall, *Greek Science in Antiquity* (Macmillan).
Cornford, Francis M., *Before and After Socrates* (Cambridge).
Cornford, Francis M., *The Origin of Attic Comedy* (Doubleday).
Cottrell, Leonard, *The Bull of Minos* (Grosset & Dunlap).
DeSantillana, Giorgio, *The Origins of Scientific Thought* (Mentor).
Devambez, Pierre, *Greek Painting* (Viking).
Dickinson, G. L., *The Greek View of Life* (Macmillan or Michigan).
Dodds, E. R., *The Greeks and the Irrational* (California).

Ehrenberg, Victor, *People of Aristophanes: A Sociology of Old Attic Comedy* (Schocken).

Ehrenberg, Victor, *The Greek State* (Norton).

Farrington, B., *Greek Science* (Penguin).

Finley, M. I., *The Ancient Greeks: An Introduction to Their Life and Thought* (Viking).

Finley, M. I., *Aspects of Antiquity: Discoveries and Controversies* (Viking).

Finley, M. I., *World of Odysseus* (Viking).

Flaceliere, Robert, *Literary History of Greece* (Mentor).

Forsdyke, John, *Greece Before Homer* (Norton).

Frankfort-Groenewegen, H. A. and B. Ashmole, *The Ancient World* (Mentor). A history of art.

Freeman, Kathleen, *The Greek City States* (Norton).

Glotz, G., *Ancient Greece at Work* (Norton).

Guthrie, William K. C., *The Greeks and Their Gods* (Beacon).

Guthrie, William K. C., *Greek Philosophers: From Thales to Aristotle* (Harper & Row).

Guthrie, William K. C., *In the Beginning: Some Greek Views on the Origins of Life and the Early State of Man* (Cornell).

Guthrie, William K. C., *Orpheus and Greek Religion* (Norton).

Hadas, Moses, *History of Greek Literature* (Columbia).

Haigh, A. E., *Tragic Drama of the Greeks* (Dover).

Hamilton, Edith, *The Greek Way* (Norton). An idealized interpretation.

Harrison, Jane, *Prolegomena to the Study of Greek Religion* (World).

Harrison, Jane, *Themis: A Study of the Social Origins of Greek Religion* (World).

Jaeger, Werner, *Paideia* (Oxford). The classic work on Greek culture and ideals. Only vol. I, *Archaic Greece*, is so far available in paperback.

Kitto, H. D. F., *The Greeks* (Penguin).

Kitto, H. D. F., *Greek Tragedy: A Literary Study* (Anchor).

Larsen, J. A. O., *Representative Government in Greek and Roman History* (California).

Lawrence, A. W., *Greek Architecture* (Penguin).

MacKendrick, Paul, *The Greek Stones Speak* (Mentor).

Michell, H., *The Economics of Ancient Greece* (Barnes & Noble).

Michell, H., *Sparta* (Cambridge).

Murray, Gilbert, *Euripides and His Age* (Oxford).

Murray, Gilbert, *Five Stages of Greek Religion* (Doubleday).

Murray, Gilbert, *The Rise of the Greek Epic* (Oxford).

Nilsson, M. P., *Greek Folk Religion* (Harper & Row).

Nilsson, M. P., *A History of Greek Religion* (Norton).

Nilsson, M. P., *Mycenaean Origin of Greek Mythology* (Norton).

Norwood, Gilbert, *Greek Comedy* (Hill & Wang).

Norwood, Gilbert, *Greek Tragedy* (Hill & Wang).

Pendleburgy, J. D. S., *The Archaeology of Crete* (Norton).

Pollitt, J. J., ed., *Art of Greece* (Prentice-Hall).

Rose, H. J. A., *A Handbook of Greek Literature* (Dutton).
Ross, W. D., *Aristotle* (Barnes & Noble).
Rostovtzeff, M. I., *Greece* (Oxford). A brief volume by the twentieth century's greatest classical historian.
Samuel, A. E., *Mycenaeans in History* (Prentice-Hall).
Scranton, R. L., *Greek Architecture* (Braziller).
Sinclair, T. A., *History of Greek Political Thought* (World).
Snell, B., *Discovery of the Mind: The Greek Origins of European Thought* (Harper & Row).
Tarn, William W., *Alexander the Great* (Beacon).
Tarn, William W., *Hellenistic Civilization* (World).
Taylor, A. E., *Aristotle* (Dover).
Taylor, A. E., *The Mind of Plato* (Michigan).
Taylor, A. E., *Socrates: The Man and His Thought* (Doubleday).
Webster, T. B. L., *From Mycenae to Homer* (Norton).
Wilcken, U., *Alexander the Great* (Norton).
Yamauchi, E. M., *Greece and Babylon: Early Contacts between the Aegean and the Near East* (Baker Books).
Zimmern, Sir Alfred, *The Greek Commonwealth: Politics and Economics in Fifth Century Athens* (Oxford).

SOURCES

Auden, W. H., *The Portable Greek Reader* (Viking).
Barnstone, Willis, trans., *Greek Lyric Poetry* (Bantam).
Bury, J. G., *The Ancient Greek Historians* (Dover).
Finley, M. I., ed., *Portable Greek Historians* (Viking).
Freeman, Kathleen, *The Murder of Herodes and Other Trials from Athenian Law Courts* (Norton).
Graves, Robert, *The Greek Myths* (Penguin).
Hadas, Moses, *Greek Drama* (Bantam).
Hadas, Moses, *Three Greek Romances* (Bobbs-Merrill).
Herodotus, *History,* numerous paperback editions.
Homer, *The Iliad* and the *Odyssey,* numerous paperback editions.
Kirk, G. S. and J. E. Raven, *The Presocratic Philosophers* (Cambridge).
Kirk, G. S., *Homer and the Epic* (Cambridge).
Lattimore, Richard, *Greek Lyrics* (Chicago).
Lattimore, Richard, *Greek Tragedies* (Chicago).
MacKendrick, Paul, and H. Howe, eds., *Classics in Translation* (Wisconsin).
Plutarch, *Lives,* several paperback editions of the brief biographies of various Greeks and Romans.
Thucydides, *The Peloponnesian War,* numerous paperback editions.
Toynbee, A. J., *Greek Civilization and Character* (Mentor).
Xenophon, *The Persian Expedition* (Penguin).

FICTION

Graves, Robert, *Hercules My Shipmate* (Pyramid).
Renault, Mary, *The King Must Die* (Pocket Books and Random House).

Republican Rome

Adcock, F. E., *Roman Political Ideas and Practice* (Michigan).

Barrow, R. H., *The Romans* (Penguin).

Brehier, E., *History of Philosophy: The Hellenistic and Roman Age* (Chicago).

Briquet, M. F., *Etruscan Art* (Tudor).

Brown, F. E., *Roman Architecture* (Braziller).

Carcopino, J., *Daily Life in Ancient Rome* (Yale).

Cowell, F. R., *Cicero and the Roman Republic* (Penguin).

Cumont, Franz, *After Life in Roman Paganism* (Dover).

Cumont, Franz, *Astrology and Religion among the Greeks and Romans* (Dover).

Cumont, Franz, *Oriental Religions in Roman Paganism* (Dover).

Dudley, D., *Civilization of Rome* (Mentor).

Duff, J. Wright, *A Literary History of Rome from the Origins to the Close of the Golden Age* (Barnes & Noble).

Fowler, William W., *Social Life at Rome in the Age of Cicero* (St. Martin's).

Frank, Tenney, *Life and Literature in the Roman Republic* (California).

Grant, Michael, *Roman History from Coins* (Gordian).

Grant, Michael, *Roman Literature* (Penguin).

Grant, Michael, *World of Rome* (Mentor).

Hadas, Moses, *A History of Latin Literature* (Columbia).

Hamilton, Edith, *The Roman Way* (Norton).

Hargreaves, Reginald, *Beyond the Rubicon: A History of Early Rome* (Mentor).

Jerome, Thomas Spencer, *Aspects of the Study of Roman History* (Putnam).

MacKendrick, Paul, *The Mute Stones Speak* (Mentor).

MacKendrick, Paul, *The Roman Mind at Work* (Van Nostrand).

Mattingly, H., *Man in the Roman Street* (Norton).

Mommsen, Theodore, *History of Rome* (Philosophical Library). A condensation of the classic history of the Roman Republic by the great nineteenth century historian.

Pallottino, M., *The Etruscans* (Penguin).

Pollitt, J. J., *Art of Rome* (Prentice-Hall).

Richardson, Emeline, ed., *Etruscan Sculptures* (Mentor).

Rostovtzeff, M. I., *Rome* (Oxford). A brief survey by the outstanding classical historian of this century.

Scullard, Howard H., *A History of the Roman World from 753 to 146 B.C.* (Barnes & Noble).

Scullard, Howard H., *From the Gracchi to Nero: A History of Rome* (Barnes & Noble).

Starr, C. G., *The Emergence of Rome* (Cornell).

Stenico, A., *Roman and Etruscan Painting* (Viking).

Syme, Sir Ronald, *The Roman Revolution* (Oxford).

Taylor, Lily Ross, *Party Politics in the Age of Caesar* (California).

Von Vacano, O. W., *Etruscans in the Ancient World* (Indiana).

Warmington, B. H., *Carthage* (Penguin).
Wheeler, Mortimer, *The Art of Rome* (Praeger).

SOURCES

Caesar, several pocketbook editions.
Cicero, *Basic Works* (Random House), and numerous other paperback selections.
Davenport, B., ed., *The Portable Roman Reader* (Viking).
Grant, M., *Roman Readings* (Penguin).
Hadas, Moses, *History of Rome* (Anchor).
Lewis, Naphtali and Meyer Reinhold, eds., *Roman Civilization: Sourcebook* (Harper & Row).
Plutarch, several paperback editions of his various lives of Roman citizens.
Roman Drama (Dell).
Roman Drama Anthology (Bobbs-Merrill).
Sinnigen, William G., *Rome* (Macmillan).

FICTION

Bryher, W., *Coin of Carthage* (Harcourt).
Duggan, Alfred, *Three's Company* (Ace).
Warner, Rex, *The Young Caesar* (Mentor).

part three

THE EMERGENCE
OF EUROPEAN
CIVILIZATION

8

The Roman Empire: Its Achievements and Failures

Octavian's defeat of Antony at Actium in 31 B.C. marked the end of a century of strife and the beginning of two centuries of the *pax Romana*, the Roman peace. There no longer remained a military power strong enough to contest Roman domination of the Mediterranean basin, and the various conquered peoples within the empire appeared willing to accept their subjugation. The Romans, wearied by the continual internal struggles for political and military control, chose to overlook past disputes out of a preference for stable leadership. The measure of Octavian's almost immediate success is indicated by the title Augustus — the most honored or revered one — which the grateful senate conferred upon him in 27 B.C. He converted this title of honor into the name by which he was regularly designated. To this name is usually added the title *imperator* (emperor) that his troops had given to him. Thus historians no longer speak of Octavian after 27 B.C. but of the Emperor Augustus.

Technically, Augustus was not an emperor but *princeps*, and his government is usually called the *principate*. As princeps, Augustus was in theory merely the leading citizen of a republican Rome. This fiction tended to obscure his real power, since he in fact controlled the city and the empire. With the example of what happened to Caesar as a constant reminder, Augustus was more than willing to keep alive the illusion of a continuing republic; it also suited his temperament, which was more that of a cautious administrator than of an innovator. Though his power rested on his control of the army, this control was not so apparent to his contemporaries, in part because Augustus him-

116

self was a poor military leader. During most of the campaigning which led to the consolidation of his position, he had been plagued with illness. As a result, his victories had not been due so much to his own battle tactics — as had been the case with Caesar and Alexander the Great — but to the military prowess of his subordinates, particularly the general Agrippa, or the strategic errors of his opponents. The Romans, who might have distrusted a brilliant general, felt they had little to fear from Augustus.

THE AUGUSTAN PROGRAM

Augustus also made certain that his real power was not obvious. He manipulated existing institutions, patching together some that might better have been discarded. He wielded the powers of *pontifex maximus*, consul, tribune, and various lesser offices even though he did not always hold them. Moreover, he knew how to gain and preserve the loyalty of subordinates who had abilities that he lacked. He was always circumspect, careful not to antagonize influential people or groups, mindful of change but hesitant to move very far. He reconstituted the senate by bringing in new men from the provinces, and he was able to give the senators an impression that they still played the key role in government. He permitted the senate to oppose him only on minor items, however; on important issues he carefully manipulated its decisions. While he allowed the senate some authority in the poorer or less important provinces, he himself managed the richer ones, as well as those that required large numbers of troops. He convinced the senate that it was necessary to station an armed force in Italy to maintain the peace, but these troops, the praetorian guard, were placed under his sole command. The only real setback to his plans for the empire came from external rather than internal forces. When Augustus tried to shorten communication lines by advancing the frontier with the Germans to the Elbe River in place of the Rhine, the Roman forces were trapped and annihilated. This defeat marked the beginning of a gradual transformation of the army from an offensive weapon to a defensive one.

To emphasize the unity of the empire, Augustus encouraged the development of religious support for his rule. He repaired innumerable temples and shrines to countless gods that had fallen into decay during the period of the civil wars, and whether he repaired old shrines or built new ones, he was careful·to link the gods with his rule. Thus, the restored temple of Mercury (the god of wealth) became Mercurius Augusta; the same was true of new temples dedicated to fortune, to peace, or to other qualities that Augustus felt the need to emphasize. To better enable non-Romans to accept his rule, Augustus encouraged the association of the cult of Rome (the personification of the Roman state) with the emperor himself. By the time of his death, each province in the Greek East, where this type of worship had long been the custom, had at least one altar dedicated to Augustus, and the imperial cult was also becoming influential in the Latin West. Legally, such worship could not be allowed on Italian soil, since it would refute Augustus' claims that he was a mere magistrate at Rome. Nevertheless, he could and did encourage the worship of his genius or spirit in Italy, and he came as close as he could to proclaiming his own divinity by elevating his adopted father Julius Caesar to the level of a deity, building a temple to him in the forum and naming the month of July after him.

Augustus also realized the value of literary support, and the period of his administration was the golden age of Latin literature. In return for imperial patronage or encouragement, Augustus expected and usually received favorable mention both of himself and his programs. Perhaps the most successful of the court poets was Publius Vergilius

Vergil reading from the *Aeneid*, detail from mosaic. (Musée National du Bardo, Tunisia)

Maro, or Vergil, whose *Aeneid* is basically a justification for Roman conquests. Running through this great epic is the idea that it was the destiny of Rome to become an empire just as it was the destiny of the family of Augustus to rule it. Vergil, fortunately, was more than a mere propagandist; he was also a great poet. The *Aeneid* is a literary classic because of its remarkable characterization of Aeneas, a refugee from the Trojan Wars who prepared for the foundation of Rome. Vergil's other great work, the *Georgics,* on which he spent some seven years is in a sense a propaganda piece for another of the Augustan programs, the attempt to turn back the clock to the ways of life and the simple faith of earlier, more rural days. Because of Vergil's rather deliberate idealization of nature, the poem retains an air of romantic unreality. Even such a favored poet as Vergil, however, was not immune from the petty intrigues of court, where a favorite one day might be dismissed the next. His *Georgics* originally ended with a panegyric to the prefect of Egypt, but when this official fell out of favor, Vergil changed his conclusion to a safer theme, an idyllic account of Orpheus and Eurydice.

Contemporary with Vergil was Quintius Horatius Flaccus (Horace), the greatest of Latin lyric poets and the author of collections of poems entitled *Odes, Satires,* and *Epodes.* While Horace was willing to suggest that Augustus was almost a god on earth, and while he is sometimes given to trite moralizing, he expressed himself, even on the most obvious theme, with such style that the end result rises above the subject matter. He remains the most quotable of Latin writers.

What poetry could do so also could prose. The best example of the prose of the period is the *History of Rome* by Titus Livius (Livy), a work that was written to glorify Rome and to inspire Roman youth with patriotic ardor and affection. Though an effective Latin stylist, Livy was not above subordinating accuracy either to get a better turn of a phrase or to put Rome in a better light. Yet in spite of such deficiencies, Livy is the chief source for early Roman history, and scholars continue to lament the loss of much of his account.

Ultimately, Augustus failed to return the Romans to the austere family morality of an earlier period and even to inspire the patriotism he wanted them to feel. His failure is most evident in the work of the poet Publius Ovidius Naso, best known as Ovid. Though Ovid escaped censure for his *Fasti* and *Metamorphoses,* audacious, swift-moving, and absorbing recountings of Greek and Roman mythology, he got into trouble with his treatment of love. In the *Art of Love,* he explained the art of seduction — stripping away romantic illusions — and in the process demonstrated the pleasure-seeking character of Augustan Rome. His failure to observe the official propaganda could only lead to difficulties, and Ovid was soon banished.

The need to banish even such minor dissenters as Ovid demonstrates that there were difficulties associated with the rule of Augustus. Augustus' difficulty in finding a successor also illustrates the kinds of problems the empire was experiencing. Obviously, the principate was built around the personality of its founder, and it is this kind of rule that is the most difficult to transfer. Augustus tried to keep the succession within his own family, but he was handicapped in this because he had only one daughter, Julia, by his second wife. Julia was married to each would-be successor in turn, first to Marcellus, a nephew, and then after his death to the faithful and loyal Agrippa, the great general. When Agrippa also died, Julia became the wife of Tiberius, the elder of Augustus' two stepsons of his third wife. Tiberius, after refusing to fall in with his stepfather's plans, was exiled. Augustus then turned to the sons of Agrippa and Julia, adopting them as his own, after first banishing their mother, his only daughter, for immoral conduct. Julia's real sin was her refusal to be used any longer as a pawn for her father's projects, but Augustus would brook no opposition. After the two boys died, only the rebellious Tiberius remained, and in spite of his misgivings, Augustus named him as his successor. Shortly after this, in 14 A.D., Augustus died, revered, respected, and still remembered today from the month of August which was named after him.

THE SUCCESSORS OF AUGUSTUS

The new emperor, Tiberius, was much less subtle than his stepfather. As a result, the Romans finally realized that they had acquired the makings of an autocracy under the trappings of a republic. Tiberius was succeeded by his adoptive grandson Gaius, better known as Caligula, whose capriciousness and violent behavior became legendary. By eliminating all possible rivals, Gaius made even his supporters uneasy, and he was assassinated after a mere four years of rule. At this juncture, the praetorian guard put Claudius, the uncle of the murdered Caligula, on the throne. Claudius had survived his nephew only by seeming to be utterly harmless, by being almost totally ineffective in everything he did. Somewhat surprisingly, however, Claudius proved to be a fairly effective ruler. He extended Roman power into Britain and reorganized the imperial civil service. His chief difficulty lay with his wives, particularly his third wife, the notorious nymphomaniac Messalina, and then after her execution, his fourth wife, Agrippina. Agrippina finally had him poisoned in order to assure the accession of her own son Nero, then sixteen, who had been adopted by Claudius. Under the direction of several well-qualified advisers, Nero's administration, while strongly autocratic in tone, was for a time both efficient and probably in the best interests of the empire. But once he took control himself, he proved to be not only totally incompetent but extremely vindictive. Threatened with overthrow by the army, he finally committed suicide. The army then moved on to the center of the stage in the first battle of the generals.

In this contest for power, the general Vespasian emerged triumphant in 69 A.D. He and his eldest son Titus together gave Rome stable and effective rule. After the death of Vespasian in 79 A.D., Titus continued the same policies until his death two years later. Vespasian's second son, Domitian, then succeeded. He was an effective but extremely arbitrary and oppressive ruler, and in his last years he executed persons on mere suspicion of disloyalty. Whether or not disloyalty was as prevalent as Domitian believed, his numerous prosecutions soon made it so. He was assassinated in 96 A.D. through the connivance of his own wife. Before the army could choose another emperor, the senate itself appointed Nerva, an elderly and able man, who prevented a revolt of the generals by wisely adopting the leading general, Trajan, as his son and successor.

During the second century, army influence was effectively curtailed through a continuous reliance on adoption. Trajan, Hadrian, Antoninus, and Marcus Aurelius succeeded one another as emperor, each adopted by his predecessor. The rule of these five men, from Nerva to Marcus Aurelius (96–180 A.D.), later came to be esteemed as the great age of imperial Rome. Unfortunately, adoption never became a fixed practice but rather was a temporary expedient put into operation when an emperor had no son to succeed him. This was not the case with the last of the so-called "good" emperors, Marcus Aurelius, whose son was routinely accepted as his successor.

The failure of sons of emperors to be good rulers was far more disastrous to the empire than the failure of emperors to have sons. The ineffective reigns of the sons could, perhaps, be traced back to the nature of their upbringing. Raising and educating a child who knew, and whose tutors and servants knew, that he might grow up to have almost absolute power was a nearly impossible task. A parent had to be continually wise and vigilant to make certain that someone did not cater to every whim of the future ruler. Few emperors had either the time or the inclination to do this, and perhaps they did not realize its necessity. Even Marcus Aurelius was unable to endow his own son with his Stoic wisdom of moderation. Thus those children who were born while their fathers were emperors, or who were young children when their fathers achieved power, usually lacked self-discipline and any concept that power entailed responsibilities. Instead, they were self-centered, accustomed to demanding what they wanted and to having their every whim gratified. Commodus, the son of Marcus Aurelius, was a much stronger individual than Gaius or Nero, sons of emperors who had come to power in the first century, but his first reaction upon inheriting the empire was to relax and enjoy what was his. With his assassination in 192 A.D., there remained no real alternative to rule by the generals.

In the struggle for succession, Septimus Severus emerged as emperor and was strong enough to found a dynasty, which ruled until 235 A.D. Severus, a Libyan of Phoenician origin, was a remorseless tyrant where his immediate interests were concerned, but he was also able and energetic. Probably only a man capable of his utter ruthlessness could have restored and kept the imperial system operating under the threats of bankruptcy and civil war which he had to face. Despotism seemed natural to Severus, and this was accompanied by a further enhancement of the military and a growing cynicism toward the public welfare. Septimus' heirs and successors, Caracalla, Elgabalus, and Severus Alexander, were almost totally incompetent, but their lack of ability was overcome by the Severi women who controlled and manipulated them. These women, Julia Domna, wife of Septimus, Julia Maesa, her sister, and the latter's two daughters, Julia Soemias and Julia Mammaea, did not hesitate to have their sons or grandsons murdered in order to keep power. Their rule was ended in 235 A.D. by an army revolt. The most noteworthy act of the Severi took place during the reign of Caracalla when citizenship was given to all free residents of the empire who had not yet received it. Unfortunately, other than giving provincials Roman legal rights, citizenship no longer had the meaning it once had.

The fifty-year period following the overthrow of the Severi family was one of nearly total demoralization as a succession of generals contended for power. Most of the thirty or so who attempted to rule either died in battle or were assassinated by military rivals. Though on the whole they were able and conscientious men, it was impossible to establish an effective rule as long as each military unit of the empire competed with the others to establish its commander as emperor. Few generals were clever or lucky enough to attract the loyalty and support of a sufficient number of soldiers to establish an effective administration. Finally, three able men managed to cling successively to power for a total of fourteen years, thereby providing a semblance of unity and effective administration.

IMPERIAL PATRONAGE AND THE ARTS

Augustus had set the pattern for imperial patronage which continued during the centuries following his death. Thus art and literature tended to reflect the style and the attitudes of the emperor. Nowhere is this more evident than in architectural works, the remains of which stand in Rome today. Rome itself was almost entirely rebuilt during the first and second centuries, aided undoubtedly by the slum clearance effect of a destructive fire during the reign of Nero. Though the Romans were much concerned that their buildings serve utilitarian needs, they did not overlook aesthetic effects. Thus we have the Coliseum built by Vespasian, the Pantheon rebuilt by Hadrian, the Forum of Trajan, and the baths of Caracalla. New buildings and works of art were commissioned in the provinces as well, and much portrait statuary of the various emperors has been found in areas that once constituted the Roman domain. Since only the emperor had the resources to commission buildings or works of art and literature, all the arts suffered when he was incapacitated or uninterested.

Individual emperors differed in their preferences for artistic or literary endeavor. Since Tiberius was hostile to writers in general, the golden age of Augustus came to a rather abrupt end. There was a revival during the first part of Nero's reign, led by Seneca, Nero's tutor and adviser. Seneca was the leading exponent of the Stoic philosophy, although he was not particularly known for practicing its precepts. In addition to his philosophical writings, Seneca was an orator and a playwright, and his tragedies are the only Roman ones that have survived. Unfortunately, they were not designed for stage presentation, but for conveying philosophical ideas, and it was this example that Rome passed on to later cultures. Once Nero reached his majority, Seneca went into eclipse; later he was forced to commit suicide for complicity in a plot against the emperor. Also suffering the same fate was Seneca's nephew, the poet Lucan. The most original writer under Nero was Petronius, who developed a new literary form, the novel. In his *Satyricon*, Petronius described the life of the freed man in the Greek areas of Italy. He too in 66 A.D. was forced to commit suicide.

Following the death of Nero there began a longer literary revival which lasted until the middle of the second century. In Latin literature, this period is sometimes called the silver age, in contrast to the golden age of Augustus. The literary masters of the period were Quintilian, the orator, Martial, the writer of satiric epigrams, and Pliny the Elder, the compiler of a massive encyclopedia of natural history. There was a brief interruption during the repressive reign of Domitian, but under the "good" emperors the silver age continued once again. The greatest prose writer of this second phase was the historian Cornelius Tacitus, the spokesman for the senatorial nobility; his histories set such a high standard for accuracy that he must be ranked with Thucydides and Polybius among ancient historians. His friend Pliny the Younger deliberately imitated Cicero in collecting and publishing his letters, which today serve as a mine of information on Roman life. The period was secure enough to tolerate a satirist, and Juvenal utilized the opportunity to attack the age in which he lived. During the second century, too, Suetonius compiled his *Lives of the Caesars*, a series of gossipy biographical narratives about the emperors which set the style for much later historical writing. By the end of the reign of Hadrian, Latin literature entered into an archaistic period as it attempted to imitate the style and content of earlier periods rather than to create something new. Most of the creative writing after this time was done by the Greeks, who, of course, wrote in their own language, as did some Romans. The emperor Marcus Aurelius, for example, chose to write his *Meditations* in Greek. Much of the new Christian literature was also written in Greek.

LAW

The most original work of the early empire was in law, perhaps the greatest contribution of Rome to Western civilization. The uniqueness of Roman law lay in the fact that it continued to grow century after century. Unwritten custom was first modified by the legislation of the assemblies and then by the opinions of the chief judicial officials, the *praetors*. New problems created new laws, so that Rome quite early developed a body of law for her noncitizen subject peoples. By the end of the republic, there was a large accumulation of law that demanded organization and codification. Moreover, the emperors wanted uniformity. This call for uniformity in the interpretation of the laws came at a time when Stoic ideals were prominent among many of the educated, including the jurists. Stoicism advocated the idea of natural law, that man had certain inalienable rights granted him by the powers that governed the universe and which could be ascertained by the power of reason. Increasingly, the jurists came to see law as consistent but flexible, the result of the continuing need to apply to current problems the pattern of general principles based upon concepts derived from natural law. The result was to free law from some of its technicalities, to give it a fairness (equity) which led Roman jurisprudence to a peak of achievement between the accession of Hadrian and the death of Severus Alexander. Three of the greatest Roman jurists and writers, Papinian, Paul, and Ulpian, served under the Severi, and the concepts they wrote into Roman law continue to represent the motivating ideals of Western civilization.

ECONOMIC CONDITIONS

As the difficulties of imperial succession became apparent, the problems of imperial administration were complicated by a scarcity of tax revenue and a shortage of manpower. Ordinarily, a long period of

peace in combination with a reasonably good government will automatically cause an increase in prosperity, which should in turn lead
to a growth in population. While Rome had some prosperous days,
most of these were in the republic or during the first century of the
principate. Even then, however, the prosperity had largely been
dependent upon the eastern Mediterranean, which had developed its
own industrial and commercial system long before the Romans took
possession of it. Much of the wealth that had come to Italy was the
outgrowth of wars and of conquests rather than of a highly developed
economy. Moreover, the Romans were never particularly interested in
business. Instead of exploiting the resources of a region, they seized
the land, levied taxes upon its population, and earned revenue by
managing it and by dispensing justice. Surplus funds were primarily
devoted either to building up an army in order to conquer more territory or to the enjoyment of the fruits of conquest and seldom to creating a merchant fleet or opening another factory as a more business-
minded people might have done. Land to a Roman was the chief means
of gaining authority and prestige and only incidentally a direct source
of income.

With such attitudes toward business, it was difficult for the Romans
to give much thought to economic matters, even though they were
able to direct and manage the conquered eastern areas much more
capably than their Hellenistic predecessors. So long as they could
continue to conquer new territories, this lack of interest in business
did not particularly matter, but by the time of the principate there was
not much more land available to seize. In effect, the plunder that had
enabled Rome to become great was no longer to be had except in very
diminished quantities, and there was a need to develop new sources of
revenue. While the establishment of the Roman roads, the curtailment
of piracy, and the building of public works were all moves in the right
direction, they were not in themselves productive operations unless
they could be linked with other enterprises to achieve economic gains.

In spite of numerous handicaps, the Romans still might not have
fallen into serious difficulties had it not been for the elements of backwardness in ancient society. Technology in the third century A.D. was
little improved over what it had been in the fifth century B.C. Unhappily, the Roman genius for large projects caused a rise in the need for
revenues that was difficult to meet. The Romans had larger and more
numerous armies, more extensive building projects, and, in general, a
greater ability to squander resources than any of their predecessors.
The very inadequacy of Roman technological development is well
demonstrated by the fact that even though they had moved into colder
areas like Great Britain and the Rhineland of Germany, they never
adjusted their home building, agriculture, or even clothing to these

changed conditions. This failure meant that great stretches of the north were scarcely populated and therefore difficult to defend.

Roman financial difficulties were accompanied by a growing arbitrariness of government. A private person had less and less recourse against an official or a soldier. If he had property that was wanted or needed by the authorities, he was quite simply done out of it. In spite of some attempts at reform, taxation was oppressive and continued to be farmed out to contractors, whose methods often included extortion and blackmail. While heavy taxes are not in themselves necessarily bad, taxes in the empire were usually levied upon the groups in society least able to bear the burden. In large measure, Roman financial difficulties stemmed from an attitude of indifference and an unawareness of alternatives. The machinery for formulating and directing the government's fiscal operations was lacking, and with no means for borrowing against future collections, the normal method of obtaining supplies to meet a crisis was confiscation or requisition. The principal alternative, and one that was also followed, called for the emperor to debase the currency. This method robbed the public at the same time that it made the solution of tomorrow's problems more difficult for everyone.

Though a great city, Rome had neither trade nor industry of consequence; in fact, the entire West was relatively poor and hence remained largely dependent upon money — gold and silver — with which to pay for the fine silks and fabrics, spices, jewelry, and other luxury goods which it imported, some coming from as far away as India. Normally, a country or an area will not long import goods for which it has to pay in gold and silver unless it mines these metals in great abundance. The wealth of Rome was not based upon great mines but on the profits of war; and when these declined, money became scarcer and the price of imported goods therefore rose. Under such conditions, a people will normally restrict its imports while seeking to meet its own needs through manufacturing or turn to building up an export market of its own. The Roman upper classes, however, had been rich for so long and able to purchase whatever struck their fancy, regardless of price, that they never noticed the difference and continued to buy at whatever price was asked. In consequence, money in the West became far too scarce to support ordinary business transactions.

SLAVERY

Roman society never ceased to be dominated by an aristocracy made up of large landholders. Though these aristocrats were not necessarily members of the same families that had dominated the early republic, their indirect power was as great. The increasing adoption of slavery in the West, a natural byproduct of success at war, in which slaves served as booty, frustrated any substantial growth of a middle class. Skilled artisans and professional people were often purchased or captured from the Hellenistic states, while common labor was the fate of many of those whom the armies spared from slaughter. Slaves lived at subsistence levels, thus depressing further the living standards of all persons other than the actual slave owners. The resultant low purchasing power of everyone but the very rich remained a major barrier to economic growth. Moreover, little upward mobility was possible, except through the army, and hence the privileged status of the aristocracy was never challenged. Such conditions also acted as a deterrent to population increase. Normally, the slave master did not wish to bother with slave children (who were unproductive) but instead preferred to purchase serviceable adults. At the same time, the low standards of living of the free workmen often made the raising of families out of the question. Since a newborn infant could be disposed of without penalty, the poor were under no pressure to keep children they might have trouble feeding.

As a result, the Roman Empire, with some exceptions (particularly in the eastern part), was an increasingly two-class society composed of the very rich and the very poor, a situation which the anarchy of the third century made rather worse than better. It was during this century that most of the surviving remnants of the small landholder or small business class disappeared in the West, a natural result of confiscations and depredations suffered alike at the hands of barbarians, marauding soldiers, and government officials seeking taxes and supplies. The rich, unless they unduly irritated the army or the emperor, could usually manage to protect themselves, while the conditions of the poor could only become worse. Whenever class divisions become as wide as they appear to have been in the third century, all understanding between the classes disappears, and the society tends to divide into societies, unable to cooperate toward the same ends or goals. In such a situation, one class or the other feels it must oppress and coerce or else be itself suppressed and coerced. The well-being of both suffers.

DEFENSE OF THE FRONTIERS

While the empire struggled with its many domestic difficulties, it also had to face increasing troubles on its borders. During the first centuries of the principate, frontier defense had not been a serious problem, but the burden of maintaining a defensive establishment increased during the second and third centuries. Some frontiers, however, were easier to defend than others. The southern frontier, for example, rested on the African deserts, which were thinly populated and not capable of supporting large armies of invaders, while the western boundary was the Atlantic Ocean. To the east, at first, lay the always annoying Parthian Empire, which, though a mere echo of the Persian Empire, repeatedly tempted ambitious Romans into projects for terminating its control over Mesopotamia and Iran. On the whole, Parthia was successful in resisting such efforts and from time to time encroached upon Roman possessions in the East. This frontier became particularly troublesome after 226 A.D., the year the Parthians were overthrown by a new Persian regime that had ambitions for recovering the lands of its ancient predecessor. Because many of these territories had been in Roman hands since the second century B.C., the Persians could fulfill these ambitions only by coming into conflict with the Romans.

The greatest problem for Rome was posed by the northern frontier, particularly the long Rhine-Danube line that separated the Germans and the Romans. The Germans, who had warred with the Romans as early as the time of Caesar, had made remarkable progress since that time, changing from a pastoral people to an agricultural one and from an illiterate society to a literate one. At the same time, German contact with the Romans had increased largely as a result of trade but also because Germans served Rome as mercenary soldiers and as slaves and because large numbers of Germans had become colonists in under-populated areas of the empire. The longer and more varied the contacts with Rome, the more the Germans learned of Roman organizational methods, weapons, and geography — and the more dangerous they became as enemies. In spite of this increased danger, the Roman generals who were continuously fighting each other in the third century solicited the help of German soldiers, so that these potential enemies came to play an increasing role in Roman domestic affairs.

THE NEW ROME

After several decades marked by wars between the generals, in 270 A.D. the general Aurelian achieved a substantial mastery of the entire empire, retaining his control for nearly five years before he was assassinated. Within a year he was succeeded by Probus, another able man who managed a six-year tenure before he was murdered. Anarchy prevailed for some three years until in 285 A.D. Diocletian seized power and kept it for twenty years before he retired unscathed, dying in retirement a decade later. Thus began what may be regarded as the last century of a united Roman Empire, the period in which the Romans became Christian, forged a complete autocracy, and shifted their capital to the Hellenistic East. In 410 A.D., the Goths captured Rome itself; and thereafter most of the western provinces fell to the control of the various intruding Germans. Any power or influence still remaining to the official government in the West was exercised by the troop commanders, usually Germans, until in 476 A.D. one of these men, Odoacer, deposed the nominal emperor in Italy, the child Romulus Augustulus, and converted the peninsula into an autonomous monarchy with himself the *de facto* king.

With these developments, the Roman Empire of Augustus passed out of existence, although in name and in fact a new empire lived on in the eastern provinces for many centuries. This eastern empire, sometimes called the later Roman Empire, was only vaguely Roman even though it was the creation of Romans, particularly Diocletian and Constantine. Diocletian in particular attempted a general overhaul of the imperial system in an effort to remedy the government's weakness and incapacity. His solution to the problems plaguing the empire was to multiply the bureaucracy and increase the civil functions of the government. The provinces, which Diocletian increased in number, were regrouped into twelve dioceses, and these in turn were formed into four prefectures. In this fashion, a hierarchy of control was created that gave the emperor some independence from the army. The system also enabled him to watch over and direct many matters that earlier had been left to local authorities or to the discretion of individuals. The long-term effect of these changes was to foster conditions that were conducive to obstructiveness, blackmail, extortion, and injustice — the very defects the new methods had been designed to correct. The system was also costly — indeed, its only merit was that it tended to lessen the importance of the army.

Roman rulers who followed Diocletian simply accepted the fact that they were autocrats, and all reminders of principate vanished. Elaborately robed, surrounded by ritual and ceremony, the emperors assumed the aura of Oriental potentates, claiming divine sanction for their acts. Their remoteness undoubtedly lessened the possibilities of assassination, but it did not solve the problem of succession, although Diocletian proposed a rather ingenious answer to this problem also. He first appointed a co-emperor, a device not without precedent, and then he divided the power by giving his colleague control in the West while he kept the East for himself. Obviously, he believed the East was more critical to successful rule than the West, because of the former's greater population, better economic development, and strategic location between the Persians and the Goths, the most obvious enemies. The implication was that the West was now expendable, that it could be sacrificed in order to hold the richer East. Diocletian had each emperor designate a successor who was associated with him in office and who took command upon his retirement or death, whereupon a new junior subordinate was appointed. This rather sensible system never worked in practice. Shortly after Diocletian's retirement, a confusing struggle broke out because one of the new emperors died after about a year, and his troops, ignoring succession procedures, reverted to the early practice of nominating their own leader — in this case Constantine, the twenty-one year old son of the dead emperor. Constantine is remembered today as the first emperor to embrace Christianity, which he did in the course of winning a six-year war with his various colleagues in the West. Thereafter, he carried on a sporadic twelve-year contest with the eastern co-Emperor, ultimately becoming sole ruler of the empire in 324 A.D. With Constantine Christianity became a legal religion in the Roman world.

Constantine soon saw the desirability of directing imperial affairs from an eastern headquarters, so he abandoned the old capital on the Tiber and founded a new Rome on the Bosporus. Usually called Constantinople, the city, which is today Istanbul, was located on the site of the ancient Greek city of Byzantium. From his new capital Constantine continued the pattern of autocracy by further exalting the ruler and extending the government's watchfulness over individuals and their personal lives, justifying these methods as means of making certain that nothing taxable escaped assessment. Central to his plans was an alliance with the newly legalized Christian Church, in which Constantine also tried to introduce the kind of uniformity pleasing to an autocrat. Toward this end he called the first ecumenical council at Nicaea in 325 A.D. Out of this meeting came a formulation of the official position of the Church on the question of the Trinity, but the council also foreshadowed the day when religious freedom in the empire would go the way of the political and economic freedoms.

After his death in 337 A.D., Constantine's three sons, Constantine II, Constantius, and Constans, immediately began fighting each other, with Constantius eventually emerging as sole emperor. He was succeeded in 361 A.D. by his cousin Julian, usually called Julian the Apostate because of his attempt to re-establish paganism as an effective rival to Christianity. Julian was killed in 364 A.D. in battle, perhaps by his own troops, and a new succession of generals struggled for power. These internal disorders were accompanied by increasing troubles on both the Persian and the northern frontier, although the new autocracy functioned well enough to allow the empire to survive. The most serious threat from the Danube frontier at this time was not that posed by the Germans but by the armies of mounted nomads known as the Huns, who had originally come from the grassland steppes of central Asia. Fortunately for the Romans, however, the chief victims of this invasion were the Germans, particularly the Goths, many of whom had been living in southern Russia.

The Hun invasion had the effect of throwing the Romans and the Germans into each other's arms, an uneasy collaboration that lasted for about a century. In 451 A.D., in a major battle near Troyes in France, the two allies successfully checked the Huns. Not long afterward the Huns lost their most qualified leader, Attila, and henceforth little is heard of them. By this time, however, the effectiveness of the Rhine-Danube boundary as a frontier between civilization and barbarism, between Latin and German, was no more. Great numbers of Germans had been admitted inside the empire by the Romans, who desperately needed their manpower. As the Hun menace receded, it became apparent that the Germans had in large measure made the Roman army their own, especially in the West, where they also held great blocks of territory. Resentful of Roman tyranny, the Germans proved to be difficult allies and had in 378 A.D., shortly after they first entered the empire, destroyed an imperial army at Adrianople.

The Romans recovered from this disaster through the leadership of Theodosius, the last person to rule as sole emperor, who managed to pacify the Goths. After him the West had its own emperor, who first ruled at Rome, then at Milan, and finally at Ravenna, while the eastern emperor ruled from Constantinople. Gradually as the West went its separate way, falling to the hands of various Germanic kings, the East discovered a new direction for itself. It had sufficient manpower reserves under its direct control not to have to draw on foreign sources; its capital, Constantinople, was a fortress and an important commercial city, a fact that allowed the East to solve its revenue problems and meet the expenses of government. The eastern portion of the Roman Empire developed into a genuinely new Christian state, usually called the Byzantine Empire, more Greek than Roman, but indebted to Rome.

CHRISTIAN BEGINNINGS

The Byzantine Empire owed much of its vitality to the influence of Christianity, which also came to be no less important in the West. The Christians, in turn, owed a great deal to the Jews, who supplied their God, their Ten Commandments, a history of mankind from the day of creation, and much else in the way of convictions concerning man's responsibilities both to the individual and to the community. But Christianity also borrowed heavily from the Greeks, whose thinking had permeated the Jewish world during the centuries since Alexander.

Christianity had its beginnings in Judea, a part of Palestine that from 6 A.D. had been a Roman province; before that time the family of Herod had ruled it as a client kingdom. A native of the region, by temperament Herod was a tyrant in the Greek style who made his position so secure that some of his successors wielded influence in northern Palestine a generation after the Romans took direct control.

Both Herod and the Romans were regarded as intruders by large numbers of Jews, who were anxious to re-establish the independence of Israel and to free Judaism from foreign contamination. This antagonism had made Palestine one of the most rebellious provinces of the Roman Empire. It was against this troubled background that Jesus was born, lived, and died, crucified by the Romans, who adjudged him seditious. His execution during the reign of Tiberius was little noticed at the time; he was just one more victim of the treason trials of that emperor. Jesus claimed to be a messiah, but what he had in mind is not made clear in any document of the period, nor was it clear to the early Christians. Technically, a messiah is one who has been anointed, or chosen for a mission, but whether his mission was in this world, in which case he might become a king, or one of a more spiritual nature, is not clear. Differing Christian views on this and other obscurities were in time dealt with by several Church councils which worked out a Christian orthodoxy based on what the clergy, mostly of Greek education, could accept. The church was in a position to enforce its decisions, so that no one today can say for sure how much Church doctrine conforms to the real teaching of Jesus.

For a generation after the crucifixion, Christianity survived more or less as another variety of Judaism. Since Jews by this time had spread throughout much of the empire, the very Jewishness of primitive Christianity facilitated its wide dissemination. Many Jews were so far removed from their origins that they had even forgotten Hebrew. The Jews in Alexandria, for example, had translated the Jewish scriptures into Greek so that they could read and understand them. This particular version of the Scriptures, known as the *Septuagint*, had great importance because it was the version known by most early Christians. No independent Latin version of the Scriptures appeared until the fourth century, when St. Jerome made a translation based upon the Greek of the Septuagint.

The early followers of Jesus, in spite of their Jewish ties, were not always welcomed in the Jewish communities. To many Jews Christianity represented a political movement in Palestine, a movement the Romans regarded as disloyal. For the Jews outside Palestine, who enjoyed some valuable privileges in the Roman state, association with the followers of the executed Jesus could only serve as an embarrassment, particularly after the Jewish rebellion broke out in Palestine in 66 A.D. These facts help to explain the alienation between Christians and Jews before the end of the first century and why Christians tended to look elsewhere for sympathy and support.

The most obvious source of support for a religion was the underprivileged in the urban centers, and Christianity became, if it had not always been, an urban movement. For two centuries, however, its success was far from spectacular as it developed its organization and doctrine. Ultimately, it successfully carried out a civilizing mission by functioning where no other institution did. It channeled into the lives of the poor or the alienated an intense meaning which the Greeks and the Hebrews in particular had discovered during past ages. It began to attract not only the displaced and the deprived but also persons of higher rank and good education whose knowledge and understanding were thus given a wide application.

ROMAN RELIGIOUS BORROWINGS

To the non-Christian Roman, Christianity could have seemed but another mystery religion. Such a faith was mysterious in the sense that its rites and beliefs were understandable only to the initiate, who had in some manner been instructed or indoctrinated as to their meaning. All of the mystery religions attempted to sustain and strengthen the individual members of their group, to provide them with a feeling of adequacy or purposefulness, and to give understanding of matters that baffle common sense or are otherwise demoralizing and frightening. They were a natural response to the needs that had arisen in the artificial world of Rome, in which exploitation had become relentless and impersonal and the future was increasingly a cause for dread. Most of the mystery religions of the empire were Hellenistic in their development, though much older in origin. Essentially Greek, Orphism, one of the major cults, had flourished in classical Greek times as well as later. Mithraism, another cult which stemmed from Persia, was a sort of Greek modification of Zoroastrianism. The worship of Isis had spread from Egypt, but in the process, it too had become a Greek religion. Manicheanism originated in Persia somewhat later than Mithraism, with its main growth taking place in the third century. All of these religions, including Christianity, had much in common, for example, belief in an afterlife, salvation for the believer, a savior, and common ceremonies such as the eucharist and baptism. Each borrowed from the other to meet common needs.

Christianity had an advantage over the other mystery religions in the immediacy of its historical messiah. Jesus was not a long-dead mystery savior but one who had lived within recent memory. Christianity also proved to be more adaptable to the demands of Hellenistic philosophy, mainly because of its Jewish background. Judaism, in fact, had already been increasingly Hellenized, although in its insistence upon Jewish dietary restrictions and circumcision it had antagonized many potential members. St. Paul, who was both a Roman citizen and a Jew, was instrumental in modifying these aspects of Christianity to better meet the needs of the gentiles, or the non-Jews. Though his

Hebrew name was Saul, he is usually known to us by his Roman name of Paulus. He had never met Jesus, but he took it upon himself to be the "Christian missionary" to the wider European community, explaining his religion in terms they could understand. The Christian explanation of the world and man's purpose therein, stemming largely from Judaism, was superior to that of other mystery religions. Many educated Greeks, influenced by Greek rationalism, came to admire, respect, and adopt Christianity for these reasons. These educated converts not only gave Christianity some measure of intellectual respectability but they also provided leadership. Over the years, they developed a Christian theology that incorporated many of the ideals of Stoicism and Epicurism so admired — if not always practiced — by the Roman upper classes, together with a good portion of Platonic philosophy. At the same time, Christianity at the popular level resembled the other mystery religions enough so that it seemed neither foreign nor unacceptable. Thus the new religion developed a rather unique appeal, and though it took several centuries, its ultimate triumph was so impressive that for many people it seemed a miracle.

THE PERSECUTIONS

Somewhat surprisingly, persecutions served to further the triumph of Christianity. From Judaism Christianity had acquired a conviction of righteousness coupled with contempt for the unrighteous and even the mighty — whether pharaoh or Roman emperor. This view, as well as the dogmatic belief on the part of Christians that theirs was the only true religion and the connection of Christianity with the revolutionary movements in Palestine, brought persecution down on the new religion. When the Romans stooped to persecution, they abandoned what had been the great virtue of paganism, its tolerance of diversity. Thus the Roman officials, trapped between the need to heed a popular outcry and their traditional practice of treating all subjects alike, elicit more pity than censure. Because of their firm monotheism, Christians shunned any pageant, public gathering, or municipal undertaking that could involve them in a pagan rite or ceremony or that threatened the acknowledgment of any god but their own. Such actions were entirely incomprehensible to the pagan mind or to members of the mystery cults. To them the Christians appeared unwilling to share in the responsibilities of managing the municipality and, by showing disrespect for the various gods, seemed to invite troubles and misfortunes to fall not only upon themselves but upon everyone else as well. Thus the public clamor concerning the Christians became loud enough to attract the attention of the imperial authorities whose concern it was to maintain order in their districts.

The Romans did not intend to allow a local disturbance to develop into a rebellion. Thus, if the Christians were found to be at the root of the uproar and if their elimination would remove the cause of the disturbance, the magistrate's duty seemed obvious. Moreover, to the Romans the Christians were seditious because they refused to pay divine honors to the emperor or to the imperial cults. Any subject who declined to render these honors was considered disloyal and deserving of punishment.

Fortunately, such persecutions were usually local affairs and did not last very long, but the dangers, nonetheless, must still have hung rather constantly over all Christians, any one of whom could be chosen for punishment any time the need arose for a scapegoat. It is not surprising that converts frequently renounced their faith when threatened by Roman magistrates; although many of them found the courage of martyrs. New to man's experience was the conviction behind a martyr's death. Only a few times in the past had ordinary people been so committed to their beliefs that they allowed themselves to be barbarously murdered when a gesture of renunciation could have saved them.

THE CHRISTIAN TRIUMPH

The dangers the Christians faced forced them to look to their own resources, encouraged them to support and assist each other, and ultimately caused them to build a kind of separate entity within the Roman state. As the empire in the third and fourth centuries lost its effectiveness and could no longer govern, defend its frontiers, or provide a fitting life for its subjects, organized Christianity, first as an extralegal body and then as a legal institution, stepped into the breach to provide social services and other functions that had previously been responsibilities of the family or the state. To the outsider watching this movement, Christian stubbornness began to take on meaning and significance as an indication that hope and faith must still exist even though the political magic that had so long been the monopoly of the Romans had evidently failed. As pagan literature declined, Christian literature sprang up to take its place; as pagan schools faltered, new Christian schools emerged; as the patronage of the emperor declined, Church patronage increased; loyalities the Roman state had once claimed increasingly shifted to the Christian Church.

It is no wonder that the emperors, looking for some means to sustain the faltering empire, turned to Christianity. Even though Christians were still a minority when Constantine adopted them, it obviously had become dangerous to exclude them from the functions of government. In fact, it was felt that their participation in imperial affairs might greatly strengthen the state. Christianity was able to adjust itself to

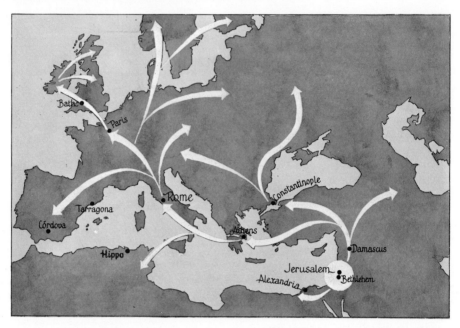

The spread of Christianity, fourth century A.D.

this new position of power so effectively that, by the end of the fourth century, it had become the only legal religion for Romans; in fact, paganism could exist only under conditions that were becoming increasingly precarious.

While it seems logical and reasonable that Christians should have one church, and therefore that a Christian empire should have a united church, beneath the apparent unity of Christianity there was wide diversity. The old language and territorial differences that the Romans had held under control revived when Rome faltered. By Constantine's time there were several Church organizations, each centered around one of the major cities — Alexandria, Rome, Antioch, and the holy city of Jerusalem. Constantinople soon became the center for another organization, albeit one much more under imperial control. Each of the centers, reflecting its variant heritage, developed a diverse opinion on what came to be regarded as doctrinal matters. The first such dispute, that of the divinity of Jesus, led Constantine to call the Council at Nicaea in 325 A.D. At this council, the Arian position, which more or less denied the divinity of Jesus, was rejected, but enforcement of the decision was another matter, and the Arians persisted for several centuries, especially in areas beyond Roman control. At best, it can be said that there were never less than two major divisions within the Church — that of the Greek East, eventually dominated by the patriarch (or pope) at Constantinople, and that of the Latin West, dominated by the pope (or patriarch) at Rome, the old capital of the empire. Much of the ancient grandeur of the empire centered around the bishop of Rome, particularly after the emperors had abandoned the city. The prestige of the pope was also increased by the belief that St. Peter had founded the church at Rome (as well as the one at Antioch). Moreover, the removal of the imperial capital from Rome, after the emperors had given special privileges to the pope, left the pope considerable freedom of action and enabled him to escape blame for the malfunctioning Roman civil administration.

Though in its early years Christianity lacked formal organization, perhaps even a priesthood, it soon developed not just one but two varieties of clergy. The first, and the earliest, were the secular clergy, who performed the routine services of supplying day-to-day leadership, eventually offering careers to men who wanted to devote their lives to church service. From these clergy an organized hierarchy evolved, patterned on the administrative divisions of the Roman state, with dioceses, provinces, and other administrative divisions. In addition, the organization had its own legal system, including courts for enforcing the laws and regulations deemed appropriate to its purposes. Such a system naturally led to an authoritarianism within Christianity that made it master of its members and remarkably able to ignore extraneous influences.

The other variety of priests were the regular clergy, or monks. Originally, the monks had been hermits and anchorites in Egypt, living apart from other people in the deserts and seeking individual salvation by rigorous self-denial, prayer, or meditation, thereby attempting to imitate the sufferings of Jesus and avoid the pollutions of the material world. Often these early anchorites fell victim to a sort of competitive asceticism — if one achieved a particularly rigorous fast or a period of uninterrupted meditation, another tried to go even further. Competition of this kind, as well as other extremes of asceticism, were soon recognized as incompatible with a true religious vocation, and, as more and more persons were attracted to the ascetic life, communities were established that followed regular rules. The Latin term for rule is *regula*, hence monks were *regular* clergy, or a body of men living by the rule. The rules set the hours of prayer, sleep, fasting, and work each monk was to do. Many communities acquired property and undertook projects that were socially useful, especially in the Latin West, where the dominant rule became that of St. Benedict, a sixth-century monk at Monte Cassino and the founder of the Benedictine Order. Under his rule, the regular clergy labored in every conceivable kind of project that seemed to need their efforts. Monasticism also attracted women, known as nuns, and the growth of convents gave women one of the first major opportunities for productive and useful work outside and beyond the home or family. The monastery and the convent came to shelter the artisan and the orphan, produced wool and manufactured wine, trained the engineer and the scholar, supplied missionaries and nurses, and produced bishops and even popes and patriarchs.

It was Christianity that preserved the contributions of Rome for the West: law, literature, art, architecture, and the Roman ways of doing things. It preserved only those customs and teachings that could be incorporated into Christianity, and those it rejected were either lost permanently or for long periods of time.

9

An Oriental Recovery: Greeks and Arabs in the Eastern Mediterranean

The term "Byzantine" is used to describe a phase of civilization and a way of life that was centered at Constantinople for some 1100 years, from 330 to 1453. Originally the area was Roman, but within three centuries it had become almost totally Greek. At first the emperor at Constantinople had laid claim to all of the Roman Empire, but by the end of the seventh century, his control was limited to Asia Minor, the Greek peninsula, and parts of Italy. Coinciding with this territorial reduction was the emergence of the Byzantine culture, which incorporated traditions from the earlier Hellenic and Hellenistic eras but which had its own unique features, particularly in the sphere of religion. Byzantine civilization served as the dominant influence on the modern Greeks, most of the peoples of the Balkan peninsula, and the Russians.

Greek had long been the prevalent language of the eastern Roman provinces, and as early as the second century A.D., Greek writers reacquired dominance in Roman scientific and philosophical writing. Unfortunately, only a small portion of this literature appeared in Latin during Roman times, which meant that the growing break between the eastern and western divisions of the empire deprived the western intellectual heritage of its main nourishment. In science, for example, much of the Greek achievement had been summarized and systematized by Ptolemy of Alexandria at the end of the second century. Ptolemy's arguments for the geocentric views of the universe dominated astronomy until the time of Galileo, and his theory of approximate calculations, the beginnings of trigonometry, represented the greatest advance in Greek mathematics. Yet Ptolemy was known mainly by reputation in the West rather than from his actual works. The same was true of Galen of Pergamum, who unified and systematized Greek anatomical and medical knowledge. Not until the full implications of the Greek accomplishments reached the West in the later Middle Ages were further significant advances made in these fields.

In literature, the outstanding pagan authors of the second century, Plutarch and Lucian, were also Greek. Plutarch's series of short biographical sketches on famous Greeks and Romans established a major new literary and historical form, while Lucian's brilliant satires dealing with pretense, pedantry, and hypocrisy rivaled anything in Greek literature. This learned tradition continued to flourish in Constantinople, as is evidenced from a long line of distinguished historians, including Procopius in the sixth century, Psellus in the eleventh century, Anna Comnena in the twelfth century, and George Phrantzes in the fifteenth century.

Increasingly, however, the Greek genius turned its attention to religion, with a number of writers attempting to explain Christianity. The first Greek Christian writer of major importance was the third-century theologian Origen. Some of Origen's thought was later deemed heretical, but he remains important because of his success in interweaving so much of pagan Greek thinking with Christianity. Much more orthodox were Athanasius, Basil, and Gregory Nazianzus, the Greek Fathers of the Church who are regarded as the formulators of Christian doctrine. Athanasius was the man most responsible for the official Church position on the Trinity, which was adopted at the Council of Nicaea in an effort to combat Arianism. Both Basil and Gregory Nazianzus wrote treatises on various questions of dogma, but they are also important because of their contributions to monasticism. Basil's guide to the monastic life set the pattern for eastern Christians, while Gregory's ascetic life served as an inspiration for many future monks. Equally important was John Chrysostom (John the Golden Mouth), an archbishop of Constantinople at the end of the fourth century who was noted as a great preacher of Christianity. He adopted the methods of Greek rhetoric to Christian concepts and made Constantinople an intellectual as well as an administrative center of religious affairs.

With Greek the medium for all of this vitality, it is apparent why the Latin overlay in the eastern Roman Empire did not last long. It is usually not until the sixth century, however, that the eastern Roman Empire comes to be called the Byzantine Empire. By that time art forms had developed that no longer showed anything Roman but instead were indicative of a radically different way of life and outlook. Perhaps most characteristic of Byzantine art are the fresco paintings in churches and monasteries. This change became evident in the reign of the Emperor Justinian, who might as easily be termed the last of the Roman emperors as the first of the Byzantine.

JUSTINIAN

Justinian was descended from a Latin-speaking peasant family in Illyria. His rise to importance came with the elevation of his uncle Justin to commander of the imperial guard. From this position, Justin rose to become emperor and was succeeded upon his death in 527 by Justinian. The new monarch was a devoted Christian and an amateur theologian who believed, nonetheless, that both Church and state should be subject to the imperial will. Just as there was one God, there was one empire, one Church, and one law; Justinian was both pope and Caesar.

In many ways, Justinian appears to have been a transitional figure. He was, for example, the last emperor whose native tongue was Latin. Under his rule, the old office of consul, a remnant of the republican period, was abolished. In 529, he confiscated the endowment of Plato's academy and prohibited the teaching of pagan philosophy, marking the end of much of the old classical intellectual tradition. Justinian also began a reorganization of the imperial government, a reorganization that was completed in the seventh century under the emperor Heraclius. The final result was a series of military districts called *themes*, in which the military commanders were also the heads of the civil government. It was also during Justinian's reign that the silkworm was introduced into the empire and as an imperial monopoly soon became a major source of income for the emperor. The first such worms had been smuggled out of China in hollow canes by Christian monks, who had learned the closely guarded secrets of silk manufacture while serving as missionaries.

Justinian devoted much of his efforts to attempting to regain political and religious unity in all of the areas formerly controlled by Rome. Upon his accession to the throne, he was recognized as emperor by the various Germanic kings, but in fact, these kings gave only lip service to the idea of imperial unity and ruled as independent monarchs. Justinian wanted real control, and the result was a series of campaigns under the direction of his trusted general and subordinate, Belisarius, which were aimed at regaining power in the west. Following some twenty years of war, the Byzantine army had defeated the Ostrogoths in Italy and the Vandals in Africa and had considerably weakened the Visigoths in Spain. Instead of strengthening the power of the emperor at Constantinople, however, the net effect was to weaken him.

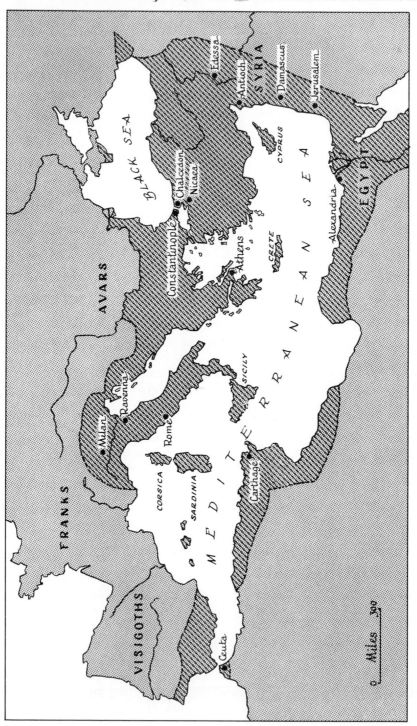

The empire of Justinian, 527–565 A.D.

JUSTINIAN'S DIFFICULTIES

The victory in Italy was achieved only at the cost of serious damage to the material welfare of the peninsula, and the resulting heavy financial burdens imposed by the Byzantine administrative system aroused bitter protests from its inhabitants. Moreover, the conquest had destroyed most of the surviving remnants of the middle class in both Africa and Italy, widening still further the economic divisions between classes in society. Of greater danger was the fact that Justinian, in order to raise troops and supplies for the west, weakened his frontier forces in the east and the north. The European frontier was infiltrated by the Bulgars and the Slavs, who gradually adapted themselves to Byzantine culture without developing any sense of loyalty to the empire. Far more dangerous was the neglect of the Asian frontier bordering on Persia. Here Justinian secured a temporary peace through payment of subsidies, but his successors suffered from the results of this policy.

The paradox of Justinian's reign is that the chief stumbling block to his ambitious dreams of unity came to be the very Christianity he was trying to promote. In fact, Christianity in Justinian's time was no more uniform than it is in the United States today. But whereas most Americans have learned to live with competing creeds, for Justinian — as for many other ancient and medieval rulers — it was imperative that all Christians have the same beliefs. From the time of Constantine, there had been attempts to settle basic differences through Church councils, but political considerations also played a major role in determining orthodoxy. The result was to classify other and entirely honest opinions as heretical, often for no better reason than geography or minority status. Since the Greek intellectuals had emphasized the importance of abstract ideas, even minor differences in concepts assumed great importance. Most of the German immigrants into the west were Arians, a belief that basically denied the divinity of Jesus. The Arian position had been declared heretical during the reign of Constantine, but the immediate effectiveness of this action can be judged from the fact that the emperor himself died as a baptized adherent of the sect. Another large group of Christians centered in North Africa in the region that is today modern Algeria and Tunisia subscribed to the Donatist heresy, which taught that Church sacraments performed by an immoral or heretical priest were invalid. The majority of the Egyptian Christians, later known as the Copts, adhered to the Monophysite belief, which held that Jesus had only one nature, divine-human, as contrasted to the orthodox interpretation of two natures, divine and human. In Syria and the surrounding areas were the Nestorians, who while teaching that Jesus was both divine and human, emphasized that it was only in the human form that Jesus had been born, lived, suffered, and died on earth. With such diverse views, the attempt to establish an orthodoxy could only fail. If an emperor tried to formulate a broad position, he ran the risk of antagonizing the Christian faithful, whereas too narrow a position meant that other and perhaps more vital business of the state had to be sacrificed in order to enforce it.

Justinian, however, was more tolerant in fact than he was in theory, probably because of the influence of his wife, the Empress Theodora, who herself was a Monophysite. Theodora is one of those rare women of the past who successfully left a distinct imprint on her age. In a period in which a woman was supposed to stay in her place, Theodora came to prominence as a personality, and much of Justinian's success has been attributed to her. Her antecedents are rather murky, although it is known that she started her career as a professional pantomime actress, a job which at that time was equated with prostitution. Regardless of her background, she became an outstanding queen, who not only checked Justinian's basic intolerance but also saved his throne during a series of riots in 532 A.D.

The riots had started as a protest on the part of the Green and the Blue factions of Constantinople over the punishment of some of their members. Originally founded in imitation of the circus parties at Rome, the Greens and the Blues soon became more than this, serving both as an urban militia and as a sort of popular assembly. Usually their protests were not particularly effective, since rivalry between them, encouraged by athletic competition, was such that they were never able to agree on joint action. When they finally did unite in 532, and almost immediately gained their demands, they were so emboldened that they attempted to seize the whole city. In the ensuing riots, much of the city was destroyed, but, largely through the tactics of Theodora, who set about to rekindle the antagonism of the groups, the riots were brought under control.

AN AGE OF SOLID ACHIEVEMENT

The very destructiveness of the riots eventually served a useful purpose. So much devastation enabled Justinian to rebuild a new and more exciting capital, and in the process there occurred an architectural revolution that led to the establishment of a new building style called Byzantine. By using a dome to cover large open areas, architects raised the worshipper's eyes upwards instead of keeping them horizontal, as had been the case in the old basilica-type churches. The great monument to this style remains the magnificent cathedral of Hagia Sophia. In it Justinian's great architect, Anthemius of Trales, successfully provided a dome for the standard three-aisled ground plan to produce an interior that is astonishingly Olympian. Even though the Turks eventually converted it to a mosque, Santa Sophia continued to serve as a model of excellence and as a pattern to be copied by subsequent builders of Orthodox churches.

An equally important achievement of Justinian's reign was the *Corpus Juris Civilis,* a codification of the Roman law by a commission of experts appointed by the emperor. The commission, headed by Trebonian, aimed not at establishing law but at reducing laws already formulated in Rome to manageable proportions. The result was published in Latin in three parts: (1) the *Code,* a summary of all laws of general validity; (2) the *Digest* (also called *Pandects*), a series of abstracts from the writings of the most famous Roman jurists arranged to amplify and explain the law, and (3) the *Institutes,* a manual designed in part to serve as a textbook for students. From the time of its promulgation, the code constituted the law of the empire and became the basis of legal instruction in the schools at Rome, Constantinople, and Berytus (Beirut). Justinian also provided for the publication of future legislation in a fourth category, the *Novels,* or new laws, but unlike the other portions of the collection, these were issued in Greek. In its extensiveness, the Justinian codification far exceeded any similar project either before or since, and it represents one of the truly monumental achievements of Western man. At the same time, it serves as an effective marker between the old Latin empire and the new Greek one.

With the death of Justinian in 565 A.D., the Roman restoration began to fall apart. Spain, which had only been partially reconquered by Justinian, was all but lost by 572 A.D. Moreover, the emperor's religious policies had so antagonized the pope in Rome that the Latin Church began to seek alternatives to domination by Constantinople. In their attempts to hold together their disparate possessions, various later emperors tried to ignore questions of religious doctrine and instead concentrated on religious practices. This attention led to the growth of iconoclasm, an imperial campaign to destroy images, that is, statues or paintings of religious figures, which were regarded as a holdover paganism. This policy further antagonized the pope at Rome and, in addition, alienated vast numbers of Christians in the East. To further complicate the difficulties, the Persians, angered by a refusal of Constantinople to continue a subsidy to them, went on the offensive at the beginning of the seventh century, sweeping everything before them. By 613 A.D., they had captured Jerusalem and were advancing on Constantinople. To cope with the crisis, the Byzantines found a remarkably strong emperor, Heraclius, who reorganized the army and administration by giving greater power to provincial governors. His reorganization, based on the theme, was perfected by his successors and is the distinguishing feature of later Byzantine administration. Once he had consolidated his position at Constantinople, Heraclius launched an attack on Persia itself without attempting to dislodge the enemy from the captured territory. By 628 A.D., the Persians had been overwhelmed. They restored to the emperor the "true Cross," which they had taken from Jerusalem, and withdrew from the lands they had conquered. Though this victory effectively destroyed Persian power, it also left an almost exhausted Byzantine Empire, which, following the death of Heraclius, once again split into warring factions. It was at this time that a new and powerful force appeared.

ISLAM

An outgrowth of the teachings of the Arab prophet, Muhammed, Islam is the third of the great monotheistic religions to originate in the Near East. While Arabia had numerous contacts with various ancient empires, it had never been conquered. Instead, as the original home of the Semitic-speaking peoples, it had periodically sent forth invaders into the more settled areas. Usually, after causing much havoc, the marauders abandoned their habits of destruction and merged with resident peoples. Some of these groups, such as the Phoenicians and the Aramaeans, retained their Semitic languages and developed civilizations of great power and influence.

Even though Arabia was clearly an intellectual backwater of the Near East, it had not been entirely isolated from the influences of neighboring cultures. The peninsula bordered a major caravan route connecting Egypt, Palestine, and Syria with India, while ports along the Red Sea, the Persian Gulf, and the Indian Ocean were important commercial depots. In fact, the peninsula in the sixth century was an area of change, where primitive institutions and ideas were being seriously undermined by more sophisticated foreign ones. Arabia was home to large numbers of Jews and had several Christian communities as well. From these external forces Muhammed's genius was able to extract something that became uniquely Arab but that also had great appeal to a variety of other peoples.

MUHAMMED

As with any major religious figure, the life of Muhammed is surrounded with mystery and legend, but there is some agreement on its basic outline. He was born in about 570 in Mecca, an important caravan city that also served as a religious center for the several tribes which inhabited western Arabia. His father Abdullah died before he was born, and his mother died before he was six years old. The boy was put under the care of his grandfather, and when he also died, an uncle,

Muhammed preaching, from an Arabic manuscript. (Edinburgh University Library)

Abu Talib, became his guardian. From such a background it should be apparent why Muhammed demonstrated great concern for widows and orphans.

Little is known about his youth, although there are traditions that he accompanied the trading caravans and had contact with Christian and Jewish missionaries. His business abilities were such that he was invited to become the caravan manager for a rich widow, Khadijah, some fifteen years his senior. When Muhammed was twenty-five, the two were married, and the forty-year-old woman bore several children, of whom three daughters survived to marriage age. Only one of them, Fatima, had children. It is through Fatima that the present-day descendants of the prophet trace their ancestry.

Some years after his marriage, around the year 610, Muhammed began to have visions and to hear supernatural voices. He became convinced that God (Allah) was calling upon him to serve as a missionary to the Arabs. He endeavored to comply but met with no great success; after several years he had converted only his wife, his freedman and adopted son Zaid, his cousin Ali, and his friend Abu Bekr. Persistence ultimately began to pay dividends, but his very success also got him in trouble with the residents of Mecca, who had previously regarded him with indifference. Part of his difficulties arose from his denunciation of idolatry, an act that represented a threat to the economic existence of Mecca, since most of the pagan shrines of Arabia, including the *Kaaba,* or the rock later sacred to Islam, were located there. Muhammed's attempt to unify the Arabs also challenged old tribal loyalties. As opposition increased, some of his followers were forced to flee to Ethiopia, where the Christian ruler offered protection. For this, the Ethiopians came to hold a special place in the opinion of all later Muslims.

Muhammed himself, in September 622, took refuge at Yathrib on the invitation of a group of sympathizers who believed his leadership would serve to lessen factionalism in that city. This *hejira,* or flight, from Mecca marks the beginning of the Islamic calendar. In Yathrib, which was soon called Medina, from Madinat al Nabi, the City of the Prophet, Islam began to catch on as a religion. At the same time, the prophetic qualities of Muhammed became subordinate to those that were necessary for a political and military leader. By mounting a series of raids upon the caravans of Mecca, Muhammed united the various factions of Medina behind his rule. Within two years, the caravan trade had been diverted to Medina, and when impoverished Meccans took up arms to counter this new threat to their existence, they were defeated. By 630, Mecca had capitulated. Muhammed returned to the city and destroyed all the idols, but he more than com-

The courtyard of the Great Mosque at Mecca, Saudi Arabia. The black silk draped edifice in the background is the Kaaba, which contains the sacred Black Stone. (Arabian American Oil Company)

pensated the citizens for this destruction by making Mecca the holy city of Islam and the *Kaaba* a sacred shrine. By the time Muhammed died in 632, nearly all of Arabia had abandoned idolatry and accepted the teachings of its prophet.

Muhammed called his religion Islam, literally submission to God. His teachings were incorporated into the *Koran,* the Arabic term for "book," which Muslims believe is a series of revelations dictated to the prophet, mostly while he was at Mecca but some while at Medina. Islam is an all-encompassing religion that specifies how a believer should act in every kind of circumstance. Much of this conduct is set forth in the Koran, although for many Muslims these rules are supplemented by a body of tradition, the *hadith,* which contains further sayings and doings of the prophet and interpretations of passages that are otherwise somewhat ambiguous.

Islamic beliefs are similar to those of both Christianity and Judaism, although they are probably closer to the latter. By Muslims Muhammed is regarded as the last in a line of prophets, some twenty-five in all, which started with Adam and includes Noah, Abraham, Moses, John the Baptist, and Jesus. Like the Jews, Muslims are forbidden to eat pork, and their religion calls for a number of purification rituals that are similar to those of orthodox Judaism. The Koran, in addition, forbids gambling, usury, and alcoholic beverages. Divorce is easy for the husband but next to impossible for the wife. Where the Christians usually observe Sunday as a holy day and the Jews Saturday, the Muslims have their public prayers on Friday. All are enjoined to recite the creed, "There is no God but Allah and Muhammed is his Prophet" five times a day while performing the accompanying prayers and ablutions. In addition, Muslims are required to give alms to the poor, to fast during the month of Ramadan (the lunar month when Muhammed first began to receive his revelations), and to make a major pilgrimage to Mecca at least once in a lifetime. Islam is a tolerant religion, with specific prohibitions against the persecution of Jews and Christians. Though Muhammed limited the number of wives to four, he himself had nine more after his first wife died. The most important of these, and his favorite, was his second wife, Aisha, whom he married when she was not quite ten years old.

THE SUCCESSORS OF MUHAMMED

When Muhammed died, his followers were faced with a major quandary, and this continuing predicament has ever since kept the Islamic world divided. Technically, Muhammed could have no successors, since he was the last — and the greatest — of the prophets; but it was his failure to designate a political and administrative successor that caused so much trouble. The Arabs, united by religion, found it increasingly difficult to find a ruler acceptable to all sections of the Islamic world. To meet the immediate need, the notables of the growing Islamic community met and selected a leader from the oldest, the most experienced, and the most trusted of Muhammed's Companions, that is, those who had joined with him before the flight from Mecca. Abu Bakr, the first caliph or administrative successor, was also Muhammed's father-in-law, the father of Aisha. It was all Abu Bakr could do to hold the warring factions of Arabia together, and to avoid a similar struggle after his death (in 634), he nominated another Companion, Umar, to succeed him as caliph. Umar, who was another of Muhammed's fathers-in-law, ruled for some ten years, and it was during his administration that the great Arab expansion began. Umar did not nominate a successor, so once again the notables met and selected still another of the Companions, Uthman, as third caliph. Uthman, who was Muhammed's son-in-law, is best remembered for the fact that it was during his reign that a committee collected, collated, and edited a final and official text of the Koran. All conflicting or variant versions were destroyed.

In spite of the success of the various Arab armies, the Arabian peninsula was far from peaceful. We can appreciate the depth of these antagonisms from the fact that Uthman was murdered in 656 after some twelve years of rule. Uthman was eighty-two at the time and had never been a particularly effective ruler, but his murder set off a whole series of further assassinations. Succeeding Uthman was Ali, the prophet's cousin and the husband of Fatima, Muhammed's daughter. In the struggle for power, Ali had made numerous enemies, notably Aisha, the most powerful widow of Muhammed, as well as the members of Uthman's clan, the Umayyads, who held him responsible for the death of his predecessor. Ali's five-year reign was marked by a series of revolts that culminated in his own murder while he was worshipping in a mosque.

With this death, Islam split into two major groupings: those who believed that the caliphate should remain in the family of Muhammed (the *shi-ites*) and those who thought a blood tie was irrelevant (the *sunni*). In general, the *shi-ites,* who are still dominant in modern Iran and parts of India and Pakistan, were more fundamentalist and sectarian in outlook. They refused to accept the hadith and instead relied almost totally upon the Koran. They first turned to Hasan, Ali's oldest son, for leadership, and then when Hasan was assassinated, they selected Husain, Ali's second son. When Husain was also killed, they were left to dispute among themselves which of the other descendants of the prophet should lead them.

The *sunni,* who constituted the majority of the adherents of Islam, turned to Muawiya for leadership. A member of Uthman's clan, governor of recently conquered Syria, and the most powerful Arab political leader, it was Muawiya who conquered Egypt and moved the capital of Islam from Medina to Damascus, and it was from Damascus that his descendants, known as the Umayyads, ruled the Islamic world until 750 A.D. In that year, the Umayyads were overthrown by the Abbasids, a family who were members of Muhammed's own Hashimite clan. The Abbasid caliphate, centered at Baghdad, ruled for some 500 years until 1258, although members of the Umayyad clan retained control of Spain beyond that date.

In spite of these family struggles and tribal animosities, Arab power expanded rapidly throughout the Mediterranean world and eastward to India. The comparative ease with which these lands were conquered can be explained by the fact that expansion, at least at first, was usually undertaken with the consent of the inhabitants. The religious dogmatism of the Byzantine rulers, as well as their fiscal policies, had alienated large numbers of their subjects, who expected — and received — better and more tolerant treatment from their Arab conquerors. Moreover, the Byzantine and Persian empires, exhausted from their prolonged warfare, were unable to mount an effective defense against the Arabs. In fact, both the Persians and the Byzantines had been utilizing Arab mercenaries, and it was a revolt of some of these mercenaries in Syria that had first led to the Islamic conquest there. Having conquered Syria, the new rulers found security impossible until they also captured Alexandria, the great Byzantine naval base. From Egypt it was not difficult to move further westward to Cyrenaica and Tripoli in modern Libya. These initial conquests brought in large amounts of booty, and the desire for further spoils, plus an awareness of Byzantine weakness, encouraged the ambitious Arab military leaders to go further. From Islam the Arabs derived the cohesiveness necessary to hold their conquests once they had been made.

The first real opposition for the Arab army was at Carthage, the Roman stronghold in Africa. The city was taken in 695 after a long and bitter siege, lost in 698, and recaptured the next year. The Arab success in this part of North Africa was due to the conversion of the Berbers, a warlike nomadic people who had never been conquered by Rome. This union of Berber and Arab quickly overcame the old outposts of Greek and Roman civilization in the area and soon led to an attack upon Spain, which was ripe for conquest because of the religious intolerance of its Visigothic rulers. One of the leaders in the conquest of Spain was a Berber named Tarik, who captured the Pillars of Hercules, one of which was renamed Djebel Tarik (Rock of Tarik), since corrupted to Gibraltar. The Muslim conquests ran out of steam against the gates of Constantinople in 718 and against the Franks in

France shortly afterwards, the first really effective opposition the Arabs had met since Carthage. In the east, after conquering an exhausted and helpless Persia and advancing to the banks of the Indus River, the Arab armies were also halted. In spite of these military defeats, Islam as a religion continued to advance and ultimately reached China, the Philippines, Malaya, and Indonesia. In the eighth century, the Arabs moved southward from Egypt into Nubia, as well as from Morocco into the Sahara, and for the first time in history central Africa was brought into direct contact with the Mediterranean world. Islam itself included among its followers persons representing every shade of skin and every variety of eye and hair coloring. As a result, the religion never drew the color bar so obvious in the more isolated and parochial Latin West. The Mediterranean Sea itself had become a Muslim lake, making direct contact between the remnants of the western parts of the Roman Empire and the eastern portion very difficult. Thus western Latin culture was further isolated from the eastern Greek civilization, and trade contacts between the two groups were greatly reduced.

THE ISLAMIC CONTRIBUTION

The most remarkable aspects of the Muslim conquest are that the Arabs managed to achieve a unity in their widely disparate territories and that they managed to develop a distinct civilization. Far from being destroyers of civilization as earlier invaders had been, the Arabs proved willing to adopt and enjoy what they themselves had not previously had. As conquerors, they did remarkably little damage and were particularly tolerant toward their Christian and Jewish subjects. They willingly adapted existing governmental institutions to their own needs and even kept the Byzantine or Persian administrators in their old jobs. Although by Muhammed's time the Arabs had just become literate, their tolerance and their active support of the arts and sciences, as well as the unifying effect of Islam, led to an outpouring of intellectual achievements. Because Islam became a major religious force much more rapidly than did Christianity, the desert Arab very quickly found himself making an accommodation with both the more sophisticated secular and the Christian philosophy of his subjects. The result was that classical Greek philosophy was absorbed into Islam, making the latter immeasurably richer. Islam soon became more sophisticated than Christianity and remained so for centuries, since no Muslim could ever isolate himself so completely in his own neighborhood as many Christians had done. The obligation to go on a pilgrimage to Mecca meant that devoted Muslims from Egypt, from Spain, from Persia, or from India could meet each other and exchange ideas before returning to their own countries. Moreover, they could easily communicate with each other, since Arabic quickly became a universal language, in part because Muhammed had prohibited the Koran from being tranlated, and therefore anyone who wanted to read it had to learn Arabic.

Perhaps even more important were the economic and commercial contacts made possible by the vast Islamic conquests. For the first time, portions of the Mediterranean world were brought into close contact with the wealthy and advanced cultures of India and the Far East. Muslim merchants, no less than pilgrims, discovered the utility of a universal language. Their business achievements were mainly responsible for keeping the Islamic world largely urban, in contrast to the western Roman Empire, which became almost totally rural.

The Greeks, the Persians, and the Hindus contributed to the Arabic cultural achievements, but the Arabs were themselves both inventive and creative. The vitality of Arabic poetry before and after the time of Muhammed is indicative of the genius of this desert people, who now also came into possession of the geometry, astronomy, logic, and medicine of the Greeks. Scholars were similarly able to draw upon Hindu learning, especially in mathematics, and upon a significant Persian literary tradition. Islamic civilization flowered during the first part of the Abbasid rule, especially under the caliphs Harun-al-Rashid and Al-Ma' Mūn at Baghdad in the ninth century. The best-known literary product of this age has come to us in the tales of Scheherazad. Most impressive, however, were the scientific achievements of the Arabs. The leading figure of the Baghdad school was the Nestorian Christian Hunayn ibn Ishaq, who with a son and a nephew translated most of the important Greek scientific writings into Syriac and Arabic. Hunayn was especially interested in medicine, and his work in this field served to encourage others. Important at a later date was Rhazes, a Persian who wrote more than two hundred works, some of which were still being used in Europe as late as the eighteenth century. A contemporary of Rhazes was the Egyptian Jew known in Western Europe as Isaac Judaeus. Perhaps the greatest of all Arabic physicians was Avicenna, whose *Canon* of medicine, written at the beginning of the eleventh century, summarized the accomplishments of Greek and Arabic learning.

In physics and mathematics, the most important figure was Al Kindi, whose work on optics broke new ground. Arabic mathematical writers learned to employ the Hindu system of numerals, particularly the zero; from them the system passed into the West, which still uses the term "Arabic numerals." The two most distinguished mathematicians were Al Khwarizmi in the ninth century and in the twelfth the poet Omar Khayyam, who did some of the theoretical work that led to analytical geometry. In philosophy, the Arabs wrestled with the problem of making religion logical. The dominant figure in this area was Averroes, a Spanish Muslim who wrote a long commentary on Aristotle's works, the translation of which was extremely important for the development of scholasticism in twelfth-century Europe. Also important was the Spanish Jew Moses ben Maimonides, whose major interests included medicine as well as philosophy. The extent of Western borrowings from Arabic learning is evident in the continuing use of such Arabic terms as alcohol, cipher, traffic, magazine, and hundreds of others.

The ability of the Arabs to assimilate the cultures they conquered is reflected in their art and architecture, particularly in the mosque. Muhammed had at first conceived of the mosque as little more than a partially roofed courtyard which offered some protection from the sun. Worshippers arranged themselves in parallel ranks facing a wall, originally in the direction of Jerusalem but later toward Mecca. From the top of the wall a man called the believers to prayer. This simple structure could take on all kinds of forms, and the Muslim world gradually developed several distinct schools of art as believers adopted their native traditions to the needs of the new religion. The minaret developed very early and became a distinguishing mark of most Muslim architecture, regardless of its style, although even today some areas are more given to building minarets than others. One style of Muslim architecture, originally established in Syria and Egypt, was based upon the Greco-Roman-Byzantine precedents in these areas. An entirely different approach developed in the Persian territories, while further east Hindu and even Chinese examples served as models. In the west, the Moorish style developed, based upon indigenous North African and Visigothic models, with an overlay of other styles from other parts of the Islamic world. Perhaps best known to us is the citadel palace of Alhambra, so called from the red-colored blocks out of which it was built. Earlier surviving examples of Muslim architectural masterpieces are the Dome of the Rock in Jerusalem and the Ummayad Mosque at Damascus. Modern Cairo contains a number of splendid examples of Islamic architecture. Since Islam, like Judaism, prohibits graven images, decoration within buildings emphasized geometrical designs and patterns, and calligraphy became a fine art with the Arabs. Though the Islamic prohibition against personalized representations encouraged the destruction of statuary and other such art forms of the past, the Muslim practice of covering wall paintings had the effect of preserving them from the elements, and thus unintentionally saving them for us to appreciate.

The transmission of architecutral ideas from one part of the Islamic world to another also led to the development of new techniques and engineering concepts. Since Syrian stone masons were imported into

Egypt and Egyptian tile setters into Spain and elsewhere, it would seem natural that the irrigation techniques common to certain parts of the Middle East were transmitted further into Asia and that crops and products indigenous to one area were often planted in another. Much of Africa was also explored during this period of Islamic dominance. In sum, the Islamic conquest opened up a new avenue for the transmission of ideas and techniques, and as these seeped into the West, at first through Spain and then elsewhere, they exerted a profound effect on Western Civilization.

10

The Birth
of Europe

In the Latin West, the Roman Empire had disappeared in all but name by the end of the fifth century. In its place there appeared various Germanic "nations." Urban life, so characteristic of the old Mediterranean civilization, had declined noticeably. This deterioration of the city was due in part to the same economic circumstances that had led to the transfer of the imperial capital of Constantinople. To compound the problem, the Germans were a rural people, hostile and suspicious of much of city life. Though Rome continued for a time to function as a western capital, gradually the government offices were transferred, first to Milan, and eventually to Ravenna, which remained an outpost of the Byzantine Empire for centuries. The chief reason that the cities continued to survive at all in the West stemmed from the Church practice of using them for administrative centers where the bishop of the diocese resided. The Church also took over many of the functions of the state in the field of education and social welfare. In fact, it was the Church that held the fragmented West together.

The literature of the period was also changing. Only the upper classes had ever demonstrated much concern for literature in Rome, and with the withdrawal of imperial patronage and the weakening of the old nobility, there was little demand or encouragement for new or creative work. Moreover, most of the schools that might have kept a literary tradition alive had been centered in the cities, which were themselves in decline. As a result, the epic and the folktale gained a prominence they had not held since Homeric times. Unlike the earlier period in Greece, however, there always remained a number of learned men — mostly clerics — who kept alive a written tradition, even though they were highly selective in what they chose to preserve.

The period from the fifth to the ninth centuries has often been called the Dark Ages, although such a designation is misleading because it implies that we do not know anything about the period and that there is nothing worth knowing. In fact, as modern historians begin to examine these years in detail, we are discovering that rather than being a period of stagnation, this era in many ways was quite the reverse. Innovations of the period were in large measure responsible for the termination of what can be considered Roman and the beginnings of what can be called European. Where the Byzantine and Arab civilizations were more or less continuations of ancient ways and concepts with a Christian or Islamic overlay, European civilization grew to be quite different, even though it also owed much to Rome, Greece, and the ancient Near East.

Culturally, what was preserved and written about was that which seemed suitable for theological and religious purposes. In this sense, early medieval civilization is a temporary break from the Greek past, where scientific and philosophical thinking had its origins. While this reorientation of learning was in part a conscious one, it also stemmed from the fact that the Romans never fully adopted Greek methods or Greek thinking, nor had they translated many important Greek works into Latin. Thus the early medieval scholar had limited access to the Greek classical heritage. Moreover, most of the literate people in the West from the fifth to the eleventh century were monks. Though they had several aims in mind, the most important task of the literary monks was the indoctrination of the faithful. In short, the bulk of the written work was not directed to a sophisticated, educated audience, as had been the case in the golden and silver ages of Latin, but was designed for oral transmission to the illiterate masses. To a large degree this work consisted of biographies of saints, collections of simple sermons, biblical stories, and other such material. The monk often regarded himself as a missionary whose business was to teach Christianity to a barbarian peasantry, and to do this he employed icons and pictorial representations as much as literature. To the modern student many of these medieval religious collections seem repetitive, boring, and innocuous, even though as historical documents they are sometimes valuable for the incidental light they throw on the customs of a people. The need for such works, however, kept literacy alive; it even led to a study of ways to carry a message more effectively to the public, which, in turn, led to a revival of Roman rhetoric and consequently the preservation of much of classical Latin. Since monks had to be literate to read and write their tracts, it was essential that monastic schools be established.

THE LATIN CHURCH FATHERS

Not all of the literature of the period was aimed at a mass audience however. As the growing Christian Church found itself forced to come to terms with the philosophical concepts of pagan literature, it began to patronize those intellectuals who could most effectively answer the questions raised by the ancients. Though the Church Fathers as a whole were products of the Greek world, the Latin West, especially in the fifth century, bred a number of the more influential of them, the most notable being St. Augustine, a teacher of rhetoric who eventually became Bishop of Hippo in North Africa. Augustine was a writer with a mission. Some Christian authors at the time of Constantine had explained the greatness of the Roman Empire on the basis of its association with, and protection by, the Christian God. Quite naturally, when the empire ran into serious difficulty, and particularly after the sack of Rome by Alaric in the year 410, the earlier interpretation caused embarrassment to Christian intellectuals. To counter the pagan attacks on Christianity that resulted, Augustine ultimately rejected the concept of material progress for the earthly city, that is, that Rome was in any way dependent upon God. He hoped the empire would continue, but he believed that the city of God — the title of his treatise — must always remain unaffected by the earthly course of events. In part, this meant that man's success or failure on earth was due to his own efforts, although Augustine weakened his case by arguing that everything was forseen by God to be the way it is. This aspect of Augustinian thought was mostly discarded by his successors, although the idea of predestination continued to recur at various times in Western history. Religiously, Augustine set the pattern for Western thinking concerning sin, grace, predestination, and free will. Intellectually, he is important because he willingly accepted the past even though he tried to reconstrue the ancient heritage in new ways. This acceptance greatly assisted the incorporation of valuable pagan elements into the intellectual foundation upon which eventually was built a new Christian civilization.

Though Augustine was the greatest of the Latin Church Fathers, both St. Jerome and St. Ambrose were almost his equal. Jerome was the man most responsible for the introduction of monasticism into the West, and though a hermit, he was an admirer of Cicero, whose rhetorical methods he utilized to popularize Christian doctrine. He is best known for his translation and adaptation of the agreed books (excluding the Apocrypha) of the Bible into Latin. His version, known as the Vulgate because it was written in vulgar or popular Latin, exerted a major influence upon both religious and secular literature throughout the medieval period. Even today the Vulgate remains the official Latin version of the Bible for Roman Catholics. Ambrose, a contemporary of Jerome and Augustine, attempted to demonstrate the superiority of the new Christian morality over the old Stoic morality of Cicero, and in the process ended up incorporating a good deal of Ciceronian thought. It was largely as a result of his work that Stoic ideals permeated so deeply into Western thinking.

Also important, but in a different way, was St. Benedict of Nursia in the sixth century, the man who drew up the rules for most forms of Western monasticism. The date traditionally given for the appearance of these rules is 529, the year Justinian closed the pagan schools of philosophy at Athens. Originally designed for his followers at Monte Cassino, Benedict's code quite naturally emphasized obedience, but the quality that made it timeless was its spirit of moderation. Benedict believed that the main obligation of a monk was to praise God in prayer with his brother monks, although, in contrast with Eastern practices, Benedict saw the value of manual labor and study. For Benedict idleness was the enemy of the soul, to be exorcised by hard work. In part it was the Benedictine emphasis on manual labor that caused so many monks to take up the task of transcribing ancient manuscripts. The endeavor also owed much to Cassiodorus, a public official and younger contemporary of Benedict, who set to work collecting Greek and Latin manuscripts from Italy and North Africa at the monastery he had founded at Squillace in southern Italy. Cassiodorus stipulated that monks spend part of their time copying and collating these as well as other books listed in his *Divine and Human Letters*. While not every Benedictine monastery devoted as much time to literature as the monks at Squillace, the preservation of Latin letters was primarily the result of such efforts.

THE GERMANIC KINGDOMS

Except in Britain, the Germanic peoples who settled within the boundaries of the old Roman Empire maintained Roman institutions, customs, and administrators for their subjects, but retained their own laws and institutions to govern themselves. Some of the German "nations" were relatively sophisticated, the Ostrogoths and the Visigoths, for example, while others such as the Franks were far more backward. By the time they entered the empire, most of the Germans had accepted Christianity, although the Franks and the Anglo-Saxons in England were still pagan. It is one of the ironies of history that Justinian, in destroying the power of the Ostrogoths in Italy and the Vandals in Africa, and seriously weakening the Visigoths in Spain, made it possible for the Franks to emerge dominant. Originally located

Clovis I, thirteenth-century French statue, detail of a doorway from the Abbey of Burgundy. (The Metropolitan Museum of Art, The Cloisters Collection, 1940)

on the north bank of the Rhine, the Franks became loyal allies of Rome in the third century. Subsequently, they took advantage of circumstances to encroach southward into the empire while also retaining their original territories outside it. At the end of the fifth century the Salian Franks, those within the empire, were united into a single unit under a king by the name of Clovis. Under the leadership of Clovis, they soon overran the Alemani, who had long controlled what is today Alsace, Baden, Wurttemberg, and northern and western Switzerland. Clovis also moved against the Ripuarian Franks, those who had remained outside of the Roman Empire. The key to his eventual success, however, was not so much his military ability as his political sensitivity, which induced him to become a Christian adhering to the pope at Rome.

Clovis approached his conversion carefully and with great calculation so as not to antagonize his pagan adherents. He first married a Catholic Christian princess of Burgundy; he then permitted his children to be baptized; and finally, in the backwash of a military triumph that he could claim was won through Christian intercession, he had himself and most of his troops baptized. This simple ceremony gave the Frankish king the support of the Catholic clergy in the remaining fragments of the West, making possible the conquest of the Burgundians and Visigoths, whose Arian Christianity left them legitimate objects of his aggression. In this fashion, the West became more Catholic, even though there is no evidence that its level of morality improved. Clovis himself was never guided by what are usually considered Christian standards. He used treachery, murder, and assassination to achieve his purposes, but backed by the proselytizing activities of various Christian missionaries, he was able to make his control unchallenged.

Unforunately for the continued growth of a stable state, Frankish kings regarded their kingdom as personal property to be divided among various heirs. When Clovis died in 511 A.D., his kingdom was divided among his four sons, who established their capitals at Metz, Orleans, Paris, and Soissons. They and their successors, collectively known as the Merovingians, continued the Frankish expansion into Aquitaine, Burgundy, Thuringia, and Bavaria. Though Frankish control was extended into areas that had never been part of the Roman Empire, the Franks themselves were only occasionally able to unify their holdings into the hands of one man. Even then government was not particularly effective, since German political institutions had not developed sufficiently to make possible the administration of the large area that had been conquered by the Merovingians. Surprisingly, however, Frankish territories held together rather well, and it was from this base that a new Europe began to take shape, a civilization quite different from that derived from Rome.

TECHNOLOGY AND SOCIAL CHANGE

There are times in history when violence and upheaval can lead to long-run benefits. Such was the early medieval world, which of necessity was a period of rebuilding, much of the old was in decay or had been destroyed. Out of the process of reconstructing there emerged a variety of new ideas that had both social and economic implications for future societies. The classical world, for example, was based upon slavery, which the medieval Western world gradually saw disappear. Undoubtedly, the decline of slavery had much to do with the depressed state of economic affairs that made slavery unprofitable — free men in this period could be employed more cheaply. In addition, the new emphasis upon the importance of manual labor, as evidenced in the regime of St. Benedict, contributed to the decline of slavery as an institution. At the same time, men were beginning to discover the potential of animal and mechanical power. Mediterranean peoples in classical times had utilized beasts of burden in the same ways as peoples of three thousand years earlier. In particular, the possibilities of the horse were little understood. Even in war, where the horse was most used, cavalry had never become more than a supplemental arm assisting the infantry, partly because horses were a luxury. They required much care, good pasturage, skilled handling, and preferred grain in their diet. The classical world needed its grain to feed the cities. Moreover, to the ancients, the ox, the cow, and the donkey seemed to be more efficient animals, and they could withstand all sorts of abuse and survive on poor forage. As a result, men had never learned how to harness or saddle a horse effectively. Only in medieval times was the stirrup invented, thus making possible the development of the heavily armed cavalrymen, who almost immediately supplanted the foot soldier. Both agriculture and land transportation were revolutionized after the ninth century when a collar was developed which enabled a horse to pull a heavy load. Earlier attempts to harness the horse had broken down when the ox yoke proved inappropriate, and thereafter a sort of breast strap had been made to serve. This device so interfered with the animal's breathing that horse power could not be used to pull anything more substantial than a light war chariot.

Classical civilization had also failed to develop the horseshoe, which greatly facilitated the shift to animal power. In fact, it seems safe to say that classical civilization, in general, preferred to assign tasks to men when it could, whereas people of the Middle Ages were more resourceful in finding ways to employ both animals and mechanical devices. Tandem harnessing allowed the medieval farmer to hitch eight oxen to a single plow, which might bear wheels and be equipped with a moldboard as opposed to the conventional scratch-type plow of the Mediterranean region. Numerous rotation systems were also devised which allowed greater variety in crop management than had the conventional two-field arrangement of prior ages. Leguminous crops such as clover and peas, while not common in the Middle Ages, were sometimes planted as a technique for preserving soil fertility. For these reasons, as well as for others having to do with climate and geography in much of Europe, agriculture came to be the full-time occupation of a whole class of people. Unlike in classical times when the farmers lived in an urban unit and commuted to the countryside, medieval farmers lived in villages where regardless of the state of business, commerce, or politics they could usually continue to exist. Unfortunately, however, there was little inducement for intellectual achievements in this society, and it was not until the growth of the new towns that the medieval world recaptured the intellectual ferment that had characterized the Greek world. In the meantime, other innovations appeared in every area of life. During this period, for example, trousers became the standard costume for the male. More important, with the development of the water mill and the windmill in the early

Middle Ages, mechanical power first began to be used effectively. The principles of both of these devices were known earlier but not widely used, probably because slaves were always available to perform arduous tasks.

PROBLEMS IN ATTAINING POLITICAL STABILITY

The main weakness of early medieval society was its inability to establish an effective political system. Economic decline, which continued well past the classical period, meant that money remained in short supply. Though the Frankish rulers were not particularly troubled by this problem as long as they could make their conquests pay, once the rate of conquest slowed down they had to face the difficulties not only of managing the remnants of the Roman bureaucracy but also of extending it into new areas without adequate funds. The problem was compounded when the Mediterranean fell almost wholly to the Muslims, who rapidly gathered most of the profitable commerce into their own hands, leaving almost nothing for the Franks. Europe became more rural, and more dependent upon barter, than it had been previously. To compensate for their lack of public revenue, Western European rulers learned to reward their servants — judges, soldiers, and others — with Church appointments. This practice burdened the clergy with personnel not only unfit to serve the cause of religion but also prone to subvert it to personal ambition or the needs of politics. Even the use of this expedient, however, did not suffice to cover all the costs of running the state. Rulers who could finance operations no other way were forced to make grants of privilege to those who could assist them from their own private resources. The result of this practice, of course, was an increase in the power of a semi-independent nobility which had additional means to challenge the authority of the king. Matters were made worse by the fact that the Merovingians took to fighting among themselves, wasting their inadequate resources on internal quarrels. The development of heavy cavalry did not improve the situation, since the effect was to give every advantage to any warrior with a handful of mounted followers and the means to keep them provisioned. Such a person found it a simple matter to overcome his less belligerent neighbors and to become a law to himself by offering to "protect" the community from his own turbulent retainers. The monarchs of the period were normally helpless before this kind of anarchy, since they needed the support of the very magnates who produced the turmoil — indeed, they even found it expedient to grant them immunity from royal interference.

The difficulties of the Merovingian rulers are summarized in the struggles between two women, Brunhild and Fredegund. Brunhild was the wife of the king of Austrasia, one of the larger of the four Merovingian states, while her sister Galswintha was married to the king of Neustria. In order to marry Galswintha, however, the king of Neustria had put aside his mistress Fredegund, a step he soon regretted. Shortly thereafter, Galswintha was murdered and Fredegund reappeared in her old position. Brunhild blamed the murder of her sister upon her brother-in-law and insisted that her husband seek revenge. The result was a prolonged struggle between Neustria and Austrasia that was marked by murder, assassination, and treachery. Brunhild kept fighting not only after the death of her husband and of Fredegund but after the loss of her sons and grandsons as well. Finally the nobles themselves grew tired of fighting and in 614 rebelled against their queen and did away with her. For all practical purposes, the Frankish monarchy became a mere formality, the pawn of various powerful families.

THE CAROLINGIANS

During the seventh century, one prominent family, known as the Carolingians, acquired a clear ascendency over the others. Beginning with control of what is today modern Belgium, its influence spread southward and eastward from these considerable holdings. Though the Carolingians suffered some early setbacks, their continuous rise dates from Pepin of Heristal, who in 687 established himself as mayor of the palace over both Neustria and Austrasia, an office that made him something of a chief counselor to the Frankish kings. It was not unusual in this period for such men to overshadow the rulers whom they served, and Pepin used his position to consolidate administration in his own hands, although he died before his objectives were completely attained. After a brief struggle among his heirs, Pepin's illegitimate but supremely capable son Charles, usually called Martel, or the Hammer, succeeded him and adopted his policies. Charles also gave aid to the Christian missionaries in the more pagan parts of his realm, and hence the expansion of Frankish power was paralleled by a growth in the influence of Christianity. One of his greatest accomplishments was his defeat of a Muslim army in the year 732 near Tours in central France. This advance marked the northernmost penetration of Islam, after which its energies were directed toward building a brilliant civilization south of the Pyrenees.

In order to build an army with contingents of mounted troops adequate to meet the Islamic invaders, Charles Martel distributed Church lands to his knights. While the Church retained legal title, the knight received the use of the land, in return for which he was obliged to give military service and counsel to the king. This device was a major step in the development of some means that would enable a centralized state to function with virtually no regular revenues. Charles was also able to eliminate the more refractory nobles, so that by the time of his death in 741, Frankish control was as centralized and effective as it had been under Clovis and his immediate successors. This centralization was threatened by the appearance of two heirs for Charles' position, but divided authority ended when Carloman retired to a monastery, leaving his brother Pepin — known as the Short — in sole command for more than twenty years. In the meantime, the Merovingian kings had deteriorated to mere perfunctory wearers of the crown, and Pepin the Short contrived to depose the last of them in order to assume the crown himself. His plan met with the approval of the pope, who was anxious to gain Frankish support in his struggle against the Lombards, a German tribe that had entered Italy in the sixth century. In early 752, when Pepin was crowned, the pope had come to France, and Pepin returned the favor by advancing into Italy, where he seized a substantial territory from the Lombards. He immediately "donated" his conquest to the pope, who thereby acquired a degree of legal sovereignty which he had formerly lacked. This "donation of Pepin" became the basis for the papal states, of which the modern Vatican is a surviving fragment.

THE PAPACY

The pope wished to encourage Carolingian power not only as a means of countering the Lombards but also in order to secure independence from the emperor at Constantinople, thereby freeing the papacy from having to deal with men whom Western Christians were coming to regard as heretical. Moreover, in the power vacuum that existed in the West, it was natural for the pope to want to increase his own influence, not only in religion but in politics as well.

As early as 452, when the city of Rome had been faced with invasion by the Huns, according to legend, Pope Leo I persuaded the Huns to leave. Whether Leo did so in fact is unimportant; the legend came to be part of papal tradition. It was under the pontificate of Gregory I during the late sixth and early seventh centuries that the papacy really emerged as an independent power. As pope, Gregory was the richest man in Italy, the overseer and business manager of large landed estates that had been given to the Church by the faithful. With this income the papacy supported clergy, churches, schools, orphanages, hospitals, monasteries, and various other similar institutions. On the basis of apostolic succession, Gregory believed himself to be the primate and chief of all Christian bishops. This claim grew out of his belief, and that of most of his predecessors, that St. Peter had founded the Church in Rome and served as its first bishop. Since the popes took Peter to be the chosen successor of Jesus, they believed that they, as the successors of St. Peter, should govern the whole Church in both the East and the West. Once subservience to the emperor at Constantinople had been denied, they could at least claim a clear right to rule the West.

More than an administrator, Gregory was also a theologian and writer, It was through his efforts that the Catholic doctrine of purgatory acquired authoritative status. In general, he dogmatized and made acceptable many of the popular beliefs associated with Catholic Christianity, including transubstantiation, or the belief that communion represents the actual body and blood of Jesus, and the existence of angels and demons. Because of the importance of Gregory in asserting papal prerogatives and in defining Church doctrine, he is usually called Gregory the Great and is often listed as the fourth of the great Latin Church Fathers with Augustine, Ambrose, and Jerome.

Though the popes who succeeded Gregory were not his match in ability, the claims he made for the papacy were never quite forgotten. When its independence was endangered first by Byzantine interference during the iconoclastic controversy and then by the Lombard invasion, the popes were more than willing to make an alliance with any power that could give them some freedom to maneuver, and the Franks at least adhered to the Roman variety of Christianity.

Pepin, who was anxious to supplant the impotent and incompetent Merovingian monarch, hesitated about taking such a step because the deposition of a king by a noble represented a dangerous precedent, and Pepin and his heirs would never be safe from the attempts of other nobles to supplant them. By having the pope, symbolically the most powerful figure in Western Christianity, anoint the king as a sign of heavenly approval, future rebellions would be much less likely. In effect, the pope and Pepin struck a bargain in which both sides stood to benefit. The pope, however, also claimed more than divine approval for his action. He believed that he also had the *secular* right to dispose of the crown, a right which he claimed was based on a document that allegedly had been given to an earlier pope by the Emperor Constantine, the so-called "donation of Constantine." This agreement had stated that because the pope had healed Constantine of leprosy, the emperor had vacated Rome, leaving the pope all the provinces, places, and districts of the West to do with as he would. The document concluded that the pope stood above empire and earthly throne as the highest and chief priest in all the Christian world. Though it was demonstrated some seven hundred years later that the document was an eighth-century forgery, its terms were evidently believed by the popes of the time, who used them to strengthen the Carolingians and themselves.

CHARLEMAGNE

Both Frankish and Carolingian power reached their height during the reign of Pepin's son Charles, who succeeded him in 768. Though Charles, best known as Charlemagne, or Charles the Great, had for a period to share his throne with his brother Carloman, the death of Carloman in 771 again left a united kingdom. Charlemagne's reign was devoted mainly to warfare; in fact, his military success is mainly what caused him to be called the Great. He was known as the destroyer of the Avars, the conqueror of the Saxons and Bavarians, and the hero of successful campaigns against the Moors. His empire included all that earlier Frankish kings had ruled, plus much more of Germany, most of Italy, and a portion of Spain. Christianity was for him the cement that could hold his conquests together. When he defeated the Saxons, he gave them the choice of Christianity or death and, in fact, executed those who refused to convert. Under this policy both Christianity and the influence of the pope spread into central Europe.

As a culmination of his military campaigns, Charlemagne was crowned emperor of the Romans by Pope Leo III on Christmas Day, 800 in a ceremony that represented another move on the part of the papacy to link up its fortunes with the powerful Franks. Leo had appealed to Charlemagne for assistance against enemies who were determined to depose him, and for this reason, the Frankish king had come to Italy. In consequence, according to the contemporary chroniclers, he was much surprised at the pope's action in making him Roman emperor. Whether this version of the story is accurate or not remains a subject of scholarly debate. What really matters is that with the coronation of Charlemagne a pope elevated a barbarian king to the august post of emperor. Though there was actually no empire in the West, and Charlemagne already controlled his own territory, the coronation marked an acceptance at the highest level of the fusion of the German, Roman, and Christian elements into a formal union. Moreover, the coronation publicly signified that the pope no longer deferred to the Byzantine emperor but instead had his own protector in the West. Charlemagne himself felt less reason to be at odds with his Byzantine counterpart, and, in fact, attempted to obtain an acknowledgment from Constantinople that in the West he was entitled to be recognized as emperor.

Historians disagree as to whether Charlemagne put little stock in his imperial title or whether he very much wanted the post even though he might have resented the way in which the pope had given it to him. At any rate, this curious anomaly of the reconstituted Roman Empire,

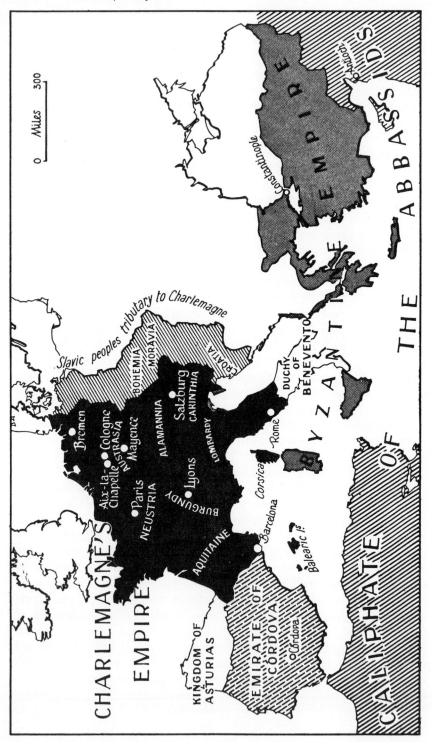

Charlemagne's empire, 800–814 A.D.

which later came to be called the Holy Roman Empire, lasted in some form for a thousand years until Napoleon finally ended it in 1806. Though historians have never tired of pointing out that it was more a loose confederation than an empire, that it was German rather than Roman, and that in no special way was it holy, it played a prominent role in the development of Western Europe. Moreover, Charlemagne quite clearly had an exalted conception of his position as ruler: in his own mind he was the anointed agent of God for the realization of God's purpose. He made no real distinction between political and religious matters in his edicts, since he regarded both as the responsibility of his government. His legislation covered almost every subject, from management of estates to education; he interfered regularly in ecclesiastical questions and was even prepared to dictate to the pope what Church doctrine should be.

In general, his government was similar to that of his Carolingian predecessors. It differed from Merovingian rule mainly because the two Pepins and the two Charleses were sufficiently strong, vigorous, and successful to command support instead of having to barter for it with grants of privileges or immunities. But money never became so plentiful that anything approaching an imperial civil service could be organized, a circumstance which meant that most subjects were forced to serve the crown without direct remuneration. Forced labor was used to maintain bridges, roads, and fortifications. Important persons had to extend hospitality to royal agents traveling on business, while local affairs were in the hands of district landlords, who at least stood to benefit if the community was well run. The chief burden continued to be military service, which more and more came to be tied in with land tenure, and anyone who held land had to equip himself for battle and serve in combat. Since this obligation became increasingly difficult for a peasant to fulfill, the responsibility necessarily fell upon certain substantial landowners whose ability to carry the burden quickly brought them a measure of privilege as well as greater capacities for coercing their lesser neighbors to their own advantage. In sum, the disintegration of empire under the Merovingians and its expansion under the Carolingians produced the same effect — the landed aristocracy grew stronger. Charlemagne attempted to dilute the power of the nobles by centralizing as much of the administration as possible in his own hands. He eliminated the office of mayor of the palace, which historically had given the nobles an overriding voice in imperial business; he created a famous corps of traveling judges (*missi dominici*) to visit the provinces and act in his name; and he adopted the practice of employing non-landowners in official positions. Nevertheless, the great landowners grew ever stronger and more influential.

THE CAROLINGIAN RENAISSANCE

It was not in the political arena but in the area of learning and scholarship that Charlemagne made his greatest contribution to history. To run even the limited bureaucracy of his empire, he had need for clerks, or learned men to carry on the record-keeping and other tasks of government. Moreover, Charlemagne considered himself something of an intellectual with an interest in both education and literature. Such an interest was much needed during this period because the political anarchy during the later years of the Merovingian era had proved utterly discouraging to letters and learning. By contrast, Charlemagne, following the example of earlier Roman emperors, became a patron of the arts and attempted to make his palace school a center of learning. In this effort he was guided by Alcuin, one of the great scholars of the time.

Alcuin had come from England, and we can trace a direct connection between the Carolingian literary revival and earlier ones in England and Ireland. Even though Britain had been conquered by the pagan Anglo-Saxons during the middle of the fifth century, before 700 A.D. it had come to be a literary center, due in large measure to the arrival on the island of learned Benedictine monks, the first of whom had been sent by Gregory the Great in 597 A.D. as missionaries. In literature, the most influential of these monks was Theodore of Tarsus, a Byzantine Greek who became Archbishop of Canterbury in 689. Theodore brought with him a number of manuscripts that served to keep alive Greek and Latin literary traditions in his island outpost. Equally important in preserving ancient literary traditions was the influence of Irish monks. Ireland had been converted to Christianity during the middle years of the fifth century by a young Briton named Succat, who had previously been taken captive to Ireland. Having escaped from servitude, he devoted himself to acquiring an education under the direction of Greek, Syrian, and Egyptian teachers. He then returned to Ireland and achieved remarkable success in converting his former captors. Today he is best known not as Succat but as St. Patrick.

The Irish Church, in part because Ireland lacked anything approaching a widespread political system, had no organization resembling the Greek or Roman Church. Each tribe had its own monastery, with leadership provided by the monastic rather than the secular clergy, although eventually the Irish Church looked to Rome for leadership. The Greek and Latin civilization brought by St. Patrick and other missionaries fused with the old Celtic culture to produce a literary awakening, a flowering of the Irish genius best exemplified by the famous *Book of Kells*. Almost immediately the Irish Church began to export missionaries, first to England and then to the Continent. In fact, most of the active missionaries of the seventh and eighth centuries, notably St. Columban, St. Gall, and St. Boniface, had some connection with either Ireland or England. It was in England that the Irish and Roman missionaries first met and fused, and the result was a stimulating intellectual revival. The most notable scholar of the period was the Venerable Bede, a seventh-century historian and chronologer, popularizer of the method for fixing dates from the birth of Christ — B.C. and A.D. — which eventually replaced methods of dating from creation or the founding of Rome.

Alcuin was an eighth-century product of this English-Irish tradition, having been a pupil and teacher at the cathedral school in York prior to becoming part of Charlemagne's entourage in 781. His main contribution at the Frankish court was in the field of education. He wrote simplified textbooks on grammar, spelling, rhetoric, and dialectics; he also demonstrated an ability to attract to the court other learned men, among whom should be mentioned the grammarian Peter of Pisa; the bibliophile Paul the Deacon; and the poet Theodulf, a Visigothic exile from Spain. In time, the school began to produce its own scholars, notably Einhard, the king's biographer. Alcuin was also important for his reform of handwriting, which resulted in the miniscule script — based on small as opposed to capital letters. This new handwriting soon replaced all competitors.

One palace school was obviously not enough to train the people of such vast territories, and it is to Charlemagne's credit that he encouraged monasteries and cathedrals to establish schools of their own. Many of them eventually did, although the monastery schools initially were the more important. Many monasteries also took up the useful practice of assembling libraries. Still, in retrospect, it is apparent that few Carolingian scholars possessed much creativity. They were both less critical and less original than their Muslim contemporaries; rather than contributing to the advancement of learning, they simply kept it alive. John the Scot (Irish were then called Scots), who came to the Continent about the middle of the ninth century from Ireland, must be noted as an exception. John, who would rank as a learned man in any society, could read Greek well enough to translate philosophical tracts into Latin, but he is important because, while he recognized the significance and authority of the Scriptures, he insisted upon the validity of reason. With this approach he helped to establish a pattern that eventually came to dominate European thinking.

The Carolingian revival was also reflected in the secular literature. Around the figure of Charlemagne there grew up a mass of legend, one of the earliest examples of which is the *Chanson de Roland*, which was put in finished form some two centuries later. This work began a cycle of romances in which the German emperor became the equal of Alexander the Great and Arthur, the legendary king of Britain.

THE FAILURE OF THE CAROLINGIANS

Charlemagne was succeeded by his son Louis, nicknamed the Pious. Though Louis, through the fortuitous death of his brother, became sole emperor, he was never able to rule effectively. Almost at once he made the serious mistake of arranging a division of his territories among his sons, extending to them an almost open invitation to begin fighting each other. The eldest, Lothair, eventually received a central portion, including the two main capitals, Aachen and Rome, a territory sometimes designated as Lothairingia, a name that still survives in the modern province of Lorraine. Another son, Louis, received the eastern territories, and the youngest son, Charles, the western. It is from the eastern and western provinces that modern Germany and France derive; the territory in between has ever since been a source of dispute between the two. In fact, it is from the ninth century that linguists can identify the beginnings of both modern French and German.

The history of the Carolingians of the ninth century is one of wars among fathers, sons, and brothers. Instead of names like Martel or the Great, these later Carolingians were memorialized as the Fat, the Simple, the German, the Bald, and the Pious. Charlemagne's administration proved to be mainly a personal achievement, and under his successors the rather tenuous centralized direction of the state quickly disappeared while power of the nobility steadily increased through usurpation and royal inaction. Not all the Carolingian difficulty, however, stemmed from internal factors. It is not impossible that these ninth-century monarchs would seem to us fairly effective rulers had not the period been cursed by a recurrence of invasions by marauding barbarians, the Magyars and Norsemen, which added to the Mediterranean depredations of the Saracens. Before their onslaughts, the fragile unity of the Franks became a jungle of disorder.

The Magyars carried out one more of the many barbarian thrusts into Europe from the plains of Asia, ever liable to occur until Russia emerged strong enough to block them. The Magyars, like the Huns, the Avars, and the Bulgars before and the Mongols after, produced a snowballing effect by sweeping up and bringing along with them many other peoples. They were subdued during the middle of the tenth century by the Saxon kings and thereafter withdrew to the region of modern Hungary, where in about the year 1000 A.D. they accepted Christianity. The Magyars today remain one of the few peoples of Europe to retain a language that derives from further Asia.

Much more disastrous were the Norsemen, also known as the

Vikings, whose raids affected all Europe. The reasons why the Vikings left Scandinavia are unclear, but historians suggest that perhaps the growth there of effective governments led to an exodus of adventurers, explorers, and settlers who were unwilling to subordinate themselves to a strong monarch. In addition, the food recources of Scandinavia have never been plentiful, and perhaps also the population increased. Moreover, the Vikings easily took to commerce and maritime enterprise, prepared to exploit the opportunities offered as either pirates or merchants. In general, the Swedes moved eastward through Russia to Constantinople, establishing trading posts along the way. The Danes and Norwegians turned to the West, where they conquered the lowland Scots and overran about half of England before Alfred the Great brought a halt to their conquests during the years just before 900. Alfred's successors eventually effected a reconquest that brought the English and the Vikings together. Ireland proved less attractive, with the result that Viking influence there never became great, but the Norwegians took possession of islands throughout the whole North Atlantic — Iceland, Greenland, and perhaps also Newfoundland. Their activities along the west Scottish coast probably also set the stage for an influx of the Scots, whose home had long been Ireland.

In Europe proper, Charlemagne had early erected a buffer state on the frontier, called the Dane march (hence the name Denmark), but he had also weakened both the Saxons and the Frisians, who occupied the region. This situation may have served to encourage an expansion by the Norse, who for two centuries harrassed and plundered coast and river settlements as far away as Gibraltar. Political disorder within the Carolingian empire probably would have made defense efforts fruitless even if the techniques employed by the marauders had been less bewildering. Lacking a navy or a naval tradition, the Franks were helpless to prevent the Vikings from coming and going as they pleased. Instead, the Franks often resorted to the practice of trying to buy off the invader with a payment of tribute, which had the effect of encouraging him to return at a future date. In 911, the king of France, Charles the Simple, found it necessary to buy off the Norse by a cession of territory along the English Channel, still known as Normandy. As Normans, the descendants of the Vikings proved astonishingly vigorous, taking a hand in every type of European enterprise — the Crusades, an eleventh-century conquest of England, the reconquest of Spain, and the invasion and occupation of southern Italy.

Muslim aggression had by no means ended with the defeat at Tours. A maritime advance in the ninth century carried the Saracens into Sicily and the Balearic Islands, and into occasional footholds on the mainland, which they used as bases for private forays and for slave trading. What still remained of Christian traffic on the Mediterranean, except for a trickle between Venice and Constantinople, was largely eliminated and did not recover much before the eleventh century.

Frankish supremacy, which had been something to reckon with during almost four centuries, sank to nothing. In the eastern part of the Carolingian territories, the Saxons, who had been notable victims of Charlemagne's fury, soon sought to build a new empire in the image of his and to make themselves heirs of the Franks and successors of Rome. At the same time, the western Franks themselves became French and attempted with signal success to develop a way of life that might shed luster upon their basic Latin heritage while at the same time functioning to the credit of their Frankish ancestry.

Supplemental Reading
for Part Three

Roman Empire*

Africa, T. W., *Rome of the Caesars* (Wiley).
Burckhardt, J., *The Age of Constantine the Great* (Random House). A
  century-old classic.
Bury, J. B., *History of the Later Roman Empire* (Dover).
Bury, J. B., *Invasion of Europe by the Barbarians* (Norton).
Chambers, Mortimer, ed., *The Fall of Rome* (Holt, Rinehart, and Win-
  ston).
Charlesworth, Martin P., *The Roman Empire* (Oxford).
Dill, S., *Roman Society from Nero to Marcus Aurelius* (World).
Duff, J. Wright, *A Literary History of Rome in the Silver Age* (Barnes
  & Noble).
Gibbon, E., *Decline and Fall of the Roman Empire.* Numerous paper-
  back abridgments of this eighteenth-century classic are available.
Glover, T. R., *The Conflict of Religions in the Early Roman Empire*
  (Beacon).
Gwynn, A., *Roman Education from Cicero to Quintilian* (Columbia).
Kagan, Donald, ed., *Decline and Fall of the Roman Empire* (Heath).
Laistner, M. L. W., *The Greater Roman Historians* (California).
Lot, Ferdinand, *The End of the Ancient World* (Harper & Row).
Mattingly, H., *Roman Imperial Civilization* (Doubleday).
Nilsson, Martin B., *Imperial Rome* (Schocken).
Richmond, I. A., *Roman Britain* (Penguin).
Starr, C. G., *Civilization and the Caesars* (Norton).
Wheeler, Sir Mortimer, *Roman Art and Architecture* (Praeger).
Wheeler, Sir Mortimer, *Rome beyond the Imperial Frontiers* (Penguin).

SOURCES

There are numerous paperback editions of Horace, Juvenal, Vergil,
  Tacitus.
Also Apuleius, *The Golden Ass,* appears under several imprints.
Petronius, *The Satyricon,* is best in Mentor.
Suetonius, *Twelve Caesars* (Penguin).

* *Some of the books listed under Republican Rome on p. 113 also deal with the
  Empire.*

FICTION

Bryher, *Roman Wall* (Random House).
Graves, Robert, *Claudius the God* (Random House).
Graves, Robert, *I Claudius* (Random House).
Vidal, Gore, *Julian* (Signet).
Yourcenar, M., *Memoirs of Hadrian* (Farrar, Strauss).

Christianity in the Roman Empire

Bainton, R. H., *Early Christianity* (Van Nostrand).
Bultman, R., *Primitive Christianity in Its Contemporary Setting* (World).
Chadwick, Henry, *The Early Church* (Penguin).
Cochrane, C. N., *Christianity and Classical Culture: A Study of Thought and Action from Augustus to Augustine* (Oxford).
Daniel-Rops, Henri, *Daily Life in the Time of Jesus* (Mentor).
Davies, J. G., *The Early Christian Church* (Anchor).
Deissman, A., *Paul: A Study in Social and Religious History* (Harper & Row).
Enslin, Morton S., *Christian Beginnings* (Harper & Row).
Frend, W. H., *Martyrdom and Persecution in the Early Church* (Doubleday).
Goodspeed, E. J., *Paul* (Abingdon).
Goodspeed, E. J., *Life of Jesus* (Harper & Row).
Harnack, A., *Outlines of the History of Dogma* (Beacon). A condensation of his monumental work which is also now available in several paperback volumes (Dover).
Jones, A. H., *Constantine and the Conversion of Rome* (Macmillan).
Laistner, M. L. W., *Christianity and Pagan Culture in the Later Roman Empire* (Cornell).
McGiffert, A. C., *A History of Christian Thought* vol. I, (Scribner).
Mattingly, H., *Christianity in the Roman Empire* (Norton).
Nock, A. D., *Conversion: The Old and the New in Religion from Alexander the Great to Augustine of Hippo* (Oxford).
Nock, A. D., *Early Gentile Christianity and Its Hellenistic Background* (Harper & Row).
Schweitzer, A., *The Mysticism of Paul the Apostle* (Seabury).
Schweitzer, A., *The Quest for the Historical Jesus* (Macmillan).
Shiel, J., *Greek Thought and the Rise of Christianity* (Barnes & Noble).

SOURCES

The Bible.
Barrett, C. K., ed., *The New Testament Background* (Harper & Row).
Bettenson, H. S., *Documents of the Christian Church* (Oxford).
Eusebius, *History of the Church* (Penguin), and other editions.

FICTION

Asch, Shalom, *The Apostle, Mary,* and other novels. A scholarly reconstruction of early Christianity. Though Mr. Asch is not a Christian, his novels are sympathetic recreations of the period.

Byzantine

Baynes, N. H. and H. Moss, *Byzantium: Introduction to East Roman Civilization* (Oxford).
Chatzidakis, M. and A. Grabar, *Byzantine and Early Medieval Painting* (Viking).
Geanakoplos, D. J., *Byzantine East and Latin West* (Harper & Row).
Guerdan, R., *Byzantium: Its Triumphs and Tragedy* (Putnam).
Hussey, Joan M., *Byzantine World* (Harper & Row).
MacDonald, W. L., *Early Christian and Byzantine Architecture* (Brazil-ler).
Rice, David Talbot, *Byzantine Art* (Penguin).
Rice, David Talbot, *Art of the Byzantine Era* (Praeger).
Runciman, S., *Byzantine Civilization* (World).
Ure, P. N., *Justinian and His Age* (Penguin).
Vasiliev, A. A., *History of the Byzantine Empire* 2 vols, (Wisconsin).
Vyronis, S., *Byzantium and Europe* (Harcourt).

SOURCES

Procopius, *History of the Wars* (Simon and Schuster).
Procopius, *Secret History* (Penguin).

FICTION

Graves, Robert, *Count Belisarius* (Pyramid).

Islam and the Arab World

Andrae, T., *Mohammed: The Man and His Faith* (Harper & Row).
Arnold, T. W., *Painting in Islam* (Dover).
Brockelmann, C., *History of the Islamic Peoples* (Putnam).
Gibb, H. A., *Mohammedanism: An Historical Survey* (Oxford).
Gibb, H. A., *Studies on the Civilization of Islam* (Beacon).
Hitti, P. K., *History of the Arabs* (St. Martin's).
Hitti, P. K., *Islam and the West* (Van Nostrand).
Hitti, P. K., *A Short History of the Arabs* (Regnery).
Hitti, P. K., *Syria: A Short History* (Macmillan).
Meyers, E. A., *Arabic Thought and the Western World in the Golden Age of Islam* (Ungar).
Smith, Wilfred Cantwell, *Islam in Modern History* (Mentor).
Von Grunebaum, G. E., *Medieval Islam* (Chicago).
Watt, W. M. and Cachia, P., *History of Islamic Spain* (Doubleday).

SOURCES

Arabian Nights, ed. J. Campbell (Viking), but there are several other editions.
Arberry, A. J., ed., *Arabic Poetry: A Primer for Students* (Cambridge).
Jeffrey, A., *Islam: Muhammad and His Religion* (Bobbs-Merrill).
The *Koran,* several paperback versions.
Rabin, C., *Arabic Reader* (Harvard).
Sommer, F. E., *Arabic Writing* (Ungar).

Early Medieval Europe

Bark, William C., *Origins of the Medieval World* (Stanford).
Belkwith, J., *Early Medieval Art* (Praeger).
Blair, Peter Hunter, *Roman Britain and Early England* (Norton).
Boissonnade, P., *Life and Work in Medieval Europe* (Harper & Row).
Bronsted, Johannes, *The Vikings* (Penguin).
Daniel-Rops, Henri, *Church in the Dark Ages* (Doubleday).
Dawson, C., *Religion and the Rise of Western Culture* (Doubleday).
Dawson, C., *The Making of Europe* (World).
Duckett, E. S., *Alfred the Great* (Chicago).
Duckett, E. S., *The Gateway to the Middle Ages* (Michigan).
Duckett, E. S., *The Wandering Saints of the Early Middle Ages* (Norton).
DuBourguet, P., *Early Christian Painting* (Viking).
Easton, S. C. and H. Wieruszowski, *Era of Charlemagne: Frankish State and Society* (Van Nostrand).
Fichtenau, H., *Carolingian Empire: The Age of Charlemagne* (Harper & Row).
Gordon, C. D., *The Age of Atilla* (Michigan).
Havighurst, A. F., *The Pirenne Thesis* (Heath).
Hoyt, R. S., ed., *Life and Thought in the Early Middle Ages* (Minnesota).
Hauser, A., *Social History of Art* vol. I, (Random House).
Hinks, R., *Carolingian Art* (Michigan).
Kitzinger, E., *Early Medieval Art* (Indiana).
Ker, W. P., *The Dark Ages* (Mentor). A history of medieval literature.
Katz, S., *Decline of Rome and the Rise of Medieval Europe* (Cornell).
Laistner, M. L. W., *Thought and Letters in Western Europe* (Cornell).
Latouche, Robert, *The Birth of Western Economy* (Harper & Row).
Morey, C. R., *Christian Art* (Norton).
Moss, H. S. B., *The Birth of the Middle Ages* (Oxford).
Pirenne, H., *Medieval Cities* (Doubleday).
Pirenne, Henri, *Mohammed and Charlemagne* (World).
Rand, E. K., *Founder of the Middle Ages* (Dover).
Robertson, Alec and Denis Stevens, eds., *The Pelican History of Music* vol. I, (Penguin).
Southern, R. W., *The Making of the Middle Ages* (Yale).
Sullivan, Richard, *The Coronation of Charlemagne* (Heath).
Sullivan, Richard, *Heirs of the Roman Empire* (Cornell).
Taylor, H. O., *The Classical Heritage of the Middle Ages* (Ungar).
Taylor, H. O., *The Emergence of Christian Culture in the West* (Harper & Row).
Trevor-Roper, Hugh, *The Rise of Christian Europe* (Harcourt).
Thrupp, S. L., *Early Medieval Society* (Appleton).
Van der Meer, F., *Augustine the Bishop* (Harper & Row).
Waddell, Helen, *The Desert Fathers* (Michigan).
Wallace-Hadrill, J. M., *The Barbarian West* (Harper & Row).
White, Lynn, *Medieval Technology and Social Change* (Oxford).
Whitelock, D., *The Beginnings of English Society* (Penguin).
Winston, R., *Charlemagne* (Random House).

SOURCES

Augustine, St., *Confessions* (Penguin).

Bede, *A History of the English Church and People* (Penguin).

Boethius, *The Consolation of Philosophy* (Ungar).

Einhard, *Life of Charlemagne* (Michigan).

Bryar, William and George L. Stengren, eds., *Rebirth of Learning* (Putnam).

Brentano, Robert, *The Early Middle Ages* (Free Press).

Cantor, Norman F., *The Medieval World* (Macmillan).

Goodrich, Norma L., *Medieval Myths* (Mentor).

Wedeck, Harry E., *Dark and Middle Ages Reader* (Putnam).

part four

EUROPEAN CIVILIZATION IN TRANSITION

11

The Medieval Response

The eastern part of the Carolingian Empire, an area roughly identical with the present state of West Germany, became the first large political unit to recover from the troubles of the ninth century. Invasions into these territories were not as severe as in other parts of western Europe, partly because they offered less plunder for the potential invader and partly because the population, organized into what came to be known as stem duchies, defended their homeland with more vigor and determination than did their western and southern contemporaries. The early decades of the tenth century witnessed the beginnings of an eastward expansion of one of these duchies, the Saxons, under the leadership of Henry the Fowler. This expansion resulted in the establishment of Brandenburg, a frontier state east of the Elbe that eventually merged with other areas to become the powerful state of Prussia. This eastward push of first the Saxons and then the Germans as a whole became characteristic of European affairs until fairly recent times. Temporarily, it had the effect of checking the Magyars and causing Henry to acquire such great power that he was acknowledged king of the Germans, a title he was able to pass on to his son Otto when he died in 936. Otto, called the Great, undertook to centralize his government, to remove the Magyars from Germany, and to revive the empire. He was so successful that in 962 he accepted the imperial crown, which had been vacated by the demise of the Carolingians.

OTTONIAN ADMINISTRATION

Administrative centralization demanded a large number of bureaucrats, and in a state with limited circulation of money, such persons

182

were difficult to find. The Carolingian experience had demonstrated the danger of putting nobles in government positions, since a noble who acquired administrative duties usually tried to pass his power on to his heirs, who then more often than not became magnates in their own right, substantially free of royal interference. In his efforts to find alternatives, Otto turned to the clergy, who were particularly useful because they were educated, their offices could not be passed on through inheritance (even though some might have children), and a monarch could always reward them by promotion within the Church hierarchy. Though in theory a bishop owed his election to the clergy and people of his diocese, in practice, any powerful ruler could nominate the successful candidate. Increasingly, this power of nomination became the prerogative of the emperor, and the German clergy proved to be his willing allies for both secular and religious reasons. In the aftermath of the ninth-century anarchy, most of the clergy believed that some sort of strong government was essential to maintain stability as well as to prevent local war lords from seizing Church property and income. A unified German state could also further missionary activity into eastern Europe, an endeavor that incidentally opened up more bishoprics for ambitious clerics. Moreover, through centralization of Church appointments in the hands of the emperor, a loyal priest could move up the ecclesiastical ladder to more important responsibilities.

In turning to the clergy for support, Otto at first deliberately ignored the pope, who was far away in Rome and whose office had become a pawn among the struggling factions in the city. During the anarchy of the last part of the ninth and first part of the tenth centuries, the papacy had sunk to the lowest levels in its history. There was a tendency to forget that the popes had once been men of great stature or that they might again be. Many of the popes of this time appear to have been little more than outright scoundrels, while others, including a number of young boys, were simply at the mercy of the warring factions. Otto, however, soon realized that some of his enemies in Germany were attempting to manipulate the papacy and that he had to act if his own control of the clergy in Germany was not to suffer. This situation caused him to enter into Italian affairs, where he established a policy of interference which he and his successors followed for three centuries of frustration. Almost continually they found themselves riding a tiger. A strong and properly moral church appeared indispensable to the orderly management of business north of the Alps, yet the head of the Church was in Rome and could be supervised only by imperial control of Rome itself. To maintain this control necessitated a dominance over the German nobles which few emperors could sustain, particularly because so much of their time and energy was siphoned off to Italy. It was a cruel dilemma that ended only when the Church found the energies and resources within its own organization to oppose the German intervention. Then, casting off the imperial protection and tutelage, the popes joined with the Italian and German enemies of the emperor to secure clerical freedom from the secular power. Such events became characteristic of Church-State relations in Germany and elsewhere for many centuries.

CHURCH REFORM

During the period of turmoil, disorder, and invasions that paralleled the deterioration of the Carolingian power, the Church suffered every kind of degradation. Churches and monasteries were a prime target for the invaders, who seized their properties and wealth. Furthermore, the anarchy offered numerous opportunities for the diversion of Church property to private use, much to the demoralization of all clergy, but especially the monks, whose ascetic ideals are difficult to achieve under the most ideal conditions. When the monastery itself was invaded and then administered by people with no religious motivation, the monastic life easily became a travesty and the monk an object of scorn and derision.

It is a measure of the inherent vitality of the monastic ideal that in spite of all obstacles the monks managed to reform themselves. Though there were numerous individual reformers in the ninth century, such as St. Benedict of Aniane, it was the tenth-century effort centered at Cluny in the Burgundy area of modern France that soon dominated the reform movement. The monastery at Cluny had been founded by William, Duke of Aquitaine, who then resigned control over it, as did the local bishop. This meant that the monks themselves could elect the abbot without extraneous interference, and the pope thus became the only outside authority over the monastery. Left to rule themselves, the monks almost at once began recovering the abstemious life characteristic of the cloister and the abbey. Invitations soon came to Cluny requesting aid in setting up new establishments or in reforming old ones. The result was the growth of almost a thousand daughter houses which came under the control of the Cluny monastery. The abbot of Cluny made periodic visits to the various houses, and if discipline was not being maintained, he or a monastic council could intervene. This centralized administration, the most effective of its time, served as a model for other Church organizations, including the papacy as well as the newly emerging secular governments.

Cluny quickly became more than a mere monastic reform. Local monks, admired for their dedication, rose to become bishops in such numbers that the Cluniacs found themselves giving as much attention to the reform of the secular Church as they were to the regular. As a consequence, a reform program took shape that, among other things, insisted upon clerical celibacy and the election of abbots and bishops by the monks and clergy themselves. Though the demand for celibacy was opposed by the vast majority of parish clergy and the reform in election procedures necessarily posed a threat to the imperial administration, most of the German emperors of the eleventh century encouraged the growth and spread of Church reform.

HILDEBRAND AND REFORM

The movement for reform of the secular Church is usually called Hildebrandine rather than Cluniac in honor of Hildebrand, a Cluniac monk who took the name of Gregory VII when he became pope. From 1046 to 1085, first as the power behind the papal throne and then after 1073 as pope, Hildebrand pushed reform. One of the first steps of the reformers was to force a break with Constantinople and the Greek Church. Though the Greek Church permitted its lower clergy to marry, had sacraments in both elements (the wafer and the wine), and differed on a whole series of minor items from the Roman Church, the real reason for the break was the rivalry between the popes and the patriarchs for control of Christians in southern Italy, parts of which continued under Byzantine control. The nominal reason for the break was over the words ex *filioque,* "and from the son," which the Latin West had provisionally added to the Nicene Creed during the time of Charlemagne. The meaning of the added words was that the Holy Spirit proceeded from the Father and from the Son, a doctrinal point with which the Greek East would agree but which it nonetheless refused to have incorporated into the Creed. The insistence upon the insertion of the phrase by the West in the eleventh century led to charges of heresy by both sides, and it was on these grounds that in 1054 the pope and patriarch excommunicated each other, formally dividing Christianity into two major groupings which still remain. The meaning of the excommunication was quite clear. A reinvigorated papacy would brook no opposition to any of its doctrinal claims.

To gain independence from continued secular interference, the Hildebrandine reformers in 1059 established a college of cardinals to choose future popes. Originally the cardinals had been the priests, deacons, and bishops attached to particularly revered churches in Rome, and most of them during Hildebrand's reign belonged to the reform party. Though the selection of a pope by the college was to be ratified by the people of Rome, the practice was clearly an attempt to exclude the emperor from any part of the procedure. Henry IV, the emperor at the time, was not yet of age, and his advisers, rather than take issue with the papacy during the trying period of a minority, made little objection.

Fearful, however, that at a later date a mature emperor might have second thoughts, Hildebrand made a political alliance with a group of Normans who had recently wrested control of southern Italy from the Saracens and Byzantines. In return for Norman support of the papacy, the popes legitimatized this seizure of power. At the same time, Pope Gregory allied himself with an assortment of dissident elements in the northern Italian towns with whom he had virtually nothing in common except opposition to the imperial pretensions in Italy.

So certain were the reformers of the rightness of their cause that they could see no reason for limiting their activities to clerical matters. Their ambitions are most evident in the *Dictatus Papae* of Gregory VII, which presented the world as a vast theocracy ruled over by the pope. Gregory believed that God, the great overlord, ruled through Jesus, who ruled through St. Peter, who in turn had delegated his power on earth to the pope. All earthly creatures were subject to the bishop of Rome — and Gregory VII, at least, attempted to act on this premise. His success depended upon what the emperor would do.

THE INVESTITURE STRUGGLE

The issue between the pope and the emperor reached an impasse in 1075. In that year, Gregory, inviting a showdown, prohibited investiture of bishops by secular officials and threatened to excommunicate those counselors and bishops loyal to Henry IV who failed to make clear their primary allegiance to the pope. The emperor, therefore, would be unable henceforth to install his loyal clerical followers in episcopal offices without prior papal approval. This attempt to free the clergy from secular deomination posed a serious threat to the emperor, since his whole administration depended upon clerical personnel whom he personally selected and could reward and promote at will. Without such officials, he was at the mercy of the feudal nobles, who, once the pope had acted, wasted little time in trying to reduce their monarch to a figurehead.

This initial revolt of the nobles was quickly quelled, whereupon Henry gathered an assembly of German Churchmen who owed their positions to him to establish the independence of the German Church from the pope. Gregory promptly frustrated this effort by excommunicating those concerned with it, including the emperor. This action led to a second and greater uprising by the nobles, who no longer felt bound by oaths of loyalty to the emperor. Helpless before this unexpected revolt, Henry was given an ultimatum to remove the excommunication or be deposed in favor of a candidate more acceptable to the nobles. The pope was invited into Germany to help the nobles decide the matter. Since crossing the mountains in the snow was dangerous, Gregory delayed at Canossa in the Apennines until spring. The emperor, who had hazarded a crossing into Italy in an attempt to prevent the pope from entering Germany, appeared before the castle gate at Canossa barefoot and without his insignia of rank, requesting an audience. For three days the pope refused the request, but as a priest he could not forever decline to receive a contrite offender nor ignore a petition for absolution. Once Henry was relieved of the ban of excommunication, he returned to Germany to reassert his control. Gregory could only go back to Rome knowing that his great hope for reforming the Church in the emperor's homeland had come to nothing.

Later writers mainly saw a triumphant Church bringing a powerful emperor to his knees, but there is little evidence that contemporary observers viewed the situation in this way. They believed that no Christian need be ashamed of submission before God's representatives. In reality, Henry lost little by his strategem, and within three or four years he effectively turned the tables on his rival by having him deposed and selecting a new pope in his place. Gregory chose to abandon Rome before the appearance of the emperor's troops in order to seek support from the Normans. When Gregory did return with his allies from southern Italy, they caused such havoc in Rome that the outraged Romans forced the pope into exile for the second time, where in 1085 he died.

For about a decade Henry enjoyed full dominance, but the latter years of his life were marked by revolts in Germany and a growing recalcitrance among Italians and the reformist clergy to accept his rule. Finally, during the reign of his son Henry V, a compromise was arranged at the Concordat of Worms in 1122. This solution followed a formula worked out several years previously in England between the archbishop St. Anselm and Henry I, which required that the bishop-elect be consecrated in his office by the pope or his representative but gave the king or emperor the right to confer the *regalia*, the lands and titles producing the essential episcopal revenues. By this agreement the Church achieved almost all it could properly demand — a veto upon bishops whom the crown might designate. It no longer had to accept persons into the upper ranks who lacked talent and training for the religious life. Unfortunately, this clerical victory played into the hands of the German nobility, who pursued their own interests at the expense of an effective central administration, ultimately leading a weakened Germany which was not effectively united until the nineteenth century.

FEUDALISM AND MANORIALISM

During the anarchy and turmoil of the ninth century, a new system of government developed which historians later called feudalism. Since the term itself appeared only after the type of government it described had decayed, there remains much controversy as to whether a particular regime was or was not feudal or even whether feudalism was unique to medieval Europe. Feudalism should be viewed as a natural and inevitable development wherever circumstances are such that effective central government has collapsed and public functions have fallen into the hands of private individuals and groups.

Since medieval feudalism was a pragmatic adaptation to many kinds of needs, there were differences from area to area and from period to period. The variety of feudalism developed in France, however, is the most studied and best understood. Some features of French feudalism can be traced back to the Roman custom of having the small landowner turn over the title of his lands to a larger holder who could more effectively deal with the demands made by the imperial officials. In return, the small landholder received protection and a kind of security; he became a tenant of the more powerful men and had to render a type of rent, usually produce, as well as a variety of services. Added to this was the German institution known as *comitatus*, a system under which a band of young men pledged unswerving loyalty to a military leader. With the increased importance of cavalry, these retainers were required to furnish horses and arms, and for this purpose they were assigned the use of various lands, although often without certainty of possession or right of inheritance. Charles Martel, for example, had assigned Church land to equip the mounted troops he needed to meet the Muslims. Because such land normally came to be granted following a formal request or prayer (*precarium*), the term "precarious tenure" at first was used to describe the system. Later the holdings were called *benefices*, a term that still implied a favor, and finally, around 1100, the word *fief* came into common usage. Anyone holding a fief was a vassal, who eventually came to have an almost hereditary right to his possessions and a status in the world that set him off from the mass of people. Potentially the vassal was the equal of the lord from whom he had originally received his honors and wealth. Lords and vassals, ranging from common knights to mighty barons, soon constituted a separate society of nobles who deferred to the king, their ultimate lord (*suzerain*), but governed themselves according to an organized pattern of rules and principles. These rules were agreed to and enforced by the nobles through a feudal court presided over by the suzerain. The prime reason for the existence of this class was to wage war, and this they did more or less interminably with each other but increasingly in a more organized fashion as gifted and successful chieftains rose to assert their control. The military power of the nobles enabled them to maintain a reign of terror throughout the countryside if they cared to do so. On the other hand, they could also be the guardians of peace.

Chance and the play of forces rather than considerations of either economics or political wisdom appear to have determined which course they usually followed.

MANORIALISM

The key to the power of the nobles was the manor, a landed property sufficient to support one horseman, his family, and the retinue necessary to render the appropriate services to the overlord. One knight might possess several manors and a great baron several dozen, depending on the terms and agreements setup between the lord and his vassal. In only a limited way did these men really "operate" their properties, for the manor became a virtually self-sustaining unit, requiring a minimum of direction from the lord's representative, the steward. The center of the manor was the house of the lord, or of his steward, which was usually fortified. Around this manor house were the houses of the tenants, most of whom were unfree peasants, although they were not slaves. These serfs, or *villeins*, as they were often called, had a large measure of responsibility for themselves, and the manorial economy was almost wholly in their hands. Under a variety of communal arrangements based on an extensive body of custom, they performed all the physical and manual tasks on the manor and kept the required cycle of operations going century after century. In return for the expenditures of about half their time working either on the lord's projects or laboring in his fields, the serfs were permitted to use most of the remaining acres to raise their own food, to graze their animals, and to scavenge wood for fuel. Beyond the manor the serfs had no rights whatever, but within it they enjoyed considerable discretion over their personal affairs. Despite an existence that seldom rose above minimal standards, and cut off from the outside because of a near cessation of commerce, the manor by drawing upon its own resources for most of its needs formed one of the most stable, resourceful, and persistently vigorous economic units in history. Its agricultural methods, which were more advanced than those of classical times, proved sufficient for a thousand years to sustain a constantly expanding and developing civilization that met and overcame a formidable series of setbacks. If the serfs showed themselves somewhat deficient in adaptability and inventiveness, they made up for it in a capacity to outlive misfortune.

THE RISE OF FEUDAL MONARCHS

Though feudalism can be considered the result of the deterioration and breakdown of a society more advanced than itself, it did not by that fact become a weak or decadent kind of barbarism. By finally assuring some sort of stability, the feudal system gave rise to a gradual growth in population and wealth which changed the nature of medieval society. By becoming established as a viable social mechanism it led to a reversal in the almost constant trend toward disintegration that had plagued the Western world from the days of Marcus Aurelius. Rudimentary states began to acquire genuine and not merely formal significance. In France, where the monarchy had become an empty institution, there was a gradual revival under the Capetians, who had shared the crown alternately with the Carolingians during most of the tenth century before acquiring sole possession through the election in 987 of Hugh Capet. Thereafter, until the death of Charles IV three hundred and forty-one years later, the Capetians successfully provided a full-grown, undisputed heir — thirteen altogether — to take over upon the death of each monarch. This lucky accident, together with an early Capetian practice of each father having his son crowned in his lifetime, firmly established the dynasty. Once the Capetians gained freedom from interference by rival magnates, they began to extend their power from the area around Paris, the Ile de France, until they controlled much of France. Their success was due in part to their ability to exploit the potential reverence that existed for the institution of kingship. This reverence was strongly buttressed by feudal theory, wherein a single, ultimate suzerain, even though he might wield no great power, provided justification and coherence for the whole system. Slowly but surely the Capetians set out to impose a measure of their authority not only over their vassals in their own county but over the counts, dukes, and clerical magnates in all of France. In 1328, the throne was inherited by another branch of the family and in 1589, by still another, but the royal authority continued its advance century by century until the French king became one of the most powerful and absolute monarchs to be found anywhere.

MONARCHY IN ENGLAND

While feudalism in France gave rise to a king with nearly unlimited discretion, in England it had an almost opposite effect. The incipient French state had failed to deal with its ninth-century disorders. The Saxon kings of Wessex in southern England, on the other hand, from the time of Alfred the Great had steadily expanded against the Danish invader until they ruled all England. Their accomplishment was surprising considering that the population of England was sparse, towns far from plentiful, and agriculture the normal means of livelihood for the majority of people. Unfortunately, Saxon achievements rested far too heavily upon the abilities of the king, and the accession of Ethelred II in 978, who lacked the qualifications of his predecessors, led to internal dissensions and disputes conducive to outside interference. In 1016, a Dane named Canute, or Knut, seized the kingdom for himself, and though this foreign interlude came to an end twenty-six years later with the death of Canute's last son, another threat materialized in 1066 when Duke William of Normandy came ashore in Kent with a large army of vassals and free lance knights.

This time the occupation proved permanent, forcing a mixture of new ingredients upon a Saxon civilization that had already developed well-intrenched and efficient machinery for local government. The Norman contribution included the continental military system characteristic of French feudalism, an adventuresome spirit in war and statecraft which moved England from the backwater to the forefront of European affairs, and the religious reforms associated with Hildebrand. William, who became known as the Conqueror, skillfully employed his conquests to establish an effective personal ascendance that soon made England the most effective monarchy in medieval Europe. Most medieval rulers functioned as suzerains, with nominal rather than real authority, but William and his successors were true sovereigns. Through feudal nobles in Britain potentially represented the same threat to the monarch that they did in France, they were more successfully brought in check by the development, under William's son Henry I, of a royal judicial system that allowed the king to maintain local control. The English rulers, however, were prevented from becoming real tyrants because of their conflicting interests on the Continent, where they held large tracts of territories in western France as vassals to the French king. Even though the English monarchs were both richer and more powerful than their French overlord, feudal ties were such that they still had to give obedience to the latter. This anomalous situation ended only after several centuries of intermittent warfare effectively limited the autocratic ambitions of the English kings.

THE CRUSADES

By the middle of the eleventh century, Europe had recovered from the invasions and anarchy that had plagued it for several hundred years. Both wealth and population had become more plentiful, and, at the same time, Europeans had become more outgoing and expansionist in their thinking. Militarily and politically, the change can be seen as early as the tenth century with the German conquest in the east and the struggle with Islam in Spain. This expansion was followed by the advance of Christian missionaries north into Scandinavia and eastward toward Poland and Hungary, in some cases preceded and in others followed, by fortune-seeking warriors. In addition, there also arose a movement to oust the Byzantines and Muslims from southern Italy. The most obvious sign of the new outlook was the growth of crusading ardor during the eleventh century. In effect, Europe became an imperialistic civilization determined to extend the sway of the Christian God and Christian beliefs against the infidel and the heretic, and incidentally to carve out new lands and business potentials for the participating leaders.

The first great offensive took place against Islam, which by the eleventh century had fallen into fragmented pieces after its earlier days of glory. For a brief time it had seemed that Seljuk Turks would once again unite all of Islam, but the first effect of the Turkish expansion was to arouse the West. Unfortunately, at the very time that the Turks became a major threat, the Byzantine Empire was on the verge of disintegration. Normans from Sicily had invaded the Greek peninsula, several Byzantine generals had proclaimed themselves independent of Constantinople, and the imperial government had proved incompetent to meet these challenges. During this crisis, the Turks had overrun and destroyed the entire Byzantine army at Manzikert in eastern Anatolia in 1071. Alexius Comenus, who seized the Byzantine throne in 1081, had rescued the empire from disintegration at the same time that the Turks themselves became involved in a dynastic struggle which caused them to neglect much of their newly conquered territory. To mount an effective offensive, Alexius needed men and supplies, for which he appealed to the West. He was totally unprepared, however, for the kind of response he received.

Pope Urban II seized upon Alexius' appeal as a means of reasserting papal power, which had temporarily been weakened by the struggle between Gregory VII and the emperor. Urban also believed that a successful campaign might heal the schism between the Greek and Roman Churches on Roman terms — and at the same time drain off some of the more truculent nobles from the West. Instead of merely sending aid to the harassed emperor, Urban conceived of a grandiose project that would not only recover recently lost Byzantine territory but would also recapture the Holy Land. After carefully setting the stage, Urban preached a crusade at Clermont in southern France in 1095, an area in which he knew he had mass support. In his speech, Urban appealed to the religious zeal of his listeners, promised absolution to those who lost their lives in these holy wars, and pointed out the great wealth awaiting them in the East. God, glory, and gold, the motivating theme of the crusade, served to drive on Western explorers, conquerors, and imperialists for the next eight hundred years. Though Urban planned and organized an effective military expedition, popular preachers, inspired by their visions of Jerusalem, went off on tangents of their own. Thousands upon thousands of poorer knights, sergeants, and lesser folk gathered up their wives, children, and belongings and set off on the road to Jerusalem, wherever that might be. Bands led by folk heroes such as Peter the Hermit or Walter the Penniless started by slaughtering the Jews in their home areas, then marched across Germany, Hungary, and into the Balkans, killing, pillaging, and marauding as they went. Since they had few provisions and less money, they believed that God must provide. Whatever they came across they took, on the ground that God had put it there for their own use. Thousands of them died, were killed, or became lost on the way, but hordes of them reached Constantinople before the main body of crusading knights had arrived. They were met by a harassed Alexius, who at first tried to give them relief and aid, but their depredations and desecrations finally forced him to transfer them across the straits to a camp in Asia Minor near the frontier. Rather than wait for the main army, they began attacking the Turks, who proceeded to slaughter them. The remnants finally joined the main body of the crusade, but the whole affair had given Alexius a rather jaundiced view of all crusaders from the West — a view that reinforced when he found several of his Norman enemies from southern Italy among the leaders of the main crusading body. To make matters worse, the crusaders not only had ideas quite different from those of Alexius on what they should do but also differed among themselves. These conflicts soon led to a parting of the ways with Alexius. In the competition for leadership, one group of crusaders established themselves in Edessa, while the main body went to besiege Antioch. Again there was a leadership struggle, but most of the crusaders went on to Jerusalem, which they captured on July 13, 1097. The victorious armies were anything but beneficent conquerors. They slaughtered most of the inhabitants of Jerusalem regardless of their religion, age, sex, or economic condition. Even after the fall of Jerusalem, the crusaders continued to dispute among themselves until four main territorial units emerged — Edessa, Antioch, Tripoli, and Jerusalem.

THE LATER CRUSADES

When news of the capture of Jerusalem reached Europe, there was an outpouring of religious enthusiasm directed toward consolidating papal power. The prestige of the papacy continued to rise during the twelfth century until the pope emerged as the most influential figure in Western Christendom. Capturing Jerusalem and holding it, however, were two different matters. New crusades were continually mounted, some minor but others major, like the second crusade of 1147. The fall of Jerusalem in 1187 to Saladin, the Sultan of Egypt, resulted in a third major crusade, in which the Holy Roman Emperor as well as the kings of England and France participated. The Muslims held on to Jerusalem, however, in large part because of personal antagonism among various crusading leaders. A fourth crusade was diverted in 1203 to Constantinople, which was soon captured and sacked, resulting in the establish-

Saladin wresting the cross from Guido Rex, from Matthew Paris'
Chronica Majora, thirteenth century. (Courtesy of the Master and
Fellows of Corpus Christi College, Cambridge)

ment of a "Latin empire" which maintained a shadowy domination
around the shores of the Aegean for half a century before the Greeks
retook the city. This first fall of Constantinople represented a major
blow to whatever hope the Christian world held for dominance in the
Near East, and though the Greeks finally recovered Constantinople, they
lost it permanently two hundred years later to the Turks.

Crusades continued sporadically through the thirteenth century, but
in 1291 the last mainland post in the Near East, Acre, was lost to Muslim
attacks. Trade had become much more active and lucrative than war,
with the merchants often successfully subverting the fighting men to
their own commercial advantages. Some of the crusading orders of
knights which grew up in the Holy Land, such as the Knights Hospital-
ler, held out defensively on Cyprus and later on Rhodes and Malta.
Others, notably the Teutonic Knights, busied themselves eastward
along the Baltic, much like American frontiersmen in the nineteenth
century, warring with the natives and seizing their land. Meanwhile, the
old pattern of conflict continued in Spain, unaffected by the troubles of
the Greeks or the Muslims, resulting in a gradual extension of Christian
dominion and the formation of several principalities. One of these units,

Portugal, the creation of Henry of Burgundy, exists today. The other states were absorbed mainly by Castile or Aragon, which in the fifteenth century combined and overran the last Muslim stronghold, Granada, and in the process joined to become modern Spain. Increasingly the popes, disappointed with the results in the Holy Land, tried to direct the crusading forces against papal enemies in Europe.

COMMERCE AND THE DEVELOPMENT OF CITIES

The crusades not only mark the beginning of Western expansion but also serve as a sort of watershed for the economic transformation of Europe. In this sense, they are symptomatic of the growing influence of international commerce, which entered into a period of rapid expansion after the crusading armies had entered the East. A Christianized northern Europe for the first time had regular and direct contact with the south. The natural communication and transportation afforded through the large rivers and the Baltic Sea soon led to the growth of a commerce based upon such commodities as fish, timber, furs, and wool. These raw materials were traded or processed in the extensive commercial and manufacturing centers which grew up in Flanders and in the Low Countries. The Swedes, for their part, earlier had developed important trade routes via Kiev on the Dnieper to Constantinople, enabling them to bypass the Muslim-controlled Mediterranean.

In southern Europe, the city of Venice, from its sandbanks at the head of the Adriatic, had from the beginning of the medieval period kept a small trade going with the Greek world, which rapidly grew in importance in the eleventh century as the Muslims began to feel the pressure in Sicily and elsewhere of adventuring bands of Normans ever on the lookout for land to plunder or conquer. Because few Mediterranean merchants had either ships or men capable of navigating the open Atlantic, most of the contact that southern Europe had with the north was through Italy, particularly through the Brenner pass into southern Germany. As Christian control of the Mediterranean increased, trade between France and Italy also rose in importance. In both cases, the Italians dominated the commerce, which brought them remarkable wealth as well as an urban culture that became extremely influential.

The Crusades further contributed to the growth of commerce by introducing Western Europeans to the more sophisticated civilizations of the East with their superior coinage, weaponry, business and tax system, and a variety of methods and resources used in the manufacture of iron, cloth, pottery, and building materials previously unknown to the West. The warrior who returned to Europe brought with him a greatly widened view of human potential as well as an immeasurably altered opinion of his own culture.

The Crusades also had the immediate effect of providing a common path along which economic growth could take place. They stimulated economic development both by channeling expenditures toward seemingly worthwhile goals and by drastically raising the level of such expenditures. Clergy and nobles, who possessed or controlled nearly all of the productive resources of Western Europe, liquidated much of their holdings in order to finance and equip a series of military adventurers. As a result shippers, money lenders, armanent suppliers, and whoever else had something a soldier needed found new commercial opportunities. From the primitive money changers who sat at their benches, (*banco,* hence the word bank) the money market grew ever more complex, with the inventions of bills of exchange, letters of credit, and the concept of limited liability, all of which further encouraged business growth. The emergence of strong monarchs and powerful city-states made it possible for money to become stabilized as the rights of coinage became concentrated into a few hands. The first Western coin to become widely circulated was the Venetian silver *groat,* first issued in 1192. Its most successful rivals in northern Europe were the *gros tournois* and *gros parisis* of the French kings. Gold also came to be used for coins, with the Florentine *florin* of 1252 serving as the standard.

With the increase in commerce, and aided by the rapid growth in population, old towns grew into thriving cities, and new towns grew up around river fords, monasteries, and strongholds. By the thirteenth century, cities from the Low Countries to the eastern end of the Baltic Sea were strong enough to form their own political unit, the Hanse, or league. For more than two centuries the Hanse acted as an important force, protecting the established commercial arrangements, only to decline in the face of the greater cohesion of the national monarchies.

Few factors were more vital to the growth of strong monarchs than the increase of commerce and the rise of cities. Kings and businessmen became natural allies. In return for royal protection, the new middle classes supplied a regular monetary revenue which enabled the monarchs to pay salaries and hire troops. The importance of this arrangement was that the king no longer had to tolerate the turbulent noblemen. Gradually, most of the functions of the nobility passed into the hands of administrative agents representing the kings or the central government, paving the way for an entirely new political and social system.

PHILOSOPHY AND LEARNING

The intellectual and cultural developments that were taking place during this period also reflected the changing social and political setting of Europe. Achievements in these areas had suffered a temporary setback with the decline in patronage of the Carolingian rulers, although Charlemagne's reforms largely kept Europe from sinking to the low intellectual level that had characterized it before this ruler came to power. The monastic and cathedral schools, especially in the eastern provinces, remained open, and though the Saxon emperors supported nothing comparable to the Carolingian palace school, they did encourage learning through ecclesiastical appointment. Their efforts in this direction were strengthened and reinforced by an influx of Greeks who accompanied the Byzantine princess Theophano, the wife of Otto II and the mother of Otto III. The artistic influence of these Greeks is still evident in the architecture of some of the surviving churches of Germany. Several bishops and abbots, including Gerbert of Aurillac, who became Pope Sylvester II, left chronicles or accounts of the time. The most interesting figure was the nun Hrotswitha from the Saxon convent of Gandersheim. Hrotswitha celebrated the deeds of Otto the Great in a poem and tried to combat the popularity of the pagan Terence by writing comedies based upon the lives of illustrious saints.

By the eleventh century, European intellectuals had acquired enough sophistication to begin dealing with some of the same problems that had plagued learned men since the time of Plato and Aristotle. Contact with Muslim knowledge, first in Spain and then in southern Italy, and later with Greek learning there and in Constantinople, brought Europe face to face with a crisis of conscience. Greek and Arabic works, particularly in medicine, astronomy, mathematics, and philosophy, together with the introduction of the Hindu enumeration system, which we call the Arabic system, caused European scholars to realize their own deficiencies. They were particularly aware of their lack of knowledge in philosophy, since the recovery of Aristotle posed a real challenge when it was suddenly realized that Aristotle was a pagan, and his thinking, however impressive, often contradicted Christian doctrine.

The dispute that brought the matter to a head was the question of universals. Two schools of thought developed in the eleventh century. One, centered around St. Anselm and William of Champeaux, maintained that universals have to be real, that there exists in the mind of God a real archetype upon which is patterned every earthly sample. This explanation, called realism, assumed that the idea of a physical entity existed before the entity itself. This view opposed by the nominalists, who under Roscellinus insisted that only the material entity was real. A universal for Roscellinus was only a descriptive name derived from the examination of several individual entities. Christian philosophy, by the nature of its basic suppositions, had to accept some version of a realist view, since the idea of the Church as a divine institution postulated the existence of universals. Realism, nonetheless, could be shown to be heretical if it could be demonstrated that it led to the denial of individual responsibility. In order to find acceptable answers to their dispute, the medieval philosophers had to re-examine many of the assumptions that had gone unchallenged since the time of the Greeks. No one did more to stoke the fires of controversy than Peter Abelard, a troublesome genius who lived and died during the first half of the twelfth century. As a student, Abelard believed, like many students before and since, that he knew more than his teachers, and he attempted to show them the fallacy of their thinking. Understandably, then, he was forced to leave the schools of Paris. He next wrote *Sic et Non* (Yes and No), in which he proposed a series of questions for which he found contradictory answers in the teachings of the Church. Abelard did nothing to reconcile these contradictions, and as a result it appeared to many people that he deliberately intended to discredit religion. It was Abelard's questioning, nevertheless, that led one of his students, Peter Lombard, to write the *Sentences,* which in its attempt to reconcile divergent opinion became the standard theological text for the later Middle Ages.

Abelard also antagonized some powerful people through his involvement with Heloise, the niece of a canon of Notre Dame. The clergyman had hired Abelard as a tutor for his niece, but Abelard and Heloise soon found that their kisses "far outnumbered reasoned words." Matters reached a climax when Heloise found she was pregnant. Abelard promised to marry her provided the marriage was kept secret. Heloise readily agreed to these terms, since if the marriage was made public all chance for Abelard's advancement as a teacher or scholar would be cut off. When Heloise's uncle made public the promise, Heloise renounced the pact and fled to a convent, where, after the birth of her child, she rose to become abbess. Her uncle, outraged at Abelard, took the law into his own hands and hired some ruffians to castrate him. Abelard then entered a monastery, where he ran into difficulty by questioning the identity of its patron saint. Next he was made abbot of another monastery, where his attempts to reform the conduct of his fellow-monks led to his own exile. He returned to Paris, where he was accused of heresy, and died before he could make an appeal to Rome. Heloise, who outlived Abelard, was later buried by his side, and both of them soon entered the province of legend.

To answer the questions raised by Abelard and others, European scholars turned to the Arabic and Greek writers. By the end of the twelfth century, most of the important works of Greek and Muslim philosophy and science had been translated into Latin, although the translations had not necessarily been made from the originals. The widening of intellectual horizons caused by the continued outpouring of new works called for new institutions, and the result was the development of the university. Originally, the term "university" implied a corporation, but gradually it became restricted to a corporation of teachers or students. Technically, both students and teachers were clerics, although since many of them never advanced beyond the level of the minor orders, they were permitted to marry. Marriage, however, was such a handicap to their professional advancement that only a minority ever entered matrimony. The two great universities after which most of the others were patterned were those at Paris and Bologna, although the medical university at Montpellier was founded at about the same time. Paris was the center for the study of the new Aristotelianism, which built upon the foundations laid by Abelard. The dominant faculty was that of theology, to which both medicine and the liberal arts were subordinate. Bologna, which was run by the students instead of the masters, as at Paris, started out as a law university. Law at Bologna had undergone much the same process as philosophy and theology at Paris. In an attempt to clarify conflicting legal doctrines, Roman law came to receive more attention, and it soon began to replace most of the existing law in Europe. Two types of law developed: civil, or secular law and canon, or religious law. This rapid growth in the development of bodies of law made possible much more sophisticated governments in Europe. Bologna also developed medical and arts universities, although they did not equal the law faculties. Universities readily proved their worth and soon multiplied rapidly, often because students and masters moved to other cities because of dissatisfaction with their treatment. Since they at first had no buildings of their own and books were scarce, it was a rather simple matter for masters and scholars, either in small or large groups, to move a whole institution. As universities became more important, kings and popes realized their value and began to establish their own. Oxford, for example, originated because English scholars were forbidden by their king to study or teach at Paris. Cambridge, on the other hand, was established as a result of a secession from Oxford which resulted from a particularly violent confrontation between students and townspeople.

The reconciliation of Aristotelian philosophy with Christian theology was accomplished through a movement known as scholasticism. The leaders of the movement were a group of thirteenth-century writers who at some time in their lives had either taught or studied at the University of Paris. The first was Albert, who moved to Paris after a distinguished teaching career at Cologne. Albert, who took as his task the Christianizing of Aristotle, attempted to comment upon all the works Aristotle had written and upon all subjects Aristotle had planned to treat or that Albert felt he should have treated. So wide was Albert's learning in Greek philosophy and in Jewish and Arabic thought and so universal were his interests that he came to be called Albertus Magnus, Albert the Great. It is at least worthy of note that only in the Middle

Ages did learning become so valued that a scholar could be so designated. Albert, however, was much more interested in Aristotle's scientific writing than in his theology, and it was one of his pupils, Thomas Aquinas, who completed the task of Christianizing Aristotle. Aquinas argued that philosophy and theology were equally valid, that they were interdependent and supplemented each other. Philosophy, he said, was derived from reason and theology from God, but he did not believe the two were necessarily contradictory. To demonstrate this thinking Aquinas attempted to fuse Aristotelian logic with Christian doctrine into one single system of order and balance. His two great works, *Summa contra Gentiles* (Summary against the Gentiles) and Summa Theologica (Summary of Theology) became the authoritative statement of Christian doctrine. To demonstrate the compatibility of divine and human knowledge, Aquinas posited some six hundred and thirty-one questions in his *Summa Theologica*. To each of these questions he gave a positive answer, based on quotations from authority as well as logic, and a negative answer, derived the same way. He then logically worked out a harmonizing conclusion compatible with what he regarded as Christian doctrine. Not satisfied, he then raised objections to his answers — some ten thousand in the *Summa Theologica* — and carefully disposed of every one. His work is a massive tribute to the powers of human reasoning and came to be accepted as the authoritative answer of the medieval Church.

St. Thomas Aquinas, however, did not entirely end the controversy over Aristotle. St. Bonaventura, for one, objected to Aquinas' preference for Aristotle over St. Augustine. Other scholars believed that the scholastic synthesis simply lacked relevance. Robert Grosseteste and Roger Bacon, for example, developed an inductive methodology which played an important part in the development of science. Still, it was the scholastic answer of Aquinas that most of medieval Europe accepted.

THE PAPACY

Rather than challenging the papacy, the new scholasticism added to weapons in the arsenal of the pope, who had become a figure of major European significance as a result of his sponsorship of the crusades. The reform movement, founded in the Cluniac monasteries, began to falter in the twelfth century, but the rise of the Cistercian monks, whose dominant figure was St. Bernard of Clairvaux, did much to reinforce it. Further strength was given by the mendicant friars in the thirteenth century. In one sense, the mendicant or begging orders differed radically from classical monasticism in that instead of withdrawing from the world, they tried to carry their faith into action. They emphasized teaching, the alleviation of the miseries of the poor, the humanization of clerical bureaucracy, and the importance of preventing rather than suppressing heresy. They were much more urban centered than the old monastic orders, and though several mendicant orders evolved, the Franciscans and Dominicans, both products of the thirteenth century, overshadowed all others. St. Francis, the founder of the former, appears to have been one of the most humane, loving, and naïve men of the medieval or any other period. Convinced of the kindness and decency of humanity, he was filled with an overwhelming love for all living things. He considered it his mission in life to alleviate suffering, a task he began by trying to live as the poor lived, begging and sharing his food with other unfortunates. He believed that only by knowing and understanding the problems of the poor could he help to overcome them. St. Dominic, though he had a similar charismatic effect on his contemporaries, was an altogether different personality type. His main concern was the growth of heresy, and he became convinced that the only weapon with which to combat it was a thoroughly educated clergy. Since his movement was designed to encourage education, the Dominicans soon became prominent in the universities. Both Albertus

Saint Francis surrounded by six scenes from his life, altarpiece. (Alinari–Art Reference Bureau)

Magnus and St. Thomas Aquinas were Dominicans. The most fascinating aspect of the development of the Dominicans and Franciscans is that though they were founded at about the same time with totally different views, the two orders grew more and more similar. The Franciscans soon became prominent in the universities through such members as St. Bonaventura, Francis Bacon, and Robert Grosseteste, while the Dominicans became more socially concerned.

The new learning became an additional tool in the hands of the Church for the furtherance of its glory in this world. Strengthened by the development of canon law, which centralized Church administration in papal hands, encouraged by the success of the crusaders, and supported by the mendicant and other monastic orders, the papacy under Innocent III (1198–1216) temporarily came to dominate Europe. Unfortunately, in attempting to maintain its new position of power and influence, the papacy tended to forget the message of St. Francis. Popes became overly concerned with buttressing conventional practices, whether in business or in politics, and the papacy soon became a symbol of wealth and affluence. Its prelates became generals, politicians, and statesmen who did not hesitate to employ religious sanctions toward material or even selfish ends. Innocent interfered in the internal affairs of various kingdoms, preached crusades against heretics, excommunicated and interdicted his political rivals, and increased Church bureaucracy. Though he left the papacy more powerful than it had ever been, he also made it extremely vulnerable. The rising townspeople and the increasingly potent monarchs were irked by the limitations imposed upon them by the papacy as well as by the special privileges enjoyed by the clergy. The end result was that the greatest days of the medieval papacy came to an end soon after they began.

SECULAR LEARNING

Literature tends to reflect the tastes of its patrons. Thus early medieval literature emphasized religious and inspirational themes because it it was directed to the priests and monks who could either read it for their own enjoyment or recount what they had read to their congregations. Church patronage was supplemented by imperial patronage during the reign of Charlemagne, but still most of the writers and their readers were Churchmen. Ordinary people tended to rely upon bards, storytellers, and minstrels, and little of their material has survived except indirectly. As Europe became more stable, there was a growth in education, a rise in literacy, and a wider demand from the reading — or listening — audience. The university student, even though he might be regarded as a cleric, wished to read something other than the required texts. A whole student literary culture centering around the beer hall developed to satisfy this extracurricular interest. The literature that so originated, called Goliardic from a mythical patron, Bishop Golias, has survived in great quantities. Like male student poetry the world over, the subjects — women and wine — are predictable. Though most of the poems and songs were by anonymous authors, many of them are nonetheless masterpieces.

Before the printing press was developed, and for several centuries afterward, no author could expect to live from the sale of his works. Only some variety of patronage, usually Church or royalty, enabled the man of letters to survive, but lesser magnates could support minstrels, jugglers, and the like. At first these patrons preferred to hear *chansons de geste,* such as the *Song of Roland,* a sort of early medieval equivalent of the modern horse opera. By the twelfth century, however, many of them demanded works that were more sophisticated, and they were supported by their women, whose enthusiasm for blood and gore had perhaps always been rather uncertain. As the original justification for the knight declined with the development of new fighting techniques, knighthood came to be identified with chivalry and its code of behavior assumed the characteristics of a sacrament. Instead of being concerned with adding notches in the heads of their battleaxes, knights became concerned with civility, with being "gentlemen," with rescuing damsels in distress. Obviously, the new chivalric code was attractive to the women, who, in the absence of the lord of the manor, often acted as patron for the wandering troubadour.

In general, women enjoyed little power, even over themselves. If they belonged to the lower classes, the most that they could get out of life was hard work in a harsh environment. If they were nuns, they were regimented by the rules of their order and supervised by male diocesan authorities. Women of the upper classes had to go along with any property to which they were attached, becoming the wives of the men chosen by their warden to possess it. In the imaginary world of romance as sung by the troubadours, however, women acquired some mystical qualities through their sisterhood with the Blessed Virgin. Paradoxically, this position allowed them to escape traditional bonds and to assume a role similar to that of the nymphs of classical paganism. They had the power to enslave the souls of men, their tutelary masters, by promising an essentially unattainable bliss.

This new chivalric literature developed in Languedoc in southern France, influenced in part by the classical Latin poet Ovid but also by Arabic influences imported into the area by the perpetual crusading enterprises going on south of the Pyrenees. The first major patron of the new literature was William, Duke of Aquitaine. The tradition was carried northward by his daughter Eleanor, who served first as queen of France and then, after her divorce, as queen of England. Her son

Richard the Lionhearted later became a symbol of the chivalric knight. Ideally, the lover in the story should hardly know the lady to whom he pledged his loyalty, since she was either married or betrothed to someone else. It was the very hopelessness of his love that carried a knight on to greater and greater deeds in his lady's name. A new interpretation was added to the traditional one in the thirteenth century by Andrew the Chaplain, Andreas Capellanus, who defined love as a passion derived from looking and thinking about the body of a person of the opposite sex. Gradually, infidelity itself became a kind of mystical sacrament. Indeed, not until fairly recent times were the opposing concepts of romantic love and marriage united. This medieval notion of romantic love, one of the most important influences of the period on modern attitudes, while it temporarily put a woman on a pedestal, it at least raised her out of the obscurity and anonymity to which she had previously been consigned. The medieval concepts are kept alive in the tales of King Arthur and his knights, as well as in numerous chronicles about the crusades, where the mystique of romantic love was combined with that of the "just" war. One of the better poets was a woman, Marie de France, although perhaps the best of the period was Chrétien de Troyes.

This chivalric approach did not particularly appeal to the rising townsmen or to the peasants. From their own experience, they knew that the knights and their ladies, no matter how hopeless their love, were arrogant, callous, and not given to charity even to themselves. Naturally, they patronized writers who chose a different subject matter. Among the most popular bourgeois stories were those with Renard, or Reynold, the Fox as hero. This sharp-witted, cunning animal, like the bourgeois he represented, overcame his rivals by using his head instead of physical force — the method associated with the nobility. Much bourgeois literature was also anticlerical. Though the first efforts were rather crude, it became more influential and sophisticated as the townspeople increased in number, wealth, and patronage.

Some peasant literature has also survived, although it was understandably much more perishable. *Der arme Heinrich* (The Poor Henry) by Hartmann von Aue is a surviving masterpiece, and the folk hero ballads centered around such figures as Robin Hood have also proved durable. It was popular rather than aristocratic taste that likewise supported the mystery plays, such as *Everyman,* which mark the beginnings of modern drama.

New and creative forms also appeared in art and architecture. Though concepts and ideas inherited from Rome had first inspired the architecture of the early Middle Ages, through modifications a uniquely medieval style, the Romanesque, gradually emerged. Romanesque buildings employed the round Roman arch, were low, and emphasized horizontal lines. The walls, designed to support the heavy stone roofs, were thick and heavy and made the interiors dim and poorly lighted. This characteristic might not have been a shortcoming in the south, where a major aim of any roofed structure was protection from the sun, but in the north such structures proved to be particularly dark and damp. Radical architectural modifications were soon made in the north leading to the style we call Gothic. Gothic architecture was a highly ingenious development that emphasized the pointed or broken arch, whereby the weight of the roof was carried on pillars instead of on the walls. As a result, since the walls did not bear weight, they could be used for windows. At the same time, the cathedral itself could rise to great heights, with flying buttresses utilized to reinforce the outward stress of the arched roof on the columns. These buttresses were soon incorporated into the church structure itself, making possible the intersection of passageways of differing widths with a great mass of floor space. Rather than decorating the wall space with frescoes or the floors with mosaics as did the Romanesque and Byzantine churches, medieval craftsmen developed and perfected the art of stained glass. Gothic cathedrals give an impression of soaring, a vertical — and heavenward — feeling enhanced by the pointed arch and augmented through the use of spires. Sculpture was also a prominent feature of Gothic churches, although it was more symbolic than realistic.

By the thirteenth century, Western civilization had reached a kind of apex, with a character all its own. It had a respectable record of achievement and promises for even greater ones. Naturally, there were still difficulties to overcome, and its promise was not to be fulfilled without a struggle.

12

Reorientation
and Transformation

By the thirteenth century, a medieval synthesis had seemingly emerged. Western Europe, united by a common Christianity, had taken the offensive against Islam, had won over to itself both the heathen Hungarians and the equally pagan Norsemen, and had sent missionaries into central and eastern Europe. Europeans themselves, enjoying new levels of prosperity in material things, were busy exploring new frontiers in the realm of ideas. Yet just as this position of growth and success had been reached, it was undermined by some of the very forces that had established it.

The papacy, for example, which had provided a unifying force, became a source of dissension as the popes found themselves heavily involved in European finance and politics. In part, this result was inevitable, since the popes were not only leaders of the Church but also secular rulers with temporal jurisdiction over the Papal States and suzerainty over such areas as Sicily and Sardinia. To maintain independence of action, the popes believed it essential to maintain their political influence in Italy. Their position was threatened at the end of the twelfth century when the Holy Roman Emperor Frederick Barbarossa, Red Beard, a member of the Hohenstaufen family, managed to unite Germany behind him, came to terms with the towns of northern Italy, and married his son, the future Henry VI, to the heiress of the Norman kingdom of southern Italy and Sicily. In the ensuing struggle to maintain papal influence in Italy, the popes managed to involve most of Europe, to curtail the power of the emperors, and to destroy effective centralized rule in Germany. In the process, they also destroyed the moral leadership of the papacy.

THE DESTRUCTION OF THE HOHENSTAUFENS

Henry VI, who had succeeded to his various positions in 1190, died in 1197 leaving a three-year-old son, the future Frederick II. The pope, Innocent III, seized this opportunity to weaken the Hohenstaufen (also known as Waibling or Ghibelline) family in German by backing a rival candidate for the imperial throne from the Welf (or Guelph) family which controlled Saxony and Bavaria. After fourteen years of civil war between Otto IV, a Guelph, and Philip, a Hohenstaufen, Otto emerged dominant. He quickly adopted the same policy toward Italy as his Hohenstaufen predecessors. Innocent then turned to the young Frederick II, who had inherited the Sicilian throne but had been excluded from the German struggle centered around his uncle. Frederick renewed the civil war with the Guelph family and with French and papal aid emerged victorious. Once on the throne, Frederick followed the same interventionist policy in Italy as his predecessors, which again led to papal intervention and civil war in Germany. Frederick was the most gifted, best educated, and most complex monarch of the medieval period. His contemporaries called him *stupor mundi,* the wonder of the word. His intellectual interests ranged from magic to science, from law to administration. He was an able general, an excellent administrator, a successful crusader, and an effective administrator, particularly in Sicily. Most of his career was spent in fighting the popes, who, fearful of his power, encouraged the rebellion of his nobles, twice excommunicated him, preached a crusade against him, and tried to encourage all of Europe to combine in a united effort to remove him from the throne. Although Frederick more than held his own until his death in 1250, the aftermath of the struggle left a confusion of warring factions in Germany, with little unity left except that provided by a common language and only nominal allegiance to the concept of an empire. After Frederick's death, the papacy successfully detached Sicily from Hohenstaufen control by inviting Charles of Anjou, brother of the French king, to mount an invasion. In 1268, the fifteen-year-old Conradino, the last of the Hohenstaufens, was beheaded at Naples through the connivance of the pope. The destruction of the Hohenstaufen family effectively ended the dominance of the Holy Roman Emperors on the European political stage. As their power and influence waned, that of various territorial rulers increased, each of whom attempted to extend his territory and authority. Initially, the most successful of these new power centers was France.

THE RISE OF FRANCE

Feudalism in France had been successfully controlled to serve the needs of the kings, and royal power was further strengthened by the growth of towns, from which the monarchs derived income to enlarge their household staff into a civil service whose loyalty was unquestioned. The biggest obstacle to royal power was the fact that a vassal, the king of England, controlled more of France than did the king. Not until the reign of Philip Augustus from 1180 to 1223 were the French kings able to curtail the growing power of this particular royal vassal. Then, by emphasizing the failure of the English king to live up to his feudal obligations, Philip was able to deprive him effectively of all of his territories in the north of France, leaving the English in control only of the territory south of the Loire River. Philip also received papal backing for a crusade against the Cathari, religious heretics with large numbers of adherents around Toulouse in southern France. In the process of stamping out the heretics, Philip managed to bring the territory directly under the control of the crown. With this new base of power, Philip's grandson, Louis IX, better known as St. Louis, found it possible to pay the role of arbiter in European affairs. St. Louis, one of the few monarchs and the only French king to achieve sainthood, earned a reputation as a pious knight, devoted crusader, and strong but fair ruler who was interested in establishing and maintaining peace. To cap his career, Louis died a martyr to his faith on a crusade. Louis' administrative ability, but not his temperament, was inherited by his grandson Philip IV, who, as the most powerful secular ruler in Europe, soon came into conflict with the pope, with a disastrous result for the papacy as well as for the cause of European unity that the popes espoused.

PHILIP AND THE POPES

The thirteenth-century popes who followed Innocent III had come to regard themselves as rulers of an international state with powers and influence that transcended the territorial limits and particular policies of all secular Christian rulers. The Church had its own law and judicial system, its own lands and financial resources, all directed by an ecclesiastical hierarchy with the pope at its head. Attempts by the popes to enforce their claims to supremacy over the state had resulted in the defeat of the German emperor as well as in a growing number of skirmishes with the other secular rulers of Europe. These conflicts culminated during the pontificate of Boniface VIII, who was installed as pope in 1294. The issue that precipitated a major struggle was whether Philip, as king of France, could tax the clergy of his realm. Official Church policy was against this practice in theory but ambiguous on it in practice, since popes had often allowed monarchs to assess clergy for support of policies in which the papacy itself was interested. Complicating matters was the fact that the Church in France — as elsewhere — controlled a large part of the wealth of the kingdom. Philip refused to keep asking papal permission to collect taxes and instead insisted that national defense in itself ought to be a sufficient justification to force a contribution from the clergy. When Philip attempted to collect, many of the more wealthy clergy and monks protested to the pope. Boniface replied with a papal bull, from the Latin *bullum,* meaning seal, stating that the clergy were not to contribute to the support of the state without the consent of the pope. Boniface did not stop there, but went on to state that those kings who did try to impose such taxes would be subject to excommunication.

Philip, as well as the English king Edward I, who was involved in the same practices, immediately retaliated. Edward simply declared that the clergy who did not contribute to the defense of the realm were outside the king's protection, that is, outlaws who were fair game for everyone. Most of the English clergy almost immediately agreed to pay their assessments. Philip was equally resourceful. Since the French Church was the main financial supporter of the papacy, Philip prohibited the export from France of all money, gold, silver, jewels, and negotiable paper intended for Rome. It is an indication of the growing importance of commerce in the thirteenth century that this measure threatened to put the papacy in financial difficulties. Though the popes had been able to defeat the imperial pretensions of the German rulers because of opposition within Germany, Boniface found no such opposition in either England or France. He had no alternative but to capitulate. After some attempts at compromise, Boniface finally agreed that in cases of emergency kings could tax Church property without papal consent. This concession was a humiliating one, and Boniface was much too proud a man to take it gracefully. He merely waited an opportunity to revenge himself on the French king who had so compromised him.

Boniface found his opportunity when Philip attempted to try a clergyman in a secular court. From the time of Constantine, two different systems of law had grown up, canon and secular. Though everyone was subject to canon or Church law in matters involving marriage, divorce, violation of oaths, and other areas of faith or morals, clergy were subjected to canon law for all their actions. By the thirteenth century, both systems of law had become highly sophisticated. The dual law system was not only a threat to an ambitious monarch, since, in effect, it recognized a state within a state, but it also led to considerable ambiguity. One problem, for example, concerned just who constituted clergy. Traditionally the question was resolved by determining whether a person could read or write Latin. Those who could were automatically judged to be clerics, subject to canon law. Such a system worked in favor of an accused person, since canon law courts were usually much more lenient for crimes against persons or property than the secular courts. Another problem was whether canon law, which claimed to be extraterritorial, could recognize treason against a particular state. This issue became a matter of extreme importance when Philip arrested a bishop on charges of treason. When the French clergy immediately demanded that the case be sent to Rome for trial, Philip reluctantly complied. Boniface, however, outraged at what he regarded as the disgraceful treatment of a bishop, and anxious to demonstrate papal authority to the French king, acted without fully considering the consequences. He revoked all taxation concessions he had made to Philip and then followed with the bull *Unam sanctam,* announcing that everyone was subject to papal authority, with those refusing to submit, such as the French king, subject to eternal damnation. Philip, outraged at what he regarded as papal interference with his royal prerogatives, laid plans for calling a general council to try Boniface on charges of heresy. When Boniface heard of these efforts, he decided to excommunicate Philip, but before the excommunication was formally isued, Philip's men had kidnapped the pope. Boniface was soon rescued, but the strain was too much for the old man, who died in October 1303, shortly after he returned in triumph to Rome.

THE DECLINE OF THE PAPACY

Immediately Philip, worried about the consequences of his actions, launched a campaign to select a pope more favorable to French interests. He was only partially successful with Benedict XI who soon died. Then, after a two-year deadlock, the archbishop of Bordeaux became pope under the name of Clement V. Clement set out for Rome from Bordeaux but somehow never reached his destination. Instead, he stopped at Avignon, a town on the east bank of the Rhone, across from what was then French territory. One of Clement's first acts was to revoke Benedict's edicts against Philip, an indication of Philip's success. Clement then proceeded not only to absolve the king and his cohorts for any complicity in the death of the pope but ordered the extermination of the Knights Templar, a crusading order that had turned to banking. Since most of the property of the order was in France, Philip's treasury received a big boost. For the next seventy years, the popes remained at Avignon, where, if they were not under French control, they nevertheless embarked upon a policy regarded as pro-French by the rest of Europe. For this reason, contemporaries called this period of papal history the Babylonian Captivity, a term modern historians find too strong. In general, the popes at Avignon were superior men, trained in the law, who completed the centralization of the Church and continued to assert papal absolutism. One reason they remained at Avignon was that Rome had become the battleground of various factions fighting for control of Italy. With the German emperors impotent and the pope in self-imposed exile, northern Italy remained in disorder for several generations. The longer the popes stayed at Avignon, the more they and their cardinals looked upon Rome as troublesome and alien territory.

Growing public opinion finally forced a return to Rome, even if only for a temporary stay. In 1377, Pope Gregory XI returned to Rome with a majority of his cardinals, only to die soon after his arrival. His death created a major crisis in Catholic Christendom. Most of the cardinals who had accompanied Gregory to Rome were French, as were all of those who had remained behind in Avignon. The Romans, fearful that the papacy might return to Avignon, demanded that an Italian be elected pope. Rather than wait for the whole sacred college to assemble, the cardinals in Rome convened in special session to decide upon a course of action. While they deliberated, Romans demonstrated outside the building demanding an Italian pope. It remains a matter of controversy whether this crowd action intimidated the cardinals; at any rate, rather than electing one of their own, they chose an Italian who was not particularly well known to them. The new pope, Urban VI, almost immediately began denouncing the personal luxuriousness of the cardinals and of his papal predecessors in Avignon. This, as well as other intemperate acts of Urban, led most of the cardinals to claim that Urban had been selected only because they feared for their lives. Shortly afterward, a majority of the cardinals left Rome and joined with the other cardinals at Avignon to choose still another pope. Clement VII, the second pope, after failing to establish himself at Rome, settled at Avignon. Thus began the period of the great schism in which there were two popes, two colleges of cardinals, and two sets of Church bureaucracies. Each pope excommunicated the other, and as each died he was succeeded in turn by another. All of Europe chose sides. France quite naturally backed the pope at Avignon, as did those states in the French orbit: Castile, Aragon, Navarre, Sicily, and Scotland. Since England was at war with France, it backed the pope at Rome, along with Flanders, the Scandinavian states, Hungary, and Poland. The German emperor supported the pope at Rome, but the German princes and towns, as did those of northern Italy, divided their loyalties. As the schism continued, numerous ingenious schemes were proposed for terminating it, but none at first seemed to work. Finally, in 1408, a majority of cardinals from both popes withdrew and held a joint session at Pisa, where, after formally deposing both popes, they elected a third — who almost immediately died. In the political struggle to find another candidate acceptable to all factions, the cardinals chose Baldassare Cosa, who as John XXIII proved particularly unsuited for the job. The fact that Cosa had made an earlier reputation as pirate, soldier, and courtier is an indication of the bankruptcy of the cardinals themselves. To make matters worse, neither of the two other popes would resign, so that after 1409 there were three popes instead of two.

CONCILIARISM

This disaster led to a renewed interest in political theory, particularly at the University of Paris. Scholars there concluded that the only solution was to call a general council entrusted with authority to settle the schism. To justify such a council, it was argued that the Church collectively was greater than its head. From this position soon came the idea that the papacy was a limited and not an absolute monarchy, subject to the control of a body representative of the whole church. European rulers, many of them acting from genuine religious motivations, others because they were plagued with growing heresy and unrest in their territories, followed through by calling a council to meet in the Swiss city of Constance in 1414. After deposing John XXIII, the Council managed to convince the countries who supported the other popes at Avignon and Rome to withdraw their support. The pope at Rome agreed to resign, in return for a high ecclesiastical appointment, but his rival at Avignon refused to do so and fled to his home in Spain, where he continued to reign, but without much influence. Martin V was then elected as the new pope to deal with a Catholic Church that was nearly united but badly in need of reform. The years of the Babylonian Captivity and the great schism had wreaked havoc. Heretical groups questioning the supremacy of the pope were appearing all over Europe, ecclesiastical abuses were widespread, and the lower clergy were demoralized. Though the Council of Constance did order the execution of Jan Hus, a Bohemian religious reformer, on charges of heresy, it did little about the abuses that Hus was protesting. Many in the Church wanted to delve deeper into these problems, but since the council had already been meeting for some four years, there was a feeling that these matters could be delayed to future councils. The papacy, however, once the schism had been healed, had no further interest in a council; rather, it feared that conciliarism would undermine the very foundations of papal power. Though Martin V had been forced to promise that he would call another council, he delayed as long as possible. By the time the council met, he was dead, and his successor immediately disbanded it. Later councils no sooner met than they were transferred to another city or disbanded.

Since no major reforms could be accomplished without the support of a council, the popes sacrificed making long overdue reforms in order to assert their supremacy over the council. Many of those supporting the concept of the council continued to meet in spite of papal opposition, even for a time electing a pope of their own. The popes eventually emerged victorious in this struggle because they were able to convince the various monarchs that the conciliar philosophy was an argument for representative government and thus a potential threat to all rulers. This argument in itself might not have been enough to win over the royal houses, but when it was coupled with concessions giving individual kings greater rights over their own national churches, they sided with the papacy. Even reform was ignored. The French clergy, for example, in a synod assembled at Bourges in 1438, issued the so-called Pragmatic Sanction, establishing the liberties of the French Church. Popes were prohibited from appointing clerics to French benefices, the payment of annates to Rome was stopped, and all judicial appeals to Rome had to first go through the French courts. In effect, the control of the Christian Church in France was turned over to the French kings. Similar concessions were made to other rulers. Though the popes remained the nominal head of the Christian Church in the West, in the aftermath of the great schism the papacy concentrated on trying to establish a power base in Italy and abandoned, at least temporarily, its attempts to be the political leader of a united Christian Europe. France, however, was in no position to assume the papal pretensions of leadership, largely because of its own struggles with England.

ENGLISH CONTRIBUTIONS

In the later Middle Ages England too was a society in transition. It was during this perod that the English developed several institutions that later had a great influence on government and jurisprudence in the United States, including the jury system, common law, and parliament. The Norman kings of England, in an effort to maintain their influence throughout their territory, had established royal courts to which any free man could bring his litigation. To assist in deciding issues of fact, the courts utilized a jury, an innovation somewhat related to Charlemagne's *missi dominici*. The English juries were first used for supplying information about local matters with which the royal agent, particularly if he were a Norman who spoke only French, might be unacquainted. The jurymen took oaths to answer truthfully the questions put to them. At first these questions dealt mainly with the community's practices concerning landholding, the answers to which the jurymen could give since they lived in the community. For example, if a person claimed to have held a piece of property for a long period of time, the jury through the collective experience of its members could well determine whether or not the claim was justified. From this beginning it was not too great a step to have a jury determine the guilt or innocence of a suspected person. Juries gradually came to supplant less sophisticated devices such as the trial by ordeal or compurgation.

The English common law was based upon many of the same assumptions as the jury system. Henry II, the first great royal lawmaker, together with his advisers, assumed that law was something to be discovered, not made. The king's duty was to furnish the procedures for enforcement. As more and more people turned to the king with their problems, new interpretations were developed which expanded both common law and royal power. Gradually, English law, like Roman law, built up a series of precedents based upon judicial opinion and interpretation. As respect for the law grew, there was an attempt to apply it to the kings instead of just their subjects. In fact, in part the Magna Carta issued in 1215 by King John grew out of such an attempt. Contrary to popular belief, John was not an evil king but simply an intemperate and unlucky one. He ran into opposition from Philip Augustus in France over his continental possessions, and in his need to finance his foreign adventures, he further alienated the English barons, Churchmen, and townsmen, who already resented his demands upon them. To further weaken his position, John had become involved with Innocent III, the most powerful of popes, over a new appointment to the see of Canterbury. To win papal support against his rebellious subjects, John finally capitulated to the pope's demands, even going so far as to turn his kingdom into a papal fief. Instead of helping John, this move only added to his troubles, since it was the new papal-supported archbishop, Stephen Langton, who advised the nobles on the provisions of the Magna Carta. Though Magna Carta has often been called the cornerstone of English — and American — liberties, it primarily set forth the privileges that nobles ought to enjoy under feudal practice; it did, however, include some provisions concerning the clergy and various lesser persons. By signing it John hoped to reduce the grievances of many of his barons and be left free to handle the others. The success of the Magna Carta in limiting the power of the king was due mostly to the fact that within a year after he had signed the document John was dead. His son Henry III, who ruled for over fifty years, was only nine when he succeeded to the throne and in no position to assert royal claims. It was during his minority, when various versions of the Magna Carta were issued, that the document took its final form. When English kings later attempted to be more absolutist, the tradition built up at this time was strong enough to hold them in check. As a result, no English ruler ever became quite as absolutist as the monarchs of France.

Parliament was also an outgrowth of the attempts of various English monarchs to deal with the problems they had to face during this period. It was a rather common medieval practice for a king who wanted to undertake an unusual or dangerous task to get the advice and consent of his council or *curia*. Since many of John's troubles as well as those of his successors had to do with money matters, ordinary common sense would suggest that it would be easier for a ruler to get financial grants if there was some consultation before money was needed. Edward I, the son of Henry III and the grandson of John, often summoned such councils and skillfully manipulated them to strengthen his own position. As different elements were included in the consultation process, there soon came to be a separation into groups. The eventual result was the growth of a two-house legislature called parliament, the name deriving from a Latin term meaning colloquium or talkfest. In one sense, parliament was a conclave of lords in a more formalized setting than the historical council; in another sense, parliament represented a broadening and deepening of public participation in the business of government. Parliamentary bodies, however, were not unique to England, since during the same time — and for many of the same reasons — similar bodies appeared in France — the Estates General — and in Spain — the Cortes — as well as in various parts of Germany and Bohemia — the Diet. Only the English model survived the medieval period as a viable body.

During the thirteenth century, English parliaments varied greatly in their composition, although in general they tended to include a specific number of knights from each shire or county; an equal number of burgesses from the cities, that is, the towns in which cathedrals were located, and the borroughs, that is, the towns that lacked cathedrals; all the prelates, or the lords spiritual; and all the magnates, or the lords temporal; and various royal officials. Sometimes representatives of the parish clergy were included, although increasingly the lower clergy met in separate clerical convocations. Parliament at first did not meet with any regularity but only when the king wanted advice or aid. Mostly the meetings dealt with financial requests, though the members also listened to petitions addressed to the king, recommending to him those they though he should approve. It is from this practice of hearing petitions that the legislative functions of parliament developed.

THE HUNDRED YEARS' WAR

The factor most responsible for the growth of parliament in England was the Hundred Years' War. This war, which actually lasted from 1337 until 1453, marked the end of many of the feudal ideals that had dominated the medieval period. Though technically the war was a continuation of the French effort to oust the English from their continental possessions, its main cause was a conflict of interests between the two great powers over Flanders. Some historians regard the Hundred Years' War as the first modern war, since it was marked by the growth of national consciousness and was fought for reasons of national interest rather than mere opportunism, at least as far as Flanders was concerned. Flanders was second only to Italy as an urban industrial and commercial center. Its prosperity was based upon the manufacture of woolen goods and the commercial opportunities provided by the Rhine, the Scheldt, and the North Sea. Though the area was under the control of the Dukes of Burgundy, they served as vassals of the French king. Most of the raw wool, however, came from England, so that economically the area was closely allied with the English kings. To complicate matters, Flemish towns such as Ypres, Bruges, Ghent, and Courtrai were centers of turmoil as the artisans and smaller merchants fought with the merchant oligarchs for control of the town government. To protect English interests, Edward III, with Flemish support, invaded northern France.

Since all the military action took place on the Continent, the English had to maintain control of the seas leading to the French and Flemish coast, a necessity that caused a continual drain on English finances. During the first stages of hostilities, large amounts of booty served to pay for the war, but as the struggle continued and the rewards decreased, the king had to make more and more concessions to an increasingly reluctant parliament in order to obtain the funds necessary for the war effort. The result was almost a stalemate, which lasted from 1373 until the accession of Henry V in 1413. Henry put new life into the war by overrunning nearly all of northern France, but he died in 1422 before he could fully secure his gains. It was on this scene that Joan of Arc, a young country girl devoted to the saints and given to hearing voices, made her appearance. In 1429, she managed to persuade the French heir to the throne, Charles VII, that a strong offensive would meet with divine approval. Charles gave her a horse, a suit of armor, a banner, and put her in charge of a small number of men who were going to relieve the siege of Orleans. The French army which had recently been reorganized, fought better than ever before, forcing the English to drop the siege. Joan continued on her campaigns, but soon was captured by a Burgundian army that sold her to their English allies for ten thousand pounds. Joan was tried and condemned to death as a witch, in part because she wore pants, although she could have been saved if Charles had been willing to intervene. The French, nonetheless, continued to press their offensive as they gained confidence in their success. By 1453, the English had been evicted from all of France except the stronghold of Calais. Flanders, however, was never taken by the French but remained instead under the control of the Counts of Burgundy, who used it to become a major power in Europe.

As the tide of war turned, England became financially exhausted and its officials corrupt and ripe for factional fights. Following the war, two baronial houses vied for the throne — that of the Lancasters, descendants of Henry IV, and that of the Yorks, which traced its ancestry back to Edward III. The struggle ended with the elimination of most of the candidates except Henry Tudor, who had only a tenuous claim to the throne. He was crowned Henry VII in 1483 and through marriage united the Lancaster and the York houses. The reign of Henry VII serves as an effective marker for the end of the old type of feudal king and the emergence of a new type of national monarch. The civil wars of the last part of the fifteenth century led to a growing support for a strong, centralized monarchy with less power for the semi-independent nobility. Absolutism in England, however, had to contend with a strong parliament and other checks to royal power, and these institutions received additional strength in the sixteenth century although more as a result of historical accident than of any deliberative scheme.

THE EMERGENCE OF MODERN SPAIN

The Spanish peninsula had undergone even more radical changes than had England. Slowly the area had been reconquered from the Arabs, until by the end of the thirteenth century five major units dominated the scene: Castile, Aragon, Portugal, Navarre, and Granada, the last still held by the Muslims. The Christian states themselves were products of unions as small individual crusading states joined together through marriage or conquest. Portugal by the thirteenth century included much the same territory as today, and any further expansion was effectively blocked by the rise of Castile. Undoubtedly, this situation encouraged the Portuguese to turn to the sea and exploration. Navarre, astride the Pyrenees, was more and more drawn into the French orbit, leaving Aragon and Castile, the two largest units, to contest for the leadership of the peninsula. Aragon, in northwestern Spain, had also become a Mediterranean power through its control of

Sardinia and Corsica and indirectly of Naples and Sicily. Competition for leadership between Aragon and Castile ended in 1469 with the marriage of Ferdinand, the son of the king of Aragon, to Isabella, the half-sister of Henry the Impotent, the king of Castile. Isabella became queen of Castile in 1474 and Ferdinand king of Aragon in 1479; thereafter the kingdoms were joined in a personal union. Almost immediately, the two monarchs began to expand their inheritance. They took advantage of war in France to annex that part of Navarre south of the Pyrenees. Next, they moved against Granada, which fell to them in 1492. With a more or less united kingdom behind them, Ferdinand and Isabella moved to the center of the European stage.

THE RISE OF THE HAPSBURGS

Equally important to the future of Europe was the rise of the house of Hapsburg. The importance of the Hapsburgs dates from the election of Rudolf of Hapsburg in 1273 as Holy Roman Emperor in order to end a twenty-three year interregnum that began with the death of Frederick II. Rudolf had been chosen by the German princes more to satisfy the formal need for an emperor than to give him any real power. To them, Rudolf seemed a perfectly harmless minor German count, although he controlled several territories in what is now Switzerland and southern Germany. As expected, Rudolf proved to be quite indifferent to imperial traditions, although he was, nonetheless, very much interested in increasing the power of his own family. One right still assigned to the German emperor was that of regranting imperial fiefs when there were no longer any heirs. During Rudolf's reign, the Babenberg house in Austria died out, after two military campaigns, Rudolf added Austria to his family's possessions. Until 1918, Austria remained under the control of the Hapsburgs.

When Rudolf died, the numerous electors of Germany turned to another obscure family. Periodically, however, Hapsburgs were strong enough to assert their right of election. Their most serious rival came to be the house of Luxemburg, which had acquired Bohemia when Henry of Luxemburg was emperor. In 1364, both families agreed to turn their inheritance over to the other in case either family died out, and after 1437, when the Luxemburg house ceased to exist, the Hapsburgs could usually claim the imperial crown as their right. Concentration of imperial power in the hands of a few families, such as the Hapsburgs or Luxemburgs, was made easier by the Golden Bull of 1356, which restricted the right of choosing the emperor to seven electors: three archbishops, whose dioceses were located along the Rhine; and four secular electors, one each from Saxony-Wittenberg, Bohemia, Brandenburg, and the Bavarian Palatinate. The Hapsburg ability to supply husbands and wives to other ruling houses and to provide heirs for themselves enabled them to spread their power throughout Europe. Through marriage, the Hapsburgs were able to gain control over Burgundy in the fifteenth century and over Spain in the sixteenth.

One major obstacle to the growing pretensions of the Hapsburgs was a group of cantons in present-day Switzerland. Since the Swiss controlled many of the most important passageways into Italy, several towns had grown rich through trade and commerce. Some of these joined together in an alliance of mutual self-help, rebelling against the domination of their overlords, the most prominent of whom were the Hapsburgs. By 1474, the Hapsburgs were forced to recognize the Swiss confederation as entirely free from their control, but it was not until 1648 that the rest of Europe extended the same recognition. In the process of their two hundred-year struggle, several non-German–speaking cantons allied themselves with the Swiss confederation. It was this alliance that led to the first multilingual modern state.

GERMANY AND THE EAST

It was in the eastern part of Germany that the foundations of the modern state were laid. The Germans expanded eastward through conquest, with the Teutonic Knights increasingly playing a leading role. The knights had originated as a German crusading group centered at the Hospital of St. Mary in Jerusalem. By the time Jerusalem fell in 1187, the knights had become a distinctive military order whose members took monastic vows, though not necessarily for life, and dedicated themselves to fighting for Christianity. In 1228, the knights were invited by a Polish prince to assist him in his campaigns against the pagan Slavic-speaking Prussians. From this base they proceeded to convert the heathen, usually at the point of the sword, and to disseminate German culture. Ambitious nobles joined the order in great numbers when it was realized that land could be had for the taking. The nobles thus recruited soon established themselves as a repressive aristocracy over the region, a dominance that lasted until World War II. Even today, under Communist rule, this particular part of Germany and Poland remains backward and depressed.

It was primarily because of the potential threat of a German conquest that the Poles accepted Catholic rather than Orthodox Christianity. By becoming Catholic they believed they could both preserve their identity and gain allies in western Europe. After the conversion of Poland, the Teutonic Knights joined with another military order, the Livonian, to move against the Lithuanians, who had remained pagans. As a result, much of north central Europe became German-oriented. In the south, German influence was spread as an aftermath of the conquest by the Turks, who, after first capturing Constantinople, had expanded into the Balkans in the last part of the fifteenth century. Here the reconquest was led by the Austrians, who thereby extended Hapsburg power over much of south central Europe.

The main obstacle to Catholic German penetration into the east came to be the emergence of an Orthodox Christian Russia. After the fall of Constantinople, the grand prince of Moscow proclaimed himself the logical successor of the Byzantine emperor, making himself the protector of all Greek Christians and his capital Moscow the new Rome. Before this action, Kiev and Novgorod had overshadowed Moscow, but Kiev had suffered from the inroads of the Mongolian nomads into southern Russia and Novgorod had been effectively isolated by the expansion of the Teutonic Knights. Moscow had been sacked and pillaged by the Golden Horde, another of the Mongol invader groups that periodically hit Europe, but there was no attempt to occupy it. Instead, the Mongols forced the princes of Moscow to become their vassals. Since the Mongols preferred the steppes of southern Russia as grazing lands for their flocks and herds, their control in the north grew more tenuous. The prince of Moscow grew to power by first becoming tribute collector for the Mongols and then, as the influence of the Golden Horde weakened, emerged as the leader of the movement to overthrow them. Moscow became a rallying point for the struggle for independence and the center of Orthodox Christianity.

ITALY

Italy, like Germany, was in the midst of political change, and after the thirteenth century no single monarch was strong enough to control the peninsula. Northern Italy, in particular, was the scene of a number of conflicts. The most powerful state was Venice, which had functioned as an independent republic from the eighth century. Through aggressive pursuit of commercial opportunities and by reason of its position as a distribution center for a variety of luxury goods, Venice had become rich enough by the fourteenth and fifteenth centuries to exert the influence of a major power. Commercially it dominated most of the eastern Mediterranean. The Venetians, however, were challenged by a number of other city-states. Genoa and Pisa on the west side of the peninsula competed vigorously in the luxury trade and profited similarly. Other cities such as Milan, Florence, and Siena were not seaports but grew wealthy through their ability to supply manufactured goods or services such as banking. For a time, these cities were more or less independent, in fact, some were even republics like Venice, but incessant strife from within and aggressive attacks from without increasingly brought them under the domination of tyrants. Some of these tyrants represented the wealthier bourgeoisie, while others claimed they held power in the name of the people. The cities were

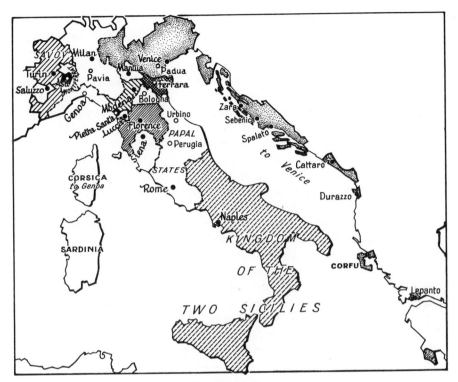

Italian cities of the Renaissance.

also continually attacking each other. Venice, for example, expanded to include Padua, while Florence subjugated Pisa, and Milan conquered Pavia. Into this picture the papacy fitted easily. Once rid of the annoying councils, the popes began the process of recovering their position as temporal princes in central Italy; their rivals were no longer the emperors or kings but the rulers of the expanding cities such as Venice, Milan, and Florence.

In southern Italy and Sicily, more traditional forms of government prevailed. The French house of Anjou, which had gained power as an ally of the papacy, was driven out of Sicily in 1285 by a massacre known as the Sicilian Vespers and was replaced by the rulers of Aragon. The Angevins managed to maintained themselves in southern Italy until 1435, when Alfonso of Aragon joined this area with Sicily, calling himself king of the two Sicilies.

UNREST AND REVOLT

The religious and political changes that were taking place in the later Middle Ages undoubtedly added to the growing unrest among the people. Other factors also contributed to this feeling of discontent. Though the feudal nobility was still politically dominant in this agricultural society, the growth of the cities had undercut its social usefulness. Income from the cities had given the monarchs the resources they needed to build up a bureaucracy and pay an army, in effect, bypassing the nobility. Instead of withering away, the nobles clung to their rights as landlords, tightening their control over the peasants and the village. In order to get money for their own rising needs, they converted services into cash and demanded monetary payment in the manorial courts. Though this practice tended to give the peasant greater discretion in his personal life, in the long run it weakened his independence by cutting out common village rights to forest, waste, meadowland, and stream. Such traditional rights had been unknown to Roman law, and, as Roman law replaced feudal law, there were fewer and fewer ways by which the peasants could peacefully assert what they regarded as their rights. Some villages bought their freedom from the lord in return for cash, but few had this much money. Others banded together as communes to force charters of liberty or some kind of self-government from their lords. Group action of this sort, however, was not usually possible. Individually, serfs could escape from their obligations by fleeing to the cities, where if they were not apprehended within a year they were recognized as free. Other serfs, as well as the poorer peasants, were recruited with the consent of their lords to join the great colonizing expeditions on the eastern frontier of Germany or to reclaim previously unused lands. Still, most of the people remained in their old villages, where even though they might no longer be regarded as serfs, they found the exactions of the local nobles becoming increasingly severe. Moreover, there was no longer the threat of anarchy to justify such a policy. The inevitable result was that many peasants broke out in revolts. Particularly hard hit by revolts were the ecclesiastical landlords, who were among the most conservative in administering their lands. Often the peasant rebels were joined by underprivileged laborers in towns who had also found their avenues of advancement closed as the more powerful townspeople organized guilds to retain control of business and industry. Flanders in 1323, for example, was torn by a peasant revolt that not only attacked the manor houses but helped to destroy unpopular patrician government in the town.

Putting even greater stress upon the peasant was the Black Death, an epidemic of bubonic plague that first hit Europe in 1348–1349 and caused a massive dislocation of all forms of human existence. A large percentage of Europeans, perhaps as many as a third of the people in some areas, died during the plague. In the consequent economic chaos, there was an increase in prices and wages, and the lower classes temporarily gained greater freedom. As conditions became stabilized, however, the ruling groups again asserted their control, and the result was increasing unrest. Adding to these difficulties was the Hundred Years' War, which was particularly hard on the French peasant, who became the victim of almost continuous scavenging attacks by noble troops and mercenary hordes. One result was the Jacquerie, a peasant revolt of 1358, which spread over much of France and was supported by the urban workers in Paris. England in 1385 was hit by a peasant revolt led by John Ball and Wat Tyler, who were also joined by urban workingmen.

HERESY

Symptomatic of the dissatisfaction with the medieval synthesis was the growth of heresy. In an age of religion, many of the dissident movements gave a religious expression to their ideals. Unfortunately, an objective account of these "heretical" movements is impossible, since the only way the doctrines of most of them are known to us is through their persecutors. One of the earliest and most controversial group of heretics were the Manicheans, or Albigensians, who believed in a dual universe of good and evil. All material things, including the organized Christian Church, they assigned to the world of evil. For them the only true church was that of the spirit. It was in order to answer the problems raised by the Albigensians that St. Dominic originated the Dominican order, but when this attempt failed to suppress the heretics, the popes preached a crusade against them. Though the crusade led to an extension of the power of the French monarchs, it did not end Manicheanism; rather, its adherents merely went underground.

Almost as powerful, although perhaps not as subversive or medieval Christian values, were the Waldensians, so called from their founder Peted Waldo of Lyons. Originally, the Waldensians had started as a movement within the Catholic Church, but when its adherents went so far as to deny the necessity for a special class of clergy, it became a heretical movement. As persecutions mounted, the Waldensians took refuge in the mountains of northern Italy, where they managed to persevere until today. It is not unfair to classify them as the oldest Protestant group in existence, since in many ways they foreshadowed Martin Luther. The successors of St. Francis also had their share of troubles. One group of Franciscans split off from the main body, or the conventual Franciscans, to form a group known as the spiritual Franciscans. Many of this group later joined with the Hussites, a heretical group, in Bohemia.

The Babylonian Captivity and the great schism added to the religious ferment and made heresies somewhat more difficult to prosecute. One of those most opposed to the papacy at Avignon was John Wyclif, a fourteenth-century master at Oxford. Wyclif emphasized a literal interpretation of the Scriptures as an antidote to the Christianized Aristotelianism of St. Thomas and other scholastics. He also ardently opposed any extension of papal power, a fact that probably enabled him to live his life in peace, since many English regarded the pope as the agent of France, and Wyclif was therefore deemed a true English patriot. He trained a band of poor priests, the Lollards, who were to spread his teachings among the people. His movement came to be regarded as subversive by the state when his teachings were blamed for the peasant revolts, although Wyclif had little to do with them. When England made peace with the pope, the Church and the state acted together to classify his followers as heretics.

The Lollards in England seem to have been closely akin to the Hussites in Bohemia. Czech scholars had studied at Oxford, where they found that Lollardism paralleled some of their own thinking. When they returned to Bohemia, the doctrines coalesced into a movement led by Jan Hus. Though Hus was a Bohemian patriot, Bohemia was not as free from foreign interference as England. Rather, Bohemia was part of the Holy Roman Empire and therefore was dominated by Germans. Even in the university, the Czechs felt they had to take a back seat to Germans. In this context, the Hussites became an instrument of the anti-German movement, with the result that the emperors devoted much of their energies to having them suppressed. When the Council of Constance met in 1414 to end the great schism, the emperor Sigmismund insisted that it deal with the question of Hus first. Hus was condemned, burned at the stake, and a crusade was preached against his followers, who nevertheless continued to exist, many of whom joined the Lutheran movement in the sixteenth century.

In dealing with these religious developments, the popes first attempted to use persuasion and education. When these tactics failed, they utilized force in the form of crusades against the heretics, which usually succeeded only in driving the movements underground. To ferret out secret sympathizers, they developed the Inquisition. Originally, the Inquisition had been under the control of the local bishop, but as heresy became widespread, tainting even the bishop, the papacy delegated enforcement to the Dominicans and Franciscans. Their job was to ferret out the heretic, secure a voluntary confession, and bring him back to the Church. Since the alleged heretic was supposed to confess his guilt without knowing of what acts or beliefs he was accused, anyone suspected of heresy immediately found himself in great difficulty. After 1252, the inquisitors were empowered to use torture to obtain the proper confession. If the heretic still failed to confess and abjure properly, he was turned over to civil authorities to be burned at the stake.

The success of the Inquisition depended upon the support of the secular rulers, and most of the worst abuses, such as those that took place in Spain, resulted when the secular ruler seized control of the Inquisition and used it to maintain political loyalty. One result of the attempt to impose a new orthodoxy was the growth of organized anti-semitism, which had existed in Europe in virulent form at least from the time of the Crusades. Jews were expelled from England in 1290, from France in 1394, and from Spain in 1492. In Spain, the Inquisition was used to ferret out any secret Jews. In parts of Italy or Germany where Jews were still allowed to live, they could not own land and could reside only in designated areas, which were forerunners of the ghetto of modern times. In addition, Jews were required to wear special colors or symbols to indicate their Jewishness.

A NEW CREATIVITY

In spite of the wars, the plagues, the schism, and the general unrest, Europeans continued to investigate and explore their surroundings. Universities multiplied and scholars grew numerous enough to supply a new level of professonalism to government, to law, to medicine, and to business. This intellectual influence penetrated into eastern and northern Europe, continuing the advance of Western culture. A new creativity was also evident in the rapid growth and development of vernacular languages. By the fourteenth century, several of these languages had developed to the point that they could be used to create masterpieces of literature. One great literary figure at this period was the Italian Dante Alighieri, whose monumental *Divine Comedy* firmly established his Florentine dialect as the literary language of Italy. Basically, the *Comedy* — the term "divine" was given to it by Dante's contemporaries — recounts a trip through hell, purgatory, and para-dise. The Roman poet Vergil served as the guide for the first two regions, but as a pagan he was forbidden to proceed to paradise. As a guide for the final stage of his journey, Dante chose Beatrice, whose only credentials for the task derived from Dante's undying love for her. As a young boy, he had fallen in love with her at first sight when she was only eight, and ever after he had worshipped her, even though each eventually married someone else. For Dante, the intensity of his passion for Beatrice was sufficient to guarantee her the immortality necessary for her role in the *Comedy*. Dante's attitude toward love reflected the chivalric yearning for the unattainable, and according to his world view, things were true simply because he believed they were true. When put in these terms, the *Divine Comedy* seems to have some of the qualities of a twentieth-century soap opera, but its in-tricate musical rhyming scheme, peerless diction, and overpowering survey of medieval beliefs and attitudes make it a masterpiece. Dante seems to imply that by striving for the highest ideals man himself can make the unknowable manifest.

The French masterpiece of the period was the *Romance of the Rose,* a collaborative effort by William of Lorris and John of Meun, who wrote at different times. Like Dante, these men too managed to write an encyclopedia of general knowledge, in this case centered around a young man who fell in love with a rose, which he finally managed to possess after a long allegorical journey. Quite different from either of these two works is the *Canterbury Tales,* an English masterpiece by Geoffrey Chaucer, a townsman and a layman who had made a career of serving the English kings. The purpose of the *Tales,* a series of stories told by a diverse band of men and women on a pilgrimage from London to Canterbury, was not so much moral edification as it was simple entertainment. Chaucer was, in many ways, the English representative of the Italian movement known as the Renaissance.

RENAISSANCE

Scholars have filled volumes arguing over whether there was such a thing as the Renaissance, but regardless of their findings, the term, first used in the nineteenth century, has become part of popular history. By the fifteenth century, man's attitudes and ideals were radically different from what they had been in the twelfth and thirteenth centuries. The earlier period is perhaps best represented by the scholastics and the later period by the humanists. In a sense, the new movement called humanism was a reaction to scholasticism, which continued to exist, with the humanists more inclined to Plato and Cicero than to Aristotle. Humanism, however, represented a diversity of interests, some of them quite contradictory. For example, though it emphasized the humanities at the expense of science, it had an important effect on the advancement of science. Humanism represented the philosophy of the new urban-oriented scholar as opposed to the scholasticism of the cleric or the chivalric ideal of the noble. Much of the support for the movement came from the aristocratic urban classes, although many important humanists stemmed from more humble backgrounds. It has often been said that humanism emphasized literature for literature's sake, yet the humanist emphasis on rhetoric was essentially practical, and individual humanists, whose style was much admired or who wrote a fine hand, served in key positions in the bureaucracy of both the Church and the state. It has been claimed that humanism was basically pagan in its outlook, yet the papacy was one of its chief supporters. Humanism also appears to have been a search for identity on the part of the Italians, who, deprived of much of their glory by the strife in Italy, looked to the ancient past, yet the movement soon pervaded all of Europe.

With the spread of humanism came a growing interest in classical authors. Latin and later Greek manuscripts became the object of a wide search, and countless numbers of them turned up in obscure monastic libraries. Many of these works were transcribed and widely disseminated, and there resulted a study of classical antiquity. The leader and founder of humanism as a movement was Petrarch, a fourteenth-century Italian who collected, transcribed, and popularized the classics. The movement was strengthened by contact with Constantinople during the fifteenth century, particularly since the Turkish threat encouraged many Greeks to come to Italy. Through increased interest in classical study, such new fields as epigraphy — the study of inscriptions — and numismatics — the study of coins — were established. Laws were also passed prohibiting the despoiling of classical monuments and buildings in Rome. New libraries, among the most important of which was that of the Vatican, were built to house the newly assembled manuscripts and archaeological finds. Rulers competed with each other to patronize the new learning, but the most influential were the Medici in Florence, the doges in Venice, and the popes in Rome.

In spite of papal support, the humanists posed a serious threat to the weakened structure of Catholic Christianity. Lorenzo Valla in the fifteenth century, for example, demonstrated that the "donation of Constantine" was a forgery because its Latin could not possibly have

Lorenzo de' Medici (1449–1492), terra-cotta bust by Andrea del Verrocchio (1435–1488). (National Gallery of Art, Washington, D.C., Samuel N. Kress Collection)

been written in the early fourth century. Even more of a threat than the scholarship of the humanists was their outlook, which emphasized this world rather than the next. It was in part to channel these energies that the papacy became a protector and patron of the humanists, encouraging them to bring their learning to bear upon problems of interest to the Church, as evidenced by the fact that Lorenzo Valla was made secretary to the pope. Secular patrons were also interested in directing humanist thought along particular lines. At Florence, for example, Lorenzo de Medici founded an academy for the study of Plato, where under the leadership of Marsiglio Ficino members of the academy attempted to interpret Christianity through Plato rather than Aristotle.

Humanism was much more than the study of Latin, since some of the most vocal humanists also wrote in the vernacular. Particularly important in this respect was Petrarch, who carried on the poetic tradition of Dante. Petrarch's younger contemporary and friend Boccaccio did for Italian prose what Dante and Petrarch had accomplished for its poetry. His most noted work, the *Decameron,* is a series of stories told by refugees from Florence at the time of the Black Death.

As humanism spread northward, it tended to become more religiously oriented, although the northern movement belongs more to the sixteenth century than to the fourteenth or fifteenth. Chaucer was undoubtedly influenced by Boccaccio, but whether he was more a medieval or a Renaissance man is still debated. His contemporary William Langland, in his allegorical *Vision of Piers Plowman,* seems to have been untouched by the new learning. François Villon, perhaps the greatest French writer of the fifteenth century, belongs more to the tradition of the Goliards than the humanists. Villon, who took a degree from the University of Paris, spent most of his adult life in wineshops and brothels, caring little for anything or anyone, suffering the vicissitudes of misery, poverty, and degradation. His *Ballade des pendu* records the conversation of a line of corpses hanging from the gibbet and talking with onlookers.

THE BREAKTHROUGH IN ART

The most impressive innovations in the later Middle Ages were not in literature but in painting and sculpture. Both Romanesque and Gothic art had been symbolic, dictated by conventions in which specified symbols were used to convey religious ideas. The purpose of such art was not realism but moral edification and inspiration. In southern Europe, walls and walls of pictures had been painted to educate the faithful, while in the north, where wall space was more limited, stained glass windows became the chief art form. Sculpture was an integral part of architecture rather than admired for its own sake. Since the main patron of the artist was the Church, artists by necessity followed religious conventions. The one area in which an artist could break away from the constraints of the Church was in manuscript illumination, which became a particularly popular art form in northern Europe. Although the illuminations themselves occupied only part of a page, the artist paid meticulous attention to details. Illustrations were often commissioned by private individuals, who soon wanted similar pictures — which included their portraits in a biblical setting — put on altar panels or in their private chapels where others might see and admire them. In Flanders, the result was a blossoming in the churches of a new kind of art in which the altar panels portrayed the same world in miniature that had appeared in the manuscripts. The fifteenth century in particular was noted for the work of the Van Eyck brothers, Hubert and Jan. These artists devised an improved oil base for mixing pigment that would allow realistic colors, thus enabling them to achieve a portraiture that still has meaning and excitement. A host of painters followed the Van Eycks — Roger van der Weyden, Hugo van der Gros, Hans Memling — with the result that almost every modern Belgian town today contains a masterpiece from this period.

Flemish painting was also closely related to Italian art. Since Italy had never adopted the Gothic cathedral, fresco painting had remained important. Usually the background in these paintings was a single tone, either blue or gold. One of the first painters to break with this custom was Giotto at the end of the thirteenth century, who attempted to put his figures in a more natural setting. Soon Giotto, as well as other artists, were striving to solve the problems of dimension and were placing new importance on light, shade, color, and composition. The eventual result of these experiments was a realistic painting of figures set in perspective. By the end of the fifteenth century, through the efforts of Masaccio, Ghirlandaio, Botticelli, and others, most of the technical problems had been overcome and the stage was set for the work of the individual geniuses who emerged in the next century. The evolution of sculpture followed similar lines, although here the attempt to achieve realism was at least in part an effort to imitate the classical figures rediscovered by the humanists. The result was a growing separation of sculpture and architecture.

TECHNOLOGICAL INNOVATION AND EXPLORATION

Coinciding with these innovations in art and literature was the invention of printing, one of the most revolutionary developments in history. Printing with movable blocks had been known in China from an early date, but apparently the methods did not spread westward. Chinese techniques for making paper came to be known in the West through the Arabs, however, and by the end of the twelfth century paper was being manufactured in the Chinese manner in Spain and southern France. These techniques spread to the rest of Europe, so that for the first time there became available a comparatively inexpensive writing material. The invention of inexpensive paper made the materials for books much cheaper, but the fact that books had to be hand copied, even though this might be done on a mass production line with one person copying the same page over and over, still made this prohibitively expensive. In the fifteenth century, several people began to apply the woodblock engraving method to book production. This technique, made possible by the invention of more improved inks, had been in use from the fourteenth century for making prints. Woodblocks still required the carving of a whole page at a time, a costly and time-consuming process, and the next step was to develop movable type, or separate letters that could be used over and over again. Books printed from movable type date from the second quarter of the fifteenth century, and the method spread rapidly. The man who perfected the technique, although he did not invent it, was the printer Johannes Gutenberg of Mainz.

Like most innovations, the potentials of movable type were not immediately realized. In fact, at first there was an attempt to make the printed book look like a handwritten one. It was not until the end of the fifteenth century that there began a kind of small-scale mass production of books, thereby opening up a whole new world of learning. Hundreds and hundreds of different titles were printed in the last few decades of the fifteenth century, particularly in Italy. The whole nature of education was affected, since rote learning decreased in importance as it became possible to record information in books. One reason for the success of the humanists is that they had access to printing presses. By the sixteenth century, reformers, radicals, and dissenters could turn to the press to disseminate their ideas, and the age of mass communication had made its first tentative appearance.

As revolutionary as printing, and with a more immediate effect on the social structure of Europe, was the development of the cannon. Gunpowder seems to have been a simultaneous invention of several different cultures in the early Middle Ages; it was found in China, among the Arabs, and at Constantinople, where "Greek" fire started other peoples on the trail of ever more combustible mixtures. Though gunpowder might have been an international development, guns themselves are Occidental in origin, appearing in large numbers during the Hundred Years' War. The cannon was not only important in itself but it was also the first explosive power machine, quite simply a one-cylinder internal combustion engine, the forerunner of the modern motor. Though cannons were not at first particularly efficient weapons of war, they at least could frighten horses and disrupt cavalry. By the end of the fifteenth century, as cannons grew more accurate and as mathematical innovations allowed a gunner to predict the trajectory, the whole nature of war changed. Mounted knights were no longer so important, although the nobles managed to retain their military status by becoming officers and administrators over a growing professional army. In the first wave of European expansion, the cannon gave the armies who used it a decided advantage over most of those they met.

Further aiding European expansion was the compass, which had reached Europe from China by the beginning of the twelfth century. Equally important was the invention of the carrack, a fully rigged, decked-over sailing ship with high bows and sufficient room for cargo, armament, stores, and crew to stay at sea for several weeks. By the end of the fifteenth century, such vessels had reached six hundred tons. Though the Vikings had earlier sailed the Atlantic, exploitation of any discoveries was dependent upon effective course plotting made possible by the compass and the astrolabe and by the safer transportation afforded by the new-type ships. Other inventions also played a major part in changing the nature of European civilization, including, for example, clocks and spectacles.

Coinciding with these developments was a renewed interest in the Far East. Numerous Christian missionaries had gone to the East since the twelfth century, followed by other Europeans, such as the Polo family, for more strictly commercial reasons. By the end of the fourteenth century, it has been estimated that there were about fifty Franciscan houses in China. There was enough interest in China that various explorers attempted to reach it without going through the Islamic lands, a route more or less monopolized by the Venetians. An obvious alternative was by way of the Atlantic, and by coincidence it was also the Atlantic states which at the end of the fifteenth century were the most unified and had the ability to channel their resources into exploration. Portugal led the way mainly because it was prevented from further expansion on the Spanish peninsula. It is also quite possible that the crusading ideal, which had dominated the thinking of the Spanish peninsula, naturally now turned toward Africa. Though the Portuguese talked a good deal about the conversion of the pagan infidel, and for a time tried to assume the offensive against Islam by moving down the coast of Africa and attacking from the south, their main interest in expansion soon became economic. Since Africa at first had little material wealth to offer, the Portuguese turned to capturing humans, who were sold as slaves. This trade became so lucrative that the Portuguese pushed further and further south in search of cheap slaves. The man who took the lead in the Portuguese exploration was the younger son of John I of Portugal, Henry, called the Navigator. Though Henry was primarily interested in building his own fortune, his expeditions incidentally gathered a great deal of information as they penetrated further down the African coast. During this period, someone inevitably conceived of the possibility of finding an all-water route to the Far East. Although Henry died in 1460, exploration was now so lucrative that the Portuguese advance continued at an even more rapid pace. By 1471, the equator had been crossed; in 1486, Bartholomew Diaz rounded the Cape of Good Hope; and in 1497, Vasco de Gama pushed on to India.

Portuguese circumnavigation of Africa was spurred on by the voyage of Columbus. Though Columbus, who was finally given backing for his voyages by Ferdinand and Isabella, is usually called the discoverer of America, he quite obviously was not, except in the sense that his voyage of 1492 led to effective exploitation and colonization, which earlier discoveries by the Viking and others had failed to accomplish. At first, the Portuguese route to India overshadowed the discovery or rediscovery of the American continent, but it was the riches of America that eventually brought the European powers world domination. At a time when the Turks were invading Europe from the southeast, Western civilization was finding new areas to conquer. This expansion, which began with a small movement, led to the gradual conquest of the whole globe. Though Europe at the end of the fifteenth century was in a sense still under siege, it had already laid the foundation for its coming period of domination. It had recovered its past and was confident of the future.

13

The End
of Religious Unity

The opening of the sixteenth century witnessed a flowering of the artistic and literary movement that had started with the Italian Renaissance. Though Italian modes and concepts continued to exercise great influence throughout the century, increasingly the age became dominated by religious controversy. In fact, the sixteenth century marks the termination of religious unity in Western Europe, a perhaps inevitable consequence of the earlier failure of the popes and emperors to maintain political unity. Much of the political history of the period centers around the ambitions of the Hapsburgs, who, with the accession of Charles V as Holy Roman Emperor in 1519, suddenly seemed destined to dominate all of Europe. They failed to do so because of the opposition of the French, the invasion of the Turks, and the appearance of Martin Luther. Though many people followed Luther because they believed he held the key to salvation, the ultimate success of his movement was due more to nonreligious than to religious reasons. Viewed in this way, Protestantism represented a reaction against the social and economic conditions of the time as well as a political and military revolt against Hapsburg pretensions.

THE HAPSBURGS

During the last years of the fifteenth century and the first few decades of the sixteenth, the Hapsburgs had extended their territory through a series of fortuitous accidents and careful marriages to include

233

the Netherlands, Spain, southern Italy, and the New World. The cornerstone of this expansion was the duchy of Burgundy, the leading commercial, industrial, intellectual, and cultural center of northern Europe. Though the dukes of Burgundy were vassals of both the French king and the German emperor for different parts of their duchy, which included Flanders, the Brabant, Holland, Zeeland, and Burgundy, they acted as independent rulers. In their attempts to consolidate their territorial boundaries through the annexation of Lorraine, the dukes became involved in a series of wars with France. Duke Charles the Bold was defeated and killed by the French in 1477, leaving a daughter Mary, the wife of the Hapsburg heir Maximilian, as his sole survivor. Most of the Burgundian territories then passed to the Hapsburgs, with others going to France. Philip, the son of Mary and Maximilian, was married to Joanna, daughter of Ferdinand and Isabella, and heiress to the Spanish throne. Their son Charles, once he reached his majority, controlled not only the Spanish and Burgundian territories but also the traditional Hapsburg possessions in central Europe. The industrial and commercial advantages of the Netherlands portion of his inheritance, the gold of the New World, which as early as 1512 had amounted to more than a million dollars a year, and the manpower of his German and Italian possessions made Charles the most powerful man in Europe. When in 1519 he was also elected Holy Roman Emperor, the Hapsburgs were seen as a major threat to independent action by many of the rulers of Europe, particularly the king of France and the pope at Rome.

France, which had finally recovered from the effects of the Hundred Years' War, had managed to annex part of Burgundy in spite of the Hapsburg succession. Encouraged by this success, the French then invaded Italy in order to contest the Hapsburg claim to the throne of Naples. As a result, the Italian peninsula, dominated by five large units centered around the cities of Milan, Venice, Florence, Naples, and Rome, became the first major battleground for the anti-Hapsburg forces. In the initial stages of the invasion, Milan, technically an imperial fief — and therefore subject to the Hapsburgs — temporarily came under French control. The Medici family in Florence, which had opposed French interference, found itself overthrown in the aftermath of the first French successes. Installed as head of a new Florentine republic by an anti-Medici faction was Girolamo Savonarola, a religious reformer later adjudged to be a heretic. The French, however, were unable to win over the Venetians, who believed that only the Hapsburgs could defeat the Turks and remove this threat to their Mediterranean possessions. Naples also remained solidly under the control of the Hapsburgs. The popes at Rome vacillated from one side to another. Eventually, the French invasion came to nothing as far as permanent territorial or military achievements were concerned, but culturally the ideas of the Italian Renaissance reached France in great force. Politically, the campaign also served to sharpen the antagonisms between the French and the Hapsburgs.

THE PAPACY AND ITALY

In the confused Italian political scene, the popes found themselves subject to all kinds of difficulties. Nepotism and simony were rampant, and the popes themselves plotted, manipulated, and fought on the same level as other secular rulers. In fact, during the pontificate of Alexander VI from 1492 to 1503, the popes became almost completely secularized rulers. Alexander VI, a member of the Borgia family, the nephew of Pope Calixtus III, had risen to power through nepotism, and by today's standards he would hardly seem suited to be a pope, since he was the father of a number of children and primarily interested in extending his family's power and influence. His daughters were married to princes whom he believed would be politically useful to him. His son, Cesare, was made a cardinal at eighteen, but later, when the family's dynastic ambitions required it, he renounced this position to become Duke of Romagna. To help Cesare expand this dukedom, Alexander appealed to Francis I of France, who was indebted to him because the pope had annulled an earlier marriage to allow the king to marry Anne of Brittany, thereby adding that territory to the possessions of the French crown. Unfortunately for the Borgia family, Alexander died before his plans had fully materialized. Within a year, Julius II, an opponent of the Borgias, was elected pope, and among his first acts was a move against the Borgias aimed at adding their family possessions to those of the papacy. Julius then began a drive to expel the French, invited in by his predecessor, from the Italian peninsula. Julius' successor, Leo X, a member of the Medici family, once again encouraged French intervention, in part because the French now promised to support the claims of the Medici family in Florence.

Obviously, in their devious struggle for political and military power for themselves or their families, the popes paid little attention to their spiritual obligations. In fact, it was by observing the activities of his papal contemporaries that Niccolo Machiavelli was moved to write the *Prince*. A Florentine and a committed Italian patriot, Machiavelli wanted a united Italy, free from foreign domination. He concluded that morality or virtue had no place in statecraft and that the only standard by which any public policy could be judged was the degree of its success. A successful and effective ruler, motivated by both selfish interests and expedience, would strengthen his power and extend his territory. Though Machiavelli's seeming cynicism has often

Niccolò Machiavelli
(1469–1527), fifteenth-
century terra cotta.
(Alinari–Art Reference
Bureau)

been criticized, he was a careful observer of the events of his own time and has proved to be an accurate prophet of the conduct of almost all rulers and states since.

THE GREAT AGE OF ITALIAN ART

While the popes of the period might have been lacking in spiritual qualities, they did demonstrate a devotion to the arts. None of them leaned more in this direction than Julius II, whose imprint is still everywhere visible in the modern Vatican. The enduring monument of his reign is St. Peter's, which he projected as the grandest and most beautiful structure in Christendom. After ruthlessly destroying an older basilica on the site, Julius hired Donato d'Agnolo, or Bramante, as architect for this new monument to papal power. Beginning in 1506, Bramante carried through the revolution in architecture that had been started by humanist admirers of Roman and Greek buildings such as Brunelleschi and Leon Battista Alberti. The success of the new style is most evident from the numerous copies and imitations of St. Peter's since constructed, including the capitol in Washington, D.C., and those in most of the states. Bramante originally laid out the new St. Peter's as a Greek cross, an effect that was visually pleasing but not quite valid structurally. This defect was not necessarily the fault of Bramante, who was unable to test his plan because Julius insisted that work start immediately and be finished as soon as possible. Neither Julius nor Bramante, however, lived to see the finished product, and Bramante's plans were modified somewhat by Michelangelo and Raphael, each of whom also served as architect for the building which still dominates Rome.

Julius was a patron of all kinds of art forms. Michelangelo Buonarotti, for example, was at heart a sculptor, and as such he completed the revolution in sculpture started by Donatello and others. With Michelangelo, sculpture was no longer simply a part of architecture but separate and distinct, valuable in its own right. Sculpture, however, need not be entirely true to nature; Michelangelo tried in his work to convey a particular meaning or thought, to which he subordinated material and physical characteristics. This quality is most evident in his *Pietà,* which conveys the grief of Mary in supporting the dead Christ, as well as in his famous statue of the young *David.* Though he regarded himself as a sculptor, Michelangelo is best known for his painting of the ceiling of the Sistine Chapel, which was commissioned by Pope Julius. Here Michelangelo concentrated on figures, almost as if making statues, and ignored background. Since both his conception of art and his personality made it difficult for him to work with others, the task of painting the three hundred ninety-four figures while lying on his back was an exhausting one that took over four years. The results justified all of his efforts, since the ceiling has come to be regarded as one of the masterpieces of world art. Michelangelo also wrote sonnets which rank among the best in Italian literature.

An older contemporary of Michelangelo was Leonardo de Vinci, whose work culminated the revolution in painting that had started earlier. One of the greatest geniuses the world has ever known, Leonardo was at once painter, architect, sculptor, engineer, scientist, mathematician, and athlete. Though trained in Florence, his first great artistic achievements were in Milan, where he went to do an equestrian statue of the Duke of Milan. This statue was never finished because Leonardo spent his time making so many studies and sketches of horses that he had to rush to make his model, which he made too large to cast in bronze. This incident effectively demonstrates the personality traits that plagued Leonardo the rest of his life and that seem so tragic to us today. Leonardo was a procrastinator who embodied the contradictory virtues of the perfectionist and the experimenter, making it almost impossible for him to finish a project. His greatest artistic achievement in Milan was the *Last Supper,* painted in oil on the walls of the refectory of Santa Maria delle Grazie. Here again Leonardo was experimenting, this time with oil paints, and failed to prepare his surface properly, so that the colors have faded. The painting was also never quite finished. Forced to leave Milan by the French invasion,

Leonardo da Vinci
(1452–1519), self
portrait. (Alinari–Art
Reference Bureau)

Leonardo turned up in the papal armies as a military engineer. His great but unfinished *Mona Lisa,* which is sometimes called the first distinctive psychological portrait, dates from this time (1506). In this work, Leonardo followed a common practice of artists of the period by posing the wife of one of his patrons as the Madonna. This portrait, as well as his other Madonnas, reveals a fundamental difference between him and Michelangelo: The latter regarded the male form, particularly the nude male, as possessing ideal beauty, while Leonard's ideal was the feminine figure. Leonardo also began to illustrate a book on anatomy, which was never published because his co-author died. His anatomical sketches were lost for hundreds of years, preventing him from being regarded as one of the founders of modern anatomical study. His other technical sketches of such modern devices as submarines and airplanes were also not published until the nineteenth century, and even then they caused tremendous excitement.

The third great artist of the period was Raphael of Urbino, who had studied in Florence under Leonardo and Michelangelo. It was under Leonardo's influence that he painted the series of Madonnas that led Pope Julius to commission him to decorate some rooms in the Vatican palace. In his Vatican paintings, Raphael showed a remarkable ability to organize large numbers of people into the limited space of a canvas. He died in 1520, at the age of thirty-seven, leaving several projects unfinished.

In addition to Florence and Rome, most of the other Italian cities had important painters or sculptors who were active during this period. Parma, for example, was the home of Correggio, who painted many of his naturalistic Madonnas there. The only city able to match Rome or Florence in patronage, however, was Venice, the center of a whole school of artists. Among them was Giorgione, who began the traditional Venetian emphasis on color. Titian, perhaps the greatest of the Venetian artists, achieved a symphony of color in his masterpiece of 1518, the *Assumption of the Virgin*. Tintoretto and Paolo Veronese continued the Venetian school in the last part of the sixteenth century, when both Rome and Florence had declined as artistic centers. Italian artists soon began to work in other parts of Europe, no longer confined to Italy. The work of the Florentine goldsmith Benvenuto Cellini, for example, was sought after by rulers throughout Europe. Cellini is also known for his autobiography, which gives an interesting but egotistic view of the time.

In literature, Italy continued to contribute a number of distinguished writers. Though authors continued to use the medieval subject matter, their work reflected quite a different attitude, as evidenced in the *Orlando Furioso* of Ludovico Ariosto, a retelling of the adventures of Charlemagne's vassal Roland. In this version of the story, Roland was driven mad by the faithlessnesse of his beloved Angelica. The master poet of this period was Torquato Tasso. His epic *Jerusalem Delivered*, which deals with the Crusades and the Christian struggle with the heretic as well as the infidel, served as a vehicle for Tasso to make an appeal for a new offensive against the Turks. The most original literary form of the time was the *Pasquinade*, a witty, personal, and malicious lampoon of people and events, which reached its highest form with Pietro Aretino.

NORTHERN HUMANISM

Inevitably, the secular activities of the early sixteenth-century popes came under attack, but more by outsiders than by Italians. The Italians themselves had mixed feelings on this matter, since most of the popes were Italian, and many of them were Italian nationalists. Moreover, in their patronage of the arts and the glorification of the Italian past, the popes played upon the patriotism of the humanistically inclined intellectuals. Though there might be discontent with particular political actions taken by the popes, there was little or no challenge to the existence of the papacy itself. In the rest of Europe, particularly in the north, the very basis of the papacy came to be questioned. Much of the protest in this area was associated with the humanist movement, which had become more religiously oriented as it moved northward. This religious preoccupation was particularly characteristic of the humanists who came into contact with schools run by the Brethren of Common Life, an order that originated with the attempt of a group of laymen to live their lives in imitation of the teachings of Jesus as set forth in the Sermon on the Mount. Reflecting their ideas is a remarkable religious work, *The Imitation of Christ,* ascribed to Thomas à Kempis and written at the end of the fifteenth century. To the Brethren and to northern humanists in general, the Greek and Roman classics were mainly valuable for elucidating the Christian religion or for instilling a purer moral conception in the lives of the people. Among the more famous pupils of the Brethren schools were Rudolf Agricola, John Wimpheling, and above all Desiderius Erasmus, who dominated the whole northern humanist movement until his death in 1538.

The illegitimate son of a priest, Erasmus was turned over to the Brethren in Deventer for his education. He later became a monk, although he never really lived in a monastery but instead, spent most of his life traveling, staying with various patrons and supporting himself with his writing. Erasmus was the first man of letters to rely entirely upon the printing press for the diffusion of his ideas, and few men before or since have exerted such a powerful influence on their contemporaries. His fame was first established by his *Adages,* published in 1500, a compilation of excerpts from classical authors that allowed men of leisure and wealth to act informed about the classics without having to read them. Still worth reading is the *Praise of Folly,* emphasizing the importance of the good life, which for Erasmus came from moderation and natural feeling without too much regard for the conventions of society. He believed that religion could serve as a guide to right living, but he was not particularly impressed by the ceremonies or institutions of Christianity. His disdain for these aspects of religion is most evident in his *Handbook of a Christian Soldier,* an attack upon the popular cult of the saints, the exhibition of relics, and numerous other aspects of the contemporary religion. In the long run, Erasmus' most important contribution was his edition of the *Greek New Testament,* based upon a collection of several Greek manuscripts. This particular work, along with that of Cardinal Ximenes in Spain, marks the beginning of modern biblical scholarship.

Desiderius Erasmus
(1466?–1536), portrait
by Hans Holbein the
Younger (1497?–1543).
(Clichés Musèes
Nationaux)

GROWING RELIGIOUS CRITICISM

In his criticism of clergy, monks, friars, popes, and Church practices in general, Erasmus was joined by other humanist writers. Ulrich von Hutten, for example, launched a direct assault on the pope for debasement of his high office, for his low morals, and for his mercenary character. Not only in German-speaking Europe but in England and elsewhere humanism became the voice for a critical examination of Church beliefs and practices. The leading humanist in England, John Colet, began to lecture on the Epistles of Paul in 1496 in an attempt to understand the texts literally. This emphasis on the meaning of the Bible was typical of northern humanists as well as of religious reformers. Not all northern humanists, however, were primarily concerned with religious practices. Guillaume Bude, the most important of the French humanists, devoted his scholarship to the study of Roman law. Still, humanist criticism of the Church was so widespread that it was carried over into the vernacular literature. François Rabelais' *Gargantua, Father of Pantagruel* is a witty, penetrating, and devastating criticism of the activities of friars, priests, and popes. Even defenders of Catholicism such as the great Spanish poet Juan Luis Vives attacked the Church for its treatment of the poor and other similar failings. Thomas More, the Englishman who was canonized because of his opposition to the policies of Henry VIII, satirized Church practices in his masterpiece, *Utopia*.

Though the masses of people were very likely unaware of the specific criticisms of the intellectuals, they could not help but be upset by the religious abuses that were in evidence all around them. This widespread discontent with the Church is perhaps confirmed by the fact that heresy continued to grow throughout this period. Almost all Christians resented the seemingly endless demand of the Church hierarchy for money. Nobles who were asked to contribute looked with envy upon the vast amounts of land held by the Church. Peasants who lived upon ecclesiastical land felt themselves to be more oppressed than their neighbors who lived upon secular estates. As a result, anyone who proposed secularization of Church lands could find a ready audience. Within the towns, there was also considerable resentment of the ecclesiastical hierarchy as the lower classes found chances for advancement blocked by the powerful guilds, which were controlled by the rich merchants and industrialists working in collaboration with Church officials. Europe was ripe for revolt, and the man who successfully launched the revolt was Martin Luther.

MARTIN LUTHER

The son of a newly rich peasant, Luther was the first member of his family to enter a university. His parents wanted him to study law, the key to high ecclesiastical or political appointments, but a personal religious crisis led the young Martin to abandon law and become a monk. Eventually, after entering the monastery, he returned to the university to study theology. After receiving a number of key ecclesiastical appointments and serving his monastery as a delegate to Rome, Luther was appointed to lecture in the newly founded university at Wittenberg. In spite of these outward signs of religious success, Luther was continually plagued by doubts concerning his own salvation. To help him in his crisis, Luther turned to the Bible, where he found his answer in the doctrine of salvation by faith. Simply stated a believer is saved by his faith in the merits of Christ's sacrifice on Calvary which had washed away the stain of man's guilt. Though Luther believed that a man who was saved would naturally do good works, he became convinced that faith and faith alone was the key to salvation.

Believing as an individual, or even discussing a possibly heretical belief with fellow-scholars, was not particularly subversive of established Christianity. Many men before Luther had not agreed with everything the Church taught, but none of them managed to reach the

Martin Luther (1483–
1546), portrait, school
of Lucas Cranach, 1546.
(Courtesy of the Busch-
Reisinger Museum,
Harvard University,
Gift, Meta and Paul J.
Sachs)

mass audience that listened to Luther. It is theoretically possible that Luther would not have been motivated to carry his doubts to the public if it had not been for the fact that the building schemes of Pope Julius II put a severe strain upon the financial resources of the papacy. To meet the need, Julius borrowed money, and then to pay his creditors, the pope proclaimed an indulgence to all who contributed toward the building of St. Peter's. An indulgence was the remission of the whole or part of the penalty imposed for a sin already forgiven. The popes believed they had the right to give such a remission because of their custody of the treasury of merit, the repository of all of the merits that Jesus, Mary, and numerous saints and martyrs had earned. Since the treasury had an excess of merits, a pope could draw from it to shorten the period penitent sinners would have to spend in purgatory, a state through which those who were saved but who had sinned would have to pass in order to expiate their sins before going on to heaven.

The situation in Germany at this time was complicated by the ambitions of Archbishop Albert of Magdeburg, who, though below the required canonical age, had been elected first as bishop of Halberstadt and then as archbishop of Magdeburg. When the archdiocese of Mainz fell vacant, Albert, then twenty-three, also laid claim to this office, a particularly powerful one, since its holder was one of the seven electors of the emperor. Albert assumed that the reigning emperor Maximilian would soon die and that his death would result in great effort and considerable expenditure of funds — most of which would end up in the pockets of the seven electors — either to prevent or secure the election of the young Charles of Hapsburg, who already controlled Burgundy, Spain, and much of Germany and Italy. Albert, unfortunately, was still under age and was further disqualified because he already held more than one benefice. The pope agreed to a dispensation, however, permitting him to hold the office in return for a cash payment of 24,000 ducats. To raise the money, Albert borrowed from the German banking firm run by the Fuggers, one of the richest families in Europe. The debt came due before Maximilian died, and the archbishop was left with finding some way to pay his creditors. To assist Albert through this financial crisis, the pope made an agreement with him that he could sell indulgences in all of his episcopal territories provided he gave half of the income he collected to the fund for building St. Peter's. John Tetzel, a Dominican supersalesman, was given responsibility for selling the indulgences in that part of Albert's territory bordering on Wittenberg. Just what Tetzel said in his sales talk is difficult at this date to reconstruct, but it is clear that in an effort to increase sales he used considerable exaggeration. Many of the people who bought indulgences from him did so under the impression that they could secure the immediate release of their dead loved ones from purgatory. Some even thought they purchased a license to sin. When the Wittenbergers returned with stories about what their indulgences permitted them to do, Martin Luther became incensed. He drew up, in Latin, some ninety-five propositions setting forth his doubts about indulgences and affixed them to the door of the castle church on the Sunday before All Saints' Day (October 31, 1517). In posting his theses, Luther was following a standard academic practice, and, as usual with academic debate, nobody paid attention to them or to him. Luther did send a few copies to some of his friends for their opinion, however, and some of these ended up in the hands of a printer, where they were soon translated and printed in German. This simple act turned a minor academic debate into a major national controversy and made Luther a hero to German-speaking Europe, which had long mistrusted the papacy. The printing press, in effect, had created a revolution in communication and Luther was both its first prophet and its first victim.

Great numbers of people rallied behind Luther's criticisms, which were not particularly heretical except for the sixth one, which held that a pope could not remit any guilt except by declaring it had been remitted by God. Archbishop Albert, angered at the drop in his revenue, sent a copy of Luther's proposition to Rome. The pope and his advisers, ignorant of the situation in Germany, misread the portents and dismissed the whole controversy as the result of the actions of a drunken German. Since this reaction was not atypical of the Italian attitude toward Germans in general, it in itself helps to explain why Luther's movement continued to grow.

As Luther refined his ideas, he became more and more opposed to the papacy. He adhered to the old conciliar notion that the Church universal was the body of the faithful and not merely the pope. With this belief, Luther approached the status of a major heretic, but there was little that could be done to curtail his activities because he enjoyed the patronage of Frederick, the Elector of Saxony. Frederick was not convinced that his most distinguished professor was wrong, and neither pope nor emperor was willing to antagonize Frederick before the issue of imperial succession had been decided, since each backed a different candidate. As a result, Luther went his own way, although he did finally participate in a long-delayed scholarly debate over his ninety-five theses with Dr. John Eck at Leipzig. Eck forced Luther to admit that some of his assumptions were similar to those of the condemned Jan Hus. Luther, however, maintained that, even though some of his ideas were similar to those of Hus, not all of Hus's positions had been declared heretical and demanded scriptural proof of his error. Increasingly, Luther — and Protestants in general — insisted that Scripture rather than philosophical, scholastic, or historical arguments be the final authority.

LUTHER'S SUCCESS

Luther for a brief time was a German hero. The German princes supported him because of what they regarded as the excessive power of the clergy. The humanists saw him as one of their own. Peasants looked to him because they felt he was one of them, opposed to the powers of the nobility, while the proletariat in the towns thought he was against the masters. It was not until 1520 that Luther was finally excommunicated; then, in a melodramatic act, he burned the bull of excommunication in a public ceremony. He then took his case directly to the nobility by denying that religious authority was superior to secular authority. He also urged massive Church reforms, including abolition of financial abuses and permission for clergy to marry.

By this time, Charles V was on the throne, so that Frederick's vote was no longer crucial. Still, the new Hapsburg emperor hesitated to intervene because he was involved in a war against France and he needed all the support he could get. Rather than act to prosecute the heretic, thus alienating Luther's supporters, Charles temporized by calling a meeting of the German Diet at Worms in 1521 to hear Luther. Luther appeared but refused to recant unless he was shown the errors of his ways in the Scriptures. After Luther and many of his followers had left, the Diet declared Luther a heretic. Frederick, anticipating such a result, had ordered Luther kidnapped for safekeeping. For nearly a year, Luther was in hiding both from his enemies and most of his friends; not even Frederick knew where he was. It was during this period of seclusion that Luther translated the New Testament into German, using the Greek version of Erasmus as a base. In a brief time, this text became a literary landmark and set the standards for all future German writing.

During Luther's absence from Wittenberg, all manner of innovations were made by his deputies, Andrew Karlstadt and Philip Melanchthon. Sacraments in both elements were given, the marriage of clergy was encouraged, and the destruction of images began. When Luther returned, even more radical revolutionaries appeared in Wittenberg from all parts of the empire demanding that Luther lead them in achieving more deep-seated social reforms. The more widespread Luther's influence became, the more confusion grew, since Luther was in the position of meaning all things to all men. Obviously, Luther could not satisfy all of his newly won followers, and as he attempted to define what he himself believed, he lost support. In a sense, Luther was naïve. He believed that there was only one true interpretation of Christianity — his own — and he felt at heart that all Christians would soon see as he did. For Luther, true reform could be carried out only by the princes and the state. Simple people could not initiate reform at all. This view represented a contradiction of the concept of the priesthood of all believers, but Luther was never much worried by his own contradictions.

The growing unrest in Germany broke out first in a series of peasant revolts. When the peasants appealed to Luther for support, he told them that righteousness was more important than justice. He held obedience to be a prime virtue, and he stated that no show of force, however justified, could ever be lawful. As the revolts continued, he turned to condemning the peasants in brutal and intemperate language, calling their rebellion a grievous sin that should be put down by force. The inevitable result was the alienation not only of most of the peasants from the Lutheran movement but of many nobles as well, since the latter blamed him for their troubles in the first place. As the problems of organizing a church forced themselves upon Luther, he further modified his earlier teachings about the priesthood of all believers to justify a new type of priest, the pastor, who, he argued, needed special training. To enforce his own views of orthodoxy, Luther more and more leaned upon the power of his princely supporters; he even went so far as to argue that all political authority was instituted by God. From this premise followed the idea that secular government was divinely inspired and held the right to manage ecclesiastical affairs. In sum, Luther ended up as one of the theorists for royal absolutism. By agreeing to princely control over the Church, he gave a doctrinal foundation to what in fact had already taken place. In spite of the falling away of much of his original support, Luther remained the dominant Protestant figure until his death in 1546.

REASONS FOR LUTHER'S SUCCESS

In many ways, Luther's beliefs were not much different from those of John Wyclif or Jan Hus or other reformers who had preceded him. Yet Luther founded an enduring religious movement while his predecessors had failed. The explanation for Luther's success lay not so much in his doctrines as in his political backing and the inability of his opponents to get at him. That this was the case is primarily a reflection of the nature of Hapsburg power. Emperor Charles V needed the support of the Lutheran princes to head off the ambitions of the French in Italy as well as elsewhere. Moreover, the popes themselves created difficulties by siding first with the French, then with the Hapsburgs, and then reversing themselves. At the same time, the Turks under Suliman the Magnificent were advancing into Europe up to the very gates of Vienna, the seat of Hapsburg power. The net result of the imperial helplessness was that those princes inclined toward Lutheranism established it in their lands, while those who were zealous Catholics tried to suppress it. Once established, Lutheranism was difficult to suppress, because the Lutheran princes, by secularizing Church property, had a vested interest in maintaining it. When the emperor temporarily felt free to move against the Lutheran princes, they organized the League of Schmalkald, a mutual defense alliance in which Philip of Hesse played a dominant part. Such an action represented open rebellion against established authority and was therefore contrary to Luther's prohibitions against revolt. Luther, however, allowed himself to be convinced that since the emperor ruled with the cooperation of the princes, the emperor had no right to impose his own will on them. Before there was much serious fighting, the Turks again invaded, forcing Charles once more to ignore his internal difficulties. The eventual result was the Peace of Augsburg, promulgated in 1555, which gave each prince the right to determine the faith of his subjects provided that faith was Lutheranism or Catholicism. Other doctrines were not to be tolerated. The agreement also stipulated that while ecclesiastical property secularized before 1552 was to remain secularized, no further secularization was to take place. In effect, the authority of a ruler to choose the religion of his subjects was recognized by both Catholics and Lutherans. The settlement is perhaps best summed up in the Latin phrase, *cuius regio eius religio,* the religion of the ruler is that of his subjects. Princes became divinely ordained rulers who were to dispose of ecclesiastical as well as secular matters, a concept that gave further theoretical support for the idea of monarchy by divine right. The notion that religion was a matter to be established by the state dominated Western thinking until the appearance of the American Constitution and the outbreak of the French Revolution.

14

The Age
of Religious
Controversy

Europe in the last part of the sixteenth century was in the midst of a full-scale religious revolt. Once the unity of Western Christendom was broken, all manner of men urged their own particular cause. The result was a divergence of opinion that permanently divided Europe into different camps. One early advocate of reform was Ulrich Zwingli, who in 1519 began preaching his doctrines in Zurich. Originally, Zwingli and Luther appeared similar in that both urged justification by faith, the repudiation of clerical celibacy and monasticism, the giving of both the bread and the wine in the Eucharist, and the use of vernacular languages in church services. Zwingli, however, was much more imbued with the humanist ethic of Erasmus and therefore more interested in life on this earth. Moreover, Zwingli was also a Swiss patriot who objected to the use of Swiss troops as mercenaries by the papacy and other rulers. Gradually, as Zwingli's views became fully developed, the differences between Luther and himself grew. To prevent any magnification of these divisions, their followers tried to bring the two men together. Any chance of union disappeared when Luther proved unwilling to compromise on any of his beliefs. Zwingli, who held many of the differences to be unimportant was, nevertheless, unwilling to follow Luther's interpretation of the Eucharist. Luther insisted on the real presence of Christ's body and blood in the Eucharist, a notion similar to the Catholic doctrine of transubstantiation, while Zwingli held that the Eucharist was more of a memorial service, symbolic of the sacrifice of Jesus. Both movements thereafter went their own way.

Zwingli was killed in 1531 while acting as a chaplain to the troops from Zurich who were fighting to establish the Zwinglian reform. The Catholics of Switzerland were backed by the Hapsburgs, but, after two short periods of warfare, both sides in 1531 agreed to peace, with the individual cantons to be given the right to decide religious beliefs. Catholics in all cantons, however, were to be guaranteed toleration, while neither Protestants nor Protestant evangelical missionary activities were to be allowed in Catholic cantons. Catholics, Lutherans, and Zwinglians all agreed, nonetheless, that the Anabaptists should be exterminated at any cost. This consensus might have resulted from the fact that the Anabaptists represented the alienated, the poor, and the powerless, while all of the others came to represent different established interests.

THE ANABAPTISTS AND OTHER GROUPS

Anabaptists had first appeared within Zwingli's own circle as the result of an effort to restore Christianity to its earlier, more primitive, and, it was therefore believed, purer form. Such an attempt led many people to the realization that the early Christian was a heartfelt believer, a minority in a pagan state, despised, rejected, and even persecuted. If this was the case with the early Christian Church, it must also be the case for Christians at all times. For the Anabaptists the implication was that the state, even though its rulers might be Christian, must by necessity be un-Christian. They therefore opposed any union of church and state. To them, true Christianity had to be particularistic, administering to the needs of the faithful who truly believed, rather than universalistic, claiming the membership of all regardless of whether they believed. The faithful were to be distinguished from the rest of the population by a strict morality, including an abstinence from alcoholic beverages, and were further separated from them by adult baptism, a visible token of their inward regeneration. Since Lutherans, Zwinglians, and Catholics accepted infant baptism, the Anabaptists appeared as rebaptizers, and hence the name that was applied to them. Because their beliefs were essentially individualistic, the Anabaptists differed widely from group to group. All sorts of doctrines have been attributed to them, and they suffered martyrdom under both Protestant and Catholic rulers. In general, however, they were pacifists, believed in a community of goods — a kind of religious communism — and lived a simple life without ostentation as they attempted to apply the precepts of Jesus to every act of their lives. Every member of the group was regarded as a missionary, and men and women periodically left their homes to go on evangelistic tours. Obviously, established authority regarded them as subversive, and in 1529, both Catholics and Lutherans agreed that the death penalty should be imposed on them. Zwingli, who usually was more tolerant of religious deviation, had some Anabaptists executed as early as 1525.

Under such harassment, the Anabaptists developed some extreme movements which predicted the imminent second coming of Christ. Thomas Münzer of Zwickau, for example, taught that a new kingdom of God was to be established in which there would be equality of social status and community of goods. When he realized the futility of attempting to establish such a community by peaceful means, Münzer urged the use of force. A large number of discontented joined with him, but most were slaughtered during the so-called Peasant Revolt of 1525. Other Anabaptist leaders included Melchior Hoffman in Swabia, Balthasar Hübmeier of Augsburg, and John Trypmaker in Amsterdam. Most successful over the long term were Jacob Hutter, who established the Hutterites, and Menno Simons, the founder of the Mennonites. Both men repudiated the excesses of Münzer in order to commit themselves and their followers to simplicity, sobriety, poverty, meekness, and suffering. Since it was almost impossible to exist in Western Europe with such views, although some of these believers managed to survive in Holland and Switzerland, most of them moved to Poland and Moravia, frontier areas of Western Christendom, and eventually migrated to Russia and the United States. Members of one of the most colorful of the Mennonite sects, the old order Amish, still wear buttonless coats — since buttons are not mentioned in the Bible — broad hats, flowing beards, and drive horse and buggies instead of cars.

Also driven to the outlying area of Europe were those reformers who continued to emphasize the humanist concept of the individual. Such a view became an increasingly difficult one to hold. Erasmus, for example, after first encouraging Luther's attacks on Catholic institutions and practices, broke with him when he realized that Lutheranism was contrary to his own tolerant humanistic ideas. Erasmus was not particularly happy with Catholicism, but he died before the religious intolerance of the age reached its heights. A few of the humanist reformers such as Sebastian Franck were closely aligned to the Anabaptists. Franck had started as a Catholic priest, then became a Lutheran minister, and finally a layman. For him the true church was to be found in each man; organized religion was unnecessary. Other individualistic reformers became antitrinitarians, such as the Spaniard Michael Servetus, who had gradually come to believe that man was almost equal to God. Jesus to him became a man like other men, and he felt that assigning him this position was not lowering Jesus but elevating man. He was burned at the stake in Geneva, where he had fled for refuge. Eventually, in order to save themselves, many of these free spirits were forced to establish some sort of religious organization. Much of the movement came to be centered around Faustus Socinus, or Sozzini, who had fled to Poland from Italy. His emphasis on critical inquiry, mystical piety, and religious liberty made his movement acceptable in the border areas between Christianity and Islam, such as in Hungary, Moravia, and Transylvania. It is here that modern Unitarianism had its origins.

JOHN CALVIN

The great leader of the second generation of Protestants was John Calvin. Born in France in 1509, Calvin was trained in the humanistic curriculum as well as in law. His father, who belonged to the bourgeois class, was excommunicated while Calvin was still a student. Shortly after this, Calvin got into difficulty over his own religious beliefs and had to flee France for Basel in Switzerland. It was at Basel, at the age of twenty-seven, that Calvin issued his *Institutes of the Christian Religion,* which he kept revising during his lifetime. Calvin's *Institutes* did for Protestantism what St. Thomas Aquinas' books had earlier done for Catholicism, although Calvin's work was much briefer and less intricate than that of Aquinas. Calvin's theology became dominant because Luther, though a powerful figure, had never reduced his intuitive religious feelings to a dogmatic system. Luther's disciple Melanchthon was capable of such a systematic work, but apparently he never felt the need for a dogmatic system, nor did Zwingli or the Anabaptists. Calvin did, however, and his world view, his definition of God, man, the Bible, and the church have dominated Protestant thought ever since. Calvin believed that God, omnipotent, omnipresent, and eternal, had created man in his own image. Original man had been sinless and immortal, but in his fall from the Garden of Eden he had become so totally depraved that his only hope for salvation lay in the grace of God. In this view, Calvin was similar to Luther, but Calvin went somewhat further than Luther in his emphasis on the notion of predestination, that is, that God had marked certain men to be saved. These were the elect, or the new Israelites, so called because God had at one time also chosen the ancient Israelites as his people. God, however, no longer selected a whole people but only individuals. Calvin did not claim to know for certain who was elected by God, but he said that the new Israelites themselves knew and that they could best be identified by their profession of faith, their upright life, and their participation in the sacrament. To be one of the elect was not enough for Calvin. It was necessary that these chosen people establish a theocracy, a holy community in which every member should make the glory of God his sole concern. Calvin sought a place to put his beliefs into practice, and he found his chance in Geneva.

Calvin believed that God's plan for salvation was set forth in the

Bible, whose every phrase and sentence was infallible. However, since much in the Bible was obscure, Scripture was to be interpreted by ministers appointed by the congregation of the faithful, although final authority rested in the faithful themselves guided by the Holy Spirit. Calvin's ideas of the holy commonwealth were enacted into law by the city council of Geneva, where Calvin had journeyed after leaving Basel. William Farrell had already established Protestantism in the city, but considerable religious turbulence still prevailed. Calvin insisted that taverns be abolished, although not alcoholic beverages; that the sabbath be kept inviolate; that card-playing, dancing, and the theatre be prohibited; and that all opponents of God's plan be removed. The thoroughness of Calvin's proposed reforms at first made the people of Geneva so resistive that the reformer was exiled. When he was recalled two years later in 1541, he was given a free hand. Most of his opponents went into exile, while the few that remained were excluded from the affairs of both the Church and the city. Calvin soon ruled Geneva almost as if he were an absolute monarch, his power cemented by the threat of execution. Some forty-eight persons, including thirty-four accused of witchcraft, were dispatched between 1542 and 1546, after which the number of executions declined radically. Many others fled. Instead of losing population, Geneva gained, for the exiles were replaced by others seeking refuge from persecution in France, Italy, England, Spain, the Low Countries, and elsewhere. Thus there came to be a sort of elite group whose dedication to the Gospel spread the fame of Calvin and Calvinism throughout Christendom. Though the model commonwealth of Geneva could not be installed everywhere, the ideal was most nearly achieved in Scotland as well as in New England. In France, Holland, and England, the Calvinists remained a minority, regarding themselves as a sort of spiritual aristocracy. In these three countries, Calvin's teachings especially appealed to the bourgeois groups, who justified their own success on the grounds that they were the elect of God. Everywhere Calvin's success led to a much more efficiently organized and reinvigorated Protestantism.

THE ENGLISH SOLUTION

Clearly, for enactment of their reforms the reformers depended upon the state, whether headed by a king, prince, or town council. In England, it was the king, Henry VIII, who led the break with Rome, although he did not by that action establish Protestantism. Since 1485, England had been under the rule of the Tudors, first Henry VII and then Henry VIII. A new type of English king, the Tudor monarch depended upon the politically powerful towns and the landed gentry for support. By the sixteenth century, the English no longer exported raw wool to the

Continent but instead used it in their own manufacturing. This economic development had created a new alliance between the landowners and the manufacturing and commercial classes, who were willing to support a strong monarch in return for internal security. These groups also cast envious eyes on the lands and wealth of the church. By moving against the power of the great nobility and by maintaining peace both at home and abroad, the Tudor monarchs endeared themselves to their supporters.

The great diplomatic coup of Henry VII was to marry his eldest son Arthur to Catherine of Aragon. As an upstart king with a disputed claim to the throne, Henry believed that such a marriage implied recognition of his family by one of the great new powers of Europe. When Arthur died before the marriage was consummated, Henry received a dispensation from the pope for Catherine to marry his second son Henry, since canon law prohibited a man from marrying his sister-in-law. The two were married in 1509, the year Henry succeeded to the throne as Henry VII. Since the Tudor dynasty had only recently been established, in order to prevent a disputed succession, it was held essential that Henry VIII produce a male heir. Though Henry and Catherine had a number of children, all save a daughter, Mary, had died in their infancy. After some eighteen years of marriage, it seemed that Catherine, who was five years older than Henry, would never give him the son the dynasty needed. Henry came to believe that God was punishing him because he had married his deceased brother's wife. His solution was to have the marriage annulled so that he could find a new queen who might give him a son. Under normal circumstances, the pope probably would have granted an annulment, since popes were inclined to sympathize with the dynastic needs of the monarchs. Unfortunately, in 1527, when Henry first began the process of securing an annulment, Charles V controlled Rome and the pope. As a nephew of Catherine, Charles was unwilling to consent to making his cousin Mary illegitimate, thereby denying her claim to the throne. The pope attempted to avoid a conflict by temporizing. As the suit dragged on over the years, Henry found himself increasingly anxious for a decision. His demands became imperative when he learned that his mistress Anne Boleyn was pregnant. Anne, an attendant to Catherine, had been encouraged in her affair with the king by her father and her powerful uncle, the Duke of Norfolk, both of whom received important benefits when the king looked favorably upon her. In 1533, unable to get the papal consent, and with Anne almost ready to deliver, Henry requested that the new Archbishop of Canterbury, Thomas Cranmer, declared his marriage to Catherine null and void. When Cranmer did so, the pope declared Cranmer's judgment illegal. The English parliament then intervened by passing the Act of Supremacy, which declared that the king himself was the supreme head of the church in England. Henry hastily married

Anne, who almost immediately gave birth to a daughter, Elizabeth. This did not help Anne, about whom Henry was having second thoughts, and the king began to look elsewhere for still another wife.

By marrying Anne, Henry had broken with the pope, but he by no means could be called a Protestant. In fact, earlier in his reign, Henry had written an anti-Lutheran tract for which he was given the title Defender of the Faith by the pope; he had also dealt rather severely with the heretics in his realm. But Henry's amorous enterprises, combined with his need for money, caused him to go further than perhaps he had originally anticipated. To gain revenue, he secularized the monastic houses in England, and by selling them or assigning their properties to others, he established a vested interest opposed to a return to Catholicism. When Henry decided to marry Jane Seymour, another former attendant of Catherine, he no longer bothered to seek a divorce. Anne was beheaded in 1536 for treason against the crown, and his former queen Catherine died in the same year. Jane Seymour, Henry's third wife, died after giving birth to the future Edward VI. Henry had three more wives before he himself died but no other children.

Both Protestants and Catholics attempted to influence Henry, but he kept his own council. Toward the end of his life he had parliament pass the Act of Succession, which stipulated that he would be succeeded by his son Edward, a sickly boy who was not expected to live very long. The act also provided that if Edward died without heirs, Henry's daughter Mary was to inherit the throne, and, if she died without issue, his daughter Elizabeth was to succeed. Thus for the first time in European history women were recognized as possible rulers in their own right. Just before he died, Henry appointed a council of regents to carry out his wishes. This body, with the Duke of Somerset as Lord Protector, and with the help of Archbishop Thomas Cranmer, led England from schism with Rome to Protestantism. Protestantism during the reign of Edward VI was a rather curious mixture of Zwinglianism, Calvinism, Lutheranism, and Catholicism, but its viability was not tested, since when Edward died, his half-sister Mary, a devoted Catholic, succeeded him. Under Mary, England was reunited with Rome. Perhaps the greatest significance of Henry's break with Rome was not its religious implications but the fact that the king was forced to turn to parliament for support. In the process, the English parliamentary system was immeasurably strengthened.

CATHOLIC REFORM

The growth and spread of Protestantism had been motivated, at least initially, by the numerous abuses within the Catholic Church. Though the reformers differed on points of doctrine, all were agreed that papal Christianity was in dire need of reform. Yet the popes themselves continued to ignore such demands until it was too late to preserve a united Church. It was not until the election of Paul III in 1534 that the first major efforts at reform were made. Paul III at first glance would not seem the kind of man who could be a dedicated reformer, since he was the father of three illegitimate sons born while he was a cardinal. He had, nonetheless, long since regretted his earlier ways and had even undergone a religious conversion. Paul's major achievement was the summoning of the Council of Trent, which in 1545 began to deal with the internal problems of Catholicism. With various interruptions, including the death of Paul, the council met until 1562. The result was a major series of reforms and innovations and a purging of many of the abuses that had long plagued the papacy. At the same time, Catholicism emerged much more intolerant of any kind of dissent than it had been before. In fact, a new dogmatism was felt in the whole intellectual climate of Europe during this period. To ferret out heresy, the Inquisition was modified and revised and, largely through its activities, Protestantism in Italy was almost exterminated. The Index of forbidden books was established in an effort to combat the newly discovered power of the printed word, and most of the writings of the reformers were put on the list. A new catechism was developed, along with a new breviary and missal, and papal government was reorganized. Most important, the Jesuit order was recognized and given control of the struggle against Protestantism. This new monastic order was an outgrowth of a movement started by St. Ignatius Loyola, who saw his group officially recognized in 1540. Through their emphasis on absolute obedience, their devotion to education, and their commitment to the papacy, the Jesuits became the nucleus of a new papal offensive against Protestantism. Numerous other orders were also founded at this time, including the Capuchins, the Gratians, the Theatines, and the Ursulines, who not only reinvigorated monasticism but also began the task of winning back to Catholicism many of the reforming princes. The new orders also carried Christianity beyond Europe itself to Asia, South America, and elsewhere, where they gave impetus to the earlier proselytizing efforts of the Dominicans and the Franciscans. Most notable among these new agents of European civilization was the Jesuit St. Francis Xavier, who established Catholic Christianity in India and Japan.

PHILIP II

Internal religious reform would have meant little if it had not been given political, military, and economic support by the Hapsburgs. The continued dominance of Catholicism in much of Europe today is due more to Spain and to the Spanish Hapsburgs than to any other force. Philip II, the son of Charles V, had divided power with his uncle

Ferdinand. When Charles abdicated from his various thrones in 1555 and 1556, Philip received Spain, the Burgundian territories, Naples and Sicily, the overlordship of Milan, and the control of the New World. Ferdinand took over Austria and the title of Holy Roman Emperor. It was in Spanish Hapsburg lands that the Inquisition was most effectively employed. At the same time, the Spanish Church remained under the firm control of the Spanish monarch. It seems natural that both Ignatius Loyola and Philip II, the leading defenders of Catholicism, were sons of Spain, since that country's crusading background and general intolerance toward its Jewish and Muslim subjects had already led to the development of an Inquisition that was copied elsewhere in Europe.

To Philip, Catholicism and Spain were one and the same. Philip was not an intolerant bigot, but an able ruler who was imprisoned and limited by his own concepts. He believed so much in his divine right to rule that he hesitated to delegate authority for fear that a wrong action might be held against him. His unwillingness to turn minor matters and decisions over to subordinates, combined with his own sense of responsibility, meant that he himself attempted to direct and regulate all public policy and governmental affairs. Though Philip labored long hours writing letters to his officials and carried on a vast correspondence, the task he imposed upon himself was impossible for anyone to achieve, and the result was a rigidity in Spanish policy which could only lead to trouble. The great tragedy was that, in attempting to destroy Protestantism, Philip seriously weakened Spain and the developing Spanish empire. By eliminating the Jew and the Moor, Philip and his predecessors nearly destroyed the Spanish middle class. Rather than using the market potential in America to rebuild Spanish industry or commerce, Philip prohibited the export of iron, leather, and cloth to these colonies, in effect, leaving the field wide open for some other country to exploit. These reactionary policies, coupled with a 10 percent sales tax, hindered the development of a strong Spanish economy. Philip's schemes to preserve Catholic and Hapsburg power were financed primarily by the gold and silver from the New World rather than from any industrial, commercial, or agricultural activities in Spain. As soon as the gold and silver exports from the New World began to decline, Spain was in trouble. Philip thus emerged as a tragic figure, a well-meaning ruler with considerable ability, who, though maintaining Catholicism, seemed to ruin everything else.

PROTESTANTISM IN THE NETHERLANDS AND IN FRANCE

Symptomatic of the growing difficulties brought about by Philip's insistence upon Catholic orthodoxy and royal absolutism was the revolt of the Netherlands. When Protestantism had first appeared in his Burgundian territories, Charles V had tried to check it by use of the Inquisition. Thousands of persons were executed or fled, but Protestantism remained a major force in the area, handicapped only by the fact that the various religious leaders could not agree upon which variety of Protestantism they would follow. The antagonism of the Protestants toward each other was subordinated only when it seemed to the people of the Netherlands that Philip was using them as a pawn in his struggle to reimpose Catholicism upon Europe. When Philip also prohibited the Netherlands from trading with the Spanish colonies, a full-scale revolt broke out. The leader of the revolt, William of Orange, who had been a Lutheran, a Catholic, and finally a Calvinist, proved to be genuinely interested in religious toleration. In that age of growing intolerance, any attempt by William to establish a measure of religious freedom was bound to fail, and the result of the revolt of the Netherlands was to divide Europe into two opposing camps, with the provinces in the north, or those closer to Germany and England, adhering to Calvinism and those in the south, who were more culturally allied with France, remaining Catholic. The northern provinces eventually came to be recognized as the United Provinces, or the Netherlands.

The factor that more than any other ruined Philip's plans to reestablish Catholicism was the consistent refusal of the French kings to support him. For a time during the reign of Henry II, who died in 1559, the Protestants in France had been hunted, harassed, and executed with great regularity. Henry was succeeded by his young son Francis II, who soon died, and was in turn succeeded by his two younger brothers, Charles IX and Henry III. The dominant power behind the scene during the reign of three young kings remained their mother, Catherine de Medici, who was determined at all costs to hold the throne for her sons. Catherine's almost fanatical dedication to this objective can be understood when it is realized that during the reign of her husband Henry II, she had been almost totally relegated to the nursery while her husband's mistress, Diane of Poitiers, held the center of the stage. All of Catherine's energies and ambitions were centered in her sons. In order to maintain some independence of action for her sons, Catherine played one faction of nobles against the other, building up the weak to take up the cause against the strong and then turning on the formerly weak. But factionalism in France was complicated by religion. One group of nobles was Protestant, or Huguenot, and was centered around Anthony of Navarre, a member of the house of Bourbon, and Gaspard and Andelot Coligny, who served as advisers to various kings. Another group of Catholic nobles looked for leadership to the house of Guise, which included the commander of the French military forces and two cardinals.

For a time during the reign of Francis II, the Catholic Guise faction appeared to be dominant. The young king supported them and so did his wife Mary Stuart, better known as Mary, Queen of Scots, who during her lifetime was queen of two countries and was executed for trying to be queen of a third. Unfortunately for the Catholic faction, Mary's husband soon died, and Mary returned to Scotland, where she ruled until she was expelled by the Protestants. Charles IX, who succeeded his brother, turned for support to the Protestant group under the leadership of Gaspard Coligny. The result was the establishment of a very limited amount of official toleration for the Huguenots. The Guises, angered at their exile from the court and fearful of any move toward toleration, turned to Philip of Spain for support. Catherine herself became worried about the growing strength of Protestantism, and she and the Guises managed to bring about a wholesale slaughter of Protestants, the St. Bartholomew's Day Massacre, August 24, 1572. This mass murder only increased antagonisms, and the result was a series of wars in which the Huguenots fought for survival, with Catherine backing first the Catholic faction and then the Protestant. When Charles IX died without issue and it became apparent that his brother Henry III would never have any children, the struggle became a full-fledged civil war which involved the Hapsburgs. This war is usually called the War of the Three Henries because of the presence of the young king Henry III, the Protestant leader Henry of Navarre, the son of Anthony, and Henry of Guise. When Henry III died, Henry of Navarre, the legitimate successor, finally converted to Catholicism in order to reduce the opposition to his reign. Henry IV, as he was now known, guaranteed the Huguenots freedom of worship in certain specified towns, a French adaptation of the principle of territorial religion already established in Germany. In order to guarantee their rights, the Huguenots were allowed to garrison some seventy-five fortified places, and Protestant judges were to sit with Catholics to assure equal justice.

ENGLAND AND THE CONTINENT

If the Hapsburgs were thwarted in the Netherlands and their attempts to interfere in France were prevented by the emergence of Henry IV, they also failed in England, though for a time it seemed that here they might meet success. Mary, the successor to Edward VI in England, had married Philip of Spain. The English parliament had consented to this union with the house of Hapsburg only on condition that Philip be specifically excluded from the throne if he and Mary had no children. Parliament also demanded that any children born of such a union would rule both in England and in the Hapsburg Burgundian territories, an area long coveted by England. Finally, Philip had to pledge that no English resources would be employed to fight Spanish or Hapsburg wars on the Continent. Under Mary, Catholicism was quickly re-established in England, although expropriated Church lands were not returned. Unfortunately, in her haste to bring England back to Rome, Mary mounted a series of persecutions which so antagonized her subjects that she was labeled Bloody Mary. Her implication in the continental schemes of her husband further antagonized her subjects. Undoubtedly, England's involvement was in part justified, since the French, in order to counter what they thought was the Hapsburg influence in England, had backed Mary Stuart, the queen of Scotland and ex-queen of France, as the real heir to the English throne. Still, the continental wars were usually seen by the English as part of the Hapsburg schemes. The result of Mary's intervention was the loss of the last remaining English possession on the Continent. Shortly after, Mary died and her half-sister Elizabeth became queen in 1558.

Elizabeth's reign was not an easy one. She was regarded as illegitimate by the Catholic Church, although the popes were willing to recognize her as legitimate if she agreed to remain a Catholic. Philip, anxious to hold on to his English alliance, even proposed marriage to her, but Elizabeth, aware of Mary's difficulties, was cautious in accepting. Moreover, the Netherlands, the natural focus of English interest on the Continent, was now in revolt against Philip. English privateers were also finding a lucrative reward in raiding Spanish treasure ships. In such a situation, Elizabeth temporized, committing herself neither to Catholicism nor to Protestantism, neither to the French nor to the Spanish cause but acting as an English patriot. The papacy finally forced her into the Protestant camp by excommunicating her in 1570. By another Act of Supremacy passed by parliament in 1559 Elizabeth had been recognized as "the supreme governor" of the Church in England, giving her the authority to direct religious affairs as she saw fit. She carried through a revision of the prayer book, eliminating some of the most obvious Protestant passages, and at the same time ordered the retention of many Catholic ceremonial customs and church decorations. Married clergy, however, were allowed, the sacrament was given in both elements, and English replaced Latin in church services. Many Protestants, especially those who had gone into exile during Mary's reign, could not accept such a Catholic form of Protestantism. They assumed the leadership of the more committed reformers, who demanded that the English church be purified of its ancient Catholic practices. As a result, they came to be called Puritans. These Protestants did not leave the Church of England but instead remained within the fold, protesting constantly and vigorously for a complete renovation. A small minority, however, left the English church altogether, and it was this group that gave birth to the small band that settled at Plymouth in America.

During Elizabeth's reign, religious divisions were fortunately kept to a minimum as far as the Protestants were concerned, in part because of the danger of a Catholic party supported by the Jesuits and the Spanish. At first, the Jesuits tried to put Mary Stuart on the throne, an effort that resulted in Mary's execution in 1587. Since Spanish opposition to Elizabeth was self-evident, the queen encouraged her privateers to step up their raids on Spanish treasure ships. Elizabeth also aided the rebellious Netherlanders. Philip II finally decided to invade England in order to eliminate what he regarded as a threat to both Catholicism and Spain. The result was the gathering of the Spanish Armada, a massive naval force sent in 1588 to invade England. The Armada was disastrously defeated because of inadequate planning, ineptness, bad weather, poor timing, and English strategy. The victory served to strengthen Elizabeth's hold on her people and at the same time further depleted Spanish resources.

THE ARTS IN THE LAST PART
OF THE SIXTEENTH CENTURY

In spite of the religious intensity of the late sixteenth century, humanist and classical ideals remained influential. All of Europe adopted the Italian modes, at least briefly. In Germany, the work of Albrecht Dürer early in the century was characterized by medieval themes rendered with a Renaissance virtuosity. In his paintings, Dürer seems to have been indebted to the Venetian school. Even more Italian was Hans Holbein, the court painter to Henry VIII, who combined the Gothic affirmity for detail with the broad brush approach of the Italians. Not all northern painters followed the Italian example, however, Pieter Bruegel of the Netherlands being the outstanding exception. Bruegel's paintings of peasant life allow us to realize in part how the peasants and ordinary people of the time lived, and for his ability to convey this world, he has often been called Peasant Bruegel. The painters who followed the Italian style were labeled Mannerists, although the term is difficult to apply to particular painters, especially those such as Domenico Theotocopuli, known as El Greco — the Greek — who introduced the Italian style to Spain. A native of Crete, El Greco studied in both Rome and Venice before settling down in Toledo. His work combined the Byzantine and the Italian styles. In his paintings, El Greco fitted his distorted figures into an almost abstract design, where light and color are not natural but are used to heighten the visual effect.

In keeping with the power of the Spanish Hapsburgs, the most impressive architectural undertaking of the late sixteenth century was the Escorial, constructed by Philip II some twenty-four miles northwest of Madrid. This combination palace, church, mausoleum, college, and monastery, built on a modified classical style, is mainly impressive because of its size; it is 774 feet long and 580 feet wide, including interior courts. Following Philip's example, every monarch in Europe had to have a great palace of his own, many of them modeled on the Escorial. Until Louis XIV built Versailles, the Escorial remained the outstanding example of monumental and lavish construction.

MUSIC

It was not until the end of the Middle Ages that musical notation had developed sufficiently for us to trace what had been accomplished in this area of the arts. We still do not quite know how the music of this period actually sounded, since the composers were accustomed to allowing considerable improvisation by the performer. We do know what instruments were used and how they were played, and through the written music, we can begin to realize the nature of sixteenth-century music. We also know that music at this time was changing as more complex forms developed and as new instruments were invented or old ones modified.

Music in the sixteenth century was predominantly of a religious nature, with the mass or the motet, a form of a capella, particularly popular. The best known and most prolific of the religious composers was Giovanni da Palestrina, whose greatest composition is usually considered to be his *Mass of Pope Marcellus*. During his lifetime, Palestrina wrote ninety-four masses and three-hundred and fifty motets, as well as numerous more secular compositions, mostly on commission from the pope. The most revolutionary development in religious music was the establishment of congregational singing by Martin Luther. Luther also wrote a number of hymns, the most famous being "A Mighty Fortress Is Our God."

The secular music of the period included songs, dances, the madrigal, and, toward the end of the period, opera. Though Palestrina was also influential in this area of music, even more significant was Claudio Monteverdi, who made so many innovations in music practice that he has been called the father of musical instrumentation. Monteverdi's system of harmony is that used in most music today. He is best noted for his operas, a form of music developed during the sixteenth century as an outgrowth of a conscious effort to imitate the music drama of the ancient Greeks. With Monteverdi opera became a unique musical form.

LITERATURE

The literature of Spain, France, and England in particular reached new heights during the last part of the sixteenth century. One of the great French literary talents, Michel de Montaigne, lived and wrote during this time. Brought up in a humanist environment and unhappy with the political and religious turmoil of his day, Montaigne retired from public life to his rural castle, where he collected books and meditated upon life. Montaigne maintained his skepticism in an age of fanaticism and his integrity when it was much easier to conform. His urbane, rational, and polished essays on numerous subjects are still worth reading. It was during this period also that Pierre de Ronsard, the dominant figure in a group of poets known as the *Pléiade,* was active. Ronsard was instrumental in developing a new form of French poetry based upon classical models; the sonnet that resulted has remained a dominant force in French literature.

A younger contemporary of Montaigne was the Spaniard Miguel de Cervantes Saavedra, whose *Don Quixote* remains one of the great pieces of world literature. A satire designed to discredit the old chivalric romances and moral conceptions that dominated Spanish thought, the work nevertheless allows the reader to feel sympathy for the absurd knight who refuses to see things as they actually are. Cervantes also wrote a number of plays, but in this field he was excelled by Lope de Vega, one of the most prolific dramatists of all time. Some five hundred of Lope's plays survive and more than that have been lost. It was through his efforts and those of his contemporary Tirso de Molina that the sixteenth century came to be viewed as the great age of Spanish drama.

So much important writing was done in England during the last part of the sixteenth century that the period is often called the Elizabethan Renaissance. One of the best known of the Elizabethan poets was Edmund Spenser, whose *Faerie Queene* established a new verse form, the so-called Spenserian stanza, as well as a new interpretation of the old legends of knights and their ladies. The *Arcadia* of Sir Philip Sidney, a contemporary of Spenser, played a significant role in the development of English prose. Sidney is also remembered for his sonnets. The chief form of literature in Elizabethan England, however, was drama. A whole series of playwrights, known collectively as the University Wits, dominated the scene. Among the best known of the group were Thomas Kyd and Christopher Marlowe. Kyd is remembered for *The Spanish Tragedy,* the prototype of the revenge tragedies of which Shakespeare was a master. Christopher Marlowe, the author of *Doctor Faustus,* was the originator of blank verse, or unrhymed iambic pentameter.

For several generations various scholars have tried to claim that William Shakespeare was really someone else, from Christopher Marlowe to Francis Bacon. The son of a well-to-do official who soon lost his fortune, Shakespeare represents the new self-made man of the Tudor age. The themes he employed, though common to his predecessors and the classics, became unique in his hands. His historical plays express the patriotism of the English during the trying days of Elizabeth, while his comedies poke fun at the foibles of his age. His genius is most evident in his tragedies, where his sensitivity to human passion gave him a world-wide reputation. In a sense, Shakespeare was a culmination of rationalism and tolerance at a time when irrationalism and intolerance seemed to be gaining everywhere. Even his female characters are individuals and assert themselves as persons more than almost any women in earlier literature. Shakespeare, however, was a man of his time in that his nationalism represents the dominant theme of a new age. By the seventeenth century, universalism was dead and in its place were the new national monarchs. Religious tensions were still growing, and one reason for the absence of any major intellectual figures in Germany was the internal strife within that country. Even in England, the English genius for drama was not to survive much beyond Shakespeare himself. Ben Jonson carried on the tradition with his great comedies, but the increasing religious tensions in England soon led to the closing of the theater and a search for new forms of expression.

Supplemental Reading
for Part Four

General and Interpretative

Artz, F. B., *From the Renaissance to Romanticism* (Chicago).

Aston, M., *The Fifteenth Century* (Holt, Rinehart and Winston).

Aston, L., *Crisis in Europe: 1560–1660* (Doubleday).

Butterfield, Herbert, *The Whig Interpretation of History* (Norton).

Cheyney, Edward P., *The Dawn of a New Era (1250–1453)* (Harper & Row).

Elliott, J. H., *Europe Divided 1559–98* (Harper & Row).

Gilmore, Myron P., *The World of Humanism 1453–1517* (Harper & Row).

Heer, Frederick, *The Medieval World* (Mentor).

Hexter, J. H., *Reappraisals in History* (Harper & Row).

Holmes, G., *Later Middle Ages* (Norton).

Muller, H. J., *Freedom in the Western World: From Dark Ages to the Rise of Democracy* (Harper & Row).

Notestein, Wallace, *The English People on the Eve of Colonization* (Harper & Row).

Painter, Sidney, *Mediaeval Society* (Cornell).

Stephenson, C., *Medieval Institutions: Selected Essays* (Cornell).

Strayer, J., *Western Europe in the Middle Ages* (Appleton).

Art, Music, and Architecture

Berenson, Bernard, *Italian Painters of the Renaissance* 2 vols., (World or Praeger).

Blunt, Anthony, *Artistic Theory in Italy 1450–1600* (Oxford).

Jantzen, H., *High Gothic: The Classic Cathedrals* (Funk & Wagnalls).

Levey, M., *Early Renaissance* (Penguin).

Lowry, B., *Renaissance Architecture* (Braziller).

Mâle, Emil, *Religious Art: From the Twelfth to Eighteenth Century* Farrar, Straus).

Murray, P., *Architecture of the Italian Renaissance* (Schocken).

Murray, P. and L., *Art of the Renaissance* (Praeger).

Panofsky, Erwin, *Gothic Architecture* (World).

Panofsky, Erwin, *Studies in Iconology: Humanistic Themes in the Art of the Renaissance* (Harper & Row).

Saalman, H., *Medieval Architecture* (Braziller).

Seay, A., *Music in the Medieval World* (Prentice-Hall).

Stechow, W., ed., *North Renaissance Art 1400–1600* (Prentice-Hall).

Steenstrup, J. C., trans. E. G. Cox, *Medieval Popular Ballads* (U. of Washington).

Stevens, D., *Tudor Church Music* (Norton).
Vallentin, Antonia, *Leonardo da Vinci* (Grosset & Dunlap).
Von Simson, *The Gothic Cathedral* (Harper & Row).

Crusades, Exploration, and the Expansion of Europe

Atiya, A. S., *Crusade, Commerce, and Culture* (Wiley).
Bannon, J., *Spanish Conquistadors: Men or Devils* (Holt, Rinehart and Winston).
Brebner, J. B., *Explorers of North America* (World).
Brundage, J. A., ed., *Crusades: Motives and Achievements* (Heath).
Diffie, B. W., *Prelude to Empire: Portugal Overseas Before Henry the Navigator* (Nebraska).
Drivers, H. E., *Americas on the Eve of Discovery* (Prentice-Hall).
Gibson, Charles, *Spain in America* (Harper & Row).
Kirkpatrick, F. A., *The Spanish Conquistadores* (World).
Morison, S. E., *Christopher Columbus* (Mentor).
Nowell, C. E., *Great Discoveries and the First Colonial Empires* (Cornell).
Parry, J. H., *Establishment of the European Hegemony 1415–1715* (Harper & Row).
Parry, J. H., *The Age of Reconnaissance* (Mentor).
Runciman, Steven, *A History of the Crusades* (Harper & Row).
Schrag, P., ed., *The European Mind and the Discovery of the New World* (Heath).
Treece, Henry, *The Crusades* (Mentor).

Economic and Social

Beard, M., *History of Business* vol. I, (Michigan).
Bennett, H. S., *Life on the English Manor* (Cambridge).
Carus-Wilson, E. M., *The Medieval Merchant Venturers* (Barnes & Noble).
Cipolla, C. M., *Guns, Sails and Empire: Technological Innovation and the Early Phases of European Expansion* (Funk & Wagnalls).
Chamberlin, E. R., *Everyday Life in Renaissance Times* (Putnam).
Coulton, G. G., *Life in the Middle Ages* 2 vols., (Cambridge).
Coulton, G. G., *Medieval Village, Manor, and Monastery* (Harper & Row).
De Roover, Raymond, *The Rise and Decline of the Medici Bank, 1397–1494* (Norton).
Holmes, U. T., Jr., *Daily Living in the Twelfth Century* (Wisconsin).
Jusserand, J. J., *English Wayfaring Life in the Middle Ages* (Barnes & Noble).
Luchaire, A., *Social France in the Time of Philip Augustus* (Harper & Row).
Mundy, J. H. and P. Risenberg, *Medieval Town* (Van Nostrand).
Pirenne, Henri, *Economic and Social History of Medieval Europe* (Harcourt).

Pirenne, Henri, *Medieval Cities* (Doubleday).

Power, E., *Medieval People* (Barnes & Noble).

Schmidt, A. J., *Yeoman in Tudor and Stuart England* (Virginia).

Tawney, Richard H., *The Agrarian Problem in the Sixteenth Century* (Harper & Row).

Tawney, Richard H., *Religion and the Rise of Capitalism* (Mentor).

Thrupp, Sylvia, *Change in Medieval Society* (Appleton).

Thrupp, Sylvia, *Merchant Class of Medieval London* (Michigan).

Weber, Max, *The Protestant Ethic and the Spirit of Capitalism* (Scribner).

Government, Politics, and Statecraft

Allen, J. W., *History of Political Thought in the Sixteenth Century* (Barnes & Noble).

Barraclough, Geoffrey, *Origins of Modern Germany* (Putnam).

Bindoff, S. T., *Tudor England* (Penguin).

Bloch, Marc, *Feudal Society* (Chicago).

Bodet, G. P., ed., *Early English Parliaments: Royal Courts, Great Councils or Representative Assemblies* (Heath).

Brandi, Karl, *The Emperor Charles V* (Humanities).

Bryce, J., *The Holy Roman Empire* (Schocken). The now classic account which is somewhat out of date.

Cam, Helen J., *England Before Elizabeth* (Harper & Row).

Davies, R. T., *The Golden Century of Spain* (Harper & Row).

Elliott, J. H., *Imperial Spain 1469–1716* (Mentor).

Fawtier, Robert, *The Capetian Kings of France* (St. Martin's).

Ganshoff, F. L., *Feudalism* (Harper & Row).

Gierke, O., *Political Theories of the Middle Ages* (Beacon).

Haskins, C. H., *The Normans in European History* (Norton).

Haskins, G. L., *The Growth of English Representative Government* (A. S. Barnes).

Hertzstein, R. E., ed., *The Holy Roman Empire in the Middle Ages* (Heath).

Hoyt, R. S., ed., *Feudal Institutions: Cause or Consequence of Decentralization* (Holt, Rinehart and Winston).

Jenkins, E., *Elizabeth the Great* (Putnam).

Kelly, Amy, *Eleanor of Aquitaine* (Random House).

Mattingly, Garret, *Catherine of Aragon* (Random House).

Mattingly, Garret, *Invincible Armada and Elizabethan England* (Virginia).

Mattingly, Garret, *Renaissance Diplomacy* (Penguin).

Myers, A. R., *England in the Late Middle Ages* (Penguin).

Neale, J. E., *Elizabeth First and Her Parliaments* (Norton).

Neale, J. E., *Queen Elizabeth* (Doubleday).

Oman, C. W., *Art of War in the Middle Ages* (Cornell).

Painter, Sidney, *Reign of King John* (Johns Hopkins).

Painter, Sidney, *Rise of the Feudal Monarchies* (Cornell).

Perroy, E., *The Hundred Years' War* (Putnam).

Petit-Dutallis, C., *Feudal Monarchy in France and England* (Harper & Row).

Pirenne, Henri, *Early Democracies in the Low Countries* (Harper & Row).

Rowse, A. L., *The England of Elizabeth* (Macmillan).

Runciman, Steven, *The Sicilian Vespers* (Penguin).

Schevill, F., *Medieval and Renaissance Florence* (Harper & Row).

Slavin, Arthur J., ed., *The New Monarchies and Representative Assemblies* (Heath).

Stephenson, Carl, *Medieval Feudalism* (Cornell).

Stenton, Doris Mary, *English Society in the Early Middle Ages* (Penguin).

Ullman, Walter, *A History of Political Thought* (Penguin).

Woodward, G. W. O., *A Short History of Sixteenth Century England* (Mentor).

Intellectual and Cultural

Adams, Henry, *Mont Saint-Michel and Chartres,* numerous paperback editions of this classic.

Baron, H., *Crisis of the Early Italian Renaissance* (Princeton).

Bolgar, R. R., *The Classical Heritage and Its Beneficiaries* (Harper & Row).

Burckhardt, Jacob., *The Civilization of the Renaissance in Italy,* numerous paperback editions. Century-old classic that started the controversy over the Renaissance.

Bush, Douglas, *The Renaissance and English Humanism* (Toronto).

Chabod, F., *Machiavelli and the Renaissance* (Harper & Row).

Copleston, F. C., *Medieval Philosophy* (Harper & Row).

Crombie, A., *Medieval and Early Modern Science* 2 vols., (Doubleday).

Dannenfeldt, K. H., ed., *Renaissance: Medieval or Modern* (Heath).

De Wulf, M., *Philosophy and Civilization in the Middle Ages* (Dover).

Ferguson, Wallace K., *The Renaissance* (Holt, Rinehart and Winston).

Ferguson, Wallace K., *The Renaissance in Historical Thought* (Harper & Row).

Gilson, E., *Heloise and Abelard* (Michigan).

Gilson, E., *Reason and Revelation in the Middle Ages* (Scribner).

Haskins, Charles Homer, *The Renaissance of the Twelfth Century* (World).

Haskins, Charles Homer, *The Rise of the Universities* (Cornell).

Hay, Denys, *Europe: The Emergence of an Idea* (Harper & Row).

Hay, Denys, *Renaissance Debate* (Holt, Rinehart and Winston).

Herlihy, D. J., *Medieval Culture and Society* (Harper & Row).

Highet, Gilbert, *The Classical Tradition: Greek and Roman Influences on Western Literature* (Oxford).

Hollister, C. Warren, ed., *Twelfth Century Renaissance* (Wiley).

Huizinga, Johan, *Erasmus and the Age of Reformation* (Harper & Row).

Huizinga, Johan, *The Waning of the Middle Ages* (Doubleday).

Jensen, D. L., ed., *Machiavelli: Cynic, Patriot or Political Scientist* (Heath).

Knowles, Dom David, *Evolution of Medieval Thought* (Random House).

Knowles, Dom David, *Saints and Scholars: Twenty-Six Medieval Characters* (Cambridge).

Kristeller, Paul O., *Renaissance Thought* (Harper & Row).

Leff, Gordon, *Medieval Thought: St. Augustine to Ockham* (Penguin).

Leff, Gordon, *Paris and Oxford Universities in the Thirteenth and Fourteenth Centuries* (Wiley).

Lewis, C. S., *The Allegory of Love: A Study in Medieval Tradition* (Oxford).

Lopez, R. S., *The Tenth Century: How Dark the Dark Ages* (Holt, Rinehart and Winston).

Lucki, Emil, *History of the Renaissance 1350–1550* (Utah). A paperback history in 5 vols. broken down by subject matter.

Martin, A. von, *Sociology of the Renaissance* (Harper & Row).

Painter, Sidney, *French Chivalry* (Cornell).

Pater, Walter, *The Renaissance* (Mentor or World).

Pennethorn, Hughes, *Witchcraft* (Penguin).

Plumb, J. H., *Italian Renaissance: A Concise Survey* (Harper & Row).

Plumb, J. H., *Renaissance Profiles* (Harper & Row).

Poole, R. L., *Illustrations of the History of Medieval Thought and Learning* (Dover).

Roeder, R., *Man of the Renaissance* (World).

Sarton, George, *Six Wings: Men of Science in the Renaissance* (Indiana).

Smith, Preserved, *Erasmus* (Dover).

Symonds, J. A., *Italian Literature*, 2 vols. (Putnam).

Taylor, H. O., *Erasmus and Luther* (Macmillan).

Taylor, H. O., *Humanism of Italy* (Macmillan).

Taylor, H. O., *Philosophy of Science in the Renaissance* (Macmillan).

Taylor, H. O., *The French Mind* (Macmillan).

Thompson, J. W., et al., *Civilization of the Renaissance* (Ungar).

Waddell, Helen, *Peter Abelard* (Compass).

Waddell, Helen, *The Wandering Scholars* (Doubleday).

Wieruszowski, H., *Medieval Universities* (Van Nostrand).

Woodward, W. H., *Vittorino da Feltre and Other Humanist Educators* (Columbia).

Religion and the Church

Bainton, Roland, *Here I Stand: A Life of Martin Luther* (Abingdon or Mentor).

Bainton, Roland, *Hunted Heretic: The Life of Michael Servetus* (Beacon).

Bainton, Roland, *Reformation of the Sixteenth Century* (Beacon).

Baldwin, M. W., *Mediaeval Church* (Cornell).

Barraclough, Geoffrey, *Medieval Papacy* (Harcourt).

Boehmer, H., *Martin Luther: Road to Reformation* (World).

Burns, Edward M., *The Counter Reformation* (Van Nostrand).

Chadwick, Owen, *The Reformation* (Penguin).

Cohn, Norman, *The Pursuit of the Millenium: Revolutionary Messianism in Medieval and Reformation Europe* (Harper & Row).

Daniel-Rops, H., *The Catholic Reformation* 2 vols., (Doubleday).

Dolan, J. P., *History of the Reformation* (Mentor).

Elton, Geoffrey, *Reformation Europe* (World).

Erikson, Erik H., *Young Man Luther* (Norton).

Harkness, Georgia, *John Calvin: The Man and His Ethics* (Abingdon).

Harbison, E. H., *The Christian Scholar in the Age of Reformation* (Scribner).

Hughes, Philip, *A Popular History of the Reformation* (Doubleday).

Jones, R. M., *The Spiritual Reformers of the Sixteenth and Seventeenth Centuries* (Beacon).

Lawson, J., *Medieval Education and the Reformation* (Humanities).

MacNeill, J. T., *History and Character of Calvinism* (Oxford).

MacFarlane, Kenneth B., *Origins of Religious Dissent in England* (Macmillan).

Mollat, G., *The Popes at Avignon, 1305–1378* (Harper & Row).

Mosse, George L., *The Reformation* (Holt, Rinehart and Winston).

Parker, T. M., *The English Reformation to 1558* (Oxford).

Pollard, A. F., *Henry Eighth* (Harper & Row).

Powell, J. M., ed., *Innocent III: Vicar of Christ or Lord of the World* (Heath).

Powicke, F. M., *Reformation in England* (Oxford).

Roth, C., *Spanish Inquisition* (Norton).

Rupp, G., *Luther's Progress to the Diet of Worms* (Harper & Row).

Smith, Preserved, *Age of Reformation* 2 vols., (Macmillan).

Spitz, Lewis W., ed., *The Reformation: Material or Spiritual* (Heath).

Sykes, Norman, *Crisis of the Reformation* (Norton).

Synan, E. A., *Popes and Jews in the Middle Ages* (Macmillan).

Williams, S., *Gregorian Epoch: Reformation, Revolution, Reaction* (Heath).

Wood, C. T., *Philip the Fair and Boniface VIII: State vs. Papacy* (Holt, Rinehart and Winston).

SOURCES

Bagley, J. J., *Sources of English Medieval History* (Penguin).

Boccaccio, *Decameron,* several paperback editions.

Calvin, John, *Institutes of Christian Religion,* ed. H. T. Ker (Westminster).

Cantor, Norman F., *The Medieval World* (Macmillan).

Cellini, *Autobiography* (Penguin), or other editions.

Chaucer, G., *The Portable Chaucer,* ed. T. Morrison (Viking).

Cohen, J. M., ed. and trans., *Diaz: The Conquest of New Spain* (Penguin).

Cohen, J. M., ed. and trans., *Zarate: The Discovery and Conquest of Peru* (Penguin).

Coulton, G. G., *Life in the Middle Ages* 2 vols., (Cambridge).

Dante, *The Portable Dante,* ed. Paolo Milano (Viking).

De Montaigne, Michel, *Autobiography* (Random House).

De Montaigne, Michel, *Essays,* several paperback selections.

Erasmus, *Praise of Folly* (Michigan).

Freemantle, Anne, ed., *The Age of Belief: The Medieval Philosophers* (Mentor).

Froissart, Jean, *Chronicles of England, France, and Spain* (Dutton), "The 100 Years War."

Hopper, V. F., and G. B. Lahen, *Medieval Mysteries, Moralities & Interludes* (Barron).

Langland, *Piers the Ploughman* (Penguin).

Lopez, R. S. and I. W. Raymond, *Medieval Trade in the Mediterranean World* (Norton).

Luther, Martin, *Selections from His Writings,* ed., J. Dillenberger (Doubleday).

Machiavelli, Niccolo, *The Prince* (Random House).

Memoirs of the Crusades: Villehardouin and de Joinville (Dutton).

More, St. Thomas, *Utopia* (Penguin).

Otto of Freising, *The Deeds of Frederick Barbarossa* (Norton).

Polo, Marco, *Travels* (Dell), or numerous other paperback editions.

Rabelais, *Gargantua and Pantagruel* (Penguin).

Ross, J. B. and M. M. McLaughlin, *The Portable Medieval Reader* (Viking).

Ross, J. B. and M. M. McLaughlin, *The Portable Renaissance Reader* (Viking).

Sherley-Price, L., ed., *The Little Flowers of St. Francis* (Penguin).

Thomas Aquinas, St., *Introduction to St. Thomas,* ed. A. C. Pegis (Random House).

Thomas à Kempis, *The Imitation of Christ,* numerous editions.

Thompson, K. F., ed., *Classics of Western Thought* vol. 2, (Harcourt).

Waddell, Helen, *Medieval Latin Lyrics* (Penguin).

Zenkovsky, S. A., ed. and trans., *Medieval Russia's Epics, Chronicles and Tales* (Dutton).

FICTION

Bolt, R., *Man For All Seasons* (Random House). A play about St. Thomas More.

Costain, T. B., *The Moneyman* (Harper). A novel of fifteenth century France.

Muntz, Hope, *The Golden Warrior, the Story of Harold and William* (Scribner).

Oldenbourgh, Zoé, *The Cornerstone* (Ballantine). The world of Philip the Fair.

Oldenbourgh, Zoé, *The World Is Not Enough* (Ballantine). A novel of the crusades.

Prescott, Hilda F. M., *Man on a Donkey* (Ballantine or Macmillan). A novel about Henry VIII.

Read, Charles, *The Cloister and the Hearth* (Simon and Schuster). A century old classic.

Shaw, Bernard, *St. Joan* (Penguin). An interesting psychological portrayal although not historically accurate.

Undset, S., *Master of Hestviken* 4 vols., (Pocket Books). Another novel of medieval Scandinavia by this Nobel prize winning author.

part five

BEGINNINGS
OF THE MODERN ERA

15

The Struggle for Dominance
in an Age of Reason

The religious struggles of the sixteenth century continued on into the seventeenth, but increasingly they served as a justification for aggrandizement, commercial exploitation, or the pursuit of dynastic supremacy. In the ensuing struggle, France temporarily emerged as the dominant power on the Continent, although both the English and the Dutch were able to challenge successfully the overseas empires of the Spanish and Portuguese. In fact, it was the increasing ability of England to control the oceans that laid the foundation for the British Empire, which began to wither away only in the last few decades. Europe itself became the battleground for the conflicting ambitions of various monarchs who were attempting to build up new national states. A brief period of fragile peace at the beginning of the century was shattered in 1618 by the outbreak of the Thirty Years' War (1618–1648), which began as a revolt against the religious policies of the German Hapsburgs. In 1609, the emperor Rudolf, one of the most tolerant of the Hapsburgs, issued a charter of religious liberty to Lutherans — but not to other Protestants — in his Bohemian and Moravian territories. This charter was abrogated by his brother and successor Matthias in 1618. Angered by this drastic revocation as well as by the implied threat to their own power, the Bohemian nobility threw the imperial governor out of a palace window in Prague, thereby igniting the struggle that ultimately engulfed all of Europe.

Religious motivations increasingly became subordinate to other considerations during the course of the war. Catholic France, for example, intervened on the side of the Protestant rebels both to weaken the power of the Hapsburgs and in the hope of extending French frontiers. Though the Protestant Swedes supported the cause of their co-religionists, they also used the opportunity to expand their power on the mainland of Europe. The Dutch were more interested in seizing the overseas possessions of the Spanish Hapsburgs than in using their resources to support the Protestant cause on the Continent. The inevitable result of the long years of religious fighting was a widespread disenchantment with narrow, doctrinal Christianity and a growing willingness to tolerate different beliefs. The fighting was terminated by a congress of nations held in Westphalia in 1648. Thus came to an end the wars of religion. Though Europeans continued to fight each other, religious differences no longer served as a justification. Politically, Westphalia marks the emergence of the Bourbons of France as the dominant power of Europe and the decline of the Hapsburgs. The Hapsburgs continued to hold Austria, and from there they were able to gain control of much of south central Europe, although they soon

Europe in 1648.

lost command of Spain, which early in the next century fell to the Bourbons. Within the Holy Roman Empire the Hapsburgs had little real power, although they still retained the imperial title. The Spanish retained their influence over much of the New World, but the religious wars and a century-long inflation caused by a massive influx of gold from the Americas had so weakened them that Spain found itself little more than a pawn in the power struggle of ambitious European monarchs. Westphalia also marked a shift northward of European power, with Holland and Sweden, followed by Russia and Brandenburg, gaining increased prominence.

In the aftermath of the Thirty Years' War Europe abandoned the cause of religious unity. Much of the disenchantment with religion was political, but it was also given impetus by a growing interest in the beliefs of non-Christian civilizations, both past and present, of which the Europeans had rather recently become aware. Even more important was the rapid growth in scientific knowledge, which soon attracted the attention of most educated people. Science developed a new body of knowledge that challenged the revealed universe of Christianity, invaded the curriculum of the schools, imposed new literary canons, and altered the world view of the philosophers. The result was a growth of religious skepticism, a hesitation to accept miracles or revelations, and an attempt to remove God to a place where He did not directly intervene in the affairs of man. European civilization became more materialistic, and the growth in population, money, and knowledge, as well as the improvement of living conditions — at least for a few — seemed to the people of the time to herald a new modern age.

THE SCIENTIFIC REVOLUTION

Though modern scholars have traced many of the developments in science to their medieval beginnings, the effect of the scientific breakthroughs in the seventeenth century still seem revolutionary. By the end of the century, Europe no longer accepted many of the basic assumptions that had been held since the time of the Greeks. The most radical change was the acceptance of a heliocentric, or sun-centered, universe in place of the old geocentric, or earth-centered, one, but developments in anatomy, physiology, medicine, mathematics, physics, and chemistry were also important. Some of the new discoveries, for example, those in anatomy, gained rapid acceptance, while others ran into more opposition and had a more difficult time, for example, those in astronomy.

Until the middle of the sixteenth century, anatomy was still based upon the teachings of Galen. The invention of printing, however, allowed the anatomist to present standardized illustrations, so that for the first time one investigator could check his findings against another, while the improvement in artistic techniques served to clarify what was being described. Gradually, anatomists began to challenge Galen, until with the publication of Andreas Vesalius' book *On the Fabric of the Human Body* in 1543 the whole system was overthrown. Though others suggested modifications of Vesalius' findings, there was no major challenge to his basic descriptions. They could be verified by any other investigator.

Nicolaus Copernicus, however, represented a different case. His *On the Revolution of the Heavenly Orbs* was posthumously published in 1543, but he offered no new evidence for his case. Rather, Copernicus merely showed that it was possible to use the same observations to demonstrate a heliocentric universe as had been used to support a geocentric one. Though the theory was an interesting one, it left many questions unanswered, and its acceptance would undermine the whole structure of science, philosophy, and religion as they were then understood. One of the few adherents of the Copernican explanation, Giordano Bruno, was burned at the stake in 1600 for advocating a plurality of worlds and an infinity of the universe, ideas that went counter to what the learned world had accepted since Aristotle. Even while the controversy over Copernicus raged, the Danish astronomer Tycho Brahe began a systematic series of observations of the heavens while serving as astronomer and astrologer first to the king of Denmark and later to the emperor. Though Brahe tried to reconcile his observations with a geocentric universe, his assistant and successor Johannes Kepler found that they gave more support to a heliocentric explanation. In the process, Kepler worked out a series of laws describing planetary motion, which he argued to be elliptical rather than circular.

While Kepler struggled with his data in Prague, Galileo Galilei in Italy was establishing mathematical explanations for ballistic trajectories, pendulum movements, and uniform acceleration. His observation that the velocity of a body falling freely in a vacuum is proportionate to the elasped time of the fall laid the foundation for modern physics. In all of his experiments and conclusions, Galileo was contradicting Aristotle, who, it seemed, could also be wrong in his astronomical suppositions. Learning of the invention of the telescope in the Netherlands, Galileo made one for himself in order to better examine the heavens. The most important of his early observations was the discovery of three of the moons of Jupiter, a finding that directly contradicted basic suppositions of Aristotle, who had taught that everything had to revolve around the earth, the center of the universe. Galileo published his theories in the *Dialogue on the Two Principal Systems of the Universe* in which he presented a series of debates between a Copernican and an Aristotelian. Though to avoid Church censure Galileo gave the decision to the Aristotelian in his book, it was quite clear that the Copernican had the better of the argument. In the resulting intense controversy, Galileo was forced by the Inquisition to retract his beliefs, although this did not end the debate.

With Galileo the controversy entered the public arena. Because the universities were under either Protestant or Catholic sponsorship, the condemnation of Galileo meant that it was difficult to continue further discussion in the established institutions of learning. Instead, the scientists turned to the newly founded academies and learned societies, which not only provided them a platform to debate the new theories but also brought the educated laymen, who also belonged to such groups, into closer contact with scientific thinking. Even though such academies and societies might challenge established learning, they were supported by various monarchs and governments in the hope that they might make discoveries that could be applied in warfare or in navigation.

Before the scientific information thus collected could be useful, mathematics itself had to develop as a means or language to explain it. To solve the problems of motion, European mathematicians learned to apply the algebra they had borrowed from the Arabs to the geometry they had inherited from the Greeks. René Descartes became an important pioneer in this field. Equally indispensable was calculus, developed concurrently by the Englishman Isaac Newton and the German Gottfried Wilhelm von Leibniz. Newton alone, however, in his epoch-making book *The Mathematical Principles of Natural Philosophy (Principia Mathematica)* developed the mathematical principles of matter in motion. His concept of the "world machine" so successfully incorporated all of the scientific knowledge of his time that it dominated European thought until challenged by the theory of relativity in this century.

Medicine also underwent rapid change, first as a result of the ideas concerning chemotherapy of Paracelsus at the beginning of the sixteenth century and then as a result of the development of a series of new surgical techniques by the French military surgeon Ambroise Paré. In a sense, Paré's techniques were a necessary response to a period marked by frequent wars, with the growing numbers of wounded forcing the military surgeon to improvise. Closely following the discoveries of Paré was William Harvey's proof of the circulation of blood, a concept that revolutionized the study of physiology. The one flaw in Harvey's proof was his inability to show a connection between arteries and veins. His supposition that such a connection must exist, however, was verified by Marcelli Malpighi's observations of capillaries later in the century.

Malpighi's proof depended upon the use of the microscope, an invention that led to even more discoveries than the telescope. The most important figure in this area was the Dutch lens maker Anton van Leeuwenhoek, who was also a pioneer in the study of microorganisms. Another Dutchman, Christian Huygens, perfected the pendulum used in clocks and developed a wave theory to explain the phenomenon of light. Modern chemistry grew out of the work of Robert Boyle, who demolished the Aristotelian notion that four elements — earth, water, air, and fire — make up the universe. Pierre de Fermat and Blaise Pascal began the mathematical study of probability; William Gilbert experimented with magnetism and electricity; and Otto von Guericke invented an air pump and demonstrated the nature of atmospheric pressure.

SCIENTIFIC PHILOSOPHY

The most immediate effect of the new discoveries was to force men to grow more skeptical and to think more critically. Francis Bacon became one of the first to suggest that new scientific discoveries required that ancient authority be discarded. None taking this advice rose to greater influence than Descartes, whose *Discourse on Method,* published in 1637, argued that any authority should be regarded with suspicion until the evidence could be analyzed and proved by meeting the test of reason. The one reality that Descartes felt he could not refute by systematic doubt, "I think, therefore I am," became the starting point for his new system of metaphysics. Inherent in Descartes' thought was the belief that the universe functioned in a rational manner which could be explained in mathematical terms. This idea received powerful stimulus with Newton's *Principia,* which appeared to demonstrate that the whole physical world functioned as a giant mathematical machine.

Though born and raised in France, Descartes did most of his work in the more tolerant atmosphere of Holland, which in the seventeenth century offered haven to scholars and scientists from all over Europe. It was in Holland that the first major Jewish philosopher of Western Europe, Baruch Spinoza, lived. Spinoza's family had fled the Inquisition in the Spanish peninsula for Holland, but, interestingly enough, Spinoza himself was excommunicated by the Jewish community in Amsterdam. He then withdrew from community activity to devote his time to a formulation of an ethic based upon scientific and mathematical principles. In his posthumously published *Ethica,* Spinoza argued that free man, led by the intellectual love of God, could rise above capricious passions through understanding them and acting upon a reasoned will. Spinoza was a Cartesian — a follower of Descartes — in that he assumed innate ideas to exist in the mind. Taking a somewhat different view was a group of men known as the empiricists, of whom the Englishman John Locke was the most influential and famous. Locke believed that the mind is not an original storehouse of ideas but instead begins as a blank tablet and builds up knowledge by recording experience. In his *Essay Concerning Human Understanding,* Locke argued that men know nothing more than they can learn from observation, and thus man is more the product of his physical environment than of a divine scheme.

Inevitably, religion itself came to be regarded as a suitable subject for investigation. Edward Herbert of Cherbury attempted through the study of comparative religion to find out the universal religious principles upon which all rational men could agree. Lord Herbert argued that the intelligent person should strive to free himself from belief in miracles and magic and be willing to guide his conduct empirically, that is, to employ reason in making decisions. Pierre Bayle, his contemporary, also lashed out against superstition, intolerance, and dogmatic assertions of religious belief. The result of these and other efforts was the growth of deism, a religious movement that recognized God as having created the universe, after which, with man's aid, let it run itself in accordance with the natural laws of physics and reason.

Many of the philosophers turned to speculation about the nature of government, which in turn led to analysis and even reform. A large number attempted justification of the existing strong monarchies. Thomas Hobbes, whose *Leviathan* appeared in 1651, became the strongest advocate of unrestrained authoritarianism. Hobbes believed that man in his "natural" state is a brute and that the only thing that raises him above the animal level is life in a society governed by a political system. Man could not in his own best interest choose anything short of total subservience to society, and the only meaningful representative of that society was the sovereign, whether king or autocrat. Somewhat more optimistic about the nature of man was the Dutch humanist Hugo Grotius, who, in order to justify the revolt of the Netherlands, had conceived of the state as an agreement among individual holders of rights. Grotius' main concern, however, lay with international relations, and in a reaction to the wars of religion, he tried to separate politics from theology. Sovereigns, he believed, should be governed by reason and natural law, their own self-interest and preservation dictating restraint.

In England, Locke amplified the concept of natural law to justify revolution. He believed that man's natural rights had existed before government, and contrary to Hobbes, man need not be a brute. Early in their history, men had come together by contract among themselves to guarantee life, liberty, and property through the establishment of civil rule. If any ruler abused his authority or failed to carry out his obligations, his subjects might revoke the contract by revolting. For Locke, effective government was limited by the consent of the governed, an idea which ever since has been used to justify the overthrow of absolutist regimes.

THE PRIMACY OF LOUIS XIV

The dominant political figure of the seventeenth century was Louis XIV, the *roi soleil,* the sun king, of France who ascended the throne at the age of five in 1643 and ruled for seventy-two years. Cardinal Mazarin, his chief minister, was the leading personality during the first part of his reign, but once Louis took power for himself in 1661, his fondness for pageantry and grandiose schemes rapidly put him at the forefront of European rulers. Though Louis had a genius for detail and an aptitude for politics, he was not as talented as some of his contemporaries; his deficiences, however, were obscured during his lifetime by the glamor in which he went about the business of governing. It was not so much what Louis did but the way in which he did things that impressed his contemporaries.

Much of the success of Louis was due to the fact that France was both larger and wealthier than any of its potential rivals. His Bourbon predecessors, Henry IV and Louis XIII, assisted by a number of able ministers such as Cardinal Richelieu and Cardinal Mazarin, had built up a rudimentary sort of centralized administration and had effectively brought the landed nobility under royal control. Moreover, the ordinary Frenchman was loyal to the crown and had a pride in national achievement, characteristics not common among the other peoples of Europe. By 1700, France had an estimated twenty million subjects, nearly three times as many as any other European power, and the lands of France were agriculturally among the richest on the Continent. Louis XIV also benefited from the growing seventeenth-century belief that a nation could be made more fruitful through better management. Though Louis had no real ideas on how to manage affairs, he did give his ministers the freedom to direct the public business to his advantage. One of the chief means of strengthening royal power was the creation of a standing army. Such an army required money, which in turn led to an attempt to replace the old feudal system of aides and fees with a system of regular revenue. Inevitably, this innovation led to more centralization and still more power for the king. It was only by such efforts that any monarch could hope to compete with the power of the Spanish Hapsburgs, whose control of the treasure of the New World gave them an influential position in European affairs.

In their attempts to rationalize government, kings and their public

Cardinal Richelieu (1585–1642), triple portrait by Philippe de Champaigne. (Reproduced by courtesy of the Trustees, The National Gallery, London)

officials ran into all sorts of obstacles. Townspeople, monks, priests, and nobles all saw their old positions threatened. To overcome such opposition, the kings usually resorted to arbitrary actions, employed force, and took the law into their own hands. They justified their tactics with the theory of the divine right of kings, which conveniently made them answerable only to God for their deeds, no matter how high-handed. Though all European rulers followed more or less the same path, the results were nowhere so spectacularly successful as in France. Louis received the reputation of wonder worker and France came to be looked upon as the land where miracles could happen. French ways came to be imitated everywhere, so much so that French itself became an international language. No small part of Louis' glamour stemmed from his generosity in patronizing artists, architects, and writers, who in turn rewarded their benefactor with praise. Paris became an intellectual center that had seldom before been equaled. Perhaps Louis' greatest achievement was the role he played in making France the cultural leader of all of Europe.

Nothing has detracted so much from Louis' ultimate reputation as his treatment of the Huguenots, who had been guaranteed their privileges by Henry IV in the Edict of Nantes in 1598. Louis' hostility toward them, originally motivated by an attempt to assert his royal prerogative, soon expressed itself in a campaign of extermination, a policy that seems contrary to the sophisticated tone of his court, as well as to his program for improving French life. Revoking the Edict in 1685, he embarked upon a campaign of persecution, the dragonnades, that included quartering troops, or dragoons, in the homes of Huguenot families until such time as they accepted Catholicism. His intolerance in the long run served to undermine French prosperity, since the Huguenots as a group were prominent in trade and manufacture. Some 200,000 of them fled France, the majority to the electorate of Brandenburg but significant numbers to Holland, England, and even to the English colonies in America, where their descendants still reside.

THE WARS OF LOUIS XIV

Louis' military endeavors proved even more damaging to the French economy, though they nominally were fought to gain territory along the northern and eastern frontiers, which were then under the control of the Spanish Hapsburgs. In a sense, however, war often seems to have been a game to Louis, who needed an occasional adventure both to fend off boredom and to keep his army in condition. His aggression began in 1667 with the assertion of some remote and tenuous claims to the Spanish Netherlands, which represented those parts of the Low Countries — mostly modern Belgium — that had not achieved independence when the Dutch did. It soon became apparent that the large and well-equipped French armies could easily defeat any forces the Spanish sent against them. So frightened were the Dutch that they joined with their former Hapsburg enemies in a coalition against the French. Leadership of the anti-French forces eventually devolved upon the young prince William of Orange, who finally persuaded Louis to accept peace in return for French control of the free county of Burgundy.

For the next dozen or so years, the grand monarch extended his kingdom by seizing bits and pieces of other peoples' lands along the French frontier until another coalition, the League of Augsburg, was formed to resist him. This time Louis found that his enemies were more than a match for him. The Austrian Hapsburgs had just recently turned back the Turks from Vienna, with the aid of John Sobieski, the king of Poland, thus enabling them to pay more attention to affairs in Germany. William of Orange in 1688 had also become king of England, ending for the time being a lengthy and bitter commercial rivalry between England and Holland and bringing the two powers into the

Louis XIV (1638–1715),
portrait by Hyacinthe
Rigaud. (Alinari–Art
Reference Bureau)

struggle against France. In spite of the coalition, Louis continued to fight until 1697, when the war ended with the Peace of Ryswick.

Almost immediately after peace was established, Louis became involved in a contest over the Spanish succession. The reigning Hapsburg monarch of Spain, Charles II, was childless. Louis' son by his Spanish wife had a claim to the throne, as did the Holy Roman Emperor and the Duke of Bavaria. Most of Europe would have preferred the Duke of Bavaria, thus breaking up the Hapsburg power without increasing that of the Bourbons. When the Duke of Bavaria died, Charles II realized that the Spanish domains faced dismemberment. In a desperate attempt to prevent division, he arranged for the succession to pass to one of Louis' grandsons, the future Philip V. By this action he angered his Austrian relatives as well as most of the other rulers of Europe. Under these circumstances, it would have been advisable for Louis to ensure the throne for his grandson by granting concessions to his opponents. Instead, with his usual lack of restraint, he took such precipitate action that he threw all of his potential opponents into each other's arms. England, Holland, and Austria joined together to nullify the succession and were able, under the military leadership of John Churchill, later Duke of Marlborough, and Prince Eugene of Savoy, repeatedly to defeat the French armies. Since the Spanish, however, stubbornly supported their new Bourbon king, the war degenerated into a deadlock, which was finally terminated by agreements negotiated at Utrecht in 1713. Philip kept his throne in Madrid, but only on the understanding that the French and Spanish thrones must never be united. The Austrians assumed possession of the Spanish Netherlands and shared with Savoy the territories that Spain had formerly held in Italy. England extended its overseas territory by taking both Nova Scotia and the Hudson Bay region in North America and keeping Gibraltar, which had been captured during the war.

Two years after the conclusion of the Peace of Utrecht, Louis died. He had outlived his own children as well as many of his grandchildren and was succeeded by a five-year-old great grandson, Louis XV. The regency brought back into power the aristocracy, which Louis, in an effort to control, had purposely allowed to grow idle and irresponsible. Moreover, during the last part of his reign, Louis had ignored many of the growing trouble spots in his kingdom, which continued to fester until the French Revolution in 1789 swept most of them away together with the monarchy itself.

BRITISH ALTERNATIVES

During much of the time that France and Louis XIV held the center of the stage, England was in the wings. The death of the childless Queen Elizabeth in 1603 brought in a new line of rulers, the Stuarts, descended from the same Mary, Queen of Scots, whom Elizabeth had executed. The accession of the Stuarts in the person of James I united the crowns of Scotland and England, although formal union did not come about until the eighteenth century. The Stuarts had little use for religious bigotry and in general attempted to rationalize governmental procedures in order to achieve more effective administration. Though England was smaller than France and lacked the wealth of its rival, it was much more tightly knit. Royal authority was enforced nearly everywhere in the realm, thus eliminating the need for the kind of autocracy that developed in France. Moreover, the English kings found autocratic rule more difficult than had Louis XIV because the legal and parliamentary struggles of the past put more limitations upon the crown. Futhermore, the great diversity of religious opinion in England made it virtually impossible to demand the kind of uniformity that Louis successfully imposed on France.

The Reformation in England had produced a new church that differed little in spirit or structure from the old one and that satisfied only a small proportion of the people. Traditional Christians were dissatisfied because England no longer looked to the pope, while the Calvinistic Puritans were unhappy because so little real change had taken place. Though the Calvinists had succeeded in gaining control of the established church in Scotland, they were hamstrung in their efforts to do the same in England. Since the Puritans formed an important element in parliament, the inevitable result of their frustration was a prolonged conflict between parliament and king over royal prerogatives. The Stuarts asserted their right to a sufficient revenue to support their administration, while their parliamentary opponents insisted upon their right to scrutinize the royal budget and to decide how the revenue could be raised. James I managed to maintain internal peace, but his son and successor Charles I in 1642 took up arms in defense of royal supremacy. This action proved disastrous. After some three years of fighting, Charles found himself prisoner of the parliamentary forces led by the Puritan Oliver Cromwell.

At this point, the Puritans found themselves isolated. The Scots, who had supported parliament, wanted to make some sort of settlement with the crown, as did most of the English, who had no wish to be rid of the king, however much they opposed his policies. Real power, however, lay with the army, which was largely composed of Puritans, some very radical, who were intent on using their victory to establish God's kingdom on earth. Seizing the initiative, the Puritans executed the king, swept away the old church, abolished the House of Lords, and, under Cromwell's masterful direction, ruled Britain for about ten years. They were unable, however, to achieve their New Jerusalem, nor did most of the English people exhibit much satisfaction with their rule. After Cromwell died, disillusionment with the Puritans soon led a new parliament to invite Charles II, the oldest son of the executed king, to take the throne. In 1660 Charles, who had been living in exile in Holland, cheerfully returned to England, and in the aftermath of the Restoration the English, so far as was convenient, forgot about their experiment in rebellion.

Obviously, the monarchy that Charles II revived differed radically from the institution in France. Charles had no command over finances beyond spending the inadequate funds allowed him by the House of Commons, and he had no power to summon a negligent official or recalcitrant subject for correction or punishment. As king he could still appoint bishops, admirals, judges, and secretaries, but he had no convenient way to check their effectiveness or to reward them for their loyalty. Charles and his brother James II did what they could to add to the power of the crown, but compared to France the country seemed to drift with the tide. In spite of this, and contrary to the political theory of the time, the kingdom prospered. Throughout the century, living conditions in Britain were superior to those elsewhere in Europe. The civil war had not left particularly great destruction, nor had it seriously interrupted overseas expansion. During the seventeenth century, the English opened up a valuable trade with the Far East, established important sugar-producing stations in the West Indies, and founded a number of self-sustaining colonies along the Atlantic seaboard of North America. A series of naval wars with the Dutch led to a growing English dominance on the seas as well as to possession of the Hudson Valley. In addition, the English extended their dominion in Ireland until it became virtually complete.

During this period, Catholicism lost much of its influence in England, although it retained a strong hold in Ireland and among some of the Highland Scots. This decline owed much to the aggressiveness of Puritanism, but it was also largely due to a growing intolerance and hostility caused by a fear of Catholic reaction, a fear that gained substance with the revocation of the Edict of Nantes and the Catholic tendencies of Charles II and James II. The mother of the kings was a Catholic French princess, while the wife of Charles, Catherine of Braganza, came from Catholic Portugal. The two monarchs had spent much of their youth at the Catholic French court, and though Charles in public adhered to the Anglican Church, he was a secret Catholic, whereas James openly espoused Catholicism. The open Catholicism of James had from 1668 on led to a vigorous agitation designed to exclude him from succeeding his childless brother. Charles, however, stubbornly resisted such efforts, and the movement gradually faded when it was realized that James himself would probably be succeeded by one of his Protestant daughters, Mary or Anne. As a result, when Charles died in 1685, James assumed the crown with no disturbance, and a revolt some weeks later was easily repressed. The new monarch, nevertheless, soon went out of his way to name Catholics to high office and to set aside the disabilities against religious dissenters — Catholics as well as non-conforming Protestants such as Unitarians. When a son was born to the new wife of James in 1688 and it seemed certain that the new heir would be raised a Catholic, the fearful Protestants were stirred to action. A number of highly placed Englishmen sent a letter to William of Orange, the husband of James's daughter Mary, promising him and his queen their support should he attempt an invasion of England. William did not need a second invitation. In November 1688, he made it ashore with about 15,000 soldiers, including 4,000 mounted troops, and caught James so unprepared that the latter could offer only a token resistance. James fled to France, where he had already sent his wife and infant son, and a hastily summoned parliament declared that he had abdicated. William and Mary were then invited to be joint sovereigns. If Mary died without heirs, William could continue to rule, but he was to be succeeded by Anne, the second daughter of the deposed James. At the same time, a bill of rights for all Englishmen was enacted into law.

THE AFTERMATH OF THE GLORIOUS REVOLUTION

All of these events make up what is known as the Glorious Revolution. They marked the end of any prospect of an English king becoming an autocrat or of basing his rule upon the theory of divine right. The bill of rights made clear that the king was responsible to parliament and held the crown only with its consent. The king, at least for another century, still had real functions and held important powers, although not enough to rule effectively without the support of parliament. During most of William's reign, which extended to 1702 (Mary died in 1694), and virtually the whole of Anne's reign, which lasted until 1714, England was at war with France. In American history, these wars are usually called King William's War and Queen Anne's War, but in Europe the main conflicts were part of Louis' grand plans that led to the War of the League of Augsburg and the War of the Spanish Succession. More or less continual warfare required large appropriations in order to maintain a permanent military establishment, and to keep track of the money, the Bank of England, the first true national bank, was founded. Parliament began to meet every year, and instead of simply voting taxes, it began appropriating funds for definite purposes. Parliament also attempted to ascertain whether the funds were spent as ordered. With the accession of George I in 1714, a German-speaking prince whose chief virtue was the fact that he was a Protestant, parliamentary responsibilities increased. George spoke no English, nor did he try very hard to learn it; he disliked life in Britain, and was generally content to let parliament have its way. At the same time, England had become the first state to turn to deficit financing in order to meet the burdens of the wars. By forcing the government to borrow money, something that had not been done before on such a scale, the English invented a national debt. Instead of being a burden to government, a national debt proved desirable, not only because it forced a streamlining of the fiscal system but also because it gave the government the means of controlling interest rates for itself as well as for other borrowers.

THE HAPSBURGS

Developments in the seventeenth century did not deal kindly with the Hapsburgs. Though the loyalty of the Hapsburgs to the popes had helped preserve Catholicism, this policy had not worked to favor the family ambitions. Spain, for example, entered into a period of severe economic distress during the Thirty Years' War from which it has not really recovered to this day. Imports of bullion from the New World declined while bit by bit French, Dutch, and English merchants began to encroach upon and seize parts of the Spanish Empire. Though Spain managed to hold on to much of its territory through the efforts of Catholic missionaries, Spaniards themselves gained little. Within Spain, the nobility grew ever more powerful, and through an alliance with the Church, managed to gain control of most of the land. Aristocratic repression of the peasants went unchecked by the increasingly hapless monarchs until vagabondage and banditry came to seem the only alternative to a life of near slavery. Eventually, the Spanish Hapsburgs were replaced by the Bourbons of France, who proved no more effective.

The Austrian Hapsburgs remained more powerful than the Spanish, although their authority in Germany continued to decline. Much of the power of this branch of the family, which also controlled Bohemia, came from its ability to seize lands formerly held by the Turks. By the end of the seventeenth century, the Hapsburgs controlled Transylvania and most of Hungary. They continued their advance into Italy until they ruled Milan, Tuscany, Naples, and Sicily; in 1704, they also annexed the Spanish Netherlands. These actions gave them control over one of the most disparate collections of territories ever assembled under a single ruler. Since the subject peoples differed widely in language, religion, and cultural level, and were spread throughout Europe, autocracy seemed almost indispensable and a centralized administration virtually impossible. In spite of the handicaps they faced, the Hapsburgs long remained a chief power on the European scene.

THE TREND TO THE NORTH

For centuries the countries of northern Europe, including France, had been increasing in importance, but their dominance had to wait until the discovery in these areas of the mineral resources, such as coal and iron, so vital to the functioning of a modern state. Even in the seventeenth century, however, it was the north that held the great timber reserves, the richer soils, and the better inland water routes. These advantages soon led the northern countries to contest the early monopoly of overseas enterprise which prior exploration had given to the Spanish and the Portuguese.

No people enjoyed greater success against Spain than the Dutch, whose religious revolt against the Spanish Hapsburgs soon became a struggle for commercial supremacy. When in 1580 the Spanish Hapsburgs had temporarily added the crown of Portugal to their collection, the Dutch managed to transfer most of the Portuguese interests in the Indian Ocean to themselves. In the aftermath, the Dutch soon dominated the Oriental spice trade, from which they received such riches that the United Provinces, also known as the Dutch Republic, became the chief naval and commercial power on the Continent.

The influence of the Swedes had also increased spectacularly after the country broke away from Denmark in the early sixteenth century. Sweden's rise to power was originally derived from its superior military tactics, based upon close-order drill, which proved unbeatable on the battlefield until other countries, particularly France, adopted its methods. The Swedes waged a series of aggressive wars against the Danes, Poles, Germans, and Austrians until they had undisputed dominion over the Baltic Sea and had become a first-rate European power. Though their intervention in the Thirty Years' War under the leadership of Gustavus Adolphus had helped the cause of Protestantism, they soon found that their newly won position was being contested by the Protestant Hohenzollern family as well as by the rulers of Russia.

The Hohenzollerns had ruled the electorate of Brandenburg, a territory around Berlin, since the fifteenth century. Though initially the region had little strategic or economic importance, the Hohenzollerns, by carefully husbanding their resources, managed to establish themselves among the ranks of the great power. The most important member of the family was Frederick William, who inherited the territory in 1640 while the Thirty Years' War raged. During the early years of his reign, Frederick William could claim dominion over little more than a devastated countryside, but with the return of peace he engaged in such a successful rebuilding program that he came to be known as the Great Elector. He created a standing army, a practice that was later imitated by Louis XIV, and then set out to find the funds to finance it. By instituting a rigorous program of government economy to apply to everything but his army, and at the same time concentrating all authority and discretion in his own hands, he managed not only to support his army but to encourage business and industrial growth. Frederick William differed from most of his contemporaries in that he seldom committed his troops to a battle, where they might be wounded or killed, until every device of diplomacy and chicanery had been tried.

In addition to Brandenburg, the Hohenzollerns had from 1609 possessed the duchy of Cleves on the Rhine in western Germany. As far to the east of Berlin, they inherited East Prussia from a collateral branch of the family. Originally, East Prussia had been conquered by the Teutonic Knights, who under the leadership of a Hohenzollern grand master had converted to Protestantism. Technically, East Prussia was not part of the Holy Roman Empire but instead enjoyed an autonomy under the nominal suzerainty of the king of Poland. Frederick William broke free of this subordination and set himself up as a sovereign duke. In 1701, his son Frederick gained the right from the

Holy Roman Emperor to rule his former Polish territories as a king. From this time on, the Hohenzollerns preferred to be known as kings of Prussia rather than electors of Brandenburg.

THE RISE OF RUSSIA

One of the ablest rulers of the seventeenth century was Peter the Great of Russia, a member of the Romanov family that had come to power in 1613. Succeeding to the throne as a child, Peter seized full authority in 1689 when he was seventeen. A physical giant with a capacity for cruelty, Peter had tremendous energy and endurance as well as enormous curiosity. Determined to free Russia from its ancient ways, Peter traveled to Western Europe to learn modern techniques and to find technicians to bring home with him. While he was abroad, he also contrived a conspiracy with the Danes, Saxons, and Poles against the Swedes, who blocked him from access to the Baltic Sea. Before he could act, Peter was forced by a revolt in 1698 to return to Russia. In the meantime, the eighteen-year-old king of Sweden, Charles XII, after learning of the plot against him, decided to break up the alliance by taking the offensive. He quickly moved his army to Denmark, forcing the Danes to desert their alliance with Russia. He then transferred his forces to the Gulf of Finland, where he defeated the Russian army at Narva. Though Charles had caught his enemies off guard, they persisted in their opposition to Swedish dominance. The result was the Great Northern War, which lasted until 1721. Though Charles was a military genius, his country had neither the resources nor the determination to continue the fight over a long period of time. Peace came after Charles was slain, probably by an assassin, in Norway. Sweden was expelled from its holdings on the European mainland and withdrew from all of its recently conquered territories except Finland.

Peter had not waited for the end of the war to get on with his other plans, which included the building of a seaport on the Baltic. Designed by Western architects and built at an exhorbitant cost in money and life, St. Petersburg — now Leningrad — came to symbolize tsarism, the moody despotism that was a marriage of Eastern practices and ceremonies with Western devices such as the standing army. To force his subjects to become more Westernized, Peter freed women from their seclusion, required his male subjects to cut their beards, and made French the language of polite conversation.

MERCANTILISM

The new rationalism that characterized seventeenth-century monarchies was also directed to economic affairs. The impetus came from attempts to imitate the economic dominance of Spain that was based on the endless flow of treasure from American mines. Other powers at first attempted to encroach on the Spanish monopoly of the American precious metals as well as to find their own supplies, and when these efforts failed, monarchs tried to find other means of building up a surplus treasury with which they could hire an army and thereby dominate Europe. The result was the evolution of the theory of mercantilism, which was based on a favorable balance of trade, or a surplus of exports over imports. The easiest way for a country to achieve a favorable balance of trade was to monopolize one or more critical products and then to exchange these for gold. Holland's effective control over the East Indies spice trade, for example, enabled the Dutch to profit at the expense of everybody who wanted cloves or cinnamon. Other nations attempted to gain monopolies over sugar, tobacco, furs, naval stores, dye stuffs, fish, tea, and Negro slaves. Such efforts required large-scale concessions to business groups, which had to be given the privilege of exploiting domestic consumers in the hopes that such rapacity could be extended to include foreign consumers as well. Wages to workingmen had to be kept at a near-starvation level so that the export price would always be low and there would be no wide-scale demand for imported products. Governments even went so far as to provide private companies with troops and ships, as well as diplomats, to help them get a stranglehold on a product that all potential buyers would have to buy from the protected company at a high price. One result was the continuing expansion of Europeans into all areas of the world.

Nations also sought to encourage and subsidize every kind of industry deemed crucial in wartime, for example, gunpowder production and shipbuilding, and to discourage by high duties the importation of whatever they thought they could do without.

No one put the mercantilistic ideas into practice more consistently than Jean-Baptiste Colbert, Louis XIV's comptroller of finances, whose twenty-year tenure of office served mainly to produce the abundant revenue the king took such pleasure in spending. Since Louis never quite understood the importance of what his minister was trying to do, Colbert was not able to carry through his plans to modernize the government, although he did promote the welfare of the business classes by building roads, improving harbor facilities, and expanding French influence overseas. Perhaps it is just as well that he died in 1683 with his work unfinished, since to effectuate mercantilism, he would have had to implement a mass of rules and standards, price-fixing, wage limitation, and a huge bureaucracy with vast potential for abuse. Moreover, if the system had been diligently enough pursued to produce the accumulation of large reserves of gold and silver, the result probably would have been as disastrous as it was in Spain, where the large treasury caused inflation and a dampening of business enterprise. In fact, to the extent that Colbert's schemes were successful, they in the long run tended to weaken the French economy by making it so rigid and inflexible that it was unable to adjust to new conditions or to adopt more advanced techniques.

In the seventeenth century, however, mercantilistic notions were rarely challenged, and nobody really examined them closely. They were standard doctrine for all rulers with any desires of bettering economic conditions. They were also in part responsible for the wars between England and Holland, with each nation trying to obtain more colonies and monopolies at the expense of the other. Mercantilism, too, produced the Acts of Trade and Navigation, which were instrumental in bringing about the American Revolution. Nevertheless, the British never incorporated mercantilism into their domestic economy to the extent the French did. In spite of a firm belief on the part of the government in the desirability of regulation and what it implied, Englishmen were free to become colonists with little help or hindrance from the king or his ministers. On the other hand, in France, the government carefully selected its colonists, assisted them in their voyages, and then tried to direct them in every way. While British settlers had to do their own fighting and pay taxes to support their government, they also enjoyed much more liberty of belief and conduct. Even in Great Britain itself, the average citizen could hire and fire, buy and sell, and change from one business to another with comparative freedom, all of which made the full-scale application of the mercantilist theory impossible. In the long run, the comparatively unmanaged British economy proved better able to exploit the numerous technological advances that led to the modern industrial state.

THE AGE OF BAROQUE

The new commercial, industrial, and political dominance of northern Europe did not immediately give the region artistic or intellectual leadership. Italy, for example, continued to be the home of vast numbers of architects, scientists, sculptors, inventors, and explorers, but as Catholicism went on the defensive, the pope was no longer able to support art and literature on the scale of his predecessors. In addition, much of the rest of the peninsula was becoming impoverished by war and lack of trade. Spain suffered even more, and Germany had been the victim of the devastation brought by the Thirty Years' War. Increasingly, the artist turned to Paris, Vienna, or London for support.

The wars, turmoil, and unrest inevitably led to a dissatisfaction with the ideas of classical simplicity that had dominated the art of the first part of the sixteenth century. Artists now attempted to convey suffering, emotion, sensuality, and spirit, often in an allegorical setting. Nowhere is the baroque more evident than in Rome, where Giovanni Bernini established the basic principles of the style and left one of its most characteristic monuments, the plaza and colonnade of St. Peter's. His use of the curved line in place of the classical straight line was widely imitated, especially in Catholic Europe. Buildings began to show curved exterior walls, twisted columns, massive facades, and ornate and sometimes grotesque statues. Bernini's altarpiece, the *Ecstasy of St. Theresa*, was also the forerunner of a new type of statuary.

It has been argued that the baroque grew out of an effort on the part of the Italians to find ecstasy and rapture in the face of the worsening economic conditions of the time and the various wars that had swept the peninsula. The painter Michelangelo Merisi da Caravaggio, perhaps because he lacked classical training in his craft, successfully managed to establish the new style before his death in 1610. His emotional subject matter as well as his color caught the mood of his fellow-Italians and was widely imitated. The trend was quickly taken up in Spain through the efforts of Jose Ribera, a student of Caravaggio, who also spread the new style in Naples. More important for Spanish painting were Francisco de Zurbaran, Diego Velasquez, and Bartolomé Murillo of Seville. Velasquez enjoyed the greatest reputation by far because of his good fortune in enjoying royal favor, although in his portraits of important persons he was not always able to give his imagination the free play so apparent in his street scenes. Murillo, who was particularly influenced by the baroque, is noted for his religious themes which emphasize a tender and sensuous piety and also for his portrayal of urchins.

Flanders, which remained Spanish until the eighteenth century, saw a revival of its earlier artistic prominence in the astonishing versatility of Peter Paul Rubens, who organized and operated until his death in 1640 an "art factory" that literally turned out hundreds of masterpieces. His chief rival in influence was Anthony Van Dyck, a younger colleague who became court painter in England and acquired fame particularly as a master of portraits.

In Holland, an impressive number of painters flourished in the seventeenth century despite the lack of royal patronage and a Dutch hostility to the baroque of the Catholic South. The United Provinces were at the height of their power and prosperity during this period, so that artists were usually able to find commissions and purchasers for their works, although the Dutch mercantile class never fully appreciated the genuine creative artists. Many of the best artists such as Jan Vermeer, Meindert Hobbema, and Jacob van Ruisdael went generally unrecognized. Franz Hals enjoyed greater fortune, lived past eighty-five, and eventually earned a pension from the town of Haarlem, but due to his

Rembrandt van Rijn
(1606–1669), self portrait.
(The Metropolitan
Museum of Art, Bequest
of Benjamin Altman,
1913)

large family and improvident habits, he too was often in financial
difficulties.

Rembrandt van Rijn, one of the great masters of all time, enjoyed a
period of genuine affluence, but the last two decades of his life were
marked by bitterness and tragedy. Rembrandt was severely criticized
by his patrons for his painting the *Night Watch* because he had placed
some figures in a shadow and had emphasized others in order to show
a particular effect of light. In effect, the *nouveaux riches* of Rembrandt's
time knew what they liked and allowed Holland's greatest painter to
labor without recognition and die in obscurity.

During the last third of the century, the court of Louis XIV provided
a degree of recognition for artists not elsewhere equalled, but the day
for painters in France was still in the future. Perhaps Louis demanded
too much conformity for the really good artists to thrive, for the French
painting of the period was characterized by mediocrity. In architecture,
the situation was quite different. The king was an imaginative builder,
as the Louvre colonnade in Paris and the palace at Versailles testify.
Colbert, whom Louis appointed to supervise the building Versailles,
successfully brought baroque emotionalism under control to produce a
monument to the sun king that has since been widely imitated. Its
exterior is classical and its gardens geometrical, only the interior of
Versailles is truly baroque. Its scale is so massive, however, that it

more than met the demands of the baroque age. Unfortunately, Versailles was not designed either for comfort or utility but to impress with its magnificence and to gather all the troublesome nobility together away from their estates. At Versailles, they would at least be under the watchful eye of the king.

MUSIC

With the perfection of stringed instruments, especially the violin at Cremona in Italy by the Amati, Stradivari, and Guarneri families, music changed radically during the seventeenth century. The Italian Arcangelo Corelli began to compose concertos and sonatas, considerably extending the repetoire of contemporary musicians. Italian music, like Italian art, moved northward, first the instruments and then the new musical forms. The Austrian Hapsburgs especially patronized the opera in their court at Vienna, which soon supplanted Venice as the leading operatic center of Europe. Other German rulers followed suit, and the result was a German tradition that together with the Italian still dominates opera today. The most significant German composer of the time was Heinrich Schütz, who died in 1672. Inevitably, the court of Louis XIV also patronized musicians, and its lasting contribution to the music of today was the development of ballet. The composer Jean Lully, by birth, an Italian, acquired a monopoly at the French court to produce operas, and his combination of opera with ballet quickly won him favor as well as a large fortune.

LITERATURE

The reign of Louis XIV, in large part because of royal patronage, is usually regarded as the golden age of French literature. Many of the great writers, however, owed little to the king, notably the outstanding poet of the period, Jean de La Fontaine, whose enormously popular and still read *Fables in Verse*, consist of sophisticated satires with animals as characters. Louis was usually portrayed as the lion, and it is by no means clear whether Louis particularly relished this satire of himself. Blaise Pascal, a scientist and mathematician, owed even less to royal patronage. He achieved his greatest influence with his *Provincial Letters*, written in defense of Jansenism, a movement opposed by the king and advocated by a group of French Catholic clergy who were disenchanted with the Jesuits and much under the influence of St. Augustine. Pascal believed that human reason could only partially provide knowledge and understanding, and his *Pensées*, published posthumously in 1670, is a classic defense of the importance of faith in the service of man's need to know and comprehend.

Much more dependent upon royal patronage was drama. With his affinity for the spectacular, the king found the stage more to his taste. Moreover, at Louis' accession, the dramatist Pierre Corneille was in his prime. Corneille's peculiar work *The Cid*, in which half a lifetime of action takes place in twenty-four hours, enjoyed great popular favor and was followed by several tragedies and at least one good comedy. Corneille's insistence that a play should have a unity of action — that is, a logical connection between successive incidents — a unity of time — usually the action should take place within a day and a night — and a unity of place or location served for a long period to inhibit French drama. The younger Jean Racine utterly eclipsed Corneille in later years, greatly to the annoyance of the latter, with a series of tragedies on classical themes — *Andromaque*, *Phèdre*, *Berenice*, and many others. Racine, however, decided when he was about forty to abandon the theater, accepted a royal sinecure, and started raising a family. During the same period, the comic theater had begun to flourish with the developing talents of Jean Baptiste Poquelin, better known as Molière, an actor as well as a playwright, whose social comedies such as *Tartuffe*, *Le Bourgeois Gentilhomme*, and *Le Misanthrope* have long enjoyed popularity.

During the period of Cromwell's rule in England, all theaters were closed, and, though they reopened after 1660, the new playwrights were not up to their predecessors. English talent seemed instead to turn to other forms of literature. The leading literary figure of the first part of the century was John Donne, a dean of St. Paul's Cathedral in London and the most outstanding of a group of metaphysical poets who attempted to examine and probe the experiences that give rise to emotions. By the middle of the century, even Donne was in disfavor with the Puritans and his place was filled by the Puritan John Milton. Supremely gifted and a figure around whom has centered interminable controversy, Milton served as apologist for the regicides of 1649 and as defender of the free press in the *Areopagitica*, a prose work which attacked his own partisans who sought to license the printing of books. His arguments have ever since proved unanswerable. Milton's masterpiece is *Paradise Lost*, which he wrote after the Restoration in order to explain why the Puritans had failed. In the process, Milton, like Dante before him, synthesized the beliefs of his time. Even though most of his readers today are not adherents of his strict variety of Protestantism, the work, in which Milton attempts to justify God's ways to man, remains a classic.

Both Milton and Pascal were transitional figures who symbolized a changing European outlook. Both represent the devoted religious advocate, but at the same time they presage later writers, Pascal in his concern for the freedom of conscience and Milton in his fight against literary censorship. The poet of the next generation, if one may use

John Dryden as an illustration, was little concerned about the word of God, and he changed his religion as convenience and the preference of his patrons seemed to dictate. Dryden wrote no plays of genuine significance, but they earned him popularity; he also lent his very considerable talents to the cause of political controversy. It is readily apparent from Dryden and others that Europeans no longer valued much that had previously been so vital to them. In England, for example, the Restoration of Charles II released the pent-up emotions of a people who had been held in check for too long, and the result was an age of debauchery. Even the amorous Samuel Pepys, whose diary records all kinds of intrigues and escapades, was appalled by the excesses of his contemporaries.

If in the minds of some people Europeans lost something by turning their backs on the mystical and the ineffable, contemporaries showed slight remorse, and the trend of opinion has since been that the gains more than outweighed the losses. Preoccupation with death and the afterworld fell away as men became interested in such practical matters as how to form a good government, educate a child, keep a business profitable, or increase the income from an estate. A Royal Society was formed in England to advance the study of natural science, and it was soon copied by the *Académie des Sciences* at Paris. Though a Louis XIV had dominated much of the seventeenth century, men of the eighteenth century spent most of their time trying to find ways to avoid such rulers in the future and to recover from the effects of Louis' excesses or those of his imitators. Europe did not change without a struggle, as is evidenced, perhaps, by the brief revival of witchcraft persecution in New England and elsewhere during this period. Yet Europeans felt they were finally beginning to understand themselves, and a new age of enlightenment seemed on the horizon.

16

Challenges
to the Old Regime

Historians have often used the term "old regime" (*ancien régime*) to describe governments of the type that ruled in eighteenth-century France. Such governments were headed by absolute monarchs and were designed mainly to satisfy the titled and privileged classes. Other groups were more or less ignored, and this lack of attention was particularly resented by the well-educated and propertied middle classes, who paid most of the taxes but were neither consulted nor permitted to hold important administrative office.

Under favorable circumstances, the absolute monarchs were able to satisfy most of their countrymen. They maintained law and order, extended and improved communication and transportation, and patronized, artists, musicians, and writers. Moreover, the upper classes, who were the advisers and companions of the monarchs, were on the whole informed, well mannered, and more likely to act as gentlemen than most of their predecessors. Though much survived of earlier barbaric practices, such as the Inquisition in Spain and public execution of criminals everywhere, soldiers were less liable to pillage, magistrates less prone to use torture, and religious dissenters less likely to be persecuted than anyone of a century earlier would have thought possible.

In fact, it was the very success of the absolute monarchs that subjected the *old regime* to increasing criticism. Many people, seemingly for the first time, began to realize the possibilities inherent in a government purposefully designed to serve the public welfare instead of accidentally doing so when the needs of the privileged classes coincided with those of the rest of society. Unfortunately, absolute monarchy was also highly dependent for its success upon the ability of the monarch. Though eighteenth-century monarchs on the whole were above average, few of them had the extraordinary ability or the tremendous capacity for hard work necessary to make the system operate most effectively. Nowhere was this more true than in France, where the eighteenth-century rulers had continually to measure up to the standards of Louis XIV. For Louis XV, who ruled from 1715 to 1774, the task was futile. Thus, in spite of the fact that the French had a higher standard of living than other peoples in Europe or that the upper classes were often genuinely concerned about the common people, the first mass assault upon the old regime came in France.

THE ENLIGHTENMENT

No group was more responsible for crystallizing the discontent of the people with the absolute monarchs than a group of intellectuals, usually called the *philosophes*, who attempted to formulate new political and social views on the basis of the discoveries and theories of science. This whole movement to popularize the new learning as the key to social and political change is known as the Enlightenment, and though it spread through Europe, it was centered in France.

Unlike earlier intellectuals, the *philosophes* were not dependent upon the patronage of a church or a king for their livelihood. Instead, they were supported by a reading public, including a large number of aristocratic women who vied with one another in inviting them to their drawing rooms, or *salons*, to engage in pleasant conversation with other guests. Since Versailles had become the real center of government in France, those noblemen who remained in Paris, as well as their wives and mistresses, had considerable leisure to promote such gatherings, which soon became a sign of distinction.

The *philosophes* believed that societies operate in accordance with natural laws as binding as the mathematical laws that govern the universe. Without intending to be revolutionary, the *philosophes* were soon at odds with many established institutions which seemed to them to have no real reason for existing and which they felt were contrary to natural law. Though the French authorities periodically censored the work of critics of the government, they did it so haphazardly and so capriciously that their action only gave added emphasis to the plea of the *philosophes* for intellectual freedom and the removal of censorship.

Educational institutions were among the first objects of criticism by the *philosophes*, who believed that only by taking control of the schools away from the Church and giving it to the state could they reorient education toward science, the practical arts, and citizenship. Their key words were "reason" and "natural," which they interpreted to mean that man, unmolested by arbitrary authority and dependent upon his own reason and observation, could find the laws that govern the universe and then act accordingly to make a better world. One of the harshest critics of the old regime in France was Baron de Montesquieu, whose *The Spirit of the Laws* was published in 1748. Montesquieu, through his study of English government, came to believe that natural law could best operate through a system of checks and balances, a principle that came to be adopted by the framers of the American Constitution. Probably the most influential writer and critic of the period was François Arouet, better known as Voltaire, who believed that the first step in reforming France was to curb the powers of the nobility. Though Voltaire was hostile to revolution and actually fearful of true democracy, he was not particularly welcome in France. As a result, he spent most of his life in England, Switzerland, or close enough to the French frontier to escape on short notice. Voltaire was intolerant only of intolerance, inhumanity, and organized religion, which he held to be responsible for the ignorance, superstition, servility, and fanaticism of the masses. Of the nearly ninety volumes comprising his complete works, many are still reprinted, especially his *Candide*, a parody of the idea that this is the best of all possible worlds.

Since the *philosophes* assumed that once man knew truth he would live in greater virtue and happiness, the gathering of knowledge became an important task. The crowning achievement of this aspect of the Enlightenment was the twenty-eight volume *Encylopédie*, edited by Denis Diderot, to which most of the French intellectuals contributed. While the political and religious articles were made carefully orthodox in order to pass the censor, the other articles — which the censors did not read — carried out a full-fledged assault on existing institutions and values, emphasizing the contradictions of the old regime. The *Encylopédie* reinforced the criticisms being aired in the *salons*, in the newly developing Masonic lodges, which were strongholds of "enlightened" attitudes, in the various scientific societies, and in the writings of popular figures such as Voltaire.

Though reformers, the *philosophes* were still more oriented toward the middle and upper classes than toward the lower. Some writers like Jean-Jacques Rousseau of Geneva, however, felt that the passions of the masses might be harnessed to useful ends. The self-educated Rousseau thought that before progress could take place a moral revolution was necessary. Such a revolution could only occur, he believed, when government itself had been transformed into an expression of popular will. As a result, some people regarded Rousseau's *Social Contract* as a call for popular revolution against monarchial and aristocratic government. In actuality, Rousseau believed that true democracy was impossible for such a large state as France, and, instead, he favored democratic assemblies as a check on the king. Moreover, he considered revolutionary cures worse than the institutions they set out to correct. In his *Confessions*, he revealed himself as few men have ever done. Tortured as he was by his own shortcomings, he still believed that man could be emancipated from his passions and eventually achieve a moral revolution. Unfortunately, this particular aspect of his teachings was used to justify all kinds of excesses. The romantic libertine Jacques Cassanova, for example, demonstrated his emancipation by seeing how many women he could seduce, while the Marquis de Sade rationalized his cruelty by claiming that since virtue was inaction, the strong man must be wholeheartedly evil.

The influence of the *philosophes* on the actual events that led up to the French Revolution is a matter of considerable debate, in part because historians are not in agreement concerning how much influence intellectual criticism has upon social upheavals. The only important *philosophe* who actually lived to see the beginning of the Revolution was the Marquis de Condorçet, who helped write the French Constitution of 1792. As the Revolution became more radical, he became suspect and was eventually eliminated. It was while hiding from the Revolutionary authorities in 1794 that he wrote his famous *Sketch of the Intellectual Progress of Mankind*. In spite of his personal difficulties, Condorçet prophesied that technology and the spread of democratic revolution would eventually lead to the perfectability of man and the equality of individuals.

THE ENLIGHTENED DESPOTS

The *philosophes* often received support and encouragement not only from the middle class and established aristocracy but also from the monarchs themselves. Without seriously analyzing what the *philosophes* were saying, many rulers imagined that they modeled their conduct and their government on such teachers. Thus they became "enlightened despots" instead of absolute monarchs, although the student of history might find it difficult to distinguish one type of ruler from the other. In general, the enlightened despots viewed themselves as pragmatic rulers and their states as secular entities rather than divinely established ones. They tried to insist that all their subjects be governed by the same law and the same officials and that they pay their share of the taxes, although they never went so far as to admit that their people could govern themselves. Nevertheless, by emphasizing that all people had legal personalities subject directly to the control of the state, the enlightened despots undoubtedly benefited the lower classes. By attempting to rationalize administration and consolidate territories, they established a growing uniformity within larger and larger areas, which increased commerce and reduced anarchy. By emphasizing state control over censorship, education, welfare, and family affairs, they eliminated many of the abuses that had crept into these areas. The so-called enlightened rulers also attempted to give considerable attention to humanitarian concerns and to promote economic well-being, but their difficulty was that all of their programs were put into practice without changing the aristocratic base of government.

One of the more successful of the enlightened despots was Frederick the Great, an extremely talented monarch and a fervent admirer of French culture, who ruled Prussia from 1740 until 1786. Frederick and Voltaire were close friends, and the two men ran a sort of mutual admiration society, which assured Frederick of a good reception among the *philosophes*. Frederick, however, also earned Voltaire's support by carrying out "enlightened" reforms, such as emancipating the peasants on his own domains, establishing freedom of the press, and abolishing torture. None of Frederick's reforms, however, altered the distribution of wealth, power, or privilege. The tax burdens were still heaviest upon the peasants and the bourgeoisie, while the landed aristocracy was largely exempt. Since such a tax policy left little money for investment in private hands, Frederick turned to government capitalism and bureaucratic paternalism as an alternative, actions that served to enhance his image as an enlightened despot even though they curtailed individual enterprise. All of Frederick's reforms were dependent upon the support of the nobility, and when the nobility felt threatened, as it did in the last part of the eighteenth century, all efforts at reform ceased. From an enlightened despotism, Prussia changed into a bulwark of traditional social order, and, following the pattern of France, became ripe for revolution itself.

Enlightened rule was established in the Hapsburg territories by Joseph II (1765–1790), the son of Maria Theresa, who first co-ruled with his mother and then in his own right. Like Frederick, Joseph managed to carry through some of the reforms advocated by the *philosophes*, including the adoption of uniform civil and penal laws in his territories and elimination of the Catholic Church monopoly over education. Church lands were taxed and the number of monasteries and bishoprics reduced. Joseph even went so far as to extend toleration to private worship, a radical revision of earlier Hapsburg policy toward Protestantism. Most of these reforms were possible because Joseph had the support of his noble advisers and administrators; when he tried to curtail noble power by freeing the serfs, he ran into solid opposition and had to retreat. As in Prussia, the nobles soon became unwilling to tolerate any further interference with their privileges. By the end of his reign, opposition to Joseph had grown so powerful that his brother and successor Leopold II was forced to cancel many of his predecessor's reforms. In the end, only Joseph's administrative reorganization, legal codification, emancipation of peasants on the royal domains, and his stimulus of medical and scientific research remained as a testimony to what he tried to accomplish. Further reform could come only by challenging the aristocratic base of Hapsburg rule.

The concepts of the Enlightenment were brought to Russia by Catherine the Great. Born into an obscure German noble family, Catherine became a major European figure through her marriage to Peter III, tsar of Russia. When Peter was murdered in 1762, Catherine became empress of Russia through the support of various nobles, who felt they could control her. Though Catherine was able to secularize much of the land of the Church and to establish hospitals, medical facilities, and other humanitarian projects with the income from these lands, she was ineffective in her attempt to reform legal procedure in Russia. She denounced serfdom, but instead of limiting it, she actually increased it by turning over confiscated Church lands — and the tenants on them — to the control of private lords. Aristocratic control over peasants was also extended into newly acquired territories. Catherine, in fact, is a good example of an enlightened but limited despot, since under her, though local government was reorganized, the power of the aristocrats was increased by exempting them from military service, personal taxation, and corporal punishment, at the same time confirming them in their right to buy and sell land freely, to trade, and to operate mines and factories. Reform was limited to what the aristocratic advisers and administrators regarded as best for themselves and for their country. As a result, serfdom reached its height under a monarch who regarded herself as an enlightened ruler. With all avenues of political expression blocked off, the only reaction of the masses to the worsening conditions was resignation or rebellion. There was a massive two-year rebellion (1773–1775), which only led to ever more brutal suppression. The peasants, resigned to their hopelessness, turned to religious and mystical solutions to their problems. The aristocrats, for their part, increasingly abandoned their homes in the vast countryside for life in St. Petersburg or Moscow, where they adopted Western ideas of the Enlightenment yet remained harshly oppressive on their own estates.

THE BRITISH ALTERNATIVE
TO THE OLD REGIME

When the *philosophes* directed their criticism at the absolute monarch, they often had English government in mind as the model for the type they wanted to establish in France and elsewhere. The situation in England differed markedly from the continental one in many ways.

For one thing, the Anglican Church was neither outstandingly rich nor in sole command of religious doctrine. In addition, the English nobility, though powerful, lacked the dominant position of their peers on the Continent, while the line between the lower nobility and the upper bourgeoisie was much more fluid. Moreover, the Puritan revolt of the seventeenth century had terminated any trend toward absolute monarchy. Thus, once the old-type absolute monarch was overthrown with the French Revolution, many of the English innovations in government came to be widely copied, in part because England represented the most successful alternative system of administration that was near at hand.

With the execution of Charles I in 1649, the British had been forced to improvise a new type of government. The Restoration had not ended the experimentation, since the subsequent kings lacked much of the power of the earlier ones. In addition, William III, who ruled from 1689 to 1702, and the first of the two Georges (1714–1760) were foreigners, while Anne, who had succeeded William, demonstrated little ability as a ruler. The British, therefore, had more than a century in which to develop administrative machinery to overcome the incompetence exhibited by the monarchs. The result was the evolution of a board of ministers, known as the cabinet, originally the cabinet council. The term "cabinet" had originally been derived from a vulgar reference to the supposed meeting place of the group, the private royal chamber that served as the equivalent of the modern bathroom.

During its formative stages, the cabinet was blamed for secretive and sinister schemes supposedly concocted against the public interest. Cabinet government, however, had no real meaning apart from parliament. Absolute monarchs had destroyed parliamentary institutions on the Continent, but the British parliament had grown and developed because the kings found it a useful institution to keep alive. After the Glorious Revolution of 1688, parliament was much too powerful for it to be abandoned. Though the English kings of the eighteenth century were not particularly strong rulers, both the exigencies of warfare and the overseas expansion that characterized the period demanded an efficient centralized government. Through history legislative bodies have not proved to be good administrative vehicles, since under such a system power is too widely diffused. It was for this reason that the cabinet system developed. At first, the cabinet was simply a committee of the king's privy council, but it soon superseded the council in function. The cabinet usually included members of the nobility and representatives of the people — the House of Commons — but never Churchmen, because Anglican clergy were too dependent upon the king for their positions to be acceptable to their colleagues in parliament. It was true that the king appointed and could remove cabinet members, but on the other hand, cabinet members did not have hereditary rights to their posts and they could be impeached, exiled, or imprisoned by order of parliament. To lessen suspicion between their councilors and parliament, the English monarchs also increasingly chose their cabinet from the legislative body, which meant that the ministers spent a good part of their energies as royal managers in parliament, defending the king's programs and keeping track of voting blocs and factions. Ultimately, it fell on one of these ministers to supervise the whole operation, becoming, in fact, the prime minister. This man became politically indispensable to the king because of his ability to secure the votes necessary for running the government. He also had to be acceptable to parliament, which could always refuse him support and thereby strip him of all his power.

Sir Robert Walpole, who headed the king's administration between 1721 and 1742, first formed the cabinet into a distinct, and effective institution of government. He so managed affairs that his colleagues cleared all their official contacts with the crown through him. This task was not particularly difficult for Walpole to carry out, however, since George I spoke no English and preferred to spend the bulk of his time on the Continent in his other kingdom of Hanover. Through his astute management of pensions, contracts, positions, and other types of patronage, combined with his able and skillful handling of the country's finances — as well as his proper deference to the crown prince, the future George II — Walpole clung to office long enough to demonstrate the potential of cabinet-type government. When he finally lost his command of votes in the House of Commons, Walpole resigned. One of his strongest opponents was William Pitt, who, in spite of royal hostility, became an influential minister for several years, Finally, the opposition of the new king, George III, so undermined his position that he resigned. Sensitive to the deterioration of royal authority, George III was determined to reassert his prerogatives and manage parliament himself. His attempts foundered with the American Revolution and finally sank with his growing insanity. Even this monarch, however, went through the motions of choosing a nominal first minister, and in 1783, he selected William Pitt, the son of the first Pitt. The younger Pitt perfected the cabinet system to the point where it became the accepted method of organizing and operating the English constitutional monarchy. Cabinet government had two main virtues: it was not particularly dependent upon the ability of the king and it eliminated the strife that had traditionally characterized relations between the executive and legislative branches of government. The cabinet system made possible a continuity of policy from reign to reign as vested interests developed to support established actions, and it provided for widened participation in national affairs by the business and professional classes.

BRITISH INNOVATIONS IN AGRICULTURE,
BUSINESS, AND ECONOMICS

Eighteenth-century England was innovative in other areas ranging from agriculture to business. Outside of England, European agriculture at the beginning of the century was not much different from what it had been for a thousand years. Crops were limited and methods were primitive, but the peasant followed the practices of previous generations. A man worked or took the day off according to village custom and not as he himself chose. He grew wheat when others grew wheat, and if others kept geese, so did he. Risks were taken collectively and not individually, making innovation difficult. If wheat ceased to be profitable, it was grown anyway, simply because all crops had been integrated into a pattern that no individual could interrupt. A good portion of everyone's livelihood depended upon common rights such as pasturage. Fences were lacking, and while the peasant might have his own vegetable garden, it was impossible for him to grow melons on a large scale on the common lands unless the whole village agreed. Such a change would have forced a reorientation of the whole cycle, which only a few families might have desired.

In England, however, agriculture had changed drastically by the beginning of the eighteenth century. Through the enclosure system, common land had over a period of several generations been fenced in and had changed into private holdings. With this system, a landlord could more easily introduce new crops, apply new agricultural techniques, and sell his surpluses for profit. Unfortunately, however, enclosure caused widespread dislocation of the peasant population as thousands of agricultural laborers and tenant farmers, denied access to the common land, were pushed off their plots and forced to hunt for new ways of earning a living. Though this experience was a traumatic one for the people concerned, the long-term result of the dislocation was the opening up of new avenues of opportunity based upon skills and experience and not on lands, family, or political connections.

The exodus of the peasants to the cities is, perhaps, one major reason why England changed so radically in the eighteenth century, but several other factors were also important. First, the English government was much more strongly influenced by the merchant classes than most other European governments, and this leaning led to the emergence of London as one of the great seaports of the world and to the development of the Bank of England. Second, since England had never had the monopolies or extensive regulation that mercantilism implied, English guilds were also much weaker than those on the Continent. Though regulation can be used to prevent the poor and the weak from being crushed by the strong and ruthless, continental monopolies did not consider this their task, and regulation in fact has usually been a way to preserve the privileged against the underprivileged. England, in effect, had a much more competitive economy than any of its continental rivals.

Competition was further increased by an eighteenth-century rebellion against any tendencies toward the managed economy that remained from the day of the mercantilist theory. This rebellion had started in France with François Quesnay and a group of thinkers known as the physiocrats, who believed that government regulation inhibited the operation of a natural law of competition. According to this theory, if restrictions were removed, there would be an increase in efficiency, particularly in agriculture, which in turn would lead to greater national well-being. The Scottish philosopher-economist Adam Smith developed these ideas further and more realistically in his famous *An Inquiry into the Nature and Causes of the Wealth of Nations* (1776). Smith believed that competition itself was a regulator that should be encouraged in place of trade restrictions, quotas, tariffs, bounties, and other devices that made up the economic management of his day. He was the prophet of laissez faire, which eventually came to be called free enterprise, and a theoretician who lent respectability and gave philosophical justification to developments already taking place in England. By the end of the eighteenth century, the British government itself was beginning to follow Smith's teachings.

These developments coincided with a series of technological and industrial innovations that were taking place in England. In part, these innovations came about as a deliberate effort to improve old procedures. Many of the innovators were products of the Scottish and dissenting Protestant schools which had been forced to develop because Oxford and Cambridge were restricted to Anglicans. These new schools reflected a strong middle class bias toward practical learning of an engineering, professional, or technical nature, and undoubtedly, this new emphasis on technical education contributed to the industrial development of England.

The major innovations were in the processing of textiles, in iron and coal production, and in the use of mechanical power. The manufacture of woolens had long been Britain's main industry and had become one of the most profitable in Western Europe. To obtain more raw wool, the English had turned over more and more of their land to sheep. Sheep, however, are particularly destructive of woodlands, and the result was that over a period of several generations England's timber resources were seriously affected. Timber was needed not only for building but for fuel and for making charcoal, an essential component in iron-making. To supplement its dwindling supply, England at first tried to secure timber through its overseas colonies, and though this source served for shipbuilding, it was much too costly as a means of obtaining ordinary fuel. Increasingly, therefore, the English turned to coal for heating houses, and inevitably, there were attempts to use coal in the smelting of iron. "Impurities" in the coal at first affected iron-making, but, through experimentation, Abraham Darby developed a method for treating coal to make coke, a process that eventually made possible a rapid expansion in iron and steel-making. As coal mining grew more extensive, a special technology was soon required to keep up with ever-increasing demands.

One special problem peculiar to English mining was drainage, since with the heavy rainfalls and high water level, mine tunnels and pits often became flooded. Shortly after 1700, Thomas Newcomen developed a simple steam engine that, though it was wasteful of fuel, could pump water out of the coal fields where fuel was cheap and plentiful. With little modification this engine was used until about 1770, when the work of James Watt increased the engine's efficiency, speed, and regularity of operation. Through the invention of the condenser, a system of valves, and the flywheel, the steam engine was not only made more efficient but could be adapted to new uses. Textile factories, for example, were freed from their dependence upon water power, and steam-run plants could be located in populous areas. Steam power was also applied to transportation. Richard Trevithick built the first effective steam locomotive in 1804, and the American Robert Fulton achieved the first commercial transportation success with his steamboat in 1807. With the opening of the Stockton and Darlington Railroad in 1825, steam power in England rapidly began to replace older forms of transportation.

Coinciding with developments in steam technology was the invention of all kinds of new machinery. Particularly important were developments in textile machinery, especially for the manufacture of cotton. Until the eighteenth century, cotton cloth had been imported from the East, principally India. As its influence in India grew, Britain began to import raw cotton to be made into cloth. Since there had been no established cotton industry in England, and since there were no communities dependent upon it with a population that might object to the introduction of new methods, the industry could locate where it pleased and escape from conventional regulations. By 1795, the English cotton industry was operating power looms and making other radical innovations in textile manufacture that many of the woolen mills also came to adopt. The pace of these developments increased when American cotton began to reach the English mills at the beginning of the nineteenth century. Steam-powered machinery, made possible by improved iron-making techniques, led to the further growth of the factory system, giving added stimulus to the urge to improve, invent, and pioneer.

This transformation from handicraft and small-scale industry to machine and factory production has long been called the Industrial Revolution. Western society was so changed by the new industrialization that by the beginning of the nineteenth century man found himself in a radically different world from that of any of his predecessors. The most notable effect of the Industrial Revolution was to make society more urban, but in so doing it gave the old regime its most serious challenge. The middle classes grew much more wealthy and influential, which soon enabled them to more than counter the privileged orders. Unfortunately, once the members of the middle class achieved power, they proceeded to ignore the needs of those less fortunate than themselves. The Industrial Revolution by breaking down the old village ways also undermined the foundations of earlier society. Masses of people were forced into the cities to fend for themselves instead of being dependent upon one another, and as their distress continued they became ripe for a continued revolution.

RELIGION AND PHILOSOPHY

The eighteenth century inevitably brought new challenges to existing beliefs. Many of the *philosophes* had sought to establish a natural religion based upon reason and free inquiry and opposed to supernaturalism. People who held these beliefs were called deists, and though they believed in God, they did not accept traditional Christianity. Many of the deists came to regard God as a sort of great clockwinder who did not intervene directly into the affairs of the world. Deism was founded upon the scientific and philosophical assumptions of Isaac Newton and John Locke, which by the end of the eighteenth century were being effectively undermined by a series of attacks. The final blow was struck by David Hume, the Scottish philosopher who ended up questioning all knowledge except individual sensory experience. Hume was particularly harsh on those thinkers who had made assumptions concerning the original state of nature. He pointed out that no man had ever observed this state and that any assumptions based on a hypothetical or theoretical concept would be impossible to prove. Turning to religion, he argued that man could not infer a divine mind as the cause of the world order — an assumption of the deists — since men did not know the objective principle of causation. Neither matter nor mind could explain orderliness, since the impressions by which man knows it are separate. Hume, instead, believed that man could know only what he learned through the study of psychology, history, anthropology, chemistry, and other disciplines.

Hume ended up a convinced skeptic, and many of the eighteenth-century figures who followed his lead became atheists. Taking a somewhat different part was Immanuel Kant, who, though rejecting Locke's doctrine of empiricism, believed that the human mind was a synthesizing agent that provided experience with the necessary categories of time, space, and causation. Kant agreed with Hume that sense could not penetrate beyond the shadow world of unreal phenomena, but he claimed that the moral and aesthetic self could. Faith for Kant then came to be based upon ethics; God he believed was the cosmic judge and policeman. Kant's reliance upon a sort of "religion of the heart" reflected his own religious background, and though he saw his system as giving a philosophical justification for believing in God, it was later adopted to justify some of the more absolutist states of the nineteenth and twentieth centuries.

Both Hume and Kant, regardless of their differences, ended up as challengers to existing religion. The questions raised by them and others caused established churches everywhere to come under attack. Though the majority of people remained within the established churches, some turned to deism, others to even more secular religions, and a large number to Pietism. Pietism taught that a moral sense within man would enable him to achieve salvation. Thus the Pietists emphasized an emotional faith of personal experience, contrition, and conversion, which was expected to transform the individual's private life. By teaching that salvation was mainly dependent upon an individual's religious and moral rebirth, the Pietists tended to undermine the emphasis of the traditional religions on sacraments and dogma. Although many Pietists were willing to render outward allegiance to the established religions, others refused to do so. Many of the German believers emigrated to the Americas, while many of those who remained behind formed lay associations for worship that were separate and distinct from the national churches. In England, where separatist movements were easier to establish than on the Continent, Pietism led to the formation of the Society of Friends, or the Quakers, a group which emphasized a private faith transcending the boundaries of creed, nationality, race, and social class. The Quakers rejected a professional clergy and insisted that their members devote their time, money, and energy to the relief of poverty, unemployment, alcoholism, slavery, and other ills. When they ran into opposition in England, large numbers of them emigrated to Pennsylvania, where they were better able to carry out their ideals. Also influenced by Pietism were the Methodists, a revivalistic English group originally organized within the Church of England by George Whitefield and the Wesley brothers, John and Charles. The Methodist belief in personal conversion led them to emphasize ethical conduct and social experience rather than a rigid doctrine and eventually caused them to be expelled from the Anglican Church.

In their emphasis on humanitarian reform, the Methodists, Quakers, and Pietists reflected a growing movement of the last part of the eighteenth century. The Italian Cesare de Beccaria, for example, urged humane treatment for convicts in his *Essay on Crimes and Punishments* (1764). The Frenchman Philippe Pinel and the Englishman William Tuke directed their efforts toward securing better treatment for the mentally ill. John Howard, another Englishman, argued for changes in prisons and hospitals. Some would-be reformers like Giovannia Battista Vico believed that an evolutionary cycle of intellectual and institutional development would eventually lead to a reform of all society. Increasingly, as the French Revolution progressed, reform became more difficult, since established governments suspected all reform as the first step toward revolution. Nowhere was this more true than in England. Joseph Priestly, one of the founders of English (and American) Unitarianism, found it convenient to leave England because of his support for the early stages of the French Revolution. Representative of the reaction that set in was Edmund Burke, who earlier in his career had championed both American independence and rights for Irishmen. His opposition to the events taking place in France is recorded in his *Reflections on the Revolution in France*, published in November 1790. Burke believed that the French experiment was dangerous, irreligious, and bound to fail because it had proceeded from abstract principles. Politics, he said, was an indissoluble partnership of succeeding generations in eternal society. The Rights of Man were a poor substitute for the experience of the landed ruling classes. Though Burke's *Reflections* temporarily opened up a great debate on the French Revolution in which various writers participated, including the American pamphleteer Thomas Paine, increasingly, fears of the French example made even discussion suspect. As a result, though the middle classes had risen to power either by revolution or co-option, the lot of the lower classes was not particularly improved during the eighteenth century.

ART AND LITERATURE

Indicative of the new status of the bourgeois was the changing literary scene. The writer no longer had to depend upon a patron but could now make a living by selling his books to a circle of readers. Literature was slowly being democratized. Since members of the newly affluent middle class wanted to know how to behave as ladies and gentlemen, there was a great vogue for essays dealing with manners, with courtesy, and with the art of letter writing. The new reading public also wanted to acquire culture, and since most of the bourgeois could not read the classics in the original, translations of them began to appear. It is apparent from his tastes that the eighteenth-century reader was in general a satisfied person, confident that he understood the laws governing the operation of the great world machine. Alexander Pope was one of the early spokesmen for this new age of the bourgeois. His translations of the *Iliad* and the *Odyssey* sold so well that he became rich. His *Essay on Man* gave a more or less deistic explanation of the world, while his *Moral Essays*, through a series of satirical portraits of his contemporaries, indicated how the well-educated man should act. Equally illustrious was Jonathan Swift, dean of St. Patrick's in Dublin, who is best remembered for his famous *Gulliver's Travels*. Swift had a strong moral sense, and his adventures of Gulliver are rather bitter satires on events taking place in his own day.

The most original literary form developed in the eighteenth century was the novel. While fiction had been written earlier, the novel represents a special kind of literature, wherein the motives of ordinary people are explored in depth in accordance with their character. The birthdate of the novel is usually given as 1740, the year Samuel Richardson published *Pamela or Virtue Rewarded*, but other writers had approached the novelistic form before this. Daniel Defoe's *Robinson Crusoe*, which appeared in 1719, is basically a novel, a form Defoe continued to develop in *Moll Flanders* and other works. Henry Fielding's *Tom Jones*, published in 1749, ranks among the great works in English literature. Fielding's work, unlike that of Richardson, still has appeal for the reader of today. Other important English novelists of the period were Laurence Stern and Tobias Smollet.

The dominant literary figure of the last part of the eighteenth century was Samuel Johnson. A poet as well as a novelist, Johnson is best remembered for his *Lives of the Poets* and his *Dictionary* of the English language. History, too, managed to become once again great literature in the hands of Edward Gibbon, whose *Decline and Fall of the Roman Empire* is still worth reading both for its style and its insights. The outstanding poet of the period was the Scottish writer Robert Burns, whose concern with nature marked the beginning of a new trend, which developed further in the Romanticism of the nineteenth century.

In France, most of the writers were caught up in the philosophical discussion of the Enlightenment, and most of *philosophes* were major literary figures. The one man who remained outside this tradition was André Chénier, a poet in an age of prose. Like so many of the French intellectuals of the time, Chénier suffered death by the guillotine. The most original and creative literature of the last part of the eighteenth century was not in French but in German. The founder of this new creative age of German literature was Gottfried Lessing. His play *Nathan the Wise* is still a clear plea for toleration of the Jews, and it along with his comedy *Minna von Barnheim* mark the beginning of modern German drama. Lessing was one of the founders of what is called the *Sturm and Drang* movement, an effort by German writers to free themselves from dependence upon French rules and to bring their literature closer to the people. The movement was encouraged by Johann Gottfried von Herder, whose chief interests were history and folklore. With subjectivity, combined with his willingness to deal with sentiment, Herder marked the start of the Romantic movement that swept all of Europe in the nineteenth century. Friedrich Schiller was also an important figure in German literature of this time. His plays were eloquent defenses of civil liberties, and his heroes were usually historical persons who championed or suffered in a great cause. The greatest of these dramas, *Wilhelm Tell*, depicted the attempts of the Swiss to escape from Austrian oppression.

The genius of German literature was Johann von Goethe. His most successful novel, *The Sorrows of the Young Werther* (1774), recounts the passions of a lovesick youth who finally killed himself with the pistol of his friend and rival. His masterpiece was the two-part poetic drama *Faust*, which he outlined in 1774 but did not completely finish until 1831. Though called a drama, it was designed more to be read than for the stage. Goethe, who spanned the eighteenth and nineteenth centuries, was undoubtedly the most influential European writer of the period, excelling in every form of literature, including the drama, the short tale, the novel, lyric poetry, and even autobiography.

Johann Wolfgang von Goethe (1749–1832), portrait by Stieler. (Ullstein Bilderdienst, Berlin)

ART

In art, the eighteenth century was the age of France, particularly the rococo style of Louis XV. More feminine and more delicate than baroque, the highly decorative rococo style is characterized by curved lines and gilded surfaces. Since every European court emulated the royal residence of the French king, French styles in art and design dominated the Continent. Typical of the period was Antoine Watteau, who painted members of the French court and various theater personalities. His successor François Boucher continued in the same fashion, but also produced mythologies, allegories, and pastorals in great quantity. France also had its painters of the Revolution, particularly Jacques Louis David, who had started out as court painter to Louis XVI. Thanks to David's canvases, many Revolutionary scenes remain vividly alive today.

The most effective painter of antiaristocratic views was the Englishman William Hogarth, the first great native-born English painter. A moral reformer interested in simple and homely virtues, Hogarth's paintings often seem to serve as illustrations for pulpit-pounding lectures. Still, they are important works of art. His series dealing with such themes as the *Harlot's Progress* or the *Rake's Progress* can be regarded as the beginnings of the English naturalistic school. England also had its aristocratic portrait painters, the most influential of whom was Sir Joshua Reynolds, who combined the French and Italian styles. The greatest of the academic portrait school was Thomas Gainsborough, whose mastery of technical details, handling of colors, and treatment of subjects set him above his contemporaries. His most famous painting, the *Blue Boy*, is symbolic of the aristocratic manner with which he portrayed his subjects.

MUSIC

The modern age of music began in the eighteenth century with Johann Sebastian Bach, a member of a family that produced many other composers and musicians. In many ways, Bach was an unlikely candidate for becoming the dominant musical figure of his time, since he spent most of his career in and near Leipzig, then sort of a parochial backwater of Europe. Moreover, the majority of his compositions were not printed during his lifetime, so that many were ultimately lost. Nonetheless, Bach managed to revolutionize music, giving it through his use of polyphony a richness and pliancy it had lacked before, though his full influence was not recognized until the nineteenth century. The complete edition of his extant works comprises some sixty volumes. Bach was primarily an organist, but his organ compositions form only a small part of his output and they are overshadowed by his compositions for keyboard string instruments, such as those that appear in *The Well-Tempered Clavichord*. Perhaps his greatest contribution was choral music, particularly his masses.

George Frederic Handel, born the same year as Bach (1685), was more in the center of the eighteenth-century musical world. After traveling around Europe, Handel settled in London, where he became a naturalized British subject. Like Bach, Handel was a practical musician, conscious of the need for popular approval. A prolific composer, he wrote some forty-six operas, which are now only rarely staged, although arias from some of them such as the *Largo* are often heard. Handel today is better remembered for his symphonies and oratorios, and in these forms he made a number of innovations.

Italian composers, so long dominant, were still important, particularly Antonio Vivaldi and Domenico Scarlatti, but they were overshadowed by their German contemporaries. In fact, it was in German-speaking Europe that the musical revolution started by Bach was carried to fruition by Joseph Haydn and Wolfgang Amadeus Mozart. Both Haydn and Mozart made Vienna the center of their activities, and the city soon became the musical capital of Europe. Many members of the Austrian nobility, as well as nobility elsewhere, maintained private orchestras, since music was still in the hands of rich patrons. The only mass audience was for church music. Conductors of these private orchestras were required to create the music necessary for the various performances, which meant that there was a continual demand for new works. It was the usual custom to commission works in batches of six, and while undoubtedly the growing demand for new works affected quality, the system did force the development of music by encouraging experimentation. In the process, a number of great works were composed. Haydn's patron was Prince Nicholas Esterhazy, who supported him in virtually any musical endeavor. In the process of writing some one hundred and four symphonies, of which fewer than a dozen are heard today with any regularity, Haydn set the form of the symphony orchestra, which has changed little since his time.

Mozart lacked the patronage of Haydn and instead spent most of his life free-lancing, which at best gave him an inadequate living. He was therefore continually forced to give lessons, write operas, or appear as soloist and composer at concerts managed by himself in order to gain money. He literally worked himself to death by the time he was 35. In spite of his comparatively short career, his musical genius extended to all fields of music. Of his twenty-two operas, several, such as *The Marriage of Figaro* and the *Magic Flute*, are still in the standard opera repertoire. He also wrote some twenty-seven string quartets, forty-nine symphonies, twenty-seven piano concertos, six violin concertos, and sixty-eight choral works.

THE EIGHTEENTH CENTURY

The eighteenth century represents one of the most innovative periods in Western civilization. During this period, almost every field of human endeavor underwent change either in content or in form. The arts were becoming less dependent upon patrons and more responsive to popular taste, or at least middle-class taste. There were widespread reforms, which, unfortunately, had primarily benefited the middle class, with only what was left over going to the masses. There was, however, a growing awareness of the individual in religion, in philosophy, and even in economics. Such was the setting of the French Revolution, which in the short run ended reform but in the long run forced radical changes, since it was impossible to reconstitute society as it had been before.

17

The French Revolution
and Its Aftermath

While many eighteenth-century European monarchs regarded themselves as "enlightened" rulers, the changes they effected did not seriously undermine the aristocratic base of government. In fact, the net effect of the teachings of the *philosophes* had been to raise the hopes of the middle class without, except in England, really giving them any major role in government. The resulting frustration on the part of this class was nowhere more in evidence than in France, the center of the Enlightenment. For some forty-nine years Louis XV ruled France without making any real effort to keep track of what was going on. The direction of the state fell into the hands of ministers or court favorites whose tenure of office was dependent not upon their ability but upon palace intrigues, the gossip of courtiers, or the good-will of the queen. In spite of the great riches of France, the government came close to bankruptcy. Further aggravating the financial instability of the government was the continued involvement of the French kings in various European wars which cost more than the country could afford.

Perhaps if the wars could have been confined to the Continent, France might not have been in such difficulty, but since the English always intervened on the opposite side, the wars became world-wide encounters. The Dutch held on to Indonesia, Portugal continued to hold a few outposts, and Spain managed to occupy a good part of the Western Hemisphere; but the struggle for control of the rest of the Far East, Africa, and the Americas was between France and England. The two powers went to war over West Indian sugar plantations, slave-shipping stations in Africa, "trading factories" in India, colonial expansion in North America, and trading rights in Spanish America. Anything that touched one of the colonial outposts affected Europe, and anything that involved Europe had ramifications all over the world.

Typical of such world-wide encounters were those set off by the war of the Austrian succession. The war began when Frederick the Great of Prussia in 1740 attempted to seize Silesia, even though he and all of the other European monarchs had agreed to recognize Maria Theresa as successor to Charles VI. No sooner had Charles died than Frederick occupied Silesia, part of Maria Theresa's Austrian inheritance. France eventually sided with Prussia in this war and England with Austria. The struggle between the two great powers was carried to North America, where it is known as King George's War. Though the war ended in 1748, the peace was only temporary.

France in the brief period of peace managed to link its territories in Louisiana and Canada by a string of forts and settlements along the north-south river systems of the eastern part of the North American continent. With the erection of Fort Duquesne (modern Pittsburgh) in 1754, the system of fortifications was complete. Shortly thereafter France became involved in a new European war that erupted when Maria Theresa attempted to regain Silesia. This time the wartime alliances were somewhat different, with Russia and France on the side of Austria and England backing Prussia. The result was the Seven Years' War, known in North America as the French and Indian War. In this conflict, the French were seriously handicapped by the lack of an adequate navy. In previous wars, when France had lost overseas territories to England, she had managed to recoup them by seizing territory on the Continent, which at the peace talks she then traded for her seized colonies. Any such plans were thwarted when Peter III, an admirer of Frederick, succeeded to the Russian throne in 1762 and withdrew Russian support just as Prussia seemed on the point of collapse. In the aftermath of the war, the French lost Canada, parts of the French West Indies, Louisiana, and most of India. England, on the other hand, lost nothing, although Frederick soon deserted his English alliance. Thus England, though victorious, was without any continental allies, a situation the rebellious American colonists soon found to their advantage.

Once the French threat in Canada and Louisiana had been removed, the American colonists grew more and more dissatisfied with the way they were treated by Great Britain. When they rebelled in 1776, most of Europe was sympathetic, in part because of the influence of the *philosophes*, but mainly because of European antagonisms toward England. As soon as the American rebels demonstrated their irrevocable split with England, France concluded a permanent alliance with the new republic. French aid, along with undercover support from Holland, Russia, and other continental powers, was the key to the American victory. None of the European powers, however, really wanted a powerful new state in North America, and, when the American peace negotiators became aware of this fact, they proceeded to ignore their continental allies and made a separate peace with England. French involvement in the American Revolution only brought France more debt and deepened the antagonisms of the French people toward their rulers. At the same time that France and England were involved in the American Revolution and its aftermath, Prussia, Austria, and Russia divided Poland among themselves in the partitions of 1772, 1793, and 1795, and Russia drove the Turks from the area around the Black Sea, thereby gaining a southern outlet on that body of water.

THE GROWING CRISIS IN FRANCE

While Americans owe a large debt to France for aiding their Revolution, the war effectively emphasized the failure of the French ruling class and caused turmoil throughout the country. French kings and their aristocratic advisers and administrators had kept France more or less continually involved in war, yet at the same time had so arranged matters that the financial burdens fell upon the middle and lower classes. The nobles not only paid no taxes but also managed to keep for themselves the pensions, jobs, sinecures, and similar perquisites which ate up most of the tax money. In an age of enlightenment, France was hamstrung by outdated administrative methods and procedures. Taxation was still based upon a farm system in which private contractors purchased the right to collect taxes, with everything they collected over their bid representing pure profit for them. Their rapacious methods led to a growing hostility toward the king, even though it was the collectors who pocketed most of the money. An internal trade tax was also levied in France, a holdover from medieval times when the country had been a collection of counties and duchies rather than a nation. Still another problem was the absence of a French national bank, which meant that there was no means for managing government debts. Even more surprising for such a great power, France not only lacked a uniform law code but also any real procedures for developing new laws. Absolute monarchy in France as developed under Louis XIV had suppressed time-honored institutions such as the Estates General, leaving all matters in the hands of the king. Thus when the king lacked determination, vigor, or resourcefulness, the system deteriorated rapidly, and there was no alternative to the monarchy except a radical revision of government. The inadequacies of the French king were increasingly resented by the middle class, who eventually came to believe that public business could never be conducted with reason and discernment by a monarch such as Louis XV. The longer he lived, the more desperate the middle class became.

The middle class, however, represented only a minority of the French population, and no overthrow of the old order could be accomplished without the collaboration of the peasants, who constituted the vast majority of the French people. The French peasants often owned their own land, were almost wholly free, and in general were more prosperous than peasants elsewhere in Europe. Yet during the last part of the eighteenth century, they too became embittered enough to revolt. Their anger was not so much directed at tax policies, the army, or their inability to rise in status, since these and similar grievances had been theirs for generations, but instead at the French nobility, who were beginning to introduce revolutionary English agricultural practices.

THE GROWTH OF PEASANT DISCONTENT

Anxious to find new sources of income as well as to rationalize old procedures, many aristocratic landowners began to employ "experts" to run their estates and to introduce agricultural reforms similar to those that in England had developed over several generations. In their haste to change practices, the nobles did not even bother to consult with their peasants; instead, they raised rents arbitrarily and increased fees or assessments on the basis of ancient privileges they discovered by searching old law books and records. At other times, they followed the English example of fencing the peasants out of the woods, where they derived their fuel and building materials, or kept them from taking their animals to what had been regarded as the common meadow. Landlords also refused to renew traditional leases and fenced in any plots that became untenanted. In any case, whether the peasant was forced to leave or to pay a higher rate for his old privileges, the landlord gained.

The peasants resisted in as many ways as they could, often turning to fence-burning, to rioting, and eventually to revolution. It was by siding with the revolutionaries in France that the traditionally conservative peasant hoped to prevent further encroachment upon his privileges. This meant that the success of the political revolution in France, guaranteeing the peasants their old rights, in the long run worked to prevent the type of farm reorganization that had taken place in England. The result was that nineteenth-century France was much more agriculturally backward than some of its continental rivals.

IMPORTANCE OF THE FRENCH REVOLUTION

The French Revolution has been studied more extensively than almost any other movement in history. In large part it has received so much attention because it became the example of what to do and what not to do either to preserve the status quo or to bring about radical change. Karl Marx studied the French Revolution, as did many other would-be revolutionaries, and when the Russian Revolution started, many of the moves and countermoves were based upon what its leaders thought had happened in France. With the French Revolution the old regime died, and the wars that resulted not only redrew the map of Europe but restructured European politics as well. Even today in France, those who champion certain Revolutionary figures arouse the animosity of others who have quite different heroes. It is particularly important that we understand what took place in the Revolution, what methods were used, and why the Revolution failed to achieve its ultimate objectives.

It would seem that when Louis XVI came to the throne in 1774 the resentment against the crown which had grown during the reign of the incompetent Louis XV would have come to an end. Louis XVI, however, in spite of his obvious capabilities, allowed his hostility toward England to get him involved in the American Revolution. He then compounded this folly by failing to support his ministers, such as Turgot (Baron de l'Aulne), whose plans for financial reform might have kept the monarchy solvent. By 1787, France was so heavily in debt that Louis was put in the position of either repudiating his financial obligations or of finding new sources of revenue. To help him find a solution, Louis finally summoned a special advisory group, the Assembly of Notables. This group of clerical and lay nobles urged many reforms, such as the legal recognition of the Protestant right to marriage and inheritance, and even some restrictions on the power of the nobles, as well as various financial reforms. Unfortunately, aristocratic opposition prevented the king from enacting any of these reforms. In still another attempt to deal with his problems, Louis summoned the Estates General, the three-house national assembly representing clergy, nobles, and common people, which had last met in 1614. After considerable debate, it was decided that the number of delegates in the third estate should equal those of the other two estates, a decision that was by no means improper, since the first two estates, the clergy and the nobles, represented less than half a million persons out of an estimated population of twenty-three million.

Elections for the third estate took place in the spring of 1789 with almost universal male suffrage, although the complicated series of electoral assemblies tended to give urban areas an overrepresentation. When the Estates General finally gathered at Versailles on May 5, 1789, the third estate, which represented those most dissatisfied with the status quo, realized that even though they were equal in numbers to the other two estates, they could be outvoted by the other two houses. They demanded a one-man, one-vote principle, which would give them an equal voice with the other houses. Their demands were opposed by the nobles, who hoped to use the problems that besieged the government as a lever to gain greater independence from the king. The reluctance of the nobles to make concessions to the third estate was shared by the higher clergy of the first estate, most of whom were nobles in their own right.

To force the issue, the third estate, dominated by business and professional men, refused to organize itself until the matter of organization was decided by a joint session of all three estates. The king or his chief minister, at this time the Swiss banker Jacques Necker, could have taken the situation in hand, and almost any program they proposed would have been put into effect. Instead, when Louis failed to assert his leadership, some members of the third estate seized the initiative by calling upon all delegates to meet with them as a national assembly. On June 17, most of the members of the third estate, together with a dozen or so clergymen from the first estate, met together and declared themselves a national assembly. Though this act was clearly illegal, Louis did almost nothing except to try to prevent a second meeting by closing the doors of the hall on the pretext that repairs were needed. Undaunted, the members retired to a nearby indoor tennis court, where, amidst much excitement, they took the famed tennis court oath binding themselves not to disband until they had written a constitution for France.

Thus openly challenged, the king finally made a show of resistance by declaring that the resolutions of the national assembly were void. When this body continued to meet, however, he not only withdrew his opposition but ordered the delegates of the first and second estates to meet with it. By now, fearing that the throne itself was in danger, Louis was playing for time so that he could collect troops in Paris and force the national assembly to disband. The possible use of troops so frightened some citizens of Paris that they set themselves up as a democratic local government known as the Commune. Fearful that the king's troops would then seize the city and destroy the precarious state of law and order that then existed, large numbers of people, including many not involved in the Commune government, began a hunt for weapons. Hearing that arms were available in the Bastille, a sort of castle inside the city which was used as both a fortress and a prison, a crowd gathered there on the morning of July 14. The group managed to pass an unguarded drawbridge to the outer court, but there they were fired upon. Angered at this attack, the mob took possession of the fort, killing the governor and several members of the garrison.

Ever since that time, the French have celebrated July 14 as Bastille Day, the day that marked the beginning of the French Revolution. The actions of the Parisians on that day effectively destroyed any plans that

Louis had to disperse the assembly. Dismissal of the national assembly would gain him nothing so long as the citizens of Paris were willing to take up arms. Moreover, almost immediately towns throughout France began to set up their own communal governments, and finally the disaffected peasantry, which had been in sporadic revolt for several weeks, broke into open rebellion. The country houses of the great nobles were attacked and many were burned, along with the records they contained. Overnight the French aristocracy found that it was no longer running the affairs of the town, the countryside, or the government. In fear of being murdered by their former subjects, many nobles and others fled France, while those who remained, perhaps out of fear, gave vigorous support to the national assembly.

THE FIRST YEARS OF CONSTITUTIONAL GOVERNMENT

The French soon found that the task of setting up a new regime that would operate better than the old one was not easy. It took two years for the national assembly to write a constitution. In the meantime it enacted the Declaration of the Rights of Man, a French bill of rights modeled on American concepts. The assembly also abolished the guilds and set about eliminating those remnants of feudalism which were largely responsible for giving the nobles the privileges they had enjoyed. Because of the collapse of the royal administration, the assembly also had to find some means of keeping the government functioning, a task made more difficult by the country's uncertain financial condition.

Louis XVI, hesitating between giving support to and opposing the events that were taking place, did not make things easier. Hopeful that moving the royal residence to Paris would improve matters, a mob, which included a large number of women, made its way to Versailles on foot in the rain during the early fall of 1789 to urge the king to return to Paris. The king allowed himself and his family to be conducted back to the Tuileries palace in Paris, and members of the national assembly soon followed. This move had an important effect upon the course of the Revolution, since it brought both the king and the national assembly under the influence of some of the more radical citizens of Paris and at the same time lessened the influence that the old aristocracy had enjoyed at Versailles.

To raise money, the national assembly expropriated much of the property of the Church, which represented about one tenth of all French land. Theoretically, the Church had justified its large holdings of land on the grounds that the income was necessary to carry out its charitable projects, although, in fact, most of the lands were set aside to support the higher clergy. The organized hierarchy thus opposed the Revolution, although the lower clergy, who received little income from Church land, did not seriously protest the expropriation after the national assembly offered to provide for them. On the basis of the prospective sale of the Church property, the government issued paper money, called *assignats*, to pay its creditors. In due course, the crown lands were also expropriated, followed by most of the land of the *emigrés*, or those nobles who had fled to foreign lands. The sequestered lands, however, did not sell very easily, simply because there was always the fear that the king or the Church might some day contrive to regain possession of them. Still, as the government's need for funds increased, more and more paper money was issued. The result was that the value of the *assignats* continued to depreciate until 1797, when the then worthless paper money was repudiated.

Since the government had offered to provide salaries for clergy, the national assembly also assumed the right to regulate religious affairs. A number of decrees passed in the summer of 1790, called the Civil Constitution of the Clergy, rearranged the ecclesiastical dioceses to correspond with the new established administrative departments, a uniform unit named after some geographical feature of the area. Bishops of the dioceses were to be elected by the popular vote of the more important residents of the department, including Protestants, Jews, and even atheists, while priests were to be chosen in the same way by members of a parish. The net effect of the reforms was to alienate a large proportion of those clergy who had heretofore supported the Revolution, and in their hostility to the changes they obtained sympathy and support from the peasantry as well as from the pope. When the clergy refused to cooperate, the assembly tried to coerce them by requiring each clergyman to take an oath of loyalty to the as yet unfinished constitution, which meant state control of the Church, before receiving his pay. The united opposition soon made the oath unenforceable, and the effect of the attempt by the assembly to control religious affairs was to alienate vast numbers of Frenchmen. The future of constitutional government thus rested primarily with the bourgeoisie, who were as much of a minority as the old aristocracy.

Finally, in 1791, the new constitution was ready, and with it France was changed into a constitutional monarchy with a one-house legislature. Much of the credit for the document goes to Count Mirabeau, one of several noblemen who had sided with the third estate. Unhappily, Mirabeau died before the constitution took effect, and the king soon demonstrated that he had no idea how a constitutional monarch should act. Louis never seemed to learn that once he had made a

Peasantry supporting
the clergy and nobility,
eighteenth-century
French cartoon. (The
Bettmann Archive, Inc.)

concession he could not change his mind and revoke it the next day. Though Louis seemed to agree to accept the new constitution, in actuality his intention was to frustrate it. The royal family attempted to flee in June to the eastern frontier, where an armed force had been assembled, but the king was recognized and conducted back to Paris.

This action proved fatal to the constitution, since it seemed unlikely that the new government could function under a king whom no one could quite trust or believe. To make conditions even more difficult for the new government, the national assembly, in a desperate effort to retrieve its lost prestige, had decreed that one of its members could serve in the new legislature. Thus the men who came to power in the autumn of 1791 did not understand the new government and lacked the experience to operate it. The new government was also handicapped by the growing disaffection of the former supporters of the Revolution. The peasants had become more and more hostile to the Revolution because they realized that the newly dominant bourgeois could not guarantee their land holdings and because they sympathized with the clergy. Even the masses in Paris were disenchanted because the national assembly had abolished labor organizations and, in addition, had deprived nonpropertied citizens of voting and office-holding privileges.

EUROPE AND THE REVOLUTION

When the new government met in 1791, it was at first dominated by groups who were intent on preserving the monarchy. Their control soon weakened, however, largely because of Austrian hostility. As the Revolution had become more and more radical, increasing numbers of French nobles fled to Austrian territory, where they encouraged Austrian fears about the spread of the Revolution. The Austrian court was also worried about the possible danger to Marie Antoinette, the wife of Louis XVI and the sister of Joseph II and Leopold II. Austrian anxieties were soon shared by Prussia, and subsequently by most states, great and small, whose aristocracy was fearful of suffering the same fate as the nobles of France. The Republicans in the French government, most of whom are known to history as Girondins because so many of their leaders came from the southern region around the Gironde River, raised the specter of Austrian intervention in the hope of embarrassing the supporters of the monarchy. Louis XVI, rather than trying to ease Austrian hostility, encouraged it, hoping that war might enable him to set aside the constitution and reassert his old powers. To this end, he allowed most of his supporters to leave office and permitted the Girondins to become part of the government. Also encouraging war was the Marquis de Lafayette, the American Revolutionary War hero and the effective commander of the French troops. Lafayette, who had been among the nobles sympathetic to the Revolution, had recently lost a contest for mayor of Paris, and there are considerable grounds for believing that he felt victories in the field would open up a larger role for him in public affairs.

As a result, in April 1792, soon after the Girondins took control of the assembly, they declared war on Austria by attacking the Austrian Netherlands (Belgium) with the support and encouragement of Louis XVI and Lafayette. The French attack was easily repelled, since the French army was totally demoralized by the years of political turmoil and most of its commissioned officers had fled France as *emigrès*. The Austrians, however, did not invade France, since they were preoccupied with Poland. Louis XVI, feeling that the war had served its purpose, replaced his discredited Girondin ministers with his own supporters, who undoubtedly sympathized with the king's feeling about the constitution. Before they could act to restore the powers of the king, the Parisian masses, the *sans culottes* — so called because workingmen did not wear gentlemen's knee breeches, or *culottes* — intervened by raiding the king's palace and upbraiding the king for his conduct. In an earlier age such an act would in all likelihood have been regarded as treasonable. Since the Parisian masses were allied with the Jacobins, a political group named after a confiscated monastery which became its headquarters, the real radicals of the Revolution, Lafayette demanded that the Jacobins apologize for the affront to the king. At the same time, the Duke of Brunswick, in command of the Prussian troops on the Rhine and acting in concert with the Austrians, was persuaded by his French *emigré* advisers to issue a statement threatening dire consequences should the royal family suffer further indignities or the French people be found bearing arms as a militia. Instead of strengthening the king's hand, the "Brunswick manifesto" caused an insurrection in Paris. The radicals seized control of the government of the Commune, and on August 10, the Tuileries was attacked and some eight-hundred defenders killed. The mob then turned on the assembly, where the king and queen had taken refuge. The assembly, out of fear, suspended the king and called a convention to frame a new constitution to be written by delegates for whom all male citizens of France would vote. In the interim, an executive committee took over the government, its most prominent member being Jacques Danton. Lafayette, upset over the treatment of the king, had attempted to come to the aid of the besieged royal couple by leading his army toward Paris. The army refused to follow him, however, and Lafayette then deserted to the Austrians. To replace him, the French turned to Charles-François Dumouriez, who reorganized and trained an army that soon became the terror of Europe. No less terrifying was the political machine that Danton established. Though the motto of Revolutionary France was liberty, equality, and fraternity, the Danton government used tyranny, oppression, and liquidation to achieve these ideals. France was saved from foreign domination, from civil war, and from aristocratic reaction, but in the process the Revolution unleashed a reign of savagery, murder, and violence.

FRANCE AS A REPUBLIC

After delaying most of the summer following the issuance of the Brunswick manifesto, the foreign armies crossed the French frontier in August 1792. To maintain Revolutionary fervor at home while the army was fighting near the frontier, Danton confined suspected persons, and then during the September massacres had thousands of them slaughtered. Nevertheless, by September 20, the Prussian advance was checked, and the next day the newly elected convention met, inaugurating another phase of the Revolution. Its first act was to declare France a republic and then to try the king for treason. Early in 1793, Louis XVI was executed on the guillotine; later the same fate befell the queen. In an attempt to undermine the religious opposition, the convention launched a full-scale assault on organized churches. As part of this program, the convention reorganized the calendar, making September 21 the first day of the new calendar, and renaming the months after typical phenomena of the times of the year, such as snow, wind, or harvest. Calendar reform was later abolished under Napoleon, but some of the other reforms made by the convention, such as the introduction of the metric system, survived to become part of established tradition.

Inevitably, most of the attention of the convention was concentrated on the war, which now involved England, Holland, Spain, Austria, Prussia, and Savoy-Sardinia, the forerunner of modern Italy. Within France, the convention faced civil war as ever more people became alienated by the extremes of the Revolution. This disaffection was soon felt in the convention itself, which was badly factionalized. The Girondins were at first the dominant party, but the Jacobins were much more cohesive and resolute. In June 1792, the Jacobin faction, assisted by the mobs of Paris, broke the power of the Girondins. By October 21, those Girondin leaders who had not escaped across the frontier were guillotined.

As justification for its conduct, the government pointed to the threat of foreign invasion. In the spring of 1793, the French army suffered severe reverses, and General Dumouriez himself deserted to the enemies of France. With disaffection rampant at home and with Europe in armed opposition, the Jacobins strained all of France to raise, equip, and train soldiers. Every man, woman, and child was expected to do something, and anyone who demonstrated even the slightest sympathy with the old regime was likely to be dealt with in summary fashion. An efficient dictatorship evolved, with power in the hands of committees, notably the one known as the Committee of Public Safety. Danton was a member, as was Lazare Carnot, the military engineer, but eventually it was dominated by Maximilien Robespierre.

The committee soon began its famed Reign of Terror. The Law of Suspects was passed, making it possible for the government to detain any person suspected of subversion. As the need for total dedication to the national effort became more pressing, the number of arrests multiplied so rapidly that the Revolutionary Tribunal concentrated on getting the accused condemned as speedily as possible, often without bothering to give him a fair trial. As the executions mounted, it seemed that the key to the success of the committee was the number of people it could eliminate. Since the victims tended to be persons of prominence, the loss to France in talent alone was devastating. Occasionally, the terror took on the nature of a massacre, especially in areas outside Paris.

Still the Revolution continued and the French armies grew ever more successful. The Jacobins, aided by Carnot's military reforms, managed to conscript, train, and put into the field over three quarters of a million men. These new Revolutionary soldiers fought with a ferocity and persistence previously unknown; they campaigned in midwinter and were willing to suffer hunger or hardship for their cause. This massive army, a forerunner of the armies of today, was more than a match for all of the troops brought against it. By 1794, the French, victorious in every sector, were no longer defending the homeland but were carrying revolution abroad, dethroning the old regimes wherever they went.

Even though internal security grew, the terror continued unabated. Some of the more extreme Jacobins and members of the Cordelier club, often known as the *Enragés*, saw the terror as a means of achieving greater social equality and fuller participation in the good life by the working classes. Robespierre, fearful of such possibilities, turned the terror on them. This action ultimately led many leaders of the convention to fear that Robespierre might next direct the terror against them. Thus on 9 Thermidor (late July), Robespierre found himself under attack in the convention. The next day, he and several of his partisans were executed, and the Reign of Terror was ended. This reaction marked the end of the Revolution as well as a return to more conservative rule. It is a historical truism that as a revolution grows more extreme it eventually reaches a point where it loses most of its supporters. Once the forward momentum is stopped, as it was with the removal of the *Enragés* by Robespierre, the revolution stops and a reaction sets in.

THE DIRECTORY

After the events of Thermidor, the French government became more conservative in outlook. The new attitude was reflected in the constitution of 1795, which provided for a two-house legislature and a plural executive called the directory. So fearful were the Jacobin regicides that free elections might bring opponents of the Revolution to power — who might attempt to restore the monarchy — that they insisted that two-thirds of the members of the new lower house be ex-convention members. While this provision was adopted, a last ditch effort was made to prevent the new directory from taking office. Several thousand rioters descended upon the convention in October 1795, but this time the mob was met by force through the resourcefulness of an artillery officer named Napoleon Bonaparte, who fired grapeshot at the crowd. Thus began Napoleon's rise to power and the end of the power of the mobs.

Though the directory governed France for four years, it solved none of the country's problems. Napoleon, however, proved to be an extremely successful general, and his army of Italy converted the Italian peninsula into a sort of French colony. Austria was forced out of the war, leaving England to carry the burden of fighting France. Napoleon then persuaded the directory to put him in charge of an expedition to Egypt as a first step in launching an attack on British India. During Napoleon's absence, the Austrians were induced by British subsidies to resume the war, and the French soon lost control of Italy. French gains in Switzerland, Germany, and Holland were also threatened. Within France, only force and chicanery enabled the directory to resist a possible restoration on the one hand and an insurrection of the Paris masses on the other.

NAPOLEON

During the summer of 1799, various plots were hatched to overthrow the directory, and one of these, in which the Abbé Sieyès was involved, planned to install Napoleon as a military strong man. Napoleon's Egyptian enterprise had proved a disaster, largely because of British control of the sea, but he had managed to escape and return to France. In spite of his defeat, Napoleon was still regarded as a victorious general by the French, who needed a popular hero during this difficult period. By November 1799, the opponents of the directory were strong enough to engineer a coup d'état and put Napoleon in power. A new constitution was drawn up which provided for a cumbersome legislature, a first consul, and two figurehead consuls. In actual fact, however, Napoleon was a military dictator, although this fact was somewhat disguised by a national plebiscite, a sort of referendum, which popularly approved the new constitution and Napoleon's position as first consul. It was while serving as first consul that Napoleon carried through the long overdue codification of French civil, criminal, and commercial law. The revision, known as the Napoleonic Codes, asserted the equality of all men before the law and provided for freedom of occupation and freedom of conscience. Though the revised codes failed to incorporate some of the more liberal ideas of the time, they proved to be a great advance over anything that Europe had known before. Since they were exported from France along with Napoleon's armies, the laws proved to be one of the most enduring influences of the Revolution on the lives of most Europeans.

In 1804, with a few strokes of his pen and another plebiscite, Napoleon converted the consulate into an empire with himself as emperor. The French Revolution, which had started out as an internal struggle for liberty, equality, and fraternity, had become a new type of imperialistic venture which proved disastrous to old regimes everywhere. Napoleon, a military and administrative genius, brought the type of order and efficiency into French government that had been missing since the days of Louis XIV. Finances were reorganized, a national bank was established, a new system of education was planned, and peace was finally made with a papacy, which had long been frightened by the Revolution. Moreover, French armies swept the battlefield so effectively that the Continent almost became Napoleon's personal property. He made and unmade states, rearranged boundaries, deposed kings, and defeated every army sent against him. Landlords, clergy, guilds, and other groups in Europe which had been accustomed to act as the ruling classes found themselves liable to be dispossessed unless they gave lip service to the Revolutionary ideals of liberty, equality, fraternity. The underprivileged throughout Europe temporarily came to look upon French conquest as a deliverance from oppression. Both Italy and Germany acquired a measure of unity not known for several hundred years; it was Napoleon who finally broke up the Holy Roman Empire as well as the ancient republic of Venice.

Napoleon's most persistent enemy was Great Britain, which was somewhat more immune to the appeal of the Revolution because in England the abuses of the old regime had never been as serious as they were on the Continent. Though the French armies could sweep much of Europe, they could not land troops in the British Isles without a large and powerful navy, and French sea power had been effectively neutralized by 1805 with the victory of Horatio Lord Nelson off Cape

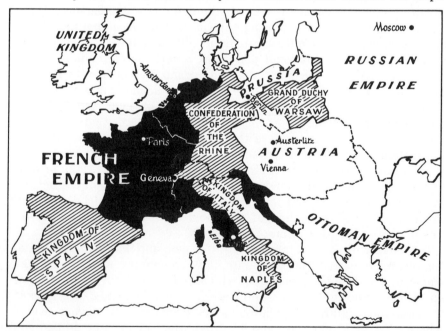

Napoleon's conquests, 1812.

Trafalgar. On the Continent itself, there was a growing disillusionment with Napoleon as many of his supporters realized that he was more interested in increasing his own power and influence than in extending liberty, equality, and fraternity to all. Napoleon's ambitions, however, only seemed to increase with his difficulties. Unable to defeat the British navy, he was determined to dominate the Continent. The eventual result was the disastrous invasion of Russia. The early onset of winter in 1812 caught the French troops unprepared either to stay in the newly captured Moscow or to retreat. Simultaneously, in the Wars of Liberation, conquered peoples throughout Europe, anxious to throw off French domination, began to revolt. By 1813, Napoleon's armies had been driven back to France; by the spring of 1814, the emperor himself was forced to abdicate.

Given control of the island of Elba near his native Corsica, Napoleon ended his first exile by escaping within less than a year. For a hundred days during the spring of 1815 he emerged as temporary master of France, but the British and Prussians soon ended his hopes by crushing his army at Waterloo in Belgium. This time Napoleon was imprisoned on St. Helena, an island in the South Atlantic far from everywhere. There he died in 1821, but all of Europe could not put the pieces together again after he had gone.

Supplemental Reading
for Part Five

General

Anderson, M. S., *Eighteenth Century Europe 1713–1789* (Oxford).
Beloff, M., *Age of Absolutism 1660–1815* (Harper & Row).
Brinton, Crane, *Anatomy of Revolution* (Random House).
Brinton, Crane, *Decade of Revolution, 1789–99* (Harper & Row).
Bruun, G., *The Enlightened Despots* (Holt, Rinehart and Winston).
Bruun, G., *Europe and the French Imperium, 1799–1814* (Harper & Row).
Clark, G. N., *The Seventeenth Century* (Oxford).
Dorn, W. L., *Competition for Empire, 1740–1763* (Harper & Row).
Friedrich, C. J., *The Age of Baroque, 1610–1660* (Harper & Row).
Gagliardo, J. G., *Enlightened Despotism* (Crowell).
Gershoy, L., *From Despotism to Revolution, 1763–1789* (Harper & Row).
Hobsbawn, E. J., *The Age of Revolution* (Mentor).
Mahan, A. T., *The Influence of Sea Power on History* (Hill & Wang).
Nussbaum, F. L., *Triumph of Science and Reason, 1660–1685* (Harper & Row).
Ogg, D., *Europe in the Seventeenth Century* (Macmillan).
Ogg, D., *Europe of the Ancien Régime* (Harper & Row).
Rabb, T. K., ed., *The Thirty Years War* (Heath).
Roberts, P., *The Quest for Security, 1715–1740* (Harper & Row).
Rutledge, J. L., *Century of Conflict: Struggle between Britain and France in Colonial America* (Popular).
Steinberg, S. H., *The Thirty Years War and the Conflict for European Hegemony, 1600–1660* (Norton).
Wedgwood, C. V., *The Thirty Years War* (Doubleday).
Wines, R., ed., *Enlightened Despotism: Reform or Reaction* (Heath).
Wolf, J. B., *The Emergence of the Great Powers, 1685–1715* (Harper & Row).

England, Empire, and Colonies

Alden, J. R., *The American Revolution* (Harper & Row).
Ashley, Maurice, *England in the Seventeenth Century* (Penguin).
Aylmer, G. E., *A Short History of 17th Century England* (Mentor).
Boyer, R. E., ed. *Oliver Cromwell and the Puritan Revolt* (Heath).
Carrington, C. E., *The British Overseas* (Cambridge).
Gooch, G. P., *English Democratic Ideas in the Seventeenth Century* (Harper & Row).
Gipson, L. H., *The Coming of the American Revolution* (Harper & Row).

Harris, R. W., *A Short History of Eighteenth Century England* (Mentor).

Hill, Christopher, *Century of Revolution* (Norton).

Hill, Christopher, *Puritanism and Revolution* (Schocken).

Keir, D. L., *The Constitutional History of Modern Britain* (Norton).

Moon, P. T., *Warren Hastings and British India* (Macmillan).

Namier, Sir Lewis, *England in the Age of the American Revolution* (St. Martin's).

Namier, Sir Lewis, *The Structure of Politics at the Accession of George III* (St. Martin's).

Notestein, W., *The English People on the Eve of Colonization, 1603–30* (Harper & Row).

Plumb, J. H., *England in the Eighteenth Century* (Penguin).

Reitan, E. A., ed., *George III: Tyrant or Constitutional Monarch* (Heath).

Rudé, G., *Wilkes and Liberty: A Social Study of 1763–1774* (Oxford).

Robertson, Charles G., *Chatham and the British Empire* (Macmillan).

Stone, L., *Social Change and Revolution in England 1540–1640* (Barnes & Noble).

Straka, G. M., ed., *The Revolution of 1688* (Heath).

Tanner, J. R., *English Constitutional Conflicts of the Seventeenth Century, 1603–1689* (Cambridge).

Taylor, P. A., ed., *Origins of the English Civil War* (Heath).

Trevelyan, G. M., *England Under the Stuarts* (Barnes & Noble).

Trevelyan, G. M., *The English Revolution, 1688–89* (Oxford).

Wedgewood, C. V., *The Life of Cromwell* (Macmillan).

France and the French Revolution

Amann, Peter, ed., *The Eighteenth Century Revolution–French or Western* (Heath).

Ashley, M., *Louis XIV and the Greatness of France* (Free Press).

Behrens, C. B. A., *The Ancien Régime* (Holt, Rinehart and Winston).

Boulenger, J. R., *The Seventeenth Century in France* (Putnam).

Brinton, Crane, *The Lives of Talleyrand* (Norton).

Butterfield, Herbert, *Napoleon* (Macmillan).

Church, W. F., ed., *The Greatness of Louis XIV: Myth or Reality* (Heath).

Church, W. F., *The Impact of Absolutism in France: National Experience under Richelieu, Mazarin, and Louis XIV* (Wiley).

Cobban, Alfred, *A History of Modern France*, vol. 1, (Penguin).

Cobban, Alfred, *A Social Interpretation of the French Revolution* (Cambridge).

Dowd, D. L., ed., *Napoleon: Was He the Heir of the Revolution* (Holt, Rinehart and Winston).

Echeverria, D., *Mirage in the West: A History of the French Image of American Society* (Princeton).

Fisher, H. A., *Napoleon* (Oxford).

Ford, F. L., *The Robe and Sword: The Regrouping of the French Aristocracy after Louis XIV* (Harper & Row).

Gershoy, Leo, *Era of the French Revolution* (Van Nostrand).

Gershoy, Leo, *French Revolution* (Holt, Rinehart and Winston).

Geyl, Peter, *Napoleon: For and Against* (Yale).

Goodwin, A., *The French Revolution* (Harper & Row).

Gottshalk, *Jean-Paul Marat: A Study in Radicalism* (Chicago).

Greenlaw, R. W., ed., *Economic Origins of the French Revolution* (Heath).

Guérard, A. L., *France in the Classical Age: Life and Death of an Ideal* (Harper & Row).

Herr, R., *Tocqueville and the Old Regime* (Princeton).

Holtman, R. B., *The Napoleonic Revolution* (Lippincott).

Kafker, F. A., and J. M. Lux, *French Revolution: Conflicting Interpretations* (Random House).

Lewis, W. H., *The Splendid Century: Some Aspects of French Life in the Reign of Louis XIV* (Doubleday).

Lefebvre, G., *The Coming of the French Revolution* (Random House).

Lefebvre, G., *Thermidorians* (Random House).

Markham, F. M. H., *Napoleon and the Awakening of Europe* (Macmillan).

Mathiez, A., *After Robespierre: The Thermidorian Reaction* (Grosset & Dunlap).

Mitford, Nancy, *Madame de Pompadour* (Pyramid).

Packard, L. B., *The Age of Louis XIV* (Holt, Rinehart and Winston).

Padover, S. K., *Life and Death of Louis XVI* (Pyramid).

Palmer, R. R., *Twelve Who Ruled* (Atheneum).

Rudé, G., *The Crowd in the French Revolution* (Oxford).

Rudé, G., ed., *Robespierre* (Prentice-Hall).

Salvemini, G., *The French Revolution* (Norton).

Syndenham, J. M., *The Girondins* (Putnam).

Thompson, J. M., *The French Revolution* (Oxford).

Thompson, J. M., *Robespierre and the French Revolution* (Macmillan).

Wedgwood, C. V., *Richelieu and the French Monarchy* (Macmillan).

Wolf, J. B., *Louis XIV* (Norton).

Other Countries

Atkinson, William C., *A History of Spain and Portugal* (Penguin).

Bruford, W. H., *Germany in the Eighteenth Century* (Cambridge).

Craig, G. A., *Politics of the Prussian Army, 1640–1945* (Oxford).

Coles, P., *Ottoman Impact on Europe* (Harcourt).

Davies, R. T., *Spain in Decline, 1621–1700* (St. Martin's).

Effendi, H., *Ottoman Egypt in the Age of the French Revolution* (Harvard).

Elliott, J. H., *Imperial Spain, 1469–1716* (Mentor).

Fay, Sidney B., *The Rise of Bradenburg–Prussia to 1786* (Holt, Rinehart and Winston).

Fletcher, C. R. L., *Gustavus Adolphus and the Thirty Years War* (Putnam).

Ford, F. L., *Strasbourg in Transition, 1648–1789* (Norton).

Geyl, Peter, *Revolt of the Netherlands* (Barnes & Noble).

Pares, Bernard, *A History of Russia* (Random House).
Raeff, Marc., ed., *Peter the Great — Reformer or Revolutionary* (Heath).
Sumner, B. H., *Peter the Great and the Emergence of Russia* (Macmillan).
Taylor, A. J. P., *The Course of German History* (Putnam).
Vernadsky, G., *History of Russia* (Yale).

Economic and Social

Ashton, T. S., *The Industrial Revolution* (Oxford).
Barber, Elinor G., *The Bourgeoisie in Eighteenth Century France* (Princeton).
Barbour, Violet, *Capitalism in Amsterdam in the Seventeenth Century* (Michigan).
Clough, S. B. and C. G. Moddie, *European Economic History* (Van Nostrand).
Deane, P. M., *The First Industrial Revolution* (Cambridge).
George, Dorothy, *England in Transition* (Penguin).
Goodwin, A., ed., *The European Nobility in the Eighteenth Century* (Harper & Row).
Hammond, J. L. and Barbara, *Town Labourer: The New Civilization 1760–1832* (Doubleday).
Hughes, T. P., *Development of Western Technology since 1500* (Macmillan).
Mantoux, P., *The Industrial Revolution in the Eighteenth Century* (Harper & Row).
Moller, H., *Population Movements in Modern European History* (Macmillan).
Minchinton, W. E., ed., *Mercantilism: System or Expedience* (Heath).
Nef, J. U., *Industry and Government in France and England* (Cornell).
Nef, J. U., *War and Human Progress: An Essay on the Rise of Industrial Civilization* (Norton).
Spiegel, H. W., *The Development of Economic Thought* (Wiley).
Taylor, Philip A. M., *The Industrial Revolution in Britain — Triumph or Disaster?* (Heath).
Toynbee, A., *Industrial Revolution* (Beacon).
Turberville, Arthur S., *English Men and Manners in the Eighteenth Century* (Oxford).
Warner, Charles K., *Agrarian Conditions in Modern European History* (Macmillan).
Williams, Gwyn A., *Artisans and Sans-Culottes* (Norton).

Intellectual: Religion, Science, Literature and the Arts

Becker, Carl, *The Heavenly City of the Eighteenth Century Philosophers* (Yale).
Brailsford, H. N., *Voltaire* (Oxford).
Bronowski, J. and Bruce Mazlish, *The Western Intellectual Tradition: From Leonardo to Hegel* (Harper & Row).

Burtt, E. A., *The Metaphysical Foundations of Modern Physical Science* (Doubleday).

Bury, J. B., *The Idea of Progress: An Inquiry into Its Origin and Growth* (Dover).

Butler, E. M., *The Tyranny of Greece over Germany* (Beacon).

Butterfield, Herbert, *The Origins of Modern Science* (Free Press).

Cassirer, Ernest, *Philosophy of the Enlightenment* (Princeton).

Cassirer, Ernst, ed., *The Question of Jean-Jacques Rousseau* (Indiana).

Church, W. F., *The Influence of the Enlightenment on the French Revolution* (Heath).

Cogniat, R., *Seventeenth Century Painting* (Random House).

Cragg, G. R., *The Church and the Age of Reason* (Penguin).

Cragg, G. R., *From Puritanism to the Age of Reason* (Cambridge).

Cranston, M., *John Locke* (British Book Centre).

D'Abro, A., *The Evolution of Scientific Thought* (Dover).

DeSantillana, Georgio, *The Crime of Galileo* (Chicago).

Einstein, A., *Mozart: His Character and Work* (Oxford).

Einstein, A., *A Short History of Music* (Random House).

Farrington, Benjamin, *Francis Bacon* (Macmillan).

Feuer, L. S., *Spinoza and the Rise of Liberalism* (Beacon).

Figgis, J. N., *The Divine Rights of Kings* (Harper & Row).

Gay, Peter, *The Enlightenment: The Rise of Modern Paganism* (Random House).

Gay, Peter, *Voltaire's Politics* (Random House).

Gierke, Otto, *Natural Law and the Theory of Society* (Beacon).

Green, F. C., *Eighteenth Century France* (Ungar).

Hall, A. R., *The Scientific Revolution* (Beacon).

Hauser, A., *Social History of Art*, vols. 2 & 3 (Random House).

Havens, G., *The Age of Ideas* (Free Press).

Hazard, P., *European Thought in the Eighteenth Century* (World).

Kaufmann, E., *Architecture in the Age of Reason* (Dover).

Koyré, A., *From the Closed World to the Infinite Universe* (Johns Hopkins).

Kronenberger, Louis, *Kings and Desperate Men: Life in Eighteenth Century England* (Random House).

Kuhn, Thomas S., *The Copernican Revolution* (Random House).

Lovejoy, Arthur, *The Great Chain of Being* (Harper & Row).

McGiffert, A. C., *Protestant Thought Before Kant* (Harper & Row).

Manuel, Frank E., *The Age of Reason* (Cornell).

Manuel, Frank E., *The Eighteenth Century Confronts the Gods* (Atheneum).

Marsak, Leonard M., *The Rise of Science* (Macmillan).

Martin, Kingsley, *French Liberal Thought in the Eighteenth Century* (Harper & Row).

Millon, H. A., *Baroque and Rococo Architecture* (Braziller).

More, L. T., *Isaac Newton* (Dover).

Nicolson, Marjorie, *Mountain Gloom and Mountain Glory* (Norton).

Nicolson, Marjorie, *Science and Imagination* (Cornell).

Palmer, R. R., *Catholics and Unbelievers in Eighteenth Century France* (Princeton).

Phostiades, W., *Eighteenth Century Painting* (Viking).

Pledge, H. T., *Science since 1500* (British Information Center).

Schweitzer, A., *J. S. Bach*, 2 vols. (Dover).

Simpson, A., *Puritanism in Old and New England* (Chicago).

Smith, Preserved, *History of Modern Culture*, 2 vols. (Macmillan).

Stephen, Leslie, *English Literature in the Eighteenth Century* (Barnes & Noble).

Stephen, Leslie, *History of English Thought in the Eighteenth Century* (Harcourt).

Trevor-Roper, H. R., *European Witch Craze in the 16th and 17th Centuries* (Harper & Row).

Wedgwood, C. V., *Poetry and Politics Under the Stuarts* (Michigan).

Wiley, Basil, *The Eighteenth Century Background* (Beacon).

Wiley, Basil, *The Seventeenth Century Background* (Doubleday).

Wolf, A., *A History of Science, Technology and Philosophy in the 17th & 18th Century*, 2 vols. (Harper & Row).

Wright, L. B., *Cultural Life of the American Colonies* (Harper & Row).

SOURCES

Bacon, Francis, *Complete Essays* (Simon and Schuster).

Berlin, Isaiah, ed., *The Age of Enlightenment* (Mentor).

Bowditch, J. and C. Ramsland, eds., *Voices of the Industrial Revolution* (Michigan).

Burke, Edmund, *Reflections on the Revolution in France* (Holt).

Defoe, D., *A Journal of the Plague Year* (Penguin or other editions). Novel or rather fictionalized account.

Descartes, René, *Discourse on Method*, numerous paperback editions.

Drake, Stillman, ed. and trans., *Discoveries and Opinions of Galileo* (Doubleday).

Fielding, Henry, *Tom Jones*, numerous paperback editions.

Forster, Robert and Elborg, *European Society in the Eighteenth Century* (Harper & Row).

Fowlie, W., ed., *Classical French Drama* (Bantam).

Goethe, J., *Sorrows of Young Werther* (Signet).

Hall, Marie Boas, *Nature and Nature's Laws: Documents of the Scientific Revolution* (Harper & Row).

Hampshire, Stuart, ed., *The Age of Reason* (Mentor).

Herold, J. C., ed., *Mind of Napoleon: A Selection from His Written and Spoken Words* (Columbia).

Hobbes, T., *Leviathan*, various editions in paperback.

Kant, *Selections*, ed. T. M. Greene (Scribner or numerous other editions).

Lewis, W. H., ed., *Memoirs of the Duc de St. Simon* (Macmillan).

Locke, John, *On Politics, Religion and Education,* ed. M. Cranston (Macmillan or numerous other editions).

Macartney, C. A., *The Hapsburg and Hohenzollern Dynasties* (Harper & Row).

Milton, John, *Areopagitica* (Appleton).

Montesquieu, Baron de, *The Spirit of Laws* (Hafner).

Pascal, B., *Pensees* (Random House).

Pepys, Samuel, *Diary,* various abridgments in paperback.

Smith, Adam, *The Wealth of Nations,* numerous editions.

Spinoza, Baruch, *Chief Works,* 2 vols. (Dover or numerous other editions).

Swift, J., *Gulliver's Travels,* numerous editions.

Tocqueville, Alexis de, *The Old Regime and the French Revolution* (Doubleday).

Voltaire, *The Portable Voltaire,* ed. by B. R. Redman (Viking) is a good selection. There are many more editions.

Young, Arthur, *Travels in France* (Doubleday). An Englishman in France before the revolution.

FICTION

Beginning in the 18th century there are contemporary novels. Other novels covering this period include the following.

Dumas, A., *The Three Musketeers,* numerous editions. Historically inaccurate novel which still has become a classic.

Forester, C. S., the various Hornblower novels (Bantam).

Hawthorne, N., *The Scarlet Letter,* numerous editions.

Hugo, Victor, *Ninety-Three* or other Hugo novels.

Manzoni, A., *Bethrothed* (Dutton).

Thackeray, J. M., *Henry Esmond* or *Vanity Fair,* several editions.

Tolstoy, L., *War and Peace.* This great classic of the Napoleonic invasion of Russia is well worth reading.

part six

THE NINETEENTH CENTURY

81

Liberalism and the Reconstruction of Europe

Liberalism has been defined as the middle class reaction to the special influence and privileges of the aristocrats under the old regime. Initially, it reflected the values of lawyers, accountants, and businessmen, but it eventually developed into a philosophy that continues to have a strong appeal for Western man.

The eighteenth-century philosopher Adam Smith came to be regarded as the prophet of the new thinking, and it was in Great Britain that liberalism was first effectively employed to free the middle classes from what they believed hampered them in their exercise of initiative. Nineteenth-century middle class liberals soon attempted to supply answers to all types of situations, to offer a remedy for every problem, to change the nature of society. Basic to a society founded on liberalism was the absence of control: monopoly companies were to be deprived of their privileges, guilds disbanded or stripped of their power to regulate, and government forced to abandon tariffs, quotas, and bounties. Reorganization was to extend to almost every area of society. Liberals, however, were not of one mind when it came to dealing with misery and suffering. One group of economists, centered around Thomas Malthus and David Ricardo, was basically pessimistic about human nature. Malthus, a clergyman, held that man's ability to procreate is greater than his ability to produce food; hence nature imposes natural checks such as wars, plagues, and famine. Building upon the assumptions of Malthus, the English banker-economist David Ricardo posited the "iron law of wages." Ricardo felt that the income of workers would always fluctuate at the subsistence level, since as soon as wages improved, workers would have larger families, increasing the supply of workers and driving down wages. Though Malthus, Ricardo, and their followers deplored misery and suffering, they became convinced that any effort on the part of government to remedy social ills would in the long run only make matters worse. Thus they not only provided a satisfactory justification for their own individual success and for the misery of the lower classes but they also advocated a policy of nonintervention.

Opposed to this pessimistic view of life were other liberals centered around Jeremy Bentham, an English lawyer, who evolved a simple criterion for deciding public policy in virtually any area — that program should be pursued that would assure the greatest happiness or good to the greatest number. Thus utility should be the guiding principle in formulating laws, eliminating poverty, or managing foreign affairs. The followers of Bentham, who included James Mill and his more famous son John Stuart Mill, came to be known as Utilitarians. The Utilitarians evolved a body of doctrine that was logically consistent yet based upon common sense. Unfortunately, they paid little attention to analyzing basic data. They viewed man as an organism motivated by pleasure, whose natural behavior consisted of seeking enjoyment and avoiding the opposite. The most logical way to attain pleasure — and the surest way to avoid pain — was to pursue wealth. As a result, for several generations, Utilitarians tended to close their minds to whatever else might be discovered about the nature of human beings as superfluous and useless, since they believed that man was already completely understood. Inevitably, both types of nineteenth-century liberals became a serious roadblock to a more scientific and realistic appreciation of the human personality as well as to discoveries in other areas of knowledge.

CONSERVATISM AND THE POSTWAR REACTION

With the defeat of Napoleon and the restoration of the French monarchy, conservatism rather than liberalism became dominant. With Edmund Burke as its prophet, conservatism had a strong English tinge, but its ideology became fully developed on the European continent through the efforts of Joseph de Maistre and the Vicomte de Bonald. In a sense, both Maistre and Bonald started out as reactionaries, striking out with fury at the *philosophes*, whom they held had introduced the poison of the Revolution. Once the poison had been eliminated, however, both men saw the need for reconstructing society and realized the impossibility of attempting to turn the clock back to the monarchy as it had been in 1789. Nonetheless, Maistre and Bonald believed that only monarchies could provide political security and that republics must always fail, since once the discipline of the monarchy, the church, and the nobility was removed, disorder, corruption, and decay would result. To them, the natural order of society was historical and traditional, while individualism and democracy were diseases that resulted in social anarchy. Wisdom in politics came from experience, which could be acquired by a discriminating study of the past and an understanding of national character as revealed in history. As a group, conservatives disliked industrialism and abhorred the impersonality of the city; instead, their values tended to be rooted in the stable society of the countryside where everyone knew everyone else and every man knew his place. Though often simply reactionaries, the more constructive of the conservatives performed the valuable task of emphasizing the importance of the community as against the rampant individualism of the more extreme liberals.

Once the Napoleonic wars ended, there was inevitably a concerted effort to eliminate liberalism, to discredit the Enlightenment, and even to establish a sort of beneficent absolutism through a new union of church and state. Least oppressive of the new regimes was that of the restored Bourbons in France. Louis XVIII, a brother of the martyred Louis XVI and uncle of the young Louis XVII, who had died in prison without ever being crowned, attempted to come to terms with a post-Revolutionary world by agreeing to rule through a constitution that provided for a legislature, religious liberty, and freedom of speech. England also avoided many of the most extreme forms of postwar reaction, although the British government for more than a decade repressed all moves to adopt more liberal policies for fear of another revolutionary outbreak.

THE AGE OF METTERNICH

Much more oppressive and longer lasting was the reaction in central and southern Europe, where the middle classes were both less numerous and less prosperous and where liberalism was tainted with Bonapartism. Personifying the reaction was the astute European politician Prince Metternich of Austria, who was so effective in his policies and so successful in holding his office that the period has often been called the age of Metternich. Ironically, Metternich was not himself a reactionary but a kind of hardheaded administrator who believed that the problems of the world could be dealt with by reasonable men acting from knowledge and common sense. Had he lived half a century earlier under the more stable conditions of the old regime, he might well have been a liberal. Instead, Metternich lived in an Austria threatened with disintegration, and the preservation of the Hapsburg Empire served as the guiding aim of his policies. Though Napoleon had abolished the Holy Roman Empire in 1806, the Hapsburg rulers of Austria continued to dominate central Europe. The reconstituted Austrian Empire not only included German-speaking peoples centered around present-day Austria but Italians in Venetia and Lombardy, Magyars in Hungary, Czechs in Bohemia, Poles in Galicia, Slovenes in Carniola, Rumanians in Transylvania, plus several other peoples. Most of these subjects harbored a strong antagonism toward their German-speaking rulers which had been encouraged by Napoleon's victories. To keep such disparate groups together, Metternich became the proponent of a policy of repression designed to curtail any popular movement or to discourage any radical changes.

When after Napoleon's defeat European statesmen attempted to put the Continent back together again at the Congress of Vienna in 1815, it was Metternich who emerged as the dominant figure. To his credit, he, along with the French minister Talleyrand, attempted to preserve the identity of France, which thus kept the territory it had held before the Revolution. This policy proved to be good politics, since it did not saddle the restored French monarchs with the problem of justifying the loss of French territory and made it possible for French rulers to join with the other leaders in settling the problems of Europe. Metternich devoted most of his energies at the Congress to attempting to re-establish Hapsburg primacy in Germany and in central and southern Europe. In place of the Holy Roman Empire, the Congress established a German confederation, the *Deutscher Bund*, made up of thirty-eight states under nominal Austrian leadership. Austria gave up its control over the southern Netherlands (Belgium) to the Dutch in compensation for the loss of Cape Colony in Africa. In return, Austria, already in control of Lombardy, took possession of the republic of Venice and was allowed to dominate the affairs of Modena, Tuscany, and Parma. These settlements made Austrian territories more contiguous and gave the Hapsburgs control over the affairs of both Italy and Germany.

Numerous other changes were made in the map of Europe. Prussia, for example, received additional German-speaking territory, mostly at the expense of Saxony, to offset losses in Poland. Poland itself became a semiautonomous part of Russia. Norway, formerly part of Denmark, was given to Sweden as a punishment to the Danes, who had clung to an alliance with France. Sweden, in turn, lost Finland to Russia. The rulers of Spain, Sardinia, and Naples were restored to their thrones, while the pope regained control over the papal territories in central Italy. Great Britain clearly dominated the seas and was content to pick up territories throughout the world rather than take any land on the Continent.

To maintain these arrangements, Russia, Prussia, Austria, and Great Britain banded together in the Quadruple Alliance and agreed to meet together in a Concert of Europe to discuss difficulties that might otherwise lead to war. In 1818, France was admitted to the group, and it then became the Quintuple Alliance. Independent of the group but often confused with it was the Holy Alliance, an effort by tsar Alexander I of Russia to get the various sovereigns to pattern their policies on Christian principles. Though the concert eventually came to be detested by European liberals because of its suppression of popular movements aimed at changing the status quo, it was a pioneering attempt to end some of the internecine wars which had plagued the Continent.

CHALLENGES TO THE STATUS QUO

Serious uprisings against the political status quo took place in 1820 in Spain and in Naples, with both revolts leading to the establishment of constitutional monarchies. A third revolt in the Piedmont, the mainland portion of the kingdom of Sardinia, failed when the ruling king abdicated in favor of his brother, who brutally suppressed it. Metternich, fearful that revolts would spread into Austrian territory, received the approval of Russia and Prussia to send Austrian troops to Naples, an action that also resulted in the restoration of absolutism and an orgy of terror and persecution. Spain, however, presented a more difficult problem, since Austria lacked a common frontier and the British feared that their support of a naval expedition would threaten their commercial dominance of the Spanish colonies in Latin America and elsewhere. Thus the matter was left up to France, which had increasingly become a bulwark of reaction through the influence of the Count of Artois. The younger brother of the childless and aging Louis XVIII, Artois belonged to a noble faction called the ultras, which aimed at restoring the old regime in every area of life. A French invasion of Spain in 1823 resulted in the restoration of royal absolutism as well as in a reign of terror against liberals. In 1824, with the accession of Artois to the French throne as Charles X, absolute monarchy again seemed to dominate Europe.

The first failure of the Concert of Europe resulted from the revolt by the Greeks against their Turkish overlords. Though Metternich saw the rebellious Greeks as merely one more gang of revolutionaries, most Europeans were much too influenced by the Greek heritage to look upon it in the same way. Moreover, the Russians were anxious to embarrass the Turks as well as to aid their fellow-Christians in a revolt against a Muslim power. Great Britain, ever anxious to extend its maritime influence, saw Greece as a possible naval base for future activities in the eastern Mediterranean. Ignoring Metternich, the new tsar Nicholas I in 1825 sent a fleet into Greek waters; in cooperation with a British fleet; this naval might managed to destroy Turkish sea power in the harbor of Navarino in 1827. France, anxious to get into the act, then sent a detachment of French troops into southern Greece while the Russians invaded from the north. The Turkish sultan saved himself from disaster by conceding independence to the Greeks in 1829. Europeans, in spite of the concert, were unable to negotiate anything without going to war.

The final blow to the concert came with a four-day outbreak in France in July 1830 which forced the reactionary Charles X to abdicate. Impetus for the revolt came from Charles's efforts to set aside the constitution provided for in 1814 with the restoration of the monarchy. The fighting, which was almost wholly limited to Paris, ended when Charles left the country. The liberal bourgeoisie then turned to a royal prince, Louis Philippe of Orleans, in order to ease European fears about a republic. Even Metternich believed that Charles X had attempted to do the absurd as well as the impossible and so was willing to accept the new king. Besides, the only alternative to accepting Louis Philippe was an invasion of France, an undertaking for which no European ruler was prepared.

Elsewhere in Europe, the French success spurred liberals to revolt against absolutism in Germany, Italy, Poland, and Belgium. In most cases, they lost rather than gained, particularly in Poland, which was fully incorporated into the Russian Empire. Most of the German states remained as authoritarian as ever, while the revolutions in Italy brought only repression enforced by Austrian troops. Liberalism did win a victory in Belgium, where an uprising took place against the Dutch, who had persistently treated their more numerous southern neighbors as colonials. Since the revolts in central Europe had kept the Prussians, Austrians, and Russians involved, the French and British were left free to deal with Belgium. Though Britain and France had fought over control of the Netherlands for centuries, the French managed to convince the English that no annexation was planned. As a result, with the support of French troops and a British naval blockade, Belgium took shape as one of the world's more important little nations.

Great Britain had never been as reactionary as the continental powers, but the success of the revolt in France frightened the British into accepting the type of change and reform so long equated with the collapse of order and decorum. The result was the Great Reform Bill of 1832, which thoroughly recast the electoral procedures for the House of Commons. The new law not only provided for an essentially uniform franchise but it also forced a redistribution of seats in accordance with population changes, thereby increasing the influence of the middle classes, who were concentrated in the cities.

ROMANTICISM AND NATIONALISM

If liberalism was a continuation of rationalism, then romanticism, like conservatism, can be called a reaction to it. Pervading romantic literature was the idea that man represented something more than the sum of his parts, that both the hardheaded member of the middle class and the objective scholar, who believed only what they could see, were overlooking essential elements of man and his world. One result of this reaction was a revival of interest in religion, which during much of the eighteenth century had been the object of general ridicule on the part of informed and educated people. Other results of the growth of romanticism ranged from an awakened interest in the Middle Ages to an abhorrence of slavery and a concern for the alleviation of suffering and injustice. Patriotism, love of country, interest in popular literature, which the romantics believed was closer to the people, and a preoccupation with folkways, which were regarded as unperverted by civilization, were all characteristics of the romantic outlook.

Politically, romanticism had its most immediate effect on the growth of nationalism. Nineteenth-century liberals as a group tended to distrust nationalism as a divisive factor in a world that was already marked by too many differences. Nationalism, however, was more than romantic sentiment, and as the conservatives would insist, the nation had a common basis in its geography, language, traditions, and political rule. Moreover, nationalism had been growing and developing in Europe for several centuries before it was recognized and described. During the eighteenth century, most intellectuals had rejected religious answers to the problems of the world in order to seek more secular ones. Increasingly in the nineteenth century, men gave to the ideals of nationalism much the same ardor and expectation that their ancestors had given to religion. The result was that new nations grew while old ones became more important in the lives of their citizens. Inevitably, governments and people came to regard themselves as self-sufficient and as laws unto themselves. Nationalism also made statesmen more parochial and more narrowly concerned with national aims and programs; eventually this approach proved to be as fruitless as the dynastic ambitions of earlier despots.

HUMANITARIANISM

Another phase of romanticism that was even more influential in the long run was a growing concern for the sufferings and misfortunes of others. Though Americans today tend to take such concern for granted as a normal and natural human sentiment, humanitarianism has in reality been mainly a development of the past two centuries, one more characteristic of Western European civilization than of those in other parts of the world. On this aspect of romanticism, liberals and humanitarians were often in agreement, even though the two groups espoused the same reforms for different reasons. Both opposed slavery, for example, but liberals did so because they regarded the institution as socially and economically inefficient, while humanitarian opposition derived from sympathy for the slave. The two groups evidenced the same cooperation in their effort to reform criminal law. In other areas, for example, child labor, the distinction between the liberals and the humanitarians was more clear-cut. Nineteenth-century liberals tended to look upon the labor of children either as good for the child's moral character or as a hardship that could not be avoided. The humanitarians, on the other hand, were outraged at the idea of small children being confined to work in mines or mills and were ready to take any measures to remedy this social evil.

The role of nineteenth-century humanitarians in lessening suffering can hardly be overestimated — on the battlefield, in hospitals, asylums, prisons, work camps, factories, the military service, schools, and in their general concern for the welfare of human beings and animals. It was in this area that the romantic impulse had its most consistent and permanent consequences, as evidenced by the fact that social reform is a continuing process. Romanticism also had the effect of tempering and providing a degree of perspective to the dogmatic rationalism that dominated so much of nineteenth-century thought. It was, for example, too much to ask men of romantic temperament to accept without question the idea that all human motivation amounts to no more than a search for pleasure. Moreover, romanticism was a major factor in furthering the acceptance of democratic government, which nearly everywhere was opposed as illogical. Many liberal politicians of the nineteenth century believed that no government could function effectively if it had always to keep one eye upon the mob, which they believed represented the least educated, the most poorly endowed, and the worst tempered elements of society. To these objections, advocates of romanticism replied that the native feelings of all men, including the underprivileged and the ill-trained, gave them a capacity for wisdom not inferior to the wisdom of scholars. In fact, at the heart of romanticism was the idea that human emotions comprise a channel of communication between the individual and the world in which he lives.

Unfortunately, in spite of its virtues, certain dangers were inherent in the romantic belief. It enabled a person to believe whatever was expedient, whatever could be dramatically presented, and whatever dogma or creed happened to be around during a crisis. It was an invitation to avoid hard thinking, careful investigation, or reasoned analysis; indeed, many of the dictatorships of the twentieth century have grown out of romantic impulses. Romanticism was at its worst when its emotionalism was linked with the parochialism of the liberals or the conservatives. The most dangerous example of this alliance is the racism that has plagued twentieth-century Western society.

ROMANTICISM IN LITERATURE

Romanticism is often said to have begun with Rousseau and then to have spread to Germany with Schiller and Goethe. During the Revolution, romanticism was somewhat suspect in France, and though it continued to influence German writing, it did not come to dominate European literature until the end of the Napoleonic wars. Giving new impetus to the romantic movement in France was Madame de Staël, a glamorous and influential woman who wrote brilliantly and fought Napoleon with equal verve. Her *De l'Allemagne*, published in 1813, finally gave the French some concept of the intellectual ferment that was taking place in Germany. By 1830, romanticism dominated French fiction. Even Heinrich Heine, the great nineteenth-century German poet, moved to Paris after the July revolution of 1830 to take a more active part in the better world he felt to be in the making. His most famous collection of poems, *The Book of Songs (Das Buch der Lieder)*, portrays his shifting feelings about the joys and sorrows of love.

At the end of the eighteenth century in England, William Wordsworth, Samuel Taylor Coleridge, and William Blake began to write a new kind of poetry, although they went unrecognized until the second decade of the nineteenth century when their work was joined by that of Percy Bysshe Shelley, George Gordon (Lord Byron), and John Keats. Byron especially seemed to incorporate the romantic hero into his own personality. Always the rebel, he encouraged legends about his wildness and debauchery and died fighting for the independence of Greece, much in the manner of the melancholy young men whom he portrayed in such works as *Childe Harold*, who continually wandered from place to place in an effort to find themselves.

THE GREAT AGE OF THE NOVEL

The nineteenth century was primarily the age of the novel. In a period of increased literacy, it was possible for a writer to reach wide audiences, and mostly these audiences liked to read novels. Though literature was still oriented toward the upper classes, in the hands of the better writers it managed to cut across class lines. The most popular writer in English of the first part of the nineteenth century was Sir Walter Scott, who in his novels managed to cover most of English and Scottish history from the twelfth to the eighteenth centuries. Though historically inaccurate, Scott's plots are full of action and suspense, with settings, events, and personages that make them easily adaptable to film. More important for the development of the novel was Jane Austen, who confined her writing to the limited world of the upper middle class gentry from which she came. In novels such as *Pride and Prejudice*, she created a vivid picture of her class, especially the women. In this aspect of her work, she reflected the new importance of women, who as a group were better educated and more literate than ever before. As a result, books that appealed to women, many of them written by women, assumed a more important place in literature. Among the most distinguished women writers were the three Brontë sisters, Charlotte, Emily, and Anne. Many of the women writers originally used male pen names, but the only English writer still so identified is Marian Evans, better known as George Eliot. She was the most philosophical of the women writers of the period and for her time held very advanced ideas. Her *Adam Bede* was one of the first psychological novels.

The most influential novelist of the period was Charles Dickens, whose works had special appeal for the emerging lower middle classes. Though Dickens' cruel fathers and employers and his virtuous heroes and heroines sometimes seem almost caricatures, his attacks on the social abuses of his time contained a great deal of power. His auto-biographical *David Copperfield* is usually regarded as his masterpiece.

In France, the dominant literary figure was Victor Hugo, the poet, dramatist, and novelist whose skill in depicting the sufferings of the poor saved his works from becoming bathed in pathos. Quite different was Théophile Gautier, who represented a reaction to Hugo's senti-mentality. Almost an exponent of art for art's sake, Gautier insisted upon careful craftsmanship and less moralizing in literature. More influ-ential was Henry Beyle, better known as Stendhal, who used fiction to portray reality. *The Red and the Black* is typical of his novels, which usually center around strong-willed, self-made men, in this case Julien Sorel, who had an ambitious career and suffered a miserable death. Stendhal is often regarded as a precursor of Honoré de Balzac, who revolutionized French fiction with his carefully documented, detailed studies of contemporary society. Balzac was a kind of transitional figure from romanticism to realism, and his work, especially the *Comédie Humaine*, represented an attempt to apply the methods of scientific study and classification to a fictional portrait of society. Like England, France also had a number of women novelists, the best known of whom was George Sand (Aurore Dupin).

Much influenced by the romantic movement was the Italian Ales-sandro Manzoni, whose *I Promessi Sposi* (The Betrothed), a study of seventeenth-century Milan, was at one time regarded by many critics as the best novel ever written. Today, however, Russian fiction of the nineteenth century is now regarded as much more important than Italian. Here literary influences from Germany planted the seeds for what was to become the great age of Russian literature. The first major figure was Alexander Pushkin, the poet who was most responsible for establishing Russian as a literary language. His *Eugeni Oniegin*, a long poem dealing with the adventures of a young man of the world who realized too late that he really desired the woman who had once offered him her love, is usually regarded as the first Russian novel. The golden age of the Russian novel began with Nikolai Gogol, whose satires of the corruption and pettiness of Russian government officials often got him into trouble. In fact, Ivan Turgenev, another Russian literary great, was exiled to his country estate for calling Gogol a great man. Turgenev is best known for his sensitive portraits of the conflicts between the young Westernized Russian intellectuals and their conservative fathers. It was Turgenev who first described *nihilism*, a nineteenth-century anarchistic movement that aimed at overthrowing all existing institutions as the essential first step in reforming the world. Nihilists also served as important figures in the novels of Fyodor Dostoevsky, one of the literary geniuses of the nineteenth century. A surprising amount of Dostoevsky's work is based upon his own experience. Many of his heroes are epileptics — as was he — and revolutionaries, plagued with poverty, sickness, and sorrow. Dostoevsky himself was condemned to death in 1849 for revolutionary activities and was actually standing before the firing squad when his sentence was commuted to hard labor in the Siberian salt mines. Though upon his return from imprisonment he was plagued by poverty and sickness, he retained his love and sympathy for mankind.

BEETHOVEN AND HIS SUCCESSORS

The effect of romanticism was greatest in music, and it was Ludwig van Beethoven who introduced the new ideals. Building upon the work of his predecessors, Beethoven became the mighty lake out of which a thousand different musical streams have poured. His genius is evident in his nine symphonies, the first of which was composed in 1800. In his early work, Beethoven followed the conventions established by Haydn and Mozart, but he ended up breaking new paths. His ninth symphony, which utilizes a choral finale, was radically different from anything that had preceded it. Beethoven's accomplishment is all the more remarkable in the light of a growing loss of hearing that began in 1798; by the time he composed his ninth symphony in the 1820s, he was totally deaf. In addition to his symphonies, Beethoven composed operas, masses, chamber music, songs, string quartets, and especially music for the piano, which in the nineteenth century became the musical instrument of the middle class. One writer has said that Bach's piano music was the Old Testament of that instrument and Beethoven's the New, although Beethoven's piano pieces were not fully appreciated until long after his death.

Musical instruments as well as musical forms were also undergoing modification. New instruments were invented and old ones perfected,

Ludwig van Beethoven (1770–1827), nineteenth-century steel engraving. (The Granger Collection)

including the flute, oboe, clarinet, saxophone, harp, and trumpet. The new forms included the romantic opera, the short piano piece, the program symphony, or symphonic poem, and the art song. The art songs, or *Lieder*, were primarily the accomplishment of Franz Schubert, a contemporary of Beethoven, who in his short life of thirty-one years not only wrote ten symphonies, a number of quartets, and piano solos but also great quantities of *Lieder*. Somewhat less important in the field than Schubert but equally precocious was Felix Mendelssohn, who composed his famous overture to Shakespeare's *A Midsummer Night's Dream* when he was only seventeen. Piano music especially was enriched by Robert Schumann's short pieces and by the longer and more complex works of Franz von Liszt and Frederick Chopin. Both Liszt and Chopin were concert virtuosos who established much of the modern piano technique. Schumann had wanted to be a concert pianist, but an injury to his finger led him to devote most of his energies to composition and writing.

Most of the current opera repertoire was composed in the nineteenth century, and the founder of romantic opera was Karl Maria von Weber.

More important was the Italian Gioacchino Rossini, who started out as a disciple of Mozart, but who, after moving to Paris, established a new romantic fashion in grand opera with his *Guillaume Tell*. For a time in the 1820s, Rossini was the most popular composer in Europe. Overshadowing all of his rivals in this field was Richard Wagner, who from 1855 until his death nearly thirty years later was the most talked about musician in Europe. Wagner attempted to fuse music with dramatic poetry, and he not only wrote the words, text, and music for his thirteen operas but established a theater devoted solely to the production of his own works. For him such a theater was essential, since he felt that only if he could control the staging, poetry, music, painting, and action could his operas achieve their true dramatic purpose. Though Wagner's colossal ego has often repelled many, the history of opera has no other major creator whose mind and music match his complexity.

Indicative of a new trend in music was the work of the French composer Hector Berlioz, who attempted to portray aural images such as the sound of nature as well as to convey various mental states. Composers also sought to capture the "people's" dances, and the most influential of the new romantic composers in this field were Josef Strauss senior and junior, who replaced the classical minuet with the popular waltz.

PAINTING AND ARCHITECTURE

Romanticism in painting became a kind of escape to strange lands or past cultures. The artist sought new or different sensations to counteract the everyday realities surrounding him. Particularly attractive were medieval themes and models, and in the hands of painters like the French master Eugene Delacroix the result could become great art, although with lesser artists the result was a dreary repetition of canvases now consigned to the storage vaults of most museums. Delacroix as a true romantic emphasized the suffering of mankind in his effort to gain freedom. Struggle of one form or another became a major theme of the romantic artist. The English landscape painters John Constable and J. M. W. Turner, for example, portrayed man pitted against nature. The romantic artists also interpreted nature in a highly emotional manner, as evidenced particularly in the works of the French painters Theodore Rousseau and Camille Corot. Quite different but in a sense more impressive is the work of Francisco Goya, whose series the *Disasters of War* is an effective sermon against man's inhumanity to man.

The architecture of the romantic period was less original than it was imitative. There was an attempt to remodel gothic structures to suit nineteenth-century conceptions of what had been truely medieval. Windsor Castle, the country house of the English kings, is an example of a nineteenth-century rebuilding of this type. The cathedral of Notre

Dame in Paris is in part a nineteenth-century restoration, as is the famous cathedral of Cologne, which was completed and modified during this period. One of the most interesting and original of the re-creations, the *Königsbau* in Munich, was based upon a fifteenth-century Florentine palace. In the process of remodeling, the ideals as well as the practices of the medieval period were often seriously violated, although a number of works in this tradition are masterpieces. Romanticism also influenced landscaping, with the formal gardens of an earlier age giving way to a sort of wild, unplanned profusion. The popularity of artificial grottoes, waterfalls, and caves, which had begun in the eighteenth century, also grew. At the same time, there was a revival of classical styles, particularly in civic monuments, as each country tried to establish its ties with the ancient Greeks and Romans.

RELIGION

Though both romanticism and liberalism were less hostile to religion than the rationalism of the eighteenth century, the various churches — particularly the Catholic — were usually allied with the forces of reaction. Since Italian nationalism threatened the territorial base of the papacy, the popes opposed the movement. Since liberalism threatened the kind of absolutism the papacy exemplified, the popes were against liberals. Liberalism also emphasized a sort of materialism that dedicated religious people found hard to accept. As a result, the popes of the nineteenth century soon became the strongest supporters of reaction and ended up condemning democracy and liberalism as well as revolution. In response to the growth of skepticism, Pope Pius IX in 1854 proclaimed the doctrine of the Immaculate Conception. Thus Catholics were taught to believe that Mary had from the instant of her conception been preserved from all stain of original sin. This proclamation was followed by the *Syllabus of Errors* of 1864, in which the pope condemned most of the intellectual and political developments of the nineteenth century. As attacks on their conservatism mounted, the popes retaliated by consolidating their control of Church machinery. The culmination of this trend was the proclamation of the principle of papal infallibility by the Vatican Council of 1869–1870, which stated that the popes, when speaking *ex cathedra*, could not err. Though twentieth-century popes modified many of the acts of Pius IX, who marked the height of papal reaction, it was not until the pontificate of John XXIII in the middle of the twentieth century that the papacy turned away from most of the pronouncements of nineteenth-century reaction. Internally, the results of papal reaction were to turn Catholics away from full support of their church; a few even joined a German-centered group known as the Old Catholics.

Protestantism, perhaps because it was strongest in countries with a developing middle class, was better able than Catholicism to come to terms with liberalism. As a result, backed by liberal businessmen and government, Protestantism entered the mission field with vigor. Though Catholicism had long maintained missions in foreign lands, the first organized Protestant effort in this area dated only from 1701, and it never became fully functioning until it won the support of liberal government and businessmen in the nineteenth century. Liberals were especially anxious to support efforts to convert heathen in Asia and Africa, and the result was a wide dissemination of Western ideas. Catholics in such countries as France and Belgium also began to receive government support for missionary activities, and the nineteenth century became the great age of the missionary. In the long run, such missionary activity served not only to undermine native institutions and establish European dominance but to equate Christianity with European business and government. As Asian and African history of recent decades indicate, these results have proved difficult to eradicate.

HISTORY AND HISTORICAL PHILOSOPHY

One vital contribution of romanticism to European thought and culture was the interest it revived in the study of the past. The result was the development of modern "scientific" historical methods which emphasize the use of archival source materials and careful criticism of documents. At the same time, there was a growing interest in philosophies of history, according to which events and people could be neatly fitted into one grand pattern. In Germany, for example, a series of philosophers attempted to erect a rational explanation for the development of civilization. Included in the group were Johann Gottfried von Herder, Johann Gottlieb Fichte, Friedrich W. Schelling, and especially Georg W. F. Hegel.

Hegel believed that the universe is not a machine but an ever-changing and growing organism; what is true today was not true yesterday, nor would it be true tomorrow. In Hegel's view, mankind is continually evolving toward a more perfect world. In attempting to explain the development of human freedom, a subject in which he was particularly interested, Hegel developed a three-step method called the dialectic. According to it, civilization began in the East and was to reach its height in the West. In the Asiatic or Eastern phase, the political history of mankind had been characterized by absolute monarchy, in which only the despot was free. The Greco-Roman world, the intermediate stage, had given freedom, but finally the Germanic European world had fused the two earlier trends to give freedom to all within the context of a strong state. For Hegel, all history could be explained by the dialectic. First an idea, or the thesis, takes form, and then its opposite, the antithesis, makes its appearance. Out of the clash comes the ultimate synthesis, which combines the best of the two and represents a further step toward progress. The new synthesis, however, soon becomes a thesis, which is opposed by a new antithesis, and the process starts all over again. This aspect of Hegelian thought also led to the growth of a kind of utopianism that gradually developed into socialism. The result was a new challenge to liberalism, one that in the long run has proved to be a more effective contestant than conservatism. Before examining the development of socialism, however, it is necessary to look at France under Louis Philippe.

19

Revolution
and the Emergence
of New Power Blocks

France, as the home of revolutionary movements, continued to hold a sort of mystic sway over the subjected and downtrodden peoples of Europe throughout most of the nineteenth century. Inevitably, political developments in France tended to set the pace for those in other countries, while failures in France foreshadowed difficulties in the rest of Europe. This was true not only in 1830 but in 1848 when Louis Philippe was overthrown. Originally brought to the throne by the revolution of 1830, Louis Philippe has often been called the citizen king even though he rendered little but lip service to the idea of constitutional monarchy. Behind the facade of a bourgeois monarch he played a rather devious game of manipulation and election-fixing that deprived the French people of any real voice in government. These policies led to a growing disenchantment on the part of the liberals, which coincided with a feeling of unrest among the workers, who were feeling the difficulties brought by growing industrialization. The industrial revolution, which resulted in the growth of factory towns, an expansion of the railroad, and a rapid urbanization, produced a variety of problems in the areas of public health, fire and police protection, unemployment, child labor, and transportation that Louis Philippe was ill equipped to handle and for which liberalism had no answer. Though the factory system demonstrated itself to be an efficient production system, it proved a poor way to distribute wealth. The rich rapidly grew richer while the poor benefited slowly if at all. Moreover, the factory system robbed the handicraftsmen, the farmers, and others of the personal control over their affairs to which they were accustomed. They could work only when the factory was open, producing only what the manager determined and not what their talents and inclination dictated. What was true in France was true in other countries undergoing industrialization.

SOCIALISM

As their disillusionment with the factory system mounted, increasing numbers of people turned to various utopian schemes that gradually came to be identified as socialism. The term "socialism," however, implies a multitude of ideas, and the socialism of the early nineteenth century was not necessarily what it is today. In fact, the ideas underlying socialism can be traced at least as far back as Plato and the early Christian Church, although modern socialism is usually regarded as a product of the industrial revolution. Generally recognized as the first modern socialist is Count Claude Henri de Saint-Simon, who believed that the rapid transformation of social and economic conditions by the scientific and industrial revolution necessitated a real science of social progress based upon thorough planning of the economy. Saint-Simon was no modern democrat who believed that all men are equal but in fact preferred enlightened despotism to democracy. Socialism to him was not to be sought by the people but to be imposed upon them by the "captains of industry," who would assert their leadership in adjusting the world to new realities. This aspect of Saint-Simon's thought was opposed by others such as Charles Fourier and Robert Owen. Fourier believed that he had a perfect plan for a harmonious society in which each person was to be placed in association according to a formula he had worked out. He promised that if people voluntarily joined his communities, all vice, crime, and unhappiness would be eliminated. Owen was more practical, although equally visionary. One result of such teachings was the growth of a number of experimental socialist communities, including Brook Farm in New England. Many of the communities were bound together by religious ties, others by more secular causes, but all of them ultimately failed.

In the 1840s in France, a number of more radical social voices urged the working classes to rise up and throw off their chains. Among the new spokesmen was Pierre-Joseph Proudhon, a man of the people, whose solution for the problems of the time was to abolish unearned increment and unproductive property. Louis Blanc, a leader of the working classes, managed to combine a Jacobin commitment to democracy with a socialist fervor, although his remedy for contemporary social ills was state-owned factories. There were other radical voices, for example, Robert de Lamennais and, in Italy, Giuseppe Mazzini, but all took their cue from events in France in 1848.

FRANCE AND THE REVOLUTION OF 1848

Louis Philippe, while recognizing the growing unrest of the French citizen, was prevented by his own liberal assumptions and those of his advisers from dealing with the basic cause of discontent. Since liberals of the period believed that the general welfare belonged to the province of laissez-faire, according to which problems were to be allowed to solve themselves or to be handled through individual benevolence and never by the government, the king felt little compulsion to act. When difficulties mounted, the only weapon the liberals could utilize was force, the method they themselves had earlier denounced when it had been used against them. Increasingly, Louis turned to breaking up public meetings, to muzzling the press, and to jailing the opposition, but never did he deal with the real problems raised by industrialization. Any effort to relieve distress would have reminded the king's bourgeois supporters of all the abuses of the old regime that they felt they had so recently escaped. Though François Guizot, the king's chief minister, was strongly committed to the liberal creed of noninterference, his policy of repression offended many of his liberal supporters. In fact, the reign of Louis Philippe demonstrated many of the contradictions contained within liberalism, and the liberals were ultimately forced to face two basic, conflicting alternatives: they could support a tyranny in an effort to maintain public order or they could abandon some of their basic ideals in favor of heretical schemes such as public assistance. Guizot and Louis Philippe chose the first course, but when they tried to use force they were answered with stronger force. As a result, the king was forced to abdicate in February 1848, an event that marked the beginning of the Revolution of 1848. Most other European countries responded to developments in France with revolutions of their own, and in Austria, Hungary, Germany, and Italy, the revolution temporarily brought new hope to those challenging the existing regime. Ultimately, the hopes proved illusory, although some reforms resulted.

With the abdication of Louis Philippe, France reverted to a republic, the so-called Second Republic. The provisional government, which ran the republic until an assembly could be brought together to frame a new government, lent a sympathetic ear to the demands of the socialist Louis Blanc, who represented the workers. Blanc proposed to replace the privately owned factories with national workshops that would guarantee minimum wages, a standard of working conditions, and old age security. The middle classes resisted the proposal, however, and the constituent assembly demonstrated soon after it met in May that it had no patience with the working class point of view. When it became apparent that all hope for the national workshops must be abandoned, the workers of Paris threw up barricades in the street. Four bloody days of fighting resulted, and this June revolt, which crushed the workers and at least temporarily discouraged the socialists from ever achieving peaceful reform, fatally discredited the republic. By becoming a party to the wholesale slaughter of their own citizens, including the archbishop of Paris, who lost his life trying to stop the fighting, the republicans so covered themselves with shame that when the first elections were held under the new constitution the man chosen president was no republican but a Bonaparte.

Louis Napoleon, the new president, was the son of Louis Bonaparte, one of the emperor's several brothers. Until his election, he had been almost a comic opera figure in French political circles and had made two unsuccessful attempts to overthrow the government. In 1840, he had been sent into exile, a circumstance that proved to be an asset for him since he was out of the country during the February revolution and had not become involved in the difficulties of the provisional government. A forty-year-old demagogue when he returned, Louis Napoleon attracted support from peasants, who remembered that his uncle had secured their land titles; from Catholics, who had detested the bourgeois monarchy; from the workers, who hated the middle class; and from active nationalists, who had considered Louis Philippe a puppet of the British. The constitution of the Second Republic provided for an executive independently elected by manhood suffrage on the American pattern. In the fall elections, Louis Napoleon won by a landslide.

NAPOLEON III AND THE SECOND EMPIRE

For three years of his four-year term Louis Napoleon served properly as president of France before seizing full power in a coup d'etat. He then declared himself Napoleon III — out of deference to the second Napoleon, the son of the emperor who had died in 1832 — beginning the period of the second empire, which lasted to 1870. During the first half of his reign, the new emperor demonstrated a decisiveness and effectiveness that was unknown under the bourgeois regime of Louis Philippe. Much of his success, however, was simply due to luck. His rule coincided with an impressive upsurge of business activity produced by gold discoveries in California and Australia. Prosperity meant increased employment for the dissatisfied laboring classes, whom Louis Napoleon further assisted by large-scale programs of public improvements. He also won the loyalty of devoted Catholics, as well as of the papacy, by sending troops to restore the pope to his patrimony from which he had been driven during the outbreak in Rome of 1848. The emperor had a talent for elegance in the tradition of Louis XIV. He and his young empress Eugénie de Montijo, whom he married shortly after he claimed the crown, maintained in grand fashion the reputation of Paris as the style, fashion, and cultural center of Europe. In the process, he rebuilt Paris so thoroughly that the city of today is still much the same as it was under the Second Empire.

Toward the end of Louis Napoleon's reign his luck ran out and his difficulties mounted. Fundamental to his growing problems was the illegitimacy of his regime. As a usurper, he could justify his rule only by results. A legitimate monarch could better withstand misfortune or the poor advice of courtiers, since his rule was founded on ancient rights and privileges, and few subjects would perpetually question whether their level of achievement justified so much exercise of privilege. Napoleon, however, had continually to face this kind of assessment. Like other dictators, he tried to weigh things in his favor by controlling public opinion. He became an expert at propaganda and at concealing his mistakes from the public. With this kind of rule, the inevitable next is the conversion of the ruler himself to the belief that what he says is true. Inevitably, when a real crisis appears the illusion is washed away and the results are disastrous.

THE FOREIGN POLICY OF NAPOLEON III

One of Napoleon's basic difficulties stemmed from his attempt to re-establish France as a great military power. In an effort to appear as a defender of Catholicism — and thereby retain conservative support — he extracted from the sultan of Turkey concessions for Catholics in the Holy Land which were not matched by concessions to Orthodox Christians. Nicholas I, the tsar of Russia, in order to force such concessions, dispatched troops into the principalities, the Turkish territories that eventually became Rumania. The ultimate result of this 1853 invasion was the Crimean War, which began when France and Great Britain entered the conflict in 1854 on behalf of the Turks to prevent the over extension of Russian influence. This war was the first to receive popular newspaper coverage. For the first time, the negligent treatment of the sick or wounded soldier was brought to public attention. The result, at least in England, was mass public outrage. Florence Nightingale appeared in the Crimea, and there followed a public recognition of the need for nursing services. The war eventually ended when Sevastopol fell after an eleven-month siege, although Napoleon's image as the masterful ruler was already beginning to tarnish.

To remain successful in war, Napoleon had to choose those causes he felt would appeal to both conservatives and liberals. He believed he had found such a cause in the attempts of the kings of Sardinia to unify Italy under their rule. Before unification could take place, however, Austria, a traditional enemy of France, had to be expelled from Italian territory. In 1859, Napoleon committed some 200,000 troops against the Austrians, who held both Venice and Milan. Napoleon captured Milan for Sardinia, only to realize that Italian nationalism, which had the support of French liberals, was anticlerical, a circumstance that terrified French conservatives. Realizing that a prolonged war could only lose him supporters from both groups, Napoleon backed off with only half a victory, and some Italian territory ceded to France, to show for a large expenditure and the loss of twenty thousand soldiers. The best long-term result of the Italian campaign was the foundation of the international Red Cross by Henri Dunant, the Geneva resident who stumbled across the battlefield at Solferino where thousands of Austrian, French, and Italian troops lay dying of their wounds without food or adequate medical services.

Anxious to bolster his position, Napoleon turned to overseas expansion. French holdings in Algeria dating from the last days of Charles X were extended. In cooperation with the British, he began an aggressive expansionist policy in China that resulted in the occupation of Vietnam and Cambodia. These achievements served to maintain his image as a masterful emperor, but once again he ran into difficulty when he seized the American Civil War as an occasion to intervene in Mexico. Mexico at that time was under the control of an anticlerical group headed by Benito Juarez. Napoleon, hoping to regain Catholic support, attempted to supplant Juarez with Maximilian, the brother of the Austrian emperor. When Maximilian ran into guerrilla opposition and the United States threatened to intervene, Napoleon was forced to withdraw in an ignominious fashion.

Napoleon might still have been able to hold his throne after such disasters if there had not been a falling off in prosperity in one of those periodic downward cycles that have so troubled Western Europe and America in the past century. Moreover, while Napoleon had been involved in Mexico, the Prussians had seized the occasion to play an increasingly important role in central Europe. Inevitably, many French government officials came to believe that the most effective way to refurbish the imperial glitter would be to assert the Gallic right to a voice in the affairs of Germany. When the emperor attempted to do so, the Prussians quickly overran the ill-prepared French army, and a second Napoleon was forced to abdicate.

HAPSBURG RULE AFTER 1848

The revolution that had overthrown the "bourgeois" monarch in France resulted in Austria in the overthrow of Metternich, who was bourgeois in no way at all. Nevertheless, the liberal antipathy toward aristocratic government and toward privilege based upon heredity or on landed properties stood behind the revolution in Vienna, as it had in Paris. The same can be said for a number of other uprisings which broke out in Germany, though a frequent element was also disappointed nationalism, characterized by a resentment of Austrian control over German affairs and a feeling that there could be no true Germany while Austria maintained its dominance in that country. In general, the revolutions of 1848 consisted of demonstrations in the capital cities by factory workers, students, and others. In Vienna, the demonstrators had the sympathy of the civic guard, a kind of militia unit, and the government proved helpless to act. After Metternich resigned and fled the country in disguise, the Emperor Ferdinand, to quiet the uprising, agreed to accept a constitution, an elected legislature, and an end to censorship of the press. In July, a convention met to determine the constitution.

In the meantime, revolutions broke out in other parts of the Austrian Empire, which beneath the seeming peace of Metternich's rule had been full of seething discontent. In the Hungarian portions, the revolt was not so much one of liberals as of nationalists who wanted self-determination. To a lesser extent this was true of revolts in the Italian portions of the empire and in Bohemia, where the Czechs wanted independence. Though Ferdinand had agreed to accept a constitution in Vienna, the imperial army moved against the rebels, and through its seizure of roads, food supplies, manpower, and communications suppressed the revolt first in Bohemia and then in Italy; finally, in the fall of 1848, the army moved into Vienna itself. Thus came to an end the work of the constitutional convention, and Ferdinand himself abdicated in favor of his eighteen-year-old nephew Franz Josef, whose reign until his death in 1916 was one of the longest in history. For a time, the army continued to hold essential power, carrying on a program of suppression in an attempt to put down liberalism and nationalism everywhere. The Hungarians under Louis Kossuth had established an independent republic, but Franz Josef successfully mobilized the Slavic dislike for the Hungarians to convince the Czechs, Croats, and other Slavic-speaking peoples to put down the rebellious Magyars. The Russians also joined with the emperor in this campaign since they feared a Hungarian success would lead to a revolt in Poland.

THE UNIFICATION OF ITALY

Revolt also broke out in 1848 in Italy. Taking advantage of the difficulties in the Italian peninsula was Charles Albert of Sardinia, the only ruler in Italy not under Austrian supervision. By proclaiming a constitution with provisions for a British-type legislature and cabinet, Charles Albert attempted to assume direction of the movement for the liberation of Italy from foreign control. His attempts led to personal disaster, since he failed to gain the support of the republicans, who had established their own regimes in Tuscany and Rome, and since he was unable effectively to challenge the Austrian troops. In order to preserve his kingdom in the face of Austrian hostility, Charles Albert abdicated in favor of his son Victor Emmanuel, who successfully concluded peace with Austria. In the long run, however, Charles Albert's action won for his family, the house of Savoy, public esteem for its support of Italian nationalism. When the republican regimes of 1848 were put down, Victor Emmanuel II, still independent in his little country, became the main hope of the Italians, who dreamed of a united Italy free from foreign domination.

Besides the kings of Sardinia, the movement for Italian unity, called the *Risorgimento* (Resurgence), produced a multitude of other heroes. One was Giuseppe Mazzini, a republican who spent much time in prison and in exile for espousing both liberalism and Italian nationalism. The founder of the Young Italy movement at Marseilles, Mazzini was a major official in the revolutionary republic in Rome until it was over-thrown by Napoleon III. An associate at Rome was the dedicated republican and soldier of good fortune Guiseppe Garibaldi, whose legendary exploits have made him the best remembered of the Italian patriots. It was Count Camillo di Cavour, however, a diplomat and the chief minister of Victor Emmanuel, who actually succeeded in putting Italy together.

While serving as chief minister, Cavour had reformed the army and modernized the administration of Sardinia. He then attempted to find some way of weakening Austrian dominance in Italian affairs, and it was through his persuasive efforts that Napoleon III had intervened in Italy. However unhappy this intervention proved for Napoleon, it marked the beginning of the unification of Italy. Victor Emmanuel annexed Lombardy, the area around Milan, and blocked Austria from effective communication with its satellites of Tuscany, Parma, and Modena. When Napoleon abandoned the Italian campaign, Cavour had resigned in disgust but soon returned to power when Tuscany, Parma, and Modena began to clamor for annexation to Sardinia. To win French support for these annexations — and to give Napoleon something to show for his efforts — Cavour and Victor Emmanuel signed over control of the area around Nice, plus Savoy, the alpine territory near Lake Geneva that had been the original home of the house of Savoy.

Cavour's next exploit was to join with Garibaldi in a project to over-throw Bourbon control in Sicily and southern Italy, an area sometimes called the Kingdom of the Two Sicilies and sometimes simply Naples. Garibaldi, who earlier had acted as a leader of irregular troops in Uruguay, gathered together a detachment of about a thousand men, called the Red Shirts, in support of a rebellion that had started near

Palermo. Officially, Cavour remained neutral about Garibaldi's expedition, but privately he facilitated its organization and departure. Somewhat to the surprise of Cavour as well as of the rest of Europe, Garibaldi rapidly overran all of Sicily, and in August 1860 crossed to the mainland of southern Italy. Cavour, fearful that Garibaldi's success might create a republican regime in southern Italy, persuaded Victor Emmanuel to intervene directly to maintain his control of the emerging Italian nation. Victor Emmanuel had to move his troops through papal dominions, but he decided that he could do this as long as he respected the city of Rome itself, since he realized that Catholics in general would appreciate that he represented a lesser threat to the Church than did Garibaldi. In effect, a hero was deprived of his laurels, but there emerged a new and genuine national state uniting the north and the south, the kingdom of Italy, although Austria still held the northeast area around Venice and Napoleon maintained a garrison of French troops in Rome. Eventual annexation of these areas was dependent upon events in Germany.

GERMANY AND 1848

The fall of Metternich and the evident helplessness of the Hapsburgs led many Germans to hope that the old regime was about to be replaced by a vastly improved new order. Many Germans were stirred by the vision of all Germans gathered into one nation with no Poles, Italians, or Czechs to mar the uniformity, but some, particularly members of the middle class, looked for a modification of the autocratic government along the lines of the English model. The hostility to tyranny and oppression that stimulated the outbreaks in Paris and Vienna also encouraged revolts in numerous German states, including Prussia, where Frederick William IV made a number of concessions similar to those made by the emperor at Vienna. Before the year was over, however, the king had recovered full command.

At the height of the revolt, the liberals of Germany came together in the famous Frankfurt Parliament, or Assembly, to begin planning for the creation of a united Germany. The task was beyond the capacity of the assembly members to achieve, however, since it required both authority and an army that they did not have. Moreover, they were not agreed on which territories the new state should include, and they lacked an effective base of operations such as Sardinia offered the nationalists in Italy. To further complicate matters, the assembly became involved in a dispute between Frederick VII of Denmark and his German subjects living in the duchies of Holstein and Schleswig. While the six hundred delegates debated, the revolution was put down in Vienna, and Austria attempted to reassert control over the German

Confederation. In desperation, the members of the assembly appealed to Frederick William, king of Prussia, who, after setting aside his concessions made under duress, nonetheless proceeded to impose a new constitution of his own drafting. Though sorely tempted to accept the crown, Frederick William finally refused because to take it meant war with Austria, which he felt he could not win, and, in addition, he was reluctant to receive the crown from such a body.

Without any real military support the liberal members of the assembly were soon dispersed by a force of arms. To Germans, particularly German liberals, the experience was shattering. Despair for any united fatherland led a significant number of them to emigrate to the United States. Those who remained saw liberalism discredited by its failure to weaken the power of the aristocracy. Moreover, in central and eastern Europe, the old regime continued, with kings and nobles enjoying as many privileges in the first part of the twentieth century as they did before the French Revolution. One of the most backward areas of Germany in this sense was Prussia, which after the failure of the Frankfurt Parliament assumed leadership of the movement for German unity. Prussian territories extended throughout Germany, including the Rhineland, but the most significant portion of the kingdom was a region east of the Elbe River that could still be described as feudal. This area contained a small liberal middle class, but the economic basis of society was rural and based upon a landlord-peasant relationship. German nationalists from this area tended to look back to the glories of Frederick the Great rather than to the vision of the future expounded by the Utilitarians in England and elsewhere.

OTTO VON BISMARCK

The weakness of the Prussian liberals was documented in the struggle to control the army. Frederick William, who had become insane and then finally died in 1861, was succeeded by his brother William, or Wilhelm, whose sole purpose in life seemed to be to improve the army. To the liberal faction in the *Landtag*, the lower house of the Prussian parliament established in 1850, armies were primarily tax eaters, liable to provoke expensive wars without materially assisting the economy. At first, the faction was strong enough to prevent approval of a tax measure that would have provided the necessary revenue to enlarge the army. The king, determined to get his way, turned to Otto von Bismarck, who felt no qualms about heading a ministry that lacked the support of the *Landtag*. Thus began one of the most famous careers in all European politics. Whatever his numerous shortcomings, it was Bismarck who brought about the unification of Germany. When in 1862 the *Landtag* refused the revenues to continue

Prince Otto von Bismarck (1815–1898), contemporary portrait by Hader. (The Bettmann Archive, Inc.)

the expansion of the army, Bismarck simply went ahead as if the money had been voted. Since the Prussian constitution did not assure ministerial subordination to a parliamentary majority, Bismarck could assume such powers as long as he had the backing of the king. After winning some military victories, he turned to the *Landtag* for acceptance of his program over the past four years. When this house gave Bismarck's policies its stamp of approval, it admitted, in effect, that the Prussian constitution was no more than a scrap of paper. The *Landtag* supported Bismarck's program because German nationalism had won out over any qualms the liberals might have had. Liberals disliked Bismarck's methods, but they approved the elimination of Hapsburg dominance which these methods had brought about.

With his accession to power Bismarck had begun to involve himself in the Schleswig-Holstein problem upon which the liberals had foundered in 1848. The Danish king, fearful of what might happen, sought to integrate these German-speaking territories into Denmark. Holstein, however, was a member of the German Confederation, a circumstance that allowed Bismarck to join with the Austrians to thwart the Danish plans. The brief war in 1864 that grew out of this conflict, in which both Austria and Prussia joined against Denmark, resulted in the Danes giving up control of the two duchies. With Holstein under Austrian control, Bismarck began to prepare for a war with Austria to remove Austrian influence in Germany. To this end he sought an alliance with Victor Emmanuel, who was anxious to drive the Austrians from Venice. Since Victor Emmanuel could not have agreed to Bismarck's plans without French connivance, Bismarck thereby assumed French neutrality. With French troops still in Rome, Napoleon was willing to remain neutral in the hope that a long, drawn-out war would result in bringing many of the southern German states into closer alliance with France. The French emperor was entirely unaware of the size of the Prussian army or of its modern equipment, which included a breech-loading "needlegun." As Bismarck hoped, Austria, after being provoked over Holstein, declared war in the summer of 1866. The Italians kept a large number of Austrians occupied in Italy, while the Prussians, after dispatching troops to take care of the Saxons, Hanoverians, Hessians, and other German states supporting Austria, concentrated their army in Bohemia. Here they defeated the Austrians at Sadowa, also called the battle of Königgrätz, on July 3. Overcome after only seven weeks of fighting, the Austrians sued for peace before any of their territories rose in rebellion. As a result of the hostilities, Italy received Venice, while Prussia emerged dominant within Germany. In place of the old Austrian-dominated confederation, there appeared a new North German federation under Prussian management. Only four south German states, Bavaria, Württemberg, Baden, and part of Hesse, remained independent.

Napoleon III was by no means pleased with the Prussian victory at Sadowa, especially as Bismarck declined to be properly appreciative of French neutrality. The chancellor, however, was clearly of the opinion that the French Empire had more shadow than substance. Bismarck believed that the advantage of Prussia could be still furthered if the south German states could, through their fear of France, be brought into closer partnership with the North German Federation, in which they had shown little interest.

THE FRANCO-PRUSSIAN WAR

Convinced that the German army could do to Napoleon what it had already done to the Austrians, the Prussians made ready such an effort and trusted Bismarck would find the occasion to go to war. Since Napoleon III still seriously underrated Prussian military strength, Bismarck had only to manipulate the circumstances under which France could be made to appear the aggressor. His opportunity came in 1870 when the Spanish, looking for a successor to the deposed Isabella II, offered the crown to Leopold of Sigmaringen, a Catholic member of the Hohenzollern family which had long ruled Prussia. French fire-eaters immediately used the issue to arouse fears that France would be surrounded by Hohenzollerns. Though Leopold was not interested in the Spanish crown and said so, the French were not happy about the situation, and Bismarck carefully fanned the flames of their discontent. His opportunity came when Napoleon attempted to extract from King William a guarantee that a Hohenzollern interest in the Spanish throne would not be revived. William, who had already made it clear that he was not empowered to speak for Prince Leopold in these matters, refused to issue such a statement.

The war party in Paris, with the connivance of newspaper interests anxious to sell more papers, made William's refusal seem an affront to the dignity of France, as Bismarck planned and hoped would happen. The result was a public clamor for war which a weakened yet frightened Napoleon found unable to resist. His decision in July 1870 to go to war over a real or imagined affront led to one of the greatest disasters ever to befall France. Unprepared for a conflict, the French people, in spite of newspaper stories to the contrary, did not want war. So poorly organized was the French army that not even half of its three-quarter million troops ever got into the field, and the majority of those that did were soon helplessly surrounded in the border fortress of Metz. Within a month from the time the first shot had been fired, most of the French troops that were left — along with the emperor — had been taken as prisoners. By September 4, the Second Empire had been terminated by an impromptu assembly of republicans who established the Third Republic. The new government continued to hold on to Paris until January 1871, when the city capitulated to the Germans. The Prussians remained in occupation until elections could be held for a new assembly that might officially end the hostilities. Though the people of Paris wanted to continue the struggle with the Germans at any cost, most Frenchmen elsewhere were determined to end the war. A majority of candidates committed to ending the war were elected, but most of them were also monarchists. The result of the election was an attempt to end the newly established French Republic, an effort that led to a rebellion of the citizens of Paris under the leadership of the Communards. By the middle of May 1871, after a two-month civil war, the assembly managed to move troops into Paris, and in the resultant slaughter the archbishop of Paris lost his life, the Hotel de Ville and the Tuileries were burned, and the city itself suffered irreparable damage. In the aftermath of the abortive revolt, the French instituted a series of political witch hunts that led to the arrest and deportation of thousands of suspected Communards without trial. Some of the more vociferous republicans lost their lives in this confrontation; in addition, by revolting while the German army was still in nominal occupation, those who supported them lost the allegiance of most of their countrymen. Ironically, the republican cause was saved by the repressive tactics used against the Parisian rebels and by the fact that in securing peace the antirepublican leaders of the national assembly agreed to the cession of Alsace-Lorraine, an action which most Frenchmen regarded as a betrayal. Even then the most important factor preventing the assembly from establishing some form of monarchy was an inability to agree upon a candidate for king. Advocates of monarchy were divided between groups supporting the Bourbons, the Orleanists — descendants of Louis Philippe — and the Bonapartes. It was not until after four years of dissension that the assembly finally agreed to accept a republican-type government, simply because this alternative seemed less dangerous to the opposing monarchical factions than giving power to their rivals. The new republic of convenience called for a president, a bicameral legislature, and a cabinet administrative unit modeled after that of the British.

THE GERMAN EMPIRE

The Franco-Prussian War had obviously succeeded beyond Bismarck's dreams. The Prussians had not only defeated France and occupied Paris but Napoleon's initial offensive enabled Bismarck to pose as protector of the south German states. These territories were thus effectively convinced of the need to join the North German Federation, and the new grouping was promptly renamed the German Empire. While the new emperor, otherwise known as the kaiser, ruled over a few Danes and a few more Poles, the overwhelming majority of his subjects were Germans. In actuality, the empire was a federal state of twenty-five little and big nations collected into a union with Prussia. Aside from the emperor, who was regulated by a constitution, the main governmental body was the *Bundesrat,* or upper house of the legislature, which had fifty-eight members appointed by the rulers of the various states. The kaiser himself, who was also king of Prussia, appointed seventeen of them; no other state had more than six. Thus with little effort the kaiser could control legislation. The lower house or *Reichstag* was more democratically elected, but other than its right to assent to new laws and new taxes, it had little power. The chancellor and other administrative officials had to answer only to the kaiser, who had full control of the army as well as of foreign affairs.

This appearance in central Europe of a new and independently powerful state, where for centuries there had only been an assortment of peoples, was sudden and disturbing to the other European powers.

France was especially fearful, since in addition to paying a large indemnity to Prussia, the German-speaking territory of Alsace and most of the French-speaking province of Lorraine were also ceded, even though they had been under French control for two centuries. France immediately sought means of revenge, marking the beginning of a rivalry between the two dominant European powers that lasted for the next seventy-five years.

OTHER EUROPEAN DEVELOPMENTS

The Prussian victory over France allowed the Italians to complete the unification of Italy, since Napoleon III had been forced to withdraw his troops from Rome and the papal states. When the Italian armies moved in, only the Vatican palace and grounds remained under papal control, although for the next fifty years the popes refused to recognize this fact.

After its defeat by Prussia, Austria underwent a reorganization. Faced with a growing tide of discontent from its many subject nationalities who witnessed the emergence of new nations such as Germany and Italy, the Hapsburgs were forced to give ground. Proposals to create some sort of federal state gained the approval of many, but instead an arrangement known as the *Ausgleich*, proposed by the Magyar leader Ferencz Deak, was adopted in 1867. The result was the creation of a dual monarchy under the title of the Austro-Hungarian Empire, wherein two linguistic groups, the Austrians and Hungarians, shared domination over the other nationalities. Two capitals, one at Vienna and the other at Budapest, were recognized. The first served as the capital for the Germans, Czechs, Poles, and Slovenes and the second for the Magyars, Slovaks, Croats, and Rumanians. The emperor Franz Josef retained sovereignty, but the two governments were independent in all matters but war, diplomacy, and finance. Since the empire was still unable to develop any real administrative machinery, Franz Josef ruled by decrees, which the army enforced when necessary. The arrangement ended the unrest of the Hungarians, but it did nothing to lessen the discontent of the other groups, and thus the Austro-Hungarian Empire remained a potentially explosive powder keg.

Russia, the other great continental power, had been slowly expanding eastward across Asia through Siberia during most of the nineteenth century, eventually coming into conflict with the Chinese and Japanese. In many ways, the Russians were isolationists in the sense that Americans were during the same period and for much the same reason. As a European power, however, Russia could not afford to ignore what was taking place in neighboring states. Moreover, since the tsar regarded himself as the protector of Orthodox Christians everywhere, he always had a pretext for interfering in Muslim Turkey, which controlled the routes from the Black Sea to the Mediterranean Sea, so long coveted by the Russians.

THE TURKS AND THE EASTERN QUESTION

Turkey, in fact, seemed to serve as a magnet for the ambitions of various European states. The once mighty Ottoman Empire had so deteriorated as to become known as the sick man of Europe. Turkish soldiers were still able fighters, but they were usually poorly led. The sultans were vicious autocrats, government officials were venal and corrupt, and nearly the whole of Turkish commerce was in the hands of foreign interests. Since Turkey was a Muslim power, few European rulers sympathized with the sultan. Indeed, any such tendency was quelled by Turkish atrocities against their numerous Christian subjects, especially the Armenians and the Bulgarians. All that kept the badly divided empire together was the unwillingness of any of the great powers to allow the others a free hand in seizing the strategically important Turkish territory that dominated the communication routes linking the three continents. Only when there was a kind of agreement among the great powers, as in the case of the Greek revolt, did the Turks lose territory, although many parts of the Ottoman Empire grew to function as more or less independent units. Increasingly, the Eastern question, or the struggle for control of Turkish-controlled territory, played an important part in European affairs. The Russians especially found pretexts to meddle in southeast Europe, although, as the Crimean War demonstrated, they did not always have a free hand.

Russia's usual reason for intervention was to aid revolts among the sultan's Christian subjects. In the 1870s, for example, the Serbs from the region of Bosnia rebelled against their Turkish overlords. They were soon joined by the Serbs in Serbia, then a Turkish satellite, and simultaneous revolts broke out in Bulgaria. Turkish efforts to end the rebellion caused so much bloodshed that in 1877 Russia was able to intervene without protest from any of the other great powers. The result of this intervention was the Treaty of San Stefano, which gave both Serbia and Rumania independence from Turkey. Under the terms of this agreement the new state of Bulgaria was created, nominally as a Turkish satellite to include about half the sultan's European possessions but in actual fact greatly dependent upon Russia. The British as well as the Austrians objected to this extension of Russian influence to the Mediterranean, whereupon the whole Balkan problem was then reworked at a general peace conference, the Congress of Berlin in 1878. In this new settlement Bulgaria was cut into segments: the Macedonian part was divided between Greece and Turkey; another portion, eastern

Rumelia, was recognized as a semi-independent Turkish possession, as was Bulgaria itself; the area around Sarajevo, in effect, Bosnia, became an Austrian satellite; the British took control of the island of Cyprus; and Russia was given Bessarabia and territory on the Black Sea.

GREAT BRITAIN

The one European power that escaped the upheaval of the period was Great Britain, which seemingly adopted more and more of the liberal concepts as government policy. In 1846, all duties were lifted from imported grain, though this measure was not designed so much to establish free trade as it was to assure supplies to feed the stricken Irish during the famine of that year and to lower the price of food to factory workers. Soon other import duties were removed in an effort to throw the home market open to foreign competition and to carry through the liberal conviction that duties acted only to buttress privilege and to bolster vested interest — which to the liberals meant landed agricultural interests. Almost immediately, England prospered, although its prosperity could not be ascribed so much to the truth of the liberal philosophy as to the gold discoveries made in 1848 and 1851 and to Britain's near-monopoly of the technology of modern industry, including steamships, railroads, machinery, and the necessary raw materials to manufacture these agents of progress. But since prosperity accidentally coincided with the adoption of free trade, it had the unfortunate effect of giving the British the belief that the liberal ideology contained the answer for making this the best of all possible worlds.

At the same time that the British economy progressed so rapidly, there was a growing agitation on the part of the lower class to improve its position in society. One of the most unique of the lower-class movements was Chartism, which resulted from a combination of demands on the part of the workingman for greater representation in politics and resentment toward a reform of the Poor Law that centralized poor relief and narrowed its scope. In addition, the lower classes were uncertain as to how the introduction of power machinery would effect them and were dissatisfied with the treatment of religious dissenters, most of whom were members of this class. The culmination of the Chartist movement was a petition presented in 1848 bearing nearly five million signatures — many of them bogus — to democratize England by establishing a secret ballot, universal manhood suffrage, and abolition of property qualifications. Though these demands were rejected by English politicians of both the Tory (Conservative) and Whig (Liberal) parties, a gradual modification came to be made in the structure of English government. The Tory party, under Sir Robert Peal, recognized the demand for humanitarian reforms, and the party continued this policy under the leadership of Benjamin Disraeli, who believed that adjustments had to be made even though he disagreed with the demands of the workingmen. The Whigs, first under Lord John Russell and Lord Henry Palmerston, but most successfully under William Gladstone, carried through a program of social reform. During the nineteenth century, the English abolished slavery, established a system of national factory inspections, reorganized local government, reformed the civil service, adopted universal compulsory education, dis-established the Anglican Church in Ireland and Wales, rebuilt the court system and the army, and gradually extended the franchise. England also put into practice the concept of the self-governing colony, which eventually led to the emergence of such independent countries as Canada and Australia. Yet in spite of its internal accomplishments, England was much less influential on the world scene in the last part of the nineteenth century than it was at the beginning as economic competition from Germany, the United States, and other new industrial powers challenged British world dominance.

The nineteenth century, however, was less marked by war than any previous period, and, because Great Britain was the acknowledged leader among the nations for most of this time, the long peace has sometimes been called the *Pax Britannica*. Though the century had its share of armed conflicts, as a general rule the wars that were fought were limited ones with limited objectives and did not involve all of the major European powers. Europe seemed to be gaining a second wind after the devastation of an earlier period. The relative impotence of France undoubtedly had much to do with keeping the peace, and Austria was in no condition to be aggressive, while Spain really no longer counted as a great power. Prussia and Russia were occupied with internal expansion, but by 1870 the situation had begun to change. Giving fuel to the growing tensions was the breakup of the Ottoman Empire, since its territories were coveted by several of the great powers. Nationalism was still rampant, and both the Austrian Empire and the Balkans supplied tinder for a major conflagration. To complicate the growing unrest, Europe was involved in a struggle for colonies all over the world. Moreover, liberalism, which had grown increasingly influential during the century, was now being challenged by harsh reality, and liberals had to admit that they did not have answers to the collection of human problems they had previously been so certain they could resolve.

20

Expansion
and Internal
Discontent

Though European civilization had been expanding almost continually
since the time of the Crusades, there were several periods when this
objective was pursued with particular intensity. The first great period
of expansion, the age of exploration from the sixteenth to the eighteenth
centuries, coincided with the growth of mercantilism. Countries did
not so much annex territory as establish trading missions or claim
exclusive trading rights. In any event, the native societies went largely
undisturbed, the chief exception being in the Americas, which were
not only commercially exploited but colonized, particularly North
America. This phase of European expansion ended with the American
and French revolutionary wars.

A second wave of expansion began in the middle of the nineteenth
century, but this time the concern was more with territory than with
products. The United States and Russia at first expanded into their
virtually unoccupied hinterlands. Other countries, lacking the unex-
plored interiors of these two nations, appropriated whatever other
region had not been taken up by other great powers. Once the United
States and Russia had fixed their new frontiers, they too joined the
rush for new territories. The Japanese, alone among Asian and African
countries, not only managed to oust the potential exploiters but
adopted Western ways and joined with the great powers in seeking
new territory. This general thirst for new territory led to a situation in
which most of the advanced nations of the world hunted for some

pretext to aggrandize themselves at the expense of backward or weaker populations that happened within their line of vision.

Though Europeans often spoke of the white man's burden, by which they meant the need to bring the benefits of Western civilizations to the rest of the world, they also justified imperialism militarily as a search for locations of strategic advantage and economically in terms of markets for the home country products, a source of raw materials, or an opportunity for investment. Missionaries served as one of the largest pressure groups in favor of imperialist expansion, and they either immediately preceded or followed economic or political penetration. In the rush to grab more and more territory, nations did not even bother to examine whether the newly annexed lands were an asset or a liability. Historical studies of the last few decades, for example, tend to show that few of the newly established colonial areas in Asia, Africa, or elsewhere ever yielded any real profits to the governments that seized them, although various individual businessmen or industrialists undoubtedly became rich. Occasionally, when the cost of ruling a colony was less than the value of what it produced, as in the case of the Congo, the results were achieved by tyrannical oppression of the natives.

Imperialism changed the world drastically. It spread Western civilization, from the alphabet to the railroads; it led to the suppression of some highly barbarous and savage customs, and in its more enlightened form it resulted in the growth of schools, hospitals, and similar institutions; in addition, it led to modifications in the status of women, the rights of children, and other humanitarian reforms. The total effect, however, was the dislocation of existing and stable societies and the eventual creation of mass discontent, which continued to grow throughout the twentieth century. For example, it was the students trained at missionary schools in China who took the lead in reforming China and in expelling Western "imperialists," including missionaries. Many of the students inevitably became Communists. Much of the unrest among "underdeveloped countries" of the world today can be accounted for by the fact that Western expansion disrupted existing societies. Moreover, imperialism abroad too often served as an excuse to divert attention away from growing internal ills within Europe.

MARXIAN SOCIALISM

Exploiting these internal discontents were the socialists, who achieved a new level of cohesion through the teachings of Karl Marx, a German who spent most of his adult life as an exile in London. Marx was a symbol of the changing nature of education, as well as of the growth of intellectual specialization, since he was one of the first major

Karl Marx (1818–1883).
(The Bettmann Archive,
Inc.)

intellectuals to obtain a doctoral degree. In fact, much of Marx's thought derived from the theoretical work of Hegel. Using Hegel's dialectic theory of progression, Marx argued that the essential factor in understanding man was the pervasive influence of material needs, and his solution to man's problems was dependent upon dialectical materialism.

Marx was disturbed by the apathy and indifference of society toward the continued prevalence of poverty and injustice. He dreamed of a revolution that would sweep out the factory owners and all economic "exploiters." Marx believed that such people were interested only in perpetuating wage slavery in order to maximize their own gains, that they were bloodsuckers living upon the misery of others. This became his thesis. As an antithesis, Marx posited the growing numbers of landless proletariat who had nothing to sell but the use of their hands. The proletariat would continue to increase, since he believed that the very covetousness of the "exploiters" would lead to a narrower and narrower ruling clique. The inevitable result would be a class struggle in which the masses of poor would join together to destroy their exploiters. Thus there would be a synthesis, a society of perfect equality. Marx believed that such developments were inevitable, that the pattern he had found from a concentrated study of history was as scientific as Newton's explanation of the universe. His economic determinism was based on the nineteenth-century assumption that there were immutable laws of social conduct just as there were immutable laws of astronomy. Most social scientists of today do not hold that there are such immutable laws, and among those that do, there is no agreement as to what these laws might be. These shortcomings, however, should not detract from the nature of Marx's achievement or of his success. Millions of people, even organized societies, came to believe that Marx was right and acted accordingly.

Marx's first major effort was a collaborative one with his long-time friend Friedrich Engels. The result, *The Communist Manifesto,* was published just before the February revolution of 1848 in Paris. This revolution came to be a dominating factor in Marx's thinking, since he regarded the revolt as the first step in the establishment of the utopia he so desired. The failure of 1848 led Marx to develop his theory further in order to explain why conservative opposition would eventually come to nothing. Marx also attempted to organize the voting strength of the ever-increasing number of factory workers. In general, the Social Democrats, who came to follow this policy, were fairly successful on the Continent, although they met with less success in England, where a combination of laboring men and dissenting Protestant groups, with a few Utilitarian liberals, established what came to be the British Labor Party. The success of the Social Democrats in the 1860s and after tended to make Marx doubt the inevitability of revolution, since as soon as the workers gained the power of the ballot, they won better wages and improved working conditions. They thus came to have such a vested interest in the established economic system that they no longer wanted it overthrown. Marx eventually came to believe that in some countries it might be possible to achieve his utopian society by the ballot box rather than through bullets, although he never entirely rejected the necessity of revolution.

The improvements in living and working conditions that disappointed the hard-core Marxists theoreticians also undermined the basic assumptions and programs of nineteenth-century liberalism. Free trade, a hallmark of the liberal program, declined in the last part of the nineteenth century as both Germany and the United States established a system of tariffs in order to build up their own factory production. Other industrial nations soon followed suit. At the same time, various social welfare programs were implemented, including mine and factory inspections, limitations upon hours of labor, and minimum wage and child labor laws. Though dogmatic liberals viewed these legislative enactments as an assault upon liberalism, the socialists who advocated these programs often received the support of conservative elements, such as the Catholic Church, which earlier had opposed the liberal program. The result was an evolution of democratic socialism or modified capitalism in most of the industrialized countries of the world.

The countries that were slowest to adjust or to modify their economic and political systems to the demands of the time were the ones most likely to be caught up in the violent revolutions of the twentieth century.

DARWINISM AND THE NEW PHYSICS

As revolutionary as Marxism, if not more so, were the ·scientific developments that took place during the nineteenth century. The first challenge to the old Newtonian view was Charles Darwin's *On the Origin of Species through Natural Selection*, first published in 1859. Where Newton seemed to say that material bodies perform the way they do because they obey laws that have some kind of force behind them, Darwin implied that evolutionary development occurs because of expedience and not out of necessity. Central to Darwin's concepts was the principle of the survival of the fittest, which stated that those traits which best enable an organism to survive are those most likely to be passed on to succeeding generations, since individuals who carry less desirable characteristics are eliminated. In effect, for Darwin, life is continually evolving into new forms, and man is not necessarily

Charles Darwin (1809–1882), portrait by John Collier. (National Portrait Gallery, London)

the final word. Like Galileo before him, Darwin ran into great opposition from many of his contemporaries and from religious groups, who felt his observations were contrary to the Scriptures. The conflict between evolution and religion has continued to our own day, although with much less force, in spite of the fact that Darwin had in part freed man from the limitations put upon him by the Newtonian universe with his insistence that the future of man is in part up to himself.

Much of the failure of Darwin's contemporaries to accept his ideas can be ascribed to their tendency to dwell in absolutes. Darwin, however, a scientist in the best sense of the word, was willing to admit that today's truth could be tomorrow's error. Though he based his conclusions on the best possible evidence and spent years of research to support his thesis before he published it, unlike Newton, he had no thought that his ideas must be valid for all time. Most people in the nineteenth century, however, were unwilling to admit the fallibility of common sense or the need for anything but the whole truth. Further challenging this preference for absolute truth was the development of modern physics, which more than anything undermined the philosophical assumptions upon which most nineteenth-century thought had been based.

Much of the work in physics derived from the discoveries of Xrays by Wilhelm Konrad Roentgen in the last decade of the nineteenth century. In attempting to explain the phenomenon, Max Planck in 1900 argued that energy was not given off smoothly, as scientists had earlier assumed, but in small bundles that he called quanta. So revolutionary was this concept that Planck himself had doubts about his own interpretation, but it proved to be the key to Albert Einstein's explanation of the hitherto incomprehensible features of the photoelectric effect. In 1905, Einstein argued that light itself must consist of quanta, or photons, and in the same year he developed his theory of relativity, which brought about a new scientific revolution.

The new physics demolished the Newtonian structure, and in the process it altered the role of science and of knowledge. Space and time, hitherto assumed to be separate and immutable, ceased to be either. When the theory was applied to philosophy, the implication was that common sense, which had so often been viewed as a criterion of truth, could now be regarded as only relative. The recognition that man's knowledge might be only partially complete, that man might never know the full truth either about the universe or himself, is perhaps the key to the intellectual accomplishments of the twentieth century. When man has only partial knowledge, he can work to gain greater understanding, and even erroneous ideas can and have led to new vistas or new approaches. Indirectly this realization led to a reappraisal of Darwin and an acceptance of his theory of evolution.

SOCIAL DARWINISM

The advances in science reflected some of the ideas developed in other disciplines and in turn were utilized in ways their originators had not intended. Darwin's principle of the survival of the fittest, for example, was seized upon by those who developed the concept that came to be called social Darwinism. For nearly two generations, men such as William Graham Sumner in the United States and Herbert Spencer in England exploited this perversion of Darwinism into a conscious anti-Marxist justification of capitalism. They and the social Darwinists in general argued that the entrepeneurs were the most fit of society and that to try to regulate them would go against all laws of nature. Conversely, any concerted effort on the part of government to assist the poor or downtrodden would tend to preserve the unfit, who could then reproduce and threaten the existence of all of society. The intellectual backing of social Darwinism combined with the political threat of socialism tended to make defenders of the status quo out of many of the individuals and groups that earlier had been in the forefront of reform.

Social Darwinism, which was never advocated by Darwin, also tended to provide a quasi-scientific underpinning for theories of racism and ethnocentrism. Disparities between countries or peoples in religion, artistic or scholarly achievement, economic advantage — in fact, in almost any area — were made to seem of genetic origin. In effect, whole societies came to be regarded as genetically inferior, and this idea was used to justify "scientifically" European dominance over the rest of the world. Jews, who had lived in Europe since Roman times, could now be shown to be inferior aliens. Northern Europeans, whose industrial superiority had become possible through abundant natural resources, ascribed their achievement to racial superiority, and even at times to an innate cultural wisdom in having chosen to be Protestants rather than Catholics.

This misuse of Darwinian ideas also served to unite liberals and conservatives as nationalists, since only by uniting could they preserve whatever could be called the indigenous elements of their society. Both groups were hostile to alterations and modifications at home and opposed to importations from abroad. These new nationalists, though often called conservatives, differed from traditional conservatives, who had been cosmopolitan and not particularly nationalistic. The result has been a continual confusion over exactly what the terms "conservative" and "liberal" mean, since there was and is no exact ideology to which each group could be assigned. One of the first results of the new ethno-centricism was a growing agitation for indepence on the part of various subjugated peoples. The Irish, who had started out demanding home rule from England, soon became involved in a struggle for complete independence. The Norwegians clamored for separation from Sweden, while the Catalonians became increasingly restive under Spanish rule. In eastern Europe, the result was pan-Slavism, representing a sort of Slavic unity against the threat of Western cultural supremacy, which was identified as worldly, decadent, materialistic, and militaristic. As the twentieth century advanced this new kind of nationalism became a potent force both within and without Europe. In many parts of the world today, hostility to anything European or American has wide appeal. In a very real sense, the pan-Arabism of today is a contemporary counterpart of the pan-Slavism of fifty years ago.

SOCIAL SCIENCES

Social Darwinism continued to have adherents well into the twentieth century, when most of its assumptions were undermined by the growth of the philosophical relativism that resulted from the work of Planck, Einstein, and others. In addition, it was challenged by new social theories which emphasized that man's nature was a reflection at least in part of his social environment. According to this view, man's integration into a community, his opportunities for individual growth and development, his economic condition, all had some effect on the kind of person he became. The study of man became a scientific enterprise in and of itself. Though Adam Smith, John Stuart Mill, Herbert Spencer, William Graham Sumner, and Karl Marx had all been concerned with man's social environment, they could more truly be called social philosophers rather than social scientists, since they were mainly concerned with finding a law of nature, a law of sociology, or a law of economics. The same was true of Auguste Comte, the founder of sociology and of positivism, who earlier in the nineteenth century had tried to formulate laws for various branches of society in an effort to remold it. Gradually, however, there came to be fewer formulations of laws and more description, classification, and collection of data, and a serious effort was made to gain understanding of the narrower aspects of man and his society.

One of the great contributors to the development of the social sciences was the Austrian physician Sigmund Freud, who began his studies in the last decade of the nineteenth century. Freud probably ran into as much opposition as did Darwin and for much the same reason, the inability of his contemporaries to appreciate what he was trying to do. Freud attempted to describe the mechanics of personality development as it actually appeared to operate instead of trying to formulate a law or say how people must operate. As man became more aware of the fact that truth could be piecemeal and relative, Freud's psychoanalytic techniques for discovering the ramifications of individual character came to be seen as genuine insights rather than as ideas based in the realm of the occult or psychic. Freud taught that individual personality develops through a series of accommodations to requirements upon which the community insists. Thus the work of Freud gave added significance to both the study of the individual and of the community in which he lives. Social scientists began to try to do realistically what had so far only been done imaginatively by the artist and the poet — to give man a comprehension of himself.

TECHNOLOGY AND SCIENCE

Coinciding with the growth in science was a rapid increase in the rate of technological innovation, which seemed to have an almost geometric progression. Some of the technological advances depended upon discoveries in science although it is often difficult to separate the theoretical from the applied scientist. Louis Pasteur, for example, through his work in applied bacteriology developed the process of pasteurization, a method for destroying pathogenic organisms. Using the theoretical work of Pasteur as a base, Joseph Lister perfected the technique of sterilization. This development was followed by the discovery of effective means of administering anesthesia, and the result was a rapid advancement in surgery. Internal medicine also benefited from the isolation of various organisms that caused many of the diseases which afflicted man. Once the disease was isolated, the physician was better able to prescribe a cure or to prevent the disease. Historians of medicine state that only since the first part of the twentieth century have the physician and surgeon finally been able to cure their patients rather than merely to ease their discomfort or help nature to cure them.

The field of electricity underwent rapid development in the nineteenth century in the aftermath of the work of Michael Faraday and James Clark Maxwell. The dynamo was perfected, opening up the possibility of obtaining electric current in large quantities at low prices, and all sorts of inventions resulted. Electricity caused a revolution in communications. First came the telegraph of Samuel Morse, then the wireless telegraph of Guglielmo Marconi, and finally the telephone of Alexander Graham Bell. Artificial lighting was introduced with the invention of the arc lamp by Sir Humphrey Davey. The incandescent lamp, made commercially successful by Thomas A. Edison, soon followed. By transmitting current and then using a reversed dynamo, the electric motor became practical. Once electricity could be converted into mechanical power, it had a multitude of new uses.

Photography was invented and perfected; rubber processing was developed; records and phonographs were invented — the list could go on and on. In fact, the last part of the nineteenth century and first part of the twentieth saw a radical change in the nature of Western civilization, and it became possible for men to do all sorts of things that earlier they had only dreamed about. As revolutionary in their implications as any of the developments were the internal combustion engine perfected by Nicholas A. Otto, and the diesel engine, invented by Rudolf Diesel. One of the earliest practical applications of the engine was to transportation with the first gasoline-powered automobile of Carl Benz. The next development in transportation was the invention of the airplane by Orville and Wilbur Wright. Interestingly, the growth and spread of the internal combustion engine served eventually to undermine European industrial dominance, since neither Germany nor France nor England had available to them the natural oil required by such engines. Though these powers soon satisfied this need by gaining control of oil resources in other parts of the world, in the long run, the internal combustion engine helped to bolster the position of the United States and Russia, which had great quantities of oil reserves. The European economy, in turn, became highly dependent upon the oil-producing countries of the Middle East and elsewhere.

Europeans of the late nineteenth century ignored the clouds that were gathering on the horizon. Populations increased, living standards rose, literacy became more widespread, agriculture grew more productive, and in spite of occasional setbacks, there was a general assumption that the world was getting better and better. Self-satisfaction prevented many of the European countries from assessing the revolutionary implications of the changes that had been taking place, and they did not stop to evaluate their position in the world in the light of the new developments.

THE VICTORIAN WRITER

This smugness was particularly characteristic of Great Britain during the last part of the reign of Queen Victoria, who ruled from 1837 to 1901. While the term "Victorian" conveys a sense of moral righteousness and physical well-being, it also implies an attempt to ignore the unpleasant facts of life. Certain things became unmentionable, and tables, for example, no longer had legs but underpinnings or supports. Women's skirts were long and even chair legs were covered; in fact, too often reality was seen through tinted glasses or distorted with gingerbread trim. The poems of Alfred Lord Tennyson have often been regarded as typically Victorian, with their tone of moralistic self-confidence, although they also carry a significant message. Tennyson's short poems especially are distinguished by their metrical skill, and they convey a kind of haunting sadness that indicates the poet understood the changes that were taking place. Robert Browning, Tennyson's contemporary, was even more aware of the changing scene, and his psychological analyses of character reflect some of the same concerns that appeared in the works of the social scientists. Even the stories of Rudyard Kipling, which have been identified with the imperialistic jingoism of the late Victorians, managed to make their more serious readers question some of the assumptions of the time. The playwright Oscar Wilde could make the Victorians laugh at their own pomposities in such works as *The Importance of Being Earnest,* while in his personal life he reflected his rebellion against the conventional moralities of his day.

This type of revolt was much more pronounced in French literature. Perhaps the greatest poet of the second half of the nineteenth century was Charles Baudelaire. In his preoccupation with death and corruption and in his willingness to face reality, Baudelaire represented a reaction to the attitudes of his age. Particularly influential were the symbolist, poets, who included Stephane Mallarmé, Paul Verlaine, and Arthur Rimbaud, in addition to Baudelaire. Their poetry attempted to reflect the fusion of the mind and the senses. The symbolists in part represent the artist withdrawn, although the French intellectual often showed himself willing to involve himself in trying to correct the social ills he saw around him. Emile Zola, for example, did not hesitate to take on the establishment either in his writings or in his private activities. His novels furnish a social document of the period and also indicate a growing relation between the social scientist and the creative artist.

An extreme form of withdrawal from the ills of society was advocated by the great Russian novelist Leo Tolstoi, whose *War and Peace* and *Anna Karenina* are classified as masterpieces of fiction. Despite the fact that he came from a wealthy noble family, Tolstoi became more and more an anarchist, deploring all man-made institutions. He eventually abandoned literature to live the simple life of a peasant in the country. Quite different from the response of Tolstoi was that of the Italian Gabriele D'Annunzio, who emphasized in both his creative writing and his personal life the idea that a writer must be commited to action. D'Annunzio, an Italian nationalist, is regarded as one of the intellectual founders of fascism.

American literature came of age in this period. Particularly influential was Mark Twain, who for many Europeans symbolized the simple life to which they longed to return. The interest in things American led to a revival of interest in Edgar Allen Poe, who had died in 1849. The French symbolists adopted Poe as one of their own and regarded him as one of the originators of the idea of art for art's sake. Poe also developed the technique of the detective story, which at the beginning of the

Count Leo Tolstoi (1828–
1910). (Prints Division,
The New York Public
Library, Astor, Lenox
and Tilden Foundations)

twentieth century became a universal form of literature, particularly
through the work of the English writer Arthur Conan Doyle. Henry
James, a native American who eventually became a British citizen, by
portraying the newly self-confident Americans in contrast with the
sophisticated and decadent aristocracy of Europe also helped to undermine the European self-image.

Social criticism was most effective on the stage, and with the plays
of the Norwegian Henrik Ibsen the whole nature of the theater was
changed. His technique, structure, methods of handling dialogue and
character strongly influenced contemporary drama, and his plays dominated the stage during his lifetime and long after. Most of Ibsen's
characters are involved in some kind of struggle against the conventions
of middle class life, and in this sense their creator was attacking the
artificial morality and self-satisfaction that characterized Victorian
society. In *Pillars of Society,* Ibsen focused on the hypocritical businessman, while the artificialities of marriage and social convention furnished
the subject of *Ghosts.* Ibsen was particularly adept at depicting women,
who were achieving revolutionary changes in status during this period,
and his *A Doll's House* is one of the first portraits of the modern

woman. Contemporary with Ibsen was August Strindberg in Sweden, who developed many of the same themes. The great defender and expounder of Ibsen in English was George Bernard Shaw.

IMPRESSIONISM

If the writer was in partial rebellion against the old ways, the artist was in full-scale revolt. In art, the new ideas came together in the movement known as Impressionism. The Impressionists were primarily interested in the possibilities of light and color in allowing the artist to capture the mind's momentary picture transmitted by the eye. One of the pioneers of the movement was Edouard Manet, who not only employed new shades and colors but posed his pictures of nudes in such common, everyday ways that the easily shocked public was aghast. Going further was Claude Monet, who attempted to apply to painting the scientific discovery that sunlight is composed of a series of colors. Instead of mixing blue and yellow to form green as artists before him had done, Monet and his successors put daubs of yellow next to daubs of blue, so that the eye rather than the artist mixed the two colors. In the course of his experimentation, Monet produced a series of canvases that reveal a rainbow of brilliant and unmixed hues. As a group, the Impressionists were reacting against the whole artistic tradition of the past. They were concerned with reproducing transitory phenomena, which they felt could be done only with a technique that remained loose and casual, and thus their pictures seem devoid of a solidity of form so evident in earlier painting. Though they were heavily criticized in their own time, the Impressionists began a revolution in art that has continued to our own time. Among the numerous major artists of the period were Camille Pissaro, Alfred Sisley, and the American James Whistler. Two of the most prominent painters of the period before World War I were Auguste Renoir and Edgar Degas, who represent different aspects of the artistic revolution. Renoir turned away from the landscapes of Monet to more informal portraits. His bright colors and his beautiful men and women give his canvases an air of unreality, as if his subjects were unaware of the ugly world around them. Renoir became the first of the Impressionists to be accepted by the Parisian upper classes. Edgar Degas used more mundane subjects — laundresses, milliners, jockeys, and particularly ballet girls, which today are among his most popular works. Degas placed greater emphasis on draftsmanship than the earlier Impressionists, an aspect of his work that was undoubtedly influenced by Chinese and Japanese art, which was beginning to be admired and copied in Europe. Combining exquisite draftsmanship with brilliant color was Henri de Toulouse Lautrec, who with a few lines and a few splashes of color managed to convey a visual impression unmatched by the detailed paintings of other artists. This same emphasis on line accompanied by alternating high and low surfaces to catch or reflect light characterized the work of the sculptor Auguste Rodin. The fleshy softness which Rodin gave to his statues with this technique is reminiscent of the effects achieved by the Impressionists in painting.

The Impressionists continued to experiment, although as their ideas became more widely accepted, certain rules of color relationship were established, particularly among the post-Impressionist artists such as Georges Seurat, who attempted to convey monumentality in carefully controlled compositions. More famous was Paul Cézanne, whose still lifes left him free to examine and probe his subject matter from all dimensions. Also regarded as a member of this group was Vincent Van Gogh, who achieved a whole new effect with the use of color. Van Gogh's paintings are bathed in sunlight and seem to have an almost frightening energy. The primitiveness implied in Van Gogh was carried to greater extremes by his friend and colleague Paul Gauguin, who in reaction against what he felt to be the decay of Europe reverted to forms of primitive expression. He himself moved to Tahiti and attempted to find a remedy for his disillusionment in an unspoiled society.

MUSIC

Music was somewhat slower in adopting new forms than were painting and sculpture. The dominant composer of the last part of the nineteenth century was probably Johannes Brahms, who was more influenced by Beethoven than by his own contemporaries. Brahms, however, appears to have been a lone wolf in his time, emphasizing substance and form instead of tone and color. Much more innovative was Richard Strauss who is best known for his symphonic poems and operas. The work of Strauss represents a continuation of the Wagnerian tradition, and his melodic and harmonic complexity are considered the highest stage of technical development in nineteenth-century musical forms. Bringing the Wagnerian technique to the symphonic field were the Austrians Gustav Mahler and Anton Bruckner. Hugo Wolf, the great composer of *Lieder*, adopted the Wagnerian idiom to song. German romanticism was exported into France, where Charles Gounod and Cesar Franck adopted it and made a music uniquely their own.

Opera continued to be a major musical form, and the most influential composer in this field was the Italian Giuseppe Verdi, who along with Wagner continues to dominate contemporary opera. Also important was Giacomo Puccini, who combined orchestral fluency with an excellent sense of the theater, and Georges Bizet, whose *Carmen* is one of the most successful operas of all time. A new form, the operatta, appeared with the work of W. S. Gilbert and Arthur Sullivan, who were not unwilling to use their music for political purposes. Occasionally their criticism of the English political scene threatened the security of various government officials, but in the process they managed to establish a new kind of light opera that continues to maintain its popularity.

Music was not unresponsive to the social changes of the nineteenth century, and nowhere is this more evident than in the attempt of the composers to convey a national identity through music. Symbolic of this movement were the great Czech patriot and composer Antonin Dvorak and the Norwegian Eduard Grieg, both of whom tried to convey native or national themes in their own music. The Russians, in particular, expressed their patriotism in music through the work of composers known as the Russian five: Mily Balakireff, Cesar Cui, Nikolai Rimski-Korsakov, Aleksandr Borodin, and Modest Musorgski. Increasingly, however, the nationalist schools became an integreated part of the European scene. It was primarily Peter Ilich Tchaikovsky who brought Russian music into the mainstream of Western culture. Tchaikovsky's melodic fluency, colorful orchestration, and sensational climaxes have made him one of the most popular of all composers. Much Russian music was composed for ballets, and it was in the nineteenth century, particularly in Russia, that ballet became a major dance form.

Impressionism, so dominant in art, also began to appear in music. The Impressionist influence is particularly evident in the work of Claude Debussy in which splashes of sound replace the splashes of color. As a result of this experimentation, Debussy is considered the founder of modern music.

RELIGION AND PHILOSOPHY

Religion in the nineteenth century became the subject of numerous analytical studies. Among the chief scholars to probe the nature of Christianity was a group centered at the University of Tübingen in Germany led by Ferdinand Christian Baur. Baur viewed Christianity as more the creation of the apostle Paul than of Jesus, whom he regarded as relatively unimportant. Baur also taught that the Gospels were chiefly mythical. These ideas were elaborated by David Friedrich Strauss, whose *Life of Jesus* appeared early in the nineteenth century. In the 1864 revision of this work, Strauss contended that the Gospel stories about Jesus were not so much myths as they were falsifications. Strauss's work was followed by that of the Frenchman Ernest Renan, who rejected any claim of Jesus either to divinity or to supernatural endowments. It was to counter these and other arguments that Albert

Schweitzer wrote *The Quest for the Historical Jesus.* Schweitzer said that whether one accepts the accounts of Jesus as true is more a matter of faith than of history, and if one wants to accept Christianity, there is more than enough evidence on which to build a belief.

In this sense, Schweitzer's conclusions were a reflection of the teachings of the German philosopher Arthur Schopenhauer, who held that while scientists could investigate and explain the realm of external phenomena, only intuition could enable one to get at reality. Schopenhauer was so pessimistic that he concluded that the worst evil that could fall anyone was to be born. The only relief that men could gain from the irrational world was through the contemplation of ideas. Writing along similar lines was Sören Kierkegaard, who, though he was little noticed in his own time, partly because he wrote in Danish, in the post-World War I period came to be acclaimed as one of the greatest Christian thinkers of all time. Kierkegaard branded as ridiculous the idea that the world is rational or that it represents the unfolding of any divine plan. Even if God had such a plan, only He could know what it is, and no individual could presume that he occupied a specific place in the known scheme of things. Rather, for Kierkegaard man was unique only because of his ability to contemplate the universe. He believed that this power, which he defined as existence, allowed man to choose what he would believe and how he would act. Kierkegaard also pointed out that it left man in a constant state of anxiety, since man had to act from day to day perpetually unsure of his actions. In this aspect of Kierkegaard's thinking modern existentialism had its beginnings.

Exercising as much influence on twentieth-century man as Kierkegaard was the German philosopher Friedrich Nietzsche, who challenged the whole institutional and ideological heritage of the West. By the often-quoted expression "God is dead," Nietzsche meant that not only the God of the Judaeo-Christian heritage but the whole realm of absolutes from Plato to his own day no longer had any relevance. Nietzsche, in a sense, was an individualist who abhorred the reduction of men to specialized functionaries and their subjugation to Christian morality. He longed for the appearance of heroic individuals, or superman, who through their disciplined struggle and sacrifice would evolve ethical concepts that were on a higher and different plane than those of the masses. Thus Nietzsche came to approve the triumph of the strong over the weak and to provide a philosophical justification for fascism, although as a nonnationalist and non-racist he probably would have been appalled by this political philosophy as it actually evolved.

Though organized religion often responded to such assaults with a growing conservatism, there were a number of religious leaders who saw the need for change. Instead of emphasizing Biblical fundamentalism, they tried to adopt the church to the needs of the modern world and to commit religion to solving the problems of contemporary life. In a sense, Albert Schweitzer was a transitional figure in this movement, since though he withdrew from the world to become a medical missionary in Africa, his action represented a commitment to a cause. In general, the result was a growing feeling among church leaders that religion should be used to bring about a better life for all men. In Protestant countries, the reformers were identified with a movement known as liberal Protestantism; within Catholicism, though receiving support from the social encyclicals of the pope, the movement was not so well organized, but still it lead to a new effort on the part of various religious orders to build hospitals, schools, and other institutions for the poor and less fortunate. New orders sprang up to meet the demands within Catholicism, and new sects, such as the Salvation Army, emerged within Protestantism. "Liberal" Protestants and Catholics also tended to accept the findings of science and of history, a circumstance that led to growing strife between the "fundamentalists" and the "modernists" that continues today, although the present struggle is not necessarily confined to the original issues.

JUDAISM

It was not Christianity but Judaism that underwent the most radical change during this period of European history. Though Jews had been in Europe since Roman times, until the French Revolution they had no political or civil rights in any of the countries except under the special dispensation of various monarchs. During the Enlightenment of the eighteenth century, the demands for religious toleration culminated in the resolution of the French national assembly of 1791 which granted full rights of citizenship to all Jews in France. Holland soon followed the French example, as did other states that came under the influence of the French Revolution. After the defeat of Napoleon, a reaction set in which temporarily made emancipation a dead issue. The various revolutions of 1848, however, served to revive the campaign for toleration. In that year, the Jews in Prussia were granted full rights of citizenship, and the same statement was agreed to by the German liberals sitting at the Frankfurt Parliament. In England, the struggle for Jewish emancipation lasted somewhat longer. It began in 1830 but was not wholly successful until 1903, when the religious tests for appointment to a professorship were removed. Austria, Hungary, Denmark, Belgium, and Rumania also granted citizenship to Jews at various times during the nineteenth century, although this did not mean the end of persecution. Russia, which then included much of Poland, the country with the largest Jewish population, did not give Jews citizenship until the Revolution of 1917. The United States, which from its foundations had separated church and state on a national level, retained forms of religious discrimination against Jews in some of the original thirteen states until after the Civil War.

Emancipation of Jews, however, did not always lessen the suspicion with which members of this group were regarded by many people. In fact, the remarkable energies and abilities that Jews devoted to all fields of endeavor led to an increasing hostility, usually called anti-Semitism. Unfortunately, Jewish emancipation also coincided with the growth of the concept of romantic nationalism and the emphasis on racial purity by various peoples. Many of the extreme nationalists tended to use Jews as scapegoats for the ills that plagued their countries. It was in part because of this continued hostility that many Jewish leaders in the last part of the nineteenth century turned to Zionism, which had as its objective the re-establishment in Palestine of the Biblical Jewish state. The leader of this movement was Theodor Herzl, an Austrian Jew, who opened negotiations with the sultan of Constantinople in 1896 to begin such a settlement. Though there had always been Jews in Palestine, this reinvigorated Zionism laid the foundations for what eventually came to be the state of Israel.

Zionism was rejected by the vast majority of European Jews in the period before the World War I. A few tried to become assimilated into the mainstream of European culture by renouncing their Jewish background. Others established Reformed Judaism, a movement that attempted to preserve Jewish culture and tradition while "modernizing" religious practices. There were, however, vast numbers of Jews who did not want to take either of these paths. Some of these established Conservative Judaism, and this group has been particularly influential in America. The majority of Jews, however, remained Orthodox, particularly in Russia and Poland, and were confined to certain prescribed areas or ghettos. Residents of such areas were subject to vast pogroms, which took place in the first part of the twentieth century in Russia and lasted until the end of World War II. Millions of Russian Jews emigrated to the United States to escape such harassment, but when the Nazi persecutions began this escape valve was closed. The Nazi machine was directed against all Jews and not just those living in the ghettos. It was the growth of such virulent anti-Semitism that led an increasing number of Jews to subscribe to Zionism, perhaps as the only alternative to annihilation.

THE DECLINE OF BRITAIN AND FRANCE

The changing nature of Western civilization that was reflected in the arts, in literature, and in the social and intellectual spheres was also

apparent in politics. From the vantage point of today, the most significant political development in the last part of the nineteenth and first
part of the twentieth centuries appears to have been the relative decline in power and influence of Great Britain and France. This is not
to say that either France or England lost population or wealth or underwent any particular crisis, but rather that both had reached more or
less simultaneously a plateau in the long course of their development.
Thus the continent, so long buffeted by the ambitions of these two
great powers, found itself under different and unfamiliar influences to
which it was difficult to adjust.

The decline in British influence must in part be explained by com-
placency. Because of their earlier industrialization, the British for more
than a century had enjoyed a near monopoly of machine production
and access to world markets. They sold high-quality merchandise
around the world in exchange for a huge variety of commodities, providing shipping, financing, insurance, and considerable technical advice as well. Other nations, however, found ways of emulating the
British, and they not only had the British experience upon which to
build but sometimes unique assets of their own. The United States
and Germany, for example, possessed superior natural resources. Since
German industrialization was from the beginning more centralized,
it was much more efficient in mounting large-scale projects than the
British. Moreover, the German worker, encouraged by social legislation which his British counterpart lacked, could be channeled into
areas of the greatest need with little dislocation. In the United States,
hordes of immigrants provided a ready and cheap source of labor that
could be easily utilized, although not so easily exploited, since the
American frontier offered an effective escape. The Japanese, who
lacked the resources of Germany, the United States, or even Great
Britain, had the advantage of being the first industrialized power in a
market area in which there were vast resources and little competition.
Moreover, the Japanese labor force proved to be not only efficient but so
undemanding that the Japanese could often undersell their competitors.

As long as the demand for manufactured products grew, the British
could act as if these new competitors did not exist. When the mid-
century rise in prices that had resulted from the California and Austral-
ian gold discoveries weakened after 1870, the British for the first time
found themselves involved in intense competition. Moreover, developing countries cut into Britain's manufacturing monopoly by attempting
to reduce imports and supply themselves. To compensate for this
change in the world market, the British expanded their foreign investment and financing. They were also able to export some raw materials,
such as coal, to the newly emerging manufacturing nations. Still, the
English economy began to slow down, and the first to feel the effects

were the working classes, who seldom had any reserves and found it difficult to learn new crafts or enterprises when the old one failed. To make matters worse, British agriculture virtually disappeared. It should be noted that the British farmers were giving an early indication of what could happen in many other countries, since the improvement of ocean transportation made it possible to ship vast quantities of American wheat to Europe. This wheat, grown on virgin land and open prairies with little labor, was far cheaper to produce and ship than any grown by European farmers. Most European governments saved their farm populations by limiting imports, but to the British any such move implied the abandonment of free trade. Rather than change the policy that the British people believed had been mainly responsible for national prosperity, the British government allowed the world's most carefully tended agricultural system to deteriorate to the point where about three quarters of the food consumed in the British Isles had to be imported. What had ruined the grain farmer soon destroyed the meat producer as refrigerated steamships proved capable of bringing beef and mutton from great distances more cheaply than the British could produce these products at home. Great Britain soon found itself dependent upon imported food, and to pay for its increasing imports it had to keep up a supply of exports, which it found increasingly difficult to do.

If the British decline was subtle and long term, and even unperceived by most, the French decline was more sudden and obvious to all. Its chief manifestation was the military defeat by the Prussians in the Franco-Prussian War of 1870, which proved to be more humiliating than devastating. Moreover, the defeat caused much dissension among factions as to the causes of the calamity, and the period was characterized by bitterness, recrimination, and a growing polarity of political ideology that has continued to plague France to the present day. No matter how the French blamed each other, the simple fact was that a united Germany had both more people and better resources than France, as well as better harbors and a more efficient system of internal communication. Earlier French dominance of Europe had been based upon the country's agricultural resources and large population, but by 1900, conditions had changed. One consequence of the French Revolution had been to fortify the system of peasant holdings against modernization. Plots remained small and ill-adapted to the use of machinery, which meant that production methods continued to follow outmoded practices that were being abandoned elsewhere. Though the peasant class in France provided a social cohesiveness that was politically important, economically it was inefficient, and France was prevented from effectively utilizing its labor force. In 1820, France had some thirty million people, more than lived either in Great Britain or in the territories that became Germany. By 1870, the population of Germany had surpassed that of France, and by 1900, Great Britain had outdistanced its rival. Though the population growth in both Great Britain and Germany slowed down in the twentieth century, both countries remained more populous than France, which no longer could dominate Europe. Now the new German Empire was stretching its wings, and Europe was in the process of realigning itself.

21

The Decline
of Western European
World Dominance

The period from 1870 to 1920 marked the culmination of Western expansion throughout the world. Yet just as this expansion reached its pinnacle, it began to crumble. The decline began with World War I, one of the bloodiest and least rational wars in all history. In the aftermath of the war, offshoots of European civilization such as the United States, fringe powers on the European scene such as Russia, and Western-influenced non-European nations such as Japan came to exercise greater and greater power. Western Europe itself, though still influential, had lost its dominance of the world.

FRANCE BEFORE THE WAR

The French Third Republic had a rather unstable history. From the first, the monarchists refused to accept the republic as anything more than an arrangement of expediency. They attempted to sabotage the government and to embarrass it whenever opportunity offered, hoping to convert it into something more to their liking. The republicans were also badly split into factions. So vigorous were the partisan disputes that sometimes no agreement could be reached on cabinet formation. The result was government instability with an almost continuous change of ministers. Many of the plots and counterplots within the French government came to a head in the Dreyfus case in the 1890s. Alfred Dreyfus, an army captain, was found guilty by a military court of selling secrets to the Germans. Ultimately, it was discovered that Drey-

fus was guilty of nothing more than being a Jew. A clique of army officers had deliberately used him as a victim in order to conceal the guilt of
another officer. For years the army tried to prevent all inquiries into the
questionable proceedings leading up to Dreyfus' conviction, and in this
suppression they were aided and supported by the high Catholic clergy
and the monarchists. Eventually, the Dreyfusards, as the captain's
partisans were called, led by Emile Zola, despite harassment and persecution, managed to expose the whole sordid mess. Dreyfus was
restored to all honor and rank in 1906, and the perpetrators and supporters of the plot were revealed. In the aftermath, there came a clean
sweep of the army command, a change that led the French military to
become a servant of the republic rather than a tool for a clique of
monarchists. In the revulsions against the part the Catholic clergy had
played in the Dreyfus case, the republicans were able to disestablish
the Church, which meant that religion no longer served as a wing of
the government but would control its own personnel and support its
own activities without state aid. In the process of disestablishment, the
Catholic Church in France lost most of its property, except for actual
church buildings, and many religious orders were shut down. This
action defeated the monarchists, and from this point on, the only danger
to the republic came from the factionalism of the republicans and not
from monarchist opponents.

Both monarchists and republicans, however, could agree on a policy
of hostility toward Germany, with both desiring the recovery of Alsace-
Lorraine — the so-called *revanche* movement. In a longe-range effort to
recover their territories, the French, after the defeat by the Prussians,
began to build up their military strength. To narrow the gap between the
population and resources of France and Germany, they began to expand
across the Mediterranean into areas in which they had gained footholds
in the 1830s. During the period before 1914, the French moved from
Algeria into Tunis and Morocco, southward across the Sahara into central Africa, and eastward to the Indian Ocean, occupying in the process
an area a dozen or more times the size of France and containing perhaps
thirty million people. French ambitions to span the continent of Africa
from east to west ran into conflict with British attempts to link South
Africa with Egypt. The result was the so-called Fashoda Incident of
1898, in which the British forced the French to withdraw. Though the
French regarded the incident as a severe defeat at the time, the result
was that it allowed the two powers to move closer together, since it
established definite British and French spheres of influence in Africa.
In addition, the French seized Madagascar in the Indian Ocean, continued to build up an Asiatic empire centered around Vietnam and Cambodia, and wound up with overseas possessions second only to those
controlled by the British.

THE NEW BALANCE OF POWER AND
THE GROWING INFLUENCE OF RUSSIA

For over two hundred years, in every European dispute France had been on one side and Great Britain on the other. To check French military power, the British had cooperated with whatever French enemies could be found, usually Austria or some German state. The creation of a united Germany altered this traditional alliance, since Germany became the most powerful continental power, with Austria increasingly pulled into the German orbit. Neither France nor Britain was able to come to terms easily with these changed circumstances, for if the British wanted to maintain a balance of power, their obvious ally, France, was their traditional enemy. Such an alliance proved difficult to achieve, but after several years of negotiation the two countries reached an understanding in the *Entente Cordiale* of 1904. Even a joint Anglo-French understanding could not be as effective as the earlier Anglo-Austrian coalition, however, since Germany could be attacked only from one side instead of two. It soon became apparent that a prerequisite for a new balance of power was the inclusion of a country that could attack Germany on its eastern frontier. This factor, then, led to the increasing importance of Russia as a European power.

The internal situation in Russia, however, the largest and most populous European state, was not conducive to the country's playing a leading role in European power politics. The Russians suspected Europeans in general, and this suspicion was matched by that of the Western Europeans, who regarded the Russians as an Asiatic people somewhat akin to the Turks. Russian alienation from Europe had been enhanced by pan-Slavism, a movement which claimed that the Slavs — the various nationality groups in Russia, plus the Poles, Serbs, and others — had a destiny of their own because of their unique racial origin. The pan-Slav nationalists disparaged other cultures, especially the liberal, progressive civilizations further west, and sought to protect what they imagined to be the peculiar and precious qualities of their own culture from "Western materialism."

The Russians were also occupied with their own expansion, extending their territory eastward to the Pacific and southward against the Turks. Other European interests in the Far East and in the Mediterranean felt threatened by this expansion, which had earlier led France and England to fight Russia in the Crimean War. Moreover, Russia's internal difficulties were not solved until after the Revolution of 1917. Though in 1900 Russian territory was nearly three times the size of the continental United States, Russian methods of transportation and communication continued to be among the most backward in Europe. The government operated with appalling inefficiency under a tsar who was a complete autocrat. Serving as administrators were the privileged nobility, who also ruled over their serfs as though they were personal possessions. Though this system must be regarded as extremely repressive, it at least had the merits of enabling the Russians to exploit large areas and to maintain an effective enough military machine to protect them from marauding enemies, who in the past had been accustomed to raid much of the vast territories of Eurasia. Internal peace was, in fact, the great accomplishment of the Russian government, since it gave security to large areas of Asia which had never known it. Peace at home however, brought special needs and demands that the Russian government seemed unable to fulfill. Most of the peoples within Russia lived at a subsistence level, and though this situation did not seriously distress the upper classes, the tsars came to realize that conditions would have to change if Russia was to grow in strength. This lesson had been effectively brought home by the Crimean War, when the large Russian army, with its poor, illiterate soldiers and primitive equipment proved no match for the well-equipped and better-trained English and French troops. Tsar Alexander II made serious efforts at reform in 1861 when he abolished serfdom, but in the long run he failed to develop adequate administrative machinery to replace the old landlord system.

If there had been time and opportunity for a large middle class to develop in Russia, the problems of backwardness might gradually have been surmounted. Though solutions were available, both the tsar and his nobility believed that any drastic action would threaten their own existence. They realized that the introduction of Western methods and technology would also introduce Western liberalism with its hostility toward nobles and autocrats. As an alternative, the new tsar Alexander III built up the secret police and employed other forms of repression in order to contain every form of subversion. At the same time, he hoped that by some miracle Russia could manage to meet its Western contemporaries on some plane of equality.

The result was a reign of repression that ended only with Russia's humiliating defeat at the hands of the Japanese in the Russo-Japanese War. This defeat deprived the Russians of a warm-water port on the Pacific and expelled them from Korea and Manchuria. More important, it provoked an internal revolution in 1905, which forced the tsar to introduce a constitution. A national assembly, called the Duma, was created with fairly substantial powers, and though its authority was much restricted over the next few years, its mere existence represented a significant new development in Russian history. Russia then began to make fairly rapid progress toward modernization, developing some of the economic potential of its vast territories. Unhappily, this development was seriously hindered by the incompetence of the tsar's government, which in 1914 further added to its difficulties by permitting the nation to stumble into hostilities against Germany.

THE GROWING INFLUENCE OF GERMANY

Otto von Bismarck served as the guiding genius of the newly established German Empire. For twenty years following the Franco-Prussian War, he attempted to maintain peace in the hope that the great powers might cease to regard Germany as an aggressor. He encouraged the French in their overseas expansion and tried to keep the Russians from looking to France for any aid or comfort. Though Bismarck could momentarily keep France occupied, his policy faced serious difficulties as long as the French seemed unlikely to forget the Prussian seizure of Alsace-Lorraine. Russia, however, was a different matter. Here Bismarck might have been more successful if it had not been for the German alliance with Austria, since the Austrians were competing with the Russians for influence in the Balkans. The Dual Alliance of 1879 between Germany and Austria-Hungary was one of the most solid-partnerships known to diplomatic history, but it also served to drive a wedge between the Germans and the Russians. Realizing this inherent difficulty, Bismarck tried to make Germany more safe from French revenge by cultivating Italy as an ally. Eventually, the Dual Alliance between Germany and Austria became the Triple Alliance and included Italy. The three countries, sometimes called the Central Powers, maintained a partnership that proved helpful to Italy in removing Austrian hostility but did little in the long run for Germany. Austria also benefited since it was able to go into the Balkans with less fear of Russia.

Bismarck demonstrated little interest in colonial ventures, but his attempts to stay out of the race for colonies ran into opposition from the German people themselves. They eventually forced Bismarck's hand by establishing trading companies, which acquired concessions in various parts of Africa and the Pacific, thereby laying a foundation for an empire. Ultimately, Bismarck went along with these concessions, which proved unfortunate for German objectives, since this policy tended to bring the British and French closed together.

Internally, Bismarck's years as imperial chancellor coincided with a period of spectacular growth in German industry, a trend that was actively encouraged by the government. Bismarck and his colleagues had little use for liberalism, including the principles of laissez-faire, and the rights of free speech and assembly. To Bismarck, an economically strong and powerful Germany was a prerequisite to military and political power and was therefore to be encouraged. In a similar way, the German ruling class was not particularly opposed to such welfare legislation as bonuses, assistance, medical care, and pensions, as well as other forms of aids for the working class family. Though Bismarck was hostile to socialism as a political movement, his years in power witnessed the introduction of a wide variety of legislation usually identified as socialistic. Meanwhile, the socialists themselves were virtually outlawed, their party meetings broken up, and their journals suppressed. Despite this suppression, when the official government hostility to the working class movements was relaxed after 1890, the German socialists were soon found to be stronger and more numerous than in any other country. By 1900, through government actions, now taken in cooperation with the socialists, the German worker found himself better off than workers anywhere else in the world. Thus the workingman in Germany tended to take an interest in the smooth operation of the factory system. This identification, which was lacking in such countries as England, perhaps also helps to explain Germany's superior achievement in the fields of industry and technology.

Germany was, however, a monarchy, and Bismarck ultimately owed his power to the king. In 1888, Bismarck's supporter Kaiser William I died and was succeeded by Frederick III, who also died soon thereafter. The crown was taken up by a second William, then twenty-nine years of age, who proceeded to undercut Bismarck's position of influence. William II was a rather unfortunate choice to head a powerful country in a time of growing international tension, since he was both impulsive and reckless and irritated many already frightened people by always talking about the excellence or superiority of anything Germany and by continually threatening to call out his troops. Once Bismarck resigned, none of William's advisers ever achieved enough power or influence over him to moderate effectively his more extreme pronouncements. As a result, William, who regarded himself as a sort of superperson, impetuously moved into situations from which it was next to impossible to extract himself. Perhaps his most fateful mistake was to allow the Russians to wander into an alliance with France in spite of the tsar's very real preference for one with Germany. Russian hostility, however, quickly grew as William involved himself in Turkish affairs, a policy the Russians viewed as a threat to their own interests in that area. William also antagonized the British, who could not understand why William would undertake to build up a large naval force when presumably Germany's potential enemies appeared to be France and Russia. When the kaiser did nothing to allay their suspicions, the British concluded that they themselves must be the future target, and initiated their own expensive effort to modernize their navy. British antagonisms were further deepened by the kaiser's expressed sympathy for the Boers in South Africa during the Boer War at the turn of the century.

When the British and French finally reached an understanding in the *Entente Cordiale* of 1904, the Germans sought to challenge the fledgling partnership by raising difficulties in Morocco. Thus the British were further convinced that the alliance was an effective counterweight to German dominance. In 1907, the British ventured still further by establishing an understanding with Russia, which since 1894 had also been allied with France. Europe, in effect, was divided into two camps, making the position of Germany, with its blustering kaiser, even more difficult.

THE LAST YEARS OF PEACE

Chances for a major conflict were increased by the weakness of most of the leaders of the European powers. Tsar Nicholas II of Russia was almost ineffective. Emperor Franz Josef of Austria-Hungary, though a better ruler, was eighty in 1910, and the government he headed can only be described as a marvel of obsolescence and bureaucratic ineptness. The French Third Republic was notoriously unstable, having gone through some fifty reshufflings of the cabinet between 1871 and 1914. Great Britain, the home of parliamentary government, was experiencing a series of domestic crises which centered around the inherent privileges of the House of Lords, the need for more radical social legislation, and the struggle for Irish independence. These conflicts exhausted governmental leaders while embittering the opposition. In Germany, the personality deficiencies of the kaiser posed a continual problem.

The spark that set Europe ablaze was tindered in the Balkans on the Austro-Hungarian border as part of the movement for Slavic nationalism. The Balkans were a storehouse of ethnic groups, which had become more and more quarrelsome as the declining Turkish Empire encouraged various rival nationalities to assert themselves. The newly independent country of Serbia, for example, attempted to include all Serbs within its borders, many of whom were under Austrian protection in Bosnia-Herzegovina. The Balkans remained comparatively quiet as long as Bosnia-Herzegovina was merely a protectorate of the Hapsburg government in Vienna, but in 1908, this peace was shattered by Austrian annexation. The Russians protested the annexation of Bosnia-Herzegovina, but when it became obvious that Germany was backing the Austrians, Russia had to withdraw. This humiliation, however, served to further draw the Russians apart from the Germans.

WHO CAUSED THE WAR?

As World War waged on, nationalist-minded writers and historians found innumerable reasons to blame Germany for the conflict. On the basis of an unfortunate remark by William II, they portrayed the contest as a diabolical plot on the part of the Germans to re-create and expand the empire of Genghis Khan and even accused Germany of using extermination to gain its objective. The term "Hun" was applied by the more jingoistic newspapers to describe German activities in the war. This simple explanation has long since been rejected, but there is still considerable debate among historians as to how the blame should be apportioned. With each new crisis, the European powers increased the size of their armies — the first Moroccan crisis of 1905–1906, the annexation of Bosnia-Herzegovina in 1908, the second Moroccan crisis in 1911, and a series of disputes in the Balkans between 1912 and 1914. This last series of crises was precipitated by the coalition of Serbia, Greece, and Bulgaria that was formed to take Macedonia from Turkey. The three Balkan powers not only captured Macedonia but most of Thrace and Albania as well. At this juncture the Austrians interfered in an attempt to prevent the Serbs from holding Albania. The Russians were thus forced to come to the aid of the Serbs, but once again German support of Austria forced the tsar to back down. Serbia, however, determined to obtain a greater share of Macedonia than was agreed upon, joined with Greece to declare war on Bulgaria. In this second contest, Bulgaria was so decisively defeated that the Turks were able to reoccupy Adrianople, which they had lost in the earlier war. The Rumanians also seized the opportunity to extend their lands along the Danube.

Increasingly, Europe took on the aspects of a major tragedy, with everyone knowing that war could break out but consoling themselves by saying it would not happen. Austrian obstinance, in large measure the root of much of Europe's difficulty, resulted from fear on the part of the Hapsburgs that concessions made to any one of the minorities would set a precedent for leniency toward the others and that the result would be the end of the empire. The more the Serbs and Croats felt the oppressiveness of the Hapsburg governors, the more unrest grew. The imperial authorities continued their repressive policies, confident that Germany would bail them out and that if war came, Germany could keep Russia neutral. The more the Germans clung to the Austrian alliance, the more they isolated themselves from the rest of Europe. The Germans began to feel themselves encircled by hostile powers without ever realizing that at least part of their difficulty might be due to their own actions, which they could have modified or corrected. As the British increasingly looked to France or Russia, the Germans realized that there was little chance that Italy would remain a loyal ally, since in any war with Britain, the long Italian seacoast and island possessions would be an open invitation to the British fleet. Thus the Germans clung more and more to the one nation they could count on — Austria-Hungary; the Hapsburgs understood the German dilemma only too well, for they exploited it ruthlessly. The situation became clear in June 1914, when the Austrian emperor's nephew and heir

Francis Ferdinand was assassinated with his wife at Sarajevo in Bosnia. It must be said that the Austrians planned poorly when they decided to send the archduke for a visit to an area where trouble was expected to break out and in fact, where he had been warned not to come. The irony of the tragedy was that Francis Ferdinand regarded himself as a liberal and might have changed Austria's repressive policies when he succeeded his uncle. The Austrians, however, set out to exploit the murder for all it was worth.

THE OUTBREAK OF WORLD WAR I

Since it appeared that the assassination was the work of Serbian-inspired terrorists, all European leaders generally supposed that Austria would seek some compensation from Serbia, even though the crime had taken place within Austrian territory and the murderer was a subject of the emperor. For nearly a month, authorities in Vienna carried on consultations with Berlin, and in these the kaiser made the fatal mistake of promising to support the Austrians in whatever course they chose to follow. This agreement later came to be known as the kaiser's blank check. With this assurance, the Austrians set about to demolish Serbia and to incorporate more of the southern Slavs into the Austro-Hungarian Empire. Though it is doubtful that Kaiser William II believed that the Austrians had anything so drastic on their minds and the Italians later complained that they were in no way consulted, the Austrians on July 23 presented an ultimatum to Serbia that would have seriously undermined the independence of the country. No nation that valued its freedom could accept such terms, and it was readily apparent that the Austrians were willing to go to war with Serbia. Since some members of the Serbian government were implicated in the assassination and others had been negligent in not reporting what they knew, the Serbians felt compelled to meet some of the Austrian demands but refused to accept any impairment of Serbian sovereignty. Vienna, therefore, in spite of the conciliatory attitude of Serbia, broke off talks and began to mobilize for war.

Europeans elsewhere were uneasy, but there was as yet no real threat of full-scale war. There were, however, serious obstacles to the maintenance of peace. First, there was the difficulty of the kaiser's blank check. When William II finally appreciated the folly of his commitment, he did not make sufficient efforts to repair the damage. He tried to prevent the Russians from calling up their troops, but the tsar felt he had to intervene on behalf of the Serbs or abandon all pretentions to a role in the Balkans. The tsar realized that if he attacked Austria-Hungary, Russia would become involved with Germany, and he knew the consequences of such an action would be disastrous. Nevertheless, he rushed to arms, thereby forcing Germany to react before France could combine with Russia to involve the Germans in a two-front war.

Perhaps France could not have prevented the war even if its government had tried. Instead, the French assured the Russians they would support them fully, an assurance that did nothing to discourage the tsar's mobilization. The Germans obviously knew that war with Russia meant war with France, but they still hoped that Great Britain would remain neutral. In the end, Britain technically entered the war, not because of commitments to France but because the German army overran Belgium in order to gain better access to France. Surprisingly, when the Austrians attempted to invade Serbia in support of their demands, the Serbians were able to expel them with little difficulty, making ironic the whole European mobilization to protect Serbian integrity. In fact, not until a German army was brought into the conflict and Bulgaria was persuaded to launch an invasion from the east was Serbia finally overrun. In retrospect, it seems that Russia might better have served its own interests and those of Serbia by rejecting military intervention and using its influence to isolate the struggle. Such a policy might have both the Germans and Bulgarians neutral, thereby giving the Serbs the one thing they needed, an opportunity to take care of themselves.

SUMMARY OF WORLD WAR I

The war of 1914–1918 was not more notably a world war than previous struggles such as the Seven Years' War of the eighteenth century. Most of the action took place in northern France and Poland. More lives were lost in this conflict than in any war before or since, however, largely because the military commanders on both sides persisted in using infantry tactics against machine gun emplacements protected by barbed wire. Several hundred thousand casualties were sometimes incurred in a single two- or three-month campaign involving only a few miles of territory. Material expenditures kept pace with the lose of life, which meant that the warring nations had to direct all of their resources to making war goods. Behind the front lines, this need produced previously undreamed levels of economic activity. The war ended when Germany, unable to mount a new offensive, had exhausted its capacity to maintain production in support of the war effort and sued for peace without actually suffering a major military reverse. Cut off from the sea by the British naval blockade, Germany was denied access to strategic and critical industrial items such as rubber, petroleum, manganese, tin, and numerous foods and drugs which could not be found in central Europe. These growing shortages, together with a real threat of starvation and the loss of several million men in the armed services, finally wore the nation down until further campaigning became pointless.

Nevertheless, the German army managed to put Russia out of the war completely in late 1917, and at different times during that year both France and Italy were also out of action. The end of 1917 found the British utterly and hopelessly stalemated in Flanders, although they did have the satisfaction of taking both Jerusalem and Baghdad from Turkey, an ally of Germany.

It was the entry of the United States with its impressive industrial system, plentiful food supplies, and vast assortment of raw materials, that ultimately led Germany to realize the hopelessness of its cause. Even before the United States officially entered the war, the Americans had been the major supplier of the Allies, since British control of the sea and of all transatlantic communication made it almost impossible for the Germans to obtain either material or emotional support in this country. Moreover, the United States, though claiming neutrality, had not really been neutral since the beginning of 1915 when it had begun to extend credit to the western Allies. It was the American insistence on the neutral's right to supply one of the belligerents that eventually caused the country to enter the war in 1917 as German submarine depredations against ships trading with Britain increased. Even though Great Britain received both manpower and resources from the various British dominions, particularly Canada, Australia, and New Zealand, it was the large-scale aid from the United States that was instrumental in giving the Allies the final victory. The American president, Woodrow Wilson, also provided the foundation for peace talks in his Fourteen Points in January 1918. Once Russia was eliminated, the Germans turned their attention to the western front, but found themselves unable to decisively defeat either the French or British, and when American reinforcements began to arrive, the Germans saw the futility of continuing the struggle. The Hapsburg Empire was already in pieces, and early in November 1918, the Germans sued for peace, and shortly after Kaiser William II abdicated.

AFTERMATH OF THE WAR

Once the war was over, there was a general desire to forget about its disruptions as much as possible and to put matters back into their accustomed patterns. The Americans used the phase "return to normalcy" to describe the immediate goal of the countries that had been involved in the war. The loss of ten million soldiers plus the devastation left by the conflict, however, made it difficult for Europeans to bury their animosities. United States losses, on the other hand, totaled only slightly more than 100,000 men, more than half of whom died of illness or accidents.

Though the war had cut down many young men in their prime, the

European birth rate increased rapidly, so that by the end of 1918 the population level had returned to what it had been before the war. Politically, the European map was much modified, although most of the changes were in central Europe and grew out of the dissolution of Austria-Hungary and the resurrection of Poland from territory that in the main had belonged to Russia. Germany remained a nation containing most of the German-speaking peoples except the Austrians, although it lost some territory to Poland on the east and to France on the west. More significant than the territorial changes were the political ones, with the Turkish, Hapsburg, Hohenzollern, and Romanov empires giving way to states that were nominally republics. The disaster of the peace was the determination on the part of the Allies to make Germany pay for a war for which others were also responsible.

Turkey lost all of its Arab provinces, leaving it little more than Asia Minor and a toehold in Europe. The left-over piece of the empire fell into the hands of an able dictator, Kemal Ataturk, who achieved a remarkable overhaul of an ancient and backward country during a nineteen-year period of domination. The state was fully secularized, church and state were separated, and as far as possible Turkish institutions were cut off from the past. The Turks received a new alphabet, a new legal system, a new pattern of marriage and divorce, new styles of clothing, a new system of weights and measures, and a new stature among nations.

THE RUSSIAN REVOLUTION

The most significant consequence of the war was the Russian Revolution of 1917. Blockaded by Germany's control of the Baltic Sea and Turkish control of the straits at Istanbul, Russia's only direct contact with friendly powers was across the trans-Siberian railroad to the ports on the Pacific. The Russian defeat, however, was due less to scarcities than to the utter inadequacy and incompetence of its government. Never did an old regime more convincingly discredit itself. The strains of the war upon Russia's inadequate industry, upon its backward agricultural system, and upon its uneducated but patriotic people were much too great. By 1917, Russian demoralization and collapse were complete. In March, the tsar, who was persuaded to abdicate, was replaced by a provisional republican-type government that derived its authority from the old Duma. The provisional government, composed of liberals who had been moderate enough to serve in the tsarist Duma yet liberal enough to encourage the abdication of the tsar, mostly represented the middle class, which amounted to about 10 percent of the Russian population. Conditions, however, had become far too critical to be handled by moderate politics, and the Russian moderates found themselves seriously handicapped by their efforts to continue fighting a hopeless and unpopular war. Those Russians who wanted more drastic change organized into soviets, or councils, that soon sprang up in almost every city of Russia. The soviet in Petrograd (St. Petersburg) from the first assumed a major role in the affairs of the capital and acted more or less as a second government. Though the soviets were more or less spontaneous movements and not initially identified with any particular organized revolutionary party, the Menshevic faction of the Russian Marxists exercised more influence than any other group. Historically, the Mensheviks represented the more moderate faction of the Russian Social Democratic party, which had split into Mensheviks, the minority, and Bolsheviks, the majority, factions in a London Congress in 1903. The Mensheviks, however, did not long prove satisfactory to the rebels because they were committed to cooperation with the provisional government, which was intent on carrying on the war. It was in this context that Vladimire Ilyich Ulyanov, better known as Lenin, a radical Marxist and the leader of the Bolshevik faction, seized his opportunity by effectively undercutting the moderate republican government.

Lenin's brother had been executed by the tsar for revolutionary activity, and Lenin himself at an early age had become a leader in the Russian Marxist movement before being exiled to Siberia, from whence he escaped to western Europe in 1899. It was Lenin who had forced the split of the Russian Marxists into two factions and who had given his own minority faction the name Bolsheviks. When Lenin arrived back in Russia from his exile in 1917, the Bolshevik faction had 80,000 members, less than the Mensheviks and considerably less than the Social Revolutionaries, a peasant socialist group. By demanding an end to the imperialist war, expropriation of the property of the larger landowners, and transfer of all power to the soviets, Lenin effectively counteracted much of the appeal of the Social Revolutionaries and the Mensheviks.

The provisional government, which was steadily losing support because of its inability to improve conditions at home or to carry on the war, attempted to broaden its base by including the left wing groups. The Bolsheviks alone refused to participate. The strongman of the new government was Alexander Kerensky, a young Social Revolutionary leader who served first as minister of war and then in July as head of the government. Before Kerensky could act effectively, the Bolsheviks gained control of the Petrograd soviet and elected Leon Trotsky as its chairman. On November 7, 1917, just before the second All Russian Congress of Soviets started meeting, the Bolsheviks seized control of Petrograd and within hours had captured or put to flight every member of the provisional government. When the Congress, which represented local councils all over the country, met that afternoon, Lenin followed through on his long-standing slogan of all power to the soviets by transferring the sovereignty of the provisional government to the Congress. In actual fact, however, the Congress found itself dominated by a council of people's commissars composed of top Bolshevik leaders. Lenin immediately arranged that the Congress promulgate two far-reaching decrees, one calling upon all belligerents to conclude an immediate peace and a second giving the peasants all the land not already in their hands. By these acts he effectively demonstrated that the Soviet regime would carry out a thorough revolutionary policy. He then moved to dismantle other reminders of the tsarist era. The power of the Russian Orthodox Church, for example, was neutralized through a separation of church and state, confiscation of church lands, and abolition of civil prerogatives of the clergy. When shortly after the Bolshevik coup the Social Revolutionaries received a clear majority of the popular vote cast in the scheduled election for a constituent assembly, Lenin's power was great enough that he refused to recognize the results and had the constituent assembly dispersed by force of arms. Gradually, the Bolsheviks extended their authority over most of the vast tsarist empire, establishing a highly sophisticated type of socialism, usually called Soviet communism. To mark the change, the nation came to be known as the Union of Soviet Socialist Republics.

Russian communism soon developed into something that even Lenin most probably never visualized — a new variety of totalitarianism which developed types of terror even the tsar might have envied. Within less than thirty years, the party of Lenin had thoroughly revitalized the Russian state, building a system so powerful and impressive that all of Europe learned to shudder at its mere mention. The evident effectiveness of Soviet methods in modernizing an appallingly backward country inspired millions of other people throughout the world. The more the Soviet example appeared to attract converts, the more fear it struck into the ruling classes in the Western world, who feared that they would find themselves trampled down as the Russian nobility had been.

THE UNITED STATES

The one power that emerged from World War I comparatively unscathed and with much greater stature was the United States. Though no country really wins a modern war, the United States survived in much the best condition, richer by far than it had been when the war started, free of an ancient foreign debt, owed mostly to England, more highly industrialized, and the world's chief creditor nation. Americans, however, apparently had no particular desire to play the role of chief world military power. As soon after the war as possible, the United States decreased the power and size of its army, putting admirals, generals, and war heroes into niches where the nation could do them honor but where they had no real function. Though politically the United States withdrew from the world scene, the country did not prevent its industrial and financial tycoons from entering world markets. Thus, while Americans perhaps visualized themselves as a symbol of peaceful democracy, uninterested in the quarrels of the old world, their economic influence became world-wide.

American government also changed. The needs of the war increased the number of government officials and so restructured American industrial society that it became highly dependent upon government policy. In this trend Americans were following the example of the British, who somewhat earlier, in spite of the teachings of classical economics, had found that government decisions have a decided effect upon business. The skillful management of the treasury, for example, became a necessity when the United States realized that though many countries owed it money, few could pay. This debt was embarrassing to European statesmen as well as to Americans, but the newly enlarged national debt gave the American government the means to manage the economy more effectively. Though it took a generaton or so for the American government to learn how to deal with a deficit — and there were many failures — the continued penetration of government into all aspects of American life might well be looked upon as a consequence of the war.

That America seemed unwilling to assume international responsibilities was nowhere more apparent than in the League of Nations, which had been created through the efforts of President Wilson. Though many of the more idealistic and grandiose plans of the American president were torpedoed by the statesmen of Europe, the League had the merit of attempting to provide a forum for international opinion without being a bulwark of reaction, as the Congress of Vienna had been earlier. Since both the United States and the Soviet Union, two of the world's most powerful nations, declined to join, the decisions of the League could not be particularly effective. The United States did join with the League in attempting to improve social conditions throughout the world, for example, in efforts directed at increasing literacy, curtailing the slave trade, and stamping out international traffic in prostitution, but it refused to do any more officially. Western European dominance had been challenged by 1920, but none of the new powers such as the Soviet Union, Japan, or the United States had as yet asserted its leadership.

Supplemental Reading
for Part Six

General

Albrecht-Carrié, *The Concert of Europe* (Harper & Row).
Albrecht-Carrié, *Europe After 1815* (Littlefield).
Artz, Frederick B., *Reaction and Revolution, 1814–1832* (Harper & Row).
Binkley, Robert C., *Realism and Nationalism, 1852–1871* (Harper & Row).
Bowle, John, *Politics and Opinion in the Nineteenth Century* (Oxford).
Bruun, Geoffrey, *Revolution and Reaction, 1848–52* (Van Nostrand).
DeRuggiero, G., *The History of European Liberalism* (Beacon).
Droz, J., *Europe between Revolutions, 1815–1848* (Harper & Row).
Gulick, E. V., *Europe's Classical Balance of Power* (Norton).
Hayes, C. J. H., *Generation of Materialism, 1871–1900* (Harper & Row).
Kissinger, Henry A., *A World Restored: The Politics of Conservatism in a Revolutionary Age* (Grosset & Dunlap).
Kranzberg, Melvin, ed., *1848: A Turning Point?* (Heath).
Kohn, Hans, *Nationalism and Realism, 1852–1879* (Van Nostrand).
Kohn, Hans, *Prophets and Peoples: Studies in 19th Century Nationalism* (Macmillan).
Langer, W. L., *European Alliances and Alignments* (Random House).
Laski, Harold J., *The Rise of European Liberalism* (Barnes & Noble).
May, Arthur, *The Age of Metternich, 1814–48* (Holt, Rinehart and Winston).
Mendenhall, T., *The Quest for a Principle of Authority in Europe, 1715 to Present* (Holt, Rinehart and Winston).
Metraux, Guy and Francois Crouzet, *The Nineteenth Century World* (Mentor).
Namier, Sir Lewis, *1848: The Revolution of the Intellectuals* (Doubleday).
Namier, Sir Lewis, *Vanquished Supremacies: Essays on European History, 1812–1918* (Harper & Row).
Nicolson, Harold, *The Congress of Vienna: A Study in Allied Unity, 1812–22* (Viking).
Robertson, Priscilla, *The Revolution of 1848* (Princeton).
Schapiro, J. S., *Liberalism: Its Meaning and History* (Van Nostrand).
Shafer, Boyd C., *Nationalism: Myth and Reality* (Harcourt).
Tuchman, Barbara, *The Guns of August* (Dell).
Viereck, Peter, *Conservatism Revisited* (Macmillan).
Webster, C. K., *The Congress of Vienna, 1814–1815* (Barnes & Noble).

England

Ausubel, Herman, *The Late Victorians* (Van Nostrand).

Birrell, Francis, *Gladstone* (Macmillan).

Bloomfield, P., *Disraeli* (British Book Centre).

Cecil, Lord David, *Melbourne* (Grosset & Dunlap).

Clark, G. Kitson, *The Making of Victorian England* (Atheneum).

Cole, G. D. H., and R. Postgate, *The British Common People, 1748–1946* (Barnes & Noble).

Dangerfield, George, *The Strange Death of Liberal England* (Putnam).

Derry, J. W., *A Short History of Nineteenth Century England* (Mentor).

Freemantle, Anne, *Little Band of Prophets* (Mentor).

Graves, Robert, *Goodbye to All That* (Doubleday).

Schuyler, Robert L., and Corinne C. West, *British Constitutional History since 1832* (Van Nostrand).

Thomson, David, *England in the Nineteenth Century* (Penguin).

Young, G. M., *Victorian England* (Oxford).

France

Brogan, Denis W., *The Development of Modern France*, vol. I (Harper & Row).

Brogan, Denis W., *The French Nation: From Napoleon to Petain* (Harper & Row).

Bury, J. P., *Napoleon III and The Second Empire* (Harper & Row).

Cobban, Alfred A., *A History of Modern France*, vols. 2 & 3, (Penguin).

Derflier, L., ed., *The Dreyfus Affair* (Heath).

Gooch, B. D., ed., *Napoleon III–Man of Destiny* (Holt, Rinehart & Winston).

Thompson, J. M., *Louis Napoleon and the Second Empire* (Norton).

William, R., *The Commune of Paris* (Wiley).

Williams, R., *The World of Napoleon III* (Macmillan).

Wolf, John B., *France, 1814–1919* (Harper & Row).

Germany and Central Europe

Craig, Gordon A., *The Politics of the Prussian Army, 1640–1945* (Oxford).

Eyck, Erich, *Bismarck and the German Empire* (Norton).

Hamerow, Theodore S., ed., *Otto von Bismarck, A Historical Assessment* (Heath).

Kohn, Hans, *Hapsburg Empire, 1804–1818* (Van Nostrand).

Kohn, Hans, *The Mind of Germany* (Harper & Row).

May, A. J., *Hapsburg Monarchy: 1867–1914* (Norton).

Pflanze, O., ed., *Unification of Germany* (Holt, Rinehart and Winston).

Pulzer, P. G. J., *The Rise of Political Anti-Semitism in Germany and Austria, 1871–1918* (Wiley).

Rosenberg, A., *Imperial Germany, 1871–1918* (Beacon).

Schwarz, H. F., ed., *Metternich: Statesman or Evil Genius* (Heath).

Stavrianos, L. S., *The Balkans, 1815–1914* (Holt, Rinehart and Winston).
Stavrianos, L. S., *Ottoman Empire: Was It the Sick Man of Europe?* (Holt, Rinehart and Winston).
Taylor, A. J. P., *Bismarck: The Man and the Statesman* (Random House).
Taylor, A. J. P., *The Course of German History* (Putnam).
Taylor, A. J. P., *Habsburg Monarchy, 1809–1918* (Harper).

Italy

Albrecht-Carrié, R., *Italy from Napoleon to Mussolini* (Columbia).
Smith, Denis Mack, *The Making of Italy, 1796–1866* (Harper & Row).
Smith, Denis Mack, *Garibaldi* (Prentice-Hall).
Whyte, A. J., *The Evolution of Modern Italy* (Norton).

Russia

Carr, E. H., *Michael Bakunin* (Random House).
Florinsky, Michael T., *The End of the Russian Empire* (Macmillan).
Karpovitch, Michael, *Imperial Russia, 1801–1917* (Holt, Rinehart and Winston).
Kohn, Hans, *Pan Slavism* (Random House).
Maynard, John, *Russia in Flux* (Macmillan).
Mosse, W. E., *Alexander II and the Modernization of Russia* (Macmillan).
Mazour, Anatole, *The First Russian Revolution* (Stanford).
Mazour, Anatole, *The Rise and Fall of the Romanovs* (Van Nostrand).
Pares, Bernard, *The Fall of the Russian Monarchy* (Random House).
Robinson, G. T., *Rural Russia* (California).
Schapiro, Leonard, *The Communist Party of the Soviet Union* (Random House).
Seton-Watson, Hugh, *The Decline of Imperial Russia* (Praeger).
Wolfe, Bertram, *Three Who Made a Revolution* (Dell).

The Americas

Cline, H. F., *Mexico: From Revolution to Evolution* (Oxford).
Haring, C. H., *Empire in Brazil* (Norton).
Hays, Samuel P., *The Response to Industrialism: 1885–1914* (Chicago).
Link, Arthur S., *Woodrow Wilson and the Progressive Era* (Harper & Row).
McDougall, R. L., *Canada's Past and Present* (Toronto).
Mowry, George E., *Theodore Roosevelt and the Progressive Movement* (Hill & Wang).
Robertson, W. S., *Rise of the Spanish American Republics* (Free Press).
Smith, Daniel M., *The Great Departure: The United States and World War I* (Wiley).

Economic and Social

Briggs, A., *The Age of Improvement* (Harper & Row).
Chambers, J. D., *Workshop of the World: British Economic History 1820–1880* (Oxford).

Cipolla, Carlo, *Economic History of World Population* (Penguin).

Clapham, John H., *The Economic Development of France and Germany, 1815–1914* (Cambridge).

Cole, G. D. H., and W. A. Filson, *British Working Class Movements* (St. Martin's).

Cole, Margaret, *The Story of Fabian Socialism* (Wiley).

Engels, Friedrich, *The Conditions of the Working Class in England* (Stanford).

Gay, Peter, *The Dilmena of Democratic Socialism* (Macmillan).

Habakkuk, H. J., *American and British Technology in the 19th Century* (Cambridge).

Hammond, John L., and Barbara, *The Rise of Modern Industry* (Harper & Row).

Hammond, John L., and Barbara, *Town Labourer: The New Civilization* (Doubleday).

Handlin, Oscar, *The Uprooted* (Grosset & Dunlap).

Hayek, F. A., ed., *Capitalism and the Historians* (Chicago).

Heilbroner, Robert L., *The Worldly Philosophers, The Lives, Times, and Ideas of the Great Economic Thinkers* (Simon and Schuster).

Henderson, W. O., *The Industrial Revolution in Europe: Germany, France, Russia, 1815–1914* (Quadrangle).

Hobsbawm, E. J., *Primitive Rebels* (Norton).

Hook, Sidney, *From Hegel to Marx* (Michigan).

Jackson, J. H., *Marx, Proudhon, and European Socialism* (Macmillan).

LeRossignol, James E., *Backgrounds to Communist Thought* (Crowell).

Lichtheim, George, *Marxism* (Praeger).

Maddison, A., *Economic Growth in the West* (Norton).

Manuel, Frank E., *Prophets of Paris: Turgot, Condorcet, Saint Simon, Fourier* (Harper & Row).

Pelling, Henry, *History of British Trade Unionism* (Penguin).

Rostow, W. W., *The Stages of Economic Growth* (Cambridge).

Sayers, R. S., *History of Economic Change in England, 1880–1939* (Oxford).

Schorske, Carl E., *German Social Democracy, 1905–1917* (Wiley).

Schumpeter, Joseph, *Capitalism, Socialism and Democracy* (Harper & Row).

Schumpeter, J. A., *Ten Great Economists* (Oxford).

Sorel, Georges, *Reflections on Violence* (Macmillan).

Soule, George, *Ideas of the Great Economists* (Mentor).

Tawney, R. H., *The Acquisitive Society* (Harcourt).

Thompson, E. P., *The Making of the English Working Class* (Random House).

Usher, A. P., *A History of Mechanical Inventions* (Beacon).

Van Laue, T., *Sergei Witte and the Industrialization of Russia* (Atheneum).

Venturi, F., *Roots of Revolution: A History of the Populist and Socialist Movements in 19th Century Russia* (Grosset & Dunlap).

Wilson, Edmund, *To the Finland Station* (Doubleday).

Woodham-Smith, C., *The Great Hunger* (Signet).

Imperialism and War

Arendt, H., *Imperialism* (Harcourt).
Easton, Stewart C., *The Rise and Fall of Western Colonialism* (Praeger).
Emerson, Rupert, *From Empire to Nation* (Beacon).
Fairbank, John K., *The United States and China* (Viking).
Falls, Cyril, *The Great War* (Putnam).
Fay, Sidney B., *The Origins of the World War*, 2 vols. (Free Press).
Feis, Herbert, *Europe, The World's Banker, 1870–1914* (Norton).
Hobson, J. A., *Imperialism* (Michigan).
Lafore, Lawrence, *The Long Fuse* (Lippincott).
Lee, D. E., ed., *The First World War–Who Was Responsible?* (Heath).
Lenin, V. I., *Imperialism: Highest Stage of Capitalism* (International).
Liddel-Hart, Basil H., *The Real War, 1914–1918* (Atlantic).
Morgan, H. W., *America's Road to Empire: The War with Spain and Overseas Expansion* (Wiley).
Nadel, G. H., and L. P. Curtis, eds., *Imperialism and Colonialism* (Macmillan).
Remak, Joachim, *The Origins of World War I* (Holt, Rinehart and Winston).
Robinson, R., *Africa and the Victorians: The Climax of Imperialism* (Doubleday).
Taylor, A. J. P., *History of the First World War* (Berkeley).
Western, J. R., *End of European Primacy, 1871–1945* (Harper & Row).
Whitaker, Arthur P., *The United States and the Independence of Latin America* (Cornell).
Winks, Robin W., ed., *British Imperialism* (Holt, Rinehart and Winston).
Woodham-Smith, C., *The Reason Why* (Dutton).

Intellectual: Religion, Science, Philosophy, Literature, and the Arts

Abrams, M. H., *The Mirror and the Lamp: Romantic Theory and the Critical Tradition* (Norton).
Aiken, Henry D., *The Age of Ideology: The 19th Century Philosophers* (Mentor).
Babbitt, Irving, *Rousseau and Romanticism* (World).
Bagehot, Walter, *Physics and Politics*, several editions of this classic.
Barzun, Jacques, *Berlioz and His Century* (World).
Barzun, Jacques, *Classic, Romantic and Modern* (Doubleday).
Barzun, Jacques, *Darwin, Marx, and Wagner* (Doubleday).
Benda, Julian, *The Betrayal of the Intellectuals* (Beacon).
Bentley, Eric, *A Century of Hero Worship* (Beacon).
Berlin, Isiah, *Karl Marx: His Life and Environment* (Oxford).
Boorstin, Daniel J., *The Genius of American Politics* (Chicago).
Bramsted, E. K., *Aristocracy and the Middle Classes in Germany: Social Types in German Literature* (Chicago).
Briggs, Asa, *Victorian People* (Harper & Row).
Brinton, Crane, *The Shaping of Modern Thought* (Prentice-Hall).

Brockway, Wallace, *Men of Music* (Simon and Schuster).
Caute, David, *The Left in Europe since 1789* (McGraw-Hill).
Clark, Kenneth, *The Gothic Revival* (Penguin).
Clive, Geoffrey, *Romantic Enlightenment: Ambiguity and Paradox in the Western Mind* (World).
Cohen, I. Bernard, *The Birth of the New Physics* (Doubleday).
Cross, R. D., *The Church and the City, 1865–1910* (Boss-Merrill).
Daniels, George, *Darwinism Comes to America* (Ginn).
De Kruif, Paul, *Microbe Hunters* (Pocket Books).
Eiseley, Lorne, *Darwin's Century* (Doubleday).
Elgar, Frank, *Van Gogh: A Study of His Life and Work* (Praeger).
Gilson, Etienne, ed., *The Church Speaks to the Modern World* (Doubleday).
Greene, John C., *The Death of Adam* (Mentor).
Griswood, H., *Ideas and Beliefs of the Victorians* (Dutton).
Hall, Calvin S., *A Primer of Freudian Psychology* (Mentor).
Hales, E. E., *The Catholic Church in the Modern World* (Doubleday).
Halévy, Elie, *The Growth of Philosophical Radicalism* (Beacon).
Himmelfarb, Gertrude, *Darwin and the Darwinian Revolution* (Doubleday).
Höffding, Harald, *A History of Modern Philosophy*, 2 vols. (Dover).
Holt, E. G., *From the Classicists to the Impressionists* (Doubleday).
Hofstadter, Richard, *Social Darwinism in American Thought* (Beacon).
Hook, Sidney, *Marx and the Marxists* (Van Nostrand).
Hughes, H. C., *Consciousness and Society* (Random House).
Huxley, Julian, *A Book That Shook the World* (Pittsburg).
Irvine, William, *Apes, Angels and Victorians* (World).
Jones, Ernest, *The Life and Work of Freud*, abridged (Doubleday).
Kennedy, Gail, ed., *Evolution and Religion* (Heath).
Kirk, Russel, *The Conservative Mind from Burke to Santayana* (Regnery).
Kohn, H., *The Making of the Modern French Mind* (Van Nostrand).
Lowenberg, B. J., ed., *Darwinism: Reaction or Reform* (Holt, Rinehart and Winston).
Mannheim, Karl, *Ideology and Utopia* (Harcourt).
Marcus, S., *The Other Victorians* (Bantam).
Merz, John Theodore, *History of European Thought in the Nineteenth Century*, 4 vols. (Dover).
Mirsky, Dmitrit P., *A History of Russian Literature to 1900* (Random House).
Newby, I. A., *Jim Crow's Defense: Anti-Negro Thought in America* (Louisiana).
Pevsner, Nikolaus, *An Outline of European Architecture* (Penguin).
Pruner, Helen Walker, *Freud, His Life and Mind* (Dell).
Reichenbach, Hans, *From Copernicus to Einstein* (Philosophical Library).
Riedel, Johannes, *Music of the Romantic Period* (Brown).
Schapiro, J. S., *Anticlericalism: Conflict between Church and State in France, Italy, and Spain* (Van Nostrand).

Schweitzer, Albert, *The Quest for the Historical Jesus* (Macmillan).

Snyder, L. L., *Idea of Racialism: Its Meaning and History* (Van Nostrand).

Sommervell, D. C., *English Thought in the 19th Century* (McKay).

Stace, W. T., *The Philosophy of Hegel* (Dover).

Strachey, Lytton, *Eminent Victorians* (Putnam).

Symons, Arthur, *The Symbolist Movement in Literature* (Dutton).

Walzel, Oskar, *German Romanticism* (Putnam).

Williams, Raymond, *Culture and Society, 1780–1950* (Doubleday).

Wilshire, Bruce, ed., *Romanticism and Evolution in the 19th Century* (Putnam).

Wilson, Edmund, *Axel's Castle: A Study in Imaginative Literature 1870–1930* (Scribner).

Wilson, R. J., *Darwinism and the American Intellectual* (Dorsey).

Woodcock, George, *Anarchism: A History of Libertarian Ideas and Movements* (World).

SOURCES *

Bagehot, Walter, *The English Constitution* (Cornell or Doubleday).

Curtin, P., ed., *Africa Remembered: Narratives by West Africans* (Wisconsin).

Darwin, Charles, *The Origin of Species*, several editions.

Freud, S., *A General Introduction to Psychoanalysis*, several editions.

Heine, Henrich, *Religion and Philosophy in Germany* (Beacon).

Kierkegaard, *Fear and Trembling* (Doubleday).

Malthus, Thomas, *On Population* (Mentor).

Marx, Karl, *The Communist Manifesto*, several editions.

Marx, Karl and Friedrich Engels, *Basic Writings on Politics and Philosophy*, ed. Lewis Feuer (Doubleday or various other editions).

Mill, John Stuart, *Autobiography* (Signet).

Mill, John Stuart, *Utilitarianism, On Liberty, and Other Writings* (World).

Miller, Perry, ed., *American Thought: Civil War to World War I* (Holt, Rinehart and Winston).

Nietzsche, *Portable Nietzsche*, ed. Walter Kaufman (Viking).

Popkins, R. H., *The Philosophical Historians* (Bobbs-Merrill).

Renan, E., *Life of Jesus* (Random House).

Spencer, Herbert, *Study of Sociology* (Michigan).

FICTION

Balzac, H. de, *Old Goriot* (Penguin).

Clavell, J., *Tai-Pan: A Novel of Hong Kong* (Dell).

Dos Passos, John, *U.S.A.* (Houghton).

Forster, E. M., *Passage to India* (Harcourt).

Galsworthy, J., *Man of Property* (Scribner).

* *Paperback editions of many of the novelists, playwrights, poets, philosophers, and others cited in the section are also available.*

Gogol, Nickolai, *Dead Souls* (Signet or other editions).
Hasek, Jaroslav, *The Good Soldier Schweik* (Signet).
Mann, Thomas, *Buddenbrooks* (Random House).
Manning, Frederic, *Her Privates We* (Berkley).
Remarque, Erich Maria, *All Quiet on the Western Front* (Crest).
Turgenev, I., *Fathers and Sons*, numerous editions.

part seven

THE TWENTIETH CENTURY

22

From World War to World War

The delegates to the peace conference who met in Paris in January 1919 faced the task of redrawing the boundaries of east-central Europe and making a peace settlement with Germany. Dominating the conference, the largest gathering of diplomats since the Congress of Vienna, were the representatives of the Big Three — Woodrow Wilson of the United States, David Lloyd George of Great Britain, and Georges Clemenceau of France — who were given an occasional assist by Vittorio Orlando of Italy. Nearly everyone at the conference was willing to agree to the American president's key fourteenth point, which called for collective security arrangements through a League of Nations, but the problems centered on Wilson's other proposals, including the establishment of democratic nation states throughout Europe with the rights of national self-determination for various ethnic groups. Wilson's Fourteen Points had been a unilateral declaration, made without consultation with the Allied leaders, and ran into conflict both with the secret treaties negotiated during the war and the realities of a postwar world. Italy's claims, for example, conflicted with those of Serbia, which by this time was known as Yugoslavia, as well as with the desires of German-speaking Austrians in the South Tyrol. When Hungary was dismembered, many Hungarians found themselves included in Rumania, Yugoslavia, or Czechoslovakia, while German-speaking Austrians were annexed to Czechoslovakia. Many other such difficulties provided agitation in the period between the two wars, but nowhere was there more trouble than in Germany.

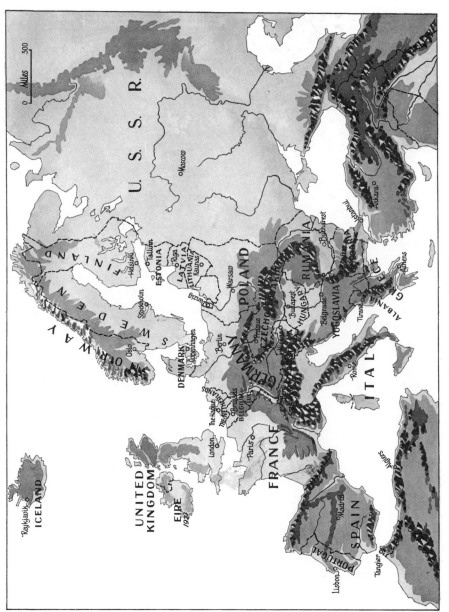

Europe around 1920.

GERMANY

German affairs during World War I had been more or less controlled by the military as the kaiser relinquished his discretionary control to General Paul von Hindenburg, and especially his more dynamic aide, Erich von Ludendorff. Though both men were competent commanders, particularly Ludendorff as chief of staff, neither had the abilities necessary for statesmen. It was their resumption of submarine warfare, for example, that led to the entry of the United States into the conflict and ultimately to Germany's defeat. When the German cause seemed hopeless, the military removed themselves from the government and a liberal aristocrat, Prince Max of Baden, formed a new government which included members of the moderate Socialists who sat in the Reichstag. This step was obviously taken to coincide with Wilson's insistence on democratic government and was designed to transform Germany into a liberal constitutional monarchy which could then negotiate for peace. Less than a month after the new government had been formed, sailors in the imperial fleet mutinied. Almost immediately following this November 3 revolt, workers' and soldiers' councils began to be formed in the larger cities much like those that had earlier sprung up in Russia. A general strike was called on November 9, and on that day William II abdicated, crossing the border into neutral Holland. A few hours later a republic was proclaimed, and within forty-eight hours German representatives had signed an armistice with the Allied commanders, ostensibly on the basis of Wilson's Fourteen Points. Later, when a democratic government had been established, Ludendorff and other generals returned to public affairs, claiming that the military had not lost the war and that worsening conditions in Germany had been brought about by the newly established republic under the control of the Social Democrats.

The Social Democrats had constituted the principle opposition to the liberals, nationalists, and conservatives who in varying degrees had embraced the Hohenzollern war regime and who therefore might be the logical group to take power when the warlike William II abidicated. The Social Democrats, however, were handicapped by the fact that they were ideological Marxists, and as a group they were suspected of being Bolsheviks, in spite of the fact that the majority of them were willing to work within a parliamentary system. The failure of the extremists, called the Spartacists, gave even further impetus to the commitment of the Social Democrats to bring about greater social welfare through parliamentary methods. The suspicion of their opponents did not lessen, however. Moreover, the Social Democrats now had to suffer as Germans for having caused the war even though they had been the most reluctant of all Germans to support the war program.

The Allied statesmen who negotiated the peace settlement with the new German government failed to recognize that the revolution of November 1918, which brought the Social Democrats to power and caused the kaiser to resign, was symbolic of a genuine revulsion against the old regime. Indeed, some of the Allies reacted to the revolution as if it represented a German conspiracy to win the peace after losing the war. The Treaty of Versailles of 1919 arranging matters between Germany and the victorious powers was not so much a treaty with the Germans as an agreement among the Allies as to what they would do about their former enemy. For one thing, the treaty blaming the Germans for causing the war stirred up widespread resentment among the German people. The Germans were also obligated to pay "reparations" for causing the war. In the past, indemnities had been a standard type of penalty imposed by a victor upon a vanquished foe, and President Wilson had expressed the opinion that such punitive damages ought to be avoided in this case, Instead, the statesmen called for reparations. While an indemnity could be any amount the victor thought he could collect, reparations were geared to the damage that was to be "repaired"; when the treaty was signed on June 1919, that amount had not been worked out.

The German representatives who were in session at Weimar formulating a republican-type constitution thus had to accept an obligation that knew no limit. When two years later the Allies finally agreed upon a sum of thirty-five billion dollars, the struggling republic was dealt a near lethal blow. The Germans tried to refuse to pay the amount, but the French sent troops to occupy part of the Ruhr until they did. On top of the war indemnity, Germany also had to retire its own war debt, which was almost unmanageable because the kaiser's war policy had depended heavily on selling bonds rather than on levying of taxes. Like the postwar governments of Austria and Hungary, the Germans canceled these debts by printing more money and thus deliberately causing an inflation. Though internal indebtedness was thus abolished, Germany's financial position became precarious as the German mark escalated to 4.2 trillion to the dollar. No amount of inflation could produce the cash demanded by the Allies, however, and when Germany defaulted on its payments for the third time, France and Belgium occupied the entire Ruhr Valley to force payment. The troops were met by a show of passive resistance, but the German government itself collapsed. The crisis finally ended when Gustav Stresemann formed a new government in September 1923 and managed to end the inflation. With a German promise to resume reparation payments in hand, the French and Belgians gradually withdrew their troops. In the aftermath of this episode, the French abandoned their effort to enforce the Versailles Treaty by military means and concentrated instead on building up their internal defenses against any future German aggression. Gradually, there was a reduction of tensions in Europe marked by the admission of Germany into the League of Nations.

Once its currency was stabilized, with American help, Germany made rapid strides. Such progress was possible because the country had suffered little physical damage during the war and thus its strong industrial system and highly skilled population were left intact. Moreover, the Versailles Treaty had forced Germany to disarm almost completely, thus freeing the country of the onerous burden of supporting a large military establishment. The one thing the country lacked was the necessary investment capital, but German potential soon attracted venturesome Americans with large war-earned surpluses to invest. The result was one of the most curious phenomena known to modern finance. With funds invested by Americans in Germany, the Germans were able to produce enough to pay reparations to Britain, France, Italy, and Belgium, who then met their obligations to the United States. Few people at the time seemed to appreciate the fact that the United States was in effect paying itself, and failed to see the link between this situation and American prosperity during the period 1924–1929. Inevitably, however, the 1929 stock market crash in the United States brought disaster when Americans became frightened and ceased their lending operations. The Germans were soon forced to halt their reparations payments, thus making it impossible for their creditors to continue making payments to the United States. Only Finland, which had remained outside of the cycle, consistently made payments after 1931.

THE UNITED STATES

While Europe struggled to recover from the ravages of the war, Americans on their part tried equally hard to forget about their involvement in the conflict. The United States had emerged from World War I as a dominant world power. Territorially, it was one of the largest nations in the world; it possessed almost unlimited natural resources; it had the world's most varied and prolific industrial establishment; and Americans had developed the technique of mass production, which made possible the production of great quantities of high-quality manufactured goods which could be sold at fairly low prices. It is no wonder that to many of the underprivileged people of the world America seemed to be a kind of promised land endowed with freedom, opportunity, and high living standards. Its brief but important role in the war, combined with the impressive idealism of

President Wilson, had forced most of the world's leaders to reassess the power of this previously ignored giant. Yet no sooner was the war over than the American people repudiated Wilson's dream and entered into a period of isolation, refusing to accept a leading role in world affairs. The United States proceeded to demobilize most of its army, to reduce its navy, and, in spite of a very low rate of taxation, to cut its national debt. At the same time, Americans constructed a coast to coast system of hard-surfaced highways, allowing the country to become the first to take full advantage of the age of the automobile. Instead of continuing their prewar concerns with the waste of natural resources, the growth of monopolies, or the exploitation of women and children, Americans went on a free-spending spree of good living known as the jazz age and became the focus of envy and imitation throughout the rest of the world.

In the aftermath of the war and with the advent of the automobile, many of the inhibitions of the past were discarded, particularly those that had restricted the activities of women. The necessity for total mobilization had everywhere given women new prominence, and as a consequence they achieved the right to vote in the United States and in parts of Europe. Though women for generations had campaigned for the suffrage, which they considered synonymous with equality, the right to vote was only the beginning of the struggle to lessen the world-wide pattern of sex discrimination that had subordinated women throughout history. At the same time, there also came a rejection of much of the morality of the past. To the conservative observer of the time, the postwar generation seemed to have an impulsive desire to trample upon the old moral standards without replacing them with anything better. The radio and the movies transmitted this spirit of rebellion across the nation, and the automobile gave young people the freedom to escape from the chaperones of the past. In making movies, building radio stations, and manufacturing cars, America seemed to show the way to much of the rest of the world. Europe in spite of itself was impressed. Yet at the same time that the old moral codes were under assault, rural America asserted itself to help impose prohibition, a Constitutional Amendment ill-suited to the temper of the time. This last-ditch stand of small-town America not only failed to raise the level of sobriety but also turned many normally law-abiding people into law-breakers who became accustomed to getting their alcoholic beverages from illegal sources. The outlawed liquor traffic supplied new funds for other forms of corruption, while the management of public affairs too often was turned over to the unedifying type of small-town businessman-politician so vividly satirized in the movies and stories of Sinclair Lewis.

Symbolic of the new America was a new type of music — jazz —

which had developed in New Orleans late in the nineteenth century among various slum dwellers, particularly Negroes. From there it worked its way northward, attracting little public attention until it reached Chicago, where it began to achieve a new aura of respectability as it left the slums and bordellos and entered into the mainstream of American life. The jazz musician demonstrated the same contempt for classical notions of harmony and instrumentation that his listeners exhibited for the moral standards of the Victorian era. Rather, he emphasized and improvised syncopated and spontaneous performances that suited both his own mood and that of his listeners. As the music acquired a variety of patterns, most of the world seemed to adopt it. Jazz musicians, both white and black, could be found in America, Europe, and Asia, everywhere spreading the image of a new and rebellious generation.

At home, however, America became almost xenophobic. Though its population and culture were only recently derived from foreign sources, legislation was enacted to curtail immigration and to exclude certain groups, such as the Japanese. Manufacturers sought to increase their tariff protection against imports by attempting to demonstrate that imported products were subversive to American values. As if to demonstrate their own schizophrenia, Americans appeared everywhere in the world while they sought to protect and isolate themselves at home. Tourists in ever-increasing numbers visited Europe, where their expenditures assisted many nations to recover from wartime deprivations. American overseas investment expanded until much of the world came to be dependent upon the United States for investment capital. In spite of itself, the United States began to play an influential role on the international scene. Though at first it had gone so far as to refuse even to acknowledge mail coming from the League of Nations headquarters in Geneva, the United States eventually established a permanent secretariat at League headquarters. While it still officially refused to join the League, the United States took an active part in the naval limitation conferences of the late 1920s. These ambiguities in America's attitude toward world affairs served only to confuse the diplomats of other countries, who never quite knew how to deal with the United States.

Yet a number of serious difficulties underlay the apparent prosperity of the United States. Matters were made worse by the unwillingness of most Americans to face up to the reality of their problems. They were much too bedazzled by their success to take into account the growing needs of an urbanized society. Industries, for example, were highly interrelated and depended upon continued operation at high levels of capacity. In addition, the American population was a mobile one, with limited resources to fall back upon in times of stress. In an earlier age, depressions could be weathered by returning to the farm, by tightening the belt, or by taking some form of charity, but in the highly interdependent American industrial complex these recourses were no longer possible. Public housing, insurance against sickness, accident, and unemployment, retirement provisions, health assistance, and other programs, all of which had come to be regarded as essential in other industrialized urban societies, were virtually nonexistent in the United States.

Moreover, much of the new wealth in the United States fell into the hands of those who were already rich. By 1929, about a third of the total income of the country was controlled by less than 5 percent of the population. Though worker efficiency had led to a 43 percent gain in production during the previous decade, wages and salaries of large numbers of workers had scarcely risen. The result was that American prosperity was largely dependent upon what the richest 5 percent of the population thought and did. As long as these people spent their money or otherwise invested it, they demonstrated their belief that the economy was "sound," and business activity continued on an acceptable level. When they failed to do these things, the results were disastrous. It seems a truism to say that in any society where an inordinate proportion of the wealth is in the hands of a tiny group who fail to realize that their actions carry serious social consequences, an entire nation can be shaken when a small minority panics.

DEPRESSION

The stock market crash of 1929 was essentially nothing more than one more sudden termination of a speculative boom that periodically took place when prospective purchasers realized that they were bidding far more for a product than the product was worth. The crash, however, understandably frightened and bewildered American economic managers, and their reaction had disastrous consequences not only in the United States but also abroad, where Americans had been supporting various kinds of private and public projects. The cessation of many American-financed operations largely terminated the export trade of the United States and threw the already weakened European finances into confusion. Since by the standards of classical economics such ills would be self-remedying as long as individuals were permitted to look to their own devices, most government authorities avoided taking any measures on the assumption that in the natural course of events, matters would right themselves. Adam Smith, however, had written for the eighteenth century, and though his insights had led to remarkable progress, they had failed to take into account the problems associated with a complex world economy based on industrialization. In fact, the bankers, by retrenching on their loans, invited what they most feared — bankruptcy — and public officials, by cutting expenditures and building up the treasury, increased unemployment. The results were devastating. In a four-year period, American trade with Europe fell off from about eleven billion dollars to approximately four billion, while Europe's foreign commerce fell from some fifteen billion dollars to one third that amount. American gross national product dropped nearly 50 percent in four years from its 1929 figure of approximately 104 billion dollars; only the outbreak of a new war in 1939 finally made recovery possible. To further complicate matters, the U.S. banking system was inadequate to meet the crisis. Long-time American fears of centralized banking had left many banks with limited resources, and with the shrinkage of business assets after 1929, the banks found themselves in further difficulty as frightened depositors began to withdraw their funds in ever-increasing numbers.

It was not until after Franklin D. Roosevelt took office in 1933 that Americans appeared willing to recognize that the government itself had to take direct action. Roosevelt proceeded to introduce long-overdue social welfare legislation, such as social security, and to commit the government to intervene directly to relieve social distress. To carry out this program, government expenditures increased from around four and a half billion dollars per year to nearly eight billion, and the national debt rose to approximately twenty billion dollars. In these policies, Roosevelt was following the prescription of the English economist John Maynard Keynes, who argued that the government itself by increasing the national debt, or engaging in deficit financing, could spend itself into prosperity, whereupon it could then raise taxes to pay off the debt. Keynes, who was interested in preserving a modified form of capitalism, seemed to propose much too radical a solution for most governments to adopt, and even in the United States it was not until the depression was over that the Keynesian solution came to be one of the dominant forces in the American economy. Great Britain at first refused to accept Keynes's prescriptions, although throughout the world, governments eventually came to adopt the Keynesian solution of massive public spending. Yet the improvement in economic conditions was due more to the outbreak of World War II than to any constructive efforts on the part of governments to end the depression.

FRANCE

The ramifications of the American depression were world-wide, in part because no other power had the financial commitments or resources of the North American colossus. This statement can be verified by a brief look at France, nominally the most triumphant of the Allies in the aftermath of World War I, since its hated enemy, Germany, was weakened and the French had recovered Alsace and Lorraine. The financial burdens of restoring the devastated areas of northern France and of converting French industry to a peacetime economy, however, proved nearly as expensive as supporting the war. France soon fell into serious economic difficulty. To make matters worse, the additions of the former Turkish and German possessions in Asia and Africa, while extending French territory, proved a financial strain and required a greater commitment of resources than France received in return. Moreover, despite the fact that they had emerged victorious, the French people still feared Germany. Though the German navy and air force had been abolished and the army reduced to 100,000 men, France felt the need to continue a vast military establishment. The French also organized the Little Entente, composed of Czechoslovakia, Rumania, and Yugoslavia, and entered into an alliance with the newly independent Poland to establish a *cordon sanitaire* in order to isolate Germany. To further protect themselves against any possible German revival, they began construction of an expensive defensive system, the Maginot Line, in northeastern France. The continuation of this costly military policy, which made no real contribution to the French industrial plant, served only to increase the national debt without giving the French people any real benefits. At the same time, the United States insisted on repayment of its loans to France. The franc proved unequal to these strains and gradually dropped in value from twenty cents in 1913 to about two cents in 1928, when the government decided on a drastic and oppressive retrenchment that stabilized it at four cents. Instead of giving a breathing spell to the French economy, this financial stabilization, by cutting government expenditures, mostly military spending, led to a recession that proved to be an unexpected opportunity to demagogues and extremists of both the left and the right, who used it to capitalize upon the discontent of the French people. The polarization of political parties in French left the government almost completely paralyzed, able only to drift from one crisis to another. Inevitably, not only was France powerless to offer help to the world when the economy of the United States collapsed, but as internal difficulties mounted, the country demonstrated itself to be almost helpless before the German invasion of World War II.

GREAT BRITAIN

Great Britain managed to escape invasion during World War I, but it had lost nearly a million men, some ten million tons of merchant marine, mainly by enemy submarine action, and had witnessed a precipitous decline in foreign investment, which was diverted to purchase imported food and supplies. Even then Great Britain had to continue to borrow money to survive, primarily from the United States, so that during the early 1920s, the interest on the national debt was more than the total annual expenditure of the government in the years before the war. Unlike France, Great Britain also had to import food materials, and thus its survival depended upon its ability to sell its manufactured products abroad. When it proved unable to do so, British difficulties were compounded.

Like the French, the British had also acquired territories from the Turks and the Germans to add to what had become the largest empire the world had yet seen. Already, however, there were indications of trouble in the empire. Ireland, for example, which had been regarded as an integral part of Great Britain, had demanded more independence in the period before the war. Though since the establishment of the Dominion of Canada in 1867 the British had allowed considerable independence to many parts of the empire, Ireland was regarded as a different case. In fact, it was only after a long series of crises that the British in 1914 reluctantly agreed to make concessions to the Irish. Home rule for the island, however, was bitterly resented by the northern (Protestant) Irish and their allies in England, who felt that Protestantism would become a minority religion in a Catholic dominion. Hardcore Protestant opposition forced the British to suspend any concessions to Ireland until Germany could be defeated. This delay led to the 1916 Easter Rebellion, staged by a nationalist minority in Dublin who demanded full independence. Though the rebellion was suppressed and its leaders imprisoned or executed, the rebels continued their agitation until finally the British split the island into two sections, one for each religious faction. In the 1930s, the southern portion became a fully independent dominion and later a separate republic; northern Ireland, on the other hand, remained closely tied to England. The Irish situation proved to be symptomatic of the increasing trouble the British would have with the Indians, the Egyptians, and various other of their subjects throughout the world.

In general, however, Great Britain's enormous empire remained comparatively peaceful. In fact, it was not so much the empire that caused problems as it was the outmoded British industrial machine. World War I had accelerated this deterioration, since it forced the British to postpone further the replacement of their aging industrial plants. When world trade resumed after the war, the British found themselves unable to compete effectively or to gain the capital to make the necessary renovation. As a result, the 1920s in Great Britain saw a pressing and continuous problem of unemployment caused by closed factories, declining shipping, and falling exports. The "nation of shop-keepers," as Napoleon had contemptuously called the country, lost many of its customers. The world no longer came to Great Britain for railroads, since most of these had been built, and in replacing old equipment the British were challenged by other industrial powers, including the United States. Shipbuilding, another large British industry, was on the decline as the countries sought ways to use the ships they had left over from World War I. Textiles, one of the mainstays of the British industrial establishment, could no longer compete even in Great Britain with the cotton mills and factories erected in India and China, which were closer to the source of supply and could hire cheaper labor. Wool remained an important part of textile manufacture, but it alone could not keep all the textile workers employed. Coal mining, another British industry, was declining as coal came to be supplanted by petroleum supplied by the Americans, and soon also by the various Middle Eastern states. Even British banking was in trouble as the British found themselves more and more dependent upon American credit. During the 1920s, the British, like the Americans, did little about their internal problems. The policies they did follow, such as restoring the pound to its prewar gold parity or insisting on the retention of free trade, tended to further weaken the British industrial establishment. In a protectionist world, British products could not compete in foreign markets without either a domestic subsidy or some kind of tariff agreement. The result was a deflation of wages within Great Britain which was accompanied by a growing unemployment.

It was not until 1931 that Britain abandoned both free trade and the gold standard, but by then the world was suffering from the effects of the American depression, As a result, the people who had invented the modern capitalist-type industrial system and who held the greatest empire in history knew scarcely any prosperity from 1920 until World War II broke out in 1939. Moreover, the British government refused to use its unemployed workers for public works projects, as was being done in the United States, but instead relied upon the dole. Thus even needed public improvements were not made. Though the Royal Navy patrolled the oceans and the British merchant fleet was still the largest in the world, the days of the empire upon which the sun never set were passing. In the aftermath of World War II, the British turned to solving their domestic problems at the expense of meeting their world commitments. From a free enterprise economy they turned more and more to government regulation in the hope that such intervention could prevent lengthy depressions and maintain reasonable levels of employment.

THE SOVIET UNION

The Soviet Union was even less prepared than France and Great Britain to act effectively when the American economy failed. Lenin had replaced the corrupt autocracy of the tsar with the equally autocratic system of one-party rule. The tsar and his family were shot, and a three-year civil war was waged and won against the adherents of conservatism and moderation. At the end of this internal struggle, little remained of the traditional order that had previously exercised control through its ownership of property or privileges based upon rank and status. During this period, the Russian economy had become totally bankrupt and millions of people had starved to death. Millions of others were saved only by the efforts of various international charitable organizations, including the League of Nations. In this continuing crisis, the Communist party took shape, and it became the driving force in the reshaping of Soviet society. Though the party included only a fraction of the Russian population, it maintained a vast surveillance over Russian affairs, and its members held the thousands of key offices necessary for the restructuring of a society in which older institutions or organizations had suffered ruin or become ineffective.

In many ways, Lenin and his colleagues seem to have been totally naïve concerning the needs of the new world they aimed to establish. They had long taught that once they had eliminated the ruling classes, which had always kept humanity in control, the natural virtue of men who had never been corrupted by wealth and power would rise to dominance. Thus a new order would begin, and men everywhere would be emancipated from their troubles. When the revolutionaries emerged victorious, they found that they commanded an effective totalitarian system dedicated to an egalitarian state, but socialism was little more than provisionally operative and their dreams were far from becoming a reality. Arguing that the Russian people had not undergone so much turmoil only to end up with the same basic structure, the Bolsheviks retained their semisecret, disciplined organization of dedicated believers which had been formed under the tsar. The Communist party also turned out to be an instrument for terror no less effective than the Committee of Public Safety which had grown out of comparable conditions during the French Revolution. At first, however, under the new economic policy, the transition to the socialist utopia was to be gradual and Russian society was pluralistic. Some private capitalism was encouraged, simply to keep the Russian state from falling into chaos, although all big industry came under government control. The party strengthened itself during this transition by encouraging dissidents to go into exile and jailing those who refused.

Under this policy, Russia began to show some signs of recovery and continued to prosper after Lenin's death in 1924. In spite of its Communist ideology, however, the changes that took place were similar to those already enacted in Western society. It was to carry through more radical programs that Stalin, who had emerged dominant after a bloody struggle, issued the first Five Year Plan. Politically, the plan represented an attempt to submerge the individual and at the same time, to destroy all existing loyalties, thereby creating the conditions in which a new type of society could emerge. Economically, the plan was a sort of engineering projection that attempted to push the economy ahead by systematically planning for every requirement. Beginning in 1928, projections called for huge capital investments, but since there was no surplus to invest, the money had to be obtained at the expense of contemporary living standards. Because the economy of the Soviet Union was mainly based on agriculture, the main source of an excess had to be those who produced and consumed food. Plans were made to recast farming practices completely by converting peasant holdings to large-scale collective and state farms. Such farms, by widespread use of machinery, would eventually increase agricultural efficiency, but the short-term result was wholesale displacement of the peasants. Massive resistance and disastrous shortages followed, and to enforce its program, the Soviet state turned to using force, exacting reprisals, and pushing forward with a relentless ferocity that cost millions of lives — some estimates running as high as twenty-five million persons.

The first Five Year Plan was followed by two more before Russia became involved in World War II. During this time, the terrorism initiated by Stalin continued. Few officials under Stalin were ever free from the likelihood that they would be denounced and shot in an effort to emphasize the necessity for complete devotion; and hanging over every Russian was the distinct possibility that the secret police, acting upon some rumor or anonymous tip, would invade his home and spirit him off. In spite of this regime of terror — or perhaps because of it — the Russian colossus managed to bring itself into the modern world. The successful repulse of the German armies served to justify the preceding era and to enhance the prestige of both the Soviet Union and the Communist party in world opinion. Even in Russia, Stalinism came to be accepted as necessary for the good of the country, although after his death his reputation changed drastically. After all, for centuries the Russian people had lived under terror and oppression and were all too familiar with the waste, inefficiency, and futility of the tsarist government. At least the Stalin variety of totalitarianism, in the minds of many, had eventually led to better conditions.

The achievements of Lenin and Stalin in remaking Russia came to be admired by radicals and would-be revolutionaries throughout the world who either were ignorant of the internal havoc taking place in Russia or justified it as a necessary evil. In emulation of the Russian model, Communist parties sprang up everywhere, but none succeeded in ruling a state for any length of time in the period before World War II. The greatest effect of these organizations, rather, was to frighten many people into joining any group that seemed to be anti-Communist, even though the parties of the right assumed the same weapons of terror as the Communists were accused of using. In a sense, the Fascist dictators of the right had the merit of being candid in their contempt for democracy. The Soviet leaders persistently claimed that Western democracy was merely a blind behind which the big capitalists could pull the strings, whereas *real* democracy was communism. The Fascists, on the other hand, simply believed that democracy represented little more than a stage in the deterioration of civilization, and that if this form of government continued, man would be fit only for slave labor camps.

ITALY: THE BEGINNINGS OF FASCISM

Italy, though a member of the victorious allied coalition, felt itself betrayed by the terms of the Versailles treaty and was bitterly resentful. The Italian armies had experienced severe losses, yet Italy failed to gain coveted areas on the east coast of the Adriatic, which remained in Yugoslavian hands. Moreover, the Italian people, who had been promised radical changes in return for their support of the war effort, became disillusioned in the aftermath of the war when long overdue reforms, particularly wide-scale land reform, failed to be enacted. To complicate matters further, the discharge of hundreds of thousands of soldiers acutely increased the Italian unemployment problem. The existing Italian government not only proved ineffective in dealing with these crises but, in addition, many of its members were suspected of feathering their own nests. Inevitably, large numbers of voters turned to the Socialists in 1919 in the hope that they would do something about postwar inflation and unemployment. Though the Socialists emerged as the strongest party, gaining one third of the seats in the national chamber of deputies, their voting power so frightened the established interests that these groups banded together to thwart most of the Socialist program without offering any constructive alternatives. As the legislature became deadlocked, the frustrated workers took matters into their own hands by staging wide-scale strikes and even seizing factories. Nationalist groups also acted on their own, and a group of volunteers under the poet Gabriele d'Annunzio occupied the

Italian-inhabited city of Fiume on the Yugoslavian coast. It was on this scene that Benito Mussolini appeared.

Mussolini was a former Socialist who had broken with his party over its opposition to Italy's entrance into the war. In the aftermath of the Russian Revolution, Mussolini abandoned socialism entirely, and in 1919 organized his followers into a paramilitary black-shirted union called the *Fasci di Combattimento.* The word *fasces,* derived from the Latin term for the ancient Roman symbol of authority, implied for Mussolini a devotion to discipline and to the state. In fact, the core of Mussolini's doctrine came to be a belief in the absolute sovereignty of the state, with the class struggle of Marxism supplanted by a national struggle of a people to achieve international power. Before Italy could achieve this objective, however, Italian workers and businessmen had to work together, abandoning their right to strike or to lock out employees. Initially, fascism was not so much an organized doctrine as it was an appeal against communism and anarchy. Unlike the doctrine of socialism, which had been built up over a long period of time, much of what came to be defined as Fascist ideology came into being only after the Fascists gained power. Mussolini's incipient party, in spite of its ambiguities, appealed to many Italians. Its militant nationalism aroused the patriotic feeling of a people who felt they had been slighted by the great powers, and its support of class interests, including those of the military, satisfied men of property and power. The emphasis of fascism on nationalism, class interests, and power in the long run made it more of a threat to capitalism than to communism. Once it gained widespread support in the troubled 1930s, fascism could be destroyed in any particular country only by external military force rather than by decay from within.

As the Italian legislature became deadlocked and found itself unable to meet the growing internal crises, more people listened to Mussolini's denunciation of the chamber of deputies as a tool of special interests. When the Socialists lost hope for achieving remedies through legislation and turned to seizing factories, Mussolini encouraged his supporters to strike back by using strong-arm methods. The Fascists broke up Socialist meetings, smashed the offices of hostile newspapers, and even assassinated some of the opposing leaders. These tactics attracted a great number of followers, and at this point, even though he continued to express contempt for the parliamentary system, Mussolini organized his own political party. In the 1921 election, the new Fascist party won some thirty-five seats, but instead of encouraging Mussolini to act within the democratic tradition, the victory enabled him to hamstring more effectively the legislative process. The more hopelessly deadlocked the legislature became, the more the shopkeepers, the middle class, and the rich flocked to fascism as the only alternative to anarchy or communism. Mussolini also gained large numbers of supporters among the young people, who became convinced that Italy was being sacrificed to selfish materialistic interests. By 1922, Mussolini's Black Shirts had become numerous enough and his supporters strong enough that he was able to drive out by force the legally elected Socialist governments in the northern industrial cities. The central government did nothing to intervene, since King Victor Emmanuel, the constitutional head of the government, sympathized with Mussolini's ultimate aims if not with his policies. After his success in the north, Mussolini planned a huge march on Rome, the seat of the government, as a protest against corruption and inaction. Victor Emmanuel was now faced with the prospect of dealing directly with the Fascists instead of merely giving them tacit support. When the prime minister was unable to secure an effective parliamentary majority for any plan to deal with Mussolini's threatened march, he urged the king to declare martial law and to meet Mussolini with force. The king answered by inviting Mussolini to become the new prime minister of a coalition government in which the Fascists were only a minority. Almost immediately, with the backing of the king, and through physically intimidating the opposition in parliament, Mussolini was given dictatorial power for a year in order to end the anarchy — for which he in part was responsible. During his dictatorial rule, Mussolini altered the election law to allow the party that received the most votes, even though it was less than a majority, to take two thirds of the seats in the chamber. A Fascist victory was thus assured, and within a few years Mussolini had virtually eliminated all opposition.

Though Mussolini was against liberalism, democracy, rationalism, socialism, and pacifism, other than his emphasis on nationalism, he offered no positive program. Once in power, however, the Fascists developed the concept of the organic state. According to this view, the state was a living and growing organism, larger and more powerful than the individual or his family. Every individual was forced to give allegiance to this new entity, which was regarded as greater than its parts and which adopted such policies as militarism, imperialism, and war as necessary to continued growth. Basically an anti-intellectual movement, fascism taught that the new order would spring from a conviction of the heart rather than from any rational or thinking process. The key to the organic state was the Fascist party headed by Mussolini, the *Duce* (leader), which was composed of people who in theory could put the needs of the country above their own desires. Thus like the Communist party of the Soviet Union, the Fascist organization was controlled by only a small fraction of the Italian people.

Mussolini's success in handling Socialist and Communist agitators, as well as in bringing internal peace to a troubled country, came to be much admired and attracted many imitators. It was not until the depression, however, that any of his emulators came to power. In part, the success of Mussolini's imitators was due to the failure of liberalism. The idea of do-nothing economic policies increasingly undermined the basis of parliamentary government throughout much of the Western world. Since neither communism nor fascism subscribed to this liberal notion, the depression offered both extremist ideologies an opportunity to demonstrate how a managed economy could perform. Communist parties grew rapidly, but their growth served only to increase the fears of the small businessmen and lower-salaried workers, who in their opposition to communism and even to socialism received the toleration and sometimes even the influential backing of veterans' organizations, the military, and some industrialists. The anti-communism of the growing Fascist movements, plus their illusion of dynamism, for many people proved to be sufficient reasons for overlooking the Fascist penchant for force and gangsterism. During the 1930s, Fascist-type regimes took form in Portugal, Spain, Austria, and Japan, although in the Japanese case, the government was managed by a clique of military personnel and not a single dictator. The most significant and the most effective authoritarian regime, however was the one that developed in Germany.

HITLER AND THE RISE OF THE NAZIS

Before Stresemann stabilized the German currency, Germany had been a country of bitterly divided antagonists. The high-ranking generals, particularly Ludendorff, resented the turn of events that left them with virtually no army and even less influence in political affairs. Many Germans who had done well under the kaiser distrusted the Social Democrats and more or less tacitly encouraged opposition to the republic, which seemed unequal to the task of governing the country. Ex-soldiers who could find nothing to do with themselves in a world at peace attempted to live by racketeering, by blackmail, and by dreaming of the lost glory of the German Empire. Among these malcontents was Adolf Hitler. In 1923, Hitler found himself jailed for nine months because of a Mussolini-like attempt to overthrow the government of Bavaria, a rowdy escapade that came to be known as the beer hall putsch. While in jail, Hitler completed *Mein Kampf* (My Struggle), the work that set forth his views of National Socialism. Hitler's failure to seize control of the Bavarian state government, as well as the fact that Germany experienced a period of prosperity after 1923, led to a temporary decline of the Nazis, as the National Socialists came to be called, and had it not been for the depression, the party would have withered away. Hitler, however, worked indefatigably for his cause. In the process, he perfected a natural gift for demagogic speech which made him strangely attractive to many people, and in imitation of Mussolini, he organized a cadre of strong-armed thugs, the brown-shirted Storm Troopers, which eventually helped him overcome the opposition. Increasingly, the Nazi program came to focus on a virulent anti-communism and a conscious hatred of Jews. By turning German resentment of their defeat in the war inward against the Jews and the Communists, Hitler had the necessary scapegoats he could blame for all of Germany's ills. By playing on the alienated and the disenchanted, and by using strong-arm tactics, he managed to keep his party in existence until the crisis of the depression immobilized the German government and created mass unemployment. In the election of September 1930, with millions unemployed and driven by feelings of helplessness, the German people turned to parties of both the right and the left. Hitler's followers gained a hundred seats in the Reichstag, making the National Socialists next in strength to the Social Democrats. The Communists also gained tremendously in this election. Since the objective of both the Communists and the Nazis was to subvert the government, the two parties could effectively hamper governmental operations at the very time when the difficulties of the Weimar Republic were most critical and required resolute action. To complicate matters further, the so-called moderate parties, the Catholic Center and the Social Democrats, so distrusted each other that they refused to cooperate to offer effective programs. In desperation, the president of the German Republic, Paul von Hidenburg, adopted the practice of ruling by presidential decree — which was technically constitutional — instead of depending upon the German parliament or his chancellor (prime minister). Hindenburg had no faith in democracy and lacked the capacity to rule effectively, yet he alone seemed able to hold Germany together. As a result, when his seven-year term was up in 1932, the eighty-year-old general was prevailed upon to run for re-election. His chief opponent was Adolf Hitler. In one of those ironies of history, the Germans found themselves having to choose between the senile Hindenburg, who suspected democracy, and Hitler, who though distasteful at least had vigor and promised to eliminate the depression.

Hindenburg won, but his victory was a hollow one, since he proved powerless to meet Germany's growing difficulties. As the depression worsened, Hitler set his Storm Troopers to breaking up the meetings and activities of the Communists and to harassing the Jews. Through his program of "action," he won the interest of many of the disgruntled army commanders upon whom Hindenburg greatly depended. Few of these military men wanted another war, but the 100,000-man army permitted by the Treaty of Versailles gave them no opportunity for advancement and denied them importance on the national scene. Though most of them disliked Hitler, they believed they could use him to achieve their ends, and Hitler was shrewd enough to let them think he was a compliant tool. Similarly, Hitler was able to convince a number of business tycoons that his leanings toward socialism were only for the gullible, and these men advanced him enough money to keep his Storm Troopers in operation. By exploiting xenophobia, anti-Semitism, fear of the Bolsheviks, and nostalgia for a less complicated past — as well as by intimidating much of their opposition — the Nazis after 1930 grew in strength. In spite of their growing power, however, the National Socialists never won a majority of the votes at the polls.

As the economic condition of Germany worsened, Hindenburg, fearful of a possible Communist gain and encouraged by his advisers, elevated Hitler to the position of chancellor. Several weeks after Hitler took office, a fire broke out in the Reichstag building in Berlin. The Nazis claimed that this action was the first step in a Communist takeover, and Hitler was able to have the constitution suspended to meet this challenge to the republic. Though the Nazi account of a Communist conspiracy was then accepted by most of the German people, historians have since demonstrated that the Communists were not involved. Even in this crisis, the Nazis were able to gain only 44 percent of the votes in the March 1933 election, yet enough Germans were frightened into believing the only alternative to Nazi rule was a Communist coup. Thus when the Nationalists joined in a coalition with the Nazis, Hitler was able to do as he pleased.

HITLER IN POWER

When Hindenburg died in 1934, Hitler proclaimed the existence of the Third Reich (empire), successor to the Holy Roman Empire and the Second Reich of the kaiser. Not convinced by the results of World War I that Germany could be overmatched, Hitler and his cohorts labored to recover German power in Europe. In the process of rearming Germany, Hitler ended the depression in his country. The unorthodox financing methods devised by his finance minister Hjalmar Schacht proved that a nation need not hesitate to do what it wanted simply because the budget did not balance — provided, of course, that it had the requisite resources, factories, and skilled labor to produce wealth. In this sense, Hitler differed from his fellow-dictator Mussolini, whom he imitated in other ways. Hitler never failed to employ the opportunities afforded him by his totalitarian position, while Mussolini, in spite of his power, never managed to overcome the depression in Italy. In fact, Mussolini increasingly became little more than a figurehead dictator while Hitler's power continued to grow.

Heinrich Himmler's Storm Troopers were free to plan and execute whatever atrocity suited their fancy, and open opposition quickly died down. The famed and feared secret police, the Gestapo, infiltrated every area of German life in order to prevent anything from happening which Nazi authorities did not sanction. At the same time, Hitler began an organized campaign to exterminate those whom he regarded as enemies of Germany: Jews, Poles, gypsies, and others. The only crime of these groups was that by Hitler's definition they were not sufficiently "Aryan." Though Hitler's program was well publicized, most of the world dismissed it until after the horrors of the mass exterminations were revealed following the German defeat in World War II. Within Germany, a large number of Germans simply closed their eyes to what was going on, preferring to believe that such atrocities could not happen in a civilized country.

THE COMING OF WORLD WAR II

In a sense, World War II was simply a continuation of World War I. On the one side were France, England, and Russia, while on the other were Germany and Austria, the latter having been incorporated into Germany in 1938. Italy and Japan, both of whom had fought on the Allied side in World War I, although neither had played a prominent part in the Allied victory, now joined with Germany. Historians are not so much concerned with debating the causes of World War II as they are with trying to explain how the Germans were willing to tolerate the ferocity, duplicity, and sheer lunacy of the Nazi program. It can be said that most Germans never realized the dangers of Hitler's program until it was too late; the majority believed that Hitler, like most other politicians, meant only a fraction of what he said. Few of the Germans who had experienced the horrors of World War I really wanted another major conflict. Though the German people can still be indicted for permitting the excesses of the Hitler regime, one wonders how the Americans, the English, or the French would have reacted if circumstances had put a Hitler in control of their own countries during the crisis of the depression. Industrial powers as a whole, in fact, seem more prone to dictatorships of the right than of the left, in spite of the fears that have been aroused in the last few decades concerning internal Communist subversion.

But even granted that the Germans were taken in by Hitler, how could the League of Nations and the rest of the world also have been deceived; In part, the answer is the same. During the whole period in which Hitler was consolidating his power, Great Britain, for example, maintained a defense establishment that assumed war would not come. Though this policy might have been justified financially, it did not necessarily represent wise statesmanship. The attitude of the United States was similar, and the failure of this country to take early action against Hitler was compounded by the fact that it was not a member of the League of Nations. Thus the League was essentially a European forum which had come to be used by the French and the British to further their own ends. With the decline of France in the 1930s, the importance of the League also dwindled, and it lost whatever status it still retained by its failure to deal with aggression in Europe, in Africa, and in the Far East.

In fact, it can be argued that World World II began in the Far East in 1931 with the deliberate and unprovoked attack by an autonomous Japanese military unit on Manchuria, which comprised China's three eastern provinces. Though the attack and occupation was not authorized by the Japanese government, officials so feared their own military clique that the army action was accepted without opposition. China, in the throes of its own national revolution, had virtually no central government and was helpless to defend itself. In 1936, the "China incident," which began as a confrontation between some Chinese and a detachment of Japanese soldiers on night exercises, developed into a full-scale Japanese effort to take over all of China, an attempt that was terminated only by the defeat of Japan in August 1945. The Japanese invasion, nonetheless, did unite the warring factions of General Chiang Kai-shek and the Communist leader Mao Tse-Tung, who resumed their civil war after the Japanese had been expelled. Only the United States made any meaningful effort to interfere with this Japanese expansion, but this action merely served to set smoldering the antagonisms that burst forth with the Japanese attack on Pearl Harbor in 1941. Most of the European powers sat on the sidelines, apparently willing to follow the traditional American policy of avoiding foreign entanglements, even though the United States was this time urging direct intervention. Moreover, Japan had withdrawn from the League of Nations, so that the member states felt no real cause to interfere.

Since Hitler had also led Germany out of the League in 1933, it was Mussolini who proved to be the most troublesome member. After having built up an image of himself as a miracle worker and then having failed to deal with the depression, Mussolini found in a policy of aggression a means of rebuilding his own ego and that of the Italian people. In 1935, he began a war with Ethiopia on the pretext that he had a grievance, and he began helping himself to that territory. The Ethiopians, whose homeland bordered on or was near the two enclaves of desert, Libya and Eritrea, acquired by Italy before World War I, appealed to the League for support against Italy. The League formally labeled Italy an aggressor and imposed sanctions on the country, but the effectiveness of these measures was dependent upon French and

British support, which was not forthcoming. World opinion condemned Mussolini, but he was not prevented from continuing his march. Encouraged by the inability of the League to deal effectively with Mussolini, Hitler in 1936 suddenly marched his troops into the Rhineland areas, which had been demilitarized by the Versallies Treaty. When this action also went uncontested, the League was revealed as nothing more than an empty shell.

Two other developments also took place in 1936. One was the formation of the so-called Axis accord, a formal agreement between Hitler and Mussolini to work together. Another accord, reached between Hitler and the Japanese, was known as the Anti-Comintern Pact, which was obviously directed at Russia. The next year Italy joined in this agreement, followed by several other European states. This anti-Communist pact served to obscure the real dangers of Fascism, since many European statesmen were deluded into believing what they fervently wanted to believe — that the main thrust of Hitler and his allies was to be directed against communism.

The second major event of 1936 was the outbreak of civil war in Spain, which resulted when the Spanish army rose in revolt against a struggling republican government that had been established in 1931 following the exile of King Alfonso XIII. The war lasted about two and a half years before the army managed to establish the Fascist-type dictatorship of General Francisco Franco. Italy and Germany supported Franco's rebels with troops and equipment, while the British, French, and Americans observed from the sidelines. The only aid the Spanish loyalists officially received was from Russia, thus making the republicans even more suspicious to the Western powers.

Encouraged by the appeasement policies of Neville Chamberlain, the British prime minister from 1937 to 1940, Hitler continued to expand his Third Reich. In 1938, Austria, which had been forbidden to join with Germany at the end of World War I, was incorporated into Hitler's state. Britain and France were much alarmed but felt unable to deal effectively with Hitler. Their failure was symbolized by their unwillingness to defend Czechoslovakia, a new state set up in the aftermath of World War I which included large concentrations of German-speaking subjects from the old Hapsburg Empire. At Munich, in September 1938, the two Western powers accepted Hitler's demand for a portion of Czechoslovakia. In March 1939, Hitler occupied the rest of Czechoslovakia. After these developments, Stalin, who more than any other ruler feared Hitler's intentions toward his country, concluded that the British and French were secretly hoping that Hitler would march eastward into the Soviet Ukraine, an action that would lock the two great European land powers into a mortal combat and thus effectively eliminate both the Communists and the Nazis from the scene. To prevent this possibility, Stalin worked out with Hitler the Nazi-Soviet nonaggression pact of August 1939. Shortly after this agreement was signed, on September 1, 1939, the Nazis invaded Poland from the west while the Russians attacked from the east. Since the French and British were committed to defend Poland, the two countries declared war on Germany and World War II was underway.

WORLD WAR II

Poland was quickly crushed by the new military tactics developed by the Germans, which included the use of fast, armored columns supported by aircraft and paratroopers to envelop opposing armed forces. In spite of the success of their *blitzkrieg*, the Germans ignored their western front until April 1940. Then, in a series of rapid campaigns that extended beyond the middle of June, the Germans overran Norway, Denmark, Holland, Belgium, and France, forcing the British off the Continent in the process. The Nazi drive then stopped, since the Germans had neither the ships nor the equipment necessary for the occupation of Britain. For a time, German bombing raids, particularly on London, caused enormous property damage and killed many civil-

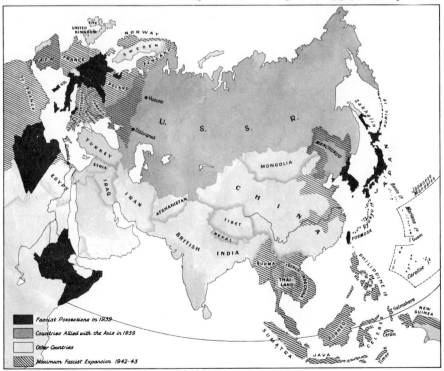

Fascist expansion in World War II, 1939–1943.

ians, but the Royal Air Force with the help of the newly perfected radar made this operation increasingly hazardous.

The quick German victory led to the replacement of Chamberlain. by the much more belligerent Winston Churchill, who quickly inspired in his countrymen a determined resistance. A year later, in the summer of 1941, abruptly dropping his attack on Great Britain, Hitler turned to the conquest of Russia, making an overt enemy out of a merely passive one. The German *blitzkrieg* overran the Ukraine and all of southern Russia, reached the Volga, and very nearly encompassed Moscow, but failed to capture most of the Russian oil fields essential to Hitler's war machine. The war then settled down to a series of sieges, particularly that around Leningrad. This phase of the war lasted for two years and consumed vast numbers of soldiers on both sides. Hitler lost some three million men, while the Russians lost twice that many. In addition, the Russians suffered civilian losses far beyond their military casualties. The murderous fighting continued during the dreaded Russian winters until 1945, when the Russians had cleared the Germans from all of southern and eastern Europe and had captured Berlin.

In the meantime, the Japanese, thinking more of themselves than of their German and Italian partners in Europe, refused to intervene against the Russians — an action that would have been disastrous for Russia — but instead provoked the United States into hostilities. By continuing an undeclared war in China and threatening to expand it southward toward Indonesia, then the Dutch East Indies colony, Japan caused increasing anxiety to those Americans who felt a responsibility for the Philippines. Moreover, France, Great Britain, and Holland could no longer defend their eastern holdings because of German occupation of their homelands. The United States began to move slowly from its policy of neutrality, giving massive aid to England and attempting to thwart Japanese expansion in the Pacific. The Japanese, misled by American efforts at appeasement, underestimated the determination of the United States to fight and in December 1941, launched a surprise attack upon the American naval base of Pearl Harbor in Honolulu. The attack not only put the base out of operation temporarily but also sank much of the American fleet. Almost immitedly, Japanese armies overran all of Southeast Asia, except Thailand, to the borders of India, captured Singapore, and occupied all of the Pacific islands, including the Philippines and northern New Guinea, as far southeastward as the Solomons.

UNITED STATES LEADERSHIP

Just as the fall of France caused the British to realize the extent of the German threat, the Japanese attack forced the United States to assume an active role in world affairs. The country might still have formally stayed out of the European conflict, but Hitler forced American entry by declaring war, leading the United States to join with Great Britain and the Soviet Union. For much of the early period of the war, America waged only a holding action against Japan by assisting the Chinese and Australians in carrying out raids and by building up a submarine fleet in Japanese waters. Instead of launching an all-out campaign in the Pacific, Americans concentrated their forces against Hitler. The Nazis soon found themselves faced with a powerful enemy who this time played a much more critical role than in 1917–1918. Americans assisted in opening up the Mediterranean, which the Axis had closed to hostile traffic in 1940, and in Great Britain they built up the daylight bombing of Germany to supplement the night bombing the British had started. In addition, the British and Americans took advantage of Hitler's preoccupation with Russia to invade North Africa in 1942, to occupy Sicily in 1943, to carry the war to the mainland of Greece, which had been invaded by Mussolini in 1940, and finally to invade Italy itself.

In June 1944, the Americans bore the brunt of the Normandy invasion. Within three months, against almost impossible odds, two million men were landed with all of their equipment and necessary supplies. Before the summer was over, Allied troops had liberated France and Belgium, and by early spring, were crossing the Rhine into Germany. The Third Reich rapidly disintegrated, but it was not until after Hitler committed suicide that all resistance ceased. On May 8, 1945, the war in Europe was officially ended. Meanwhile, the Japanese, in spite of determined resistance, had been losing the Pacific war. Submarines very nearly obliterated the Japanese merchant marine, and the United States developed highly effective amphibious techniques to recover conquered islands. Reoccupation of the Philippines was begun in 1944, at about the same time that intensive raids upon Tokyo became possible with the American seizure of the Marianas. The Japanese navy was so reduced as to be unable to protect the home islands, and by mid-1945, with the cessation of hostilities in Europe, it became apparent that operations in Asia could have but one conclusion. Still the military autocrats in Japan continued to fight, but American scientific enterprise, with notable assistance from scientists who had fled Hitler and Mussolini, developed the atomic bomb. Two atomic bombs were dropped within three days of each other early in August 1945 over the Japanese cities of Hiroshima and Nagasaki, killing about 75,000 people each time. A few days later, the Japanese surrendered. The Japanese capitulation came largely as the result of the efforts of Emperor Hirohito, who had been interested in ending the war earlier and whose task was made easier by American employment of the atomic bomb.

Whether Hirohito and the growing antimilitary group in Japan would
have been successful in their effort had the atomic bomb not been used
has been a subject for much debate, but it was obvious in the summer
of 1945 that further resistance was useless.

At the end of World War II, Japan was stripped of its empire, Germany was divided and occupied, and fascism was destroyed. While
victorious, Great Britain was exhausted, and France had been reconstituted only by outside intervention. Thus the Soviet Union, whose
armies occupied much of eastern Europe, in spite of its enormous
losses and damages, emerged the dominant power on the Continent.
With the destruction of Japan, the Russians had also been able to extend their power into Asia. China, the obvious alternative to Japanese
domination in the Far East or to further Russian penetration, had been
recognized as one of the great powers by the Allies. No sooner had
peace been established, however, than the Chinese resumed their civil
war, thereby giving the Russians much more influence than they might
otherwise have had. Comparatively untouched at home by the ravages
of the war, the United States loomed above the rest of the world as an
economic and military giant whose power was capped by its sole possession of the atomic bomb. This new position of power had been
anticipated by President Franklin Roosevelt, the principal leader of
the victorious coalition, who in 1944 had proposed a new international
organization to be known as the United Nations. Though modeled on
the League of Nations, the United Nations was set up to do much less
than the League had attempted. Its chief function was to serve as an
instrument that would enable the United States, and to a lesser extent
the Soviet Union, along with France, Britain, and China, the wartime
Allies, to maintain world order.

RUSSIAN-AMERICAN RELATIONS

The Soviet Union, however, was a Communist state that had been
forced into an alliance with the United States by a common enemy. At
best, the alliance was an uneasy one, and its success in part was dependent upon the ability of President Roosevelt to win Stalin over to
his various proposals. When the American president died shortly
before the end of the war, relations between the two powers began to
deteriorate. Almost immediately, Winston Churchill, who had always
feared Soviet ambitions, proposed to the new American president
Harry Truman that understandings reached earlier with the Russians
concerning German occupation zones be repudiated. Though Truman
initially rejected this proposal, he later joined with Great Britain and
France in converting the Western occupation zones in Germany into an
independent state. The antagonisms and fears of the West toward

Soviet intentions grew as Stalin failed as promised to provide for free elections in the Russian-occupied areas of Poland, Rumania, Bulgaria, and Hungary. When Communist-supported guerrilla fighters threatened the Western-oriented government of Greece in 1947, America felt forced to intervene more directly. Truman responded first by dispatching military and economic aid to the Greek government and later by beginning the rearmament of West Germany. The result was the new American policy of "containment," which pledged military assistance to any regime threatened by "armed minorities or by outside pressure." Even before the Communists, who represented the largest party, seized control of the Czechoslovakian government in February 1948, Truman had launched the Marshall Plan, a multibillion dollar program of economic aid to Western Europe to prevent such takeovers. The United States also concluded a twelve-nation military alliance, the North Atlantic Treaty Organization (NATO). All of these actions constituted the beginning of the Cold War.

In their effort to prevent Communist subversion, Americans often threw their support behind any force that opposed communism, ignoring their own revolutionary tradition. Change in any part of the world was frequently identified with communism as Americans became fearful of any challenge to the status quo. Though reformers were not usually communists, extremism was encouraged by American opposition, so that for many people the only alternative to the status quo seemed to be communism. While many Americans seemed to believe that Stalin desired to march across Western Europe, there is little objective evidence to indicate that the Soviet Union was planning a military attack on the West. Undoubtedly Stalin hoped for Communist advances in France, Italy, Austria, and other countries that had been devastated by the war, but he was in no position to impose such governments. The people of the Soviet Union had suffered more than those in any of the Allied countries and were so absorbed in rebuilding their battered homeland that they were in no condition to undertake a major military struggle. The Russian government was also aware of the American monopoly of the atomic bomb and could only assume that the United States was willing to use it against future enemies. In fact, instead of forcing an open confrontation with the United States, the Soviet Union devoted much of its energy to building an atomic bomb of its own, and its success in so doing in 1949 caused a wave of anti-Communist hysteria in the United States, most associated with the name of Senator Joseph McCarthy of Wisconsin. Many Americans believed that the Soviet success was due to Russan espionage, little realizing that the Russians, in spite of their rigid dogmatism, had developed an outstanding scientific establishment. When in 1952 the United States detonated its first hydrogen, or fusion bomb, the

Russians followed with their own a year later. In 1957, the Russian Sputnik rocket was launched into outer space, pre-empting, for a time, American dominance in this area. Finally, the two great powers realized the dangers of the continued Cold War when each side became capable of virtually destroying the other. Then a sort of balance of terror was struck that allowed the two superpowers once again to deal with each other. This new phase of Soviet-American relations was aided by the death of Joseph Stalin and the coming to power of Nikita Khrushchev.

Even before tensions between the two powers began to relax, the apparent monolithic Communist structure in eastern Europe showed signs of weakening. The first country to break with Russia was Yugoslavia, under the direction of Marshal Joseph Broz Tito, who had risen to power through successful guerrilla actions against the Germans. A Communist, Tito nevertheless insisted on running his own country without Russian interference. Gradually, other Soviet satellites began to seek their own national identities and interests within a Communist framework — at least as far as the Soviet Union would permit. Communism found itself confronted with the same national interests that had ruined all earlier universalistic movements, including Christianity — which also had been unable to preserve unity. The most significant development was the growing power of China, which in 1949 had fallen to the Communists with the victory of Mao Tse-tung over Chiang Kai-shek. American attempts to isolate the Chinese Communists forced the Chinese to become almost totally dependent upon Russian aid, but as the Chinese government gained stability and power — including possession of its own atomic bomb — it began to act independently of the Russians. Soon, in fact, the Chinese began to compete with the Soviet Union for the allegiance of uncommitted peoples throughout the world.

At the same time that the Russian Communist monolith appeared to be weakening, so did American domination of the United Nations and the non-Communist world. This tendency was manifested particularly in 1950, when the North Koreans invaded South Korea in violation of a 1945 occupation-zone line. The United States, which had received control of South Korea in the aftermath of the war with Japan, was able to capitalize upon a Soviet boycott of the United Nations to obtain the backing of that body for a united defense of South Korea. Increasingly, the United Nations became disenchanted with this action, especially after the American military commander General Douglas MacArthur, instead of trying to re-establish the old armistice line, set out to invade North Korea. This action brought China into the picture, and the result was a severe setback to United Nations troops, which were mostly Americans. While the armistice line was eventually restored, U.S. actions in Korea led to considerable resentment against American domination and to a reassessment of the role of the United Nations. There was also a realignment of power blocs in the United Nations resulting from the disintegration of the Western alliance and the admission of dozens of new member states, many of whom came to identify the United States with colonialism. Both Great Britain, which shared atomic secrets with the United States, and France developed their own atomic bombs. With less need for the American umbrella of nuclear deterrence, the various European powers attempted to re-assert their old positions of influence. After 1958, France, under President Charles de Gaulle, attempted to follow an independent policy, even going so far as to force the removal of NATO headquarters from Paris. With American encouragement, the continental Western European countries had also developed a Common Market among themselves which allowed them to compete with the American industrial colossus.

23

Problems
and Prospects

So far in this book we have attempted to demonstrate that cultural developments in any period in history are closely related to economic, political, and social events. Yet while intellectual and cultural achievements reflect trends and events, those who build the culture — the artists, the musicians, the writers, and others — can also act upon society. If in the last part of the twentieth century society seems to be in transition, then so are the traditional forms and styles of expression. The period has been characterized by a searching for new styles on the part of the artists, and on the part of the various governments by attempts to establish new norms in the hope that society as a whole will conform to specific ideals. Art and literature have been particularly exploited by Communist and Fascist regimes, but similar attempts have been made by certain dogmatic groups in the Free World. The anti-intellectualism of the Fascists was nearly matched by the insistence of the Communist upon socialist realism. In neither case did the effort result in great art or great literature; instead, by forcing nonconformists into the silence of exile, such regimes curtailed or hindered their own national development. Art and literature proved to be subject to greater consorship and restriction than music, perhaps because this art form, on the surface at least, seemed less threatening to the status quo. The devoted musician could also continue to play the classics, so that even the most restrictive of countries continued to produce masters. All of this is not to say that great works were not produced in totalitarian countries but that such works were usually

452

denied public recognition and were circulated surreptitiously among selected groups. Such was the case of Boris Pasternak in the Soviet Union, who kept alive his literary skills by officially translating Shakespeare and Goethe. He managed to have published his antiestablishment masterpiece *Dr. Zhivago* only by smuggling it out of Russia during a time of thaw in the Cold War, and the novel has still not been published in Russia. In recent years, Soviet artists and writers have enjoyed somewhat more freedom of expression, although in this respect the future for artists remains uncertain.

As education has become more widespread, tastes have changed in almost every area of the world. Growing literacy has opened up vast new audiences for the printed word, especially in the Western world. As the number of college graduates has increased, the painter, the writer, and the composer have been forced to take into account the broader horizons of their audience. At the same time, urbanization has led to ever more specialization in all aspects of life, making it increasingly difficult for the creative person to find a base from which he can project his ideas. The large number of people engaged in the arts today has also made it difficult for one artist, writer, or composer to reach all segments of a potential audience — or to reach any at all. Recognition often seems to be dependent upon exploitation or manipulation of public opinion, which to the creative personality is usually repugnant. Instead of allowing their work to be sold like furniture in a mass media campaign, more and more artists and writers have become introspective and subjective, writing, painting, or composing for themselves and their group rather than for a large audience. Perhaps more so than in any other period, the contemporary artist believes in the importance of preserving his integrity as an artist.

THE WRITER IN A CHANGING WORLD

Twentieth-century literature has been characterized particularly by the attempt of authors to see their characters as unique, to be comprehended only through their own personal experience. Where earlier writers controlled their stories from without, furnishing dialogue and action, the modern writer attempts to delve into the private thoughts of his characters. The trend can be traced back to the nineteenth century, one of the key figures in its development was Marcel Proust, who in his sixteen volumes of *Remembrances of Things Past* summed up upper-class French society in the decade before World War I. Proust's story, told in the first person, mixes an examination of the narrator's shifting desires and jealousies with exhaustive description and recitation. The narrator, his memory stimulated by certain past associations such as a strain of music or a taste of a certain pastry, summons up and comments upon people and places he has known. No one merely acts or speaks in Proust's works, but each phrase and each room or building which comes from the unconscious mind are broken up for analysis and blended with other associations. A single moment can swell into pages, an afternoon can fill a book.

More radical and even more influential in the English-speaking world than Proust was James Joyce, the Irish stream-of-consciousness author. By examining his own experience, Joyce sought to understand the human problems of his time. His *Ulysses* is a modern restructuring of Homer's *Odyssey,* in which the hero Leopold Bloom is Ulysses and his erotic and faithless wife Molly a new Penelope. The book closes with a lengthy, unpunctuated reverie of the sex-obsessed Molly, and because of this passage the work has until very recently been banned in much of the English-speaking world. Though on first reading Joyce seems to be a jumble of sense and nonsense and of the past, present, and future, in its whole his work is awe-inspiring. Joyce forces upon his readers a new point of view in every area of life. Born a Catholic in Ireland, Joyce left his homeland, abandoned his Catholicism, and committed himself to the life of the writer in exile.

The artist in exile, in fact, seemed to characterize the period between the two wars. The pre-eminent poet of the period was the American-born T. S. Eliot, who found a spiritual home in England. In his reaction to the spiritually barren and frustrating world in which he felt he lived, Eliot turned to religion to find a secure place for himself. His poetry increasingly reflected traditional Christian symbols and images. Even poets who remained in the land of their birth seemed to be in exile. William Butler Yeats, who utilized indigenous Irish materials to fashion his verse, engaged in an earnest search for mystical experience to replace the faith that he had lost. Unlike Eliot, Yeats never really found a satisfactory answer to his quest.

One of the most influential American novelists was Ernest Hemingway, who also spent much af his career as an expatriot in Paris or as a war correspondent. Hemingway's works focus largely upon the violence and evil in society, often symbolized in his tales of hunting and war. His ability to glorify tough and brutal characters, to report realistically on drinking, sexual promiscuity, physical sensation, and violent death established the mode and manners of fictional realism in English literature. His constant need to assert himself through energetic pilgrimages around the world is perhaps indicative of an artist who was unable to come to terms with life as it was taking place around him. Yet the exile often did not even leave his own country. William Faulkner, by withdrawing from the main literary and artistic centers and concentrating on the decadence and abnormality that characterized some parts of the Deep South, expressed his alienation from contemporary society in a different way than did Hemingway. Even when an author such as Sinclair Lewis remained in society, his bitter satires on the smugness, hypocrisy, and bigotry around him were indications of his estrangement from his world. The English novelist D. H. Lawrence also spent much of his life away from home and in *Lady Chatterley's Lover* attempted to find in physical passion the meaning of life he felt was missing in the industrialized society of the twentieth century.

Not all of the exiles, however, were voluntary. The rise of fascism and communism and their demands for conformity forced many people to become involuntary exiles. This trend was accentuated by the disruption of World War II. The German novelist Thomas Mann left Nazi Germany for Switzerland in 1933 and eventually settled in the United States. Perhaps because of his own experience, Mann came to view the creative artist as a sort of social aberration and looked upon the twentieth century as a period of great decadence.

Some writers suffered ostracism because of their personal habits or beliefs. André Gide, for example, was violently attacked for his justification of homosexuality in *Corydon* (1924), although toward the end of his life he began to receive some of the honors long denied him, and in 1947, he was awarded the Nobel prize. Nikos Kazantzakis, the modern Greek writer, not only had his work suppressed in Greece but was publicly denounced by the Greek Orthodox Church and was denied passports to travel abroad for much of his life. In spite of these restrictions, Kazantzakis developed the despised street-and-peasant Greek into a worthy literary language and managed to support himself by translations from various modern languages. Most of his fame has come posthumously. The same was true of Franz Kafka, who died in comparative obscurity in 1924. One of the most influential German writers of the twentieth century, Kafka concentrated on relating the experience of man in an unintelligible universe and his difficulties in coming to terms with a remote, incomprehensible power.

The dominant English-speaking playwright of the first half of the twentieth century was George Bernard Shaw, who delighted in making satirical attacks on social convention. Increasingly, however, this type of drama was succeeded by the more introspective and subjective plays of such writers as Eugene O'Neill. Perhaps more influential than O'Neill has been Jean Anouilh, whose work is usually divided into four main groups: the dark plays, the rosy plays, the grating plays, and the glittering plays; most commercially successful have been his witty and lively comedies, or his rosy plays. His dark plays, however, with their emphasis on the futility and despair in the world, have influenced the theater of the absurd, which attempts to reflect the meaninglessness of life and the failure of human communication. The best-known writers in this field are Eugene Ionesco, a half-Rumanian and half-French writer, and the Irishman Samuel Beckett, who spent most of his life in exile.

If the writer was alienated from his culture, he was also attempting to find roots. As Eliot found satisfaction in a return to Christianity, other artists found answers to their search in folk cultures of the past — such as Gaelic in Ireland — in the newly emerging states — such as Israel — or in emphasizing the importance of being a Negro — in both Africa and the United States — or in examining their Indian background — as in Mexico. Two of the most influential writers have been the Frenchmen Jean-Paul Sartre and Albert Camus. Sartre can better be discussed under philosophy, but his compatriot Camus looked upon himself as a moralist and not a philosopher. Camus' favorite themes, the absurdity of life and the irrational nature of the world, appear in many of his novels and in this sense are reflective of the concerns of other writers. Feeling that religious belief was impossible, however, Camus tried to define the basic tenets of aesthetic humanism.

The Soviet Union was notably absent from the world literary scene as the Stalin government attempted to dictate artistic style and themes, although not all Communist countries were so repressive. For example, one of the most innovative of modern dramatists was the German Bertold Brecht, who fled Germany in 1935 and eventually arrived in the United States. When the World War II was over, Brecht returned to a divided Germany and settled in East Berlin, where his drama with a message received support from the Communist government. Brecht must be regarded as one of the influential creators in modern drama, blazing a different path from that of O'Neill, Anouilh, or Beckett.

HISTORY AS LITERATURE

As the cultivated citizen of the world became worried about what was taking place around him, history as a form of literature once again assumed major importance. The revival dates from the nineteenth century and probably coincided as well with the increased purchasing power of the literate middle classes. During this period, history thrived on both romanticism and nationalism, but historians finally rebelled against these approaches and instead undertook to follow the creed of realism. In his search for realism, the historian sought objectivity, or "historicism." The seminal figure in this movement was the German Leopold von Ranke, who trained a generation of scholars at Berlin in the middle of the nineteenth century. Von Ranke's influence soon reached into most of the Western world. Historicism taught that the historian could accept as real only that which is tangibly demonstrated, that the true model for the historian should be the natural scientist instead of the man of letters. The best historian would write history as it actually happened. In practice, this attempt proved to be impossible, since it is one thing to strive for objectivity and quite another to create a genuine account of an occurrence from its surviving evidence. To make this point, the historian had to borrow back from the man of letters the creative writing that earlier generations of historians had rejected. Still, however, by attempting to objectify his own impressions through an examination of evidence the historian did become somewhat less subjective.

As the novelist turned to introspection, history and biography replaced the old-fashioned novel in recreating the past and even in telling a good story. The historian, however, by adapting the critical tools of his profession, made his work subject to critical attack by other historians, who used the same tools and had access to the same information. This need to undergo critical scrutiny has tended to keep the historian from being too rash in his generalizations and in a sense has led to a better understanding of historical events and personalities.

Much of the best work in history, however, is not reflected in generalized accounts of Western civilization or even in wide-ranging books dealing with specific events. Instead, in history, as in other scholarly fields, the most learned and accurate work is done in the specialized monograph, read usually by other professionals in the field. The problem of communicating this specialized knowledge to public is one that has not yet been solved. In a sense, this is the function of the critic — one who attempts to draw from specialized knowledge and apply it to specific problems. Unfortunately, even the critic's audience is limited to the readers of the better-quality newspapers or magazines.

THE PHILOSOPHER AS CRITIC

One task of the philosopher is not only to find flaws in any system of beliefs, but, if possible, to propose new or better systems. The blow to old systems and absolutes mounted by Nietzsche and others led to attempts to build new systems. Alfred North Whitehead and Bertrand Russell attempted to reform logic by adapting it to a mathematical model; for example, instead of saying "all men are mortal," they expressed the same idea by writing $(x) (Fx \supset Gx)$. In transcribing the equation, if any x is an F (man), then x is a G (mortal). With this new notation it became possible to simplify logical techniques. John Dewey, on the other hand, wanted philosophy to utilize the experimental procedures developed by science. The logical extension of this system was the philosophy of Ludwig Wittgenstein, who held that the meaning of a statement is determined by its relation to some possible fact. The growth of logical positivism, as it came to be called, set one pattern in philosophical thinking. Another pattern led to the growth of existentialism. The existentialist saw man as being submerged and depersonalized by the forces of modern society. To counter his helplessness, the existentialists attempted to awaken in man a sense of his individuality and to offer the possibility of living an authentic life. The French writer and philosopher Sartre mirrored in his own person many of the changes that took place in existential thought. His philosophy started out as a highly individualistic one, but Sartre, through his own experience in the French Resistance against the Nazis, came to believe that personal commitment and action are essential to genuine living. Even in extreme situations, Sartre has said, man possesses the liberty of saying no, and this freedom to say no is his ultimate defense against being swallowed up as a person. Sartre held that each man's existence was prior to an essence or abstraction and that to realize himself, each man must live according to his own values in the face of an aimless and painful universe. Even if the world is absurd, then the first requirement of the individual is to recognize the absurdity and man's freedom within it.

THE ALIENATED ARTIST

There is some indication that the artist now is less alienated from society than was the case at the turn of the century. Though Pablo Picasso, perhaps the most influential artist in the last fifty years, is an exile from his native Spain, he is not cut off from society in the way that a writer, who depends upon his ability to use words, would be. Art in this sense is universal, although exactly what constitutes great art varies from culture to culture and from age to age. Picasso had the satisfaction not only of being able to reject much of the artistic standards of the past but also of finding that his rejection ultimately became successful. Though since mid-nineteenth century, artists had turned their back on the past, large numbers of the avant garde had died poor and hungry. The popular artists were those that, with few exceptions later generations rejected. Perhaps for this reason, it is too early to assess the ultimate value of Picasso's works. Still, Picasso has had enormous influence on other artists. Starting out as an Impressionist, Picasso painted the poor, the derelict, and the alienated, but continued to experiment with forms and to discover new facets of his art. He, along with Georges Braques, developed cubism, one of the most fertile movements in twentieth-century art. Building upon the work of Cézanne, the cubists attempted to reduce natural subjects to their component cubes, cones, and cylinders, to break down and reorder nature. With this approach, Picasso led a full-scale revolt against the artistic values of his time, and his innovations rapidly attained success. In fact, his results were so widely imitated that the artist was forced to make new "discoveries" or find new materials to keep up with his imitators.

Even totally nonobjective painters soon won over an audience. The pioneer in this field was the Russian Vassily Kandinsky, who in 1910 painted what is generally considered to be the first nonobjective painting. Much of Kandinsky's early work was done in Munich, but with the outbreak of World War I, the artist left Germany to return to his native Russia, where he rose to an influential position after the Revolution of 1917. In 1921, however, Kandinsky returned to Munich, where with Paul Klee and others he brought the abstract movement to flower. With the rise of Hitler, most of the abstract painters had to flee, and abstractionism spread rapidly, particularly in the United States. The abstractionists insisted that painting should contain no preconceived pattern but instead ought to express the artist's reactions to the canvas, responding subconsciously to his strong inner tensions.

Still another art movement was surrealism, which attempted to achieve a sort of superrealism through the juxtaposition and combination of verbal images and physical objects usually considered incongruous. Though the Italian Giorgio di Chirco was the first important surrealistic painter, the Spaniard Salvador Dali achieved the most fame. Both the surrealists and the abstractionists were more or less deliberately removed from "people's" art, but there were also artists who set out to reflect the popular art of the common man. Such was the case with the Mexicans Diego Rivera and Jose Clemente Orozco, who depicted social conditions of the modern world, and presented in graphic detail the struggles of peasants and workers. Though these artists did not follow the conventions of the past, there was nothing unintelligible about their art.

Even in sculpture, conventional representations were abandoned. The pioneer in this form was the Frenchman Auguste Rodin, whose ideas were carried further by Jacob Epstein and Ivan Mestrovic. Epstein represented still another artist in exile, since though he was born in New York, he spent most of his career in England. Mestrovic was a Yugoslav who lived most of his life in the United States. On the other hand, the Englishman Henry Moore remained in his homeland. Regardless of where they lived, however, the new breed of sculptor accepted commissions from all over the world. One of Moore's most noteworthy commissions was at the University of Chicago, where he commemorated the first successful atomic pile by a work that could represent both an atomic cloud and the skull of man.

ARCHITECTURE

Part of the revolution in art was due to the appearance of new materials, new techniques, and perfection in the use of new colors. Nowhere was the revolution more apparent than in architecture, an art form that requires the insight of the artist and the technical skill of the engineer. The revolution in architecture began in the last part of the nineteenth century as designers and builders scorned imitation of the gothic cathedral, the Greek temple, and other designs of the past. No architects were more influential in the evolution of new design than Louis Sullivan and his pupil Frank Lloyd Wright, who together dominated the field for some eight decades. Most of Sullivan's work was done in Chicago at the end of the nineteenth and beginning of the twentieth centuries. Wright started in Chicago, but his work appeared all over the world, although the bulk of it was centered in the Midwest. Together Sullivan and Wright concluded that the machine is here to stay and that the architect bears a responsibility to utilize whatever kind of beauty the machine is capable of producing; in essence, form should follow function. This functional architecture was bare of ornament for the sake of ornamentation, but it was, nonetheless, decorative in its use of materials. The first effect of the new architecture was to deprive the artist and sculptor of the murals and trim that earlier had been prime sources for commissions; Wright especially insisted that beauty was in the character of the building materials themselves. Since his structures were designed around the needs and desires of the individuals who occupied them, Wright called his style organic.

Strongly influenced by Wright was Walter Gropius, the founder of the famous Bauhaus art school in Germany. Like many other creative Germans, Gropius was forced to emigrate during the Nazi era. His Bauhaus, which emphasized that good design in itself insures beauty, became the basis for the international style that proved to be especially well adapted to large buildings, factories, and offices. The most successful exponent of the Bauhaus school was Ludwig Mies van der Rohe, who, like Gropius, emigrated to the United States, where he created the new campus for the Illinois Institute of Technology. Mies van der Rohe's classic buildings were soon seen to be easy to mass produce, guaranteeing the greatest space at the smallest cost, and the result in many major cities was blocks of giant skyscrapers covered with sheets of glass. Though these buildings paid lip service to the ideals of Gropius and Mies van der Rohe, they became undistinguished and monotonous when the builders cut corners on materials, used poor design, and replicated the same structure in block after block. As a result, architects began to turn away from the international style to seek a more imaginative, even if less efficient, design. The French architect Le Corbusier produced some striking examples of the new type of architecture, which appeared to reject the machine. Other architects have attempted to find new forms by incorporating machine designs in their own structures. Even though many contemporary architects subordinate function to evocative form, like Sullivan and Wright, most of them have abandoned the backward-looking imitativeness of the past and are committed to an architecture that is modern in spirit and materials. Interestingly, some of the most creative work in this new spirit is being done in such countries as India, Japan, Egypt, Israel, and other areas that have not previously been a part of the Western artistic tradition.

CLASSICS VERSUS THE MASSES

Music mirrored the developments in art and literature, although the composer for the most part was never as removed from his audience as some other creative artists. Perhaps the major exception to this generalization was the American Charles Ives, whose genius is just now beginning to be appreciated. Ives not only removed himself from the public but also from most other musicians. The artist in his isolation had communicated with his fellow-artist and the writer with a few select disciples, but Ives was apart from both. He was a pioneer, however, and his theories that several musical units of an ensemble could proceed independently of each other, as well as his freedom in tonality, rhythm, and harmony, were later adopted by other composers. More immediately successful, and working in some of the same areas as Ives, was Arnold Schönberg. This Viennese composer, who later was forced to flee to the United States, was one of the early masters in expressionism. Schönberg sought to record musically his innermost unconscious feelings, and to do this, he abandoned traditional tonality, stressing melodic distortions and chance coincidences of notes. On first listening, his compositions sound harshly discordant, but as one becomes accustomed to such tones, they begin to sound melodious. This approach offered a new potential for the composer. Interestingly, many of the innovators were Russians, both pre- and post-Revolution. It might be that Soviet insistence on socialist realism was not as inhibiting to the composer as it was to the writer or painter. Igor Stravinsky, who started as an Impressionist composer, turned to the creative dissonances in the style of Schönberg and then returned to a new classic form. He left Russia after the Revolution, but his compatriot Serge Prokofiev who had left Russia as a young man, returned there after the Revolution. Prokofiev's work is marked by bold harmonic clashes and original rhythmic style in the spirit of Schönberg, although it is never quite as daring. Dimitri Shostakovich, the most prominent of the composers trained and educated in the Soviet Union, has managed to continue his musical experimentation within the Russian state. He has experienced several periods of ostracism, but he has never suffered the persecutions that have been directed at the nonconforming writer or artist. France, the home of Debussy, also continued to contribute major musical figures, for example, Darius Milhaud.

Impressionism and expressionism in music also led to a growth of interpretive dance. Ballet, which had been developed by the French, had so deteriorated by 1850 that it had lost most of its following. Its revival was almost wholly the work of the Russians, who kept it alive and perfected new forms. This new Russian form of ballet reached the West in 1909, when Sergei Diaghilev brought a company of Russian dancers to Paris. Diaghilev remained there the rest of his life as founder and director of the Ballet Russe. By the 1930s, his ballets had become so popular that his disciples established ballet companies in both Great Britain and the United States. With ballet as a base, a new form of dance evolved in the United States, called modern dance, which Isadora Duncan and Martha Graham did much to popularize.

The most revolutionary impact on music was the development of the phonograph, which made the concert artist a figure of mass appeal. Singers like Enrico Caruso or pianists such as Ignace Paderewski could cut across class lines and reach wider audiences than before. The phonograph, however, also served to widen the gap between "popular" and classical music. Popular artists such as Guy Lombardo or Frank Sinatra seemed to have little connection with serious ones. Though some forms of jazz did seem to bridge the two groups, especially as some of the innovations of Schönberg found their way into classical music, it was not until popular music adopted the new harmonic forms that the two kinds of music came closer together. Particularly influential in this respect were George Gershwin and Kurt Weill. One group that has been most successful in pioneering new sounds has been the Beatles, who gained fame as a popular singing group with a mass following. Nonetheless, the group has proved to be extremely innovative in applying advanced techniques of musicology to their compositions.

SCIENCE AND TECHNOLOGY

The past few decades of the twentieth century have been dominated, however, by the scientist and the engineer rather than by the artist. This is true not only with regard to the impact of scientists on society but also in terms of the sheer numbers of technical experts working today. In fact, more scientists and engineers are now active than the total of all who lived in the past. The result has been an outpouring of new discoveries and inventions that are rapidly changing every area of life as well as man's conception of himself and his universe. Scientific progress has not necessarily been characterized by a steady stream of new discoveries; rather, advances have come in spurts, with first one field and then another making major breakthroughs. In the period between 1920 and 1945, it was the physicists who took the lead, developing electron accelerators and sophisticated mathematical theory that enabled them to penetrate the atom. The new physics achieved its most dramatic practical application with the development of the atomic bomb under an international team of scientists led by the Italian refugee Enrico Fermi. The United States in this period became the home of great numbers of scientists, largely because of the Nazi expansion in Europe. Not only did Albert Einstein come to the United States but also such people as the Dane Nils Bohr, the Hungarian Leo Szilard, and a host of others who were influential in the development of the atomic bomb. These refugees also assured the United States an important role in other areas of scientific endeavor.

During the last two decades, far-reaching advances have been made in biology and genetics. In 1953, Francis H. C. Crick and James D. Watson, with the help of Maurice Wilkins, were able to suggest a physico-chemical model for the molecule that carries genetic information from cell to cell. Since that time, a large number of geneticists, many of them Americans, have won Nobel prizes for their contributions in this field. As chemical definitions of life became known, speculation grew concerning the origin of such a molecule, with many scientists suggesting the possibility of the existence of life elsewhere in the universe. Practical application of this new theoretical understanding of genetic mechanisms has only begun, but it appears possible that in the future man will be able to manipulate and change human genetic characteristics. This area of science thus holds the potential for changing even the nature of mankind.

The major technological breakthrough has been the invention of the electronic computer to solve both practical and theoretical problems. Pioneer models of computers were built during World War II, but until the relatively short-lived vacuum tubes could be replaced by the more dependable transistors, development in this area was handicapped. Beginning in the 1950s, however, computers came to be widely used by both government and industry, permitting the sorting, manipulation, and retrieval of enormous amounts of information in short periods. Since computers can be programed to make calculations that otherwise take months, if not years, they have been of inestimable value in aiding scientific research. By making possible quantitative answers, the computer has also aided the work of sociologists, political scientists, and even historians, who can now test their theories in areas never before possible. The immediate practical uses of the computer in giving census information, sorting data, and correlating information are readily apparent.

Another area that has gained tremendously in the last few decades is geophysics. Space exploration since 1957, including the moon landing of 1969, has opened up vast new horizons, providing man with all kinds of information concerning electrical and other phenomena. New methods of exploring the ocean depths as well as the interior of the earth have extended the range and accuracy of the data at the disposal of the scientist. The most immediate practical application of this information has been to improve weather prediction. Some experiments in the field of geophysics have also shown a discrepancy between light sources and radio sources in the universe, although the meaning of this discovery is not yet clear.

Man himself has benefited tremendously from advances in medicine, with discoveries in immunization leading to the development of preventive medicine. Many contagious diseases can now be controlled, while other major illnesses can be made less severe by the use of such drugs as penicillin and other antibiotics. Laser beams have made possible more delicate eye operations, while other technical discoveries have made it possible to use transplanted and artificial human organs. Although medical progress has lengthened the human lifespan, it has had the unfortunate effect of creating larger and larger populations in a world in which most of the people still lack enough to eat.

ADJUSTMENTS IN RELIGION

Religion, that most conservative of institutions which attempts to preserve some of the highest ideals of man, has had to change drastically in order to meet the demands of the twentieth century. As traditional Western images of God crumbled with the outpouring of scientific findings and historical scholarship, and as secularism grew in part because of the growth of urbanization and industrialization, the vision of reality expressed in the Bible and other religious sources of the past seemed to be less and less credible to more and more people. To exist, religion had to create an imagery compatible with contemporary knowledge. This subject, indeed, has been the particular concern of Martin Buber, Paul Tillich, and other contemporary theologians of various religions. An outgrowth of work in this area has been the "God is dead" school of religious thinking, which rests on the idea that true religion stems not so much from man's belief in God as from man's commitment to his fellow-man and his willingness to act upon this commitment.

A byproduct of the challenge to existing religious ideas has been a lessening of sectarian differences, which has resulted, in part, from the realization that organized religion in the West was being undermined by Marxism as well as by secularism. Fearful that interfaith antagonisms would serve only to strengthen secularism, Protestantism began to grope for unity through the World Council of Churches in 1948. The Eastern Orthodox groups were included from the beginning, but Roman Catholicism did not join the ecumenical movement until 1958 when Pope John XXIII gave the impetus. Jewish-Christian dialogues have also become common, and the ecumenical movement has even indicated a willingness to encompass the religions of the East.

POLITICAL ADJUSTMENTS

The most obvious political change in Western civilization in the twentieth century has been the decline in the influence of monarchs. World War I led to the unseating of monarchs in Germany, Austria-Hungary, Russia, and Turkey, and World War II saw many of the remaining ones either exiled or forced to readjust to a different role. Those who seemed best able to survive were the monarchs who patterned themselves after the British, Scandinavian, or Dutch rulers, who became little more than symbolic figureheads in their own countries. Parliamentary bodies, modeled on those of England and France, came to be increasingly dominant not only in Europe but throughout the world, although the road from the establishment of a parliament to the beginnings of effective democracy is a long one.

The period since World War II has also been marked by a growth in nationalism, particularly in areas of the world formerly held by Western powers. Even in Europe, the feelings of national identification that emerged in the aftermath of the World War I remain strong and appear even among such long quiescent peoples as the Scots and Welsh in Great Britain, the Bretons in France, the Slovaks in Czechoslovakia and the Basques in Spain. Yet Europe, in part to meet the challenge of the two great superpowers, the Soviet Union and the United States, has attempted to heal many of the old nationalist controversies by emphasizing a European ideal, the most successful example of which is the European Common Market.

THE END OF COLONIALISM

In the aftermath of World War II, Europe underwent a radical readjustment in its assessment of its own future. Europeans had first to accept the fact that they no longer dominated the world, and this realization caused psychological traumas as deep as any inflicted by the war itself. Since the Crusades, Europeans had been on the offensive, bringing more and more peoples under their influence politically, militarily, economically, and culturally. The last great wave of conquest in the nineteenth century had resulted in Western control of most of the world. The underdeveloped peoples who were annexed or protected had reacted with awe, confusion, or hatred, but felt helpless before European might. World War II brought about a change in this attitude as colonials witnessed the defeat and occupation of France, Holland, and Belgium, three of the great colonial powers, and the occupation of many of the Asian territories of the British and the Americans by the Japanese, who though equally imperialistic, were not European. The result was the unleashing of a wave of anti-European nationalism after the war that caught Western powers off guard. Events moved so rapidly that even nationalist-minded agitators found themselves unable to control them.

Great Britain, which held the largest colonial empire, in some ways, was most successful in divesting itself of its holdings. The British Commonwealth of Nations evolved into a loose confederation of self-governing nations which included Canada, New Zealand, Australia, and South Africa. The British had even been able to accept the total separation of southern Ireland. India, however, proved more troublesome since the Indians themselves were bitterly divided by language, religion, and class distinctions and could not agree on anything but independence. Moreover, India was one of the few areas in the empire that had proved extremely profitable for the British to control. For a time, it seemed that Mahatma Gandhi, an impressively influential moralist who was also an effective politician, might be able to unite all India behind himself and his Congress party. His demand for immediate independence, combined with his nonviolent methods, elevated him to a position of leadership not only in India but in the world. In spite of the efforts of Gandhi, however, the only force that united the people of India was hostility to British rule. When the British Labor party, which had come to power in 1945, agreed to satisfy Indian demands for independence, the disunity became apparent. Though the British hung on in the hope of finding an acceptable solution, when it became apparent that this was not possible, in June 1948 they simply agreed to abandon the country. The result was a division of the area into India, which was predominantly Hindu, and the geographically split Pakistan, which was mainly Muslim. The division immediately led to large-scale massacres. Though India still has the second largest Muslim population in the world and includes large numbers of other minorities from Parsees to Christians, the hostility

Mahatma Gandhi (1869–
1948). (Prints Division,
The New York Public
Library, Astor, Lenox
and Tilden Foundations)

between the two former parts of India continues even though both
joined the Commonwealth Association.

The British were somewhat more successful in granting independence to Ceylon, Burma, and Malaya, although in the last case there
was considerable antagonism between the Chinese population of Singapore and the rest of Malaya. The eventual result was the separation
of Singapore from the new country. In Africa, too, the British took
appropriate steps to prepare their colonies for independence, ending
their treaty rights with Egypt in 1954 — though only after a war — and
granting independence to Ghana in 1957 and later to other areas. One
of the most troublesome areas was Palestine, which was inhabited
by both Muslims and Christian Arabs as well as Jews. During World
War I, the British had agreed to recognize both the establishment of a
Jewish national homeland in the Holy Land and an independent Arab
state. In the aftermath of Hitler's campaign to exterminate the Jews,
the demand for a separate Jewish state gained momentum. The British,
anxious to keep their influence among the Arabs, who controlled vast
quantities of petroleum resources, and aware of their contradictory
promises, proved reluctant to establish an independent Israel. As a
result, Great Britain found itself in the position of fighting against

many of the survivors of Hitler's concentration camps; finally, in 1948, the British simply abandoned the struggle and let the Arabs and Israelis fight it out. Israel won this battle for independence, but its Arab neighbors still refused to recognize the country, as the continued warfare between the two groups demonstrates. Economically, however, Israel became one of the most successful of the former British-controlled areas, largely because it received massive payments from Germany as symbolic compensation for the millions of executed Jews as well as large-scale American capital investment. Trouble also brewed in other parts of Africa where the British and other colonial powers had divided up territories without considering tribal loyalties or regional conflicts. When many of these areas were given independence as a united country, old tribal animosities led to near-anarchy and civil war, particularly in Nigeria. The British also experienced problems in Rhodesia, where a small colony of Europeans tried to maintain dominance over the more numerous natives.

OTHER COLONIAL POWERS

France initially attempted to take a different tack in dealing with its colonies by integrating the various territories into the government of continental France. Such a policy had the advantage of giving status to those colonials who had been educated in French schools or who admired French culture, but it had the disadvantage of excluding the majority of the native population from participation. After long, drawn-out guerrilla wars in Indochina and Algeria, France also finally agreed to give these former colonies their independence. Portions of Indochina — Laos and Cambodia — won their independence in 1954, but Vietnam was partitioned by an international conference. When the French withdrew, the United States gradually intervened in Vietnam on the assumption that this was the only way to prevent a Communist take-over. The net effect of the American policy was probably to increase Chinese Communist influence in all of Southeast Asia, since the various ex-colonials turned for support to China in order to oppose U.S. intervention. Tunisia and Morocco became independent in 1956, several other colonies in Africa gained their independence in 1959, and finally Algeria, which had large numbers of European settlers, was granted its freedom in 1962. President Charles de Gaulle proved to be most successful in dismantling the French colonial holdings and at the same time in preventing an uprising of the rightists in France, who believed the end of the empire signified a decline in French prestige. By establishing the French Community, the counterpart of the British Commonwealth, de Gaulle also managed to maintain French influence in many of the former colonies. Particularly helpful to many of the

African colonies was the fact that they were allowed to retain associate membership in the European Common Market, a considerable economic boon.

The United States also broke up most of its colonial empire after the war by giving independence to the Philippines, commonwealth status to Puerto Rico, and statehood to Hawaii and Alaska. The smaller colonial states, notably the Netherlands, Belgium, and Portugal, tried at first to regain or hold on to their colonies in the aftermath of World War II. The Dutch, however, were almost immediately faced with a crisis in the East Indies, and by 1949, were forced to recognize the newly formed state of Indonesia, with a population many times larger than that of the Netherlands itself. Belgium refused to make preparations for the ultimate independence of the Congo, but in 1960, it was finally forced to grant freedom to its African subjects. The inevitable result was widespread anarchy since the natives of the Congo were totally unprepared to assume the task of running a government. The Portuguese, the weakest of the colonial powers, were able to retain most of their colonies, which were both less valuable and more primitive that those of other countries. India managed to annex the Portuguese colony of Goa with no opposition, but China continued to allow Macao to exist on sufferance, as it did the British colony of Hong Kong. In Angola and Mozambique, the Portuguese turned to repressive tactics, causing them to be ostracized throughout Africa. In this policy, they joined the Union of South Africa, which still controls many of the German territories under a mandate from the old League of Nations. Like Portugal, it rules with an iron hand, although South African policies are much more racist than those of the Portuguese.

PROBLEMS OF THE EX-COLONIALS

As many of the emerging nations discovered, independence did not immediately solve their problems. In fact, many of the new countries are only now beginning to appreciate the extent of their problems, since for a long period they tended to blame the occupying powers for all internal difficulties. Ignorance, primitive economies, and even widespread corruption were all said to result from imperialism. While it is true that even comparatively enlightened colonial powers caused problems, they were not usually the ones that aroused protest on the part of the native populations. By introducing Western medical practices, for example, the British, French, Americans, and others tended to encourage rapid population growth in countries whose resources were already strained. Even after the Western powers withdrew, the population increase continued, so that one of the major problems of our time is providing an adequate food supply for people the world over. Unless solutions can be found quickly, the result will be increasing starvation as the world population continues to grow. Birth control methods and devices offer some hope, but before these can be effective, massive educational programs have to be launched, and there is little evidence that this effort is being made on anything but a token scale.

By blaming the imperialist powers for all of their ills, the ex-colonials tended to believe that independence was synonymous with utopia. They soon found, however, that not only did all of the old problems continue to exist but that these were compounded by the inefficiency of the new government and a serious lack of investment capital. The new states then found themselves caught in a vicious cycle. To increase agricultural productivity, they had to mechanize their farms, but such an undertaking required investment capital, which few countries had available. Moreover, where agricultural machinery was introduced, the result was the displacement of large numbers of villagers, who were then forced to move to the city where they could not find work. Here they became an unstable element which encouraged the rise of various demagogues. Increasingly, governments in the ex-colonial areas tended to discourage mechanized agriculture until they could offer alternative employment to those who would be displaced by the new methods.

The feelings of helplessness that the new governments experienced as they attempted to deal with their internal problems came to be reflected in the United Nations, where, at least in the General Assembly, the newly independent powers were seated as equals with their old colonial masters. The voting power of these areas changed the nature of the United Nations by increasing the number of countries that remained uncommitted to either the United States or the Soviet Union but that were willing to do anything to gain power for themselves and some sort of assistance for their countrymen.

OTHER PROBLEMS OF THE UNDERDEVELOPED WORLD

In general, the underdeveloped countries leaned more toward centralized state planning than free enterprise capitalism. Unfortunately, large numbers of Americans associated any kind of state planning with communism, and this attitude served to increase the antagonism between the United States and the underdeveloped areas. In their anxiety to combat the spread of Communist influence, Americans sometimes forgot that the Western liberal hostility to communism was not shared by all peoples of the world. Neither Hinduism nor Buddhism, for example, opposed the Communist system in the same way as organized Christianity. It was only among the Islamic powers, where communism was equated with atheism, that some of the same hostility appeared. Americans were also surprised when the various newly developing countries, many only recently freed from colonial rule, looked upon American investment in much the same way they had regarded occupation by the imperialist powers. Many of the new states became almost paranoiac about outside interference in their affairs, although they welcomed support for projects they themselves selected. While they wanted the United States and other countries to provide them with money and armaments, they did not wish to account for how the money was to be spent or to what purposes the armaments were to be used. Often money sent under these conditions ended up in the pockets of officials, while the arms were used to suppress genuine popular protest. If the regime seemed to be sufficiently anti-Communist, the American government rarely cut off the funds. Even when countries were willing to give the United States some kind of control over American money spent in the country, most of them refused to identify with American foreign policy and many refused to join the various anti-Communist alliances, such as the Southeast Asia Treaty Organization (SEATO), which the United States made a condition for receiving aid.

Many of the older yet underdeveloped countries of the world, notably those of Latin America, also began to express resentment against what they regarded as their economic exploitation by outside interests. More than half a century ago, Mexico attempted to exclude American economic domination, but much of the rest of the southern hemisphere has only recently awakened to the fact that most of its business and industry have been controlled by foreign interests. Even in these countries, there has been a tendency to blame the United States, Great Britain, and other industrial countries for current problems. Brazil, for example, holds vast potential, but widespread poverty, the indifference of the ruling clique, and poor governmental leadership are more responsible for the country's backwardness than anything any outside power has done in the country.

It has been a common practice in the contemporary political world for underdeveloped countries to nationalize industries controlled by outside interests. In resisting such action, the United States, which controls much of the world's wealth, has often found itself forced to side with reactionary forces whose only merit is that they are anti-Communist. The result has been to increase hostility toward the United States among the underdeveloped countries and to make America the bulwark of the status quo. United States-Cuban relations are illustrative of these problems. Cuba, though independent since 1898, was still under the economic control of foreigners, primarily Americans, until Fidel Castro's revolution of 1958 and the subsequent nationalization of much foreign property. Whether Castro was originally a Communist has often been debated, but it seems clear that once he aroused American antagonisms through his nationalization policy, his only alternative was to seek support from the Communist bloc. Castro's success in these tactics has inspired other rulers of underdeveloped countries to try to launch their own revolutionary movements in the hope of matching Cuban accomplishments. In their haste to come to terms with the modern world, backward nations find themselves handicapped by outmoded social systems, by inadequate educational systems, and by well-established ruling classes, leading many reformers to turn to ever more radical solutions.

Underdeveloped peoples of the world want the kind of life that peoples in the richer countries enjoy and that they so often see depicted in films and on television. As they begin to realize the possibility of satisfying some of their wants, the result is a revolution of rising expectations. Spurred by mounting national pride and aroused by Hollywood films, the poor fail to see why they should not share in the good things of life. They want more of everything now for themselves and their children, unable to realize that it takes time, even for a country rich in resources, to achieve economic growth.

THE URBAN REVOLUTION

Today's world is a changed world from that of the past. In many ways the most revolutionary change has been growing urbanization. In the past century, millions of people throughout the world have migrated from the country to ever-larger cities. By 1960, over 20 percent of the world's people were living in cities with populations of over 100,000. In countries such as the United States, where the urban trend has been strongest, only 5 percent of the population is presently engaged in agriculture, and similar patterns are beginning to emerge throughout the world. Such concentration of population has speeded up communication and in the process has broken down much of the old isolation between areas and peoples — making it easier, in turn, to organize mass movements among the disenchanted.

Urbanization and the new technology have also been held largely responsible for the so-called generation gap so publicized in recent years, with young people throughout the world seeking to abandon the ways of the past in virtually every sphere of life. The shift from the settled life of the country village to the unsettled one of the modern urban complex has taken place within one or two generations, with the result that many young people today feel cut off from the past of their parents and grandparents.

Technology has also made human labor less important as machines take over more and more of the functions once reserved for brains and muscles. The result has been a fundamental challenge to traditional attitudes toward work and leisure, a trend that in highly developed societies has proved as disruptive of the old norms as any change that has taken place in Western civilization.

Urbanization has also demanded more centralized control in all aspects of human affairs. The old-style village had a life of its own which went on for generations with little change. Urban living, however, has forced large numbers of strangers into closer proximity, making necessary increased governmental regulation in many spheres. Centralized direction also becomes more important as the extended family structure breaks down and is replaced by a smaller unit, the nuclear family. Services that members of the family used to render to each other now must be performed by outside agencies. Even the United States, which has long emphasized individual enterprise, has found it necessary to turn more and more to central planning to meet the problems of a complex urban society.

Technology and urbanization together have served to widen the gap between the "haves" and the "have nots" in all societies. In the United States, for example, large numbers of people still live at or near poverty levels. Many of these people are members of groups that have traditionally been discriminated against in American life, such as Negroes, Mexican-Americans, Indians, and Appalachian whites, but others are the aged or the sick, who in an earlier period would have been sheltered by the family. The situation of many of these groups is likely to worsen unless efforts are made to provide them with educational and employment opportunities. In the United States, in recent years, high school drop-outs, and even young people who have completed their secondary education, have found it increasingly difficult to obtain jobs in today's automated world. Hardest hit by the changing employment standards has been the Negro, who, despite civil rights legislation during the administrations of Dwight D. Eisenhower, John F. Kennedy, and Lyndon B. Johnson, in actuality finds himself little better off today because of economic and educational disadvantages. In sharp contrast to the United States, Sweden has experienced much success in dealing with its underprivileged citizens, and despite its cradle to grave security program, has managed to keep many of the better aspects of the capitalist system.

On the world scene, the United States and other major industrial countries now hold a much higher proportion of the world's wealth than they did twenty years ago; and by itself, the United States is the richest and most powerful nation the world has yet seen. Thus comparatively few people and countries have enjoyed the benefits of twentieth-century technology. While perhaps several hundred million people are living better today than at any time in the past, the rest of the world comparatively is worse off than ever. Since most of those who enjoy high standards of living are concentrated in the United States and the countries of Western Europe, resentment in underdeveloped countries can only grow.

THE CHANGED ROLE OF THE MILITARY

The Cold War has turned the contemporary world into an armed camp, with the United States, the Soviet Union, and now China providing military-aid programs to almost all of the underdeveloped countries of the world. One result of this situation has been the rise of military dictators in these backward areas, some of whom were or are committed to social change, such as Gamal Abdul Nasser in Egypt, while others, notably those in many Latin American countries, seek only to preserve the status quo. To many of the underdeveloped countries, arms shipments offer an opportunity to commit acts of aggression against their opponents. India and Pakistan, for example, who fought a brief war in 1967, were both armed by the United States; and Turkey and Greece, who came close to war in 1965, were not only both armed by the United States but were military allies whom this country was committed to defend. With the underdeveloped countries on a perpetual quest for arms, vast quantities of the world's resources have been diverted from being used for much-needed internal improvements in backward areas.

Some historians have argued that the arms race among the underdeveloped countries is not in itself a bad thing, since it has forced these nations to face the realities of the twentieth century. They point out that men who know practically nothing about machinery must learn how to use and maintain such military necessities as trucks, tanks, artillery, telephones, radios, and other sophisticated equipment. When these men enter civilian life, it is argued, they should be able to apply these skills to more productive tasks. This theory has not worked out in practice, however, since most of the resources in these countries are committed to the military, and only a small percentage of soldiers learn anything that has practical application in civilian life. Moreover, the arms race has served to make the underdeveloped countries depend more closely on the major powers, since only the large industrial countries have the resources to produce sophisticated weapons and planes or to supply their purchasers with spare parts. Though an underdeveloped country can easily establish an army after it has gained independence, its rulers soon find that their freedom of action is limited by the need to purchase spare parts, which they can often not afford or which the industrial countries are reluctant to sell them. While they can make do during a short-term war, as their equipment begins to break down, they are forced to appeal to the great powers. The joint attempt of India and the United Arab Republic to make a jet plane so far has not resulted in much more than a model, because to produce the plane, key parts and machinery must be purchased from the great powers. Such equipment is expensive, and even England and France have found it necessary to combine their financial resources to begin planning for the aircraft of the future.

POSTSCRIPT

Obviously, the world today is in ferment, as is the United States itself. Largely because of the war in Vietnam, Americans came to realize that even the great power of the United States was not equal to being the world's policeman and began to question the nature of U.S. commitments across the world. The international problems of the United States have been compounded in recent years by a growing gap in the country's balance of trade. At home, Americans have been troubled by unemployment and continued racial unrest. In recent decades, the United States, like other great powers earlier, has had to make some hard decisions concerning its role in world affairs. Soviet communism today does not seem as threatening as it did twenty years ago, although Soviet ambitions appear to be much the same. Communist China, however, poses a new kind of threat, one the U.S. government long ignored by refusing to recognize the existence of this world power. Cuba, once under American influence, has demonstrated open hostility to the United States while attempting to export revolution to much of Latin America. In the United States itself, Negroes, and to a lesser extent other minority groups such as Indians and Mexican-Americans, are demanding a greater share of American prosperity. These are some of the problems that Americans today must solve with alacrity.

Man, however, has come a long way from the Stone Age, although there is as yet no assurance that he will not destroy himself, either by nuclear holocaust or genetic mutation or by reproducing himself beyond the world's food supply or polluting the earth he lives on. The sad fact is that though man has become the master of the earth, he has not managed to master himself. Civilization has made its greatest strides in the last thousand years, and in the last three centuries, man's rate of development seems almost to have increased by geometric progression. Much of this progress has taken place in what today we call Western civilization. The result has been that though Western man can now reach the moon or fly around the world without seeing the sun set, many peoples of the world still live under conditions that are little better than those of four thousand years ago. The "haves" grow richer while the "have nots" grow more numerous. The historian Arnold Toynbee has said that the best remedy for contemporary problems would be a new universal religion that would do for the twentieth century what Christianity did for the fourth century. Inherent in this suggestion is Toynbee's belief that Western civilization is now in the same stage of history as the Roman Empire in the fourth century. While Toynbee's solution has appealed to some people, few have attempted to follow it. Many have turned to communism for an answer, others to existentialism, with its belief in commitment, or to humanism, a sort of secular religion, or to anarchy, which is based on the premise that existing institutions must be destroyed before man can build new ones. Some of the disenchanted have found answers in the religions of the East or within their own religious tradition. In the long run successful answers can come only from a willingness to examine, change, and reform existing institutions, even to abolish some.

The human experience has demonstrated tremendous potential, and in the past, those people and leaders who have had the courage, the patience, and the wisdom to encourage man to live up to his potential have opened vast doorways to the future. Though we concentrate upon our own anxieties, it might be well to remember that mankind in the past has always had anxieties, and even many of the same fears that we have now. In many ways, most of us in the Western world are better off than any of our predecessors. History can obviously be made — even though some of its makers seem to be more its victims than its conquerors. No age has been more exciting than our own, and none has demanded more of its heroes.

Supplemental Reading
for Part Seven

General

Archer, Jules, *The Dictators* (Bantam).

Arendt, Hannah, *Antisemitism* or *The Origins of Totalitarianism* (Harcourt or World).

Arendt, Hannah, *The Human Condition: A Study of the Central Dilemmas Facing Modern Man* (Doubleday).

Aron, Raymond, *The Century of Total War* (Beacon).

Bailey, Sydney D., *The United Nations: A Short Political Guide* (Praeger).

Barraclough, Geoffrey, *An Introduction to Contemporary History* (Penguin).

Borsody, Stephen, *The Tragedy of Central Europe* (Macmillan).

Brown, Harrison, *The Challenge of Man's Future* (Viking).

Brown, Harrison, and others, *The Next Hundred Years* (Viking).

Bunting, G. R., and M. J. Lee, eds., *The Evolution of the United Nations* (Pergamon).

Cantor, Norman F. and Michael S. Werthman, *The History of Popular Culture since 1815* (Macmillan).

Cantor, Norman F., and Michael S. Werthman, *The Twentieth Century* (Crowell).

Carr, E. H., *German-Soviet Relations between the Two World Wars, 1919–1939* (Harper & Row).

Carr, E. H., *International Relations between the Two World Wars, 1919–1939* (Harper & Row).

Calder, Nigel, ed., *The World in 1984*, 2. vols. (Penguin).

Churchill, Winston, *The Second World War*, 6 vols. (Bantam).

Coyle, David Cushman, *The United Nations and How It Works* (Mentor).

Craig, Gordon A., *Europe since 1914* (Holt, Rinehart and Winston).

Craig, Gordon A., and Felix Gilbert, *The Diplomats, 1919–1939*, 2 vols. (Atheneum).

Eisenhower, Dwight D., *Crusade in Europe* (Avon or Doubleday).

Fuller, Buckminster, *Utopia or Oblivion: The Prospect for Humanity* (Bantam).

Gatzke, Hans W., *The Present in Perspective* (Random House).

Greene, N., *Fascism: An Anthology* (Crowell).

Heilbroner, Robert, *The Future as History* (Harper & Row).

Hersey, John, *Hiroshima* (Bantam).

Hitchcock, William R., *The Twentieth Century: The Great Issues* (Wadsworth).

Hook, Sidney, *Marx and the Marxists: The Ambiguous Legacy* (Van-Nostrand).

Leckie, Robert, *Conflict: The History of the Korean War* (Avon).

Lettis, R. and W. E. Morris, eds., *The Hungarian Revolt* (Scribner).

Lichtheim, George, *The New Europe* (Praeger).

Lukacs, John A., *A New History of the Cold War* (Doubleday).

McNeill, William H., *The Contemporary World* (Scott, Foresman).

McNeill, William H., *Past and Future* (Chicago).

Millis, Walter, *Arms and Men* (Mentor).

Milosz, Czeslaw, *The Captive Mind* (Random House).

Namier, L. B., *Facing East: Essays on Germany, the Balkans, and Russia in the Twentieth Century* (Harper & Row).

Neumann, S., *Permanent Revolution: Totalitarianism in the Age of International Civil War* (Praeger).

Nolte, Ernst, *Three Faces of Fascism* (Holt, Rinehart and Winston).

Popper, K. R., *The Open Society and Its Enemies* (Harper & Row).

Seton-Watson, Hugh, *Neither War nor Peace: The Struggle for Power in the Postwar World* (Praeger).

Seton-Watson, Hugh, *The New Imperialism* (Putnam).

Snell, J. L., ed., *The Meaning of Yalta* (Louisiana).

Snyder, Louis L., *The War: A Concise History, 1939–1945* (Dell).

Spitz, David, *Patterns of Anti-Democratic Thought* (Free Press).

Strachey, John, *The End of Empire* (Random House).

Talmon, Jacob L., *The Origins of Totalitarian Democracy* (Praeger).

Taylor, A. J. P., *From Sarajevo to Postdam* (Harcourt).

Treadgold, D. W., *Soviet and Chinese Communism: Similarities and Differences* (U. of Wash.).

Wagar, W. Warren, *The City of Man* (Penguin).

Weber, Eugen, *Varieties of Fascism: Doctrines of Revolution in the 20th Century* (Van Nostrand).

Wheeler-Bennet, J. W., *Munich: Prologue to Tragedy* (Random House).

Willis, F. R., *France, Germany and the New Europe* (Oxford).

Wilmot, Chester, *The Struggle for Europe: History of World War II* (Harper & Row).

Wiskeman, Elizabeth, *Europe of the Dictators, 1919–1945* (Harper & Row).

Zagoria, Donal S., *The Sino Soviet Conflict* (Atheneum).

Europe

ENGLAND

Graves, Robert, and Alan Hodge, *The Long Weekend, 1918–1939* (Norton).

Havighurst, Alfred E., *Twentieth Century Britain* (Harper & Row).

Jarman, T. L., *A Short History of 20th Century England* (Mentor).

Sampson, Anthony, *The Anatomy of Britain Today* (Harper & Row).

Thomson, David, *England in the Twentieth Century* (Penguin).

FRANCE

Langer, William L., *Our Vichy Gamble* (Norton).
Luethy, Herman, *France against Herself* (World).
Osgood, S. M., ed., *The Fall of France, 1940* (Heath).
Pickles, Dorothy, *The Fifth French Republic* (Praeger).
Thomson, David, *Democracy in France since 1870* (Oxford).
Werth, Alexander, *De Gaulle* (Penguin).
Werth, Alexander, *France, 1940–1955* (Beacon).
Wolfer, Arnold, *Britain and France between Two Wars* (Norton).
Wright, G., *Rural Revolution in France* (Stanford).

GERMANY

Bullock, Alan, *Hitler: A Study in Tyranny* (Harper & Row).
Craig, Gordon A., *From Bismarck to Adenauer: Aspects of German Statecraft* (Harper & Row).
Dehio, Ludwig, *Germany and World Politics in the 20th Century* (Norton).
Eyck, Erich, *A History of the Weimar Republic* (Wiley).
Frank, Anne, *The Diary of a Young Girl* (Pocket Books).
Fromm, Erich, *Escape from Freedom* (Avon).
Gatzke, Hans W., *Stresemann and the Rearmament of Germany* (Norton).
Halperin, S. W., *Germany Tried Democracy* (Norton).
Hartman, F. H., *Germany between East and West: Reunification Problem* (Prentice-Hall).
Kogon, Eugen, *Theory and Practice of Hell* (Berkeley).
Meineck, Friedrich, *The German Catastrophe* (Beacon).
Mosse, George L., *The Crisis of German Ideology: Intellectual Origins of the Third Reich* (Grosset & Dunlap).
Neumann, Franz, *Behemoth: The Structure and Practice of National Socialism* (Harper & Row).
Schoenbaum, D., *Hitler's Social Revolution: Class and Status in Nazi Germany* (Doubleday).
Shirer, William L., *The Rise and Fall of the Third Reich* (Crest).
Snyder, L. L., *Hitler and Nazism* (Bantam).
Stern, Fritz, *The Politics of Cultural Despair* (Doubleday).
Trevor-Roper, H. R., *The Last Days of Hitler* (Macmillan).
Viereck, Peter, *Metapolitics, The Roots of the Nazi Mind* (Putnam).
Von Klemperer, Klemens, *Germany's New Conservatism and Dilemma in the 20th Century* (Princeton).
Wheeler-Bennet, J. W., *Nemesis of Power: The German Army in Politics* (Viking).

ITALY

Fermi, Laura, *Mussolini* (Chicago).
Finer, Herman, *Mussolini's Italy* (Grosset & Dunlap).
Kirkpatric, Sir Ivone A., *Mussolini: A Study in Power* (Avon).

SOVIET UNION

Bauer, Raymond A., *How the Soviet System Works* (Random House).

Carr, E. H., *History of Soviet Russia: Bolshevik Revolution, 1917–1923,* 3 vols. (Penguin).

Chamberlin, W. H., ed., *The Russian Revolution,* 2 vols. (Grosset & Dunlap).

Daniels, Robert V., *The Stalin Revolution* (Heath).

Deutscher, Isaac, *Stalin: A Political Biography* (Oxford).

Deutscher, Isaac, *Trotsky,* 3 vols. (Random House).

Deutscher, Isaac, *Unfinished Revolution, Russia, 1917–1967* (Oxford).

Fischer, Louis, *Life of Lenin* (Harper & Row).

Fischer, Louis, *Fifty Years of Soviet Communism* (Popular).

Fischer-Galati, Stephen, ed., *Eastern Europe in the Sixties* (Praeger).

Gunther, John, *Inside Russia Today* (Pyramid).

Kennan, George F., *Soviet Foreign Policy, 1917–1941* (Van Nostrand).

McNeal, Robert H., *The Bolshevik Tradition: Lenin, Stalin, Kruschchev* (Prentice-Hall).

Reshetar, John S., Jr., *A Concise History of the Communist Party of the Soviet Union* (Praeger).

Rostow, W. W., and Rozek, E. J., *The Dynamics of Soviet Society* (Mentor).

Schapiro, Leonard, *Government and Politics of the Soviet Union* (Random House).

Schapiro, Leonard, *The Communist Party of the Soviet Union* (Random House).

Schapiro, Leonard, *The Origins of the Communist Autocracy* (Praeger).

Scott, Derek J. R., *Russian Political Institutions* (Praeger).

Shub, David, *Lenin* (Penguin).

Seton-Watson, Hugh, *Eastern Europe between the Wars, 1918–1941* (Harper & Row).

Seton-Watson, Hugh, *From Lenin to Khrushchev: The History of World Communism* (Praeger).

Trotsky, Leon, *The History of the Russian Revolution* (Doubleday).

OTHER COUNTRIES

Childs, M. W., *Sweden, The Middle Way* (Yale).

Eyck, G. F., *Benelux Countries* (Van Nostrand).

Jackson, Gabriel, ed., *Spanish Civil War* (Heath).

Orwell, George, *Homage to Catalonia* (Beacon).

Payne, Stanley G., *Franco's Spain* (Crowell).

Thomas, Hugh, *The Spanish Civil War* (Harper & Row).

West, Rebecca, *Black Lamb and Grey Falcon,* 2 vols. (Viking).

Asia

Clubb, Oliver Edmund, *Twentieth Century China* (Columbia).

Fischer, Louis, *Life of Mahatma Gandhi* (Macmillan).

Fitzgerald, C. P., *The Birth of Communist China* (Penguin).

Grant, Bruce, *Indonesia* (Penguin).
Reischauer, Edwin O., *Japan Past and Present* (Random House).
Robinson, Joan, *The Cultural Revolution in China* (Penguin).
Schwartz, Benjamin, *Chinese Communism and the Rise of Mao* (Harper & Row).
Snow, Edgar, *Red Star over China* (Grove).
Spear, Percival, *A History of India* (Penguin).
Storry, Richard, *A History of Modern Japan* (Penguin).

Africa

Arikpo, Okoi, *The Development of Modern Nigeria* (Penguin).
Duffy, James, *Portugal in Africa* (Penguin).
Hatch, John, *Africa Today — and Tomorrow* (Praeger).
Hatch, John, *A History of Post-War Africa* (Praeger).
Hepple, Alexander, *Verwoerd* (Penguin).
Hughes, A. J., *East Africa — the Search for Unity* (Penguin).
Lengyel, E., *Africa, Past, Present and Future* (Oxford).
Oliver, Roland and J. D. Fage, *A Short History of Africa* (Penguin).

Middle East, North Africa

Brace, R. M., *Morocco, Algeria, Tunisia* (Prentice-Hall).
Fischer, C. A. and F. Krinsky, *Middle East in Crisis* (Syracuse).
Halpern, Manfred, *The Politics of Social Change in the Middle East and North Africa* (Princeton).
Kirk, George, *A Short History of the Middle East* (Praeger).
Lerner, D., *The Passing of Traditional Society: Modernizing the Middle East* (Free Press).
Lewis, Bernard, *The Emergence of Modern Turkey* (Oxford).
Prittie, Terence, *Israel: Miracle in the Desert* (Penguin).

Latin America and Canada

Dame, Hartley F., *Latin America 1969* (Stryker-Post).
Draper, Theodore, *Castro's Revolution: Myth and Realities* (Praeger).
Gunther, John, *Inside Latin America* (Pocket Books).
Harrison, W. E., *Canada in World Affairs* (Oxford).
Jackson, D. Bruce, *Castro, The Kremlin, and Communism in Latin America* (Johns Hopkins).
Lieuwen, Edwin, *Arms and Politics in Latin America* (Praeger).
Lieuwen, Edwin, *Generals vs. Presidents: Neomilitarism in Latin America* (Praeger).
Nehemkis, Peter, *Latin America: Myth and Reality* (Mentor).
Nun, José, *Latin America: Politics of Modernization* (Institute for International Studies).

United States

Allen, Frederick Lewis, *Only Yesterday* (Harper & Row).
Allen, Frederick Lewis, *Since Yesterday* (Bantam).

Alperowitz, G., *Atomic Diplomacy: Hiroshima and Pottsdam* (Random House).

Bailey, T. A., *Woodrow Wilson and the Lost Peace* (Quadrangle).

Beloff, Max, *The United States and the Unity of Europe* (Random House).

Bernstein, Irving, *The Lean Years* (Penguin).

Burns, J. M., *Roosevelt: The Lion and the Fox* (Harcourt).

Clark, K. B., *Dark Ghetto: Dilemmas of Social Power* (Harper & Row).

Fairbank, John K., *The United States and China* (Viking).

Feis, Herbert, *The Diplomacy of the Dollar, 1919–1932* (Norton).

Feis, Herbert, *The Road to Pearl Harbor* (Atheneum).

Harrington, Michael, *Toward A Democratic Left* (Penguin).

Hughes, H. S., *The United States and Italy* (Norton).

Hofstadter, Richard, *The American Political Tradition* (Random House).

Keller, Morton, ed., *The New Deal: What Was It?* (Holt, Rinehart and Winston).

Kennan, George F., *American Diplomacy: 1900–1950* (Mentor).

Kennan, George F., *Realities of American Foreign Policy* (Norton).

Kissinger, Henry A., *The Necessity for Choice: Prospects of American Foreign Policy* (Doubleday).

Kissinger, Henry A., *Troubled Partnership: A Re-Appraisal of the Atlantic Alliance* (Doubleday).

Leuchtenburg, William E., *The Perils of Prosperity, 1914–1932* (Chicago).

Rozwenc, E. C. and K. Lindfors, eds., *Containment and the Origins of the Cold War* (Heath).

Social and Economic

Bagdikian, Ben H., *In the Midst of Plenty* (Mentor).

Blaustein, Arthur and Roser Woock, eds., *Man against Poverty* (Random House).

Boulding, Kenneth, *The Meaning of the Twentieth Century* (Harper & Row).

Burnham, James, *The Managerial Revolution* (Indiana).

Clough, S. and Moodie, T. and C., *Economic History of Europe* (Harper & Row).

Crosland, C. A., *The Future of Socialism* (Schocken).

Dales, John H., *Pollution, Property and Prices* (Toronto).

Djilas, Milovan, *The New Class* (Praeger).

Dowd, D. F., *Modern Economic Problems in Historical Perspecitve* (Heath).

Ehrlich, P. R., *Population Bomb* (Ballantine).

Galbraith, J. K., *The Great Crash* (Houghton).

Galbraith, J. K., *The New Industrial State* (Signet).

Goldman, M. I., *Comparative Economic Systems* (Random House).

Harrington, Michael, *The Other America* (Penguin).

Hauser, P. M., ed., *The Population Dilemma* (Prentice-Hall).

Heilbroner, Robert L., *The Great Ascent: The Struggle for Economic Development in Our Time* (Harper & Row).

Landsberg, H. H., *Natural Resources for U. S. Growth* (Johns Hopkins).
Lockwood, William, *The Economic Development of Japan* (Princeton).
Mead, Margaret, ed., *Cultural Patterns and Technical Change* (Mentor).
Mills, C. Wright, *White Collar* (Oxford).
Mitrany, David, *Marx against the Peasant* (Macmillan).
Mumford, Lewis, *The City in History: Its Origins, Its Transformations, and Its Prospects* (Harcourt).
Myrdal, G., *Beyond the Welfare State* (Yale).
Myrdal, G., *Challenge to Affluence* (Random House).
Saarinen, E., *The City, Its Growth, Its Decay, Its Future* (MIT Press).
Shonfield, Andrew, *Modern Capitalism* (Oxford).
Toffler, Alving, *The Culture Consumers: Art and Affluence in America* (Penguin).
Udall, S. L., *Quiet Crisis* (Avon).
Ward, Barbara, *The Rich Nations and the Poor Nations* (Norton).
Whyte, William H., *The Organization Man* (Doubleday).
Wingert, N., *Natural Resources and the Political Struggle* (Random House).
Wolfson, M., *A Reappraisal of Marxian Economics* (Penguin).

Intellectual: Religion, Science, Philosophy, Literature, and the Arts

Ayer, A. J., ed., *Logical Positivism* (Free Press).
Barth, Karl, *Credo* (Scribner).
Baumer, Franklin L., *Religion and the Rise of Scepticism* (Harcourt).
Bell, Daniel, *The End of Ideology* (Free Press).
Bergson, Henri, *Two Sources of Morality and Religion* (Doubleday).
Blake, Peter, *Frank Lloyd Wright* (Penguin).
Blake, Peter, *Le Corbusier* (Penguin).
Bowra, C. M., *The Heritage of Symbolism* (St. Martin's).
Brenan, G., *The Literature of the Spanish People* (World).
Buber, Martin, *I and Thou* (Scribner).
Bultmann, Rudolf, *Existence and Faith* (World).
Cohen, J. M., *Poetry of This Age* (Harper & Row).
Collaer, P., *A History of Modern Music* (Grosset & Dunlap).
Copland, A., *Music and Imagination* (Mentor).
Copleston, F., *Contemporary Philosophy* (Newman).
Cowell, H. and S., *Charles Ives and His Music* (Oxford).
Crossman, R. H. S., *The God That Failed* (Bantam).
Dawson, Christopher, *The Dynamics of World History* (Mentor).
Dewey, John, *Reconstruction in Philosophy* (Beacon).
Eddington, Arthur, *The Nature of the Physical World* (Michigan).
Ehrlich, Paul R., Richard W. Holm, and Peter N. Raven, *Papers on Evolution* (Littlefield).
Eliade, Mircea, *Myths, Dreams and Mysteries* (Harper & Row).
Eliade, Mircea, *Patterns in Comparative Religion* (World).
Empson, William, *Seven Types of Ambiguity* (New Directions).

Fermi, Laura, *Atoms in the Family* (Chicago).

Fowlie, Wallace, *The Age of Surrealism* (Indiana).

Frankel, Charles, *The Case for Modern Man* (Beacon).

Gill, Jerry H., *Philosophy Today* (Macmillan).

Goodman, Paul, *Growing Up Absurd* (Random House).

Grene, Marjorie, *Toward a Unity of Knowledge* (International University Press).

Haas, W. P., *Contemporary Arts* (Thomist).

Haftmann, Werner, *Painting in the Twentieth Century*, 2 vols. (Praeger).

Harrod, R. F., *The Life of John Maynard Keynes* (St. Martin's).

Hays, H. R., *From Ape to Angel* (Putnam).

Heidegger, Martin, *Existence and Being* (Regnery).

Heisenberg, W., *Physics and Philosophy: The Revolution in Modern Science* (Harper & Row).

Hoggart, Richard, *The Uses of Literacy* (Beacon).

Humphrey, Robert, *Stream of Consciousness in the Modern Novel* (California).

Jeans, James, *The Growth of Physical Science* (Premier).

Kaufman, Walter, *Existentialism from Dostoyevsky to Sartre* (World).

Keene, Donald, *Japanese Literature* (Grove).

Kracauer, Siegfried, *From Caligari to Hitler: A Psychological History of German Film* (Princeton).

Leepa, A., *Challenge of Modern Art* (A. S. Barnes).

Marty, Martin, *Varieties of Unbelief* (Doubleday).

Metraux, Guy S. and François Crouzet, *Religions and the Promise of the 20th Century* (Mentor).

Mosse, G. L., *Nazi Culture: Intellectual, Cultural and Social Life in the Third Reich* (Grosset & Dunlap).

Neill, Stephen, *A History of Christian Missions* (Penguin).

Neumann, John von, *The Computer and the Brain* (Yale).

Niebuhr, Reinhold, *The Children of Light and the Children of Darkness* (Scribner).

Northrup, F. S. C., *The Meeting of East and West* (Macmillan).

Ong, Walter J., ed., *Knowledge and the Future of Man* (Simon and Schuster).

Ortega y Gasset, José, *The Revolt of the Masses* (Norton).

Plumb, J. H., *Crisis in the Humanities* (Penguin).

Read, Herbert, *Concise History of Modern Painting* (Praeger).

Reichenbach, Hans, *The Rise of Scientific Philosophy* (California).

Reinisch, L., ed., *Theologians of Our Time* (Notre Dame).

Riesman, David, *Individualism Reconsidered* (Free Press).

Riesman, David, *The Lonely Crowd* (Yale).

Sartre, Jean Paul, *Existentialism and Human Emotions* (Philosophical Library).

Schlenoff, N., *Art in the Modern World* (Bantam).

Simpson, George G., *The Meaning of Evolution* (Yale).

Snow, C. P., *The Two Cultures and the Scientific Revolution* (Mentor).

Stebbing, L. S., *Philosophy and the Physicists* (Dover).

Struve, G., and others, *A Century of Russian Prose and Verse* (Harcourt).

Teilhard de Chardin, Pierre, *The Phenomenon of Man* (Harper & Row).

Tillich, Paul, *Biblical Religion and the Search for Ultimate Reality* (Chicago).

Ulanov, B., *History of Jazz in America* (Viking).

Wagar, W. Warren, *Science, Faith, and Man* (Harper & Row).

Weil, Simone, *Waiting for God* (Putnam).

Weil, Simone, *The Need for Roots* (Beacon).

Wiener, Norbert, *Cybernetics* (MIT Press).

SOURCES *

Daniels, Robert V., *Documentary History of Communism* (Random House).

Gandhi, *The Story of My Experiments with Truth* (Beacon).

Hitler, *Mein Kampf* (Houghton).

John XXIII, Pope, *Mater et Magister* (Paulist Press).

Kohn, Hans, *The Modern World* (Macmillan).

Lincoln, W. B., *Documents in World History since 1945* (Chandler).

Nehru, Jawaharlal, *Toward Freedom: An Autobiography* (Beacon).

Trotsky, Leon, *My Life* (Grosset & Dunlap).

Weeks, Robert P., *Machines and the Man* (Appleton).

White, Morton, ed., *The Age of Analysis: Twentieth Century Philosophers* (Mentor).

FICTION

Buck, Pearl, *The Good Earth* (Pocket Books).

Grass, Günter, *The Tin Drum* (Pantheon or Fawcett).

Heller, Joseph, *Catch-22* (Dell).

Koestler, Arthur, *Darkness at Noon* (Bantam).

Malraux, André, *Man's Fate* (Random House).

Orwell, George, *1984* (Signet).

Pasternak, Boris, *Doctor Zhivago* (Signet).

Paton, Alan, *Cry the Beloved Country* (Scribner).

Mann, Thomas, *The Magic Mountain* (Random House).

Solzhenitsyn, Alexander, *One Day in the Life of Ivan Denisovich* (Signet or Praeger).

Steinbeck, John, *The Grapes of Wrath* (Bantam).

Wilder, Thornton, *The Bridge of San Luis Rey* (Simon and Schuster).

Wright, Richard, *Native Son* (Harper & Row).

Zamiatin, Evgenii I, *We* (Dutton).

* *Paperback editions of many of the novelists, playwrights, poets, philosophers, and others cited in the section are also available, and some have been indicated elsewhere in the bibliography.*

A BRIEF NOTE ON FURTHER READING

Paperbacks, at best, cover only a small part of the vast history of Western civilization. For the student who desires to read further, a most helpful tool is the *Guide to Historical Literature*, prepared by the *American Historical Association* under the direction of George F. Howe (1961). This can be supplemented by the bibliographies and reviews in current learned journals such as the *American Historical Review, Journal of Modern History, Speculum, Renaissance Quarterly, Classical Philology*, or others. Also helpful are the comprehensive Cambridge histories which include *The Cambridge Ancient History* (8 vols.), *The Cambridge Medieval History* (8 vols.), and *The Cambridge Modern History* (13 vols.), which is currently being revised as *The New Cambridge Modern History*. The student should consult S. H. Steinberg, *Historical Tables 58 B.C.–A.D. 1965* (St. Martin's) as well as a good historical atlas. Recommended are the *Historical Atlas of the World* edited by R. R. Palmer (Rand McNally) and the *European History Atlas* edited by J. H. Breasted, Carl F. Huth, and Samuel B. Harding (Denoyer-Gepper). All three of these last books are also available in paperback.

Index

UNIVERSITY OF CONNECTICUT · GROTON, CONN. — SOUTHEASTERN BRANCH

DATE DUE

MAR 10 71
MAY 8 '75

DEMCO 38-297